Liberal Arts Mathematics
A Florida Course

The Consortium for Foundation Mathematics

Ralph Bertelle — *Columbia-Greene Community College*
Judith Bloch — *University of Rochester*
Roy Cameron — *SUNY Cobleskill*
Carolyn Curley — *Erie Community College–South Campus*
Ernie Danforth — *Corning Community College*
Brian Gray — *Howard Community College*
Arlene Kleinstein — *SUNY Farmingdale*
Kathleen Milligan — *Monroe Community College*
Patricia Pacitti — *SUNY Oswego*
Rick Patrick — *Adirondack Community College*
Renan Sezer — *LaGuardia Community College*
Patricia Shuart — *Polk Community College*
Sylvia Svitak — *Queensborough Community College*
Assad J. Thompson — *LaGuardia Community College*

Excerpts taken from

Mathematical Models with Applications, **Texas** Edition
by the Consortium for Foundation Mathematics

Mathematics in Action: Algebraic Graphical and Trigonometric Problem Solving
by the Consortium for Foundation Mathematics

Mathematics in Action: Algebraic, Graphical, and Numerical Problem Solving
by the Consortium for Foundation Mathematics

Custom Publishing

New York   Boston   San Francisco
London   Toronto   Sydney   Tokyo   Singapore   Madrid
Mexico City   Munich   Paris   Cape Town   Hong Kong   Montreal

Cover Art: Courtesy of Photodisc/Getty Images.

Excerpts taken from:

Mathematical Models with Applications, Texas Edition
by The Consortium for Foundation Mathematics
Copyright © 2008 by Pearson Education, Inc.
Published by Addison-Wesley
Boston, Massachusetts 02116

Mathematics in Action: Algebraic, Graphical, and Trigonometric Problem Solving
by The Consortium for Foundation Mathematics
Copyright © 2008 by Pearson Education, Inc.
Published by Addison-Wesley

Mathematics in Action: Algebraic, Graphical, and Numerical Problem Solving
by The Consortium for Foundation Mathematics
Copyright © 2008 by Pearson Education, Inc.
Published by Addison-Wesley

Printed in the United States of America

2 3 4 5 6 7 8 9 10 V357 14 13 12 11 10

2009360178

CF

Please visit our website at *www.pearsonschool.com/Advanced*

ISBN 10: 0-558-20307-8
ISBN 13: 978-0-558-20307-8

Contents

CHAPTER 2   LINEAR FUNCTION MODELS AND PROBLEM SOLVING   165

To the Teacher

Our Vision

Liberal Arts Mathematics: A Florida Course is intended to build on previous mathematics courses and to place emphasis on bringing about a deeper understanding of those mathematical relationships that will help students gain mathematical literacy in the real world, show the connection between algebra, geometry, and statistics, and simultaneously help them build a strong foundation for future study in mathematics and other disciplines. The main goals for this textbook are to teach students how to **problem solve**, **communicate**, and **reason** mathematically; make **mathematical connections**; create and interpret mathematical **representations** and **models**; and make efficient and appropriate use of **technology** to solve problems. *Liberal Arts Mathematics: A Florida Course* is based on the principle that students learn mathematics best by doing mathematics within a meaningful context. In keeping with this premise, students solve problems in a series of realistic situations, or investigations, from which the crucial need for mathematics arises. *Liberal Arts Mathematics: A Florida Course* guides students toward developing a sense of independence and taking responsibility for their own learning. Students are encouraged to construct, reflect on, apply, and describe their own mathematical models, which they use to solve meaningful problems. We see this as the key to bridging the gap between abstraction and application and as the basis for transfer learning. Appropriate technology is integrated throughout the book, allowing students to interpret real-life data verbally, numerically, symbolically, and graphically.

We expect that by using *Liberal Arts Mathematics: A Florida Course* that all students will be able to achieve the following goals:

- Develop mathematical intuition and a relevant base of mathematical knowledge.
- Gain experiences that connect classroom learning with real-world applications.
- Learn to work in groups as well as independently.
- Increase knowledge of mathematics through explorations with appropriate technology.
- Develop a positive attitude about learning and using mathematics.
- Build techniques of reasoning for effective problem solving.
- Learn to apply, display, and communicate knowledge through alternative means of assessment, such as mathematical portfolios and journal writing.

 In addition, this textbook can be used to help students prepare for local testing requirements. A chart on the following pages correlates the Florida Course Benchmarks for the Liberal Arts Mathematics course to the corresponding chapters and sections in this text.

Our vision for your students is to join the growing number of students using our approach who have discovered that mathematics is an essential and learnable survival skill for the 21st century.

Pedagogical Features

The pedagogical core of *Liberal Arts Mathematics: A Florida Course* is a series of guided-discovery activities in which students work in groups to discover mathematical principles embedded in realistic situations. The key principles of each activity or investigation are highlighted and summarized at the activity's conclusion. Each activity is followed by exercises that reinforce the concepts and skills revealed in the activity.

Each chapter contains regular activities along with project activities that relate to particular topics. The activities may require more than just paper, pencil, and calculator. They may also require measurements and data collection and are ideal for in-class group work. The project activities are designed to allow students to explore specific topics in greater depth, either individually or in groups. For specific suggestions on how to use the two types of activities, we strongly encourage you to refer to the *Teacher's Resource Guide* that accompanies this text.

Occurring naturally as summary and review are the What Have I Learned? and How Can I Practice? exercises. The What Have I Learned? exercises are designed to help students pull together the key concepts of the section. The How Can I Practice? exercises are primarily designed to provide additional practice with the numeric, graphical, and algebraic skills of the section. Taken as a whole, these exercises give students the tools they need to bridge the gaps between abstraction, skills, and application.

Additionally, each chapter ends with a summary that contains a brief description of the concepts and skills discussed in the chapter, plus examples illustrating these concepts and skills. The concepts and skills are also cross-referenced to the activity in which they appear, making the format easier to follow for those students who are unfamiliar with our approach. Each chapter also ends with a Gateway Review, providing students with an opportunity to check their understanding of the chapter's concepts and skills.

Supplements
The following supplements are available to qualified adopters.

Teacher Supplements

Annotated Teacher's Edition   0-558-20308-6

This special version of the student text provides answers to all exercises directly beneath each problem.

Teacher's Resource Guide/Printed Test Bank   0-558-20310-8

This valuable teaching resource includes the following materials:
- Teaching notes for each chapter. These notes are ideal for those using the *Liberal Arts Mathematics: A Florida Course* approach for the first time.
- Extra practice skills worksheets for topics with which students typically have difficulty.
- Sample chapter tests and final exams for in-class and take-home use by individual students and groups.
- Sample journal topics for the students to write comments and observations about the course are included for each chapter.

- Transparency masters of graphs, charts, and data used throughout the book.
- A section discussing learning in groups with questions and answers for teachers trying collaborative learning for the first time.
- Information about incorporating technology in the classroom, including sample graphing calculator assignments.
- Answers to the exercises contained in the *Student Extra Practice Workbook.*

TestGen with QuizMaster   ISBN   0-558-20722-7

TestGen enables teachers to build, edit, print, and administer tests using a computerized bank of questions developed to cover all the objectives of the text. TestGen is algorithmically based so that multiple, yet equal, versions of the same question or test can be generated at the click of a button. Teachers can also modify test bank questions or add new questions by using the built-in question editor, which allows users to create graphs, import graphics, insert math notation, and insert variable numbers or text. Tests can be printed or administered online via the Web or other network. Many questions in TestGen can be expressed in a short-answer or multiple-choice form, giving teachers greater flexibility in their test preparation. TestGen comes packaged with QuizMaster, which allows students to take tests on a local area network. The software is available on a dual-platform Windows/Macintosh CD-ROM.

Supplements for Teachers and Students

MathXL® for School Tutorials on CD   ISBN   0-558-20818-5

Included with each student edition is an interactive tutorial CD-ROM that provides algorithmically generated practice exercises that are correlated to the skills covered in the textbook. Every practice exercise is accompanied by an example and a guided solution designed to involve students in the solution process. The software provides helpful feedback for incorrect answers and can generate printed summaries of students' progress.

MathXL® for School www.MathXLforSchool.com   (Optional for Purchase Only)

MathXL® for School is a powerful online homework, tutorial, and assessment program. With MathXL, teachers can create, edit, and assign online homework and tests using algorithmically generated exercises correlated to the basic skills of the textbook. They can also create and assign their own online exercises and import TestGen tests for added flexibility. All student work is tracked in MathXL® for School's online gradebook. Students can take chapter tests in MathXL and receive personalized study plans based on their test results. The study plan diagnoses weaknesses and links students directly to tutorial exercises for the basic skill they need to study and retest. For additional information, visit our web site at www.mathxlforschool.com.

Student Extra Practice Workbook   ISBN   0-558-20309-4
(Optional for Purchase Only)

The *Student Extra Practice Workbook* is designed to provide students with additional opportunities to practice the basic skills covered in the text. The workbook is made up of a series of worksheets that include skill maintenance exercises for concepts and skills that tend to be challenging for students. Answers to the extra practice worksheets are provided in the *Teacher's Resource Guide/Printed Test Bank.*

Acknowledgments

A special thank-you to our families for their unwavering support and sacrifice, which enabled us to make this text a reality.

To the Student

The book in your hands is most likely very different from any mathematics textbook you have seen before. In this book, you will take an active role in developing the important ideas of mathematical modeling. It is the belief of the authors that students learn mathematics best when they are actively involved in solving problems that are meaningful to them.

Problem Solving and Mathematical Reasoning: The text is primarily a collection of situations drawn from real life. Each situation leads to one or more problems. By answering a series of questions and solving each part of the problem, you will be using and learning one or more mathematical ideas. Sometimes, these will be basic skills that build on your knowledge of arithmetic and algebra. Other times, they will be new concepts that are more general and far reaching. The important point is that you won't be asked to master a skill until you see a real need for that skill as part of solving a realistic application.

Communication: Another important aspect of this text and the course you are taking is the benefit gained by collaborating with your classmates. Much of your work in class will result from being a member of a team. Working in small groups, you will help each other work through a problem situation. While you may feel uncomfortable working this way at first, there are several reasons we believe it is appropriate in this course. First, it is part of the learning-by-doing philosophy. You will be talking about mathematics, needing to express your thoughts in words. This is a key to learning. Secondly, you will be developing skills that will be very valuable when you leave the classroom. Currently, many jobs and careers require the ability to collaborate within a team environment. Your teacher will provide you with more specific information about this collaboration.

Representation and Technology: One more fundamental part of this course is that you will have access to appropriate technology. You will have access to calculators and some form of graphics tool—either a calculator or computer. Technology is an integral part of our world, and learning to use technology and recognizing what the results of the technology represent goes hand in hand with learning mathematics. Your work in this course will help prepare you for whatever career you pursue.

This course will help you develop both the mathematical and general skills necessary in today's workplace, such as organization, problem solving, communication, reasoning, representation, and collaborative skills. In addition, this book will help preprare you to be successful on your local exam. By keeping up with your work and following the suggested organization of the text, you will gain a valuable resource that will serve you well in the future. With hard work and dedication, you will be ready for the next step.

The Consortium for Foundation Mathematics

Liberal Arts Mathematics Correlation

LIBERAL ARTS MATHEMATICS COURSE BENCHMARKS	LIBERAL ARTS MATHEMATICS: A FLORIDA COURSE TEXTBOOK REFERENCES
LA.910.1.6.1 The student will use new vocabulary that is introduced and taught directly.	21, 29, 44–46, 50–52, 58–60, 117, 135–136, 168, 178, 181, 191–193, 201, 204–205, 207, 234, 258, 303, 375, 385, 387, 404, 435, 453, 474, 477, 490, 500–501, 503, 513, 516, 551–552, 615, 642, 647, 756, 760, 767, 779, 796, 821
LA.910.4.2.1 The student will write in a variety of informational/expository forms, including a variety of technical documents (e.g., how-to manuals, procedures, assembly directions).	2, 10, 38, 174, 262, 266, 282, 289, 424, 492, 494, 566, 651, 775, 782, 833
MA.912.A.1.3 Simplify real number expressions using the laws of exponents.	449–457, 457–459, 460, 462, 465–466
MA.912.A.1.4 Perform operations on real numbers (including integer exponents, radicals, percents, scientific notation, absolute value, rational numbers, irrational numbers) using multistep and real-world problems.	13, 30, 33, 89, 314, 608–610, 613–614, 688, 809, 813
MA.912.A.1.8 Use the zero product property of real numbers in a variety of contexts to identify solutions to equations.	403–404, 406, 407–409, 464
MA.912.A.2.1 Create a graph to represent a real-world situation.	46–47, 55, 56, 62, 66, 68, 79–80, 82, 114–115, 122–123, 243, 260–261, 301, 329–332, 364, 366, 370, 374, 384, 396, 410, 414, 489, 491, 493, 497, 499, 512
MA.912.A.2.2 Interpret a graph representing a real-world situation.	47–49, 59–62, 69–70, 79–80, 82, 84–85, 112–114, 115–116, 119–120, 243, 301, 329–332, 365, 366, 370, 374, 384, 396, 410, 414, 489, 491, 493, 497

LIBERAL ARTS MATHEMATICS COURSE BENCHMARKS	LIBERAL ARTS MATHEMATICS: A FLORIDA COURSE TEXTBOOK REFERENCES
MA.912.A.2.3 Describe the concept of a function, use function notation, determine whether a given relation is a function, and link equations to functions.	44–45, 51, 52–54, 57–58, 60–65, 68–69, 117–118, 121, 125–126, 150, 155, 193, 213, 216–217, 220, 378, 380, 503, 507–508, 514
MA.912.A.3.3 Solve literal equations for a specified variable.	98–99, 103, 105–106, 153, 202, 206, 208, 231–232, 234, 342, 350, 352–353, 648
MA.912.A.3.4 Solve and graph simple and compound inequalities in one variable and be able to justify each step in a solution.	302–309, 310–315, 316, 337–339, 345–346, 359–360
MA.912.A.3.5 Symbolically represent and solve multistep and real-world applications that involve linear equations and inequalities.	16, 62, 82, 84, 86–88, 90–91, 95, 97, 100–103, 107–108, 139, 144–146, 156–160, 316–319, 320–325, 326–332, 334, 339–340, 564–565, 618, 634, 638, 648–649
MA.912.A.3.7 Rewrite equations of a line into slope-intercept form and standard form.	202, 206, 208, 231–232, 234, 242, 350, 352–353
MA.912.A.3.8 Graph a line given any of the following information: a table of values, the x- and y-intercepts, two points, the slope and a point, the equation of the line in slope-intercept form, standard form, or point-slope form.	194–195, 198, 199, 200, 203–204, 205–208, 209–213, 216, 223, 227–228, 352–353, 495
MA.912.A.3.9 Determine the slope, x-intercept, and y-intercept of a line given its graph, its equation, or two points on the line.	193–195, 196, 197–200, 203, 206–208, 212, 213, 216, 223, 227, 229, 230, 233, 235, 240, 349, 350, 351–352, 504, 507, 535, 693
MA.912.A.3.10 Write an equation of a line given any of the following information: two points on the line, its slope and one point on the line, or its graph. Also, find an equation of a new line parallel to a given line, or perpendicular to a given line, through a given point on the new line.	131, 192, 200–201, 203, 207–208, 223, 225–226, 228–231, 234–235, 237–238, 240–241, 276–278, 349, 351, 535
MA.912.A.3.11 Write an equation of a line that models a data set and use the equation or the graph to make predictions. Describe the slope of the line in terms of the data, recognizing that the slope is the rate of change.	203, 223, 225–226, 228–231, 237, 239, 241, 243–244, 245–246, 249, 250, 253–254, 278, 349, 354–355, 535
MA.912.A.3.13 Use a graph to approximate the solution of a system of linear equations or inequalities in two variables with and without technology.	280–281, 283–284, 286–292, 293, 300–301, 320–324, 326–332, 334, 335–337, 339–340, 345–347, 357–361
MA.912.A.7.2 Solve quadratic equations over the real numbers by factoring and by using the quadratic formula.	408–409, 411–416, 419, 422, 430–432, 464–465, 469, 664

LIBERAL ARTS MATHEMATICS COURSE BENCHMARKS	LIBERAL ARTS MATHEMATICS: A FLORIDA COURSE TEXTBOOK REFERENCES
MA.912.G.1.1 Find the lengths and midpoints of line segments in two-dimensional coordinate systems.	235–236, 241, 355, 608–610, 613–614, 688
MA.912.G.1.4 Use coordinate geometry to find slopes, parallel lines, perpendicular lines, and equations of lines.	131, 181–184, 188–189, 192, 200–201, 203, 207–208, 223, 225–226, 228–231, 233–235, 237–241, 273–274, 276–278, 351, 355, 504, 507
MA.912.G.2.3 Use properties of congruent and similar polygons to solve mathematical or real-world problems.	615–619, 619–622, 623–626, 627–629, 630–632, 638–641, 682, 689–690
MA.912.G.2.5 Explain the derivation and apply formulas for perimeter and area of polygons (triangles, quadrilaterals, pentagons, and so forth).	13–14, 17–18, 39, 92, 97, 103–104, 150, 201, 395–396, 409, 446, 459, 552–557, 559, 560, 561–566, 568–569, 570–574, 575–582, 583–587, 588–589, 590–592, 593–594, 597
MA.912.G.2.7 Determine how changes in dimensions affect the perimeter and area of common geometric figures.	446, 568–569, 571, 573–574, 587, 590, 592, 689–690
MA.912.G.3.1 Describe, classify, and compare relationships among quadrilaterals including the square, rectangle, rhombus, parallelogram, trapezoid, and kite.	551, 554–557, 560, 563–565, 576–577, 579–581
MA.912.G.4.4 Use properties of congruent and similar triangles to solve problems involving lengths and areas.	615–619, 619–622, 623–626, 627–629, 630–632, 638–640, 682, 689–690
MA.912.G.5.3 Use special right triangles (30°-60°-90° and 45°-45°-90°) to solve problems.	623–626, 627–629, 630–632, 640
MA.912.G.5.4 Solve real-world problems involving right triangles.	372, 607, 611–613, 623–625, 627–629, 630–632, 640, 687
MA.912.G.7.5 Explain and use formulas for lateral area, surface area, and volume of solids.	160–161, 449–450, 453–454, 459, 642–644, 645–646, 647–650, 651–653, 654–657, 657–660, 661–663, 673–675, 676–678, 682–684, 690–691
MA.912.G.7.7 Determine how changes in dimensions affect the surface area and volume of common geometric solids.	453–454, 459, 643, 646, 653, 655, 657, 658–660, 674–675
MA.912.G.8.2 Use a variety of problem-solving strategies, such as drawing a diagram, making a chart, guess-and-check, solving a simpler problem, writing an equation, and working backwards.	1–5, 6–9, 10–16, 17–18, 62, 79, 82–84, 86–88, 90–91, 95, 97, 100–103, 107–108, 144–145, 152, 158, 262, 287–289, 293–294, 396, 409, 420, 512, 515, 523, 526, 568, 569, 649

LIBERAL ARTS MATHEMATICS COURSE BENCHMARKS	LIBERAL ARTS MATHEMATICS: A FLORIDA COURSE TEXTBOOK REFERENCES
MA.912.G.8.3 Determine whether a solution is reasonable in the context of the original situation.	11–12, 16, 95, 114, 145, 262, 422, 517, 529, 548, 549, 588, 625, 644, 654, 656, 754, 828
MA.912.S.3.1 Read and interpret data presented in various formats. Determine whether data is presented in appropriate format, and identify possible corrections. Formats to include: • Bar graphs • Line graphs • stem-and-leaf plots • circle graphs • histograms • box and whiskers plots • scatter plots • cumulative frequency (ogive) graphs	79–80, 165, 243, 246, 249–250, 252, 255–257, 260–261, 263–265, 289, 355, 417, 420–423, 433, 499, 530, 532, 534–535, 543, 550, 696-699, 700–708, 709–710, 712-714, 716–719, 721, 724, 731, 733, 735, 748–751, 783, 786–787, 789, 790, 800–802, cumulative frequency (ogive) graphs are covered in the *Teacher's Resource Guide/Printed Test Bank.*
MA.912.S.3.2 Collect, organize, and analyze data sets; determine the best format for the data and present visual summaries from the following: • bar graphs • line graphs • stem-and-leaf plots • circle graphs • histograms • box and whisker plots • scatter plots • cumulative frequency (ogive) graphs	79–80, 243–250, 253, 255–258, 263–265, 289, 417–418, 420–424, 433, 531–532, 534–535, 543, 550, 709–712, 714–715, 720–730, 737, 752–753, 788–789, 790, 801, 803, 807–808, cumulative frequency (ogive) graphs are covered in the *Teacher's Resource Guide/Printed Test Bank.*
MA.912.S.3.3 Calculate and interpret measures of the center of a set of data, including mean, median, and weighted mean, and use these measures to make comparisons among sets of data.	731–738, 739–746, 747, 752–753, 783, 790, 792, 803, 807–808
MA.912.S.3.5 Calculate and interpret the range and quartiles of a set of data.	736, 783–789, 800, 803, 808

CHAPTER 1

Introduction to Problem Solving and Mathematical Models

ACTIVITY 1.1
Wild about Harry

OBJECTIVES

1. Practice communication skills.

2. Organize information.

3. Write a solution in sentences.

4. Develop problem-solving skills.

The last *Harry Potter* novel has just arrived and by 11:00 A.M. a line has formed outside the crowded bookstore. Knowing you have class at noon, you ask the guard at the door how long you can expect to wait. She provides you with the following information: She is permitted to let 6 people into the bookstore only after 6 people have left; customers are leaving at the rate of 2 customers per minute; and she has just let 6 new customers in. Also, each customer spends an average of 15 minutes browsing at books and 10 minutes waiting in line to check out.

Currently 38 people are ahead of you in line. You know that it is a 10-minute walk to your noon class. Can you buy your book and still expect to make it to your noon class on time? Use the following questions to guide you in solving this problem.

1. What was your initial reaction after reading the problem?

2. Have you ever worked on a problem such as this before?

3. Organizing the information will help you solve the problem.

   a. How many customers must leave the bookstore before the guard allows more to enter?

   b. How many customers per minute leave the bookstore?

   c. How many minutes are there between groups of customers entering the bookstore?

   d. How long will you stand in line outside the bookstore?

e. Now finish solving the problem and answer the question: How early or late for your noon class will you be?

4. In complete sentences, write what you did to solve this problem. Then, explain your solution to a classmate.

SUMMARY
Activity 1.1

Steps in Problem Solving

1. Sort out the relevant information and organize it.

2. Discuss the problem with others to increase your understanding of the problem.

3. Write your solution in complete sentences to review your steps and check your answer.

EXERCISES
Activity 1.1

1. Think about the various approaches you and your classmates used to solve Activity 1.1, Wild about Harry. Choose the approach that is best for you, and describe it in complete sentences.

2. What mathematical operations and skills did you use?

ACTIVITY 1.2
The Classroom

OBJECTIVES

1. Organize information.
2. Develop problem-solving strategies.
   • Draw a picture.
   • Recognize a pattern.
   • Do a simpler problem.
3. Communicate problem-solving ideas.

The Handshake

This mathematics course involves working with other students in the class, so form a group of three, four, or five students. Introduce yourself to every other student in your group with a firm handshake. Share some information about yourself with the other members of your group.

1. How many people are in your group?

2. How many handshakes in all were there in your group?

3. Discuss how your group determined the number of handshakes. Be sure everyone understands and agrees with the method and the answer. Write the explanation of the method here.

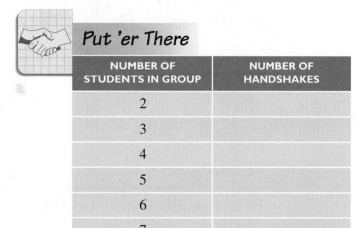

Put 'er There

NUMBER OF STUDENTS IN GROUP	NUMBER OF HANDSHAKES
2	
3	
4	
5	
6	
7	

4. Share your findings with the other groups, and fill in the chart.

5. a. Describe a rule for determining the number of handshakes in a group of seven students.

b. Describe a rule for determining the number of handshakes in a class of *n* students.

6. If each student shakes hands with each other student, how many handshakes will be needed in your class?

7. Is shaking hands during class time a practical way for students to introduce themselves? Explain.

George Polya's book, *How to Solve It*, outlines a four-step process for solving problems.

1. Understand the problem (determine what is involved).
2. Devise a plan (look for connections to obtain the idea of a solution).
3. Carry out the plan.
4. Look back at the completed solution (review and discuss it).

8. Describe how your experiences with the handshake problem correspond with Polya's suggestions.

The Classroom

The tables in your classroom have square tops. Four students can comfortably sit at each table with ample working space. Putting tables together in clusters as shown will allow students to work in larger groups.

9. Construct a table of values for the number of tables and the corresponding total number of students.

NUMBER OF SQUARE TABLES IN EACH CLUSTER	TOTAL NUMBER OF STUDENTS
1	4
2	6

10. How many students can sit around a cluster of 7 square tables?

11. Describe the pattern that connects the number of square tables in a cluster and the total number of students that can be seated. Write a rule in sentences that will determine the total number of students that can sit in a cluster of a given number of square tables.

12. There are 24 students in a science course at your school.

    a. How many tables must be put together to seat a group of six students?

    b. How many clusters of tables are needed?

13. Discuss the best way to arrange the square tables into clusters given the number of students in your class.

SUMMARY
Activity 1.2

1. Problem-solving strategies include the following:
   - discussing the problem
   - organizing information
   - drawing a picture
   - recognizing patterns
   - doing a simpler problem

2. George Polya's book, *How to Solve It,* outlines **a four-step process for solving problems**.
   i. Understand the problem (determine what is involved).
   ii. Devise a plan (look for connections to obtain the idea of a solution).
   iii. Carry out the plan.
   iv. Look back at the completed solution (review and discuss it).

EXERCISES
Activity 1.2

1. At the opening session of the United States Supreme Court, each justice shakes hands with all the others.

   a. How many justices are there?

   b. How many handshakes do they make?

2. Identify how the numbers are generated in this triangular arrangement, known as Pascal's triangle. Fill in the missing numbers.

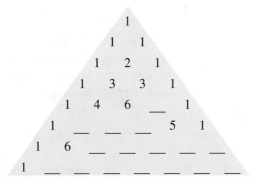

3. An **arithmetic sequence** is a list of numbers in which consecutive numbers share a common difference. Each number after the first is calculated by adding the common difference to the preceding number. For example, the arithmetic sequence 1, 4, 7, 10, . . . has 3 as its common difference. Identify the common difference in each arithmetic sequence that follows.

   a. 2, 4, 6, 8, 10, . . .

   b. 1, 3, 5, 7, 9, 11, . . .

   c. 26, 31, 36, 41, 46, . . .

4. A **geometric sequence** is a list of numbers in which consecutive numbers share a common ratio. Each number after the first is calculated by multiplying the preceding number by the common ratio. For example, 1, 3, 9, 27, . . . has 3 as its common ratio. Identify the common ratio in each geometric sequence that follows.

   a. 2, 4, 8, 16, 32, . . .

   b. 1, 5, 25, 125, 625, . . .

5. The operations needed to get from one number to the next in a sequence can be more complex. Describe a relationship shared by consecutive numbers in the following sequences.

   a. 2, 4, 16, 256, . . .

   b. 2, 5, 11, 23, 47, . . .

   c. 1, 2, 5, 14, 41, 122, . . .

6. In biology lab, you conduct the following experiment. You put two rabbits in a large caged area. In the first month, the pair produces no offspring (rabbits need a month to reach adulthood). At the end of the second month, the pair produces exactly one new pair of rabbits (one male and one female). The result makes you wonder how many male/female pairs you might have if you continue the experiment and each existing pair of rabbits produces a new pair each month, starting after their first month. The numbers for the first four months are calculated and recorded for you in the following table. The arrows in the table illustrate that the number of pairs produced in a given month equals the number of pairs that existed at the beginning of the preceding month. Continue the pattern and fill in the rest of the table.

Hare Today

MONTH	NUMBER OF PAIRS AT THE BEGINNING OF THE MONTH	NUMBER OF NEW PAIRS PRODUCED	TOTAL NUMBER OF PAIRS AT THE END OF THE MONTH
1	1	0	1
2	1	1	2
3	2	1	3
4	3	2	5
5			
6			
7			
8			

The list of numbers in the second column is called the **Fibonacci sequence**. This problem on the reproduction of rabbits first appeared in 1202 in the mathematics text *Liber Abaci*, written by Leonardo of Pisa (nicknamed Fibonacci). Using the first two numbers, 1 and 1, as a starting point, describe how the next number is generated. Your rule should generate the rest of the numbers shown in the sequence in column two.

7. If you shift all the numbers in Pascal's triangle so that all the 1's are in the same column, you get the following triangle.

a. Add the numbers crossed by each arrow. Put the sums at the tip of the arrow.

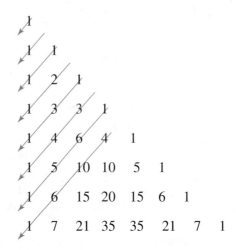

b. What is the name of the sequence formed by these sums?

8. There are some interesting patterns within the Fibonacci sequence itself. Take any number in the sequence and multiply it by itself, and then subtract the product of the number immediately before it and the number immediately after it. What is the result? Pick another number and follow the same procedure. What result do you obtain? Try two more numbers in the sequence.

For example, choose 5.　　For example, choose 3.

$5 \cdot 5 = 25$　　　　　　$3 \cdot 3 = 9$

$3 \cdot 8 = 24$　　　　　　$2 \cdot 5 = 10$

$25 - 24 = 1$　　　　　　$9 - 10 = -1$

9. a. Complete the following table by performing the following sequence of operations on the original number: Multiply the number by 4, add 12 to the product, divide the sum by 2, and subtract 6 from the quotient.

ORIGINAL NUMBER	RESULT OF SEQUENCE OF OPERATIONS
2	
5	
10	
15	

b. There is a hidden pattern in the sequence of operations that causes the original number and the result of the sequence of operations to always have the same relationship. What relationship do you observe between the number and the result?

Based on the specific examples in part a, you might conclude that if you follow the given sequence of operations on *any* number, the result would always be twice the original number. Arriving at a general conclusion from specific examples is a type of reasoning called **inductive reasoning** or **induction**. However, this type of reasoning does not prove that the general conclusion is true for all numbers.

c. Generalize the situation in part a by choosing a variable to represent the original number. Use x as your variable and perform the sequence of operations on the variable x. Simplify the resulting algebraic expression.

d. What general conclusion is proven in part c?

The type of reasoning used in parts c and d is called **deductive reasoning** or **deduction**. Deductive reasoning is used to prove conjectures true or false.

ACTIVITY 1.3

Make Me an
Offer

OBJECTIVES

1. Use the basic steps for problem solving.

2. Translate verbal statements into algebraic equations.

3. Use the basic principles of algebra to solve real-world problems.

4. Use formulas to solve problems.

Many students believe "I can do math. I just can't do word problems." In reality, you learn mathematics so you can solve practical problems in everyday life and in science, business, technology, medicine, and most other fields.

On a personal level, you solve problems every day by calculating the delivery charge for an online order, remembering a birthday, or figuring out how to get more exercise. Most everyday problems don't require algebra, or even arithmetic, to be solved. But the basic steps and methods for solving any problem can be discussed and understood. In the process you will, with practice, become a better problem solver.

Solve the following problem any way you can, making notes of your thinking as you work. In the space provided, record your work on the left side. On the right side, jot down in a few sentences what you are thinking as you work on the problem.

"Night Train" Henson's Contract

1. "Night Train" Henson is negotiating a new contract with his team. He wants $800,000 for the year with an additional $6000 for every game he starts. His team offered $10,000 for every game he starts, but only $700,000 for a base salary. How many games would he need to start in order to make more with the team's offer?

SOLUTION TO THE PROBLEM	YOUR THINKING

2. Talk about and compare your methods for solving the above problem with classmates or your group. As a group, write down the steps you all went through from the very beginning to the end of your problem solving.

PROCEDURE: Basic Steps for Problem Solving

Solving any problem generally requires the following four steps:

1. Understand the problem.

2. Develop a strategy for solving the problem. (Devise a plan.)

3. Execute your strategy to solve the problem. (Carry out the plan.)

4. Check your solution for correctness. (Look back at the completed solution.)

3. How do these four steps compare to your group's solutions? How do your group's answers compare with other groups' answers?

Let's consider each of the steps 1 through 4.

Step 1. Understand the problem.   This step may seem obvious, but many times this is the most important step and is the one that commonly leads to errors. Read the problem carefully, as many times as necessary. Draw some diagrams to help you visualize the situation. Get an explanation from available resources if you are unsure of any details.

4. List some strategies you could use to make sure you understand the "Night Train" Henson problem.

Step 2. Develop a strategy for solving the problem.   Once you understand the problem, it may not be at all clear what strategy is required. Practice and experience are the best guides. Algebra is often useful for solving a math problem but is not always required.

5. How many different strategies were tried in your group for solving the "Night Train" problem? Describe one or two of them.

Step 3. Execute your strategy to solve the problem.   Once you have decided on a strategy, carrying it out is sometimes the easiest step in the process. If you really understand the problem and are clear on your strategy, the solution should happen almost automatically.

6. When you decided on a strategy, how confident did you feel about your solution?

Step 4. Check your solution for correctness.   This last step is *critically important*. Your solution must be reasonable, it must answer the question, and most importantly, it must be correct.

7. Are you absolutely confident your solution is correct? If so, how do you know?

Solution: "Night Train" Henson's Contract

As beginning problem solvers, you may find it useful to develop a consistent strategy. Let's examine one possible way you can solve "Night Train's" problem by applying some algebra tools.

Step 1. Understand the problem. If you understand the problem, you will realize that "Night Train" needs to make $100,000 more with the team's offer (800,000 − 700,000) to make up for the difference in base salary. So he must start enough games to make up for this difference. Otherwise, he should not want the team's offer.

Step 2. Develop a strategy for solving the problem. Recall that a **variable**, usually represented by a letter, is a quantity or quality that may change in value from one particular instance to another. In this situation, you could let the variable x represent the number of games "Night Train" needs to start to make the same amount of money with either offer. Then we note that he would make $4000 more for each game started with the team's offer. So $4000 for each game started times the number of games started must equal $100,000.

Step 3. Execute your strategy for solving the problem. You can translate the statement above into an equation, then apply the fundamental principle of solving equations to obtain the number of games.

$$4000x = 100{,}000$$
$$4000x \div 4000 = 100{,}000 \div 4000$$
$$x = 25$$

Your answer would be: "Night Train needs to start in more than 25 games to make more with the team's offer."

Step 4. Check your solution for correctness. This answer seems reasonable but to check it you should refer back to the original statement of the problem. If "Night Train" starts in exactly 25 games his salary for the two offers can be calculated.

Night Train's demand: $800,000 + $6000 × 25 = $950,000
Team's offer: $700,000 + $10,000 × 25 = $950,000

If he starts in 26 games, the team's offer is $960,000 and "Night Train's" demand is $956,000.

This confirms our solution.

There are other ways to solve this problem. But this gives you an example of how algebra can be used. Use algebra in a similar way to solve the following problems. Be sure to follow the four steps of problem solving.

Additional Problems to Solve

8. You need to open a checking account and decide to shop around for a bank. SunState Bank has an account with a $10 monthly charge plus 25 cents per check. Farmer's Bank will charge you $12 per month, with a 20 cent charge per check. How many checks would you need to write each month to make Farmer's Bank the better deal?

Step 1. Understand the problem.

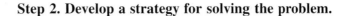

Step 2. Develop a strategy for solving the problem.

Step 3. Execute your strategy to solve the problem.

Step 4. Check your solution for correctness.

9. The perimeter of a rectangular citrus grove is 2400 feet. If the width is 800 feet, how long is the citrus grove?

Step 1. Understand the problem.

Step 2. Develop a strategy for solving the problem.

Step 3. Execute your strategy to solve the problem.

Step 4. Check your solution for correctness.

Formulas

The solution to Problem 9 involved the relationship between a rectangle's perimeter and its length and width. Stated in words, the perimeter is the sum of twice the width and twice the length. This can be translated into an equation involving letters called a **formula**. If P represents the perimeter, w represents the width, and l represents the length, the stated relationship can be written as

$$P = 2w + 2l.$$

Formulas are useful in many business applications. For Problems 10–12,

 a. First, choose appropriate letters to represent each variable quantity and write what each letter represents.

 b. Use the letters to translate each stated relationship into a symbolic formula.

 c. Use the formula to solve the exercise.

 10. Net income is equal to the total revenue from selling an item minus the cost of producing the item. Determine the net income if the revenue from a business is $400,000 and the cost is $156,800.

 11. Net pay is the difference between a worker's gross income and his or her deductions. A person's gross income for the year was $65,000 and their total deductions were $12,860. What was their net pay for the year?

12. Annual depreciation equals the difference between the original cost of an item and its remaining value, divided by its estimated life in years. Determine the annual depreciation of a new car that costs $25,000, has an estimated life of ten years, and a remaining value of $2000.

Formulas are also found in the sciences. In Problems 13–15, use the given formulas to solve each problem.

13. In general, temperature is measured using either the Celsius (C) or Fahrenheit (F) scales. To convert from degrees Celsius to degrees Fahrenheit, use the following formula.

$$F = \frac{9C}{5} + 32$$

   a. Use the formula to convert 20°C into degrees F.

   b. 100°C is equal to how many degrees F?

14. To convert from degrees F to degrees C, use the following formula.

$$C = 5(F - 32) \div 9$$

   a. Use the formula to convert 86°F into degrees C.

   b. What is a temperature of 41 degrees F equal to in degrees C?

15. The distance an object travels is determined by how fast it goes and for how long it moves. If an object's speed remains constant, the formula is $d = r \cdot t$, where d is the distance, r is the speed, and t is the time.

a. If you drive at 50 miles per hour for 5 hours, how far will you have traveled?

b. A satellite is orbiting the Earth at the rate of 25 kilometers per minute. How far will it travel in two hours?

Orbits at 25 km per minute

SUMMARY
Activity 1.3

The Four Steps of Problem Solving

Step 1. Understand the problem.

a. Read the problem completely and carefully.

b. Draw a sketch of the problem, if possible.

Step 2. Develop a strategy for solving the problem.

a. Identify and list everything you know about the problem, including relevant formulas. Add labels to the diagram if you have one.

b. Identify and list what you want to know.

Step 3. Execute your strategy to solve the problem.

a. Write an equation that relates the known quantities and the unknowns.

b. Solve the equation.

Step 4. Check your solution for correctness.

a. Is your answer reasonable?

b. Is your answer correct? (Does it answer the original question? Does it agree with all the given information?)

EXERCISES
Activity 1.3

In Exercises 1–10, solve the following problems by applying the four steps of problem solving. Use the strategy of solving an algebra equation for each problem.

1. In preparing for a family trip, your assignment is to research the travel arrangements. You determine that to rent a car with unlimited mileage will cost $75 per day. If your parents have budgeted $600 for car rental, how many days can your family drive?

2. You need to drive 440 miles to get to your cousin's wedding. How fast must you drive to get there in 8 hours?

3. Your goal is to save $1200 to pay for next year's books and fees. How much must you save each month if you have 5 months to accomplish your goal?

4. You have enough wallpaper to cover 240 square feet. If your walls are 8 feet high, what wall length can you paper?

5. In your part-time job selling kitchen knives, you have two different sets available. The better set sells for $35, the cheaper set for $20. Last week, you sold more of the cheaper set, in fact twice as many as the better sets. Your receipts for the week totaled $525. How many of the better sets did you sell?

6. A rectangle that has an area of 357 square inches is 17 inches wide. How long is the rectangle?

7. A rectangular field is five times longer than it is wide. If the field's perimeter is 540 feet, what are the dimensions (length and width) of the field?

8. In your part-time job, your hours vary each week. Last month, you worked 22 hours the first week, 25 hours the second week, 14 hours during week three, and 19 hours in week four. Your gross pay for those four weeks was $960.

  a. Let p represent your hourly pay rate. Write the equation for your gross pay over these four weeks.

  b. Solve the equation in part a to determine your hourly pay rate.

9. Over the first three months of the year, you sold 12, 15, and 21 SuperPix digital cameras. The total in sales was $18,960.

  a. Let p represent the price of one SuperPix digital camera. Write the equation for your total in sales over these three months.

b. Solve the equation in part a to find the retail price of a SuperPix digital camera.

10. Evaluate each formula for the given value(s).

    a. $d = r \cdot t$, where $r = 35$ and $t = 6$

    b. $F = ma$, where $m = 120$ and $a = 25$

    c. $V = lwh$, where $l = 100$, $w = 5$, and $h = 25$

    d. $F = \dfrac{mv^2}{r}$, where $m = 200$, $v = 25$, and $r = 125$

    e. $A = \dfrac{(t_1 + t_2 + t_3)}{3}$, where $t_1 = 76$, $t_2 = 83$, and $t_3 = 81$

ACTIVITY 1.4
Proportional
Reasoning

The following table summarizes Michael Jordan's statistics during the six games of one of his National Basketball Association (NBA) championship series.

OBJECTIVES

1. Use proportional reasoning as a problem-solving strategy.
2. Write a proportion and then solve the resulting proportion.

GAME	POINTS	FIELD GOALS	FREE THROWS
1	28	9 out of 18	9 out of 10
2	29	9 out of 22	10 out of 16
3	36	11 out of 23	11 out of 11
4	23	6 out of 19	11 out of 13
5	26	11 out of 22	4 out of 5
6	22	5 out of 19	11 out of 12

1. What was his points-per-game average over the six-game series?

2. In which game did he score the most points?

3. In which game(s) did he score the most field goals? The most free throws?

Problem 3 focused on the *actual* number of Jordan's successful field goals and free throws in these six games. Another way of assessing Jordan's performance is to *compare* the number of successful shots to the total number of attempts for each game. This comparison gives you information on the *relative* success of his shooting. For example, in each of games 1 and 2, Jordan made 9 field goals. Relatively speaking, you could argue that he was more successful in game 1 because he made 9 out of 18 attempts; in game 2, he only made 9 out of 22 attempts.

4. Use the free-throw data from the six games to express Jordan's *relative* performance in the given comparison formats (verbal, fraction, division, and decimal). The data from the first game have been entered for you.

Jordan's Relative Free-Throw Performance

	VERBAL	FRACTION	DIVISION	DECIMAL
GAME 1	9 out of 10	$\frac{9}{10}$	$9 \div 10$ or $10\overline{)9}$	0.90
GAME 2				
GAME 3				
GAME 4				
GAME 5				
GAME 6				

5. a. For which of the six games was his relative free-throw performance highest?

b. Which comparison format did you use to answer part a? Why?

6. For which of the six games was Jordan's *actual* free-throw performance the lowest?

7. For which of the six games was Jordan's *relative* free-throw performance the lowest?

When relative comparisons using quotients are made between different values or quantities of the same kind (e.g., number of baskets to number of baskets), the comparison is called a **ratio**. Ratios can be expressed in several forms—verbal, fraction, division, or decimal, as you saw in Problem 4.

Proportional reasoning is the ability to recognize when two ratios are equivalent, that is, when equivalent ratios represent the same relative performance level.

DEFINITION

Two ratios are said to be **equivalent** if the ratios have equal numerical (e.g., decimal or fraction) values. The mathematical statement that two ratios are equivalent is called a **proportion.** In fraction form, the proportion is written $\frac{a}{b} = \frac{c}{d}$.

You can determine *equivalent* ratios the same way you determine equivalent fractions. For example, 3 out of 4 is equivalent to 6 out of 8, because $\frac{3}{4} \cdot \frac{2}{2} = \frac{6}{8}$.

8. Fill in the blanks in each of the following proportions.

a. 3 out of 4 is equivalent to _____ out of 12

b. 3 out of 4 is equivalent to _____ out of 32

c. 3 out of 4 is equivalent to _____ out of 100

d. Write the resulting proportion from part c using a fraction format.

9. a. Explain why the following ratios are equivalent.

    i. 27 out of 75   **ii.** 63 out of 175   **iii.** 36 out of 100

b. Write each ratio in fraction form.

c. Determine the reduced form of the equivalent fractions from part b.

d. With which of the equivalent ratios in part a do you feel most comfortable? Explain.

The number 100 is a very familiar quantity of comparison: There are 100 cents in a dollar and frequently 100 points on a test. Therefore, people feel most comfortable with a ratio such as 70 out of 100 or 36 out of 100.

The phrase "out of 100" is commonly referred to by its Latin equivalent, *percent*. Per means "division" and cent means "100," so **percent** means "divide by 100."

Therefore, 70 out of 100 can be rephrased as 70 percent and written in the familiar notation 70%, which equals $70 \div 100 = \frac{70}{100} = 0.70$. Similarly, 36 out of 100 can be rephrased as 36 percent and written in the familiar notation

$$36\% = 36 \div 100 = \frac{36}{100} = 0.36.$$

10. Complete the following table using Michael Jordan's field goal data from the beginning of the activity.

Jordan's Relative Field Goal Performance

	VERBAL	FRACTION	DECIMAL	PERCENT
GAME 1	9 out of 18	$\frac{9}{18}$	0.50	50%
GAME 2				
GAME 3				
GAME 4				
GAME 5				
GAME 6				

Solving Proportions

In an effort to increase the education level of their police officers, many municipalities are requiring new recruits to have at least a two-year college degree. A recent survey indicated that 1 out of 5 officers in the New York City Police Department (NYPD) holds a four-year college degree. There were approximately 41,000 NYPD officers when the survey was conducted.

To calculate the number of four-year college degree holders, you can start with the proportion statement

$$1 \text{ out of } 5 = \underline{\quad ? \quad} \text{ out of } 41,000.$$

This proportion can be written in fraction form as

$$\frac{1}{5} = \frac{n}{41,000},$$

where n is the unknown quantity of the proportion.

> One method of solving proportions uses the fact that the two mathematical statements
>
> $$\frac{a}{b} = \frac{c}{d} \quad \text{and} \quad a \cdot d = b \cdot c$$
>
> are equivalent.

Transforming the statement on the left (containing two fractions) into the statement on the right is commonly called **cross multiplication** because the numerator of the first fraction is multiplied by the denominator of the second and the numerator of the second fraction is multiplied by the denominator of the first.

You can use cross multiplication to solve proportions as demonstrated in Example 1:

Example 1   *Solve the proportion* $\dfrac{2}{5} = \dfrac{n}{6000}$.

SOLUTION

Original proportion: $\dfrac{2}{5} = \dfrac{n}{6000}$

Cross multiply: $2 \cdot 6000 = 5 \cdot n$

Divide both sides by 5: $\dfrac{2 \cdot 6000}{5} = \dfrac{\cancel{5} \cdot n}{\cancel{5}}$

Simplify: $2400 = n$

11. Use the cross-multiplication method to solve the following proportion:

$$\frac{1}{5} = \frac{n}{41,000}$$

12. Solve the following proportions.

a. 2 out of 3 = _____ out of 36

b. $\dfrac{2}{3} = \dfrac{n}{45}$

Application

New York State has taken a leading position in raising the standards of its high school graduates. In the year 2003, every graduate needed to pass a series of rigorous subject-matter tests called Regents exams. Currently, your cousin lives in a New York State county in which only 6 out of 10 graduates receive Regents diplomas.

13. If 5400 students in your cousin's county earned a Regents diploma last year, estimate (without actually doing a calculation) the total number of high school graduates in that county last year.

This situation differs from the previous NYPD situation because the total number is not known. The 5400 represents that part of the total number of high school graduates who earned a Regents diploma. Written as a proportion,

6 out of 10 = 5400 out of ___?___

14. a. Rewrite this proportion in fraction form. Let n represent the unknown.

b. To determine the total number of students, use cross multiplication to calculate the unknown denominator in part a.

15. Solve these proportions.

a. 2 out of 3 = 80 out of _____.

b. $\dfrac{2}{3} = \dfrac{216}{n}$

SUMMARY
Activity 1.4

1. When comparisons using quotients are made between different quantities of the same kind, the comparison is called a **ratio**.

2. Ratios can be expressed verbally (4 out of 5), as a fraction $\frac{4}{5}$, as a division $(5\overline{)4}\,)$, as a decimal (0.80), or as a percent (80%).

3. Two ratios are said to be equivalent if the ratios have equal numerical values. The mathematical statement that two ratios are equivalent is called a **proportion**.

4. A proportion expressed in fraction form, $\frac{a}{b} = \frac{c}{d}$, is equivalent to the statement $ad = bc$.

5. Problems that involve **proportional reasoning** usually include a known ratio $\frac{a}{b}$ and a given piece of information, either a "part" or a "total" value, resulting in the following proportion:

$$\frac{a}{b} = \frac{part}{total}$$

The missing value can be determined by cross multiplying and solving the resulting equation.

EXERCISES
Activity 1.4

1. Here are your scores on three graded assignments. On which assignment did you perform best?

   a. 25 out of 30   **b.** 30 out of 40   **c.** 18 out of 25

2. At competitive colleges, the admissions office often compares the number of students accepted to the total number of applications received. This comparison is known as the *selectivity index*. The admissions office also compares the number of students who actually attend to the number of students who have been accepted for admission. This comparison is known as the *yield*. Complete the following table to determine the selectivity index and yield (in percent format) for colleges A, B, and C.

	NUMBER OF APPLICANTS	NUMBER ACCEPTED	NUMBER ATTENDING	SELECTIVITY INDEX	YIELD (AS A %)
COLLEGE A	5500	3500	1000		
COLLEGE B	8500	4800	2100		
COLLEGE C	4200	3200	900		

Which college do you think is the most competitive? The least competitive? Explain.

3. Solve each proportion for the unknown quantity.

   a. $\dfrac{2}{3} = \dfrac{x}{48}$ 　　　　　　 b. $\dfrac{5}{8} = \dfrac{120}{x}$ 　　　　　　 c. $\dfrac{3}{20} = \dfrac{x}{3500}$

In Exercises 4–12, write a proportion that represents the situation and then determine the unknown value in the proportion.

4. A conservationist can estimate the total number of a certain type of fish in a lake by using a technique called "capture-mark-recapture." Suppose a conservationist marks and releases 100 rainbow trout into a lake. A week later, she nets 50 trout in the lake and finds 3 marked fish. An estimate of the number of rainbow trout in the lake can be determined by assuming that the proportion of marked fish in the sample taken is the same as the proportion of marked fish in the total population of rainbow trout in the lake. Use this information to estimate the population of rainbow trout in the lake.

5. The school taxes on a house assessed at $210,000 are $2340. At the same tax rate, what are the taxes (to the nearest dollar) on a house assessed at $275,000?

6. According to the 2000 U.S. Census, 7 out of every 25 homes are heated by electricity. At this rate, predict how many homes in a community of 12,000 would be heated by electricity.

7. A hybrid car can travel 45 miles on one gallon of gas. Determine the amount of gas needed for a 500 mile trip.

8. A normal 10 cc specimen of human blood contains 1.2 g of hemoglobin. How much hemoglobin would 16 cc of the same blood contain?

9. The ratio of the weight of an object on Mars to the weight of an object on Earth is 0.4 to 1. How much would a 170 pound astronaut weigh on Mars?

10. The ancient Greeks thought that the most pleasing shape for a rectangle was one for which the ratio of length to width was 8 to 5. This ratio is called the Golden Ratio. If the length of a rectangular painting is 20 inches, determine the width of the painting in order for the length and width of the painting to have the Golden Ratio.

11. The designers of sport shoes assume that the force exerted on the soles of shoes during a basketball jump shot is proportional to the weight of the person jumping. A 140-pound athlete exerts a force of 1960 pounds on his shoe soles when he returns to the court floor after a jump. Determine the force that a 270-pound professional basketball player exerts on the soles of his shoes when he returns to the court floor after shooting a jump shot.

12. Your high school softball team won 80% of the games it played this year. If your team won 20 games, how many games did it play?

ACTIVITY 1.5
Fuel Economy

OBJECTIVES

1. Apply rates directly to solve problems.

2. Use proportions to solve problems.

3. Use unit or dimensional analysis to solve problems.

You are excited about purchasing a reliable used car for your commute to high school. Concerned about the cost of driving, you do some research on the Internet and come across a Web site that lists fuel efficiency, in miles per gallon (mpg), for five cars that you are considering. You record the mpg for city and highway driving in the following table.

1. a. For each of the cars listed in the following table, how many city miles can you travel per week on five gallons of gasoline? Explain the calculation you will do to obtain the answers. Record your answers in the third column of the table.

Fuel for Thought

MAKE/MODEL	CITY MPG	CITY MILES ON 5 GAL OF GAS	HIGHWAY MPG	GAL NEEDED TO DRIVE 304 MILES	FUEL TANK CAPACITY IN GAL
Chevrolet Cobalt	32		41		13.2
Ford Focus	28		36		13.2
Honda Civic	33		39		13.2
Hyundai Accent	28		36		11.9
Toyota Corolla	34		41		11.9

b. The roundtrip drive to your high school is 29 city miles, which you do five days a week. Which of the cars would get you to school each week on five gallons of gas?

2. Suppose your roundtrip commute to a summer job would be 304 highway miles per week. How many gallons of gas would each of the cars require? Explain the calculation you do to obtain the answers. Record your answers to the nearest tenths in the fifth column of the above table.

Rates and Unit Analysis

Miles per gallon (mpg) is an example of a rate. Mathematically, a **rate** is a comparison of two quantities that have different units of measurement. Numerically, you calculate with rates as you would with ratios. Paying attention to what happens to the units of measurement during the calculation is critical to determining the unit of the result.

> **DEFINITION**
>
> A **rate** is a comparison, expressed as a quotient, of two quantities that have different units of measurement.
>
> **Unit analysis** (sometimes called *dimensional analysis*) uses units of measurement as a guide in setting up a calculation or writing an equation involving one or more rates. When the calculation or equation is set up properly, the result is an answer with the appropriate units of measurement.

There are two common methods for solving problems involving rates. One method is to apply the known rate directly by multiplication or division. The second method is to set up and solve a proportion equation. In each method, you use the units of measurement as a guide in setting up the calculation or writing the appropriate equation. Example 1 demonstrates these two methods.

Example 1

Direct Method: Apply a known rate directly by multiplication or division to solve a problem.

In Problem 1, the known rate is miles per gallon. You can write miles per gallon in fraction form, $\dfrac{\text{number of miles}}{1 \text{ gal}}$. The fuel economy rating for the Chevrolet Cobalt is $\dfrac{32 \text{ miles}}{1 \text{ gal}}$. To determine how many city miles you can travel on five gallons of gasoline, you multiply the known rate by 5 gal as follows:

$$\frac{32 \text{ miles}}{1 \text{ gal}} \cdot 5 \text{ gal} = 160 \text{ miles}$$

Notice that the unit of measurement, gallon, occurs in both the numerator and the denominator. You divide out common units of measurement in the same way that you divide out common numerical factors.

Proportion Method: Set up and solve a proportion.

Form two fractions, $\dfrac{a}{b}$ and $\dfrac{c}{d}$, set them equal to one another and solve the resulting proportion.

Step 1. The first fraction, $\dfrac{a}{b}$, is the known rate. Its numerator represents one measurement unit and its denominator the other unit. In Problem 1, the known rate is $\dfrac{32 \text{ miles}}{1 \text{ gallon}}$.

Step 2. To determine the second fraction, $\dfrac{c}{d}$, the measurement unit of the numerator c must have the same unit as the numerator of the known rate (miles). The denominator d must have the same measurement unit as the denominator of the known rate (gallons).

You know that you have five gallons of gas. Therefore, five gallons is the denominator d. The unknown is the number of miles that you can drive on five gallons.

Represent the unknown in the numerator by a symbol such as x. The numerator c is x miles. Therefore, the fraction $\frac{c}{d}$ is

$$\frac{x \text{ miles}}{5 \text{ gallons}}.$$

Step 3. Set the two fractions $\frac{a}{b}$ and $\frac{c}{d}$ equal to each other to obtain a proportion, $\frac{a}{b} = \frac{c}{d}$. In Problem 1, the proportion is

$$\frac{32 \text{ miles}}{1 \text{ gallon}} = \frac{x \text{ miles}}{5 \text{ gallons}}.$$

Step 4. Solve $\frac{32}{1} = \frac{x}{5}$ to obtain $x = 160$ miles.

Therefore, in the Chevrolet Cobalt, you can drive 160 miles on five gallons of gas.

3. Solve the following problems by using both methods demonstrated in Example 1 and compare the results.

   a. The gas tank of a Ford Focus holds 13.2 gallons. How many highway miles can you travel on a full tank of gas?

   b. The Toyota Corolla gas tank holds 11.9 gallons. Is it possible to travel as far on the highway in this car as in the Ford Focus?

In Problem 2, you were asked to determine how many gallons of gas were required to drive 304 highway miles. Using the direct method, you may have known to divide the total miles by the miles per gallon. For example, in the case of the Honda Civic,

$$\frac{304}{39} = 7.8 \text{ gallons}.$$

One way to be sure the problem is set up correctly is to use the units of measurement. In Problem 2, you are determining the number of gallons. Set up the calculation so that miles will divide out and the remaining measurement unit will be gallons.

$$304 \text{ ~~miles~~} \cdot \frac{1 \text{ gallon}}{39 \text{ ~~miles~~}} = \frac{304}{39} \text{ gallons} = 7.8 \text{ gallons}$$

This example shows that a rate may be expressed in two ways. For miles and gallons, the rate can be expressed as $\dfrac{\text{miles}}{\text{gallon}}$ or as $\dfrac{\text{gallon}}{\text{miles}}$. To solve a problem, you choose the form so that all measurement units can be divided out except the measurement unit of the answer.

Alternatively, you may have set up a proportion.

$$\frac{39 \text{ miles}}{1 \text{ gallon}} = \frac{304 \text{ miles}}{x \text{ gallons}}$$
$$39x = 304$$
$$x = \frac{304}{39}$$
$$x = 7.8 \text{ gallons}$$

4. After you purchase your car, you would like to take a trip to see a good friend in another state. The highway distance is approximately 560 miles. Solve the following problems by the direct method and by the proportion method, and compare your results.

   a. If you bought the Hyundai Accent, how many gallons of gas would you need to make the round trip?

   b. How many tanks of gas would you need for the trip?

PROCEDURE: **Methods for Solving Problems Involving Rates**

Direct Method: Multiply and Divide by the Known Rate

1. Identify the unit of the result.
2. Set up the calculation so the appropriate units will divide out, leaving the unit of the result.
3. Multiply or divide the numbers as usual to obtain the numerical part of the result.
4. Divide out the common units to obtain the unit of the answer.

Proportion Method: Set Up and Solve a Proportion

1. Identify the known rate, and write it in fractional form.
2. Identify the given information and the quantity to be determined.
3. Write a second fraction, placing the given information and the quantity x in the same positions as their units in the known rate.
4. Equate the two fractions to obtain a proportion.
5. Solve the equation for x, affixing the correct unit to the numerical result.

Using Unit Analysis to Solve a Problem

5. You are on a part of a 1500-mile trip where gas stations are far apart. Your car is averaging 40 miles per gallon and you are traveling at 60 miles per hour (mph). The fuel tank holds twelve gallons of gas, and you just filled the tank. How long is it before you have to fill the tank again?

   You can solve this problem in two parts, as follows:

   a. Determine how many miles you can travel on one tank of gas.

   b. Use the result of part a to determine how many hours you can drive before you have to fill the tank again.

Problem 5 is an example of applying consecutive rates to solve a problem. Part a was the first step and part b was the second step. Alternatively, you can also determine the answer in a *single calculation* by considering what the measurement unit of the answer should be. In this case, it is hours per tank. Therefore, you will need to set up the calculation so that you can divide out miles and gallons.

$$\frac{40 \text{ miles}}{1 \text{ gal}} \cdot \frac{12 \text{ gal}}{1 \text{ tank}} \cdot \frac{1 \text{ hour}}{60 \text{ miles}} = \frac{8 \text{ hours}}{1 \text{ tank}}$$

Notice that miles and gallons divide out to leave hours per tank as the measurement unit of the answer.

PROCEDURE: Using Unit Analysis to Solve Problems

To apply consecutive rates:

1. Identify the measurement unit of the result.
2. Set up the sequence of multiplications so that the appropriate units divide out, leaving the appropriate measurement unit of the result.
3. Multiply and divide the numbers as usual to obtain the numerical part of the result.
4. Check that the appropriate measurement units divide out, leaving the expected unit for the result.

---

6. You have been driving for several hours and notice that your car's 13.2-gallon fuel tank registers half empty. How many more miles can you travel if your car is averaging 55 miles per gallon?

Unit Conversion

In many countries, distance is measured in kilometers (km) and gasoline in liters. A mile is equivalent to 1.609 kilometers, and a liter is equivalent to 0.264 gallons. Each of these equivalences can be treated as a rate and written in fraction form. Thus, the fact that a mile is equivalent to 1.609 kilometers is written as $\frac{1.609 \text{ km}}{1 \text{ mile}}$ or $\frac{1 \text{ mile}}{1.609 \text{ km}}$. Using the fraction form, you can convert one measurement unit to another by applying multiplication or division directly, or you can use a proportion.

7. Your friend joins you on a trip through Canada, where gasoline is measured in liters and distance in kilometers.

   a. Write the equivalence of liters and gallons in fraction form.

   b. If you bought 20 liters of gas, how many gallons did you buy?

8. To keep track of mileage and fuel needs in Canada, your friend suggests that you convert your car's miles per gallon into kilometers per liter. Your car's highway fuel efficiency is 45 miles per gallon. What is its fuel efficiency in kilometers per liter?

SUMMARY
Activity 1.5

1. A **rate** is a comparison, expressed as a quotient, of two quantities that have different units of measurement.

2. **Unit analysis** (sometimes called *dimensional analysis*) uses units of measurement as a guide in setting up a calculation or writing an equation involving one or more rates. When the calculation or equation is set up properly, the result is an answer with the appropriate units of measurement.

3. Two common methods to solve problems involving rates:

   Direct Method: Multiply or divide directly by rates to solve problems:

   1. Identify the measurement unit of the result.

   2. Set up the calculation so that the appropriate measurement units will divide out, leaving the unit of the result.

   3. Multiply or divide the numbers as usual to obtain the numerical part of the result.

   4. Divide out the common measurement units to obtain the unit of the answer.

Proportion Method: Set up and solve a proportion

1. Identify the known rate, and write it in fractional form.

2. Identify the given information and the unknown quantity to be determined.

3. Write a second fraction, placing the given information and unknown quantity x in the same position as the measurement units in the known rate.

4. Equate the two fractions to obtain a proportion.

5. Solve the equation for x, affixing the correct unit to the numerical result.

4. Applying several rates consecutively:

1. Identify the measurement unit of the result.

2. Set up the sequence of multiplications so the appropriate measurement units divide out, leaving the unit of the result.

3. Multiply and divide the numbers as usual to obtain the numerical part of the result.

4. Check that the appropriate measurement units divide out, leaving the expected unit of the result.

EXERCISES
Activity 1.5

Appendix

Use the conversion tables in Appendix B of this textbook for conversion equivalencies.

1. The length of a football playing field is 100 yards between the opposing goal lines. What is the length of the football field in feet?

2. The distance between New York City, New York, and Los Angeles, California, is approximately 4485 kilometers. What is the distance between these two major cities in miles?

3. The aorta is the largest artery in the human body. In the average adult, the aorta attains a maximum diameter of about 1.18 inches where it adjoins the heart. What is the maximum diameter of the aorta in centimeters? In millimeters?

4. In the Himalaya Mountains along the border of Tibet and Nepal, Mount Everest reaches a record height of 29,035 feet. How high is Mt. Everest in miles? In kilometers? In meters?

5. The average weight of a mature human brain is approximately 1400 grams. What is the equivalent weight in kilograms? In pounds?

6. Approximately 4.5 liters of blood circulates in the body of the average human adult. How many quarts of blood does the average person have? How many pints?

7. How many seconds are in a day? In a week? In a year?

8. The following places are three of the wettest locations on Earth. For each site, determine the rainfall in centimeters per year. Record your results in the third column of the table.

Looks Like Rain

LOCATIONS	ANNUAL RAINFALL (IN INCHES)	ANNUAL RAINFALL (IN cm)
Mawsynram, Meghalaya, India	467	
Tutenendo, Colombia	463.5	
Mt. Waialeale, Kauai, Hawaii	410	

9. Jewelry is commonly weighed in carats. Five carats is equivalent to one gram. How many grams of gold are contained in a 24-carat gold chain? How many ounces?

10. Tissues of living organisms consist primarily of organic compounds; that is, they contain carbon molecules known as proteins, carbohydrates, and fats. A healthy human body is approximately 18% carbon by weight. Determine how many pounds of carbon your own body contains. How many kilograms?

Activities 1.1–1.5   What Have I Learned?

Activities 1.1 through 1.5 gave you an opportunity to develop some problem-solving strategies. Apply the skills you used in this section to solve the following problems:

1. Your last class for the day is over! As you grab a water bottle and settle down to read a chapter of text for tomorrow's class, you notice a group of students forming a circle outside and beginning to randomly kick an odd-looking ball from person to person. You notice that there are 12 students in the circle and that they are able to keep the object in the air as they kick it. Sometimes they kick it to the person next to them; other times they kick it to someone across the circle.

    a. Suppose each student kicks the Hacky-Sack (you've discovered the odd-looking ball has a name) exactly once to each of the others in the circle. How many total kicks would that take? Explain your method.

    b. One student in the circle invites you and another student to join them for a total of 14. How many kicks would it now take if each student kicks the Hacky-Sack exactly once to each of the others? How do you arrive at your answer?

    c. George Polya's book, *How to Solve It,* outlines a four-step process for solving problems.

        i.   Understand the problem (determine what is involved).

        ii. Devise a plan (look for connections to obtain the idea of a solution).

        iii. Carry out the plan.

        iv. Look back at the completed solution (review and discuss it).

        Describe how your procedures in parts a and b correspond with Polya's suggestions.

2. You are assigned to read *War and Peace* for your literature class. The edition you have contains 1232 pages. You time yourself and estimate that you can read 12 pages in one hour. You have five days before your exam on this book. Will you be able to finish reading it before the exam?

3. On a 40-question practice test for this course, you answered 32 questions correctly. On the test itself, you correctly answered 16 out of 20 questions. Does this mean that you did better on the practice test than you did on the test itself? Explain.

4. In the 2000 U.S. Census, Florida's total population was 15,982,378 persons and 183 out of every 1000 residents were 65 years and older. Show how you would determine the actual number of Florida residents who were 65 years or older in 2000.

5. Submit two articles from a newspaper, magazine, or the Internet, in which ratios and proportions are used. Write a brief summary explaining how the ratios and proportions are used in each article.

Activities 1.1–1.5 **How Can I Practice?**

1. Solve the following problem by applying the four steps of problem solving given in Activity 1.3. Use the strategy for solving an algebraic equation.

   Your average reading speed is 160 words per minute. There are approximately 800 words on each page of the textbook you need to read. Approximately how long will it take you to read 50 pages of your textbook?

2. You need to buy grass seed for a new lawn. The lawn will cover a rectangular plot that is 60 feet by 90 feet. Each ounce of grass seed will cover 120 square feet.

   a. How many ounces of grass seed will you need to buy?

   b. If the grass seed you want only comes in one-pound bags, how many bags will you need to buy?

3. Translate each statement into a formula.

   a. The total weekly earnings equal $12 per hour times the number of hours worked.

   b. The total time traveled equals the distance traveled divided by the average speed.

   c. The distance between two cities, measured in feet, is equal to the distance measured in miles times 5280 feet per mile.

4. Use your formulas in Exercise 3 to answer the following questions.

   a. If you make $12 per hour, what will your earnings be in a week when you work 35 hours?

   b. If you earned $336 last week (still assuming $12 per hour), how many hours did you work?

   c. If you travel 480 miles at an average speed of 40 miles per hour, for how many hours were you traveling?

   d. The distance between Dallas and Houston is 244 miles. How far is the distance in feet?

5. What will the temperature be in degrees Fahrenheit when it is 40° Celsius outside? Use the formula $F = (9C \div 5) + 32$.

6. Solve the following proportions.

   a. 3 out of 5 = _____ out of 20   **b.** $\frac{3}{5} = \frac{n}{765}$

   c. $\frac{3}{5} = \frac{27}{n}$ **d.** $\frac{3}{5} = \frac{1134}{n}$

In Exercises 7–15, write a proportion that represents the situation and then determine the unknown value in the proportion.

7. You correctly answered two-thirds of the questions on your history exam. There were 75 questions on the exam. How many questions did you answer correctly?

8. During a recent infestation by beetles, $\frac{2}{3}$ of the ash trees in a local park were destroyed. If 120 trees were destroyed, how many ash trees were originally in the park?

9. Your high school freshman class consists of 760 students. In recent years, only 4 out of 7 students actually graduated in four years. Approximately how many of your classmates are expected to graduate in four years?

10. Your car averages 380 miles on a 14-gallon tank of gas. You run out of gas on a deserted highway, but you have $\frac{1}{2}$ gallon of lawn mower gas with you. Will you be able to reach the nearest gas station 15 miles away?

11. As part of your job as a quality-control inspector in a factory you can check 16 parts in 3 minutes. How long will it take you to check 80 parts?

12. Your car averages about 27 miles per gallon on highways. With gasoline priced at \$2.599 per gallon, how much will you expect to spend on gasoline during your 500-mile trip?

13. You currently earn \$11.50 per hour. Assuming that you work 40-hour weeks with no raises, what total gross salary will you earn in the next five years?

14. You are traveling at 75 miles per hour on a straight stretch of highway in Nevada. It is noon now. When will you arrive at the next town 120 miles away?

15. To estimate the size of the grizzly bear population in a national park, rangers tagged and released 12 grizzly bears into the park. A few months later, 2 out of 21 grizzly bears sighted were tagged. Assuming the proportion of tagged bears in the population, estimate the number of grizzly bears in the population of this national park.

ACTIVITY 1.6
Florida Heat

OBJECTIVES

1. Identify input and output in situations involving two variable quantities.

2. Identify a functional relationship between two variables.

3. Identify the independent and dependent variables.

4. Use a table to numerically represent a functional relationship between two variables.

5. Represent a functional relationship between two variables graphically.

6. Identify trends in data pairs that are represented numerically and graphically, including increasing and decreasing.

A key step in the problem-solving process is to look for relationships and connections between the variable quantities in a given situation. Problems encountered in the world around us, including the environment, medicine, economics, and the Internet, are often very complicated and contain several variables. In this text, you will primarily deal with situations that contain two variables. In many of these situations, the variables will have a special relationship called a **function**.

Function

It is July, and you have just moved to Tallahassee, Florida. The area is in the middle of a heat spell. The high temperature for each of the last 5 days has exceeded 100°F. You are curious about the temperatures you will experience while living in Florida. You discover that the National Weather Service has calculated the average monthly high temperatures in Tallahassee over the period from 1971 to 2000. This information is shown in the following table. Note that January is represented by 1, February is represented by 2, and so forth.

MONTH OF THE YEAR	1	2	3	4	5	6	7	8	9	10	11	12
AVERAGE MONTHLY HIGH TEMPERATURE, °F	56.8	63.0	70.9	78.8	86.8	92.7	94.3	92.8	86.1	77.4	65.9	58.4

Source: The Weather Channel

This situation involves two variables, the month and the average monthly high temperature. Typically, one variable is designated as the **input** and the other is called the **output**. The input is the value given first, and the output is the value that corresponds to, or is determined by, the given input value. The input variable is often represented by the letter x. The output variable is frequently represented by the letter y.

1. In the temperature situation, identify the input variable and the output variable.

2. **a.** For an input of 7 (July), what is the average high temperature (output)?

b. For an input of 1 (January), what is the average high temperature (output)?

c. For each value of input (month), how many different outputs (average high temperature) are there?

The set of data in the table is an example of a **mathematical function**.

> **DEFINITION**
> A **function** is a correspondence between an input variable and an output variable that assigns a single, unique output value to each input value. Therefore, for a function, any given input value has exactly one corresponding output value. If x represents the input variable and y represents the output variable, then the function assigns a single, unique y-value to each x-value.

3. Explain how the data in the previous table fit the description of a function.

A functional relationship is stated as follows: "The output variable is a function of the input variable." Using x for the input variable and y for the output variable, then the functional relationship is stated "y is a function of x." Because the input for the temperature function is the month and the output is the average high temperature for that month, you write that the average high temperature is a function of the month.

Example 1 *Consider the following table listing the official high temperature (in °F) in the village of Lake Placid, New York, during the first week of January. Note that the date has been designated the input and the high temperature on that date the output. Is the high temperature a function of the date?*

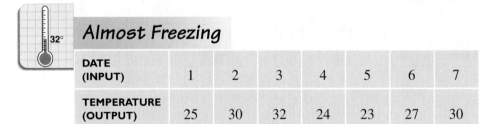

Almost Freezing

DATE (INPUT)	1	2	3	4	5	6	7
TEMPERATURE (OUTPUT)	25	30	32	24	23	27	30

SOLUTION

From this table, you observe that the high temperature is a function of the date. For each date there is exactly one high temperature. The relationship in this example can be visualized as follows:

DATE (INPUT)	TEMPERATURE (OUTPUT)
1 ⟶	25
2 ⟶	30
3 ⟶	32
4 ⟶	24
5 ⟶	23
6 ⟶	27
7 ⟶	30

If d represents the input (date) and T represents the output (temperature), then T is a function of d.

Example 2   *Determine if the amount of postage for a letter is a function of the weight of the letter. Give a reason for your answer.*

SOLUTION

Yes, the situation does describe a function. The weight of the letter is the input and the amount of postage is the output. Each letter has one weight. This weight determines the postage necessary for the letter. There is only one amount of postage for each letter. Therefore, for each value of input (weight of the letter) there is one output (postage). Note that if w represents the input (weight of the letter) and p represents the output (postage), then p is a function of w.

4. Determine whether or not each situation describes a function. Give a reason for your answer.

    a. The amount of property tax you have to pay is a function of the assessed value of the house.

    b. The weight of a letter in ounces is a function of the postage paid for mailing the letter.

> DEFINITION
>
> For all functions, the input variable is called the **independent** variable and the output variable is called the **dependent** variable. If x represents the input variable and y represents the output variable, then x is the independent variable and y is the dependent variable.

5. The independent variable in Example 1 is the date. The dependent variable is the temperature. Identify the independent and dependent variables in Example 2.

Representing Functions Numerically

The input/output pairing in the temperature function on page 44 is presented as a **table of matched pairs**. In such a situation, the function is defined **numerically**. Another way to define a function numerically is as a set of **ordered pairs**.

> DEFINITION
>
> An **ordered pair** of numbers consists of two numbers written in the form
>
> $$(x, y),$$
>
> where x represents the independent variable and y represents the dependent variable. The order in which they are listed *is* significant.

> Example 3 *The ordered pair (3, 4) is distinct from the ordered pair (4, 3). In the ordered pair (3, 4), 3 is the x-value and 4 is the y-value. In the ordered pair (4, 3), 4 is the x-value and 3 is the y-value.*

DEFINITION

A function may be defined **numerically** as a set of ordered pairs (x, y), where x represents the input and y represents the output. No two ordered pairs have the same x-value and different y-values.

---

6. Write three other ordered pairs for the Florida temperature function.

Representing Functions Graphically

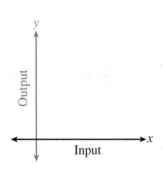

You may have seen an ordered pair before as the coordinates of a point in a **rectangular coordinate system**, typically using ordered pairs of the form (x, y), where x is the input (independent variable) and y is the output (dependent variable). The first value, the horizontal coordinate, indicates the directed distance (right or left) from the vertical axis. The second value, the vertical coordinate, indicates the directed distance (up or down) from the horizontal axis.

The variables may not always be represented by x and y, but the horizontal axis will always be the input axis and the vertical axis will always be the output axis.

7. Plot each ordered pair in the Florida temperature table on the following grid. Set your axes and scales by noting the smallest and largest values for both input and output. Label each axis by the variable name. *Remember, the scale for the horizontal axis does not have to be the same as the scale for the vertical axis. However, each scale (vertical and horizontal) must be divided into equal intervals.*

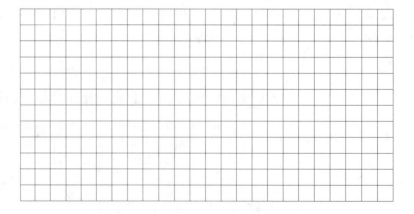

The preceding graph, which consists of a set of labeled axes and 12 points, presents the same information that is in the Florida temperature table on page 43, but in a different way. It shows the information as a graph and therefore defines the function **graphically**.

8. In Example 1, the high temperature in Lake Placid is a function of the date.

   a. Convert to ordered pairs all the values in the Almost Freezing table on page 44.

   b. Plot each ordered pair as a point on an appropriately scaled and labeled set of coordinate axes.

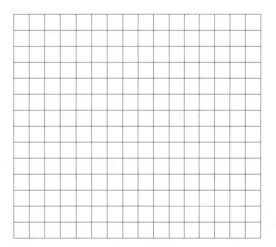

More Graphing

Living on Earth's surface, you experience a relatively narrow range of temperatures. You may know what $-20°F$ (or $-28.9°C$) feels like on a bitterly cold winter day. Or you may have sweated through $100°F$ (or $37.8°C$) during summer heatwaves. If you were to travel below Earth's surface and above Earth's atmosphere, you would discover a wider range of temperatures. The following graph displays a relationship between the altitude and temperature. Note that the altitude is measured from Earth's surface. That is, Earth's surface is at altitude 0.

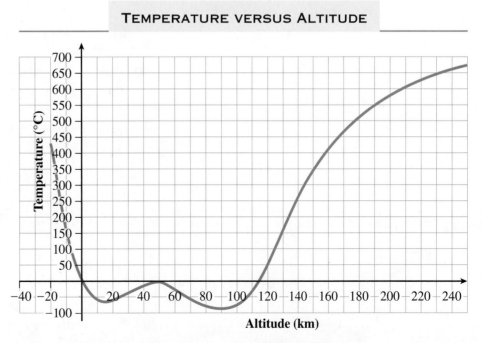

TEMPERATURE VERSUS ALTITUDE

Use this graph to answer Problem 9.

9. a. With what variable and units of measure is the horizontal axis labeled?

b. What is the practical significance of the positive values of this quantity?

c. What is the practical significance of the negative values of this quantity?

d. How many kilometers are represented between the tick marks on the horizontal axis?

10. a. With what variable and units of measure is the vertical axis labeled?

b. What is the practical significance of the positive values of this quantity?

c. What is the practical significance of the negative values of this quantity?

d. How many degrees Celsius are represented between the tick marks on the vertical axis?

Recall, the two perpendicular coordinate axes divide the plane into four **quadrants**. The quadrants are labeled counterclockwise, using Roman numerals, with quadrant I being the upper-right quadrant.

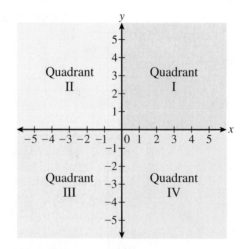

11. The following graph displays eight points selected from the Temperature versus Altitude graph on page 47.

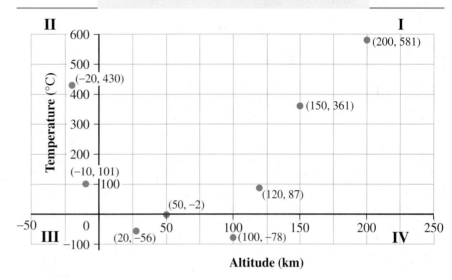

a. What is the practical meaning of the point with coordinates (150, 361)?

b. What is the practical meaning of the point with coordinates (100, −78)?

c. What is the practical meaning of the point with coordinates (−20, 430)?

d. In which quadrant are the points (120, 87), (150, 361), and (200, 581) located?

e. In which quadrant are the points (−10, 101) and (−20, 430) located?

f. In which quadrant are the points (20, −56) and (100, −78) located?

g. Are there any points located in quadrant III? What is the significance of your answer?

Increasing and Decreasing Functions

There are many other advantages to having the function in graphical form. For example, you are often interested in determining how the output values change as the input values increase.

> **DEFINITION**
>
> A function is **increasing** if its graph goes up to the right, **decreasing** if its graph goes down to the right, and **constant** if its graph is horizontal. In each case, you are viewing the graph as a point moves along the curve from left to right, that is, as the input values increase.

Example 4

   a. The graph of this function is always increasing. The graph rises from left to right.

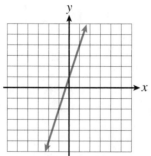

   b. The graph of this function is decreasing because its graph falls from left to right.

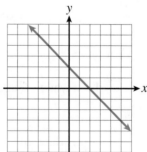

   c. The graph of this function is constant, because the graph goes neither up nor down. The y-value is always 3 no matter what the x-value is.

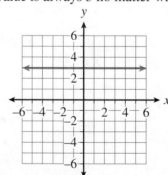

12. Is the following function increasing, decreasing, or constant over the domain displayed in the window?

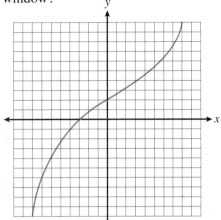

---

1. A **variable**, usually represented by a letter, is a quantity that may change in value from one particular instance to another.

2. In a situation involving two variables, one variable is designated the **input** and the other the **output**. The input is the value given first, and the output is the value that corresponds to or is determined by the given input value.

3. A **function** is a correspondence relating an input variable (*independent variable*) and an output variable (*dependent variable*) so that a single, unique output value is assigned to each input value. In such a case, you state that the output variable is a function of the input variable.

4. An **ordered pair** of numbers consists of two numbers written in the form

(*input value*, *output value*).

The order in which they are listed *is* significant.

5. Functions may be defined **numerically** using ordered pairs of numbers. The ordered pairs are always given in the form (input value, output value). These can be displayed as a table of values or points on a graph. For each input value, there is one and only one corresponding output value.

6. When a function is represented **graphically**, the *x* and *y* data pairs are represented as plotted points on a grid called a *rectangular coordinate system*. The *x*-variable is referenced on the horizontal axis. The *y*-variable is referenced on the vertical axis.

7. The two perpendicular coordinate axes divide the plane into four **quadrants**. The quadrants are labeled counterclockwise, using Roman numerals, with quadrant I being the upper-right quadrant.

8. A function is **increasing** if its graph rises to the right, **decreasing** if its graph falls to the right, and **constant** if its graph is horizontal.

1. The weights and heights of six mathematics students are given in the following table:

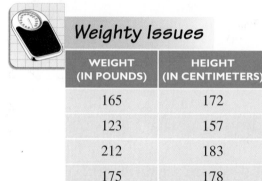

Weighty Issues

WEIGHT (IN POUNDS)	HEIGHT (IN CENTIMETERS)
165	172
123	157
212	183
175	178
165	163
147	167

   a. In the statement "Height is a function of weight," which variable is the input and which is the output?

   b. Is height a function of weight for the six students? Explain using the definition of function.

   c. In the statement "Weight is a function of height," which variable is the input and which is the output?

   d. Is weight a function of height for the six students? Explain using the definition of function.

   e. For all students, is weight a function of height? Explain.

For Exercises 2–7, determine whether or not each of the situations describes a function. Give a reason for your answer. For each functional relationship, determine the independent and dependent variables.

2. **a.** The amount of federal income tax you pay is a function of your taxable income.

b. The value of your car is a function of the total mileage on the car.

3. a. The letter grade in this class is a function of your numerical grade.

b. The numerical grade in this class is a function of the letter grade.

4. a. The input is any number and the output is the square of the number.

b. The square of a number is the input and the output is the number.

5. In the following table, elevation is the input and amount of snowfall is the output.

ELEVATION (IN FEET)	SNOWFALL (IN INCHES)
2000	4
3000	6
4000	9
5000	12

6. Number of hours using the Internet is the input variable, and the monthly cost for the Internet service is $19.95, regardless of the number of hours of usage.

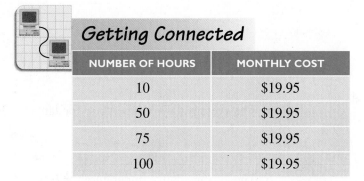

Getting Connected

NUMBER OF HOURS	MONTHLY COST
10	$19.95
50	$19.95
75	$19.95
100	$19.95

7. Each of the following tables defines a relationship between an input x and an output y. Which of the relationships represent functions? Explain your answers.

a.

x	−8	−3	0	6	9	15	24	38	100
y	24	4	9	72	−14	−16	53	29	7

b.

x	−8	−5	0	6	9	15	24	24	100
y	24	4	9	72	14	−16	53	29	7

c.

x	−8	−3	0	6	9	15	24	38	100
y	24	4	9	72	4	−16	53	24	7

8. You work for the National Weather Service and are asked to study the average daily temperatures in Anchorage, Alaska. You calculate the mean of the average daily temperatures for each month. You decide to place the information on a graph in which the date is the input and the temperature is the output. You also decide that January 1950 will correspond to the month 0 as indicated by the dot on the input scale. Determine the quadrant in which you would plot the points that correspond to the following data.

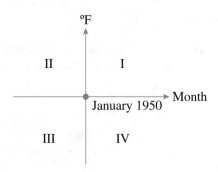

a. The average daily temperature for January 1936 was −15°F.

b. The average daily temperature for July 1963 was 63°F.

c. The average daily temperature for July 1910 was 71°F.

d. The average daily temperature for January 1982 was –21°F.

9. Measurements in wells and mines have shown that the temperatures within the earth generally increase with depth. The following table shows average temperatures for several depths below sea level.

A Hot Topic

DEPTH (km) BELOW SEA LEVEL	0	25	50	75	100	150	200
TEMPERATURE (°C)	20	600	1000	1250	1400	1700	1800

a. Represent the data from the table graphically on the grid following part d. Place depth along the horizontal axis and temperature along the vertical axis.

b. How many units does each tick mark on the horizontal axis represent?

c. How many units does each tick mark on the vertical axis represent?

d. Explain your reasons for selecting the particular scales that you used.

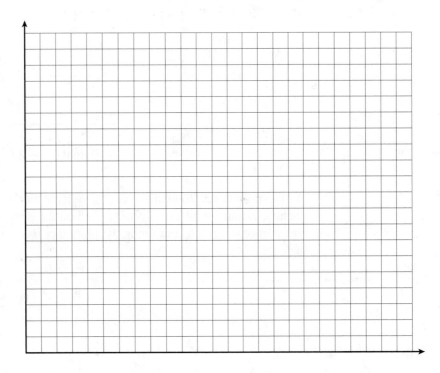

e. Which representation (table or graph) presents the information and trends in this data more clearly? Explain your choice.

10. The following table presents the average recommended weights for given heights for 25- to 29-year-old medium-framed women (wearing 1-inch heels and 3 pounds of clothing). Consider height to be the input variable and weight to be the output variable. As ordered pairs, height and weight take on the form (h, w). Designate the horizontal (input) axis as the h-axis and the vertical (output) axis as the w-axis. Since all values of the data are positive, the points will lie in quadrant I only.

h, HEIGHT (in.)	58	60	62	64	66	68	70	72
w, WEIGHT (lb)	115	119	125	131	137	143	149	155

Plot the ordered pairs in the height–weight table on the following grid. Note the consistent spacing between tick marks on each axis. The distance between tick marks on the horizontal axis represents 2 inches. On the vertical axis the distance between tick marks represents 5 pounds.

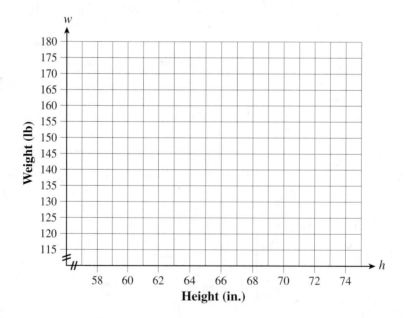

Note: The slash marks (//) near the origin indicate that the interval from 0 to 56 on the horizontal axis and the interval from 0 to 115 on the vertical axis are not shown. That is, only the part of the graph containing the plotted points is shown.

ACTIVITY 1.7
Fill 'er Up

OBJECTIVES

1. Write the equation to define a function.

2. Determine the domain and range of a function.

3. Identify the independent and the dependent variables of a function.

You probably need to fill your car with gas more often than you would like, so you drive around looking for the best price per gallon.

1. There are two variables that determine the cost of a fill-up. What are they? Be specific.

2. The cost of a gallon of gas has fluctuated greatly over recent years. For the purpose of this activity, suppose the local gas station is selling gas at a price of $2.47 $\frac{9}{10}$ per gallon. Now one of the variables in Problem 1 will become a constant. The value of a constant will not vary throughout the problem. The cost of a fill-up is now dependent on only one variable, the number of gallons of gas pumped.

   a. Complete the following table:

NUMBER OF GALLONS	5	8	10	14
COST OF FILL-UP				

   b. Is the cost of a fill-up a function of the number of gallons pumped? Explain.

   c. Identify the independent and dependent variables.

3. **a.** Write a statement that describes how the cost of a fill-up is determined.

   b. Let g represent the number of gallons of gasoline pumped and c represent the cost of the fill-up. Translate the verbal statement (a relationship between variables stated in words) in part a into a symbolic statement (an equation) that expresses c in terms of g.

Defining Functions by a Symbolic Rule (Equation)

The symbolic rule (equation) $c = 2.479g$ represents the third method of defining a function. Recall that the other two methods are numerically (tables and ordered pairs) and graphically.

4. **a.** Use the given equation to determine the cost of a fill-up that required 8 gallons of gas.

   b. Explain the steps that you used to determine the cost in part a.

Function notation is an efficient and convenient way of representing the dependent variable. The equation $c = 2.479g$ may be written using the function notation by replacing the dependent variable c with $f(g)$ as follows:

$$f(g) = 2.479g, \text{ where } c = f(g)$$

The letter f in the notation $f(g)$ represents the name of the function. The letter within the parentheses always represents the independent variable. The notation $f(g)$ is simply another way of representing the dependent variable c. Remember,

$$c = f(g) = 2.479g.$$

Now, the cost of 5 gallons of gas can be represented by $f(5)$. To evaluate $f(5)$, substitute 5 for g in $f(g) = 2.479g$ as follows:

$$f(5) = 2.479(5) = 12.395$$

The results can be written as $f(5) = 12.395$ or as the ordered pair $(5, 12.395)$. Therefore, 5 gallons of gas will cost \$12.40 (rounded to the nearest cent).

5. a. Write the cost of 8 gallons of gas using function notation and evaluate. Write the result as an ordered pair.

b. Use the equation for the cost-of-fill-up function to evaluate $f(12)$, and write a sentence describing its meaning. Write the result as an ordered pair.

Real Numbers

The numbers that you will be using as input and output values in this text will be real numbers. A **real number** is any rational or irrational number.

A rational number is any number that can be expressed as the quotient of two integers (negative and positive counting numbers as well as zero).

Example 1   *Rational numbers include the following:*

$$\frac{3}{4} \quad -\frac{7}{8} \quad 2\frac{1}{3} = \frac{7}{3} \quad 5 = \frac{5}{1} \quad 0 = \frac{0}{1} \quad -3\frac{1}{4} = -3.25 \quad \frac{2}{3} = 0.666\ldots = 0.\overline{6}$$

An irrational number is a real number that cannot be expressed as a quotient of two integers.

Example 2   *Irrational numbers include* $\sqrt{2}, -\sqrt{7}, \sqrt[3]{5}, \pi$.

All of the numbers in Examples 1 and 2 are real numbers. A real number can be represented as a point on the number line.

Domain and Range

6. Can any real number be substituted for the variable g in the cost of fill-up function? Describe the values of g that make sense and explain why they do.

> **DEFINITION**
>
> The collection of all possible values of the independent variable is called the **domain** of the function. The **practical domain** is the collection of replacement values of the independent variable that makes practical sense in the context of the problem.

Example 3   *The practical domain in Problem 6 is the real numbers 0 through 20, assuming that 20 gallons is the maximum capacity of your gas tank. The value of g would be 0 if your gas tank is totally full and 20 if your gas tank is totally empty.*

Following is the graph of the cost-of-fill-up function defined by $c = 2.479g$ over its practical domain.

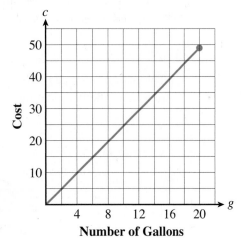

Number of Gallons

The domain for the general function defined by $c = 2.479g$, with no connection to the context of the problem, is the set of all real numbers, since any real number can be substituted for g in $2.479g$. Following is a graph of $c = 2.479g$ for any real number g.

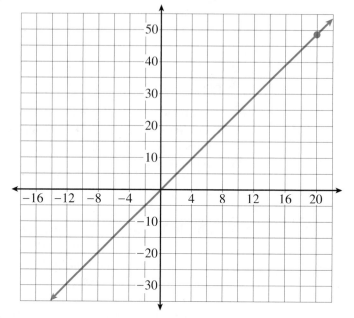

When a value from the domain is substituted for the independent variable and the corresponding output is evaluated, the result is a value of the dependent variable.

DEFINITION

The collection of all possible values of the dependent variable is the **range** of the function. The practical range corresponds to the practical domain.

Example 4   *Consider the following table that gives the percentage of mothers in the workforce with children under the age of 6 from 1999 to 2004.*

YEAR	PERCENTAGE
1999	64.4
2000	65.3
2001	64.4
2002	64.1
2003	62.9
2004	62.2

Source: U.S. Department of Labor

Although the table contains only six pairs of numbers, it represents a function. The input or independent variable is the year, and the output or dependent variable is the percentage. The domain of the function is {1999, 2000, 2001, 2002, 2003, 2004} because these are all the input values. The range of the function is {62.2, 62.9, 64.1, 64.4, 65.3} because this is the set of all of the output values. Note that although 64.4 occurs twice in the table as an output value, it is listed only once in the range.

7. a. What is the practical range for the cost function defined by $f(g) = 2.479g$ if the practical domain is 0 to 20?

b. What is the range of this function if it has no connection to the context of the problem?

8. Use the form of the gas cost of fill-up function, $f(g) = 2.479g$, to evaluate $f(0), f(5), f(10), f(15)$, and $f(20)$, and complete the following table. Note that the variable g increases by 5 units. In such a case, you say that g increases by an **increment** of 5 units.

NUMBER OF GALLONS OF GAS NEEDED, g	COST OF FILL-UP, $f(g)$
0	
5	
10	
15	
20	

A numerical form of the cost of fill-up function is a table or a collection of ordered pairs. When a function is defined using an equation, you can use technology to generate the table. The TI-83/84 Plus calculator is a function grapher. The y variables Y_1, Y_2, and so on represent function output (dependent) variables. The input, or independent variable, is represented by x. The steps to build tables with the TI-83/84 Plus can be found in Appendix A.

Appendix

9. Use your graphing calculator to generate a table of values for the function represented by $f(g) = 2.479g$ to check your values in the table in Problem 8. The screens on your calculator should appear as follows:

 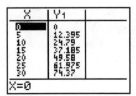

Gross Pay Function

10. If you work for an hourly wage, your gross pay is a function of the number of hours that you work.

a. What is the independent variable? What is the dependent variable?

b. If you earn $8 per hour, complete the following table:

NUMBER OF HOURS	0	3	5	7	10	12
GROSS PAY						

c. Plot the ordered pairs determined in part b on an appropriately scaled and labeled set of axes.

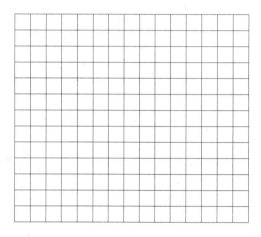

d. Let n represent the number of hours worked and $f(n)$ represent the gross pay. Write an equation for $f(n)$ in terms of n.

e. Evaluate $f(10)$ and write a sentence explaining the meaning of $f(10)$.

f. What are the practical domain and the practical range of the function? Explain.

SUMMARY
Activity 1.7

1. **Independent variable** is another name for the input variable of a function.

2. **Dependent variable** is another name for the output variable of a function.

3. The collection of all possible replacement values for the independent variable is called the **domain of the function.** The **practical domain** is the collection of replacement values of the independent variable that makes practical sense in the context of the problem.

4. The collection of all values of the dependent variable of a function is called the **range of the function.** When a function describes a real situation or phenomenon, its range is often called the **practical range** of the function.

5. When a function is represented by an equation, the function may also be written in **function notation.** For example, given $y = 2x + 3$, you can replace y with $f(x)$ and rewrite the equation as $f(x) = 2x + 3$.

In Exercises 1 and 2,

a. *Identify the independent and dependent variables.*

b. *Let x represent the independent variable. Use function notation to represent the dependent variable.*

c. *Translate the written statement into an equation.*

1. Sales tax is a function of the price of an item. The amount of sales tax is 0.08 times the price of the item. Use h to represent the function.

2. The Fahrenheit measure of temperature is a function of the Celsius measure. The Fahrenheit measure is 32 more than 9/5 times the Celsius measure. Use g to represent the function.

For each function in Exercises 3–5, evaluate $f(2), f(-3.2),$ and $f(a)$.

3. $f(d) = 2d - 5$

4. $f(t) = -16t^2 + 7.8t + 12$

5. $f(x) = 4$

In Exercises 6–8, construct a table of values of four ordered pairs for the given function. Check your results using the table feature of your graphing calculator.

6. $g(x) = x^2$. Start the independent variable x at 3 and use an increment of 2.

x	g(x)

7. $h(x) = \dfrac{1}{x}$. Start the x-values at 10 and use an increment of 10.

x	h(x)

8. $f(x) = 3.5x + 6$. Start the x-values at 0 and use an increment of 5.

x	f(x)

9. a. The distance you travel while hiking is a function of how fast you hike and how long you hike at this rate. You usually maintain a speed of three miles per hour while hiking. Write a statement that describes how the distance that you travel is determined.

b. Identify the independent and dependent variables of this function.

c. Write the statement in part a using function notation. Let t represent the independent variable. Let h represent the function, and $h(t)$ the dependent variable.

d. Use the equation from part c to determine the distance traveled in four hours.

e. Evaluate $h(7)$ and write a sentence describing its meaning. Write the result as an ordered pair.

f. Determine the domain and range of the general function.

g. Determine the practical domain and the practical range of the function.

h. Use your calculator to generate a table of values beginning at zero with an increment of 0.5.

x	g(x)

10. Determine the domain and range of each function.

a. $\{(-2, 4), (0, 3), (5, 8), (8, 11)\}$

b. $\{(-6, 5), (-2, 5), (0, 5), (3, 5)\}$

11. According to the AAA, it costs approximately $0.689 per mile to own and operate a car. The total cost is a function of the number of miles driven and can be represented by the function defined by $C = 0.689m$. When you finally take your car to the junk-yard, the odometer reads 157,200 miles.

a. Identify the input variable.

b. Identify the output variable.

c. Use f to represent the function and rewrite $C = 0.689m$ using function notation.

d. Evaluate $f(10,000)$ and write a sentence describing its meaning. Write the result as an ordered pair.

e. Use the table feature of your calculator to create a table of values with a beginning input of 0. Use increments of 50,000 miles.

f. What is the practical domain for this situation?

g. What is the practical range for this situation?

12. To change a Celsius temperature to Fahrenheit, use the formula $F = 1.8C + 32$. You are concerned only with temperatures between freezing and boiling.

a. What is the practical domain of the function?

b. What is the practical range of the function?

13. Your high school service organization has volunteered to help with Spring Cleanup Day at a youth summer camp. You have been assigned the job of supplying paint for the exterior of the bunkhouses. You discover that 1 gallon of paint will cover 400 square feet of flat surface.

a. If n represents the number of gallons of paint you supply and s represents the number of square feet you can cover with the paint, complete the following table:

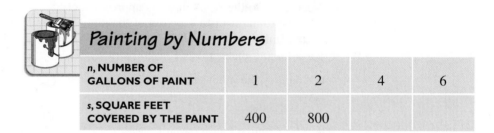

Painting by Numbers

n, NUMBER OF GALLONS OF PAINT	1	2	4	6
s, SQUARE FEET COVERED BY THE PAINT	400	800		

b. Let n be the independent variable and s be the dependent variable. Plot the ordered pairs determined in part a on an appropriately scaled and labeled set of axes.

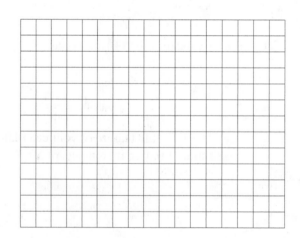

   c. Let *s* be represented by $f(n)$, where *f* is the name of the function. Determine $f(6)$.

   d. Write a sentence explaining the meaning of $f(4) = 1600$.

14. Give an example of a function that you may encounter in your daily life or that describes something about the world around you.

   a. Identify the independent and the dependent variables.

   b. Write the function in the form "output is a function of the input."

   c. Explain how the example fits the definition of a function.

ACTIVITY 1.8
Mathematical
Modeling

OBJECTIVES

1. Identify a mathematical model.

2. Solve problems using formulas as models.

3. Develop a function model to solve a problem.

4. Recognize patterns and trends between two variables using tables as models.

After an automobile accident, the investigating police officers often estimate the speed of the vehicle by measuring the length of the tire skid distance. The following table gives the average skid distances for an automobile with good tires on dry pavement.

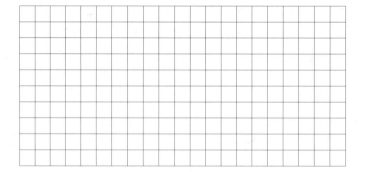

The Long and Short of It

SKID DISTANCE (FEET)	SPEED (MPH)
28	25
54	35
89	45
132	55
184	65
244	75
313	85
390	95

1. Does the table data define speed as a function of skid distance? Explain using the definition of function.

2. Identify the independent variable and the dependent variable.

3. Plot the data as ordered pairs on an appropriately scaled and labeled set of coordinate axes. Remember, the values of the independent variable appear along the horizontal axis, and the values of the dependent variable appear along the vertical axis.

After a particular accident, a skid distance was measured to be 200 feet. From the table, the investigating officer knows that the speed of the vehicle was between 65 and 75 miles per hour. She would, however, like to be able to be more precise in reporting the speed. One way of getting values that are not listed in the table is to use a graph or equation of a function that best fits the actual data.

Note that the points on the graph in Problem 3 do not appear to lie exactly on a specific curve. However, calculators use a special mathematical process to produce an equation that best fits actual data. From the data in the table, The Long and Short of It, the TI-83/84 Plus can be used to generate the following equation:

$$y = -0.00029x^2 + 0.31x + 18.6 \text{ (coefficients are rounded), (eq. 1)}$$

where x represents the skid distance in feet and y represents the speed in miles per hour. The process for generating such equations is covered in later activities.

Appendix

4. a. Enter the function equation above into your calculator. For help with the TI-83/84 Plus, see Appendix A. The screen should appear as follows:

b. The values in the table, The Long and Short of It, can help to set appropriate window values in your calculator to view the graph. Starting at a minimum skid distance of 0, a reasonable maximum value of the skid distance in this situation would be 450 feet. Beginning at a minimum speed of 0, a reasonable maximum speed value would be 100 mph. Using these settings, the window screen should appear as follows:

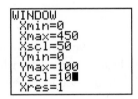

c. Display your graph using the window settings from part b. Your graph should resemble the following:

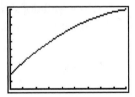

5. a. By pressing the trace button and the left and right arrow keys, you can display the x-y values of points on the graph on the bottom of the display. Use the trace feature of your calculator to approximate the speed of the car when the length of the skid distance is 200 feet. You can obtain the exact value for any x-value between Xmin and Xmax by entering the x-value while in trace mode and pressing (ENTER). Your screen should appear as follows:

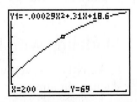

    b. Use your calculator to verify the result in part a by evaluating
$-0.00029(200)^2 + 0.31(200) + 18.6$.

The equation $y = -0.00029x^2 + 0.31x + 18.6$ is called a **mathematical model**. A mathematical model is a mathematical form, such as a formula, an equation, a graph, or a table, that fits or approximates the important features of a given situation. Such models can then be used to estimate, make predictions, and draw conclusions about the given situation.

The process of developing a mathematical model to represent a given situation involves several steps. First, you need to identify the problem and develop a well-defined question about what you want to know. For example, in the automobile accident situation, can you determine the speed of the car when the brakes are applied?

Next, you look for relationships and connections between the variables that are involved in the situation. You may also need to make assumptions about the situation before you begin to construct the mathematical model.

    6. What are some of the variable quantities present in determining what you want to know in the automobile accident situation? What assumptions did you make?

Using your mathematical and problem-solving skills, you can now translate the features and relationships you have identified into a mathematical model. The model can be used to answer the questions that you originally raised.

Finally, you need to verify that the mathematical model you have developed accurately represents the situation under investigation.

    7. How well does the mathematical model (equation 1) determine the speed of the car for a given skid distance? Explain how you came to this conclusion.

Note that one way to verify the accuracy of your mathematical model is to collect data and compare the data to the results predicted by the model. In the speed and skid-distance situation, the use of data actually helped you determine the model. By observing patterns revealed by the data and graph, an appropriate model was developed.

The process just described to develop a mathematical model is called **mathematical modeling**. The development and use of mathematical models to help solve simple to extremely complicated problems is a very important use of mathematics.

Modeling with Formulas

In Activity 1.3, you used formulas to model situations in geometry, business, and science. In almost every field of study, you are likely to encounter formulas that relate two or more variables represented by letters. Problems 8 and 9 feature formulas used in the health field.

8. Medical researchers have determined that for exercise to be beneficial, a person's target heart rate while exercising, R, in beats per minute, can be approximated by the formulas

$$R = 143 - 0.65a \text{ for women}$$

$$R = 165 - 0.75a \text{ for men},$$

where a represents the person's age.

a. If the target heart rate for a woman is 130 beats per minute, how old is she?

b. If the target heart rate for a man is 135 beats per minute, how old is he?

9. The basal energy rate is the daily amount of energy (measured in calories) needed by the body at rest to maintain body temperature and the basic life processes of respiration, cell metabolism, circulation, and glandular activity. As you may suspect, the basal energy rate differs for individuals, depending on their gender, age, height, and weight. The formula for the basal energy rate for men is

$$B = 655.096 + 9.563W + 1.85H - 4.676A,$$

where B is the basal energy rate (in calories), W is the weight (in kilograms), H is the height (in centimeters), and A is the age (in years).

a. A male patient is 70 years old, weighs 55 kilograms, and is 172 centimeters tall. A total daily caloric intake of 1000 calories is prescribed for him. Determine if he is being properly fed.

b. A man is 178 centimeters tall and weighs 84 kilograms. If his basal energy rate is 1500 calories, how old is the man?

Tables as Models

In Activity 1.6, you encountered several tables of matched pairs of values for situations involving two variables. These tables serve as models that help represent the relationship between the quantities involved. Patterns are revealed and often lead to an equation that can model the relationship more completely.

For example, you feel colder on a windy cold day than the air temperature indicates. This is commonly referred to as windchill.

10. Suppose the wind is a constant 20 mph. The following table gives the wind chill temperature (how cold your skin feels) for various air temperatures.

AIR TEMPERATURE °F	40	30	20	10	0	−10	−20
WINDCHILL TEMPERATURE (20-MPH WIND)	30	17	4	−9	−22	−35	−48

    a. What relationship do you observe between the windchill temperature and the air temperature?

    b. Estimate the windchill temperature for an air temperature of −30°F.

    c. If the windchill speed is 30 mph, how would you expect the windchill temperatures in the table to change?

11. The following windchill chart has been published by the National Weather Service. Note that the formula used to generate the table values is based on scientific knowledge and experiments.

Windchill Chart

Temperature (°F)

Wind (mph)	40	35	30	25	20	15	10	5	0	−5	−10	−15	−20	−25	−30	−35	−40	−45
5	36	31	25	19	13	7	1	−5	−11	−16	−22	−28	−34	−40	−46	−52	−57	−63
10	34	27	21	15	9	3	−4	−10	−16	−22	−28	−35	−41	−47	−53	−59	−66	−72
15	32	25	19	13	6	0	−7	−13	−19	−26	−32	−39	−45	−51	−58	−64	−71	−77
20	30	24	17	11	4	−2	−9	−15	−22	−29	−35	−42	−48	−55	−61	−68	−74	−81
25	29	23	16	9	3	−4	−11	−17	−24	−31	−37	−44	−51	−58	−64	−71	−78	−84
30	28	22	15	8	1	−5	−12	−19	−26	−33	−39	−46	−53	−60	−67	−73	−80	−87
35	28	21	14	7	0	−7	−14	−21	−27	−34	−41	−48	−55	−62	−69	−76	−82	−89
40	27	20	13	6	−1	−8	−15	−22	−29	−36	−43	−50	−57	−64	−71	−78	−84	−91
45	26	20	12	5	−2	−9	−16	−23	−30	−37	−44	−51	−58	−65	−72	−79	−86	−93
50	26	19	12	4	−3	−10	−17	−24	−31	−38	−45	−52	−60	−67	−74	−81	−88	−95
55	25	18	11	4	−3	−11	−18	−25	−32	−39	−46	−54	−61	−68	−75	−82	−89	−97
60	25	17	10	3	−4	−11	−19	−26	−33	−40	−48	−55	−62	−69	−76	−84	−91	−98

Frostbite Times: 30 minutes   10 minutes   5 minutes

Windchill (°F) = 35.74 + 0.6215T − 35.75(V^{0.16}) + 0.4275T(V^{0.16})

Where, *T* = Air Temperature (°F)   *V* = Wind Speed (mph)

a. In the windchill chart, locate the table values in Problem 10.

b. If the wind is blowing at 30 mph, use the windchill chart to complete the following table.

AIR TEMPERATURE °F	40	30	20	10	0	−10	−20
WINDCHILL TEMPERATURE (30-MPH WIND)							

c. If the wind speed is 40 mph, what is the windchill temperature if the air temperature is −20°F?

Modeling with Functions

Many of the mathematical models you will use to solve problems in this course will be function models. As you learned in Activities 1.5 and 1.6, functions can be represented by tables, graphs, and equations. Problem 12 gives you a sample of how to develop a function model to solve a problem.

12. As part of a community service project at your high school, you are organizing a fund-raiser at the neighborhood roller rink. Money raised will benefit a summer camp for children with special needs. The admission charge is $4.50 per person, $2.00 of which is used to pay the rink's rental fee. The remainder is donated to the summer camp fund.

a. State a question that you want answered in this situation.

b. What two variables are involved in this problem?

c. Which variable can best be designated as the dependent variable? As the independent variable?

d. Complete the following table.

INDEPENDENT VARIABLE	1	2	3	4	5	6	7	8
DEPENDENT VARIABLE								

e. State in words the relationship between the independent and dependent variables.

f. Let *x* represent the number attending and *y* represent the amount donated. Translate the written statement in part e as an equation.

g. If 91 tickets are sold, use the equation model developed in part f to determine the amount donated to the summer camp fund.

h. If the maximum capacity of the rink is 200 people, what is the maximum amount that can be donated?

You will learn more about using graphs as mathematical models in Activity 1.13.

SUMMARY
Activity 1.8

1. A **mathematical model** is a mathematical form, such as a formula, an equation, a graph, or a table, that fits or approximates the important features of a given situation.

2. **Mathematical modeling** is the process of developing a mathematical model for a given situation.

EXERCISES
Activity 1.8

1. The speed, s, of an ant (in centimeters per second) is related to the temperature, t (in degrees Celsius), by the formula

$$s = 0.167t - 0.67.$$

a. If the temperature is 40°C, how fast is the ant moving?

b. If an ant is moving at 4 centimeters per second, what is the temperature?

2. The pressure, p, of water (in pounds per square inch) at a depth of d feet below the surface is given by the formula

$$p = 15 + \frac{15}{33}d.$$

a. If a diver is 100 feet below the surface, what is the pressure of the water on the diver?

b. On November 14, 1993, Francisco Ferreras reached a record depth for breath-held diving. During the dive, he experienced a pressure of 201 pounds per square inch. What was his record depth?

3. The following formula is used by the National Football League (NFL) to calculate quarterback ratings:

$$R = \frac{250C + 12.5Y + 1000T - 1250I + 6.25A}{3A},$$

where R = quarterback rating
$\quad A$ = passes attempted
$\quad C$ = passes completed
$\quad Y$ = passing yardage
$\quad T$ = touchdown passes
$\quad I$ = number of interceptions

In the 2005–2006 regular season, Tom Brady, quarterback for the New England Patriots, and Brett Favre, for the Green Bay Packers, had the following player statistics:

PLAYER	PASSES ATTEMPTED	PASSES COMPLETED	PASSING YARDAGE	NUMBER OF TOUCHDOWN PASSES	NUMBER OF INTERCEPTIONS
Tom Brady	530	334	4110	26	14
Brett Favre	607	372	3881	20	29

a. Determine the quarterback rating for Tom Brady for the 2005–2006 NFL football season.

b. Determine the quarterback rating for Brett Favre.

c. Visit www.nfl.com and select the Stats menu to obtain the rating of your favorite quarterback in the current regular season.

4. a. You want to invest money in order to receive the best return. You have two options.

Option 1: Invest at 6% simple annual interest for 10 years.

Option 2: Invest at 5% interest compounded annually.

The following tables model the growth of $2000 over a 10-year period using the two options.

	NUMBER OF YEARS									
	1	2	3	4	5	6	7	8	9	10
6% SIMPLE ANNUAL INTEREST	2120	2240	2360	2480	2600	2720	2840	2960	3080	3200
5% COMPOUNDED ANNUALLY	2100	2205	2315.30	2431	2552.60	2680.20	2814.20	2954.90	3102.70	3257.80

Describe any trends or patterns that you observe in the data.

b. The amount of your investment in option 1 can be determined by the following formula

$$A = P + Prt,$$

where A = amount of the investment
P = principal or amount invested
r = annual percentage rate (expressed as a decimal)
t = number of years invested

Use the formula to determine the amount of your $2000 investment in option 1 after 20 years. What is the total amount of interest earned?

c. The amount of your investment in option 2 can be determined by

$$A = P(1 + r)^t,$$

where A = amount of the investment
P = principal
r = annual percentage rate (expressed as a decimal)
t = number of years invested

Use the formula to determine the amount of your $2000 investment in option 2 after 20 years.

d. Which option would you choose? Explain.

5. The following table gives the number of people infected by the flu over a given number of months.

NUMBER OF MONTHS	0	1	2	3	4	5
NUMBER OF PEOPLE INFECTED	1	5	13	33	78	180

Describe any trends or patterns that you observe.

6. The value of almost everything you own (assets), such as a car, computer, or house, depreciates (goes down) over time. When an asset's value decreases by a fixed amount each year, the depreciation is called straight-line depreciation.

Suppose your truck has an initial value of $12,400 and depreciates $820 per year.

a. State a question that you might want answered in this situation.

b. What two variables are involved in this problem?

c. Which variable can best be designated as the dependent variable? As the independent variable?

d. Complete the following table.

INDEPENDENT VARIABLE	1	2	3	4	5
DEPENDENT VARIABLE					

e. State in words the relationship between the independent and dependent variables.

f. Use appropriate letters to represent the variables involved and translate the written statement in part e as an equation.

g. If you plan to keep the truck for 7 years, determine the value of the truck at the end of this period. Explain the process you used.

h. What assumption was made regarding the rate of depreciation of the truck? Does this seem reasonable?

ACTIVITY 1.9
Fund-Raiser
Revisited

OBJECTIVES

1. Solve an equation numerically.

2. Solve an equation graphically.

3. Distinguish between a situation represented by a graph of distinct points versus a continuous graph.

In Problem 12 of Activity 1.8 you developed the following equation to model the fund-raiser situation:

$$y = 2.50x$$

where x represents the number of admission tickets sold and y represents the amount of money donated to the summer camp fund.

Since the variable y is written by itself on one side, you say the equation is "solved for y."

Evaluating an Algebraic Expression

In the following example, you are asked to determine a value for the dependent variable y for a given value of the independent variable x.

Example 1 *Use the equation $y = 2.5x$ to determine the amount of money raised if 84 tickets are sold. Stated another way, determine y for a value of $x = 84$.*

SOLUTION:

Step 1: Substitute 84 for x in the equation $y = 2.5x$:

$$y = 2.50(84)$$

Step 2: Perform the arithmetic operations on the right-hand side to obtain the y-value:

$$y = \$210$$

Note that the expression $2.50x$ has been **evaluated** for $x = 84$ to obtain the corresponding y-value.

Appendix

A graphing calculator is an excellent tool for generating x-y tables. Instructions for generating tables using a TI-83/84 Plus are given in Appendix A.

1. Use the equation $y = 2.50x$ to complete the table. Verify using the table feature of a graphing calculator.

x, NUMBER OF TICKETS SOLD	y, AMOUNT RAISED ($)
26	
94	
278	

Solving Equations Numerically and Graphically

Suppose the goal is to raise a total of at least $200 for the summer camp fund. You can determine how many tickets to sell to raise $200 by replacing y with 200 in $y = 2.50x$ to produce the **equation**

$$200 = 2.50x.$$

The problem now is to solve the equation for x. There are three different methods for solving such equations: numerical, graphical, and algebraic. The numerical and graphical methods are often quite useful but frequently overlooked. Problems 2 and 3 will illustrate the numerical and graphical solution techniques.

2. a. Use a table of values to estimate how many tickets must be sold to raise $200. Begin by estimating a value for x so that the expression $2.50x$ is close to 200. For example, $x = 100$ tickets produces a value of 250. In this case, increase or decrease your guesses for x until you obtain 200.

x, NUMBER OF TICKETS SOLD	y, AMOUNT RAISED ($)

This approach, consisting of a guess, check, and repeat, is a **numerical method** for solving the equation $200 = 2.50x$ for x.

b. List at least one disadvantage of solving an equation numerically.

3. Recall that the practical domain for x (number of tickets sold) of the summer camp situation is 0, 1, 2, 3, . . ., 200. Some of the x-y pairs are shown in the following graph.

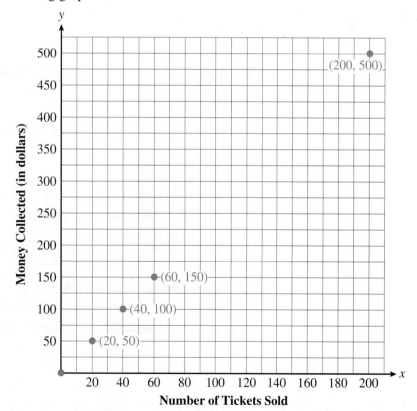

a. The point (60, 150) lies on the graph. Interpret the meaning of the coordinates 60 and 150 in the fund-raiser situation.

b. Connect the points on the graph in Problem 3 to form a line. Use this line to estimate how many tickets must be sold to raise at least $200. Remember, you need to determine x when $y = 200$.

c. Explain the process you used in part b.

The approach in part b is the **graphical method** for solving the equation $200 = 2.50x$ for x.

d. List at least one disadvantage to using a graphing approach to solving an equation.

In Problem 3b, the points of the scatterplot were connected to form a smooth continuous line. This was done as a graphing aid to help solve the given equation graphically. The practical domain of the fund-raiser function is 0, 1, 2, …, 200. Therefore, the graph of the fund-raiser function consists of just distinct points.

4. Consider the general equation $y = 2.50x$ where x is not restricted to whole numbers as it is for number of tickets sold.

a. What is the replacement set for the input variable x?

b. Complete the following table for selected input values.

x	y = 2.50x
−100	
−75	
−50	
−25	
0	
25	
50	
75	
100	

c. The points from the table in part b are plotted on the following grid and a straight line is drawn through them. Compare the graph with the graph of y = 2.50x in Problem 3b where the input x represents the number of tickets sold.

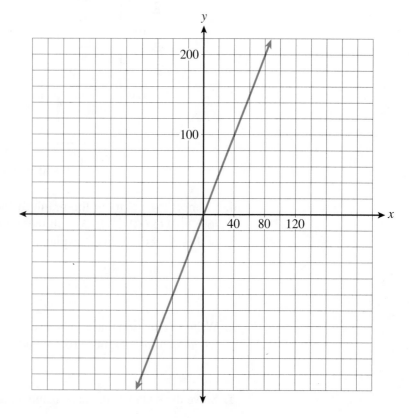

5. The recommended weight of an adult male can be approximated by the formula

$$w = 5.5h - 220,$$

where w = recommended weight

h = height in inches.

a. What is a possible practical domain for the weight function defined by the given formula?

b. Complete the following table. If you are using a graphing calculator, remember to replace the independent variable *h* with *x* and the dependent variable *w* with *y*.

h, HEIGHT IN INCHES	60	64	68	72	76	80
w, WEIGHT IN POUNDS						

c. Plot the points determined in part b.

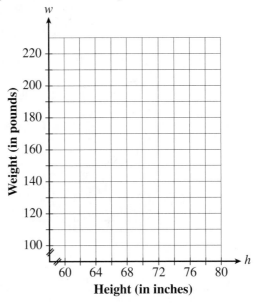

d. Connect the points in the graph to form a continuous line segment from (60, 110) to (80, 220). Are all the points on this line segment on the graph of the weight function? Explain.

e. Write an equation that can be used to determine the height of a male whose recommended weight is 165 pounds.

f. Solve the equation in part e using a numerical approach.

g. Solve the equation in part e using a graphical approach.

1. To solve an equation using a **numerical approach**, use a guess, check, and repeat process.

2. To solve an equation using a **graphical approach**, read the appropriate coordinates on the graph of the equation relating x and y.

3. A **solution** of an equation containing one variable is a replacement value for the variable that produces equal values on both sides of the equation.

4. A graph is said to be **continuous** if you can place your pencil on any point on the graph and then trace the entire graph without lifting the pencil off the paper. The graph has no breaks or holes.

1. Your local gas station is having a super sale and is selling regular unleaded gasoline for three hours at $1.239 per gallon.

   a. Let x be the independent variable representing the number of gallons purchased. Let C be the dependent variable representing the total cost of the fuel. Write an equation relating x and C.

   b. What is the practical domain for x?

   c. Use the equation from part a to complete the following table.

x, NUMBER OF GALLONS PURCHASED	5	10	15	20
c, TOTAL COST OF THE PURCHASE				

    d. You have only $10 with you. Use the equation from part a to write an equation that can be used to determine how many gallons you can purchase.

    e. Solve your equation from part d using a numerical approach.

    f. The graph of the equation determined in part a is given below. Use the graph to estimate the number of gallons you can purchase with $10.

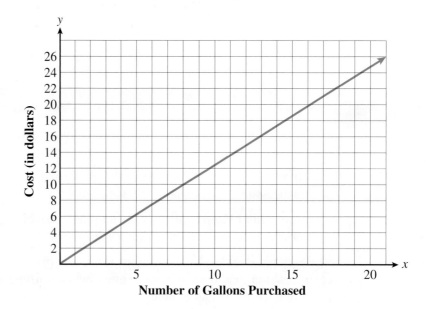

Number of Gallons Purchased

2. You are president of the high school band booster club. You have arranged for the school's jazz band to perform at a local coffee shop for three hours. In exchange for the performance, the booster club will receive three-quarters of the shop's gross receipts during that three-hour period.

    a. Let x be the independent variable representing the gross receipts of the coffee shop during the performance. Let y be the dependent variable representing the share of the gross receipts that the coffee shop will donate to the band boosters. Write an equation relating x and y.

x, TOTAL GROSS RECEIPTS ($)	250	500	750	1000
y, BOOSTERS' SHARE ($)				

    b. Use the equation from part a to complete the following table.

    c. If the coffee shop presents you with a check for $650, what were the gross receipts during the performance? Estimate your answer using a numerical approach.

d. The graph of the equation determined in part a is given below. Use a graphical approach to estimate the gross receipts from part c.

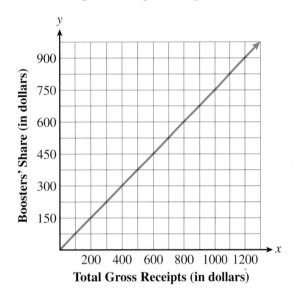

3. A tennis ball is dropped from an upper floor of the Sears Tower in Chicago. The following table gives the ball's distance from ground level at a given time after it is dropped.

TIME (SEC)	1	2	3	4	5	6	7
DISTANCE (FT)	1398	1350	1270	1158	1014	838	630

The ball was dropped from a height of 1414 feet. Use the information in the table to approximate the time when the ball will have fallen half the height it was dropped from.

4. a. The depth (inches) of water that accumulates in the spring soil from melted snow can be determined by dividing the cumulative winter snowfall (inches) by 12. Translate this statement into an equation, using I for the accumulated inches of water and n for the inches of fallen snow.

b. Determine the amount of water that accumulates in the soil if 25 inches of snow falls.

c. Write an equation that can be used to determine the total amount of winter snow that accumulates 6 inches of water in the soil.

d. Solve the equation in part c using a numerical approach.

e. Solve the equation in part c using a graphing approach.

ACTIVITY 1.10
Leasing a Copier

OBJECTIVES

1. Develop a mathematical model in the form of an equation.

2. Solve an equation using an algebraic approach.

As part of a summer program at your high school, you are an intern in a law office. You are asked by the office manager to gather some information about leasing a copy machine for the office. The sales representative at Western Supply Company recommends a 50-copy/minute copier to satisfy the office's copying needs. The copier leases for $455 per month, plus 1.5 cents a copy. Maintenance fees are covered in the monthly charge. The lawyers would own the copier after 39 months.

1. a. The total monthly cost depends upon the number of copies made. Identify the independent and dependent variables.

b. Write a statement in words to determine the total monthly cost in terms of the number of copies made during the month.

c. Complete the following table.

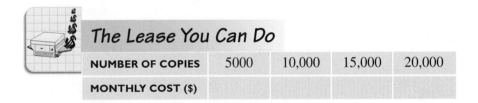

The Lease You Can Do

NUMBER OF COPIES	5000	10,000	15,000	20,000
MONTHLY COST ($)				

d. Translate the statement in part b into an equation. Let n represent the number of copies made during the month and c represent the total monthly cost.

2. a. Use the result obtained in Problem 1d to determine the monthly cost if 12,000 copies are made.

b. Is 12,000 a replacement value for the independent or for the dependent variable?

In Problem 2, you determined the cost by evaluating the expression $0.015n + 455$ for $n = 12,000$.

3. Suppose the monthly budget for leasing the copier is $800.

a. Is 800 a value for n or a value for c?

b. If the monthly budget is $800, write an equation that can be used to determine the number of copies in the month.

4. Use the result in Problem 1d to write an equation that can be used to determine the number, n, of copies that can be made with a monthly budget of $c = 800$.

Notice in Problem 4 that n is not isolated by itself on one side of the equation. To isolate n, you need to undo two operations: the addition of 455 and the multiplication by 0.015. You do this by reversing the sequence of operations, replacing each operation by its inverse.

Example 1 *The following example illustrates a systematic algebraic procedure by undoing two operations to solve an equation.*

Solve for x: $120 = 3x + 90$

$$120 = 3x + 90$$
$$\underline{-90 \qquad\quad -90}$$
$$30 = 3x$$

Step 1: To undo the addition by 90, subtract 90 from each side of the equation.

$$\frac{30}{3} = \frac{3x}{3}$$
$$10 = x$$

Step 2: To undo the multiplication of 3, divide each side of the equation by 3.

The variable x has been isolated on the right side with coefficient 1; the solution is 10.

Check:
$$120 \stackrel{?}{=} 3\,(10) + 90$$
$$120 \stackrel{?}{=} 30 + 90$$
$$120 = 120$$

Note that the algebraic procedure emphasizes that an equation can be thought of as a scale whose arms are in balance. The equals sign can be thought of as the balancing point.

As you perform the appropriate inverse operation to solve the equation $120 = 3x + 90$ for x, you *must* maintain the balance as you perform each step in the process. If you subtract 90 from one side, then you must subtract 90 from the other side. Similarly, if you divide one side by 3, then you must divide the other side by 3.

5. a. Solve the equation in Problem 4 using the algebraic procedure outlined in Example 1.

b. Verify your answer in part a using either a numerical or graphical approach.

6. For each of the following, substitute the given value of y and use an algebraic approach to solve the resulting equation for x.

   a. If $y = 3x - 5$ and $y = 10$, determine x.

   b. If $y = 30 - 2x$ and $y = 24$, determine x.

   c. If $y = \frac{3}{4}x - 21$ and $y = -9$, determine x.

   d. If $-2x + 15 = y$ and $y = -3$, determine x.

SUMMARY
Activity 1.10

1. The goal of **solving an equation** of the form $ax + b = c$, where $a \neq 0$, for the variable x is to isolate the variable x (with coefficient 1) on one side of the equation.

2. Use **inverse operations** to isolate the variable. Apply the inverse operations in the following order:

   Step 1: Undo the addition of b by subtracting b from each side of the equation; undo the subtraction of b by adding b to each side of the equation.

   Step 2: Undo the multiplication of the variable x by the nonzero coefficient a by dividing each side of the equation by a.

EXERCISES
Activity 1.10

1. A long-distance telephone plan costs $4.95 a month, plus 10 cents per minute, or part thereof, for any long-distance call made during the month.

   a. Write a statement to determine the total monthly cost for your long-distance calls for the month.

   b. Translate the statement in part a into an equation, using c to represent the total monthly cost and n to represent the total number of long-distance minutes for the month.

   c. Determine the monthly cost if 250 minutes of long-distance calls are made.

d. If you budget $50 per month for long-distance calls, how many minutes can you call in the month?

2. You are considering taking some courses at your local community college on a part-time basis for the upcoming school year. For a student who carries fewer than twelve credits (the full-time minimum), the tuition is $155 for each credit hour taken. All students, part-time or full-time, must pay a $20 parking fee for the semester. This fixed fee is added directly to your tuition and is included in your total bill.

a. Complete the following table, where t represents the total bill and n represents the number of credit hours taken.

NUMBER OF CREDIT HOURS, n	1	2	3	4	5	6
TOTAL BILL, t ($)						

b. Write an equation to determine the total bill, t, for a student carrying fewer than twelve credit hours. Use n to represent the number of hours taken for the semester.

c. Determine the total bill if you take nine credit hours.

d. Suppose you have $1000 to spend on the total bill. How many credit hours can you carry for the semester?

3. The senior class is organizing an entertainment night to benefit charities in the community. You are a member of the budget committee for the class project. The committee suggests a $10 per person admission donation for food, nonalcoholic beverages, and entertainment. The committee determines that the fixed costs for the event (food, drinks, posters, tickets, etc.) will total $2100. The high school is donating the use of the gymnasium for the evening.

a. The total revenue (gross income before expenses are deducted) depends on the number, n, of students who attend. Write an expression in terms of n that represents the total revenue if n students attend.

b. Profit is the net income after expenses are deducted. Write an equation expressing the profit, p, in terms of the number, n, of students who attend.

c. If the gymnasium holds a maximum of 700 people, what is the maximum amount of money that can be donated to charity?

d. Suppose that the members of the committee want to be able to donate at least $1500 to community charities. How many students must attend in order to have a profit of $1500?

4. When an asset depreciates by a fixed amount per year, the depreciation is called straight-line depreciation (see Problem 6 on page 77). Suppose a car has an initial value of $15,000 and depreciates $950 per year.

a. Let v represent the value of the car after t years. Write an equation that expresses v in terms of t.

b. What is the value of the car after four years?

c. How long will it take for the value of the car to decrease to $10,000?

5. The cost, c, in dollars, of mailing a priority overnight package weighing one pound or more is given by the formula $c = 2.085x + 15.08$, where x represents the weight of the package in pounds.

a. Determine the cost of mailing a package that weighs 10 pounds.

b. Determine the weight of a package that costs $56.78 to mail.

6. Archaeologists and forensic scientists use the length of human bones to estimate the height of individuals. A person's height, h, in centimeters, can be determined from the length of the femur, f (the bone from the knee to the hip socket), in centimeters, using the following formulas:

Man: $h = 69.089 + 2.238f$

Woman: $h = 61.412 + 2.317f$

a. A partial skeleton of a man is found. The femur measures 50 centimeters. How tall was the man?

b. What is the length of the femur for a woman who is 150 centimeters tall?

7. Let p represent the perimeter of an isosceles triangle that has two equal sides of length a and a third side of length b. The formula for the perimeter is $p = 2a + b$. Determine the length of the equal side of an isosceles triangle having perimeter of $\frac{3}{4}$ yard and a third side measuring $\frac{1}{3}$ yard.

8. The recommended weight of an adult male is given by the formula $w = \frac{11}{2}h - 220$, where w represents his recommended weight in pounds and h represents his height in inches. Determine the height of a man whose recommended weight is 165 pounds.

9. Even though housing prices have been declining in many parts of the country, in your neighborhood they have been increasing steadily since you bought your home in 2000. The relationship between the market value of your home and the length of time you have been living there can be expressed algebraically by the rule

$$V = 130,000 + 3500x,$$

where x is the length of time (in years) in your home and V is the market value (in dollars).

a. Complete the following table:

YEAR	x	MARKET VALUE
2000		
2005		
2008		

b. Determine the value of your home in 2010.

c. In which year will the value of your home reach $186,000?

10. Use an algebraic approach to solve each of the following equations for x.

a. $10 = 2x + 12$

b. $-27 = -5x - 7$

c. $3x - 26 = -14$

d. $24 - 2x = 38$

e. $5x - 15 = 15$

f. $-4x + 8 = 8$

g. $12 + \dfrac{1}{5}x = 9$

h. $\dfrac{2}{3}x - 12 = 0$

i. $0.25x - 14.5 = 10$

j. $5 = 2.5x - 20$

ACTIVITY 1.11

Comparing
Energy Costs

An architect is hired to design a home. She obtains the following information regarding the installation and operating costs of two types of heating systems: solar and electric.

OBJECTIVES

1. Develop mathematical models to solve problems.

2. Write and solve equations of the form
$ax + b = cx + d$.

3. Use the distributive property to solve equations involving grouping symbols.

4. Solve formulas for a specified variable.

Some Like It Hot

TYPE OF HEATING SYSTEM	INSTALLATION COST	OPERATING COST PER YEAR
Solar	$25,600	$200
Electric	$5500	$1600

1. **a.** Determine the total cost of the solar heating system after five years of use.

   b. Write a statement for the total cost of the solar heating system in terms of the number of years of use.

   c. Let x represent the number of years of use and c represent the total cost of the solar heating system. Translate the statement in part b into an equation.

   d. Use the equation from part c to complete the following table:

NUMBER OF YEARS IN USE, x	5	10	15	20
TOTAL COST, c				

2. **a.** Determine the total cost of the electric heating system after five years of use.

   b. Write a statement for the total cost of the electric heating system in terms of the number of years of use.

   c. Let x represent the number of years of use and c represent the total cost of the electric heating system. Translate the statement in part b into an equation.

   d. Use the equation from part c to complete the following table:

NUMBER OF YEARS IN USE, x	5	10	15	20
TOTAL COST, c				

The installation cost of solar heating is much more than that of the electric system, but the operating cost per year of the solar system is much lower. Therefore, it is reasonable to think that the total cost for the electric system will eventually "catch up" and surpass the total cost of the solar system.

3. Compare the table values for total heating costs in Problems 1d and 2d. Estimate in what year the total cost for electric heating will "catch up" and surpass the total cost for solar heating. Explain.

4. The year in which the total costs of the two heating systems are equal can be determined algebraically. Write an equation you can solve to determine when the total heating costs are the same by setting the expressions in the symbolic rules in Problems 1c and 2c equal to each other.

The following example demonstrates a systematic algebraic procedure that you can use to solve equations similar to the equation in Problem 4. Remember that your goal is to isolate the variable on one side of the equation with coefficient 1 by applying the appropriate inverse operations.

Example 1 *Solve for x: $2x + 14 = 8x + 2$*

SOLUTION

First, add and/or subtract terms appropriately so that all terms involving the variable are on one side of the equals sign and all other terms are on the other side.

$$2x + 14 = 8x + 2 \qquad \text{Subtract } 8x \text{ from both sides and combine like terms.}$$
$$\underline{-8x \qquad\quad -8x}$$
$$-6x + 14 = 2$$
$$\underline{\qquad -14 = -14} \qquad \text{Subtract 14 from each side and combine like terms.}$$
$$-6x \qquad\;\; = -12$$
$$\frac{-6x}{-6} = \frac{-12}{-6} \qquad \text{Divide each side by } -6, \text{ the coefficient of } x.$$
$$x = 2$$

Check: $2(2) + 14 = 8(2) + 2$
$$4 + 14 = 16 + 2$$
$$18 = 18$$

5. In Example 1, the variable terms are combined on the left side of the equation. Solve the equation $2x + 14 = 8x + 2$ by combining the variable terms on the right side.

6. a. Solve the equation in Problem 4 for x.

b. Interpret what your answer in part a represents in the context of the heating system situation.

Purchasing a Car

You are interested in purchasing a new car and have narrowed the choice to a Honda Accord LX (4 cylinder) and a Passat GLS (4 cylinder). Being concerned about the value of the car depreciating over time, you search the Internet and obtain the following information:

Driven Down

MODEL OF CAR (2009)	MARKET SUGGESTED RETAIL PRICE (MSRP) ($)	ANNUAL DEPRECIATION ($)
Accord LX	20,925	1730
Passat GLS	24,995	2420

7. a. Complete the following table:

YEARS THE CAR IS OWNED	VALUE OF ACCORD LX ($)	VALUE OF PASSAT GLS ($)
1		
2		
3		

b. Will the value of the Passat GLS ever be lower than the value of the Accord LX? Explain.

c. Let v represent the value of the car after x years of ownership. Write a symbolic rule to determine v in terms of x for the Accord LX.

d. Write a symbolic rule to determine v in terms of x for the Passat GLS.

e. Write an equation to determine when the value of the Accord LX will equal the value of the Passat GLS.

f. Solve the equation in part e.

NBA Basketball Court

You and your friend are avid professional basketball fans and discover that your math teacher shares your enthusiasm for basketball. During a mathematics class, your instructor tells you that the perimeter of an NBA basketball court is 288 feet and the length is 44 feet more than its width. He challenges you to use your algebra skills to determine the dimensions of the court. To solve the problem, you and your friend use the following plan.

8. a. Let w represent the width of the court. Write an expression for the length in terms of the width, w.

b. Using the formula for perimeter of a rectangle, $P = 2l + 2w$, and the information given to obtain an equation containing just the variable w.

c. Solve the equation you obtained in part b by first applying the distributive property and then combining like terms in the expression involving w.

d. What are the dimensions of an NBA basketball court?

Solving Formulas for a Specified Variable

9. Windchill temperature, w, produced by a 30-mile-per-hour wind at various Fahrenheit degrees can be modeled by the formula

$$w = 1.6t - 49.$$

a. Use the formula $w = 1.6t - 49$ to determine the windchill temperature if the air temperature is 7°F.

b. On a cool day in Tampa, the wind is blowing at 30 miles per hour. If the windchill temperature is reported to be 39°F, then what is the air temperature on that day? Use the formula $w = 1.6t - 49$.

The formula $w = 1.6t - 49$ is said to be solved for w in terms of t because the variable w is isolated by itself on one side of the equation. To determine the windchill temperature, w, for air temperature $t = 7$°F (Problem 9a), you simply substitute 7 for t in $1.6t - 49$ and do the arithmetic:

$$w = 1.6(7) - 49 = -37.8°F$$

In Problem 9b, you needed to determine the air temperature, t, for a given windchill temperature. In this case, you substitute 39 for w in $w = 1.6t - 49$ and then solve the resulting equation for t.

If you had to determine the corresponding t-value for several different w-values, you would have to solve several equations for t. It is much more convenient and efficient to solve the original formula $w = 1.6t - 49$ for t and then use the new equation to determine values of t.

Example 2 *Solving the formula $w = 1.6t - 49$ for t is similar to solving the equation* $-18 = 1.6t - 49$ *for t.*

$$-18 = 1.6t - 49$$
$$\underline{+49 \qquad\quad +49}$$
$$31 = 1.6t$$

$$\frac{31}{1.6} = \frac{1.6t}{1.6}$$

$$19.4 \approx t$$

$$w = 1.6t - 49$$
$$\underline{+49 \qquad\quad +49} \qquad \text{Add 49 to each side.}$$
$$w + 49 = 1.6t$$

$$\frac{w + 49}{1.6} = \frac{1.6t}{1.6} \qquad \text{Divide each side by 1.6.}$$

$$\frac{w + 49}{1.6} = t$$

The new formula is $t = \dfrac{w + 49}{1.6}$ or $t = \dfrac{w}{1.6} + \dfrac{49}{1.6}$, which is equivalent to $t = 0.625w + 30.625$.

To solve the equation $w = 1.6t - 49$ for t means to isolate the variable t (with coefficient 1) on one side of the equation, with all other terms on the opposite side.

10. Redo Problem 9b using the new formula derived in Example 2 that expresses *t* in terms of *w*.

11. a. If the wind speed is 15 miles per hour, the windchill can be approximated by the formula $w = 1.4t - 32$, where *t* is the air temperature in degrees Fahrenheit. Solve the formula for *t*.

b. Use the new formula from part a to determine the air temperature, *t*, if the windchill temperature is $-10°$F.

12. Solve each of the following formulas for the specified variable.

a. $A = lw$ for *w*   **b.** $p = c + m$ for *m*

c. $P = 2l + 2w$ for *l*   **d.** $R = 165 - 0.75a$ for *a*

e. $V = \pi r^2 h$ for *h*   **f.** $P = 2l + 2w$ for *w*

g. $V(P + a) = k$ for *P*

Additional Practice

13. Solve each of the following equations for *x*. Remember to check your result in the original equation.

a. $2x + 9 = 5x - 12$ **b.** $21 - x = -3 - 5x$

c. $2(x - 3) = -8$ **d.** $2(x - 4) + 6 = 4x - 7$

SUMMARY
Activity 1.11

1. General strategy for solving equations for a variable, such as x.

- Remove parentheses, if necessary, by applying the distributive property.

- Combine like terms that appear on the same side of the equation.

- Write the equation so that the product of the coefficient and the variable is on one side and all other numbers and variables are on the other side. This is generally accomplished by adding and/or subtracting terms so that all terms involving the variable you are solving for are on one side of the equation and all terms involving numbers and other variables appear on the other side.

- Solve for the variable by dividing each side of the equation by the nonzero coefficient of the variable.

- Check the result in the original equation to be sure that the value of the variable produces a true statement.

2. To solve a **formula** for a variable, isolate that variable (with coefficient 1) on one side of the equation with all other terms on the "opposite" side.

EXERCISES
Activity 1.11

1. You need to rent a truck so you contact two local rental companies and acquire the following information for the one-day cost of renting a truck:

Company 1: $39.95 per day, plus $0.19 per mile

Company 2: $19.95 per day, plus $0.49 per mile

Let x represent the number of miles driven in one day and C represent the total daily rental cost ($).

a. Write an equation that represents the total daily rental cost from company 1 in terms of the number of miles driven.

b. Write an equation that represents the total daily rental cost from company 2 in terms of the number of miles driven.

c. Write an equation to determine for what mileage the one-day rental cost would be the same.

d. Solve the equation you obtained in part c.

e. For which mileages would company 2 have the lower price?

2. You are considering installing a security system in your new house. You gather the following information about similar security systems from two local home security dealers:

Dealer 1: $3560 to install and $15 per month monitoring fee

Dealer 2: $2850 to install and $28 per month for monitoring

You see that the initial cost of the security system from dealer 1 is much higher than that of the system from dealer 2 but that the monitoring fee is lower. You want to determine which is the better system for your needs.

Let x represent the number of months that you have the security system and C represent the cumulative cost ($).

a. Write an equation that represents the total cost of the system from dealer 1 in terms of the number of months you have the system.

b. Write an equation that represents the total cost of the system from dealer 2 in terms of the number of months you have the system.

c. Write an equation to determine the number of months for which the total cost of the systems will be equal.

d. Solve the equation in part c.

e. If you plan to live in the house and use the system for ten years, which system would be less expensive?

3. You are able to get three summer jobs to help save for future college expenses. In your job as a cashier, you work twenty hours per week and earn $6.50 per hour. Your second and third jobs are both at a local hospital. There you earn $8.50 per hour as a payroll clerk and $6.00 per hour as an aide. You always work ten hours fewer per week as an aide than you do as the payroll clerk. Your total weekly salary depends on the number of hours that you work at each job.

a. Determine the independent and dependent variables for this situation.

b. Explain how you calculate the total amount earned each week.

c. If x represents the number of hours that you work as a payroll clerk, represent the number of hours that you work as an aide in terms of x.

d. Write an equation that describes the total amount you earn each week. Use x to represent the input variable and y to represent the output variable. Simplify the expression as much as possible.

e. If you work twelve hours as a payroll clerk, how much will you make in one week?

f. What is a practical domain for x? Would eight hours at your payroll job be a realistic replacement value? What about fifty hours?

g. When you don't work as an aide, what is your total weekly salary?

h. If you plan to earn a total of $505 in one week from all jobs, how many hours would you have to work at each job? Is the total number of hours worked realistic? Explain.

    i. Solve the equation in part d for x in terms of y. When would it be useful to have the equation in this form?

4. A florist sells roses for $1.50 each and carnations for $0.85 each. Suppose you purchase a bouquet of one dozen flowers consisting of roses and carnations.

    a. Let x represent the number of roses purchased. Write an expression in terms of x that represents the number of carnations purchased.

    b. Write an expression that represents the cost of purchasing x roses.

    c. Write an expression that represents the cost of purchasing the carnations.

    d. What does the sum of the expressions in parts b and c represent?

    e. Suppose you are willing to spend $14.75. Write an equation that can be used to determine the number of roses that can be included in a bouquet of one dozen flowers consisting of roses and carnations.

    f. Solve the equation in part e to determine the number of roses and the number of carnations in the bouquet.

5. The viewing window of a certain calculator is in the shape of a rectangle.

    a. Let w represent the width of the viewing window in centimeters. If the window is 5 centimeters longer than it is wide, write an expression in terms of w for the length of the viewing window.

    b. Write a symbolic rule that represents the perimeter, P, of the viewing window in terms of w.

c. If the perimeter of the viewing window is 26 centimeters, determine the dimensions of the window.

Solve the equations in Exercises 6–17.

6. $5x - 4 = 3x - 6$

7. $3x - 14 = 6x + 4$

8. $0.5x + 9 = 4.5x + 17$

9. $4x - 10 = -2x + 8$

10. $0.3x - 5.5 = 0.2x + 2.6$

11. $4 - 0.025x = 0.1 - 0.05x$

12. $5t + 3 = 2(t + 6)$

13. $3(w + 2) = w - 14$

14. $21 + 3(x - 4) = 4(x + 5)$

15. $2(x + 3) = 5(2x + 1) + 4x$

16. $500 = 0.75x - (750 + 0.25x)$ **17.** $1.5x + 3(22 - x) = 70$

18. The National Weather Service reports the daily temperature in degrees Fahrenheit. The scientific community, as well as Canada and most of Europe, reports temperature in degrees Celsius. The Celsius, C, and Fahrenheit, F, temperature readings are related by the formula

$$F = 1.8C + 32.$$

a. Determine the Fahrenheit reading corresponding to the temperature at which water boils, 100°C.

b. Solve the formula $F = 1.8C + 32$ for C.

c. Use the new formula from part b to answer part a.

19. The number of women enrolled in college has steadily increased. The following table gives the enrollment, in millions, of women in a given year.

Women in College

YEAR	1970	1975	1980	1985	1990	1995	2000	2001
NUMBER ENROLLED IN MILLIONS	3.54	5.04	6.22	6.43	7.54	7.92	8.59	8.97

Source: U.S. Department of Education, National Center for Education Statistics

Let t represent the number of years since 1970. The number N (in millions) of women enrolled in college can be modeled by the formula

$$N = 0.158t + 4.092.$$

a. Estimate in what year women's college enrollment will reach 11 million.

b. Solve the equation $N = 0.158t + 4.092$ for t.

c. Use the new formula in part b to estimate the year in which women's enrollment will reach 12 million.

Solve each of the following formulas for the specified variable.

20. $E = IR$ for I

21. $C = 2\pi r$ for r

22. $P = 2a + b$ for b

23. $P = R - C$ for R

24. $P = 2l + 2w$ for w

25. $R = 143 - 0.65a$ for a

26. $A = P + Prt$ for r

27. $y = mx + b$ for m

28. $m = g - vt^2$ for g

29. $m = g - vt^2$ for v

PROJECT ACTIVITY 1.12
Summer Job Opportunities

OBJECTIVE

Use problem-solving skills to make decisions based on solutions of mathematical models.

You will be attending college this fall, so it is important for you to find a summer job that pays well. Luckily, the classified section of your newspaper lists numerous summer job opportunities in sales, road construction, and food service. The advertisements for all these positions welcome applications from high school students. All positions involve the same 10-week period during the summer.

Sales

A new electronics store opened recently. There are several sales associate positions that pay an hourly rate of $7.25 plus a 5% commission based on your total weekly sales. You would be guaranteed at least 30 hours of work per week but not more than 40 hours.

Construction

Your state's highway department hires students every summer to help with road construction projects. The hourly rate is $13.50 with the possibility of up to 10 hours per week in overtime, for which you would be paid time and a half. Of course, the work is totally dependent on good weather, and so the number of hours that you would work per week could vary.

Restaurants

Local restaurants experience an increase in business during the summer. There are several positions for waitstaff. The hourly rate is $3.60, and the weekly tip total ranges from $300 to $850. You are told that you can expect a weekly average of approximately $520 in tips. You would be scheduled to work five dinner shifts of 6.5 hours each for a total of 32.5 hours per week. However, on slow nights you might be sent home early, perhaps after working only 5 hours. Thus, your total weekly hours might be fewer than 32.5.

All of the jobs would provide an interesting summer experience. Your personal preferences might favor one position over another. Keep in mind that you will probably have a lot of college expenses.

1. At the electronics store, sales associates average $8000 in sales each week.

   a. Based on the expected weekly average of $8000 in sales, calculate your gross weekly paycheck (before any taxes or other deductions) if you worked a full 40-hour week in sales.

   b. Use the average weekly sales figure of $8000 and write an equation for your weekly earnings, s, where x represents the total number of hours you would work.

    c. What would be your gross paycheck for the week if you worked 30 hours and still managed to sell $8000 in merchandise?

    d. You are told that you would typically work 35 hours per week if your total electronic sales do average $8000. Calculate your typical gross paycheck for a week.

    e. You calculate that to pay college expenses for the upcoming academic year, you need to gross at least $675 a week. How many hours would you have to work in sales each week? Assume that you would sell $8000 in merchandise.

2. In the construction job, you would average a 40-hour workweek.

    a. Calculate your gross paycheck for a typical 40-hour workweek.

    b. Write an equation for your weekly salary, s, for a week with no overtime. Let x represent the total number of hours worked.

    c. If the weather is ideal for a week, you can expect to work 10 hours in overtime (over and above the regular 40-hour workweek). Determine your total gross pay for a week with 10 hours of overtime.

    d. The equation in part b can be used to determine the weekly salary, s, when x, the total number of hours worked, is less than or equal to 40 (no overtime). Write an equation to determine your weekly salary, s, if x is greater than 40 hours.

e. Suppose it turns out to be a gorgeous summer and your supervisor says that you can work as many hours as you want. If you are able to gross $800 a week, you will be able to afford to buy a computer. How many hours would you have to work each week to achieve your goal?

3. The restaurant job involves working a maximum of five dinner shifts of 6.5 hours each.

   a. Calculate what your gross paycheck would be for an exceptionally busy week of five 6.5-hour dinner shifts and $850 in tips.

   b. Calculate what your gross paycheck would be for an exceptionally slow week of five 5-hour dinner shifts and only $300 in tips.

   c. Calculate what your gross paycheck would be for a typical week of five 6.5-hour dinner shifts and $520 in tips.

   d. Use $520 as your typical weekly total for tips, and write a symbolic rule for your gross weekly salary, s, where x represents the number of hours.

   e. Calculate what your gross paycheck would be for a 27-hour week and $520 in tips.

   f. During the holiday week of July 4, you are asked to work an extra dinner shift. You are told to expect $280 in tips for that night alone. Assuming a typical workweek for the rest of the week, would working that extra dinner shift enable you to gross at least $950?

4. You would like to make an informed decision in choosing one of the three positions. Based on all the information you have about the three jobs, fill in the following table.

REGULAR PAY OVERTIME HOLIDAY VACATION *Totally Gross*	LOWEST WEEKLY GROSS PAYCHECK	TYPICAL WEEKLY GROSS PAYCHECK	HIGHEST WEEKLY GROSS PAYCHECK
SALES ASSOCIATE			
CONSTRUCTION WORKER			
WAITSTAFF			

5. Money may be the biggest factor in making your decision. But it is summer, and it would be nice to enjoy what you are doing. Discuss the advantages and disadvantages of each position. What would be your personal choice? Why?

6. You decide that you would prefer an indoor job. Use the equations you developed for the sales job in Problem 1b and for the restaurant position in Problem 3d to calculate how many hours you would have to work in each job to receive the same weekly salary.

ACTIVITY 1.13
Graphs Tell Stories

OBJECTIVES

1. Describe in words what a graph tells you about a given situation.
2. Sketch a graph that best represents the situation described in words.
3. Identify increasing, decreasing, and constant parts of a graph.
4. Identify minimum and maximum points on a graph.
5. Identify a functional relationship graphically using the vertical line test.

The expression "A picture is worth a thousand words" is a cliché, but it is true. Mathematical models are often easier to understand when presented in visual form. To understand such pictures, you need to practice going back and forth between graphs and word descriptions.

Every graph shows how the independent and dependent variables change in relation to one another. As you read a graph from left to right, the *x*-variable is increasing in value. The graph indicates the change in the *y*-values (increasing, decreasing, or constant) as the *x*-values increase.

Graphs are always constructed so that as you read the graph from left to right, the *x*-variable increases in value. The graph shows the change (increasing, decreasing, or constant) in the *y*-values as the *x*-values increase.

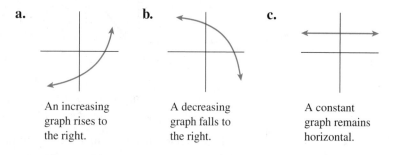

a. An increasing graph rises to the right.

b. A decreasing graph falls to the right.

c. A constant graph remains horizontal.

If a graph increases and then decreases, the point where the graph changes from rising to falling is called a **maximum point**. The *y*-value of this point is called a **local maximum value**. If a graph decreases and then increases, the point where the graph changes from falling to rising is called a **minimum point**. The *y*-value of this point is called a **local minimum value**.

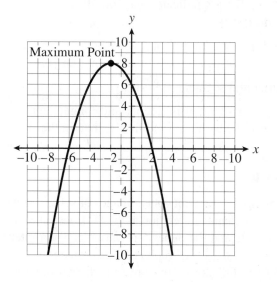

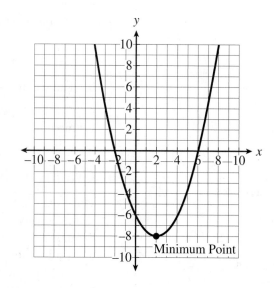

Example 1 *The following graph describes your walk from the parking lot to the library.*

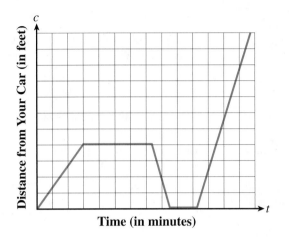

As you read this graph from left to right, it shows how your distance from your car changes as time passes. One possible scenario this graph describes is as follows:

You leave your car and walk at a steady pace toward the library. You meet some friends and stop to chat for a while. You realize that you forgot something and quickly return to your car. After rummaging around for a while, you hurry off to the library.

How did anyone come up with this from the graph? Look at the graph in sections.

a. The first increasing line segment indicates you are moving away from your car because the time and the distance are increasing.

b. The first horizontal section indicates that your distance from the car is constant, so you are standing still.

c. The decreasing line segment indicates your distance from the car is decreasing. When it reaches the horizontal axis, it tells you that you are back at your car.

d. The second horizontal segment indicates you stay at your car for a time.

e. The final increasing segment is steeper and longer than the first, so you are moving away from the car faster and farther than in the first segment.

Graphs to Stories

The graphs in Problems 1–4 present visual images of several situations. Each graph shows how the *y*-values change in relation to the *x*-values. In each situation, identify the independent variable and the dependent variable. Then interpret the situation; that is, describe in words what the graph is telling you about the situation. Indicate whether the graph rises, falls, or is constant and whether the graph reaches either a minimum (smallest) or maximum (largest) *y*-value.

1. A person's core body temperature (°F) in relation to time of day.

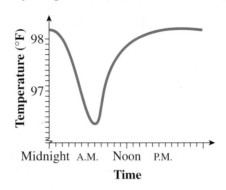

a. Independent: _____ Dependent: _____

b. Interpretation:

2. Performance of a simple task in relation to interest level.

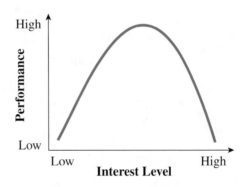

a. Independent: _____ Dependent: _____

b. Interpretation:

3. Net profit of a particular business in relation to time given quarterly.

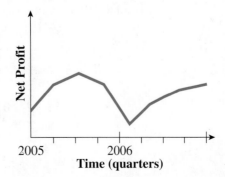

a. Independent: _____   Dependent: _____

b. Interpretation:

4. Annual gross income in relation to number of years.

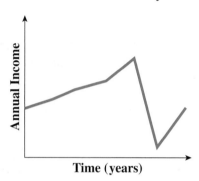

a. Independent: _____   Dependent: _____

b. Interpretation:

Stories to Graphs

In Problems 5 and 6, sketch a graph that best represents the situation described. Note that in many cases the actual values are unknown, so you will need to estimate what seems reasonable to you. Remember to label your axes and identify the independent/dependent variables.

5. You drive to visit your parents, who live 100 miles away. Your average speed is 50 miles per hour. On arrival, you stay for five hours and then return home, again at an average speed of 50 miles per hour. Graph your distance from home, from the time you leave until you return home.

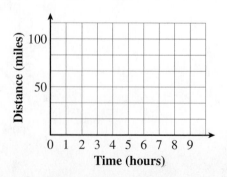

6. You just started a new job that pays 6 dollars per hour, with a raise of 2 dollars per hour every six months. After one and a half years, you receive a promotion that gives you a wage increase of 5 dollars per hour, but your next raise won't come for another year. Sketch a graph of your wage over your first *two and a half* years.

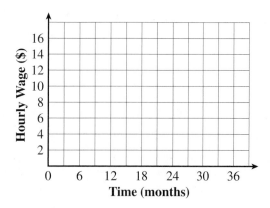

Representing Functions Graphically

Although each of the graphs in Problems 1–6 has a different shape and different properties, they all reflect a functional relationship between the independent and dependent variables. In the following problem, you will explore this special relationship or correspondence more closely.

7. **a.** Use the graph in Problem 1 to complete the following table. Estimate the temperature for each value of time.

TIME OF DAY	1 A.M.	5 A.M.	7 A.M.	10 A.M.	12 NOON	1 P.M.
BODY TEMPERATURE (°F)						

b. How many corresponding temperatures are assigned to any one particular time?

For any specific time of day, there is one and only one corresponding temperature. Therefore, the body temperature is a function of the time of day.

8. The following graph shows the distance from home over a 9-hour period as described in Problem 5.

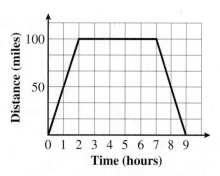

a. Use the graph to complete the following table.

TIME (hours)	1	3	4	8	9
DISTANCE FROM HOME (miles)					

b. Is the distance from home a function of the time on the trip? Explain.

9. The following graph shows the height of a roller coaster as it moves away from its starting point and goes through its first loop.

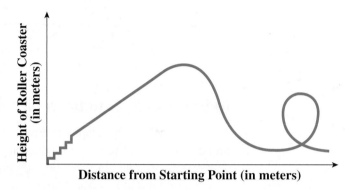

Is the height of the roller coaster a function of the distance of the coaster from the starting point?

Vertical Line Test

You can determine directly from a graph whether or not there is a functional relationship between the two variables.

10. **a.** Refer to the graph in Problem 1 on page 113, and select any specific time of day along the horizontal (*x*) axis. Then move straight up or down (vertically) from that value of time to locate the corresponding point on the graph. How many points do you locate for any given time?

b. If you locate only one point in part a, explain why this would mean that body temperature is a function of the time of day.

c. If you had located more than one point on the graph in part a, explain why this would mean that body temperature is not a function of time.

The procedure in Problem 10 is referred to as the **vertical line test**.

> **DEFINITION**
>
> In the **vertical line test**, a graph represents a function if any vertical line drawn through the graph intersects the graph no more than once.

11. Use the vertical line test on the graphs in Problems 2 through 4 to verify that each graph represents a function.

12. Use the vertical line test to determine which of the following graphs represent functions. Explain.

a.

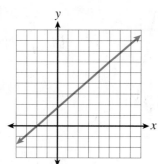

b.

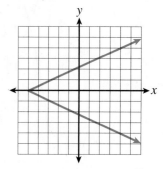

c.

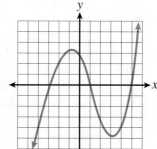

d.

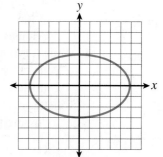

SUMMARY
Activity 1.13

1. In the **vertical line test**, a graph represents a function if any vertical line drawn through the graph intersects the graph no more than once.

2. If a graph increases and then decreases, the point where the graph changes from rising to falling is called a **maximum point**. The y-value of this point is called a **local maximum value**. If a graph decreases and then increases, the point where the graph changes from falling to rising is called a **minimum point**. The y-value of this point is called a **local minimum value**.

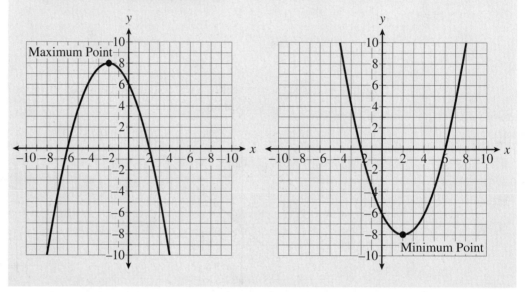

EXERCISES
Activity 1.13

1. You are a technician at the local power plant and you have been asked to prepare a report that compares the output and efficiency of the six generators in your sector. Each generator has a graph that shows output of the generator as a function of time over the previous week, Monday through Sunday. You take all the paperwork home for the night (your supervisor wants this report on his desk at 7:00 A.M.) and to your dismay your cat scatters your pile of papers out of the neat order in which you left them. Unfortunately, the graphs for generators A through F were not labeled (you will know better next time!). You recall some information and find evidence elsewhere for the following facts:

   • Generators A and D were the only ones that maintained a fairly steady output.

   • Generator B was shut down for a little more than two days during midweek.

   • Generator C experienced a slow decrease in output during the entire week.

   • On Tuesday morning, there was a problem with generator E that was corrected in a few hours.

   • Generator D was the most productive over the entire week.

Match each graph with its corresponding generator. Explain in complete sentences how you arrive at your answers.

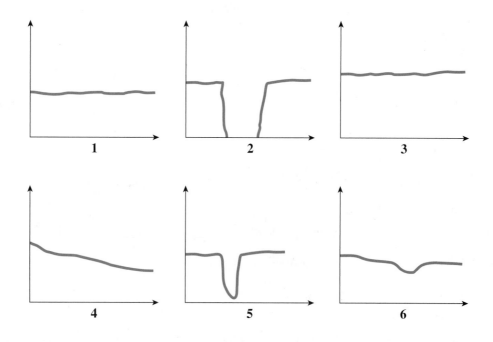

In Exercises 2 and 3, identify the independent variable and the dependent variable. Then interpret the situation being represented. Indicate whether the graph rises, falls, or is constant and whether the graph reaches either a minimum (smallest) or maximum (largest) output value.

2. Time required to complete a task in relation to number of times the task is attempted.

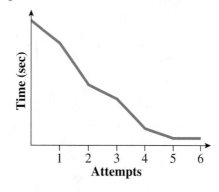

a. Independent: _____   Dependent: _____

b. Interpretation:

3. Number of units sold in relation to selling price.

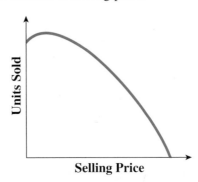

    a. Independent: _____   Dependent: _____

    b. Interpretation:

4. You leave home on Friday afternoon for your weekend getaway. Heavy traffic slows you down for the first half of your trip, but you make good time by the end. Express your distance from home as a function of time.

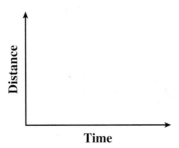

5. Your small business started slowly, losing money in its first 2 years, then breaking even in year three. By the fourth year, you made as much as you lost in the first year and then doubled your profits each of the next 2 years. Graph your profit as the output and time as the input.

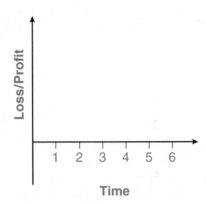

6. Use the vertical line test to determine which of the following graphs represents a function. Explain your answer.

a.

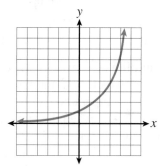

b.

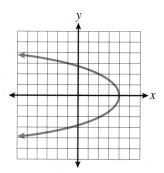

c.

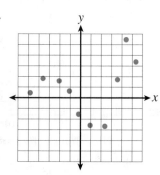

ACTIVITY 1.14

Heating
Schedule

The cost of fuel oil is rising and is affecting the school district's budget. In order to save money, the building maintenance supervisor of the high school has decided to keep the building warm only during school hours.

1. Sketch a graph that best represents the following building heating schedule, which begins at midnight.

At midnight, the building temperature is 55°F. This temperature remains constant until 4 A.M., at which time the temperature of the building steadily increases. By 7 A.M., the temperature is 68°F. The temperature is maintained at a constant 68°F until 7 P.M., when the temperature begins a steady decrease. By 10 P.M., the temperature is back to 55°F.

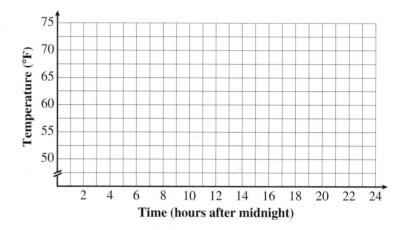

Now, suppose the building maintenance supervisor is instructed by the Board of Education to increase the temperature of the building by a constant 3°F.

2. **a.** On the graph in Problem 1, sketch a graph that represents the new building heat schedule over a 24-hour period, starting at midnight.

   b. Describe how the graph in part a can be obtained from the original graph of the building heating schedule in Problem 1.

The graph of the new heating schedule in Problem 2 represents a **vertical shift** of the original graph. The graph has been shifted vertically upward by 3 units.

3. The heating schedule for a warehouse is represented by the following graph.

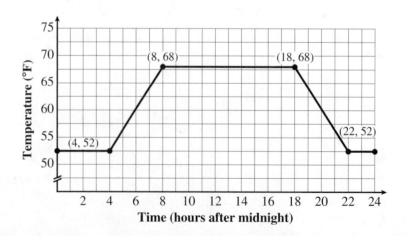

a. As a cost saving measure, the building superintendent decides to drop the temperature of the warehouse by 2°F. Using the given graph, sketch a graph that represents the new heat schedule.

b. Describe how the graph of the new heating schedule can be obtained from the original graph.

Horizontal Shift

4. The following graph represents the heating schedule in an office building.

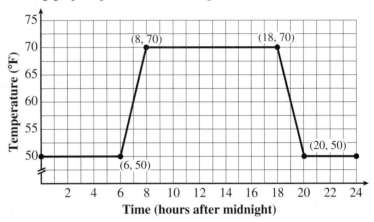

The building superintendent needs to change the heating schedule by moving everything two hours earlier.

a. On the given graph, sketch a graph that represents the new heating schedule. Describe the new schedule in words.

b. Describe how the graph of the new heating schedule can be obtained from the original graph.

The graph of the new heating schedule in Problem 4 represents a **horizontal shift** of the original graph. The original graph has been shifted two units horizontally to the left.

5. a. The heating schedule for the warehouse in Problem 3 is delayed by 2 hours. Sketch a graph that represents the new heating schedule.

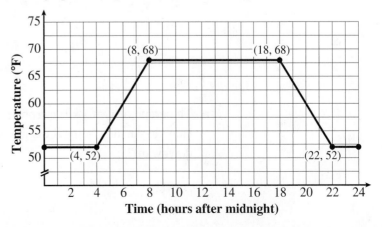

b. Describe how the graphs of the new and original heating schedule are related.

Function Formulas for a Graph Resulting from Vertical or Horizontal Shift

6. a. Use a graphing calculator to graph the squaring function, defined by $y = x^2$, in a standard window. The screen should appear as follows:

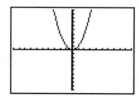

Note: The squaring function is an example of a quadratic function. Quadratic functions are studied in detail in Chapter 3.

b. Graph $y_2 = x^2 + 2$ on the same coordinate axis as $y = x^2$ in part a.

c. Describe how the graph for $y_2 = x^2 + 2$ can be obtained from the graph of $y = x^2$.

d. Now, let $y_3 = x^2 - 3$. Use a graphing calculator to graph the function defined by this equation. Describe how the graph can be obtained from the graph of $y = x^2$.

e. The graph of $y = x^2 + c$ represents a vertical shift of the graph of $y = x^2$. How do you determine if the graph is shifted vertically upward or vertically downward?

7. a. Use a graphing calculator to sketch a graph of $y_2 = (x + 2)^2$ on the same coordinate axis as $y = x^2$. The screen should appear as follows:

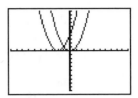

b. Does the graph of $y_2 = (x + 2)^2$ represent a shift of the graph $y = x^2$? If yes, describe the type of shift.

c. Use a graphing calculator to sketch a graph of $y_3 = (x - 4)^2$ on the same coordinate axis as $y = x^2$. Describe how the graph of $y_3 = (x - 4)^2$ can be obtained from the graph of $y = x^2$.

d. The graph of $y = (x + c)^2$ represents a horizontal shift of the graph of $y = x^2$. How do you determine if the shift is to the right or left?

In Problem 6b, adding 2 to the output (the square of a number) results in a vertical shift of the graph of the squaring function. Using function notation, if $y = f(x) = x^2$, then

$$y = x^2 + 2 = f(x) + 2 \text{ is the upward vertical shift of } y = f(x) = x^2.$$

Since $y = f(x) + 2$ involves a change to the output value, $f(x)$, vertical shifts result from "outside" changes to the function.

In Problem 7b, adding 2 to the input value x **before** the squaring is done results in a horizontal shift of the graph of the squaring function. Using function notation, if $y = f(x) = x^2$, then

$$y = (x + 2)^2 = f(x + 2) \text{ is a horizontal shift to the left of } y = f(x) = x^2.$$

Since $y = f(x + 2)$ involves a change to the input value, x, horizontal shifts result from "inside" changes to the function.

The results from Problems 6 and 7 can be generalized as follows:

In general,

1. If a function is defined by $y = f(x)$, and c is a constant, then the graph of $y = f(x) + c$ is the graph of $y = f(x)$ shifted vertically $|c|$ units. If $c > 0$, then the shift is upward. If $c < 0$, then the shift is downward.

2. If a function is defined by $y = f(x)$, and c is a constant, then the graph of $y = f(x + c)$ is the graph of $y = f(x)$ shifted horizontally $|c|$ units. If $c > 0$, then the shift is to the left. If $c < 0$, the shift is to the right.

A vertical or horizontal shift of the graph of a function is called a **translation**. A translation does not change the shape of the graph. It translates (moves) the graph into a new position in the plane.

8. The graph of the absolute value function, defined by $y = |x|$, is

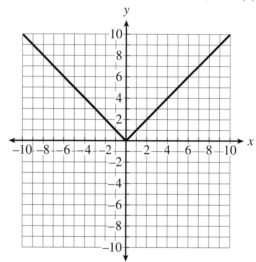

Determine the graph of each of the following translations of the absolute value function. Describe the shift in words. Verify your results using a graphing calculator.

Note: Absolute value functions are discussed in more detail in Chapter 2.

a. $y = |x| + 5$ **b.** $y = |x + 5|$

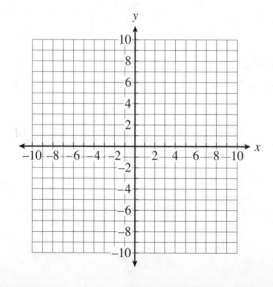   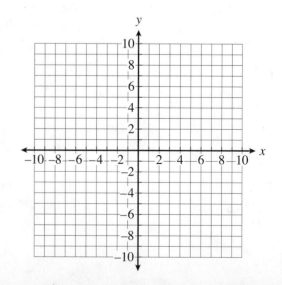

c. $y = |x| - 2$ **d.** $y = |x - 2|$

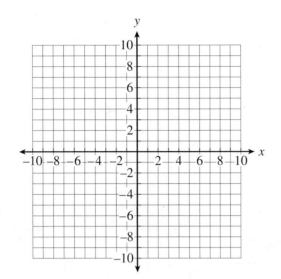   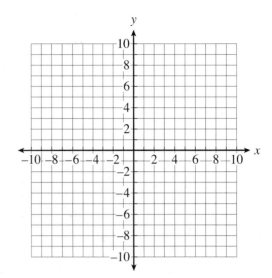

9. The graph of the squaring function, defined by $y = x^2$, is translated (shifted) in parts a–d. Write the equation of the resulting graph.

   a. vertical shift of the graph 3 units upward

   b. vertical shift of the graph 5 units downward

   c. horizontal shift of the graph 2 units to the left

   d. horizontal shift of the graph 4 units to the right

10. The graph of $y = (x - 3)^2 + 5$ involves a vertical and horizontal shift of the graph of $y = x^2$. Use the patterns discussed in this activity to sketch the graph. Verify using a graphing calculator.

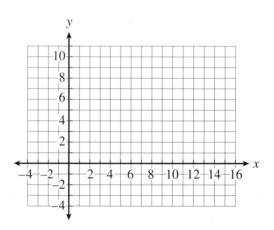

1. In a **vertical shift** of a graph, a positive constant is added to (upward shift) or subtracted from (downward shift) each output value. As a result, the graph is moved vertically upward or vertically downward.

2. In a **horizontal shift** of a graph, a positive constant is first added to (shift left) or subtracted from (shift right) each input value. As a result, the graph is moved horizontally to the left or horizontally to the right.

3. In general, if a function is defined by $y = f(x)$, and c is a constant, then the graph of

   i. $y = f(x) + c$ is the graph of $y = f(x)$ shifted vertically $|c|$ units. If $c > 0$, then the shift is upward. If $c < 0$, then the shift is downward.

   ii. $y = f(x + c)$ is the graph of $y = f(x)$ shifted horizontally $|c|$ units. If $c > 0$, then the shift is to the left. If $c < 0$, the shift is to the right.

4. A vertical or horizontal shift of the graph of a function is called a **translation**. A translation does not change the shape of the graph. It translates (moves) the graph into a new position in the coordinate plane.

EXERCISES
Activity 1.14

1. The graph of the absolute value function is given in Problem 8 on page 126.

   Match each of the graphs in parts a–d with the corresponding shift of the graph of the absolute value function from i–iv.

   i. vertical shift of the graph 3 units upward

   ii. vertical shift of the graph 3 units downward

   iii. horizontal shift of the graph 3 units to the right

   iv. horizontal shift of the graph 3 units to the left

   a.

   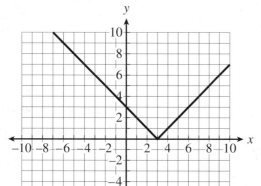

   b.

   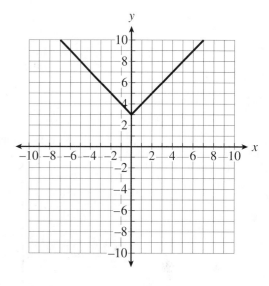

   c.

   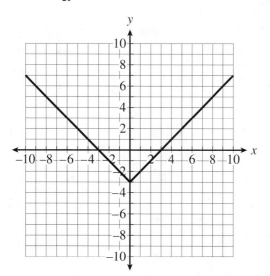

   d.

   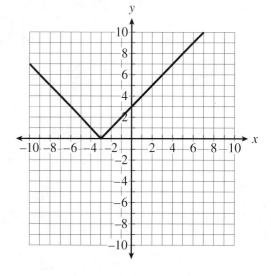

2. In parts a–d, sketch a new graph by performing the specified shift on the given graph.

    a. Vertical shift of the graph
3 units downward.

    b. Horizontal shift of the graph
2 units to the right.

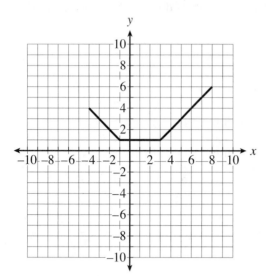

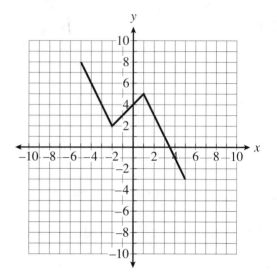

    c. Vertical shift of the graph
4 units upward.

    d. Horizontal shift of the graph
3 units to the left.

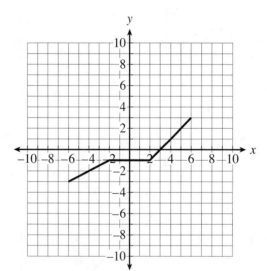

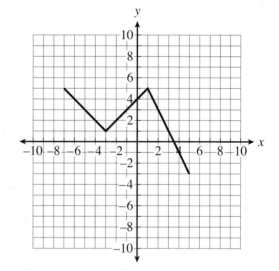

3. The graphs below are horizontal translations of the basic squaring function, $f(x) = x^2$. Write the equation for each function. Check your answer by graphing on your calculator.

a.   **b.**

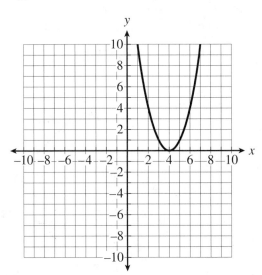   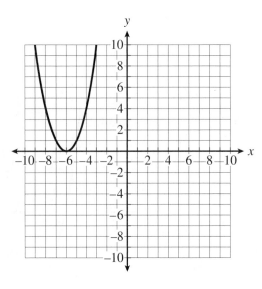

4. Given the graph of $y = f(x)$, translate as indicated by the given equation to graph a new function in parts a–c.

a. $y = f(x) - 3$ **b.** $y = f(x + 2)$ **c.** $y = f(x) + 2$

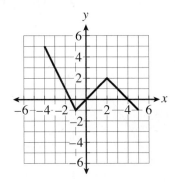   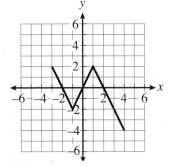   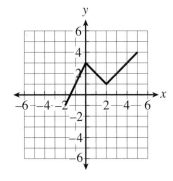

5. Describe in words how the graph of the basic absolute value function will be translated in each case. Check by graphing on your calculator.

  a. $y = |x - 5|$

  b. $y = |x| - 7$

  c. $y = 2 + |x + 4|$

6. Write the equation for each described function. Check by graphing on your calculator.

  a. The squaring function shifted down 8 units.

  b. The absolute value function shifted to the left 4 units.

  c. The linear function $y = 3x$ shifted to the right 5 units.

d. The squaring function shifted up 3 units and to the left 6 units.

7. Each of the following graphs represents the translation of the indicated basic function. Write the equation for each graph. Check by graphing on your calculator.

a. Translation of $y = x^2$

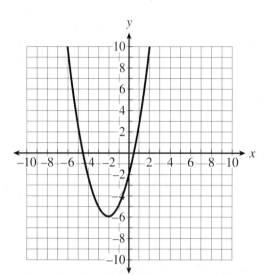

b. Translation of $y = |x|$

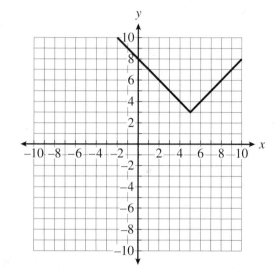

8. A computer technician charges a flat fee of $50 for an on-site service call and $75 per hour thereafter. The following graph represents the total cost c as a function of the number of hours.

a. What is the equation for this function?

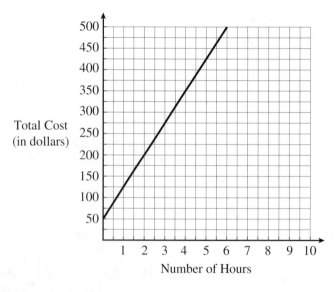

b. Suppose the flat fee for an on-site service increases by 20 dollars. How does the increase affect the cost?

c. Sketch a graph of the new cost function.

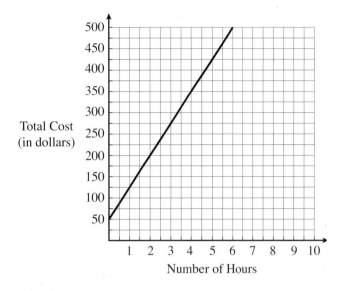

d. Describe how the new graph can be obtained from the original graph.

e. Write an equation for the new cost function in part c.

9. The speed limits over a four mile stretch of country road are represented by the following graph.

   If all the speed limits are to be reduced by 5 MPH, sketch the new graph and describe how it is obtained from the original graph.

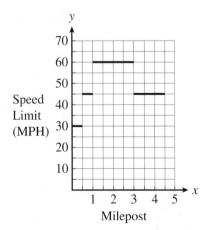

10. A new car depreciates in value over time. Assuming a straight-line depreciation, the car will decrease in value the same amount every year. If a car is purchased in 2005 for $32,000 and decreases in value $2000 every year, the graph shows the car's value, where x represents the years since purchase.

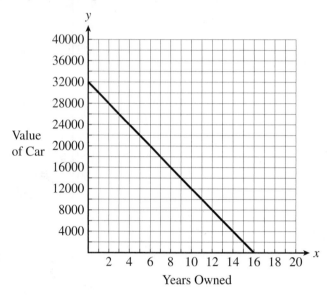

a. What is the equation for this function?

b. If you want the independent variable x to be the actual year instead of the number of years since 2005, how would the graph be shifted?

c. Write the equation for this translated function, where x represents the actual year.

Activities 1.6–1.14   What Have I Learned?

1. What is the mathematical definition of a function? Give a real-life example and explain how this example satisfies the definition of a function.

2. Describe how you can tell from a graph when a function is increasing and when it is decreasing.

3. Identify four different ways that a function can be defined. Give an example of each.

4. Use a newspaper to find at least 4 examples of functions and report your findings back to the class. For each example, you should do the following:

   a. Explain how the example satisfies the definition of a function.

   b. Describe how the function is defined (see Problem 3).

   c. Identify the independent and dependent variables.

   d. Determine the domain of the function.

5. The notation $g(t)$ represents the weight (in grams) of a melting ice cube t minutes after being removed from the freezer. Interpret the meaning of $g(10) = 4$.

6. The graph of $y = |x + 2| - 3$ involves a horizontal and vertical shift of the graph of the function defined by $y = |x|$.

   a. Sketch a graph of $y = |x + 2| - 3$ by first doing a horizontal shift of the graph of $y = |x|$, followed by a vertical shift of the graph resulting from the horizontal shift.

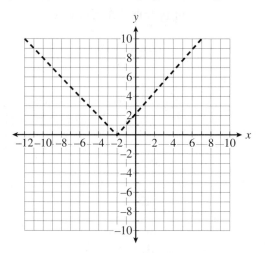

   b. Now, sketch a graph of $y = |x + 2| - 3$ by first doing the vertical shift of the graph of $y = |x|$, followed by the horizontal shift.

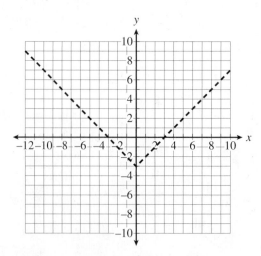

   c. Compare the graphs in parts a and b.

Activities 1.6–1.14 **How Can I Practice?**

1. You bought a company in 2006 and have tracked the company's profits and losses from its beginning in 2000 to the present. You decide to graph the information where the number of years since 2006 is the x-variable and profit or loss for the year is the y-variable. Note that the year 2006 corresponds to 0 on the x-axis. Determine the quadrant or axis on which you would plot the points that correspond to the following data. If your answer is on an axis, indicate between which quadrants the point is located.

   a. The loss in 2003 was $1500.

   b. The profit in 2007 was $6000.

   c. The loss in 2009 was $1000.

   d. In 2002, there was no profit or loss.

   e. The profit in 2000 was $500.

   f. The loss in 2006 was $800.

2. Fish need oxygen to live, just as you do. The amount of dissolved oxygen (D.O.) in water is measured in parts per million (ppm). Trout need a minimum of 6 ppm to live.

   The data in the table shows the relationship between the temperature of the water and the amount of dissolved oxygen present.

TEMP (°C)	11	16	21	26	31
D.O. (in ppm)	10.2	8.6	7.7	7.0	6.4

   a. Represent the data in the table graphically. Place temperature along the horizontal axis and dissolved oxygen along the vertical axis.

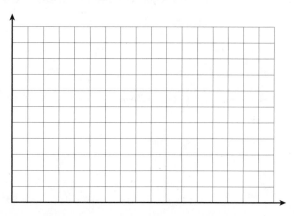

b. What general trend do you notice in the data?

c. In which of the 5-degree temperature intervals given in the table does the dissolved oxygen content change the most?

d. Which representation (table or graph) presents the information and trends more clearly?

3. When you were born, your uncle invested $1000 for you in a local bank. Your bank has compounded the interest continuously at a rate of 6%. The following graph shows how your investment grows.

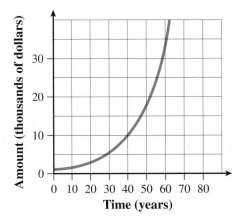

a. Which variable is the independent variable?

b. How much money did you have when you were 10 years old?

c. Estimate in what year your original investment will have doubled.

d. If your share of your college tuition bill is estimated to be $2600 in the first year of college, will you have enough to pay the bill with these funds? (Assume that you attend when you are eighteen.) Explain.

4. You decide to lose weight and will cut down on your calories to lose 2 pounds a week. Suppose that your present weight is 180 pounds. Sketch a graph covering twenty weeks showing your projected weight loss. Describe your graph. If you stick to your plan, how much will you weigh in three months (13 weeks)?

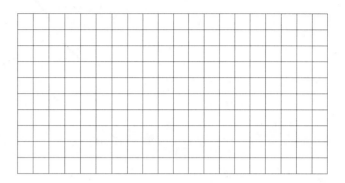

5. A taxicab driver charges a flat rate of $2.50 plus $1.50 per mile. The fare F (in dollars) is a function of the distance driven, x (in miles). The driver wants to display a table for her customers to show approximate fares for different locations within the city.

a. Write an equation for F in terms of x.

b. Use the equation to complete the following table:

x	0.25	0.5	0.75	1.0	1.5	2.0	3.0	5.0	10.0
F									

6. Interpret each situation represented by the following graphs. That is, describe in words what the graph is saying about the relationship between the variables. Indicate what occurs when either a minimum or maximum value is reached.

a. Hours of daylight per day in relation to time of year.

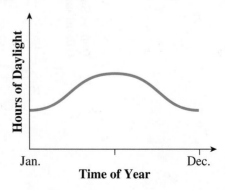

b. Population of fish in a pond in relation to the number of years since stocking.

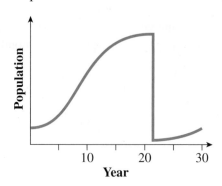

c. Distance from home (in miles) in relation to driving time (in hours).

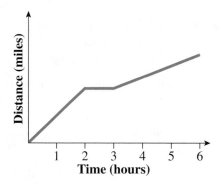

d. Amount of money saved per month in relation to amount of money earned.

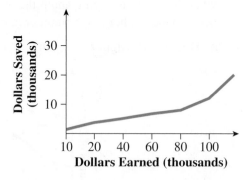

7. In the following situations, determine the independent and dependent variables and then sketch a graph that best describes the situation. Remember to label the axes with the names of the variables.

   a. Sketch a graph that approximates average temperatures where you live as a function of the number of months since January.

   Independent variable:_____

   Dependent variable: _____

   b. If you don't study, you would expect to do poorly on the next test. If you study several hours, you should do quite well, but if you study for too many more hours, your test score will probably not improve. Sketch a graph of your test score as a function of study time.

   Independent variable: _____   Dependent variable: _____

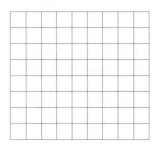

In Exercises 8–15, solve each equation for x.

8. $2(x + 4) = 12$

9. $3x + 2(x - 6) = x + 4$

10. $\frac{1}{3}(2x + 3) = 3(x + 1)$

11. $(2x - 5) - (4 - 3x) = 11$

12. $\frac{1}{2}x + \frac{1}{3}x + 5 = x$

13. $1.50x + 0.85(12 - x) = 14.75$

14. $-7 = -3(x - 7) + 2x + 1$

15. $2[6x - 7(x - 1)] = 5x - 21$

16. The cost of printing a brochure to advertise your lawn-care business is a flat fee of $10 plus $0.08 per copy. Let C represent the total cost of printing and x represent the number of copies you order.

a. Write an equation that expresses the relationship between C and x.

b. Organize the data into a table of values. Begin with 1000 copies, increase by increments of 1000, and end with 5000 copies.

NUMBER OF COPIES, x	TOTAL COST ($), C

c. Graph the data obtained in part b. Use a straightedge to connect the points and extend the graph. Scale the axes appropriately so that you can plot the ordered pair corresponding to 10,000 copies.

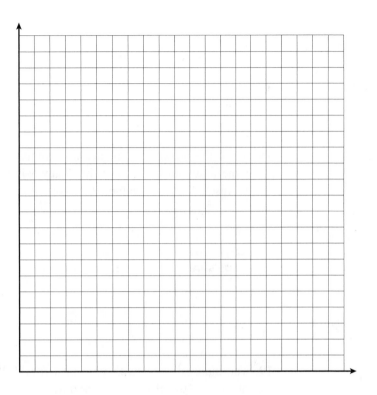

d. What is the total cost of printing 8000 copies?

e. You have $500 to spend on advertising. How many copies can you have printed for that amount?

17. Solve each of the following equations for the given variable:

    a. $d = rt$ for r **b.** $P = a + b + c$ for b

c. $A = P + Prt$ for r **d.** $y = 4x - 5$ for x

e. $w = \dfrac{4}{7}h + 3$ for h

18. A volatile stock began the last week of the year worth x dollars per share. The following table shows the changes during that week. If you own 30 shares, write an equation that represents the total value, V, of your stock at the end of the week.

DAY	1	2	3	4	5
CHANGE IN VALUE/SHARE	Doubled	Lost 10	Tripled	Gained 12	Lost half its value

19. You planned a trip with your best friend. You had only four days for your trip and planned to travel x hours each day.

The first day, you stopped for sightseeing and lost two hours of travel time. The second day, you gained one hour because you did not stop for lunch. On the third day, you traveled well into the night and doubled your planned travel time. On the fourth day, you traveled only a fourth of the time you planned because your friend was sick. You averaged 45 miles per hour for the first two days and 48 miles per hour for the last two days.

a. How many hours, in terms of x, did you travel the first two days?

b. How many hours, in terms of x, did you travel the last two days?

c. Express the total distance, D, traveled over the four days as an equation in terms of x. Simplify the equation. Recall that distance = average rate · time.

d. Write an equation that expresses the total distance, y, you would have traveled had you traveled exactly x hours each day at the average speeds indicated above. Simplify the equation.

e. If you anticipated traveling for seven hours each day, how many miles did you actually go on your trip?

f. How many miles would you have gone had you traveled exactly seven hours each day?

20. You read about a full-time summer position in sales at the Cameron-Dylan Furniture Store. The job pays $260 per week plus 20% commission on sales over $1000.

a. Explain how you would calculate the total amount earned each week.

b. Let x represent the dollar amount of sales for the week. Write a symbolic rule that expresses your earnings, E, for the week in terms of x.

c. Write an equation to determine how much furniture you must sell to have a gross salary of $500 for the week.

d. Solve the equation in part c.

e. Is the total amount of sales reasonable? Explain

21. As a prospective employee in a furniture store, you are offered a choice of salary. The following table shows your options:

OPTION 1	$100 per week	Plus 30% of all sales
OPTION 2	$150 per week	Plus 15% of all sales

a. Write an equation to represent the total salary, S, for option 1 if the total sales are x dollars per week.

b. Write an equation to represent the total salary, S, for option 2 if the total sales are x dollars per week.

    c. Write an equation that you could use to determine how much you would have to sell in a week to earn the same salary under both plans.

    d. Solve the equation in part c. Interpret your result.

    e. What is the common salary for the amount of sales found in part d?

    f. Graph the two equations from parts a and b on the following grid. Locate the point of the common salary and use the graph to determine which option provides the larger salary for furniture sales of more than $333 per week.

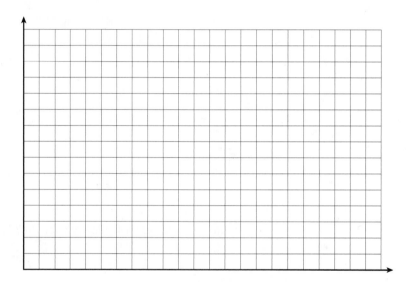

22. A triathlon includes swimming, long-distance running, and cycling.

    a. Let *x* represent the number of miles the competitors swim. If the long-distance run is 10 miles longer than the distance swum, write an expression that represents the distance the competitors run in the event.

    b. The distance the athletes cycle is 55 miles longer than they run. Use the result in part a to write an expression in terms of *x* that represents the cycling distance of the race.

c. Write an expression that represents the total distance of all three phases of the triathlon. Simplify the expression.

d. If the total distance of the triathlon is 120 miles, write and solve an equation to determine x. Interpret the result.

e. What are the lengths of the running and cycling portions of the race?

23. The following graph is a sketch of the step function. Note that an open circle indicates that the point is not included in the graph.

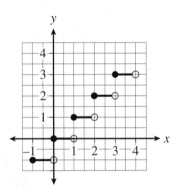

In parts a–d, sketch a new graph of the step function by performing the specified translation.

a. Vertical shift of the graph 1 unit upward.

b. Vertical shift of the graph 1 unit downward.

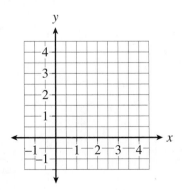

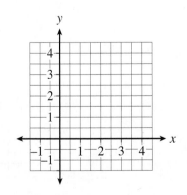

c. Horizontal shift of the graph 1 unit to the right.

d. Horizontal shift of the graph 1 unit to the left.

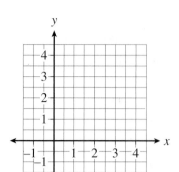

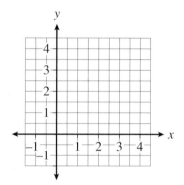

24. The graph of the function defined by $y = f(x)$ is

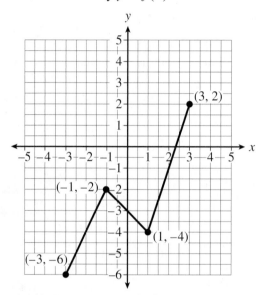

Sketch a graph of each function defined by the given equation. Describe the type of shift that was performed on the original graph.

a. $y = f(x) + 3$

b. $y = f(x + 3)$

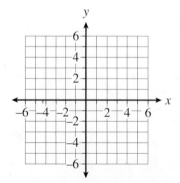

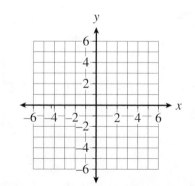

Summary

The bracketed numbers following each concept indicate the activity in which the concept is discussed.

CONCEPT / SKILL	DESCRIPTION	EXAMPLE
Problem solving [1.2], [1.3]	Problem-solving strategies include: • discussing the problem • organizing information • drawing a picture • recognizing patterns • doing a simpler problem	You drive for 2 hours at an average speed of 47 mph. How far do you travel? $d = rt$ $d = \dfrac{47 \text{ mi}}{\text{hr}} \cdot 2 \text{ hr} = 94 \text{ mi}$
Variable [1.3]	A quantity or quality that may change in value from one particular instance to another, usually represented by a letter. When a variable describes an actual quantity, its values must include the unit of measurement of that quantity.	The number of miles you drive in a week is a variable. Its value may (and usually does) change from one week to the next. x and y are commonly used to represent variables.
Formulas [1.3]	A formula shows the arithmetic relationship between two or more quantities; each quantity is represented by a letter or symbol.	$F = ma$ for $m = 120$ and $a = 25$ $F = 120 \cdot 25 = 3000$
Applying a known ratio to a given piece of information [1.4]	Total · known ratio = unknown part Part ÷ known ratio = unknown total	Forty percent of the 350 children play an instrument; 40% is the known ratio; 350 is the total. $350 \times 0.40 = 140$ A total of 140 children play an instrument. Twenty-four children, constituting 30% of the marching band, play the saxophone; 30% is the known ratio, 24 is the part. $24 \div 0.30 = 80$ A total of 80 children are in the marching band.
Solving a proportion [1.4]	$\dfrac{a}{b} = \dfrac{c}{d}, b \neq 0, d \neq 0$ Equivalently, $a \cdot d = b \cdot c$	$\dfrac{7}{30} = \dfrac{x}{4140}$ $30 \cdot x = 7 \cdot 4140$ $x = \dfrac{7 \cdot 4140}{30} = 966$
Using unit (or dimensional) analysis to solve conversion problems [1.5]	1. Identify the unit of the result. 2. Set up the sequence of multiplications so the appropriate units cancel, leaving the unit of the result. 3. Multiply and divide the numbers as usual to obtain the numerical part of the result. 4. Check that the appropriate units cancel, leaving the expected unit of the result.	To convert your height of 70 inches to centimeters: $70 \text{ in.} \cdot \dfrac{2.54 \text{ cm}}{1 \text{ inch}} = 177.8 \text{ cm}$

Input variable [1.6]	The input variable, often represented by x, is the value given first in a relationship.	In the relationship between the perimeter and the side of a square, $P = 4s$, s is the input variable.
Output variable [1.6]	The output, often represented by y, is the value that corresponds to or is determined by the given input value (x).	In the relationship between the perimeter and the side of a square, $P = 4s$, P is the output variable.
Function [1.6]	A function is a correspondence between an input (x) variable and an output (y) variable that assigns a single, unique output value (y) to each input value (x).	See Example 1 in Activity 1.6.
Ordered pair [1.6]	An ordered pair of numbers consists of two numbers written in the form (x, y), where x is the input and y is the output. The order in which they are listed is significant.	(2, 3) is an ordered pair. In this pair, 2 is the input and 3 is the output.
Verbally defined function [1.6]	A function is defined verbally when it is defined using words.	The high temperature in Miami, Florida, is a function of the day of the year, because for each day there is one high temperature.
Graphically defined function [1.6]	A function is defined graphically when the x-variable is represented on the horizontal axis and the y-variable on the vertical axis.	
Numerically defined function [1.6]	A function is defined numerically using ordered pairs or presented as a table of matched pairs.	See Example 1 in Activity 1.6.
Horizontal axis [1.6]	In graphing an x-y relationship, the variable x is referenced on the horizontal axis (often called the x-axis).	
Vertical axis [1.6]	In graphing an x-y relationship, the variable y is referenced on the vertical axis (often called the y-axis).	
Rectangular coordinate system [1.6]	Allows every point in the plane to be identified by an ordered pair of numbers, determined by the distance of the point from two perpendicular number lines (called coordinate axes) that intersect at their respective 0 values, the origin.	

Scaling [1.6]	Setting the same distance between each pair of adjacent tick marks on an axis.	 −4 −3 −2 −1 0 1 2 3 4 Scale is 1
Quadrants [1.6]	Two perpendicular coordinate axes divide the plane into four quadrants, labeled counterclockwise with quadrant I being the upper-right quadrant.	
Point in the plane [1.6]	Points that are identified by an ordered pair of numbers (x, y) in which x represents the horizontal distance from the origin and y represents the vertical distance from the origin.	$(2, 30)$ are the coordinates of a point in the first quadrant located 2 units to the right and 30 units above the origin.
Independent variable [1.7]	Independent variable is another name for the x-variable (the input) of a function.	See Example 4 in Activity 1.7.
Dependent variable [1.7]	Dependent variable is another name for the y-variable (the ouput) of a function.	See Example 4 in Activity 1.7.
Domain of a function [1.7]	The domain of the function is the collection of all replacement values for the independent variable.	See Example 4 in Activity 1.7.
Practical domain of a function [1.7]	The practical domain is the collection of replacement values of the independent variable that makes practical sense in the context of the situation.	See Example 3 in Activity 1.7.
Range of a function [1.7]	The range of a function is the collection of all dependent variable values of a function.	See Example 3 in Activity 1.7.
Practical range of a function [1.7]	The practical range is the collection of all dependent variable values that make practical sense in the context of the situation.	See Example 3 in Activity 1.7.
Mathematical model [1.8]	A mathematical model is a mathematical structure such as a formula, a graph, or a table, that fits or approximates the important features of a given situation.	See Problems 8 and 10 in Activity 1.8.
Solution of an equation [1.9]	The solution of an equation is a replacement value for the variable that makes both sides of the equation equal in value.	3 is a solution of the equation $4x − 5 = 7$.

Solve an equation using a numerical approach [1.9]	To solve an equation using a numerical approach, use a guess, check, and repeat process. This process can be automated using the table feature of a graphing calculator.	$4x - 7 = 5$ try $x = 2, 4(2) - 7 = 1$ (too low) try $x = 4, 4(4) - 7 = 9$ (too high) try $x = 3, 4(3) - 7 = 5$ (This is it!)
Solve an equation graphically [1.9]	To solve an equation graphically, first graph the equation. Then locate the point that has the desired value as its y-coordinate. The value of the x-coordinate of that point is the solution to the equation.	Solve $-2x + 3 = 5$ 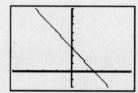 The output value is 5 when the input value is -1. Therefore, -1 is the solution.
Evaluate an algebraic expression [1.9]	To evaluate an algebraic expression, replace the variable(s) by its (their) assigned value(s) and perform the indicated arithmetic operation(s).	Evaluate $3x^2 - 2x + 4$ when $x = 2$. $3(2)^2 - 2(2) + 4$ $3 \cdot 4 - 4 + 4$ $12 - 4 + 4$ 12
Isolate a variable in an equation [1.9], [1.10]	Write the equation so that the variable you are solving for is on one side and all other numbers and variables are on the other side.	The variable y is isolated in the equation $y = 3x + 25$.
How to solve an equation for a given variable [1.9], [1.10]	Add and/or subtract appropriate terms so that all terms involving the variable you are solving for are on one side of the equation and all terms involving numbers and other variables appear on the other side. Then combine like terms and finally divide and/or multiply by the coefficient of the variable.	$4x + 7 + 5x = 7 + 2x - 13$ $9x + 7 = 2x - 6$ $7x = -13$ $x = -13/7$
Solve an equation algebraically for a specified variable [1.9], [1.10]	An algebraic approach to solving an equation is complete when the variable of interest is alone on one side of the equation with coefficient 1 and the other side is simplified.	$4x + 7 + 5x = 7 + 2x - 13$ $9x + 7 = 2x - 6$ $7x = -13$ $x = -13/7$

Solve a formula for a given variable [1.11]	To solve a formula, collect the term containing the variable of interest on one side of the equation, with all other terms on the other side. Then, divide both sides of the equation by the coefficient of the variable.	$2(a + b) = 8 - 5a$ for a $2a + 2b = 8 - 5a$ $2a + 5a = 8 - 2b$ $7a = 8 - 2b$ $a = \dfrac{8 - 2b}{7}$
Distributive property [1.11]	$\underbrace{a \cdot (b + c)}_{\text{factored form}} = \underbrace{a \cdot b + a \cdot c}_{\text{expanded form}}$	$4(x + 6) = 4 \cdot x + 4 \cdot 6$ $\qquad\quad = 4x + 24$
General strategy for solving equations algebraically [1.11]	General strategy for solving an equation algebraically: 1. Simplify the expressions on each side of the equation. 2. Collect the variable term on one side of the equation. 3. Solve for the variable by dividing each side of the equation by the coefficient of the variable. 4. Check your result in the original equation.	$3(2x - 5) + 2x = 9$ $6x - 15 + 2x = 9$ $8x - 15 = 9$ $8x = 24$ $x = 3$ Check: $\quad 3(2 \cdot 3 - 5) + 2 \cdot 3$ $= 3(6 - 5) + 6$ $= 3 \cdot 1 + 6$ $= 9$
Vertical line test [1.13]	In the **vertical line test**, a graph represents a function if any vertical line drawn through the graph intersects the graph no more than once.	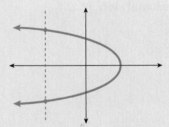 This graph is not a function.
Increasing function [1.13]	The graph of an increasing function rises to the right.	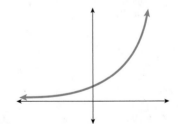
Decreasing function [1.13]	The graph of a decreasing function falls to the right.	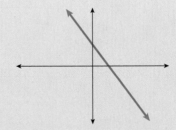

Constant function [1.13]

The graph of a constant function is a horizontal line.

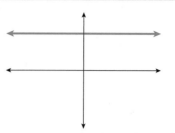

Vertical shift [1.14]

A positive constant is added to (upward shift) or subtracted from (downward shift) each output value. As a result, the graph is moved vertically upward or vertically downward.

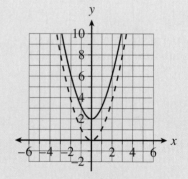

Vertical shift of the graph of $y = x^2$ 2 units upward.

Horizontal shift [1.14]

A positive constant is first added to (shift left) or subtracted from (shift right) each input value. As a result, the graph is moved horizontally to the left or horizontally to the right.

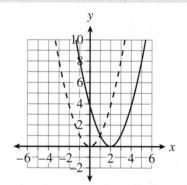

Horizontal shift of the graph of $y = x^2$ 2 units to the right.

Gateway Review

1. Determine whether each of the following is a function.

   a. The loudness of the stereo system is a function of the position of the volume dial.

   b. $\{(2, 9), (3, 10), (2, -9)\}$

   c.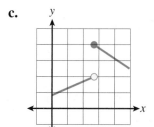

2. For an average yard, the fertilizer costs $20. You charge $8 per hour to do yard work. If x represents the number of hours worked on the yard, and y represents the total cost, including fertilizer, complete the following table:

x	0	2	3	5	7
y					

   a. Is the total cost a function of the hours worked? Explain.

   b. What is the independent variable?

   c. Which is the dependent variable?

   d. Which value(s) of the domain would not be realistic for this situation? Explain.

3. As a real estate salesperson you earn a small salary plus a percentage of the selling price of each house you sell. If your salary is $100 a week plus 3.5% of the selling price of each house sold, what must your total annual home sales be for you to gross $30,000 in one year? Assume that you work 50 weeks per year.

4. Use the formula $I = Prt$ to evaluate I, given the following information.

   a. $P = \$2000, r = 5\%, t = 1$

   b. $P = \$3000, r = 6\%, t = 2$

5. Use the formula $P = 2(w + l)$ to evaluate P for the following information.

   a. $w = 2.8$ and $l = 3.4$

   b. $w = 7\frac{1}{3}$ and $l = 8\frac{1}{4}$

6. Solve the given equations, and check your results.

   a. $4(x + 5) - x = 80$ **b.** $-5(x - 3) + 2x = 6$

   c. $38 = 57 - (x + 32)$ **d.** $-13 + 4(3x + 5) = 7$

   e. $5x + 3(2x - 8) = 2(x + 6)$

   f. $-4x - 2(5x - 7) + 2 = -3(3x + 5) - 4$

   g. $-32 + 6(3x + 4) = -(-5x + 38) + 3x$

7. You visit some relatives in Syracuse, New York. You want to drive to Buffalo to see Niagara Falls. The cost of renting a car for a day is $25 plus 15 cents per mile.

   a. Identify the independent variable.

   b. Identify the dependent variable.

   c. Use x to represent the independent variable and y to represent the dependent variable. Write an equation rule that models the daily rental cost in terms of the number of miles driven.

   d. Complete the following table:

e. Plot the points from the table in part d. Then draw the line through all five points.

x	100	200	300	400	500
y					

(Make sure you label your axes and use appropriate scaling.)

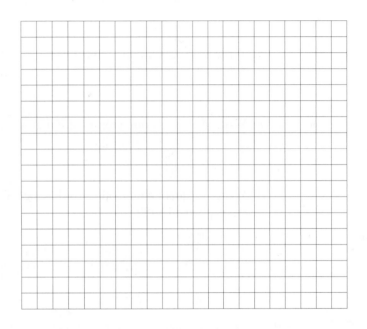

f. The distance from Syracuse to Buffalo is 153 miles. Estimate from the graph in part e how much it will cost to travel from Buffalo to Syracuse and back.

g. Use the mathematical model in part c to determine the exact cost of this trip.

h. You have budgeted $115 for car rental for your day trip. Use your graph to estimate the greatest number of miles you can travel in the day and not exceed your allotted budget? Estimate from your graph.

i. Use the mathematical model in part c to determine the exact number of miles you can travel in the day and not exceed $115.

j. What are realistic replacement values for the independent variable if you rent the car for only one day?

8. The proceeds from your high school talent show to benefit a local charity totaled $950. Since the seats were all taken, you know that 500 people attended. The cost per ticket was $1.50 for students and $2.50 for adults. Unfortunately, you misplaced the ticket stubs that would indicate how many students and how many adults attended. You need this information for accounting purposes and future planning.

    a. Let n represent the number of students who attended. Write an expression in terms of n to represent the number of adults who attended.

    b. Write an expression in terms of n that will represent the proceeds from the student tickets.

    c. Write an expression in terms of n that will represent the proceeds from the adult tickets.

    d. Write an equation that indicates that the total proceeds from the student and adult tickets totaled $950.

    e. How many student tickets and how many adult tickets were sold?

9. You have an opportunity to be the manager of a day camp for the summer. You know that your fixed costs for operating the camp are $600 per week, even if there are no campers. Each camper who attends costs the management $10 per week. The camp charges each camper $40 per week.

    Let x represent the number of campers.

    a. Write an equation in terms of x that represents the total cost, C, of running the camp per week.

    b. Write an equation in terms of x that represents the total income (revenue), R, from the campers per week.

    c. Write an equation in terms of x that represents the total profit, P, from the campers per week.

    d. How many campers must attend for the camp to break even with revenue and costs?

e. The camp would like to make a profit of $600. How many campers must enroll to make that profit?

f. How much money would the camp lose if only 10 campers attend?

g. Use your graphing calculator to graph the revenue and cost equations. Compare the break-even point from the graph (point of intersection) with your answer in part d.

10. Solve each of the following equations for the specified variable.

    a. $I = Prt$, for P

    b. $f = v + at$, for t

    c. $2x - 3y = 7$, for y

11. You contact the local print shop to produce a commemorative booklet for your high school theater group. It is the group's twenty-fifth anniversary, and in the booklet you want a short history plus a description of all the theater productions for the past 25 years. It costs $750 to typeset the booklet and 25 cents for each copy produced.

    a. Write a mathematical model that gives the total cost, C, in terms of the number, x, of booklets produced.

    b. Use the equation from part a to determine the total cost of producing 500 booklets.

    c. How many booklets can be produced for $1000?

d. Suppose the booklets are sold for 75 cents each. Write an equation for the total revenue, *R*, from the sale of *x* booklets.

e. How many booklets must be sold to break even? That is, for what value of *x* is the total cost of production equal to the total amount of revenue?

f. How many booklets must be sold to make a $500 profit?

12. You are designing a cylindrical container as new packaging for a popular brand of coffee. The current package is a cylinder with a diameter of 4 inches and a height of 5.5 inches. The volume of a cylinder is given by the formula

$$V = \pi r^2 h,$$

where *V* is the volume (in cubic inches), *r* is the radius (in inches), and *h* is the height (in inches).

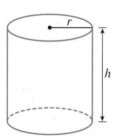

How much coffee does the current container hold? Round your answer to the nearest tenth of a cubic inch.

13. You have been asked to alter the dimensions of the container in Problem 12 so that the new package will contain less coffee. To save money, the company plans to sell the new package for the same price as before.

You will do this in one of two ways:

  i. By increasing the diameter and decreasing the height by $\frac{1}{2}$ inch each (resulting in a slightly wider and shorter can) or

  ii. By decreasing the diameter and increasing the height by $\frac{1}{2}$ inch each (resulting in a slightly narrower and taller can).

a. Determine which new design, if either, will result in a package that holds less coffee than the current one.

b. By what percent will you have decreased the volume?

14. In parts a–d, sketch a graph of the new function resulting from the specified translation of the given graph.

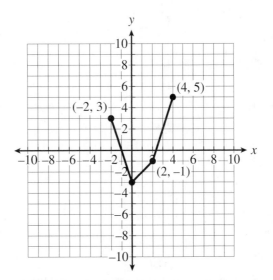

a. Vertical shift of the graph 3 units downward.

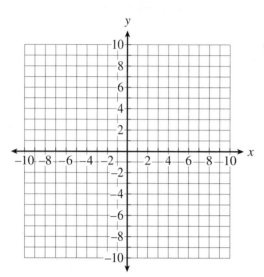

b. Vertical shift of the graph 5 units upward.

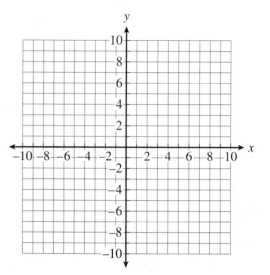

c. Horizontal shift of the graph 2 units to the left.

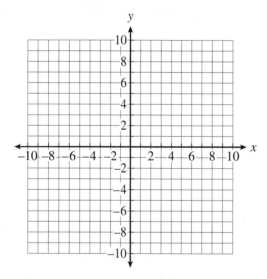

d. Horizontal shift of the graph 4 units to the right.

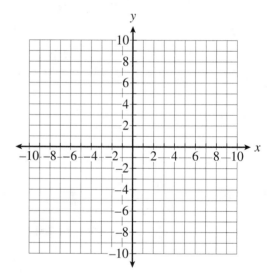

15. The graph of the function defined by $y = g(x)$ is

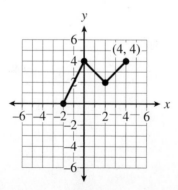

Sketch a graph of each of the following functions defined by the given equation. Describe the type of shift that you performed on the original graph.

a. $y = g(x) - 2$

A vertical shift of the graph of $y = g(x)$ 2 units downward.

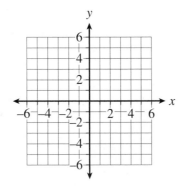

b. $y = g(x - 2)$

A horizontal shift of the graph of $y = g(x)$ 2 units to the right.

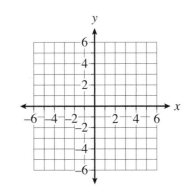

CHAPTER 2

Linear Function Models and Problem Solving

ACTIVITY 2.1
How Fast Did
You Lose?

OBJECTIVE

1. Determine the average rate of change.

You are a member of a health and fitness club. The club's registered dietitian and your personal trainer helped you develop a special eight-week diet and exercise program. The data in the following table represents your weight, w, as a function of time, t, over an eight-week period.

Time Weights for No One

TIME (weeks)	0	1	2	3	4	5	6	7	8
WEIGHT (lb)	140	136	133	131	130	127	127	130	126

1. a. Plot the data points using ordered pairs of the form (t, w). For example, $(3, 131)$ is a data point that represents your weight at the end of the third week.

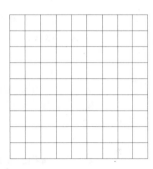

The resulting graph of points in Problem 1 is called a **scatterplot**.

b. What is the practical domain of this function?

   c. What is the practical range of this function?

2. a. What was your weight at the beginning of the program?

   b. What was your weight at the end of the first week?

3. To see how the diet and exercise program is working for you, you analyze your weekly weight changes during the eight-week period.

   a. During which week(s) does your weight increase?

   b. During which week(s) does your weight decrease?

   c. During which week(s) does your weight remain unchanged?

Average Rate of Change

4. Your weight decreases during each of the first five weeks of the program.

   a. Determine the actual change in your weight over the first five weeks of the program by subtracting your initial weight from your weight at the end of the first five weeks.

   b. What is the sign (positive or negative) of your answer? What is the significance of this sign?

   c. Determine the change in the t-value over the first five weeks; that is, from $t = 0$ to $t = 5$.

   d. Write the ratio of the change in weight from part a to the change in time in part c. Interpret the meaning of this ratio.

The change in weight describes how much weight you have gained or lost, but it does not tell how quickly you shed those pounds. That is, a loss of 3 pounds in one week is more impressive than a loss of 3 pounds over a month's time. Dividing the change in weight by the change in time gives an average rate at which you have lost weight over this period of time. Its units are weight units per time unit—in this case, pounds per week.

The ratio in Problem 4d,

$$\frac{-13 \text{ pounds}}{5 \text{ weeks}} = -2.6 \text{ pounds per week},$$

is called the **average rate of change** of weight with respect to time over the first five weeks of the program. It can be interpreted as an average loss of 2.6 pounds each week for the first five weeks of the program.

Delta Notation

The change in the values of a variable is so important that special symbolic notation has been developed to denote it.

The uppercase Greek letter delta Δ is used with a variable's name to represent a change in the value of the variable from a starting point to an ending point.

For example in Problem 4, the notation Δw represents the change in value of the dependent variable, weight w. It is calculated by subtracting the initial value of w, denoted by w_1, from the final value of w, denoted by w_2. Symbolically, this change is represented by

$$\Delta w = w_2 - w_1.$$

In the case of Problem 4a, the change in weight over the first five weeks can be calculated as:

$$\Delta w = w_2 - w_1 = 127 - 140 = -13 \text{ lb}$$

In the same way, the change in value of the independent variable, time (t), is written as Δt and is calculated by subtracting the initial value of t, denoted by t_1, from the final value of t, denoted by t_2. Symbolically, this change is represented by

$$\Delta t = t_2 - t_1.$$

In Problem 4c, the change in the number of weeks can be written using Δ notation as follows:

$$\Delta t = t_2 - t_1 = 5 - 0 = 5 \text{ weeks}$$

The average rate of change of weight over the first five weeks of the program can now be symbolically written as follows:

$$\frac{\Delta w}{\Delta t} = \frac{-13}{5} = -2.6 \text{ lb per week}$$

Note that the symbol Δ for delta is the Greek version of d, for difference, the result of a subtraction that produces the change in value.

5. Using Δ notation, determine the average rate of change of weight over the last four weeks of the program.

> **DEFINITION**
>
> The ratio $\frac{\Delta w}{\Delta t}$ is called the **average rate of change** of weight, w, with respect to weeks, t. In general, the average rate of change is
>
> $$\frac{\Delta w}{\Delta t} = \frac{w_2 - w_1}{t_2 - t_1},$$
>
> where (t_1, w_1) is the initial point and (t_2, w_2) is the final point.

Graphical Interpretation of the Average Rate of Change

6. a. On the graph in Problem 1, connect the points (0, 140) and (5, 127) with a line segment. Does the line segment rise, fall, or remain horizontal as you follow it from left to right?

b. Recall that the average rate of change over the first five weeks was -2.6 pounds per week. What does the average rate of change tell you about the line segment drawn in part a?

7. a. Determine the average rate of change of your weight over the time period from $t = 5$ to $t = 7$ weeks. Include the appropriate sign and units.

b. Interpret the rate in part a with respect to your diet.

c. On the graph in Problem 1, connect the points (5, 127) and (7, 130) with a line segment. Does the line segment rise, fall, or remain horizontal as you follow it from left to right?

d. How is the average rate of change of weight over the given two-week period related to the line segment you drew in part c?

8. a. At what rate is your weight changing during the sixth week of your diet; that is, from $t = 5$ to $t = 6$?

b. Interpret the rate in part a with respect to your diet.

c. Connect the points (5, 127) and (6, 127) on the graph with a line segment. Does the line segment rise, fall, or remain horizontal as you follow it from left to right?

d. How is the average rate of change in part a related to the line segment drawn in part c?

9. a. What is the average rate of change of your weight over the period from $t = 4$ to $t = 7$ weeks?

b. Explain how the rate in part a reflects the progress of your diet over those three weeks.

SUMMARY
Activity 2.1

1. Let y_1 represent the corresponding value for the x_1 and y_2 represent the corresponding value for the x_2. As the variable x changes in value from x_1 to x_2,

a. the change in x is represented by $\Delta x = x_2 - x_1$

b. the change in y is represented by $\Delta y = y_2 - y_1$

2. The quotient $\dfrac{\Delta y}{\Delta x} = \dfrac{y_2 - y_1}{x_2 - x_1}$ is called the **average rate of change** of y with respect to x over the x-interval from x_1 to x_2. The units of measurement of the quantity $\dfrac{\Delta y}{\Delta x}$ are y-*units* per x-*unit*.

3. The line segment connecting the points (x_1, y_1) and (x_2, y_2)

a. increases from left to right if $\dfrac{\Delta y}{\Delta x} > 0$

b. decreases from left to right if $\dfrac{\Delta y}{\Delta x} < 0$

c. remains constant if $\dfrac{\Delta y}{\Delta x} = 0$

1. For the years between 1900 and 2000, the following table presents the median ages (output) of U.S. men at the time when they first married.

INPUT, year	1900	1910	1920	1930	1940	1950	1960	1970	1980	1990	2000
OUTPUT, age	25.9	25.1	24.6	24.3	24.3	22.8	22.8	23.2	24.7	26.1	26.8

   a. During which decade(s) did the median age at first marriage increase for men?

   b. During which decade(s) did the median age at first marriage decrease?

   c. During which decade(s) did the median age at first marriage remain unchanged?

   d. During which decade(s) was the change in median age at first marriage the greatest?

2. Graph the data from Exercise 1, and connect consecutive points with line segments. Then answer the following questions using the graph.

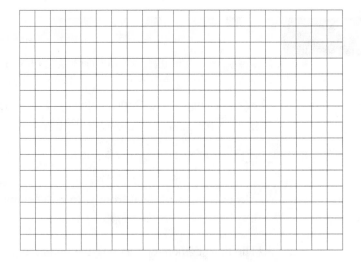

   a. During which decade(s) is your graph increasing?

b. During which decade(s) is the graph decreasing?

c. During which decade(s) is your graph horizontal?

d. During which decade(s) is the graph the steepest?

e. Compare the answers of the corresponding parts (a–d) of Exercises 1 and 2. What is the relationship between the sign of the output change for a given input interval and the direction (rising, falling, horizontal) of the graph in that interval?

Use the data in Exercise 1 to answer Exercises 3–6.

3. a. Determine the average rate of change in median age per year from 1950 to 1990.

b. Describe what the average rate of change in part a represents in this situation.

c. Determine the average rate of change in median age per year from 1930 to 1960.

4. During what decade period did the average age increase the most?

5. a. What does it mean in this situation if the average rate of change is negative?

b. Determine at least one ten-year period when the average rate of change is negative.

c. What trend would you observe in the graph if the average rate of change were negative? That is, would the graph increase, decrease, or remain constant?

6. a. Is the average rate of change zero over any ten-year period? If so, when?

b. What does an average rate of change of zero mean in this situation?

c. What trend would you observe in the graph during this period? That is, would the graph go up, go down, or be horizontal?

The following table gives information about new hotel construction in the U.S. from 1997 to 2001:

YEAR, t	1997	1998	1999	2000	2001
HOTELS CONSTRUCTED, h	1476	1519	1402	1246	1047

Use the table of data to answer Exercises 7 and 8.

7. Plot the data points using ordered pairs of the form (t, h).

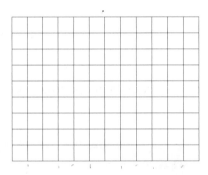

8. a. Determine the average rate of change of new hotel construction from 1997 to 1998.

b. Determine the average rate of change from 1998 to 1999.

c. Compare the average rate of change from 1997 to 1998 with the rate of change from 1998 to 1999.

d. When the average rate of change is negative, what trend will you observe in the graph? What does that mean in this situation?

9. Between 1960 and 2003, the size and shape of automobiles in the United States have changed almost annually. The amount of fuel consumed by these vehicles has also changed. The following table describes the average fuel consumed per year per passenger car in gallons of gasoline.

YEAR, t	1960	1970	1980	1990	1995	2000	2002	2003
GALLONS CONSUMED PER PASSENGER CAR (average)	668	760	576	520	530	547	555	550

a. Determine the average rate of change, in gallons of fuel used per passenger car, from 1960 to 1970.

b. Determine the average rate of change, in gallons of gas per year, from 1960 to 1990.

c. Determine the average rate of change, in gallons of gas per year, from 1995 to 2003.

d. Determine the average rate of change, in gallons of gas per year, between 1960 and 2003.

e. What does the result in part d mean in this situation?

10. The National Weather Service recorded the following temperatures one February day in Chicago:

TIME OF DAY	10 A.M.	12 NOON	2 P.M.	4 P.M.	6 P.M.	8 P.M.	10 P.M.
TEMPERATURE (°F)	30	35	36	36	34	30	28

a. Determine the average rate of change (including units and sign) of temperature with respect to time over the entire twelve-hour period given in the table.

b. Over which period(s) of time is the average rate of change zero? What, if anything, can you conclude about the actual temperature fluctuation within this period?

c. What is the average rate of change of temperature with respect to time over the evening hours from 6 P.M. to 10 P.M.? Interpret this value (including units and sign) in a complete sentence.

d. Write a brief paragraph describing the temperature and its fluctuations during the twelve-hour period in the table.

ACTIVITY 2.2
The Snowy Tree
Cricket

OBJECTIVES

1. Identify linear functions by a constant average rate of change.

2. Interpret slope as an average rate of change.

3. Determine the slope of the line drawn through two points.

4. Identify increasing and decreasing linear functions using slope.

5. Identify parallel lines using slope.

One of the more familiar late-evening sounds during the summer is the rhythmic chirping of a male cricket. Of particular interest is the snowy tree cricket, sometimes called the temperature cricket. It is very sensitive to temperature, speeding up or slowing down its chirping as the temperature rises or falls. The following data shows how the number of chirps per minute of the snowy tree cricket is related to temperature.

Timely Noise

T, TEMPERATURE (°F)	N, NUMBER OF CHIRPS/MINUTE
55	60
60	80
65	100
70	120
75	140
80	160

1. Crickets are usually silent when the temperature falls below 55°F. What is a possible practical domain for the snowy tree cricket function?

2. **a.** Determine the average rate of change of the number of chirps per minute with respect to temperature as the temperature increases from 55°F to 60°F.

   b. What are the units of measure of this rate of change?

3. **a.** How does the average rate of change determined in Problem 2 compare with the average rate of change as the temperature increases from 65°F to 80°F?

   b. Determine the average rate of change of number of chirps per minute with respect to temperature for the temperature intervals given in the following table. The results from Problems 1 and 2 are already recorded. Add several more of your own choice. List all your results in the table.

TEMPERATURE INCREASES	AVERAGE RATE OF CHANGE (number of chirps/minute with respect to temperature)
From 55° to 60 °F	4
From 60° to 80 °F	4
From 55° to 75 °F	
From 65° to 80 °F	

c. What can you conclude about the average rate of increase in the number of chirps per minute for any particular increase in temperature?

4. For any 7° increase in temperature, what is the expected increase in chirps per minute?

5. Plot the data pairs (temperature, chirps per minute) from the table preceding Problem 1. What type of graph is suggested by the pattern of points?

Note: Use a double slash (//) to indicate that the horizontal axis has been compressed between 0 and 50 and the vertical axis between 0 and 60.

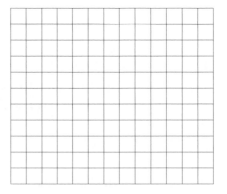

Linear Functions

If the average rate of change in *x* with respect to *y* remains constant (stays the same) for *any* two points in a data set, the points will lie on a straight line. That is, *y* is a **linear** function of *x*. Conversely, if all the points of a data set lie on a straight line when graphed, the average rate of change of *y* with respect to *x* will be constant for any two data points.

6. From the graph in Problem 5, would you conclude that the number of chirps per minute is a linear function of the temperature? Explain.

As you will see in the following activities, many situations in the world around us can be modeled by linear functions.

Slope of a Line

You have seen that the average rate of change between any two points on a line is always the same constant value. This value has a geometric interpretation as well—it describes the "steepness" of the line and is called the **slope** of the line.

7. a. What is the slope of the line in the snowy tree cricket situation?

b. Because the slope of this line is positive, what can you conclude about the direction of the line as the independent variable (temperature) increases in value?

c. What is the practical meaning of slope in this situation?

The slope of a line is often denoted by the letter *m*. It can be determined by selecting *any* two points on the line and calculating the average rate of change between them. That is, if (x_1, y_1) and (x_2, y_2) represent two points on a line, then the slope of the line is calculated by the following formula:

$$m = slope = \frac{\Delta y}{\Delta x} = \frac{y_2 - y_1}{x_2 - x_1}, \text{ and where } x_1 \neq x_2$$

Example 1   *Determine the slope of the line containing the points (1, −2) and (3, 8).*

SOLUTION

Let $x_1 = 1$, $y_1 = -2$, $x_2 = 3$, and $y_2 = 8$; so

$$m = \frac{y_2 - y_1}{x_2 - x_1} = \frac{8 - (-2)}{3 - 1} = \frac{10}{2} = \frac{5}{1} = 5.$$

8. Determine the slope of the line in the snowy tree cricket situation using delta notation. Select any two points from the table preceding Problem 1 for (x_1, y_1) and (x_2, y_2).

On a graph, slope is the ratio of two distances. The Δy represents a vertical distance (rise) from one point to another point on the same line. The Δx represents a horizontal distance (run) between the same points. For example, in the snowy tree cricket situation, the slope of the line between the points (55, 60) and (56, 64) as well as between (56, 64) and (57, 68) is $\frac{4}{1}$, as shown on the following graph.

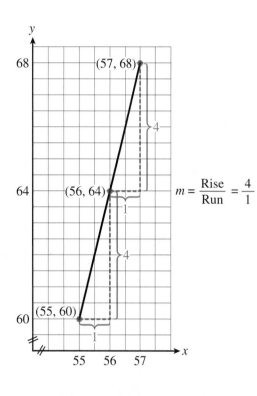

$$m = \frac{\text{Rise}}{\text{Run}} = \frac{4}{1}$$

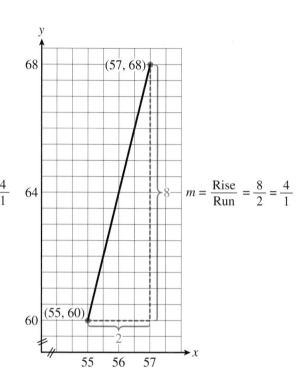

$$m = \frac{\text{Rise}}{\text{Run}} = \frac{8}{2} = \frac{4}{1}$$

DEFINITION

From its geometric meaning, slope may be determined from a graph by the formula

$$m = \text{slope} = \frac{\text{rise}}{\text{run}} = \frac{\text{distance up } (+) \text{ or down } (-)}{\text{distance right } (+) \text{ or left } (-)}.$$

The slope can be used to locate additional points on a graph, as demonstrated in Problem 9.

9. a. Consider the line containing the point $(-6, 4)$ and having slope $\dfrac{3}{4}$. Plot the point and then determine two additional points on the line. Draw a line through these points.

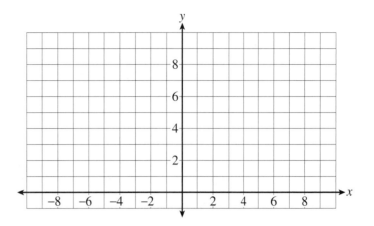

b. Which line increases most rapidly: a line with slope 3 or a line having slope $\frac{3}{4}$? Explain.

> The graph of a line having positive slope rises from left to right. Such a line represents an **increasing function**.

Decreasing Linear Function

While on a trip, you notice that the video screen on the airplane, in addition to showing movies and news, records your altitude (in kilometers) above the ground. As the plane starts its descent (at time $x = 0$), you record the following data:

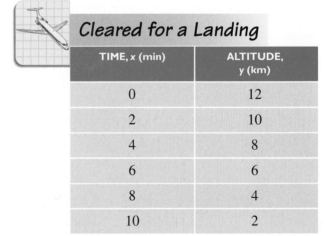

Cleared for a Landing

TIME, x (min)	ALTITUDE, y (km)
0	12
2	10
4	8
6	6
8	4
10	2

10. a. What is the average rate of change in the altitude of the plane from two to six minutes into the descent? Pay careful attention to the sign of this rate of change.

b. What are the units of measurement of this average rate of change?

c. Determine the average rate of change over several other input intervals.

d. What is the significance of the signs of these average rates of change?

e. Based on your calculation in parts a and c, do you think that the data lie on a single straight line? Explain.

f. What is the practical meaning of slope in this situation?

g. By how much does the altitude of the plane change for each three-minute change in time during the descent?

11. a. Plot the data points from the table preceding Problem 10, and verify that the points lie on a line. What is the slope of the line?

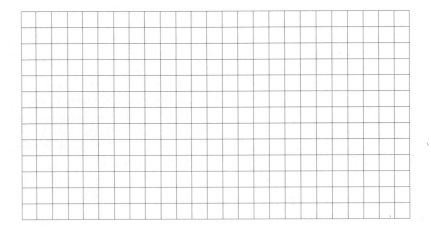

b. Explain to a classmate the method you used to determine the slope in part a.

12. a. The slope of the line for the descent function in this activity is negative. What does this tell you about how the altitude changes as the time increases in value?

b. Is the descent function an increasing or decreasing function?

Parallel Lines

13. a. Two lines, denoted by l_1 and l_2, contain the given points. Sketch a graph of each line on the following coordinate axes.

l_1: $(-2, -3), (2, 5)$ l_2: $(-1, -5), (3, 3)$

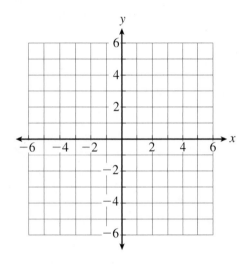

b. What can you say about the graphs of the two lines?

c. Determine and then compare the slopes of the two lines.

d. By inspection of the graph in part a, estimate the y-intercepts of the two lines. How do they compare?

> **DEFINITION**
>
> Two lines are parallel if they never intersect, no matter how far you extend the lines in either direction. Parallel lines have equal slopes but different y-intercepts.

14. Are the two lines in Problem 13 parallel? Explain.

Note that if two lines have equal y-intercepts as well as equal slopes, the graphs are exactly the same and the two lines are said to **coincide**.

SUMMARY
Activity 2.2

1. A **linear function** is one whose average rate of change of y with respect to x from any one data point to any other data point is always the same (constant) value.

2. The **graph** of a linear function is a line whose slope is the constant rate of change of the function.

3. The **slope of a line segment** joining two points (x_1, y_1) and (x_2, y_2) is denoted by m and can be calculated using the formula $m = \dfrac{\Delta y}{\Delta x} = \dfrac{y_2 - y_1}{x_2 - x_1}$. Geometrically, Δy represents a vertical distance (rise), and Δx represents a horizontal distance (run).

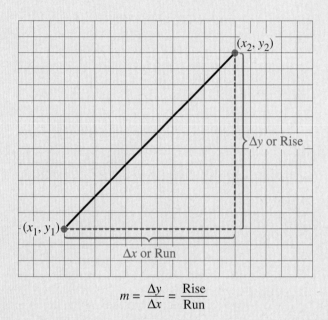

$$m = \frac{\Delta y}{\Delta x} = \frac{\text{Rise}}{\text{Run}}$$

Therefore, $m = \dfrac{\Delta y}{\Delta x} = \dfrac{\text{rise}}{\text{run}}$.

4. The graph of every linear function with **positive slope** is an increasing line, rising to the right. The function is then said to be an **increasing function**.

5. The graph of every linear function with **negative slope** is an decreasing line, falling to the right. The function is called a **decreasing function**.

6. Two lines are parallel if they never intersect, no matter how far you extend the lines in either direction. Parallel lines have equal slopes but different y-intercepts.

1. In a science lab, you collect the following sets of data. Which of the four data sets are linear functions? If linear, determine the slope.

a.

TIME (sec)	0	10	20	30	40
TEMPERATURE (°C)	12	17	22	27	32

b.

TIME (sec)	0	10	20	30	40
TEMPERATURE (°C)	41	23	5	−10	−20

c.

TIME (sec)	3	5	8	10	15
TEMPERATURE (°C)	12	16	24	28	36

d.

TIME (sec)	3	9	12	18	21
TEMPERATURE (°C)	25	23	22	20	19

2. a. You are a member of a health and fitness club. A special diet-and-exercise program has been developed for you by the club's registered dietitian and your personal trainer. You weigh 181 pounds and would like to lose 2 pounds every week. Complete the following table of values for your desired weight each week:

N, NUMBER OF WEEKS	0	1	2	3	4
W, DESIRED WEIGHT (lb)					

b. Plot the data points.

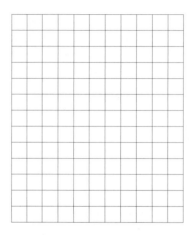

c. Explain why your desired weight is a linear function of time. What is the slope of the line containing the five data points?

d. What is the practical meaning of slope in this situation?

e. How long will it take to reach your ideal weight of 168 pounds?

3. Your aerobics instructor informs you that to receive full physical benefit from exercising, your heart rate must be maintained at a certain level for at least twelve minutes. The proper exercise heart rate for a healthy person, called the *target heart rate*, is determined by the person's age. The relationship between these two quantities is illustrated by the data in the following table.

A, AGE (years)	20	30	40	50	60
R, TARGET HEART RATE (beats per minute)	140	133	126	119	112

a. Does the data in the table indicate that the target heart rate is a linear function of age? Explain.

b. What is the slope of the line for this data? What are the units?

c. What is the practical domain for age, A?

d. Plot the data points on coordinate axes where both axes start with zero. Connect the points with a line.

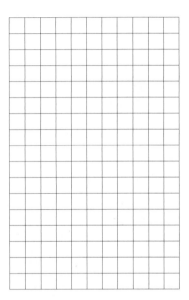

4. Determine the slope of each of the following lines:

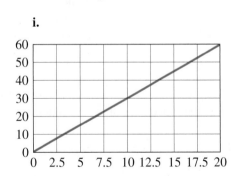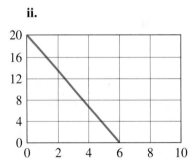

5. Each question refers to the graph that accompanies it.

a. How fast is the car traveling? Explain how you obtained your result.

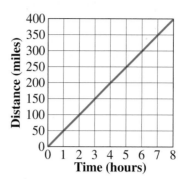

b. How can you determine visually from the following graph which car is going faster? Verify your answer to the first question by calculating the speed of each car.

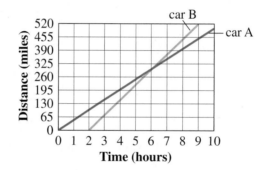

c. Describe in words the movement of the car that is represented by the following graph:

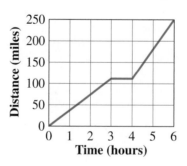

6. a. Determine the slope of each of the following lines:

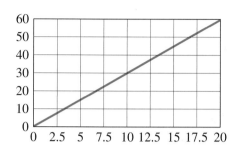 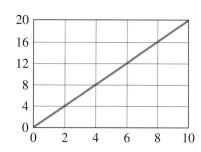 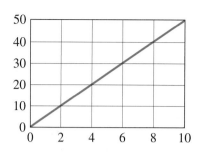

b. At first glance, the three graphs in part a may appear to represent the same line. Do they?

7. For each of the following, determine three additional points on the line. Then sketch a graph of the line.

a. A line contains the point $(-5, 10)$ and has slope $\frac{2}{3}$.

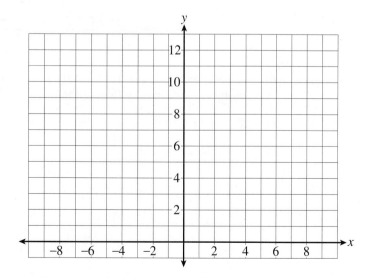

b. A line contains the point $(3, -4)$ and has slope 5.

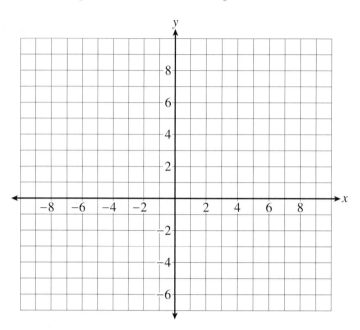

8. The concept of slope arises in many practical applications. When designing and building roads, engineers and surveyors need to be concerned about the grade of the road. The grade, usually expressed as a percent, is one way to describe the steepness of the finished surface of the road. For example, a 5% grade means that the road has a slope (rise over run) of $0.05 = \dfrac{5}{100}$.

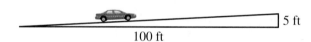

100 ft 5 ft

a. If a road has a 5% upward grade over a 1000-foot run, how much higher will you be at the end of that run than at the beginning?

b. What is the grade of a road that rises 26 feet over a distance of 500 feet?

9. The American National Standards Institute (ANSI) requires that the slope for a wheelchair ramp does not exceed $\frac{1}{12}$.

   a. Does a ramp that is 160 inches long and 10 inches high meet the requirements of ANSI? Explain.

   b. A ramp for a wheelchair must be 20 inches high. Determine the minimum length of the ramp so that it meets the ANSI requirement.

   c. Are there any wheelchair ramps in your school? If so, determine a way to measure the slope. What is the slope?

10. Determine if the given pair of lines is parallel. Verify your conclusion by sketching a graph of each pair of lines.

   a. l_1: $(-1, 1), (1, 7)$

      l_2: $(-2, -5), (1, 4)$

   b. l_1: $(-2, -5), (1, 4)$

      l_2: $(-1, 7), (2, 1)$

   c. l_1: $(-2, 2), (4, -1)$

      l_2: $(4, -5), (2, -4)$

   d. l_1: $(2, -3), (1, -1)$

      l_2: $(-1, 3), (2, -3)$

      Hint: Determine *y*-intercepts from a sketch.

ACTIVITY 2.3

Depreciation

OBJECTIVES

1. Identify whether a situation can be modeled by a linear function.

2. Determine *x*- and *y*-intercepts of a graph.

3. Identify the practical meaning of *x*- and *y*-intercepts.

4. Develop the slope-intercept model of an equation of a line.

5. Use the slope-intercept formula to determine *x*- and *y*-intercepts.

6. Determine the zeros of a linear function.

You have decided to buy a new Honda Accord LX, but you are concerned about the value of the car depreciating over time. You search the Internet and obtain the following information:

2010 Accord LX

- Suggested retail price: $20,025
- Depreciation per year: $1,385 (assume constant)

1. a. Complete the following table in which *V* represents the value of the car after *n* years of ownership.

Accordingly

n, YEARS	*V*, VALUE IN DOLLARS
0	
1	
2	
3	
5	
8	

b. Is the value of the car a function of the number of years of ownership? Explain.

c. What is the independent variable? What is the dependent variable?

2. a. Select two ordered pairs of the form (*n*, *V*) from the table in Problem 1 and determine the average rate of change.

b. What are the units of measure of the average rate of change?

c. What is the practical meaning of the sign of the average rate of change?

d. Select two different ordered pairs and compute the average rate of change.

e. Select two ordered pairs not used in parts a or d, and compute the average rate of change.

f. Using the results in parts a, d, and e, what can you infer about the average rate of change over any interval of time?

3. a. Is the value, *V*, of the car a linear function of the number of years, *n*, of ownership? Explain using the definition of linear function.

b. Is this function increasing, decreasing, or constant?

Graph of a Linear Function

4. Consider the ordered pairs of the form (*n*, *V*), and plot each ordered pair in Problem 1 on an appropriately scaled and labeled set of axes. Connect the points to see if there is a pattern.

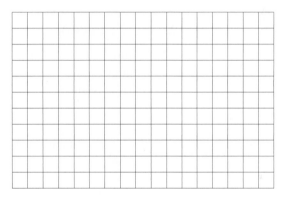

The graph of a linear function is a nonvertical line. Remember that the constant average rate of change is called the **slope** of the line and is denoted by the letter *m*.

5. a. What is the slope of the line graphed in Problem 4?

b. What is the relationship between the slope of the line and the average rate of change?

c. What is the practical meaning of slope in this situation?

Vertical Intercept (*y*-intercept)

> **DEFINITION**
>
> In general, the **vertical intercept** is the point where the graph crosses, or intercepts, the vertical axis. If the dependent variable is represented by *y*, the vertical intercept is called the **y-intercept**. The corresponding *x*-value of the *y*-intercept is always zero.

6. a. Using the table of data in Problem 1 or the graph in Problem 4, determine the *V*-intercept. Note that the dependent variable in the car depreciation situation is represented by *V*, the value of the car. Therefore, the vertical intercept is called the *V*-intercept.

b. What is the practical meaning of the *V*-intercept in this situation? Include units.

Slope-Intercept Form of a Linear Equation

7. a. Review how you determined the value, *V*, of the car in Problem 1 for a given number of years, *n*, of ownership. Write an equation for *V* in terms of *n* that models this situation.

b. Use your graphing calculator to sketch a graph of this equation. Use the window Xmin = −2, Xmax = 16, Ymin = −500, and Ymax = 25,000.

c. How does this graph compare to your graph in Problem 4?

8. Recall that the slope of your line is $m = -1385$ and the *V*-intercept is (0, 20,025). How is this information contained in the equation of the line you determined in Problem 7a?

> **DEFINITION**
>
> The coordinates of all points (x, y) on the line with slope *m* and *y*-intercept $(0, b)$ satisfy the equation
>
> $$y = mx + b \quad \text{or} \quad y = b + mx.$$
>
> This is called the **slope-intercept form** of the equation of a line.

Note that the coefficient of x, which is m, is the *slope* of the line. The constant term, b, is the *y-coordinate of the y-intercept*. If $f(x)$ replaces y, the equation $y = mx + b$ can be written as

$$f(x) = mx + b.$$

Example 1 *The slope-intercept form of the equation of the line with slope 3 and vertical intercept $(0, -6)$ is $y = 3x - 6$. Using function notation and replacing y with $f(x)$, the equation becomes $f(x) = 3x - 6$.*

9. Identify the slope and y-intercept of the line whose equation is given. Write the y-intercept as an ordered pair.

a. $y = -2x + 5$ **b.** $s = \frac{3}{4}t + 2$

c. $q = 2 - r$ **d.** $y = \frac{5}{6} + \frac{x}{3}$

Horizontal Intercept (*x*-intercept)

DEFINITION

In general, a **horizontal intercept** of a graph is a point where the graph meets or crosses the horizontal axis. If the independent variable is represented by x, the horizontal intercept is called the **x-intercept**. The y-value of the x-intercept is always zero.

Example 2 *Consider the equation $y = 2x - 10$.*

a. The y-intercept occurs where the line crosses the vertical axis, i.e., where $x = 0$. Letting $x = 0$, $y = 2(0) - 10$ or $y = -10$. The y-intercept is $(0, -10)$.

b. The x-intercept occurs where the line crosses the horizontal axis, that is, where $y = 0$.

Letting $y = 0$,

$$\begin{aligned} 0 &= 2x - 10 \\ +10 & +10 \qquad \text{Add 10 to each side.} \\ \hline 10 &= 2x \\ \frac{10}{2} &= \frac{2x}{2} \qquad \text{Divide each side by 2.} \\ 5 &= x \end{aligned}$$

Therefore, the x-intercept is $(5, 0)$.

c. You can now sketch a graph of $y = 2x - 10$ by plotting the x- and y-intercepts and connecting the points.

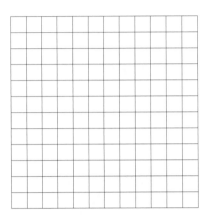

10. a. Determine the n-intercept of the graph of the car value equation

$$V = -1385n + 20{,}025.$$

b. What is the practical significance of the n-intercept? Include units.

Converting Celsius to Fahrenheit

11. The temperature on a warm summer day may be 27°. Your refrigerator is set at 5°. You set your oven to 180° to cook a turkey. If these temperatures seem strange, it is because they are measured on the *Celsius scale*. If the TV weather forecaster says it is going to be 65°F tomorrow, you know what that temperature will feel like and you can dress accordingly. How should you dress if the reporter says it will be 10°C? Most of us need to convert Celsius to Fahrenheit so we can better understand the temperature. The equation that relates Celsius measure to Fahrenheit measure is

$$F = 1.8C + 32,$$

where C is the Celsius measure and F is the Fahrenheit measure.

a. Use the equation to complete the following table:

C	−10	0	5	10	27	100
F						

b. Sketch a graph of the equation $F = 1.8C + 32$ by plotting the ordered pairs in part a.

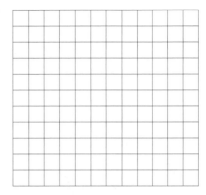

c. Determine the average rate of change of F as C increases from 0 to 100.

d. What is the slope of the line? How does the slope compare to the average rate of change in part c?

e. Is the function increasing, decreasing, or constant?

f. Determine the intercepts of the graph using the equation of the line. Verify your results using the graph of the line.

g. What is the practical significance of each intercept in this situation?

Zeros of a Function

The x-values of the x-intercepts of a function's graph are called the **zeros** of the function. To determine the zeros of a function defined by $f(x) = 2x - 6$, proceed as if you were trying to determine the x-intercepts of the graph. Simply set $f(x) = 0$ and solve for x.

12. Determine the zeros of the function defined by $f(x) = 2x - 6$.

SUMMARY
Activity 2.3

1. A function for which the average rate of change between any pair of points remains constant is called a **linear function**.

2. The graph of a linear function is a nonvertical line. The constant average rate of change is called the **slope** and is denoted by the letter m (from the French verb *monter*, "to climb" or "rise").

3. The **slope** of a line segment joining two points (x_1, y_1) and (x_2, y_2) is denoted by m and is defined by $m = \dfrac{y_2 - y_1}{x_2 - x_1}$, where $x_1 \neq x_2$.

4. The **y-intercept** $(0, b)$ of a graph is the point where the graph crosses the y-axis. The **x-intercept** $(a, 0)$ of a graph is the point where the graph crosses the x-axis.

5. The x-value of the x-intercept of the graph of a function is called a **zero** of the function.

6. The slope-intercept form of the equation of a line is $y = mx + b$.

7. To determine the b-value of the y-intercept $(0, b)$ from $y = mx + b$, set $x = 0$ and solve for y.

8. To determine the a-value of the x-intercept $(a, 0)$ from $y = mx + b$, set $y = 0$ and solve for x.

9. If the **slope** of a linear function is **positive**, the graph of the function increases (rises to the right).

10. If the **slope** of a linear function is **negative**, the graph of the function decreases (falls to the right).

EXERCISES
Activity 2.3

1. Determine whether the following functions are linear. If they are, determine the constant average rate of change, called the slope of the line.

a.

x	y
0	−1
1	9
2	19

b.

x	2	4	6
y	11	8	−1

c. $\{(-2, 18), (2, 9), (6, 0)\}$

2. Determine whether the following tables contain data that represent a linear function. Assume that the first row of the table is the x-variable and the second row is the y-variable. Explain your reasoning.

a. You owe your grandmother $1000. She paid for your first semester at community college. The conditions of the loan are that you must pay her back the whole amount in one payment using a simple interest rate of 6% per year. She doesn't care in which year you pay her. The table contains data values to represent how much money you will owe your grandmother one, two, three, or four years later.

YEAR	1	2	3	4
AMOUNT OWED (in $)	1060	1120	1180	1240

b. You decide to invest $1000 of your 401(k) funds into an account that pays 5.5% interest compounded continuously. The table contains data that represent the amount an initial investment of $1000 is worth at the end of each year.

YEAR	1	2	3	4	5
TOTAL INVESTMENT (in $)	1057	1116	1179	1246	1317

3. You belong to a health and fitness center. You and your friends are enrolled in the center's weight-loss program. The charts contain data that represent the weight over a four-week period for you and your two friends. Determine which charts contain data that is linear and explain why.

a.

WEEK	1	2	3	4
WEIGHT (in lb)	150	147	144	141

b.

WEEK	1	2	3	4
WEIGHT (in lb)	183	178	174	171

c.

WEEK	1	2	3	4
WEIGHT (in lb)	160	160	160	160

4. Consider the equation $y = -2x + 5$.

a. Construct a table of five ordered pairs that satisfy the equation.

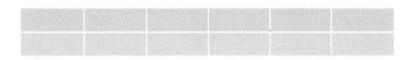

b. What is the slope of the line represented by the equation?

c. What is the y-intercept?

d. What is the x-intercept?

e. Sketch a graph of the line using each of the following methods:

Method 1: Plot the five ordered pairs.

Method 2: Plot one point and use the slope to obtain additional points on the line.

Method 3: Plot the intercepts.

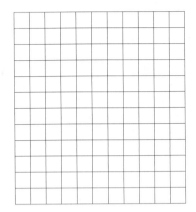 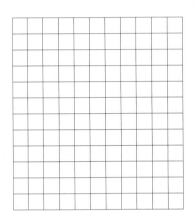 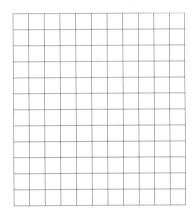

5. a. Determine the slope of the line that goes through the points $(2, -7)$ and $(0, 5)$.

b. Determine the y-intercept of this line.

c. What is the equation of the line through these points? Write the equation in function notation.

d. What is the x-intercept?

6. A car is traveling on a highway. The distance (in miles) from its destination and the time (in hours) is given by the equation $d = 420 - 65t$.

a. What is the d-intercept of the line?

b. What is the practical meaning of the d-intercept?

c. What is the slope of the line represented by the equation?

d. What is the practical meaning of the slope determined in part c?

e. What is the *t*-intercept?

f. What is the practical domain of this function?

g. Graph the equation, both by hand and with your graphing calculator, to verify your answers.

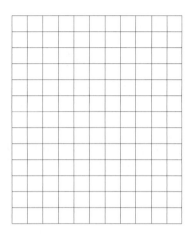

7. The following table gives a jet's height above the ground (in feet) as a function of time (in seconds) as the jet makes its landing approach to the runway:

t (in seconds)	h (in feet)
0	3500
5	3000
10	2500
15	2000
20	1500
25	1000

a. Is this function linear? Explain.

b. Calculate the slope using the formula $m = \dfrac{\Delta h}{\Delta t}$.

c. What is the significance of the sign of the slope in part b?

d. Determine where the graph crosses the *h*-axis.

e. Write the equation in slope-intercept form.

f. Determine the t-intercept. What is its significance in this situation?

8. Determine the zeros of the function whose equation is given.

a. $y = 4x + 2$

b. $y = \dfrac{x}{2} - 3$

9. a. Use your graphing calculator to graph the linear functions defined by the following equations: $y = 2x - 3$, $y = 2x$, $y = 2x + 2$, $y = 2x + 5$. Discuss the similarities and the differences of the graphs.

b. Use your graphing calculator to graph the linear functions defined by the following equations: $y = x - 2$, $y = 2x - 2$, $y = -x - 2$, $y = -2$. Discuss the similarities and the differences in the graphs.

c. Use your graphing calculator to graph the linear functions defined by the following equations: $y = 3x$, $y = -2x$, $y = \frac{1}{2}x$, $y = -5x$. Discuss the similarities and differences in the graphs.

ACTIVITY 2.4
Skateboard Heaven

OBJECTIVES

1. Write an equation of a line in standard form $Ax + By = C$.

2. Write the slope-intercept form of a linear equation given the standard form.

3. Determine the slope and the equation of a horizontal and vertical line.

Your town has just authorized funding to build a new ramp and pathways for skateboarding. For security, the ramp and pathways must have a rectangular fence surrounding them. The money allocated in the budget for fencing will be enough to purchase 350 feet of fence. The only stipulation is that the width must be between 35 and 60 feet to properly enclose the new ramp. The length will depend on the width you choose. Your task is to determine the length and width of the rectangular region so that you use all of the fencing.

1. a. What does the value of 350 represent with regard to the rectangular region?

   b. Using x to represent the width and y to represent the length, write an equation for the perimeter of this rectangular region.

   c. The linear equation in part b should be in the form of $Ax + By = C$. Identify the values of the constants A, B, and C in the equation.

DEFINITION

When a linear equation is written in the form $Ax + By = C$, it is said to be in **standard form**, where A, B, C represent constants, and A and B cannot both be zero.

Example 1   *Sometimes, it is advantageous to rewrite a linear equation given in general form as its equivalent slope-intercept form. For example, consider the equation $3x + 7y = 5$. To write this equation in the slope-intercept form, you need to solve for y as follows.*

$$3x + 7y = 5$$
$$\underline{-3x \qquad\quad -3x}$$ Add $-3x$ to each side of the equation.
$$7y = -3x + 5$$

$$\frac{7y}{7} = \frac{-3x}{7} + \frac{5}{7}$$ Divide each side of the equation by 7, the coefficient of y.

$$y = -\tfrac{3}{7}x + \tfrac{5}{7}$$

2. a. Rewrite the equation from Problem 1b in slope-intercept form by solving the equation for y in terms of x.

b. What is the slope of the line represented by the equation you wrote in part a? What is the practical meaning of the slope in this situation?

c. What is the y-intercept of the line represented by the equation you determined in part a? What is the practical meaning of the y-intercept in this situation?

d. What is the practical domain and range of this function?

3. a. Determine the corresponding y-value for $x = 35$ using $2x + 2y = 350$ (standard form of the equation of a line).

b. Determine the corresponding y-value for $x = 35$ using $y = -x + 175$ (slope-intercept form of the equation of a line).

c. Was it more convenient to use the standard form or the slope-intercept form to determine a y-value given $x = 35$? Explain.

d. Complete the table to determine some possible lengths and widths for the rectangular region.

x	35	40	50	60
y				

Equations of a Horizontal Line

If either A, the coefficient of x, or B, the coefficient of y, in the standard form $Ax + By = C$ equals zero, a special situation arises. You will explore this in the following problems.

4. a. When the ramp for skateboarding is complete, you and your friends will be able to pay a monthly fee of $12.50 to use the ramp for as many hours as you wish. Complete the table of values below where x is the number of hours per month that each person who pays the fee uses the ramp and y is the total cost per month for each person.

x, TIME (in hours)	5	10	15	20
y, COST (in $)				

b. Use the data points from the table to sketch the graph.

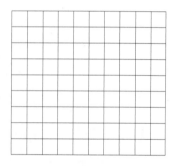

c. Describe the graph in words.

d. Choose two ordered pairs from part a and determine the slope, m, of the line. What is the practical meaning of the slope in this situation?

e. What are the intercepts (vertical and horizontal) of the line (if they exist)?

f. Write the equation of this line in slope-intercept form, $y = mx + b$.

g. Change the equation from part f to the general form $Ax + By = C$, and identify A, B, and C. Note that when there is no input variable appearing in an equation, its coefficient is understood to be zero.

h. The equation of the horizontal line in part b is $y = 12.50$. Does this make sense? Explain.

> **DEFINITION**
>
> A graph in which the output y is a constant or, equivalently, $f(x)$ is a constant, is a **horizontal line**. The equation of a horizontal line is $y = c$ (or $f(x) = c$), where c is some fixed real number. The slope of any horizontal line is zero.

5. Determine three ordered pairs that satisfy each of the following equations. Then sketch the graph of each constant function on the same coordinate axes.

   a. $y = -2$ **b.** $f(x) = 1$

   c. $g(x) = \frac{5}{2}$

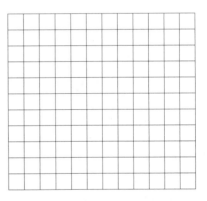

Undefined Slope

6. You apply for a part-time job at the skateboarding rink to help cover your weekly expenses. The following table gives your weekly salary, x, and corresponding weekly expenses, y, for a typical month.

x, WEEKLY SALARY IN DOLLARS	70	70	70	70
y, WEEKLY EXPENSES IN DOLLARS	45	35	50	60

   a. Sketch a graph of the given data points.

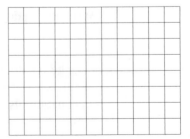

b. Describe the graph in words.

c. Choose two ordered pairs from the table and determine the slope, *m*.

d. What are the intercepts of the line (if they exist)?

e. Is *y* a function of *x*? Explain using the definition of a function.

f. Do the ordered pairs in the table satisfy the equation $x = 70$? Explain why or why not.

g. Write the equation $x = 70$ in $Ax + By = C$ form. Identify A, B, and C.

h. Can you graph the equation $x = 70$ using your graphing calculator? Explain.

DEFINITION

A graph in which x is a constant is a **vertical line**. The equation of a vertical line is $x = a$, where a is some fixed real number. The slope of a vertical line is **undefined**.

---

7. Determine three ordered pairs that satisfy each of the following equations, and then sketch each graph.

a. $x = -2$ **b.** $x = 4$ **c.** $x = \dfrac{5}{2}$

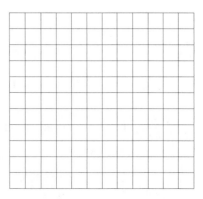

SUMMARY
Activity 2.4

1. The **standard form** of a linear equation is $Ax + By = C$, where A, B, and C are constants, and A and B are not both zero.

2. The graph of $y = c$ or $f(x) = c$ is a **horizontal line**. In this case, f is called a constant function. Every point on this line has a y-coordinate equal to c. A horizontal line has slope of zero.

3. The graph of $x = a$ is a **vertical line**. Every point on this line has an x-coordinate equal to a. The slope of a vertical line is undefined.

EXERCISES
Activity 2.4

1. Write the following linear equations in slope-intercept form. Determine the slope and vertical intercept of each line.

   a. $2x - y = 3$ **b.** $x + y = -2$

   c. $2x - 3y = 7$ **d.** $-x + 2y = 4$

   e. $0x + 3y = 12$

2. **a.** Sketch the graph of the horizontal line through the point $(-2, 3)$.

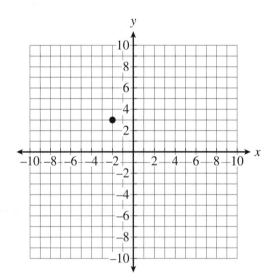

   b. Write the equation of a horizontal line through the point $(-2, 3)$.

   c. What is the slope of the line?

   d. Does the graph represent a function? Explain.

3. a. Sketch the graph of the vertical line through $(-2, 3)$.

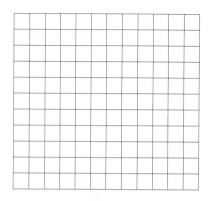

b. Does the graph represent a function? Explain.

c. Write the equation of a vertical line through the point $(-2, 3)$.

d. What is the slope of the line?

4. Explain the difference between a line with a zero slope and a line with an undefined slope.

5. You are retained as a consultant for a major computer company. You receive $2000 per month as a fee no matter how many hours you work.

a. Using x to represent the number of hours you work each month, write an equation to represent the total amount received from the company each month.

b. Complete the following table of values.

x, HOURS WORKED PER MONTH	15	25	35
y, FEE PER MONTH (in $)			

c. Use your graphing calculator to sketch the graph of this function.

d. What is the slope of the line? What is the practical meaning of the slope in this situation?

e. Describe the graph of the function.

6. You are working in the purchasing department of an appliance retailer. This month you are stocking up on washers and dryers. Your supervisor informs you that your budget this month is $10,000. You know that the average wholesale cost of the washer over the past year has been $250, while the average wholesale cost of a dryer has been $200.

a. If *w* represents the number of washers you can purchase, write an expression that represents the amount you can spend on washers.

b. If *d* represents the number of dryers you can purchase, write an expression that represents the amount you can spend on dryers.

c. Write a linear equation in general form that relates the number of washers and dryers you can expect to purchase with your budget.

d. Solve your equation in part c for *d*. In other words, express the number of dryers you can expect to purchase as a function of the number of washers you can expect to purchase.

e. What is the horizontal intercept for this function? What is its practical meaning in this situation?

f. What is the vertical intercept for this function? What is its practical meaning in this situation?

g. What is the slope of this function? What is its significance in this situation?

h. Use your graphing calculator to graph the function in part d. What part of this graph is relevant to this situation?

i. What are the practical domain and range of this situation?

ACTIVITY 2.5

Family of
Functions

OBJECTIVES

1. Identify the effect of changes in the equation of a line on its graph.

2. Identify the effect of changes in the graph of a line on its equation.

3. Identify the change in the graph and equation of a basic function as a translation, reflection, or vertical stretch or shrink.

A primary objective of this textbook is to help you develop a familiarity with the graphs, equations, and properties of a variety of functions, including linear, quadratic, and exponential. You will group these functions into families and identify the similarities within a family and the differences between families.

The family of functions being investigated in this chapter is linear functions. As you have discovered in previous activities, there are strong relationships between the equation of a line and its corresponding graph. Recognizing such relationships will help you identify patterns in the equations and graphs of other families of functions.

Vertical and Horizontal Shifts Revisited

1. Determine the slope and intercepts of the line having equation $y = 2x$.

2. **a.** Using a graphing calculator, sketch a graph in the standard window of each of the following. What do you observe?

$$y_1 = 2x, y_2 = 2x + 2, y_3 = 2x + 6$$

b. Now, sketch a graph of each of the following. What do you observe?

$$y_1 = 2x, y_2 = 2x - 3, y_3 = 2x - 5$$

c. The equations in parts a and b are of the form $y = 2x + c$, where c is a constant. What is the effect of c on the graph of $y = 2x$?

d. The graph of $y = 2x + 6$ is a vertical shift of the graph of $y = 2x$ upward by 6 units. As a result, which intercept of the graph is changed by exactly 6 units?

e. Does adding a constant c to the output value have any effect on the slope of the line?

3. a. Use a graphing calculator to sketch a graph of $y_1 = 2x$, $y_2 = 2(x + 1)$, $y_3 = 2(x + 4)$, and $y_4 = 2(x + 5.5)$. What do you observe?

b. The equations in part a are of the form $y = 2(x + c)$, where $c > 0$. What is the effect of c on the graph of $y = 2x$?

c. Describe how the graph of $y = 2(x - 3)$ can be obtained from the graph of $y = 2x$. Verify using a graphing calculator.

d. The graph of $y = 2(x + 4)$ is a horizontal shift of the graph $y = 2x$ horizontally to the left 4 units. As a result, which intercept of the graph of $y = 2x$ changed by 4 units?

e. Does adding a constant c to the input x have any effect on the slope of the line $y = 2x$?

Now, look carefully at the graphs of $y_1 = 2x$, $y_2 = 2x + 6$, $y_3 = 2(x + 3)$ from Problems 2 and 3. Note that a horizontal shift 3 units to the left of the graph of $y = 2x$ results in the same graph as a vertical shift upward 6 units. Is this true for all functions? Problem 4 uses the squaring function to demonstrate that this is not generally true.

4. a. Using a graphing calculator, sketch a graph of each of the following in the standard window:

$$y_1 = x^2, y_2 = x^2 + 6, y_3 = (x + 3)^2$$

b. For the squaring function, does a horizontal shift 3 units to the left of the graph result in the same graph as a vertical shift 6 units upward?

Reflections

5. a. Consider the linear function defined by $y = x$. Using a graphing calculator, graph the equation $y = -x$ in the same standard window as $y = x$. What do you observe?

> The graph of $y = -x$ is a **reflection** of the graph of $y = x$ across the x-axis.

b. When a graph is reflected across the x-axis, the x-value of each point remains the same. What happens to the corresponding y-values?

> In general, if the graph of $y = f(x)$ is reflected across the x-axis, then the equation of the resulting graph is $y = -f(x)$. The graphs of $y = f(x)$ and $y = -f(x)$ are mirror images across the x-axis. The y-values of the graph of $y = f(x)$ change in sign. The x-values remain the same.

6. Reflect each of the following graphs across the x-axis. If a formula is given for the graph, write the equation of the reflected graph. Where possible, verify using a graphing calculator.

a. $y = 2x$ **b.** $y = x^2$

c.

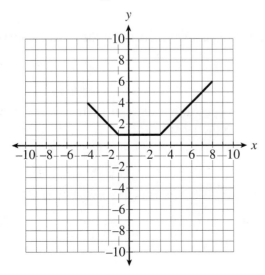

d.

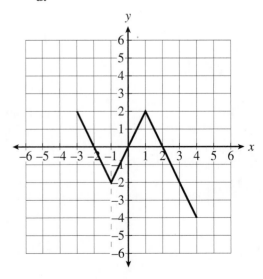

7. a. Determine the slope and intercepts of the graph of $y = f(x) = 3x + 6$.

b. Graph the function defined by $y = 3x + 6$. Verify using a graphing calculator.

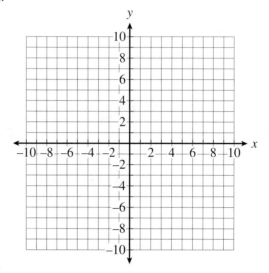

c. On the graph in part b, reflect the graph of $y = 3x + 6$ across the x-axis.

d. Write the equation of the reflected graph in part c.

e. Use a graphing calculator to verify the graph in part d.

f. Determine the slope and intercepts of the reflected graph.

g. Compare the slopes and intercepts of the graph of $y = 3x + 6$ and its reflection across the x-axis.

8. Consider the graph of the function defined by $y = f(x) = 3x + 6$ in Problem 7.

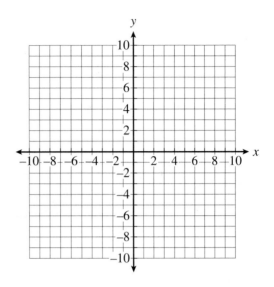

a. Determine an equation for $y_2 = f(-x)$. That is, replace x with $-x$ in the equation for f.

b. Determine the slope and intercepts of the graph of $y_2 = f(-x)$.

c. Sketch a graph of $y = f(-x)$ on the same coordinate axis as $y = f(x)$.

d. How can the graph of $y = f(-x)$ be obtained from the graph of $y = f(x)$?

The graph of $y_2 = f(-x) = -3x + 6$ is a reflection of the graph of $y = f(x) = 3x + 6$ across the y-axis.

e. When a graph is reflected across the y-axis, the y-values of each point remain the same. What happens to the corresponding x-values?

f. Compare the slopes and intercepts of the graph of $f(x) = 3x + 6$ and its reflection across the y-axis $f(-x) = -3x + 6$.

9. Reflect each of the following across the y-axis. If a formula is given for the graph, write the equation of the reflected graph. Where possible, verify using a graphing calculator.

a. $y = 2x - 8$ **b.** $y = x^2$

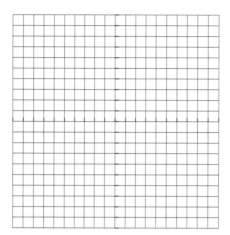 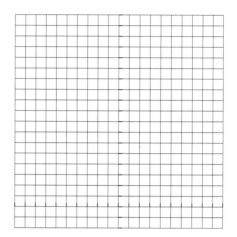

c.

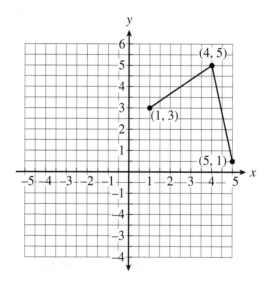

Vertical Stretch and Shrink of a Graph

You have just purchased a stereo system that includes an amplifier. The purpose of the amplifier is to take the signal from a component part (such as the compact disc player) and boost the signal in order to power a set of speakers.

The following graph shows a situation where a sound has been amplified 5 times.

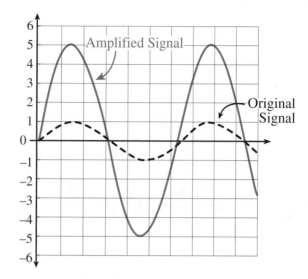

The transformation of the graph of the original signal into the graph of the amplified signal is called a **vertical stretch**. Note that the height of the graph of the amplified signal is 5 times as high as the original signal. The number 5 is called the **stretch factor**. Therefore, if $y = g(x)$ is the equation of the original signal, the equation of the amplified graph is $y = 5\, g(x)$.

In general, if the graph of $y = f(x)$ is vertically stretched by a factor of a, then the equation of the stretched graph is $y = a\, f(x)$. The number a is called the stretch factor. The y-value of each point in the graph of $y = f(x)$ is multiplied by a factor of a. The x-values remain fixed.

How does a vertical stretch of the graph of a line affect the properties of the graph?

10. a. Using a graphing calculator, sketch a graph of each of the following in a standard window. What do you observe?

$$y_1 = x, \, y_2 = 2x, \, y_3 = 5x$$

b. How does the vertical stretch of the graph of $y = x$ affect its graph?

11. a. Determine the slope and intercepts of the graph of $y = g(x) = 2x + 3$.

b. Graph the function defined by $y = 2x + 3$. Verify using a graphing calculator.

c. Write an equation that represents a vertical stretch of the graph of $y = 2x + 3$ by a factor of 3.

d. Graph the line having equation in part c on the same coordinate axis as the graph of $y = 2x + 3$. Verify using a graphing calculator.

e. Determine the slope and intercepts of the vertically stretched graph.

f. Compare the slopes and intercepts with the graph of the original function.

12. a. Using a graphing calculator, sketch a graph of each of the following in a standard window:

$$y_1 = x, y_2 = 0.5x$$

b. Is the graph of $y = 0.5x$ a vertical stretch of the graph of $y = x$? Explain.

In general, if a is a positive constant, then the graph of $y = a f(x)$ is the graph of $y = f(x)$

    i. vertically shrunk by a factor of a, if $0 < a < 1$.
   ii. vertically stretched by a factor of a, if $a > 1$.

Vertical and horizontal shifts (also called translations), reflections, and vertical stretches and shrinks are all examples of **transformations**. These are ways in which the graph of a given function can be changed or transformed.

13. If the graph of a line is vertically stretched or shrunk, explain why the *x*-intercept of the line is not affected? See Problem 11f.

14. The graph of $y = -2x + 1$ can be interpreted as a combination of transformations of the graph of $y = x$. Sketch a graph of $y = -2x + 1$ by performing the following changes in the graph of $y = x$: First, a vertical stretch; second, a reflection; last, a vertical shift. Each transformation should be performed in the natural order of operations. Verify using a graphing calculator.

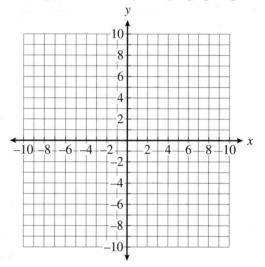

The transformations discussed in this activity can be applied to the graph of any function, as you will see in subsequent activities, as well as some of the exercises that follow.

15. Consider the basic absolute value function, $f(x) = |x|$, which is then changed by four transformations described in parts a–d. To determine the final equation for this function, you will consider one transformation at a time.

   a. Graph the basic absolute value function that has been shifted 3 units to the left.

   Write the equation for the absolute value function that has been shifted 3 units to the left.

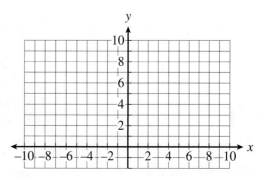

b. Graph the function in part a, which is then stretched vertically by a factor of 2.

Write the equation for the function in part a, which is then stretched vertically by a factor of 2.

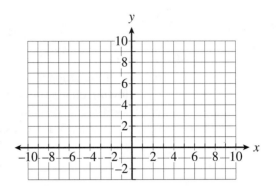

c. Graph the function in part b, which is then reflected across the x-axis.

Write the equation for the function in part b, which is then reflected across the x-axis.

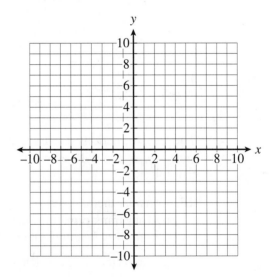

d. Finally, graph the function in part c, which is then shifted upward 5 units. Write the equation for this final graph.

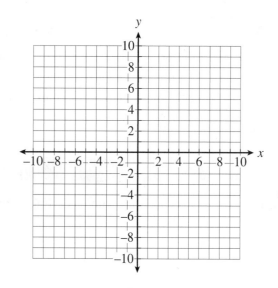

e. Check your final function by graphing the equation on your calculator.

SUMMARY
Activity 2.5

1. In a **vertical shift** of a graph, a positive constant is added to (upward shift) or subtracted from (downward shift) each output value. As a result, the graph is moved vertically upward or vertically downward.

2. In a **horizontal shift** of a graph, a positive constant is first added to (shift left) or subtracted from (shift right) each input value. As a result, the graph is moved horizontally to the left or horizontally to the right.

3. In general, if a function is defined by $y = f(x)$, and c is a constant, then the graph of

   i. $y = f(x) + c$ is the graph of $y = f(x)$ shifted vertically $|c|$ units. If $c > 0$, then the shift is upward. If $c < 0$, then the shift is downward.

   ii. $y = f(x + c)$ is the graph of $y = f(x)$ shifted horizontally $|c|$ units. If $c > 0$, then the shift is to the left. If $c < 0$, the shift is to the right.

4. The graph of $y = -x$ is a **reflection** of the graph of $y = x$ across the x-axis.

5. If the graph of $y = f(x)$ is reflected across the x-axis, then the equation of the resulting graph is $y = -f(x)$. The graphs of $y = f(x)$ and $y = -f(x)$ are mirror images across the x-axis. The y-value of each point in the original graph changes sign. The x-value of each point remains the same.

6. If the graph of $y = f(x)$ is reflected across the y-axis, then the equation of the resulting graph is $y = f(-x)$. The graphs of $y = f(x)$ and $y = f(-x)$ are mirror images across the y-axis. The x-value of each point in the original graph changes sign. The y-value of each point remains the same.

7. If the graph of $y = f(x)$ is vertically stretched by a factor of $a > 0$, then the equation of the stretched graph is $y = af(x)$. The number a is called the **stretch factor**. The y-value of each point in the graph of $y = f(x)$ is multiplied by a factor of a. The x-values remain fixed.

8. In general, if a function is defined by $y = f(x)$, and a is a positive constant, then the graph of

   i. $y = af(x)$ is the graph of $y = f(x)$ vertically shrunk by a factor of a, if $0 < |a| < 1$.

   ii. $y = af(x)$ is the graph of $y = f(x)$ vertically stretched by a factor of a, if $a > 1$.

9. Vertical and horizontal shifts (also called translations), reflections, and vertical stretches and shrinks are all examples of **transformations**.

EXERCISES
Activity 2.5

1. Describe in words how the basic linear function, $f(x) = x$, is transformed by each equation.

   a. $y = 3x$

   b. $y = x - 4$

   c. $y = -x$

   d. $y = \dfrac{1}{2}x + 3$

2. Write the equation for the basic squaring function, $f(x) = x^2$, that has been transformed by

   a. reflecting across the x-axis.

   b. shifting down 6 units.

   c. stretching vertically by a factor of 4.

   d. shifting right 3 units and shrinking vertically by a factor of $\frac{1}{3}$.

   Check each equation by graphing on your calculator.

3. For each function graphed below, sketch the graph of the new function after it is transformed as described.

    a. Shift left 3 and reflect across *x*-axis.

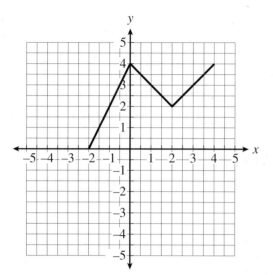

    b. Stretch vertically by a factor of 2, then shift down 3 units.

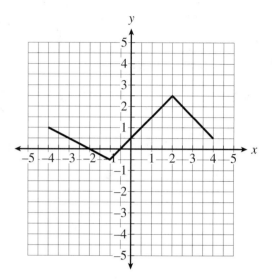

4. For each of the following linear function graphs, describe how $f(x) = x$ is transformed, write the equation for the line, and then check by graphing on your calculator.

    a.

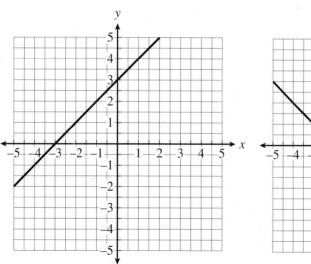

    b.

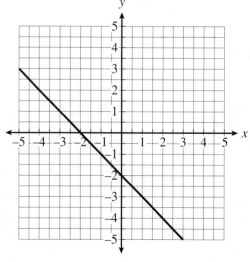

c.

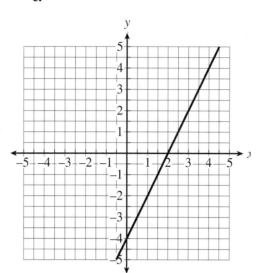

d.

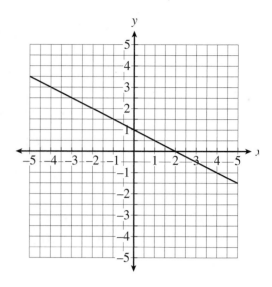

5. If the point $(3, -5)$ is on the graph of $y = f(x)$ and the graph is transformed with a vertical stretch by a factor of 5, then reflected across the x-axis, what must be the coordinates of one point on the new graph?

6. If the point $(-2, 8)$ is on the graph of $y = f(x)$ and the graph is transformed with a vertical shrink by a factor of $\frac{1}{2}$ then shifted down 5 units, what must be the coordinates of one point on the new graph?

7. If the point $(-5, 2)$ is on the graph of $y = f(x)$ and the graph is transformed with a horizontal shift of 3 units to the right, then a reflection across the x-axis, what must be the coordinates of one point on the new graph?

ACTIVITY 2.6
Predicting
Population

OBJECTIVES

1. Write an equation for a linear function given its slope and *y*-intercept.

2. Write linear functions in slope-intercept form
$y = mx + b$.

3. Determine the relative error in a measurement or prediction using a linear model.

4. Interpret the slope and *y*-intercept of linear functions in contextual situations.

5. Use the slope-intercept form of linear equations to solve problems.

According to the U.S. Bureau of the Census, the population of the United States was approximately 132 million in 1940 and 151 million in 1950.

For this activity, assume that the rate of change of population with respect to time is a constant value over the decade from 1940 to 1950. This means you are assuming that the relationship between the independent variable time and the dependent variable population is linear.

1. **a.** Write the given data as ordered pairs of the form $(t, P(t))$, where *t* is the number of years since 1940 and $P(t)$ is the corresponding population, in millions.

   b. Plot the two data points, and draw a straight line through them. Label the horizontal axis from 0 to 25 and the vertical axis from 130 to 180.

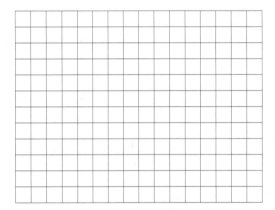

2. **a.** What is the average rate of change of population from $t = 0$ (1940) to $t = 10$ (1950)?

   b. What is the slope of the line connecting the two points in part a? What is the practical meaning of the slope in this situation?

3. What is the *P*-intercept of this line? What is the practical meaning of this intercept in this situation?

4. **a.** Use the slope and *P*-intercept from Problems 2 and 3 to write an equation for the line.

b. Assume that the average rate of change you determined in Problem 2 stays the same through 1960. Use the equation in part a to predict the U.S. population in 1960. Also estimate the population in 1960 from the graph.

The **error** in a prediction is the difference between the observed value (actual value that was measured) and the predicted value. The **relative error** of a prediction is the ratio of the error to the observed value. That is,

$$\text{relative error} = \frac{\text{observed value} - \text{predicted value}}{\text{observed value}} = \frac{\text{error}}{\text{observed value}}.$$

5. a. The relative error is usually reported as a percent. The actual U.S. population in 1960 was approximately 179 million. What is the *relative error* (expressed as a percent) in your prediction?

b. What do you think was the cause of your prediction error?

6. You want to develop a population model based on more recent data. The U.S. population was approximately 249 million in 1990 and 281 million in 2000.

a. Plot these data points using ordered pairs of the form $(t, P(t))$, where t is the number of years since 1990 (now, $t = 0$ corresponds to 1990). Draw a line through the points.

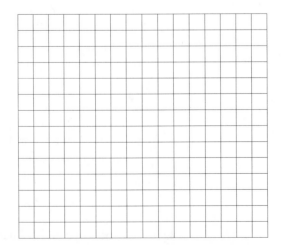

b. Determine the slope of the line in part a. What is the practical meaning of the slope in this situation? How does this slope compare with the slope in Problem 2?

c. In which decade, 1940–1950 or 1990–2000, did the U.S. population increase more rapidly? Explain your answer in terms of slope.

d. Determine the P-intercept of the line in part a.

e. Write the equation of the line in part a.

7. a. Use the equation $P(t) = 3.2t + 249$, also called a linear model, developed in Problem 6 to predict the population in 2010. What assumptions do you make about the average rate of change of the population in this prediction?

b. According to the linear model in $P(t) = 3.2t + 249$, in what year will the population be 350 million?

SUMMARY
Activity 2.6

1. The **error** in a prediction is the difference between the observed value and the predicted value. The **relative error** in prediction is the ratio of the error to the observed value. That is,

$$\text{relative error} = \frac{\text{observed value} - \text{predicted value}}{\text{observed value}} = \frac{\text{error}}{\text{observed value}}.$$

Relative error is usually reported as a percent.

1. a. Use the equation $P(t) = 3.2t + 249$ developed in Problem 6 to predict the U.S. population in the year 2005. What assumptions are you making about the rate of change of the population in this prediction? Recall that t is the number of years since 1990.

b. The actual U.S. population in 2005 was approximately 296 million. What is the relative error in your prediction?

c. What do you think was the cause of the prediction error?

2. a. According to the U.S. Bureau of the Census, the population of California in 2000 was approximately 34.10 million and was increasing at a rate of approximately 630,000 people per year. Let $P(t)$ represent the California population (in millions) and t represent the number of years since 2000. Complete the following table.

t	P(t) (in millions)
0	
1	
2	

b. What information in part a indicates that the California population growth is linear with respect to time? What are the slope and vertical intercept of the graph of the population data?

c. Write a linear function rule for $P(t)$ in terms of t.

d. Use the linear function in part c to estimate the population of California in 2004.

e. Population data from the State of California Department of Finance is used by California state agencies in developing their programs and policies. The Department of Finance estimated that the population of California in 2004 was approximately 36.59 million. Determine the relative error (as a percent) between your prediction in part d and the estimate actually used by the state of California.

f. Use the linear model from part c to predict the population of California in 2010.

3. a. The population of the Miami metropolitan area was approximately 2.3 million in 2000 and 5.4 million in 2007. This information is summarized in the accompanying table, where t is the number of years since 2000 and $P(t)$ represents the population (in millions) at a given time t.

t	P(t)
0	2.3
7	5.4

Assume that the average rate of change of the population over this seven-year period is constant. Determine this average rate.

b. Plot the two data points, and draw a line through them.

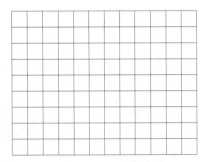

c. Determine the slope and P-intercept of the line in part b.

d. Write an equation to model Miami's population, $P(t)$ (in millions), in terms of t.

   e. Use this linear model to predict Miami's population in 2020.

4. a. The population of Portland, Oregon, was 2.39 in 1990 and 2.36 million in 2000. If t represents the number of years since 1990, and $P(t)$ represents the population (in millions) at a given time, t, summarize the given information in the accompanying table.

t	$P(t)$

   b. Plot the two data points on appropriately scaled and labeled coordinate axes. Draw a line connecting the points.

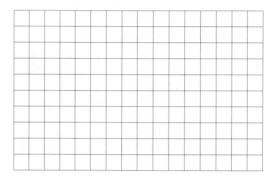

   c. What is the slope of the line? What is the practical meaning of the slope in this situation?

   d. What is the P-intercept of the line? What is the practical meaning of the intercept in this situation?

   e. Write an equation to model Portland's population, $P(t)$, in terms of t.

   f. Use this linear model to predict the population of Portland in 2020.

5. In each part, determine the equation of the line for the given information:

  a. Two points on a line are (0, 4) and (7, 18). Use the points to first determine the slope and y-intercept. Then write the equation of the line.

  b. The graph has y-intercept (0, 6) and contains the point (2, 1).

6. a. In 1990, the rate of change of the world population was approximately 0.09125 billion per year (or approximately 1 million people every four days). The world population was estimated to be 5.3 billion in 1990. Write an equation to model the population, P (in billions), in terms of t, where t is the number of years since 1990 ($t = 0$ corresponds to 1990).

  b. Use the linear model to predict the world population in 2020.

  c. According to the model, when will the population of the world be double the 1990 population?

ACTIVITY 2.7

Housing Prices

Despite the decrease in housing prices in recent years, there has been a steady increase in housing values in your neighborhood since 2000. The house across the street sold for $125,000 in 2003, and then sold again in 2007 for $150,000. This data can be written in a table, where n represents the number of years since 2000 and P represents the sale price of a typical house in your neighborhood.

NUMBER OF YEARS SINCE 2000, n	HOUSING PRICE (thousands of $), P
3	125
7	150

1. Plot the two points on the grid below, and sketch the line containing them. Extend the line so that it intersects the P-axis. Scale the n-axis to include the period of years from 2000 to 2010 (from $n = 0$ to $n = 10$). Scale the P-axis by increments of 25, starting at 0 and continuing through 250.

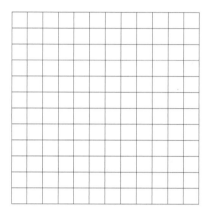

2. **a.** Use the points in the table to determine the slope of the line. What are its units of measurement?

   b. What is the practical meaning of the slope in this situation?

If you assume that the average rate of increase of housing prices remains constant, then the price, P, of the house is a linear function of the number, n, of years since 2000. Therefore, the relationship between P and n can be modeled by an equation written in the slope-intercept form, $P = mn + b$.

3. **a.** What is the value of the slope m (see Problem 2)?

   b. Write the equation $P = mn + b$, replacing m with its value.

c. Use the ordered pair (3, 125) from the table and rewrite the equation in part b by replacing P and n with the appropriate values in the ordered pair.

d. Solve the equation in part c for b, the P-intercept of the graph of the line.

e. Interpret the value of the P-intercept b in the housing price function.

f. Finally, rewrite the equation $P = mn + b$, replacing b and m with their respective values.

In Problem 3, you determined a linear equation in the slope-intercept form, using two ordered pairs that satisfy the equation. You determined the slope m in part 3a and the vertical intercept b in part 3d. There is a general method for writing a linear equation from two ordered pairs using the slope formula.

Let (h, k) be a known point on a line and let (x, y) be any other point on the line. The slope m of the line is determined by the two ordered pairs, (h, k) and (x, y).

$$m = \frac{\Delta y}{\Delta x} = \frac{y - k}{x - h}, \text{ so}$$
$$y - k = m(x - h)$$

The last equation, $y - k = m(x - h)$, gives a linear equation in **point-slope form**.

Example 1   *Write an equation of the linear function whose graph is a line containing the points $(-1, 3)$ and $(2, 9)$.*

SOLUTION

Step 1. Determine the slope of the line.

$$m = \frac{9 - 3}{2 - (-1)} = \frac{6}{3} = 2$$

Step 2. Choose any point on the line and substitute for h and k. Using the point-slope form $y - k = m(x - h)$ with $m = 2$ and $(h, k) = (-1, 3)$, you have

$$y - 3 = 2(x - (-1))$$
$$y - 3 = 2(x + 1)$$

Step 3. Solve the equation in step 2 for y.

$$y = 3 + 2x + 2, \text{ or } y = 2x + 5$$

Since the independent and dependent variables for the housing price function are n and P respectively, the point-slope form for the line is $p - k = m(n - h)$.

4. a. Use the ordered pair (3, 125) for (h, k) and $m = 6.25$ to write the point-slope form of the housing price function.

b. Simplify the right side of the point-slope form of the equation, solve for *P*, and compare the result to the slope-intercept form in Problem 3f.

c. Repeat parts a and b using the ordered pair (7, 150) for (*h*, *k*).

Problem 4 demonstrates that you obtain the same equation of the line regardless of which point you use for (*h*, *k*).

5. The basal energy requirement is the daily number of calories that a person needs to maintain basic life processes. For a 20-year-old male who weighs 75 kilograms and is 190.5 centimeters tall, the basal energy requirement is 1952 calories. If his weight increases to 95 kilograms, he will require 2226 calories.

The given information is summarized in the following table.

20-YEAR-OLD MALE, 190.5 CENTIMETERS TALL		
w, WEIGHT (kg)	75	95
B, BASAL ENERGY REQUIREMENT (cals)	1952	2226

a. Assume that the basal energy requirement, *B*, is a linear function of weight, *w* for a 20-year-old male who is 190.5 cm tall. Determine the slope of the line containing the two points indicated in the above table.

b. What is the practical meaning of the slope in the context of this situation?

c. Using the point-slope form, determine an equation that expresses *B* in terms of *w* for a 20-year-old, 190.5 cm tall male.

d. Does the *B*-intercept have any practical meaning in this situation? Determine the practical domain of the basal energy function.

Perpendicular Lines

6. a. Consider two lines with equations $y_1 = -2x + 3$ and $y_2 = \dfrac{1}{2}x + 4$. Without graphing, are the lines parallel? Explain. *Hint:* Compare the slopes.

b. Use a graphing calculator to sketch a graph of each line on the same coordinate axes. What do you observe?

If the slopes of the two lines are different, the lines will intersect at some point. The two lines in Problem 6 intersect in a special way to form four angles of equal size. Such an angle is called a **right angle** and measures 90°. In a diagram, right angles are usually designated as follows:

Perpendicular Lines

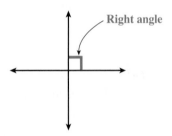

Right angle

Two lines that intersect at right angles are called **perpendicular lines**. The slopes of perpendicular lines are related in a special way. Problem 7 demonstrates this relationship.

7. a. Multiply the slopes of the two perpendicular lines in Problem 6.

b. Two lines having equations $y_1 = \dfrac{2}{3}x - \dfrac{1}{2}$ and $y_2 = -\dfrac{3}{2}x + 4$ are perpendicular. Determine the slope of each line and then multiply the slopes.

c. Compare the results from parts a and b.

d. Use your observation from part c to determine if the following lines are perpendicular:

$$y_1 = -4x + 3 \text{ and } y_2 = \dfrac{1}{4}x - 2$$

If the product of two numbers is -1, then the numbers are called **negative reciprocals**.

> **DEFINITION**
>
> Two lines are perpendicular if their slopes are negative reciprocals. Stated symbolically, if m_1 and m_2 represent the slopes of two lines l_1 and l_2 respectively, then l_1 is perpendicular to l_2 if $m_1 \cdot m_2 = -1$.

In certain situations, you need to determine the equation of a line perpendicular to a given line. The following is an example of such a problem.

Example 2   *Determine the equation of the line perpendicular to the line with equation $2x - y = -3$ and passing through the point $(-1, 5)$.*

SOLUTION

Step 1. Write the equation of the given line in the form $y = mx + b$.

Solving $2x - y = -3$ for y, you have

$$2x - y = -3$$
$$-y = -2x - 3$$
$$y = 2x + 3.$$

Step 2. Determine the slope of the unknown line.

The slope of the given line $y = 2x + 3$ is 2. Therefore, the slope of the unknown line is $-\dfrac{1}{2}$, since $2\left(-\dfrac{1}{2}\right) = -1$.

Step 3. Use the point-slope form of a line to determine the equation of the unknown line.

The unknown line contains the point $(-1, 5)$ and has slope $-\dfrac{1}{2}$.

Substituting $-\dfrac{1}{2}$ for m, -1 for h, and 5 for k, you have

$$y - k = m(x - h)$$
$$y - (5) = -\frac{1}{2}(x - (-1))$$
$$y - 5 = -\frac{1}{2}x - \frac{1}{2}.$$

8. Determine the equation of the line perpendicular to the line having equation $y = \dfrac{1}{5}x - 2$ and passing through the point $(2, -3)$.

9. a. Sketch a graph of a line segment having endpoints $(0, -2)$ and $(2, 6)$. Determine the slope of the line segment.

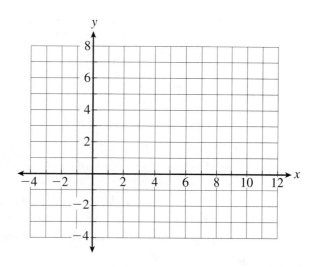

b. The point located exactly halfway between the endpoints of a line segment is called the **midpoint**. For a line segment with endpoints (x_1, y_1) and (x_2, y_2), the midpoint of the line segment has the following coordinates:

$$\left(\frac{x_1 + x_2}{2}, \frac{y_1 + y_2}{2} \right)$$

Determine the midpoint of the line segment in part a.

c. Determine the slope of the line perpendicular to the line segment in part a.

d. Determine the equation of the line perpendicular to the line segment in part a that passes through the midpoint of the line segment. Such a line is called a **perpendicular bisector**.

e. Sketch a graph of the perpendicular bisector of the line segment in part a.

SUMMARY
Activity 2.7

1. To determine the equation of a line when two points on the line are known:

   Step 1. Determine the **slope** of the line: $m = \dfrac{\Delta y}{\Delta x}$.

   Step 2. If the x-value of one of the points is zero, then b is the y-value of this point (y-intercept) and you can write the equation in **slope-intercept form**, $y = mx + b$.

   Step 3. If neither point has an x-value of zero, then choose one of the points as (h, k) and write the equation in **point-slope form**, $y - k = m(x - h)$. Then, solve for y.

2. If the product of two numbers is -1, then the numbers are called **negative reciprocals**.

3. Two lines are **perpendicular** if their slopes are negative reciprocals. Stated symbolically, if m_1 and m_2 represent the slopes of two lines l_1 and l_2 respectively, then l_1 is perpendicular to l_2 if $m_1 \cdot m_2 = -1$.

4. The point located exactly halfway between the endpoints of a line segment is called the **midpoint** of the line segment. If the line segment has endpoints (x_1, y_1) and (x_2, y_2), then the midpoint of the line segment has the following coordinates:

$$\left(\frac{x_1 + x_2}{2}, \frac{y_1 + y_2}{2} \right)$$

5. A line perpendicular to a line segment that passes through the midpoint of the line segment called a **perpendicular bisector**.

EXERCISES
Activity 2.7

1. Federal income tax paid by an individual single taxpayer is a function of taxable income. The following table represents the 2005 federal tax for various taxable incomes.

i, TAXABLE INCOME ($)	15,000	16,500	18,000	19,500	21,000	22,500	24,000
t, 2005 FEDERAL TAX ($)	1,889	2,114	2,339	2,564	2,789	3,014	3,239

   a. Plot the data points, with taxable income i as input and 2005 tax t as output. Scale the input axis from $0 to $24,000 and the output axis from $0 to $4000. Explain why the relationship is linear.

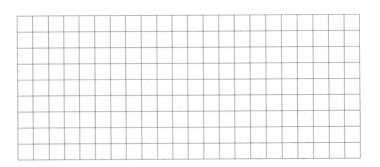

b. Determine the slope of the line. What is the practical meaning of the slope?

c. Use the point-slope form to write an equation to model this situation. Use the variable i to represent the taxable income and the variable t to represent the federal tax owed.

d. What is the t-intercept? Does it make sense?

e. Use the equation from part c to determine the federal tax owed by a college student having a taxable income of $\$8600$ in 2005.

f. Use the equation from part c to determine the taxable income of a single person who paid $1686 in federal taxes for 2005.

In Exercises 2–8, determine the equation of the line that has the given slope and passes through the given point. Then sketch a graph of the line.

2. $m = 3$, through the point $(2, 6)$ **3.** $m = -1$, through the point $(5, 0)$

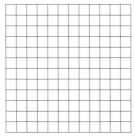
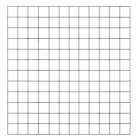

4. $m = 7$, through the point $(-3, -5)$ **5.** $m = 0.5$, through the point $(8, 0.5)$

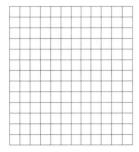   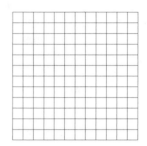

6. $m = 0$, through the point $(5, 2)$ **7.** $m = -4.2$, through the point $(-4, 6.8)$

8. Undefined slope, through the point $(2, -3)$

In Exercises 9–14, determine the equation of the line that passes through the given points. Use the table feature of a graphing calculator to confirm that the coordinates of both points satisfy your equation.

9. $(2, 6)$ and $(4, 16)$ **10.** $(-5, 10)$ and $(5, -10)$

11. $(3, 18)$ and $(8, 33)$ **12.** $(0, 6)$ and $(-10, 0)$

13. (10, 2) and (−3, 2)

14. (3.5, 8.2) and (3.5, 7.3)

15. You have just been offered your first job. The following table gives the salary schedule for the first few years of employment. Bonuses are not included. Let s represent your salary after x years of employment.

YEARS OF EMPLOYMENT, x	SALARY, s ($)
0	32,500
1	34,125
2	35,750
3	37,375

a. Is the salary a linear function of the years of employment? Explain.

b. What is the practical domain for the input variable x?

c. Scale and label the axes appropriately and plot the points from the table on the following grid.

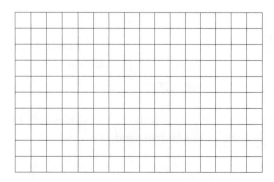

d. Determine the slope of the line containing the points.

    e. What is the practical meaning of the slope in this situation?

    f. Write an equation to determine the salary, s, after x years of employment.

    g. What is the s-intercept? What is the practical meaning of the intercept in this situation?

    h. Assume that the rate of increase in your salary remains the same. Use the equation model to determine your salary after eight years of employment.

16. The following table gives the distance, d, in miles of a boat from a marina as a linear function of time, t, in hours.

t (in hours)	d (in miles)
2	75
4	145

    a. Determine the slope of the line. What is the practical meaning of slope in this situation?

    b. Write the equation of the line in slope-intercept form.

17. According to the Hudson Institute, from 1980 to 2000, the number of U.S. lawyers increased, in thousands, from 506 to 1026.

    a. The number of U.S. lawyers is a function of the number of years since 1980 (use 0 to represent the year 1980, 1 to represent 1981, and so forth). Write the two ordered pairs describing this situation.

    b. Assume that this function is linear, and write the slope-intercept equation of the line that represents this data.

    c. What is the practical meaning of the slope in this equation? (Remember, your slope is in thousands.)

    d. How many lawyers were there in the United States in 1995?

18. Straight-line depreciation helps spread the cost of new equipment over a number of years. The value of your company's copy machine after 1 year will be $14,700 and after 4 years will be $4800.

    a. Write a linear function that will determine the value of the copy machine for any specified year.

    b. The salvage value is the value of the equipment when it gets replaced. What will be the salvage value of the copier if you plan to replace it after 5 years?

In Exercises 19–21, determine whether the lines are parallel, perpendicular, or neither.

19. $y = -2x + 6$
    $y = 2x - 1$

20. $x - 3y = -2$
    $6x - 18y = 3$

21. $y = -\dfrac{5}{3}x + 4$

       $y = \dfrac{3}{5}x - \dfrac{2}{5}$

22. Write an equation of the line containing the point $(-2, 1)$ and perpendicular to the line having equation $3x + 5y = 4$.

In Exercises 23–24, write an equation of each line satisfying the given conditions.

23. Passes through the point $(3, -2)$ and is

    a. perpendicular to the line $x - 4y = 6$.   **b.** parallel to the line $x - 4y = 6$.

24. Passes through the point $(5, -4)$ and is

    a. parallel to the line $y + 10 = 0$.   **b.** perpendicular to the line $y + 10 = 0$.

25. Determine the equation of the perpendicular bisector of the line segment having endpoints $(3, -1)$ and $(-5, 1)$.

ACTIVITY 2.8
Body Fat
Percentage

OBJECTIVES

1. **Construct scatterplots from sets of data pairs.**

2. **Recognize when patterns of points in a scatterplot have a linear form.**

3. **Recognize when the pattern in the scatterplot shows that the two variables are positively related or negatively related.**

4. **Identify individual data points, called outliers, that fall outside the general pattern of the other data.**

5. **Estimate and draw a line of best fit through a set of points in a scatterplot.**

6. **Determine residuals between the actual value and the predicted value for each point in the data set.**

7. **Use a graphing calculator to determine a line of best fit by the least-squares method.**

8. **Measure the strength of the correlation (association) by a correlation coefficient.**

9. **Recognize that a strong correlation does not necessarily imply a linear, or a cause-and-effect, relationship.**

Your body fat percentage is simply the percentage of fat your body contains. If you weigh 150 pounds and have a 10% body fat, your body consists of 15 pounds of fat and 135 pounds of lean body mass (bone, muscle, organs, tissue, blood, etc.).

A certain amount of fat is essential to bodily functions. Fat regulates body temperature, cushions and insulates organs and tissues, and is the main form of the body's energy storage. The American Council on Exercise has established the following categories for females and males based upon body fat percentage.

CLASSIFICATION	FEMALE (% fat)	MALE (% fat)
Essential Fat	10–12%	2–4%
Athletes	14–20%	6–13%
Fitness	21–24%	14–17%
Acceptable	25–31%	18–25%
Obese	32% plus	25% plus

Hydrostatic measurement (body composition analysis through immersion of a person's body in water) is considered the most accurate method of determining body fat percentage. However, in most clinical or applied situations, underwater weighing is not practical.

A group of researchers is searching for alternative methods to measure body fat percentage. They first investigate if there is an association between body fat percentage and a person's weight. The body fat percentage of 19 male subjects is accurately determined using hydrostatic weighing method. Then, each subject is weighed, using a traditional scale. The results are recorded in the following table.

w, Weight (pounds)	175	181	200	159	195	192	205	173	187	188	240	175	168	246	160	215	155	146	219
y, Body Fat %	16	21	25	6	22	30	32	21	25	19	15	22	9	38	14	27	12	10	30

1. Plot the data points as ordered pairs of the form (w, y) on an appropriately scaled and labeled coordinate axis.

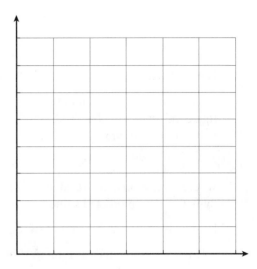

In this situation, you are interested in determining if body fat percentage is related to body weight. The graph in Problem 1, called a **scatterplot**, is an ideal tool to identify patterns in the relationship between two variables.

2. **a.** Does there appear to be a linear relationship between weight w and body fat percentage y?

   b. As body weight increases, what is the general trend in the values of the body fat percentage?

   c. Identify any data points that fall outside the general trend or pattern of the other data points. Such data points are called **outliers**. Explain.

3. **a.** Use a straightedge to draw a single line through the points (175, 16) and (200, 25). This line can be used to represent the linear trend in the data.

   b. Determine the slope of the line in part a.

   c. Determine the equation of the line.

d. Use the linear model in part c to predict the body fat percentage of a male weighing 192 pounds. How does the predicted value compare to the actual value of 30%?

Residuals

In almost every situation in which predictions are made from data, it is important to investigate the residuals. **Residuals** are the difference between the actual value and the predicted value for each point in your data. Symbolically stated, you have

$$E = y - \hat{y},$$

where E represents the residual, y is the actual value of the dependent variable, and $\hat{y}$, read "y-hat", is the predicted value for a given x.

Residuals represent the error between the actual value and the value predicted by the model.

4. a. Determine the residual in Problem 3d.

b. If a residual is positive, what does that tell you about the predicted value?

5. a. Determine the residual for a body weight of 168 pounds.

b. If the residual is negative, what does that tell you about the prediction?

c. What if the residual error is zero? What must be true about the predicted value of body fat percentage?

6. The residuals can be used to determine how well a particular line fits the data.

a. Determine all the residuals for the body fat versus weight data using the linear model from Problem 3. Use your graphing calculator to create a table to easily display the values. On the TI-83/84 Plus, enter the body fat percentage data by first pressing STAT and choosing Edit. Then, enter the weight data (w-values) in L_1 and the body fat % data in L_2. Your equation can be entered in L_3, and then using $L_4 = L_2 - L_3$, the residuals will appear in L_4. (See Appendix A for TI-83/84 Plus procedures.)

Appendix

Record the predicted body fat % values and corresponding residuals in the following table.

Weight (pounds) w	Body Fat % y	Predicted Body Fat % $\hat{y}$	Residual $E = y - \hat{y}$	E^2
175	16			
181	21			
200	25			
159	6			
195	22			
192	30			
205	32			
173	21			
187	25			
188	19			
240	15			
175	22			
168	9			
246	38			
160	14			
215	27			
155	12			
146	10			
219	30			

b. If the line is a good estimate of the linear pattern, there should be approximately half the points above the line and half below. Is that the case with your line?

c. The sum of all the residuals should be close to zero, if the line is a reasonably good fit. What is the sum of the residuals in this case? (Use sum(L_4) on TI-83/84 Plus.)

Regression Line

There is an established method for determining the line of best fit. The method depends on calculus to find the line that will have the smallest possible sum of all the squares of the residuals. The line that is determined by this method is called the **least squares regression line**.

7. a. Determine the squares of the residuals in Problem 6. You can use the TI-83/84 Plus again by entering the list $L_5 = L_4^2$. Record your results in the last column of the table in Problem 6. Then use sum (L_5) to determine the sums of the squares of the residuals.

b. The regression line can be determined with your calculator by pressing $\boxed{\text{STAT}}$, choosing CALC and option 4: LinReg($ax + b$), rounding the coefficients to four decimal places. Your screen should appear as follows:

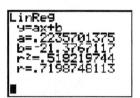

c. When you use the calculator to find the regression line, the residuals have already been calculated and stored for you. They are in a list, which can be found under LIST (2nd $\boxed{\text{STAT}}$) then scroll down under the NAMES menu until you see RESID. Determine the sum of the residuals and the sum of the squares of the residuals for the regression line model. Then compare with the results in Problems 6c and 7a.

Note that the sum of the squares of the residuals for any other linear model will be greater than what you found for the regression line. Hence the name, least squares regression line.

8. a. Produce the scatterplot for the body fat versus weight data, along with the graph of the regression line and the original line from Problem 3. (See Appendix A for TI-83/84 Plus procedures.) Your screen should appear as follows:

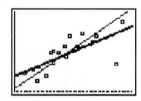

b. Describe how the two lines compare. What do you think might be the cause of any significant differences?

c. Use the regression line model to predict the body fat percentage for a male who weighs 225 pounds.

d. Interpret the practical meaning of the slope of the regression line in this context.

Linear Correlation

When a linear pattern is evident in a scatterplot, there is said to be a linear correlation between the two variables. (When the word correlation appears by itself, it usually means **linear** correlation.) Your calculator window in Problem 7b should have included a value for r, called the **correlation coefficient** as shown below. (If it didn't, see Appendix A to enter DiagnosticOn.)

$$r = 0.7198748113 \text{ or } r = 0.72$$

Note that the correlation coefficient is generally rounded to the nearest hundredth.

The value of the correlation coefficient indicates how strong a linear relationship exists between the two variables under consideration. The value of r ranges between -1 and 1. When the value of r is closer to zero, you would conclude that there is little or no linear correlation. The closer r is to either 1 or -1 the stronger the linear correlation between the two variables.

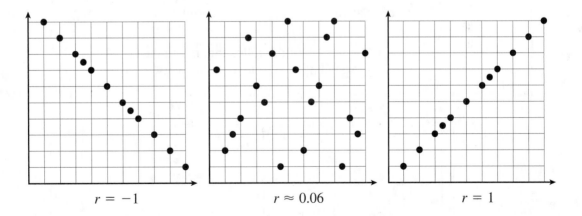

$r = -1$ $r \approx 0.06$ $r = 1$

If $r = 1$, then all the data points lie exactly on a straight line with positive slope. In this case there is a perfect positive correlation. If $r = -1$, then all the decreasing data points lie exactly on a straight line with negative slope. In this case there is a perfect negative correlation. The strength of the correlation is generally best described by both the correlation coefficient and a visual interpretation of the scatterplot. The following scatterplots with their respective correlation coefficients should help make this clear.

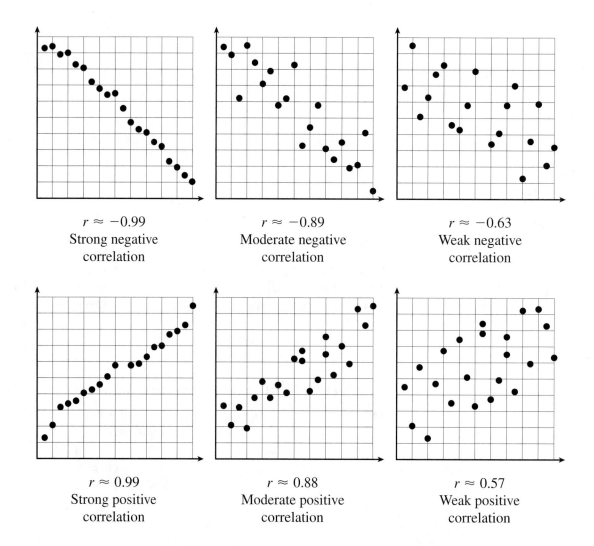

$r \approx -0.99$
Strong negative
correlation

$r \approx -0.89$
Moderate negative
correlation

$r \approx -0.63$
Weak negative
correlation

$r \approx 0.99$
Strong positive
correlation

$r \approx 0.88$
Moderate positive
correlation

$r \approx 0.57$
Weak positive
correlation

9. For each of the following, match the correlation coefficient r with the corresponding scatterplot of data points.

a. $r = 0.84$ **b.** $r = 0.53$ **c.** $r = -0.45$

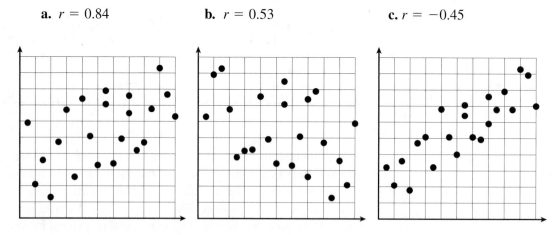

Be careful. The correlation coefficient can be dramatically affected by outlying values, as demonstrated in Problem 10.

10. Recall from Problem 2c that the outlier for the body fat versus weight data was the point (240,15). The correlation coefficient from Problem 7b was $r = 0.72$.

   a. Recalculate the regression line and correlation coefficient when the outlier is removed from the data. What significant differences do you observe?

   b. Use your new regression line to predict the body fat percentage of a 225-pound male, and compare with your result from Problem 8c, when you used the old regression line model.

A correlation coefficient value of $r = 0.85$ suggests a moderately strong linear association between two variables. However, as demonstrated in Problem 11, a line may not be the best model or representation of the data.

11. a. Produce a scatterplot for the following table of values. How would you describe the association between x and y?

x	0.5	0.5	1	1	1.5	2	2.5	3	3.5	4	4.5	5	5	5.5	5.5	6	6.5	7	7	7.5	8	8
y	3.2	2.9	2.5	2.1	2.6	1.8	2.6	2.2	3.2	2.9	3.1	3.6	4	4.1	3.1	3.9	4.9	4.6	5.3	6.3	7.4	6.2

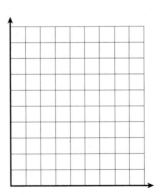

   b. Determine the regression line equation and correlation coefficient. Does the coefficient confirm what you said in part a?

   c. Graph the regression line with the scatterplot. Do you think a different graph might better describe the pattern seen in the scatterplot?

Regression Line Revisited

12. The research group is trying to determine a better predictor of body fat percentage. In addition to the weight of each of the 19 male subjects, the waist size of each subject was measured and recorded.

w, WAIST (inches)	32	36	38	33	39	40	41	35	38	33	40	36	32	44	33	41	34	34	44
y, BODY FAT %	16	21	25	6	22	30	32	21	25	19	15	22	9	38	14	27	12	10	30

a. Plot the data points as ordered pairs of the form (w, y) on an appropriately scaled and labeled coordinate axis.

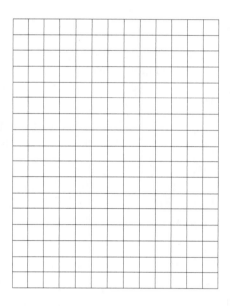

b. Describe any patterns you observe in the scatterplot.

c. Use the linear regression feature of a graphing calculator to determine the equation of the regression line in this situation. What does the slope of this line tell you?

d. Determine the value of the correlation coefficient in this situation. What does it tell you about the relationship between waist size and body fat percentage?

e. Is waist size or body weight a more reliable predictor of body fat percentage? Explain.

Cause-and-Effect Relationships

A strong correlation between two variables does not necessarily mean that a cause-and-effect relationship exists between the two variables. For example, there is a strong positive correlation between height and weight. However, an increase in height does not necessarily cause an increase in weight. There are many other variables that could cause the increase in weight such as gender, age, or body type. Such variables are often called **lurking variables**, hidden in the background and not explicitly measured.

13. a. Suppose your home is heated with natural gas. There is a strong positive correlation between the amount of natural gas usage and the outside temperature. Is there a cause-and-effect relationship between these two variables? Explain.

b. In a 2002 publication, *The Natural History of the Rich*, the author claimed a positive correlation between people with two cars and a longer life span. Is there a cause-and-effect relationship between the number of cars you own and length of life? Explain.

SUMMARY
Activity 2.8

1. A **scatterplot** is a graph of individual data points, useful in determining visually how two variables may be related.

2. An **outlier** is a data point that lies far outside the general pattern of points in a scatterplot.

3. A line that lies within the middle of a linear pattern of data points in a scatterplot is sometimes called a **line of best fit**.

4. A **correlation coefficient**, r, measures how strongly two related variables follow a linear pattern. The value of r ranges between -1 and 1. When the value of r is closer to zero, you would conclude that there is little or no linear correlation. The closer r is to either 1 or -1, the stronger the linear correlation between the two variables. If $r < 0$, a negative correlation, then the linear pattern follows a negative slope. If $r > 0$, a positive correlation, then the linear pattern follows a positive slope.

5. A **residual** is the vertical distance between a data point and a best-fit line. In other words, it is the *error* between an actual data value and a value predicted by the linear model, $E = y - \hat{y}$, where E represents the residual, y is the actual value of the dependent variable, and $\hat{y}$, read "y-hat," is the predicted value for a given x.

6. A **regression line** is considered to be the best fit line for paired data. It is determined by the least squares method, meaning the sum of the squares of the residuals is as small as possible for the regression line, when compared to any other line.

EXERCISES
Activity 2.8

1. For each of the following, determine if there is a positive or negative correlation between the independent variable x and the dependent variable y.

   a. x = age of a child, y = height of a child

   b. x = age of a car, y = resale value of the car

2. During the spring and summer, a concession stand at a community Little League baseball field sells soft drinks and other refreshments. To prepare for the season, the concession owner refers to the previous year's files, in which he had recorded the daily soft drink sales (in gallons) and the average daily temperature (in Fahrenheit degrees). The data is shown in the table.

t, TEMPERATURE (°F)	g, SOFT DRINK SALES (gal)
52	35
55	42
61	50
66	53
72	66
75	68
77	72
84	80
90	84
94	91
97	95

   a. Plot the data points as ordered pairs of the form (t, g).

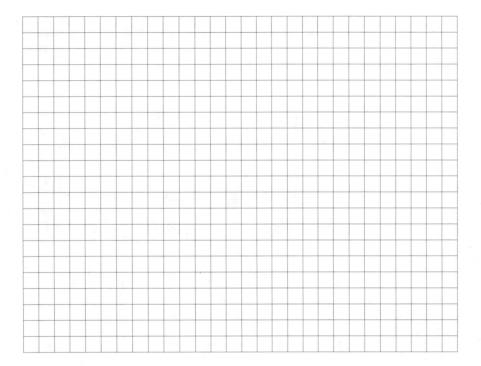

b. Does there appear to be a linear trend between the temperature, t, and the soft drink sales, g? Is there an exact linear fit?

c. Use a straightedge to draw a line of best fit through the points (84, 80) and (66, 53).

d. Use the coordinates of two points in part c to determine the slope of your line.

e. What is the equation of this line?

f. Complete the following table.

t, TEMPERATURE	ACTUAL SALES	g, PREDICTED SALES	RESIDUALS
52	35		
55	42		
61	50		
66	53		
72	66		
75	68		
77	72		
84	80		
90	84		
94	91		
97	95		

3. a. Use your graphing calculator's statistics menu to determine the equation for the regression line in the situation in Exercise 2.

b. Determine the residuals for the regression line in part a. Proceed as you did in Exercise 2f.

t, TEMPERATURE	ACTUAL SALES	G(t), PREDICTED SALES	RESIDUALS
52	35		
55	42		
61	50		
66	53		
72	66		
75	68		
77	72		
84	80		
90	84		
94	91		
97	95		

c. Compare the residual errors of your line of best fit in Problem 2f with the error of the least-squares regression line in part b.

d. Determine the correlation coefficient.

4. In 1966, the U.S. Surgeon General's health warnings began appearing on cigarette packages. The following data seems to demonstrate that public awareness of the health hazards of smoking has had some effect on consumption of cigarettes.

	YEAR							
	1997	1998	1999	2000	2001	2002	2003	2004
% of total population 18 and older who smoke	24.7	24.1	23.5	23.2	22.7	22.4	21.6	20.9

Source: U.S. National Center for Health Statistics.

a. Plot the given data as ordered pairs of the form (t, P), where t is the number of years since 1997 and P is the percent of the total population (18 and older) who smoke. Appropriately scale and label the coordinate axes.

b. Determine the equation of the regression line that best represents the data.

c. Use the equation to predict the percent of the total population 18 and older that will smoke in 2010.

5. The number of Internet users in the United States has increased steadily over the past several years, as indicated in the following table.

YEAR	NUMBER OF INTERNET USERS IN U.S. (in millions)
2000	121
2001	127
2002	140
2003	146
2004	156
2005	163

a. Plot the data points on an appropriately scaled and labeled coordinate axis. Let *x* represent the number of years since 2000.

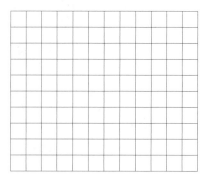

b. Use your graphing calculator's statistics menu (STAT) to determine the equation of the regression line.

c. What is the slope of the line in part b? What is the practical meaning of the slope?

d. Use the linear model from part b to predict when the number of Internet users in the U.S. will reach 220 million. How confident are you in this prediction?

ACTIVITY 2.9

College Tuition

The following graphic contains the average tuition and required fees for all 4-year colleges from 1987 through 2003.

OBJECTIVES

1. Determine the equation of a regression line using a graphing calculator.

2. Use the regression equation to interpolate and extrapolate.

College Costs

YEAR	1987	1992	1996	1999	2001	2003
COST	$5964	$8238	$10,330	$11,888	$12,922	$14,504

1. a. Let t, the number of years since 1987, represent the independent variable and c, the average cost, the dependent variable. Determine an appropriate scale, and plot the data points from the accompanying table. Therefore, $t = 0$ corresponds to the year 1987, $t = 5$ to 1992, $t = 9$ to 1996, and so on.

b. Describe any patterns in the scatterplot.

2. a. Enter the tuition data into your calculator by pressing ⟨STAT⟩ and choosing EDIT.

b. Enter the year data in L1 and the tuition data in L2.

c. Determine the regression line by pressing STAT, choosing CALC and option 4: LinReg($ax + b$).

```
EDIT CALC TESTS
1:1-Var Stats
2:2-Var Stats
3:Med-Med
4:LinReg(ax+b)
5:QuadReg
6:CubicReg
7↓QuartReg
```

d. Write the result, rounding the coefficients to three decimal places.

e. Determine the correlation coefficient.

3. Now use the regression equation you determined in Problem 2 to model the tuition data. Use the table feature on your graphing calculator to determine the model's predicted output in the following table.

INPUT, t	ACTUAL OUTPUT, c	MODEL'S PREDICTED OUTPUT
0	5964	5754
5	8238	8372
9	10,330	10,466
12	11,888	12,037
14	12,922	13,084
16	14,504	14,131

DEFINITION

Using a regression model to predict an output within the boundaries of the input values of the given data is called **interpolation**. Using a regression model to predict an output outside the boundaries of the input values of the given data is called **extrapolation**. In general, interpolation is more reliable than extrapolation.

4. a. Use the regression equation to predict the average tuition and fees at all 4-year colleges in 1993 ($t = 6$). Is this an example of interpolation or extrapolation?

b. Use the regression equation to predict the average tuition and fees at all 4-year colleges in 2005. Is this an example of interpolation or extrapolation?

c. Use the regression line to estimate the year in which average tuition and fees will be at least $20,000.

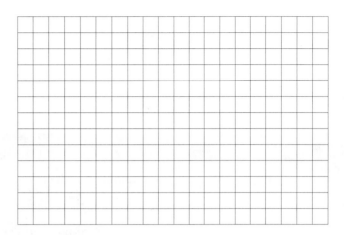

5. Over the past quarter century, the number of bachelor's degrees conferred by degree-granting institutions has steadily increased. The following table contains data on the number of bachelor's degrees (in thousands) earned by women in a given year. The input t represents the number of years since 1977.

	YEAR						
	1977	1981	1985	1990	1995	2000	2004
t, NUMBER OF YEARS SINCE 1977	0	4	8	13	18	23	27
$f(t)$, NUMBER OF DEGREES IN THOUSANDS	423	465	492	558	634	708	775

a. Sketch a scatterplot of the given data.

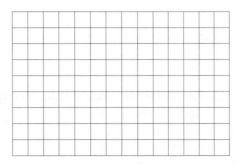

b. Enter the data into your graphing calculator, and determine a linear regression model to represent the data. Write the result here.

c. What is the slope of the line? What is the practical meaning of the slope in this situation?

d. Use the regression model to predict the number of bachelor's degrees that will be granted in the year 2010.

SUMMARY
Activity 2.9

1. The linear regression equation is the linear equation that "best fits" a set of data.

2. The regression line is a mathematical model for the data.

3. **Interpolation** is the process of using a regression equation to predict a value of y for an x-value that lies within the boundaries of the given data.

4. **Extrapolation** is the process of using a regression equation to predict a value of y for an x-value that lies outside the boundaries of the given data.

EXERCISES
Activity 2.9

1. a. Plot the following data:

x	0	3	6	9	12	15	18
y	−0.8	6.3	13.1	19.6	27.0	33.5	40.8

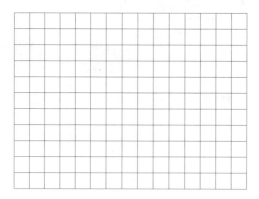

b. With a straightedge, draw a line that you think looks like the line of best fit. Does this data appear to be linear?

c. Use your graphing calculator to determine the equation of the regression line. Write the result below.

d. Use your equation from part c to predict the value of y when $x = 10$.

e. Use your equation from part c to predict the value of y when $x = 25$.

f. Which prediction, in part d or e, would be more accurate? Explain.

2. Public debt increased at a relatively constant rate from 1986 to 1996. The following table gives the average debt per capita (in thousands of dollars) for selected years, where $t = 0$ corresponds to the year 1986:

t (in years since 1986)	0	2	4	6	8	10
d (in thousands of dollars)	8.77	10.53	13.00	15.85	18.02	19.81

Source: Bureau of Public Debt, U.S. Department of the Treasury

a. Plot the data.

b. Use your graphing calculator to determine the equation of the regression line. Write the result here.

c. What is the slope of the line? What is the practical meaning of slope in this situation?

d. Use your regression line to determine the average debt of an individual in 1990 ($t = 4$). Compare your result with the actual value of $13,000 in 1990.

e. Would you use the regression equation to predict the average debt of an individual in 2012?

f. What is the process called that you used to make the prediction in part e?

Collecting and Analyzing Data

3. One measure of how well the American economy is doing is the number of new houses built in a given year. Your economics teacher has asked the class to investigate trends in new home construction in recent years and to predict the number of new homes that will be constructed in 2010.

Use the U.S. Bureau of the Census* as a resource to obtain the latest data available on new home construction from 2000 to 2008. Work with a group and be prepared to give an oral presentation of your findings to the class. The presentation should include visual displays showing any tables, scatterplots, regression equations, and graphs used in the problem-solving process.

Each member of the group should submit a report of the group's findings. The report should contain the following information:

a. The source(s) of the data.

b. A description of the dependent and independent variables.

c. A table and scatterplot of the data.

d. Identification of any patterns in the scatterplot.

e. A linear regression equation and correlation coefficient for the data.

f. A table of residuals between the actual data values and values predicted by the linear model and a description of whether it is reasonable to use a linear equation to model the data.

g. A prediction of the number of new homes to be constructed in 2010 and a description of the level of confidence in this prediction.

h. A conclusion of the data analysis process.

---

* The U.S. Bureau of the Census gathers large amounts of data about the United States and its population. This information is published in the *Statistical Abstract of the United States*. The publication is available on the Internet as well as in print form at most libraries. This is an excellent source of data on a variety of topics.

LAB ACTIVITY 2.10
Measuring Up

OBJECTIVES

1. Collect and organize data in a table.
2. Plot data in a scatterplot.
3. Recognize linear patterns in paired data.
4. Determine a linear regression equation.

Variables arise in many common measurements. Your height is one measurement that has probably been recorded frequently from the day you were born. In this project, you are asked to pair up and make the following body measurements: height (*h*); arm span (*a*), the distance between the tips of your two middle fingers with arms outstretched; wrist circumference (*w*); foot length (*f*); and neck circumference (*n*). For consistency, measure the lengths in inches.

1. Gather the data for your entire class, and record it in the following table:

Inch by Inch

STUDENT	HEIGHT (h)	ARM SPAN (a)	WRIST (w)	FOOT (f)	NECK (n)	

2. What are some relationships you can identify, based on a visual inspection of the data? For example, how do the heights relate to the arm spans?

3. Construct a scatterplot for heights versus arm span on the grid below, carefully labeling the axes and marking the scales. Does the scatterplot confirm what you may have guessed in Problem 2?

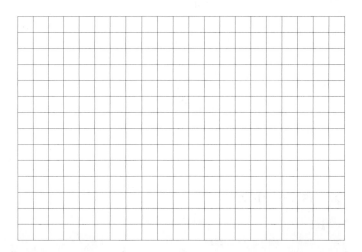

4. Use your calculator to create scatterplots for the following pairs of data, and state whether or not there appears to be a linear relationship. Comment on how the scatterplots either confirm or go against the observations you made in Problem 2.

VARIABLES	LINEAR RELATIONSHIP?
Height versus Foot Length	
Arm Span versus Wrist	
Foot Length versus Neck Circumference	

5. Determine a linear regression equation to represent the relationship between the two variables in Problems 3 and 4 that show the strongest linear pattern.

Predicting Height from Bone Length

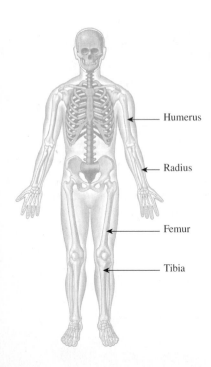

Humerus

Radius

Femur

Tibia

An anthropologist studies human physical traits, place of origin, social structure, and culture. Anthropologists are often searching for the remains of people who lived many years ago. A forensic scientist studies the evidence from a crime scene in order to help solve a crime. Both of these groups of scientists use various characteristics and measurements of the human skeletal remains to help determine physical traits such as height, as well as racial and gender differences.

In the average person, there is a strong relationship between height and the length of two major arm bones (the humerus and the radius), as well as the length of the two major leg bones (the femur and the tibia).

Anthropologists and forensic scientists can closely estimate a person's height from the length of just one of these major bones.

6. Each member of the class should measure his or her leg from the center of the kneecap to the bone on the outside of the hip. This is the length of the femur. Record the results in the appropriate place in the last column of the table in Problem 1.

a. If you want to predict height from the length of the femur, which variable should represent the independent variable? Explain.

b. Make a scatterplot of the data on a carefully scaled and labeled coordinate axes.

c. Describe any patterns you observe in the scatterplot.

d. Determine the correlation coefficient. Describe any correlation between the two variables.

e. Determine the equation of the regression line for the data.

f. Use the equation of the regression line in part e to predict the height of a person whose femur measures 17 inches.

g. Anthropologists have developed the following formula to predict the height of a male based on the length of his femur:

$$h = 1.888L + 32.010$$

where h represents the height in inches and L represents the length of the femur in inches. Use the formula to determine the height of the person whose femur measures 17 inches.

h. Compare your results from parts f and g. What might explain the difference between the height you obtained using the regression formula in part f and the height using the formula in part g?

i. Determine the regression line equation for femur length vs. height using just the male data from Problem 1. How does this new regression line equation compare with the formula $h = 1.888L + 32.010$ used by anthropologists?

7. a. Determine the linear regression equation (femur length vs. height) for the female data in Problem 1.

b. Compare your results to the formula used by anthropologists:

$$h = 1.945x + 28.679$$

where h represents height in inches and x represents femur length in inches.

8. The work of Dr. Mildred Trotter (1899–1991) in skeletal biology led to the development of formulas used to estimate a person's height based on bone length. Her research also led to discoveries about the growth, racial and gender differences, and aging of the human skeleton. Write a brief report on the life and accomplishments of this remarkable scientist.

What Have I Learned?

1. What must be true about the average rate of change between any two points on the graph of an increasing function?

2. You are told that the average rate of change of a particular function is always negative. What can you conclude about the graph of that function and why?

3. Describe a step-by-step procedure for determining the average rate of change between any two points on the graph of a function. Use the points represented by (85, 350) and (89, 400) in your explanation.

4. A line is given by the equation $y = -4x + 10$.

a. Determine its x- and y-intercepts algebraically from the equation.

b. Use your graphing calculator to confirm these intercepts.

5. a. Does the slope of the line having the equation $4x + 2y = 3$ have a value of 4? Why or why not?

    b. Solve the equation in part a for y so that it is in the form $y = mx + b$.

    c. What is its slope?

6. Explain the difference between a line with zero slope and a line with an undefined slope.

7. Describe how you recognize that a function is linear when it is given

    a. graphically.

    b. as an equation involving x and y.

    c. numerically in a table.

8. Do vertical lines represent functions? Explain.

9. Explain the difference between the slopes of lines that are parallel and the slopes of lines that are perpendicular.

Activities 2.1–2.10 **How Can I Practice?**

1. As part of your special diet and exercise program, you record your weight at the beginning of the program and each week thereafter. The following data gives your weight, w, over a five-month period:

MONTHS (t)	0	1	2	3	4	5
WEIGHT, w (lb)	196	183	180	177	174	171

a. Sketch a graph of the data on appropriately scaled and labeled axes.

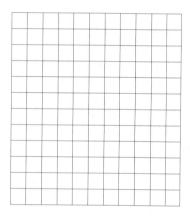

b. Determine the average rate of change of your weight during the first three months. Be sure to include the units of measurement of this rate.

c. Determine the average rate of change during the five-month period.

d. On the graph in part a, connect the points (0, 196) and (3, 177) with a line segment. Does the line segment increase, decrease, or remain horizontal as you follow the line left to right?

e. What is the practical meaning of the average rate of change in this situation?

f. What can you say about the average rate of change of weight during any of the time intervals in this situation?

2. A function is linear because the rate of change of y with respect to x from point to point is constant. Use this idea to determine the missing x and y values in each table, assuming that each table represents a linear function.

a.

x	y
1	4
2	5
3	

b.

x	y
1	4
3	8
5	

c.

x	y
0	4
5	9
10	

d.

x	y
−1	3
0	8
	13
2	

e.

x	y
−3	11
0	8
3	
	2

f.

x	y
−2	−5
0	−8
	−11
4	

g. Explain how you used the idea of constant rate of change to determine the values in the tables.

3. The pitch of a roof is an example of slope in a practical setting. The roof slope is usually expressed as a ratio of rise over run. For example, in the building shown, the pitch is 6 to 24 or in fraction form as $\frac{1}{4}$.

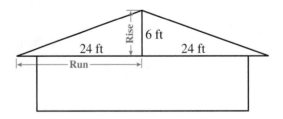

a. If a roof has a pitch of 5 to 16, how high will the roof rise over a 24-foot run?

b. If a roof's slope is 0.25, how high will the roof rise over a 16-foot run?

c. What is the slope of a roof that rises 12 feet over a run of 30 feet?

4. Determine whether any of the following tables contain data that represent a linear function. In each case, give a reason for your answer.

a. You make an investment of $100 at 5% interest compounded semiannually. The following table represents the amount of money you will have at the end of each year.

TIME (years)	AMOUNT ($)
1	105.06
2	110.38
3	115.97
4	121.84

b. A cable TV company charges a $45 installation fee and $28 per month for basic cable service. The table values represent the total usage cost since installation.

NUMBER OF MONTHS	6	12	18	24	36
TOTAL COST ($)	213	381	549	717	1053

c. For a fee of $20 a month, you have unlimited video rental. Values in the table represent the relationship between the number of videos you rented each month and the monthly fee.

NUMBER OF RENTALS	10	15	12	9	2
COST ($)	20	20	20	20	20

5. After stopping your car at a stop sign, you accelerate at a constant rate for a period of time. The speed of your car is a function of the time since you left the stop sign. The following table shows your speedometer reading each second for the next 7 seconds:

t, TIME (sec)	s, SPEED (mph)
0	0
1	11
2	22
3	33
4	44
5	55
6	55
7	55

a. Graph the data using ordered pairs of the form (t, s).

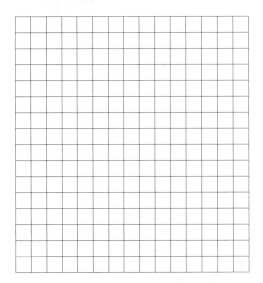

b. For what values of t is the graph increasing?

c. What is the slope of the line segment during the period of acceleration?

d. What is the practical meaning of the slope in this situation?

e. For what values of t is the speed a constant? What is the slope of the line connecting the points of constant speed?

6. a. The three lines shown in the following graphs appear to be different. Calculate the slope of each line.

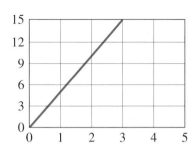 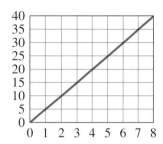 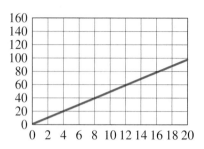

b. Do the three graphs represent the same linear model? Explain.

7. a. Determine the slope of the line $y = -3x - 2$.

b. Determine the slope of the line $2x - 4y = 10$.

c. Determine the slope of the line from the following graph:

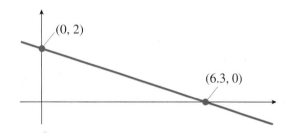

d. Determine whether the lines are parallel, perpendicular, or neither.

i. $y = -5x + 4$ **ii.** $y = \dfrac{2}{5}x + 1$ **iii.** $3x - y = -2$

     $y = 5x - 2$ $y = -\dfrac{5}{2}x - 3$ $6x - 2y = 8$

8. Determine the *x*- and *y*-intercepts for the graph of each of the following:

    a. $y = 2x - 6$ **b.** $y = -\dfrac{3}{2}x + 10$

    c. $y = 10$ **d.** $x = 5$

9. Determine the equation of each line.

    a. The line passes through the points $(2, 0)$ and $(0, -5)$.

    b. The slope is 7, and the line passes through the point $\left(0, \dfrac{1}{2}\right)$.

    c. The slope is 0, and the line passes through the point $(2, -4)$.

10. Sketch a graph of each of the following. Use your graphing calculator to verify your graphs.

    a. $y = 3x - 6$

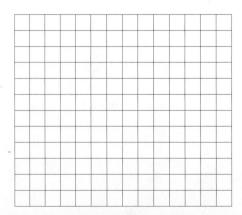

b. $y = -2x + 10$

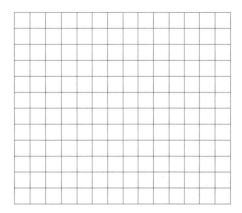

11. Write each equation in slope-intercept form to discover what the graphs have in common. Use your graphing calculator to verify your graphs.

    a. $3x - y = 0$ **b.** $y = 3x - 4$ **c.** $y - 3x = 6$

    d. Describe how the graphs in parts b and c can be obtained from the graph of $y = 3x$ in part a.

In Problems 12–15, determine the slope and the x- and y-intercepts of each line.

12. $y = 2x + 1$ 13. $y = 4 - x$

14. **a.** $y = -2$ **b.** $x = 2$

15. $3x + 2y = -10$

16. Find the equation of the line that passes through the points $(0, 4)$ and $(-5, 0)$.

17. Identify the independent and dependent variables, and write a linear equation model for each of the following situations. Then give the practical meaning of the slope and vertical intercept in each situation.

   a. You make a down payment of $50 and pay $10 per month for your new computer.

   b. You pay $16,000 for a new car whose value decreases by $1500 each year.

18. Suppose you enter Interstate 90 in Montana and drive at a constant speed of 75 miles per hour.

   a. Write a linear model that represents the total distance, $d(t)$, traveled on the highway as a function of time, t, in hours.

   b. Sketch a graph of the function. What are the slope and d-intercept of the line? What is the practical meaning of the slope?

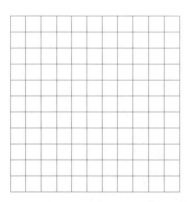

    c. How long would you need to drive at 75 miles per hour to travel a total of 400 miles?

    d. You start out at 10:00 A.M. and drive for three hours at a constant speed of 75 miles per hour. You are hungry and stop for lunch. One hour later you resume your travel, driving steadily at 60 miles per hour until 6 P.M., when you reach your destination. How far will you have traveled? Sketch a graph that shows the distance traveled as a function of time.

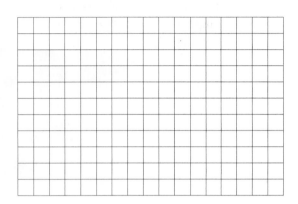

19. Determine the equation of the line passing through each pair of points.

    a. $(0, 6)$ and $(4, 14)$ **b.** $(-9, -7)$ and $(-7, -3)$

20. Determine the equation of the line shown on the following graph:

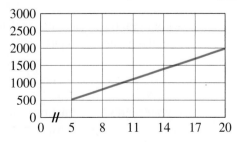

21. Write the equation of the line satisfying the given conditions.

    a. Passes through the point (2, 1) and is parallel to the line having equation
$6x - 2y = 3$.

    b. Passes through the point (3, 7) and is perpendicular to $4x - y = 3$.

22. On an average winter day in Chicago, the Auto Club receives 125 calls from people who need help starting their cars. The number of calls varies, however, depending on the temperature. Here is some data giving the number of calls as a function of the temperature (in degrees Celsius).

TEMPERATURE (°C)	NUMBER OF AUTO CLUB SERVICE CALLS
−12	250
−6	190
0	140
4	125
9	100

    a. Sketch the given data on an appropriately scaled and labeled coordinate axes.

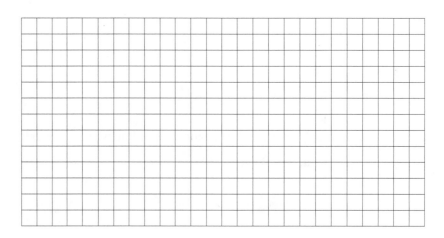

    b. Use your graphing calculator to determine the equation of the regression line for the data in the preceding table.

    c. Use your regression equation from part b, $y = -7.11x + 153.9$, to determine how many service calls the Auto Club can expect if the temperature drops to −20°C.

ACTIVITY 2.11
Business
Checking Account

In setting up your part-time business, you have two choices for a checking account at the local bank.

	MONTHLY FEE	TRANSACTION FEE
REGULAR	$11.00	$0.17 for each transaction
BASIC	$8.50	$0.22 for each transaction in excess of 20

OBJECTIVES

1. Solve a system of two linear equations numerically.

2. Solve a system of two linear equations graphically.

3. Solve a system of two linear equations using the substitution method.

4. Recognize the connections between the three methods of solution.

5. Interpret the solution to a system of two linear equations in terms of the problem's content.

1. If you anticipate making about 50 transactions each month, which checking account will be more economical?

2. Let x represent the number of transactions. Write an equation that expresses the total monthly cost, C, of the regular account in terms of x.

3. The equation model for the basic account is not expressed as easily, because the transaction fee does not apply to the first 20 transactions. Assuming that you will write at least 20 checks per month, determine a model for this situation.

4. **a.** Complete the following table for each account, showing the monthly cost for 20, 50, 100, 150, 200, 250, and 300 transactions. Estimate the number of transactions for which the cost of the two accounts comes the closest. If you have a graphing calculator, use the table feature to complete the table.

Checking In

NUMBER OF TRANSACTIONS	20	50	100	150	200	250	300
COST OF REGULAR ($)	14.40	19.50					
COST OF BASIC ($)	8.50	15.10					

b. Use the table feature of the graphing calculator to determine the *x*-value that produces two identical *y*-values. What is that value?

5. a. Graph the cost equation for each account on the same coordinate axes. Plot the data points for $x \geq 20$ and then use a straightedge to draw a line connecting each set of points. Be sure to properly scale and label the axes.

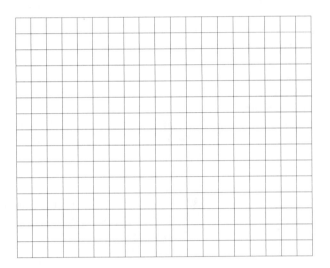

b. Estimate the coordinates of the point where the lines intersect. What is the significance of this point?

Appendix

c. Verify your results from part b using your graphing calculator. Use the trace or intersect feature of the graphing calculator. See Appendix A for the procedure for the TI-83/84 Plus. Your final screens should appear as follows:

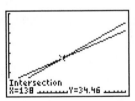

System of Two Linear Equations

Two linear equations that relate the same two variables are called a **system of linear equations**. The two cost equations from Problems 2 and 3 form a system of two linear equations,

$$C = 0.17x + 11$$
$$C = 0.22x + 4.10,$$

where $x \geq 20$.

The **solution** of a system is the set of all ordered pairs that satisfy both equations. If the system has exactly one solution, the system is called **consistent**. The solution to the cost system is (138, 34.46). This solution represents the specific number of transactions ($x = 138$) that produce identical costs in both accounts ($34.46).

In Problem 4, you solved the cost system **numerically** by completing a table and noting the value of the input that resulted in the same output. In Problem 5, you solved the cost system **graphically** by determining the coordinates of the point of intersection.

You can also determine an exact solution by solving the system of equations **algebraically**. In Problem 6, you will explore one method—the **substitution method**—for solving systems of equations algebraically.

Substitution Method for Solving a System of Two Linear Equations

Consider the following system of two linear equations:

$$y = 3x - 10$$
$$y = 5x + 14$$

To solve this system, you need to determine for what value of x are the corresponding y-values the same. The goal of the substitution method is to write a single equation involving just one variable.

6. a. Use the two linear equations in the preceding system to write a single equation involving just one variable.

b. Solve the equation in part a for the variable.

c. Use the result in part b to determine the corresponding value for the other variable in the system.

d. Write the solution to this system as an ordered pair.

e. Verify this solution numerically as well as graphically using the intersection feature of your graphing calculator.

7. The algebraic process used in Problem 6 is called the **substitution method** for solving a system of two linear equations. Write a summary of this procedure.

8. a. Using the substitution method, solve the following system of checking account cost functions:

$$C = 0.17x + 11$$
$$C = 0.22x + 4.10$$

    b. Compare your result with the answers obtained using a numerical approach (Problem 4) and a graphing approach (Problem 5).

    c. Summarize your results by describing under what circumstances the basic account is preferable to the regular account.

9. The part-time business is growing to a full-time operation. You need to purchase a car for deliveries.

    a. An American car costs $13,600 and depreciates $500 a year. Write an equation to determine the resale value, V, of the car after x years of use.

    b. A Japanese car costs $16,000 and depreciates $800 a year. Write an equation to determine the resale value, V, of this car after x years of use.

    c. Write a system of two linear equations that can be used to determine in how many years both cars will have the same resale value.

d. Solve this system numerically by completing the following table.

NUMBER OF YEARS	VALUE OF AMERICAN CAR ($)	VALUE OF JAPANESE CAR ($)
1		
5		
8		
10		
12		

e. Solve the system graphically.

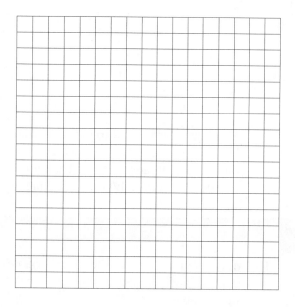

f. Solve the system algebraically using the substitution method.

g. Compare the results in parts d, e, and f.

Does every system of equations have exactly one solution? Attempt to solve the system in Problem 10 algebraically. Explain your result using a graphical interpretation.

10. $y = 2x + 2$
$y = 2x - 1$

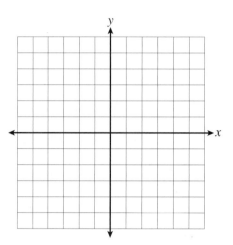

The linear system in Problem 10 is said to be **inconsistent**. There is no solution because the lines never intersect. Graphically, the slopes of the lines are equal, but the x-intercepts are different. Therefore, the graphs are **parallel lines**. Solving such a system algebraically results in a false equation such as $2 = -1$.

SUMMARY
Activity 2.11

1. Two equations that relate the same variables are called a **system of equations**. The solution of a system of equations is the set of all ordered pairs that satisfy both equations.

2. If x is the independent variable and y the dependent variable, then a system of two linear equations is often written in the form
$$y = ax + b$$
$$y = cx + d.$$

3. There are three standard methods for solving a system of equations:
    1. **Numerical method:** Make a table of values for both equations. Identify or estimate the x-value that produces the same y-value for both equations.
    2. **Graphical method:** Graph both equations on the same grid. If the two lines intersect, the coordinates of the point of intersection represent the solution of the system.
    3. **Substitution method:** Replace (or *substitute*) the variable y in one equation with its algebraic expression in x from the other equation. Solve for x. Substitute this x-value into either function rule to determine the corresponding y-value.

4. A linear system is **consistent** if there is at least one solution, the point of intersection of the graphs.

5. A linear system is **inconsistent** if there is no solution; the lines are parallel.

EXERCISES
Activity 2.11

1. Two companies sell software products. In 2008, company A had total sales of $17.2 million. Its marketing department projects that sales will increase $1.5 million per year for the next several years. Company B had total sales of $9.6 million of software products in 2008 and projects that its sales will increase an average of $2.3 million each year.

   Let n represent the number of years since 2008.

   a. Write an equation that represents the total sales (in millions of dollars), s, of company A since 2008.

   b. Write an equation that represents the total sales (in millions of dollars), s, of company B since 2008.

   c. The two equations in parts a and b form a system. Solve this system to determine the year in which the total sales of both companies will be the same.

2. You are considering installing a security system in your new house. You gather the following information from two local home security dealers for similar security systems.

   Dealer 1 charges $3565 to install and $15 per month for a monitoring fee and dealer 2 charges $2850 to install and $28 per month for a monitoring fee.

   Although the initial fee of dealer 1 is much higher than that of dealer 2, the monitoring fee is lower.

   Let n represent the number of months you have the security system.

   a. Write an equation that represents the total cost, c, of the system with dealer 1.

   b. Write an equation that represents the total cost, c, of the system with dealer 2.

   c. Solve the system of equations that results from parts a and b to determine in how many months the total cost of the systems will be equal.

d. Describe a circumstance under which the first security system would be preferable to the second system. Assume the two systems are identical except for the installation costs and fees.

Use substitution to determine algebraically the exact solution to each system of equations in Exercises 3–7. Use the table feature or graphing capability of your calculator to verify these solutions.

3. $p = q - 2$
$p = -1.5q + 3$

4. $n = -2m + 9$
$n = 3m - 11$

5. $y = 1.5x - 8$
$y = -0.25x + 2.5$

6. $z = 3w - 1$
$z = -3w - 1$

7. $y = -3x + 2$
    $y = -3x + 3$

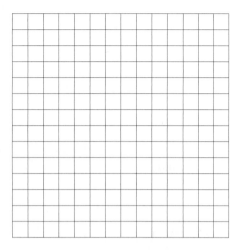

8. You like to drive to a special store to buy your favorite gourmet jelly beans for a low price of $1.30 a pound. However, your best friend points out that you are spending about $3 on gas every time you drive to that store and that you might as well buy your jelly beans at your local supermarket for $2.10 a pound. You decide to show him that you are getting enough of those jelly beans to make it worth the trip.

  a. Let x represent the number of pounds of jelly beans you purchase. Write an equation to determine the total cost, C, if you purchase the jelly beans at the specialty store. Remember to include the cost of the gas.

  b. Write an equation to determine the cost, C, if you purchase the jelly beans at the local supermarket.

  c. The two equations in parts a and b form a system of two linear equations. Solve this system using an algebraic approach.

d. Verify your solution using a numerical (table) and graphing approach.

e. How many pounds of jelly beans must you buy to make it worth the trip to the specialty store?

9. Your mother wants to hire someone to prune the trees and shrubs. One service she calls charges a $15 consultation fee plus $8 an hour for the actual work. A neighbor's son says he does not include a consulting fee, but he charges $10 an hour for the work.

a. Write an equation that describes the pruning service's charge, C, as a function of h, the number of hours worked.

b. Write an equation that describes the neigbor's charge, C, as a function of h, the number of hours worked.

c. Whom should your mother hire for a 3-hour job?

d. When, if at all, would it be more economical to hire the other service? Set up and solve a system of equations to answer this question.

e. Use your graphing calculator to verify your results.

10. You and your friend are going rollerblading at a local park. There is a 5-mile path along the lake that begins at the concession stand. You rollerblade at a rate of 10 miles per hour, and your friend rollerblades at 8 miles per hour. You start rollerblading at the concession stand. Your friend starts farther down the path, 0.5 mile from the concession stand.

  a. Write an equation that models your distance from the concession stand as a function of time. What are the units of the input variable? output variable? (Recall that distance $=$ rate $\cdot$ time.)

  b. Write an equation that models your friend's distance from the concession stand as a function of time.

  c. How long will it take you to catch up to your friend? In that time, how far will you have rollerbladed?

  d. Use your graphing calculator to verify your results.

Collecting and Analyzing Data

11. The women's world record time in the 400-meter run is decreasing at a faster rate than the men's record time. A similar occurrence is happening in many events, including the men's and women's Olympic 500-meter speed skating and world record times in the 1500-meter run.

Choose one of these competitions and use linear functions to model the data for the women's event and for the men's event. Use the models to estimate when the women's record time will equal the men's record time.

Work in a group and be prepared to give a presentation to the class. The presentation should include visual displays showing the tables, scatterplots, and equations used in the problem-solving process. Be sure to identify the source of your data.

**PROJECT
ACTIVITY 2.12**
Modeling a
Business

You are employed by a company that manufactures solar collector panels. To remain competitive, the company must consider many variables and make many decisions. Two major concerns are those variables and decisions that affect operating expenses (or costs) of making the product and those that affect the gross income (or revenue) from selling the product.

OBJECTIVES

1. Solve a system of two linear equations by any method.
2. Determine the break-even point of a linear system algebraically and graphically.
3. Interpret break-even points in contextual situations.

Costs such as rent, insurance, and utilities for the operation of the company are called *fixed costs*. These costs generally remain constant over a short period of time and must be paid whether or not any items are manufactured. Other costs, such as materials and labor, are called *variable costs*. These expenses depend directly on the number of items produced.

1. The records of the company show that fixed costs over the past year have averaged $8000 per month. In addition, each panel manufactured costs the company $95 in materials and $55 in labor. Write an equation for the total cost, $C(n)$, of producing n solar collector panels in one month.

2. A marketing survey indicates that the company can sell all the panels it produces if the panels are priced at $350 each. The revenue (gross income) is the amount of money collected from the sale of the product. Write an equation for the revenue, $R(n)$, from selling n solar collector panels in one month.

3. **a.** Complete the following table:

Sky Light

n, NUMBER OF SOLAR PANELS	0	10	20	30	40	50	60
$C(n)$, TOTAL COST ($)							
$R(n)$, TOTAL REVENUE ($)							

b. Sketch a graph of the cost and revenue functions using the same set of coordinate axes.

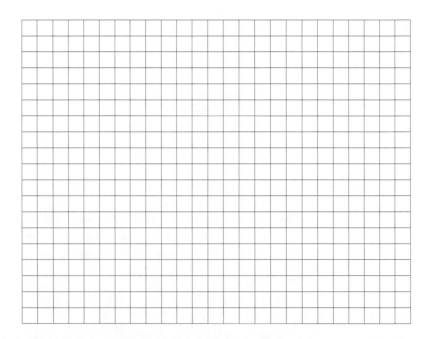

4. The point at which the cost and revenue functions are equal is called the *break-even point*.

   a. Estimate the break-even point on the graph.

   b. What system of equations must be solved to determine the break-even point for your company?

   c. Solve the system algebraically to determine the exact break-even point.

   d. Does your graph confirm the algebraic solution in part b?

5. Revenue exceeds costs when the graph of the revenue function is above the graph of the cost function. For what values of n is $R(n)$ greater than $C(n)$? What do these values represent in this situation?

6. *Profit* is defined as revenue minus cost.

   a. Determine the profit when 25 panels are sold. What does the sign of your answer signify?

   b. Determine the profit when 60 panels are sold.

   c. Write an equation for the profit, $P(n)$, made by selling n solar panels in one month.

d. Use your result in part c to compute the profit for selling 25 and 60 panels. How do your results compare with the answers in parts a and b?

7. a. Sketch a graph of the profit function $P(n) = 200n - 8000$.

b. Determine the intercepts of the graph. What is the meaning of each intercept in this situation?

c. What is the slope of the line? What is the practical meaning of slope in this situation?

EXERCISES
Activity 2.12

1. A company will break even when its revenue, R, exactly equals its cost, C. C and R depend on x, the number of bundles sold.

   You are the manager of a small company producing interlocking paving blocks, called pavers, for driveways. You sell the pavers in bundles that cost $200; each bundle contains 144 pavers. The total cost in dollars, $C(x)$, of producing x bundles of pavers is modeled by $C(x) = 160x + 1000$.

   a. Write an equation for the revenue function in dollars, R, from the sale of the pavers.

   b. Determine the slope and the C-intercept of the cost function. Explain the practical meaning of each in this situation.

   c. Determine the slope and the R-intercept of the revenue function. Explain the practical meaning of each in this situation.

   d. Graph the two functions from parts b and c on the same set of axes. Estimate the break-even point from the graph. Express your answer as an ordered pair, giving units. Check your estimate of the break-even point by graphing the two functions on your graphing calculator.

   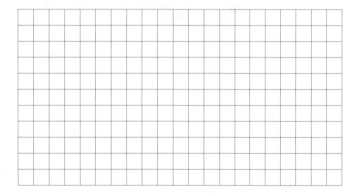

e. Determine the exact break-even point algebraically. If your algebraic solution does not approximate your answer from the graph in part d, explain why.

f. How many bundles of pavers does the company have to sell for it to break even?

g. What is the total cost to the company when you break even? Verify that the cost and revenue values are equal at the break-even point.

h. For what values of *x* will your revenue exceed your cost?

i. As manager, what factors do you have to consider when deciding how many pavers to make?

j. If you knew you could sell only 30 bundles of pavers, would you make them? Consider how much it would cost you and how much you would make. What if you could sell only 20 bundles?

ACTIVITY 2.13
Healthy Lifestyle

OBJECTIVES

1. Solve a 2 × 2 linear system algebraically using the substitution method and the addition method.
2. Solve equations containing parentheses.

You are trying to maintain a healthy lifestyle. You eat a well-balanced diet and follow a regular schedule of exercise. One of your favorite exercise activities is a combination of walking and jogging in a nearby park.

On one particular day, it takes you 1.3 hours to walk and jog a total of 5.5 miles in the park. You are curious about the amount of time you spent walking and the amount of time you spent jogging during the workout.

Let x represent the time you walked and y represent the time you jogged.

1. Write an equation, using x and y, for the total time of your walk/jog workout in the park.

2. **a.** If you walk at 3 miles per hour, write an expression that represents the distance you walked.

 b. If you jog at 5 miles per hour, write an expression that represents the distance you jogged.

 c. Write an equation for the total distance you walked/jogged in the park.

The situation just described can be represented by the following system.

$$x + y = 1.3$$
$$3x + 5y = 5.5$$

Note that each equation in this system is in standard form $Ax + By = C$, where A, B, and C are constants, A and B both not zero. One approach to solving this system is to solve each equation for one variable in terms of the other and then use the substitution method.

3. **a.** Solve each of the equations in the system above for y.

 b. Solve the system in part a using the substitution method.

 c. Check your answer graphically using your graphing calculator. You may want to use the window Xmin = −2.5, Xmax = 2.5, Ymin = −2.5, and Ymax = 2.5.

Addition Method

Sometimes it is more convenient to leave each equation in the linear system in standard form ($Ax + By = C$) rather than solving for one variable in terms of the other. Look again at the original system.

$$x + y = 1.3 \quad \text{(eq. 1)}$$
$$3x + 5y = 5.5 \quad \text{(eq. 2)}$$

If you apply the addition principle of algebra by adding the two equations (left side to left side and right side to right side), you may be able to obtain a single equation containing only one variable.

$$x + y = 1.3 \quad \text{(eq. 1)}$$
$$\underline{3x + 5y = 5.5 \quad \text{(eq. 2)}}$$
$$4x + 6y = 6.8$$

In this case, adding the equations does not eliminate a variable. But if you multiply both sides of equation 1 by -5, the coefficients of y will be opposite, and the variable y can be eliminated.

$$-5(x + y) = -5(1.3) \rightarrow \quad -5x - 5y = -6.5$$
$$3x + 5y = 5.5 \qquad\qquad \underline{3x + 5y = 5.5}$$
$$-2x + 0 \;= -1$$

Add the corresponding sides of the equation.

Solving the resulting equation, $-2x = -1$, for x, you have

$$-2x = -1$$
$$x = \tfrac{1}{2} = 0.5.$$

Substituting for x in $x + y = 1.3$, you have

$$0.5 + y = 1.3$$
$$\text{or } y = 0.8.$$

This method of solving systems algebraically is called the **addition method**.

To solve a 2×2 linear system by the addition method,

1. line up the like terms in each equation vertically;
2. if necessary, multiply one or both equations by constants so that the coefficients of one of the variables are opposites;
3. add the corresponding sides of the two equations.

4. Solve the following system again using the addition method. Multiply the appropriate equation by the appropriate factor to eliminate x and solve for y first.

$$x + y = 1.3$$
$$3x + 5y = 5.5$$

Not all systems will have convenient coefficients, and you may need to multiply one or both equations by a factor that will produce coefficients of the same variable that are additive inverses, or opposites.

5. Consider solving the following system with the addition method.

$$-2x + 5y = -16$$
$$3x + 2y = 5$$

a. Identify which variable you wish to eliminate. Multiply the appropriate equation by the appropriate factor so that the coefficients of your chosen variable are opposite. Show the two equations after you multiply by the factor. (Remember to multiply both sides of the equation by the factor.)

b. Add the two equations to eliminate the chosen variable.

c. Solve the resulting linear equation.

d. Determine the complete solution. Remember to check by substituting into both of the original equations.

Substitution Method Revisited

The substitution method of solving a 2×2 system of linear equations is generally used when each equation in the system is solved for one variable in terms of the other. However, it can be convenient to use the substitution method when only one of the equations is solved for a variable.

Note: As you solve a system such as the walk/jog system using the substitution method (see Example 1), you will encounter an equation involving parentheses. It would be an equation like

$$2(3x - 7) + 9 = -x + 2.$$

To solve this equation, you first simplify the expression on the left-hand side.

$$2(3x - 7) + 9 = -x + 2$$
$$6x - 14 + 9 = -x + 2$$
$$6x - 5 = -x + 2$$

Use the addition principle to move all x-terms to one side,

$$6x - 5 = -x + 2$$
$$\underline{+x \qquad\quad +x}$$
$$7x - 5 = \qquad 2$$

Using the addition principle again to isolate the x-term, you have

$$7x - 5 = 2$$
$$\underline{+\ 5 \quad\ +5}$$
$$7x\quad\ = 7$$

or $x = 1$.

Example 1 *In the walk/jog system,*

$$x + y = 1.3 \quad \textbf{(eq. 1)}$$
$$3x + 5y = 5.5 \quad \textbf{(eq. 2)}$$

you could solve equation 1 for y and then substitute for y in equation 2 as follows:

Step 1. Solve $x + y = 1.3$ for y.

$$y = 1.3 - x$$

Step 2. Substitute $1.3 - x$ for y in equation 2.

$$3x + 5(1.3 - x) = 5.5$$

Step 3. Solve the resulting equation for x.

$$3x + 5(1.3 - x) = 5.5 \qquad \text{Remove the parentheses by applying the distributive property.}$$

$$3x + 6.5 - 5x = 5.5 \qquad \text{Collect like terms on the same side.}$$

$$-2x + 6.5 = 5.5$$

$$\underline{-\ 6.5 - 6.5} \qquad \text{Add the opposite of 6.5 to both sides.}$$

$$-2x = -1 \qquad \text{Divide each side by } -2.$$

$$\frac{-2x}{-2} = \frac{-1}{-2}$$

$$x = 0.5$$

Step 4. From equation 1, $y = 0.8$ as before.

---

6. a. Solve the following linear system using the substitution method in which you solve only one of the equations for a variable.

$$x - y = 5$$
$$4x + 5y = -7$$

b. Check your answer in part a by solving the system using the addition method.

SUMMARY
Activity 2.13

1. There are two methods for solving a 2×2 system of linear equations algebraically:

   a. the substitution method and

   b. the addition method

2. To solve linear systems by substitution,

   Step 1. solve one or both equations for a variable;

   Step 2. substitute the expression that represents the variable in one equation for that variable in the other equation;

   Step 3. solve the resulting equation for the remaining variable;

   Step 4. substitute the value from step 3 into one of the original equations, and solve for the other variable.

3. To solve linear systems by addition with equations written in the form $Ax + By = C$,

   Step 1. multiply one equation or both equations by the number(s) that will make the coefficients of one of the variables opposite;

   Step 2. add the two equations to eliminate one variable and solve the resulting equation;

   Step 3. substitute the value from step 2 into one of the original equations, and solve for the other variable.

EXERCISES
Activity 2.13

1. Solve each of the following equations.

   a. $5(x + 3) + 4 = 6x - 1 - 5x$

   b. $-3(1 - 2x) - 3(x - 4) = -5 - 4x$

   c. $2(x + 3) - 4x = 5x + 2$

2. Solve the following systems algebraically using the substitution method.

a. $y = 3x + 1$
$y = 6x - 0.5$

b. $y = 3x + 7$
$2x - 5y = 4$

c. $2x + 3y = 5$
$-2x + y = -9$

d. $4x + y = 10$
$2x + 3y = -5$

3. Solve the following systems algebraically using the addition method.

a. $y = 2x + 3$
$y = -x + 6$

b. $2x + y = 1$
$-x + y = -5$

4. Solve the system both graphically and algebraically.

$$3x + y = -18$$
$$5x - 2y = -8$$

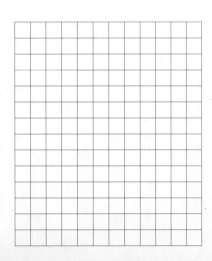

5. A catering service placed an order for eight centerpieces and five glasses, and the bill was $106. For the wedding reception, they were short one centerpiece and six glasses and had to reorder. This order came to $24. Let x represent the cost of one centerpiece, and let y represent the cost of one glass.

   a. Write a system of equations that represents both orders.

   b. Solve the system using the substitution method. Interpret your solution.

   c. Check your result in part b using the addition method.

   d. Use your graphing calculator to solve the system.

ACTIVITY 2.14

How Long Can You Live?

OBJECTIVES

1. Solve linear inequalities in one variable numerically and graphically.

2. Use properties of inequalities to solve linear inequalities in one variable algebraically.

3. Solve compound inequalities in one variable algebraically and graphically.

4. Use interval notation to represent a set of real numbers by an inequality.

Life expectancy in the United States is steadily increasing, and the number of Americans aged 100 or older will exceed 850,000 by the middle of this century. Medical advancements have been a primary reason for Americans living longer. Another factor has been the increased awareness of maintaining a healthy lifestyle.

The life expectancies at birth for men and women born after 1975 in the United States can be modeled by the following functions.

$$W(x) = 0.106x + 77.01$$
$$M(x) = 0.200x + 68.94,$$

where $W(x)$ represents the life expectancy for women, $M(x)$ represents the life expectancy for men, and x represents the number of years since 1975 that the person was born. That is, $x = 0$ corresponds to the year 1975, $x = 5$ corresponds to 1980, and so forth.

1. a. Complete the following table.

Counting the Years	YEAR					
	1975	1980	1985	1990	1995	2000
x, YEARS SINCE 1975	0	5	10	15	20	25
W(x)						
M(x)						

b. For people born between 1975 and 2000, do men or women have the greater life expectancy?

c. Is the life expectancy of men or women increasing more rapidly? Explain using slope.

You would like to determine in what birth years the life expectancy of men is greater than that of women. The phrase "greater than" indicates a mathematical relationship called an **inequality**. Symbolically, the relationship can be represented by

$$\underbrace{M(x)}_{\substack{\text{Life expectancy} \\ \text{for men}}} \quad \underbrace{>}_{\text{is greater than}} \quad \underbrace{W(x)}_{\substack{\text{life expectancy} \\ \text{for women.}}}$$

Other commonly used phrases that indicate inequalities are given in the following example.

Example 1

STATEMENT, WHERE x REPRESENTS A REAL NUMBER	TRANSLATION TO AN INEQUALITY
x is greater than 10	$x > 10$ or $10 < x$
x is less than 10	$x < 10$ or $10 > x$
x is at least 10	$x \geq 10$ (also read, "x is greater than or equal to 10")
x is at most 10	$x \leq 10$ (also read, "x is less than or equal to 10")

2. Substitute the appropriate expressions for $M(x)$ and $W(x)$ in $M(x) > W(x)$ to obtain an inequality involving x that can be used to determine the birth years for which the life expectancy of men is greater than that of women.

Solving Inequalities in One Variable Numerically and Graphically

DEFINITION

Solving an inequality in one variable is the process of determining the values of the variable that make the inequality a true statement. These values are called the **solutions** of the inequality.

3. Solve the inequality in Problem 2 numerically. That is, continue to construct a table of values (see Problem 1) until you determine the values of the years x (inputs) for which $0.200x + 68.94 > 0.106x + 77.01$. Use the table feature of your graphing calculator.

Therefore, if the trends given by the equations for $M(x)$ and $W(x)$ continue, the approximate solution to the inequality $M(x) > W(x)$ is $x > 86$. That is, according to the models, after the year 2062, men will live longer than women.

4. Now, solve the inequality $0.200x + 68.94 > 0.106x + 77.01$ graphically.

   a. Use your graphing calculator to sketch a graph of $M(x) = 0.200x + 68.94$ and $W(x) = 0.106x + 77.01$ on the same coordinate axis.

 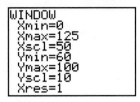 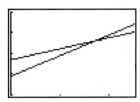

   b. Determine the point of intersection of the two graphs using the intersect feature of your graphing calculator. What does the point represent in this situation?

To solve the inequality $M(x) > W(x)$ graphically, you need to determine the values of x for which the graph of $M(x) = 0.200x + 68.94$ is above the graph of

$$W(x) = 0.106x + 77.01.$$

   c. Use the graph to solve $M(x) > W(x)$. How does your solution compare to the solution in Problem 3?

5. a. Write an inequality to determine the birth years of women whose life expectancy is at least 85.

   b. Solve the inequality numerically, using the table feature of your graphing calculator.

   c. Use your graphing calculator to solve this inequality graphically.

Solving Inequalities in One Variable Algebraically

The process of solving an inequality in one variable algebraically is very similar to solving an equation in one variable algebraically. Your goal is to isolate the variable on one side of the inequality symbol. You isolate the variable in an **equation** by performing the same operations to both sides of the equation so as not to upset the **balance**. You isolate the variable in an **inequality** by performing the same operations to both sides so as not to upset the **imbalance**.

6. a. Write the statement "15 is greater than 6" as an inequality.

b. Add 5 to each side of $15 > 6$. Is the resulting inequality a true statement? (That is, is the left side still greater than the right side?)

c. Subtract 10 from each side of $15 > 6$. Is the resulting inequality a true statement?

d. Multiply each side of $15 > 6$ by 4. Is the resulting inequality true?

e. Multiply each side of $15 > 6$ by -2. Is the left side still greater than the right side?

f. Reverse the direction of the inequality symbol in part e. Is the new inequality a true statement?

Problem 6 demonstrates two very important properties of inequalities.

> **Property 1:** If $a < b$ represents a true inequality, then if
>
> **i.** the same quantity is added to or subtracted from both sides
>
> or
>
> **ii.** both sides are multiplied or divided by the same *positive number*, then the resulting inequality remains a true statement and the direction of the inequality symbol remains the same.

For example, because $-4 < 10$, then

i. $-4 + 5 < 10 + 5$ or $1 < 15$ is true;

$-4 - 3 < 10 - 3$ or $-7 < 7$ is true.

ii. $-4(6) < 10(6)$ or $-24 < 60$ is true;

$\frac{-4}{2} < \frac{10}{2}$ or $-2 < 5$ is true.

> **Property 2:** If $a < b$ represents a true inequality, then if both sides are multiplied or divided by the same *negative number*, then the inequality symbol in the resulting inequality statement must be reversed ($<$ to $>$ or $>$ to $<$) in order for the resulting statement to be true.

For example, because $-4 < 10$, then $-4(-5) > 10(-5)$ or $20 > -50$.

Because $-4 < 10$, then $\dfrac{-4}{-2} > \dfrac{10}{-2}$ or $2 > -5$.

Properties 1 and 2 will be true if $a < b$ is replaced by $a \leq b$, $a > b$, or $a \geq b$.

The following example demonstrates how properties of inequalities can be used to solve an inequality algebraically.

Example 2   *Solve* $3(x - 4) > 5(x - 2) - 8$.

SOLUTION

$3(x - 4) > 5(x - 2) - 8$ **Apply the distributive property.**

$3x - 12 > 5x - 10 - 8$ **Combine like terms on the right side.**

$3x - 12 > 5x - 18$

$\dfrac{-5x \qquad\quad -5x}{-2x - 12 > -18}$ **Subtract 5x from both sides; the direction of the inequality symbol remains the same.**

$\dfrac{+12 \quad\ +12}{}$ **Add 12 to both sides; the direction of the inequality does not change.**

$\dfrac{-2x}{-2} > \dfrac{-6}{-2}$ **Divide both sides by −2; the direction is reversed!**

$x < 3$

Therefore, from Example 2, any number less than 3 is a solution to the inequality $3(x - 4) > 5(x - 2) - 8$. The solution set can be represented on a number line by shading all points to the left of 3:

The open circle at 3 indicates that 3 is *not* a solution. A closed circle indicates that the number beneath the closed circle *is* a solution. The arrow shows that the solutions extend indefinitely to the left.

7. Solve the inequality $0.200x + 68.94 > 0.106x + 77.01$ algebraically to determine the birth years in which men will be expected to live longer than women. How does your solution compare to the solutions determined numerically and graphically in Problems 3 and 4c?

Compound Inequality

You have joined a health and fitness club. Your aerobics instructor recommends that to achieve the most cardiovascular benefit from your workout, you should maintain a target heart rate between a lower and upper range of values while exercising. These values depend on your age.

8. If the variable a represents your age, then the lower and upper values for a target heart rate are determined by the following:

$$\text{lower value: } 0.72(220 - a)$$
$$\text{upper value: } 0.87(220 - a)$$

    a. Determine your lower value.

    b. Determine your upper value.

For the most cardiovascular benefit, a 20-year-old's target heart rate should be between 144 and 174. The phrase "between 144 and 174" means the target heart rate should be greater than 144 *and* less than 174. Symbolically, this combination or **compound inequality** is written as

$$144 < \text{target heart rate } and \text{ target heart rate} < 174.$$

This statement is written more compactly as $144 < \text{pulse rate} < 174$.

The numbers that satisfy this compound inequality can be represented on a number line as

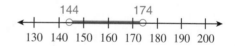

Other commonly used phrases that indicate compound inequalities involving the word *and* are given in the following example.

Example 3

STATEMENT, WHERE x REPRESENTS A REAL NUMBER	TRANSLATION TO A COMPOUND INEQUALITY
x is greater than or equal to 10 and less than 20	$10 \leq x < 20$
x is greater than 10 and less than or equal to 20	$10 < x \leq 20$
x is from 10 to 20 inclusive	$10 \leq x \leq 20$

9. Recall that the life expectancy for men is given by the expression $0.200x + 68.94$, where x represents the number of years since 1975. Use this expression to write a compound inequality that can be used to determine in what birth years men will be expected to live into their 80s.

The following example demonstrates how to solve a compound linear inequality algebraically and graphically.

Example 4   a. *Solve* $-4 < 3x + 5 \leq 11$ *using an algebraic approach.*

SOLUTION

Note that the compound inequality has three parts: left: -4, middle: $3x + 5$, and right: 11. To solve this inequality, isolate the variable in the middle part.

$$-4 < 3x + 5 \leq 11$$

| -5 | | -5 | -5 | Subtract 5 from each part. |

$$-9 < 3x \leq 6$$

$$-\frac{9}{3} < \frac{3x}{3} \leq \frac{6}{3} \qquad \text{Divide each part by 3.}$$

$$-3 < x \leq 2$$

The solution can be represented on a number line as follows.

b. *Solve* $-4 < 3x + 5 \leq 11$ *using a graphical approach.*

SOLUTION

First, graph each part of the inequality on the same coordinate axes.

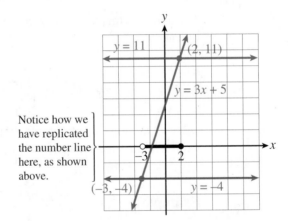

Notice how we have replicated the number line here, as shown above.

You need to determine values of x for which the graph of $y_2 = 3x + 5$ is above the graph of $y_1 = -4$ and on or below the graph of $y_3 = 11$. Using the graphs, verify that the solution is $-3 < x \leq 2$.

10. a. Solve the compound inequality $80 \leq 0.200x + 68.94 < 90$ from Problem 9 to determine in what birth years men will be expected to live into their 80s.

b. Verify your results in part a by solving the compound inequality graphically. Use the window from Problem 4a.

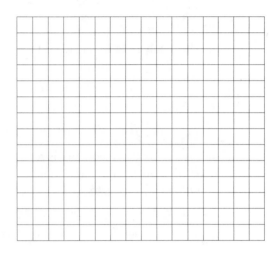

Interval Notation

Interval notation is an alternative method to represent a set of real numbers described by an inequality. The **closed interval** $[-3, 4]$ represents all real numbers x for which $-3 \leq x \leq 4$. The square brackets [and] indicate that the endpoints of the interval are included. The **open interval** $(-3, 4)$ represents all real numbers x for which $-3 < x < 4$. Note that the parentheses (and) indicate that the endpoints are not included. The interval $(-3, 4]$ is said to be **half-open** or **half-closed**. The interval is open at -3 (endpoint not included) and closed at 4 (endpoint included).

Suppose you want to represent the set of real numbers x for which x is greater than 3. The symbol $+\infty$ (positive infinity) is used to indicate **unboundedness** in the positive direction. Therefore, the interval $(3, +\infty)$ represents all real numbers x for which $x > 3$. Note that $+\infty$ is always open.

The symbol $-\infty$ (negative infinity) is used to represent unboundedness in the negative direction. Therefore, the interval $(-\infty, 5]$ represents all real numbers x for which $x \leq 5$.

11. In parts a–d, express each inequality in interval notation.

    a. $-5 \leq x \leq 10$ **b.** $4 \leq x < 8.5$ **c.** $x > -2$ **d.** $x \leq 3.75$

    In parts e–h, express each of the following using inequalities.

    e. $(-6, 4]$ **f.** $(-\infty, 1.5]$ **g.** $(-2, 2)$ **h.** $(-3, +\infty)$

SUMMARY
Activity 2.14

1. The **solution set** of an inequality in one variable is the set of all values of the variable that satisfy the inequality.

2. The direction of an inequality is not changed when

   i. The same quantity is added to or subtracted from both sides of the inequality. Stated algebraically,

   $$\text{If } a < b, \text{ then } a + c < b + c \text{ and } a - c < b - c.$$

   ii. Both sides of an inequality are multiplied or divided by the same positive number.

   $$\text{If } a < b, \text{ then } ac < bc, \text{ and } \frac{a}{c} < \frac{b}{c}, \text{ whenever } c > 0.$$

3. The direction of an inequality is reversed if both sides of an inequality are multiplied by or divided by the same negative number. These properties can be written symbolically as

   i. If $a < b$, then $ac > bc$, where $c < 0$;

   ii. If $a < b$, then $\frac{a}{c} > \frac{b}{c}$, where $c < 0$.

   The two properties of inequalities (parts 2 and 3 above) will still be true if $a < b$ is replaced by $a \le b$, $a > b$, or $a \ge b$.

4. Inequalities such as $f(x) < g(x)$ can be solved using three different methods:

   i. A **numerical approach**, in which a table of input-output pairs is used to determine values of x for which $f(x) < g(x)$;

   ii. A **graphical approach**, in which values of x are located so that the graph of f is below the graph of g;

   iii. An **algebraic approach**, in which the properties of inequalities are used to isolate the variable.

   Similar statements can be made for solving inequalities of the form $f(x) \le g(x)$, $f(x) > g(x)$, and $f(x) \ge g(x)$.

EXERCISES
Activity 2.14

In Exercises 1–6, translate the given statement into an algebraic inequality or compound inequality.

1. To avoid an additional charge, the sum of the length, l, width, w, and depth, d, of a piece of luggage to be checked on a commercial airline can be at most 61 inches.

2. A PG-13 movie rating means that your age, a, must be at least 13 years for you to view the movie.

3. The cost, $C(A)$, of renting a car from company A is less expensive than the cost $C(B)$ of renting from company B.

4. The label on a bottle of film developer states that the temperature, t, of the contents must be kept between 68° and 77° Fahrenheit.

5. You are in a certain tax bracket if your taxable income, i, is over $24,650, but not over $59,750.

6. The range of temperature, t, on the surface of Mars is from $-140°C$ to $28°C$.

Solve Exercises 7–10 graphically and algebraically.

7. $3x > -6$ 8. $3 - 2x \leq 5$

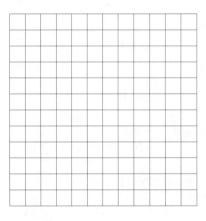

9. $x + 2 > 3x - 8$ 10. $5x - 1 < 2x + 11$

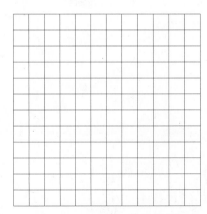
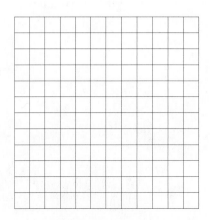

Solve Exercises 11–14 algebraically.

11. $8 - x \geq 5(8 - x)$

12. $5 - x < 2(x - 3) + 5$

13. $\frac{x}{2} + 1 \leq 3x + 2$

14. $0.5x + 3 \geq 2x - 1.5$

Solve Exercises 15–16 graphically and algebraically.

15. $1 < 3x - 2 < 4$

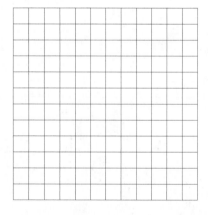

16. $-2 < \frac{x}{3} + 1 < 5$

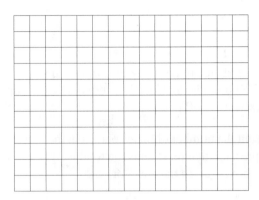

17. The consumption of cigarettes is declining. If t represents the number of years since 1985, then the consumption, C, is modeled by

$$C = -14.25t + 598.69,$$

where C represents the number of billions of cigarettes smoked per year.

a. Write an inequality that can be used to determine the first year in which cigarette consumption is less than 200 billion cigarettes per year.

b. Solve the inequality in part a using an algebraic as well as a graphical approach.

18. You contact two local rental companies and obtain the following information for the one-day cost of renting a truck:

Company 1: $40.95 per day plus $0.19 per mile

Company 2: $19.95 per day plus $0.49 per mile

Let n represent the total number of miles driven in one day.

a. Write an expression to determine the total cost, C, of renting a truck for n days from company 1.

b. Write an expression to determine the total cost, C, of renting a truck for n days from company 2.

c. Use the expressions in parts a and b to write an inequality that can be used to deter-mine for what number of miles it is less expensive to rent the truck from company 2.

d. Solve the inequality.

19. The sign on the elevator in a seven-story building states that the maximum weight it can carry is 1200 pounds. You need to move a large shipment of books to the sixth floor. Each box weighs 60 pounds.

   a. Let n represent the number of boxes placed in the elevator. If you weigh 150 pounds, write an expression that represents the total weight in the elevator. Assume that only you and the boxes are in the elevator.

   b. Using the expression in part a, write an inequality that can be used to determine the maximum number of boxes that you can place in the elevator at one time.

   c. Solve the inequality.

20. The following equation is used in meteorology to determine the temperature humidity index T:
$$T = \tfrac{2}{5}(w + 80) + 15,$$

   where w represents the wet-bulb thermometer reading. For what values of w would T range from 70 to 75?

21. The temperature readings in the United States have ranged from a record low of $-79.8°F$ (Alaska, January 23, 1971) to a record high of $134°F$ (California, July 10, 1913).

   a. If F represents the Fahrenheit temperature, write a compound inequality that represents the interval of temperatures (in °F) in the United States.

   b. Recall that Fahrenheit and Celsius degrees are related by the formula
$$F = 1.8C + 32.$$

   Rewrite the compound inequality in part a to determine the temperature range in degrees Celsius.

   c. Solve the compound inequality.

22. You are enrolled in a half-year wellness course. You achieved grades of 70, 86, 81, and 83 on the first four exams. The final exam counts the same as the four exams already given.

   a. If x represents the grade on the final exam, write an expression that represents your course average.

   b. If your average is greater than or equal to 80 and less than 90, you will earn a B in the course. Using the expression from part a for your course average, write a compound inequality that must be satisfied to earn a B.

   c. Solve the inequality.

ACTIVITY 2.15

Will Trees Grow?

OBJECTIVES

1. Graph a linear inequality in two variables.

2. Solve a system of linear inequalities in two variables graphically.

3. Determine the corner points of the solution set of a system of linear inequalities.

While researching a term paper on global climate change, you discover a mathematical model that gives the relationship between temperature and amount of precipitation that is necessary for trees to grow. If t represents the average annual temperature in °F, and p represents the annual precipitation in inches, then

$$t \geq 35$$
$$5t - 7p < 70.$$

Source: Miller and Thompson, *Elements of Meteorology*.

These inequalities form a **system of inequalities in two variables**. The solution of the system is the set of all ordered pairs of the form (t, p) that make each of the inequalities in the system a true statement.

1. **a.** Will trees grow in a region in which the average annual temperature is 22°F and the annual precipitation is 30 inches?

   b. Will trees grow if the average annual temperature is 55°F and the annual precipitation is 20 inches?

   c. In Sydney, Australia, the average annual temperature is 64°F and the annual precipitation is 48 inches. Will trees grow in Sydney?

Actually, there are an infinite number of pairs of values for temperature t and amount of precipitation p for which trees will grow. Although it is not possible to list all the possible combinations, you can visualize all the solution pairs by graphing the solution set of the system. You will return to the Will Trees Grow? system later in this activity.

Solving a Linear Inequality in Two Variables by Graphing

To determine the solution set for a system of linear inequalities in two variables, you begin by graphing the solutions of each of the inequalities in the system. Problem 2 guides you through the process of graphing a linear equality.

2. a. To obtain the graph of $4x - 2y \geq 8$, first replace the inequality symbol $\geq$ with an equal sign and sketch a graph of the resulting equation.

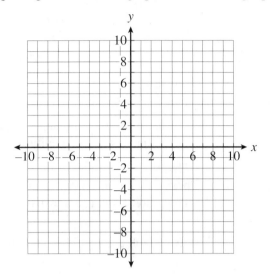

Note that the line $4x - 2y = 8$ divides the coordinate plane into three sets of points:

    1. Points *on* the line that satisfy the equation $4x - 2y = 8$

    2. Points *below* the line that satisfy the inequality $4x - 2y > 8$

    3. Points *above* the line that satisfy the inequality $4x - 2y < 8$

A **half-plane** is a set of points on one side of a line. Therefore, the set of points above the line $4x - 2y = 8$ is a half-plane. The set of points below the line is also a half-plane. The solution set to a linear inequality will include all the points in one half-plane or the other.

    b. Select a point in the half-plane below the line $4x - 2y = 8$. Use this test point to determine if the points in the half-plane are in the solution set of the inequality $4x - 2y \geq 8$.

c. Determine if the points in the half-plane above the line $4x - 2y = 8$ are solutions to the inequality $4x - 2y \geq 8$.

d. Shade the half-plane in the graph in part a that contains the test point that makes the inequality $4x - 2y \geq 8$ a true statement.

Therefore, the graph of the solution of the inequality $4x - 2y \geq 8$ is the set of all points on the line $4x - 2y = 8$ and in the half-plane below the line $4x - 2y = 8$. The graph gives you a visual representation of the solution set.

3. Graph the solution to the linear inequality $2x + 3y < 6$.

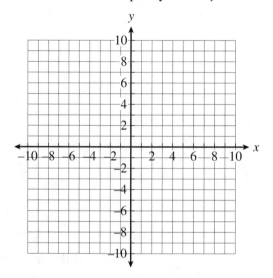

You may have discovered several patterns while graphing the inequalities in Problems 2 and 3. First, if the inequality symbol is $\leq$ or $\geq$, the points along the line are solutions to the inequality and the line is drawn solid. If the inequality symbol is $<$ or $>$, the corresponding line is drawn dashed, indicating that points along the line are not solutions to the inequality.

When the inequality **is written in slope-intercept** form (solved for *y*), another pattern is observed.

i. $y < mx + b$ or $y \leq mx + b$ means the half-plane **below** the line $y = mx + b$ is shaded.

ii. $y > mx + b$ or $y \geq mx + b$ means the half-plane **above** the line $y = mx + b$ is shaded.

4. Redo Problem 2 using the given patterns. Compare your results.

5. You can use the TI-83/84 Plus to graph a linear inequality such as $4x - 2y \geq 8$.

a. Replace the inequality symbol with an equal sign and solve the corresponding equation $4x - 2y = 8$ for *y*.

b. Enter the equation in part a into the calculator and show the graph in the standard window. Your screen should appear as follows:

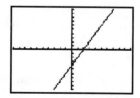

c. To shade the half-plane below the line, press $y =$ and move the cursor to the extreme left. Next press ENTER key as many times as necessary to change the icon to ◣. Then graph to obtain the following screen:

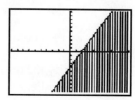

6. Use the graphing calculator to verify the results in Problem 3.

Solving a System of Linear Inequalities by Graphing

Recall that the solution to a system of linear **equations** is the point of intersection of the graphs of each line in the system. The (x, y) coordinates of the point of intersection makes each equation in the system a true statement. The solution to a system of linear **inequalities** such as

$$4x - 2y \geq 8$$
$$2x + 3y < 6$$

is the intersection of the solutions for each of the inequalities in the system. Therefore, to determine the solution set for a system of linear inequalities, you begin by graphing the solutions of each of the inequalities in the system.

7. a. Use the results from Problems 2 and 3 to graph the solution set of the inequalities $4x - 2y \geq 8$ and $2x + 3y < 6$ on the following coordinate system:

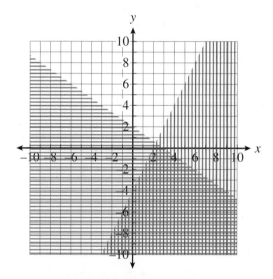

The solution of the system inequalities

$$4x - 2y \geq 8$$
$$2x + 3y < 6$$

is the intersection (if any) of all the solution regions of the inequalities in the system.

b. Graph the solution set of the system

$$4x - 2y \geq 8$$
$$2x + 3y < 6$$

on the coordinate system in part a.

c. Verify the results in part b using the graphing calculator. After solving each inequality for y, enter the corresponding equations in Y_1 and Y_2. Determine the intersection of the boundary lines using CALC feature. Shade the regions determined by each inequality. The solution set is that portion of the graph that is shaded twice. Your screen should appear as follows:

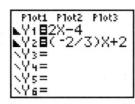 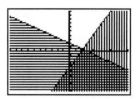

Note: The calculator does not draw dashed lines.

8. Solve each of the following systems of linear inequalities using a graphing approach. Verify using a graphing calculator.

   a. $3x + 2y \geq 16$
   $x - 2y \leq 0$

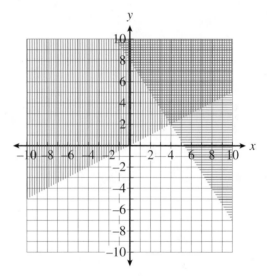

b. $y \leq -3x + 9$

$y \geq 2x - 3$

$x \geq 0$

$y \geq 0$

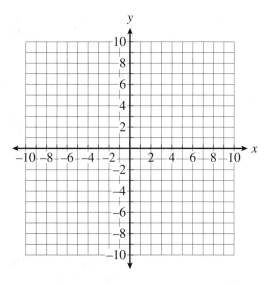

c. $y > 2x + 4$

$y \leq 2x - 6$

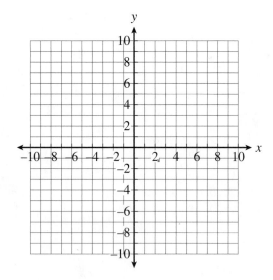

Corner Points

The graph of the system of inequalities in Problem 8a is

$$3x + 2y \geq 16$$
$$x - 2y \leq 0$$

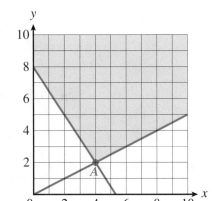

The point A of the intersection of the boundary lines of the shaded region is called a **corner point**.

9. a. Determine the coordinates of the corner point A in Problem 8a.

   b. Is the corner point in part a solution of the given system of inequalities in Problem 8b? Explain.

10. By observing the boundary lines, determine if the corner point in Problem 7 is a solution to the system of inequalities.

11. Determine the corner points of the system in Problem 8b.

12. Return to the system of linear inequalities encountered in the Will the Trees Grow? situation,

$$t \geq 35$$
$$5t - 7p < 70,$$

where t represents the average annual temperature in °F, and p represents the annual precipitation in inches.

a. Graph the given system of inequalities. Determine ordered pairs of the form (t, p).

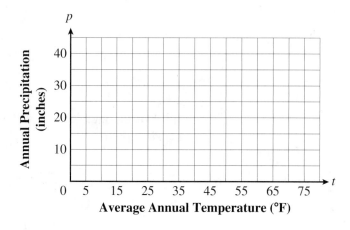

b. Determine the corner point. What is the significance of the point in this situation?

c. Determine whether or not trees will grow in each of the following regions.

REGION	AVERAGE TEMPERATURE (°F)	ANNUAL PRECIPITATION (inches)	(t, p)	CONCLUSION
Baghdad, Iraq	73	6		.
Fairbanks, Alaska	29	14		
Lima, Peru	66	1		
Aden, Yemen				

Now, go to additional regions (such as Aden, Yemen) and confirm whether trees will grow there (without artificial support) by inspecting the graph of the system and by direct substitution.

SUMMARY
Activity 2.15

1. An inequality of the form $Ax + By < C$, where A and B cannot both equal zero, is called a **linear inequality in two variables**. The symbol $<$ can be replaced by $>$, $\leq$ or $\geq$.

2. The solution set of a linear inequality in two variables x and y is the collection of all the ordered pairs (x, y) whose coordinates satisfy the given inequality.

3. A **half-plane** is the set of all points on one side of a line.

4. To graph a linear inequality in two variables,
   i. Replace the inequality symbol with an equal sign and graph the resulting line. Draw a solid line if the inequality symbol is $\leq$ or $\geq$. If the inequality symbol is $<$ or $>$, draw a dashed line.
   ii. Select a test point not on the line and substitute its coordinates into the inequality. If the resulting statement is true, shade in the area on the same side of the line as the test point. If the resulting statement is false, shade in the area on the opposite side of the line as the test point.

5. Two or more linear inequalities in two variables make up a **system of linear inequalities**.

6. The solution set of a system of linear inequalities in two variables is the collection of all ordered pairs whose coordinates satisfy each linear inequality in the system.

7. To graph a system of linear inequalities in two variables,
   i. Graph each linear inequality in the system.
   ii. The graph of the system is the intersection (overlap) of the shaded areas representing the solutions of the linear inequalities in the system, and any solid line common to all the inequalities in the system.

8. The points determined by the intersection of the boundary lines of the graph of a system of linear inequalities are called **corner points**.

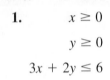

In Exercises 1–7, solve each of the systems of linear inequalities using a graphing approach. Verify using a graphing calculator.

1.

$$x \geq 0$$

$$y \geq 0$$

$$3x + 2y \leq 6$$

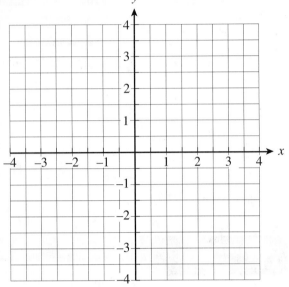

2. $x + y \leq 5$

$$2x + y \geq 4$$

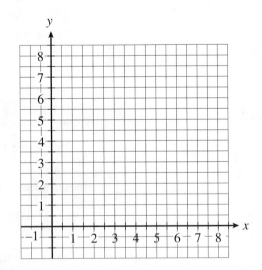

3. $y < x + 3$

   $y \geq -2x + 6$

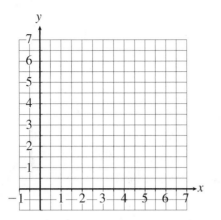

4. $-x + 2y \leq 10$

   $2x - y \geq -4$

   $y \leq 8$

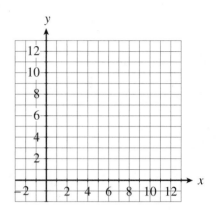

5. $2x - y \leq 0$

   $2x + y \geq 4$

   $-2x + 3y \leq 12$

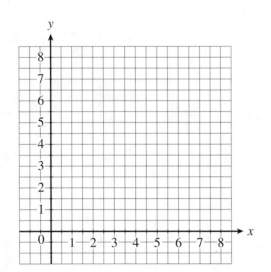

6. $x - 3y \leq 6$

   $x - 3y > -6$

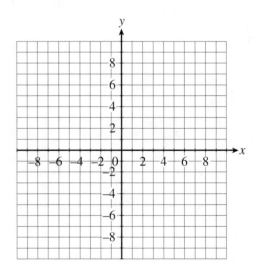

7. $x - 3y \geq 6$

$x - 3y < -6$

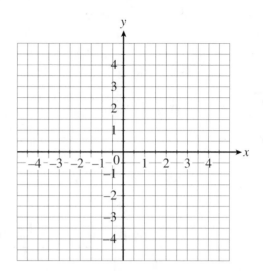

In Exercises 8–10, graph the given system of linear inequalities. Then, determine the corner points of the graph of the solution set.

8. $x \geq 1$

$y \geq 0$

$2x + y \geq 4$

9. $y \geq 0$

$y \leq 4$

$x \geq 0$

$x + y \leq 5$

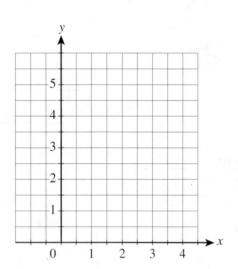

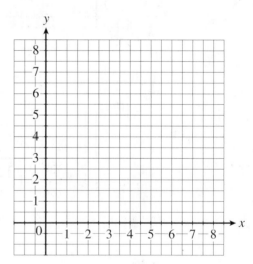

10. $3x - 5y \geq -10$
$x + y \geq 6$
$x \leq 5$

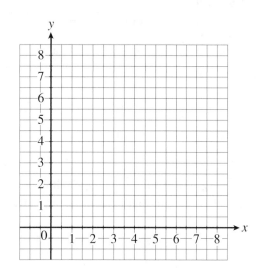

11. According to Miller and Thompson in their book *Elements of Meteorology*, grasslands will occur if the following system of inequalities is satisfied:

$$t \geq 35$$
$$5t - 7p \geq 70$$
$$3t - 35p \leq -140,$$

where t represents the average annual temperature in °F, and p represents the annual precipitation in inches.

a. Will grass grow in a region in which the average annual temperature is 40°F and the annual precipitation is 30 inches?

b. Graph the solution to the given system of linear inequalities.

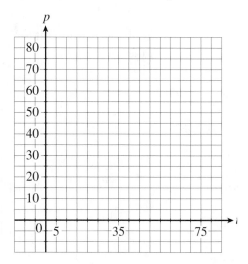

    c. Determine the corner points.

12. The following mathematical model gives a relationship between a person's height and weight that is recommended for a healthy weight:

$$h > 0$$
$$w > 0$$
$$25h - 7w \leq 800$$
$$5h - w \geq 170,$$

where h represents height in inches, and w represents weight in pounds.

    a. Your friend is 5 feet 7 inches tall and weighs 150 pounds. Is this a healthy weight for your friend? Explain.

    b. According to the model, is 175 pounds a healthy weight for someone who is 6 feet tall? Explain.

    c. Graph the solution set to the given system of linear inequalities. Use ordered pairs of the form (w, h).

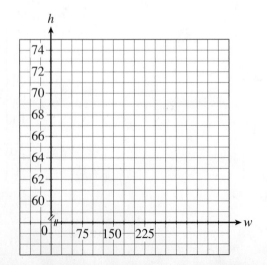

13. The local university requires that students applying for admission must have a combined SAT verbal and math score of at least 1150. The college of arts and sciences has an additional requirement that the verbal score must be at least 550.

    a. Write a system of linear inequalities that gives the requirements (constraints) to be admitted to the college of arts and sciences.

    b. The maximum score on the verbal part of the SAT is 800. The maximum score on the math portion of the SAT is also 800. Write two linear inequalities that express the constraints on the SAT scores.

    c. The total system that describes the SAT requirements for admission to the college of arts and sciences is the combination of inequalities in parts a and b. Solve this system by graphing.

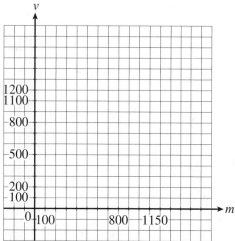

    d. Determine two different combinations of verbal and math scores that satisfy the admission requirements to the college of arts and sciences.

14. A course in graphic design is being offered in the evening at the local high school. Because of limited space in the lab, the course is limited to 16 students. In order for the high school to cover expenses to run the course, at least $2800 must be received in student fees. The high school charges $280 per student if you are a resident student (live in the town where the high school is located). Students who live outside the town are charged $400 for the course.

    a. Could a combination of 10 in-town students and 8 out-of-town students enroll in the course? Explain.

b. Could a combination of 6 in-town students and 2 out-of-town students enroll in the class? Explain.

c. Let *x* represent the number of in-town students enrolled in the class and *y* represent the number of out-of-town students enrolled. Write a system of linear inequalities that describes the constraints (limitations or restrictions) placed on *x* and *y* in this situation.

d. Solve the system in part c by graphing.

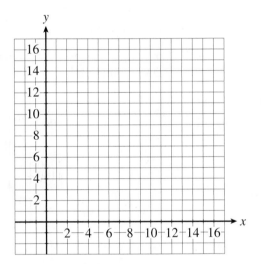

e. Give one combination of students (number of in-town and number of out-of-town) that could enroll in the class so that the constraints on the numbers and what they paid are satisfied.

f. Write an equation that gives the total amount of tuition, denoted by *T*, in terms of *x* and *y*.

Activities 2.11–2.15 What Have I Learned?

1. What is meant by a *solution to a system of linear equations*? How is a solution represented algebraically? Graphically?

2. Typically, a linear system of equations has one unique solution. Under what conditions is this not the case?

3. In this section, you solved 2×2 linear systems four ways. List them. Give an advantage of each approach.

4. Describe a procedure that will combine the following two linear equations in three variables into a single linear equation in two variables.

$$2x + 3y - 5z = 10$$
$$3x - 2y + 2z = 4$$

5. Explain when the addition method would be more efficient to use than the substitution method as you solve a system of linear equations algebraically.

6. In solving an inequality, explain when you would change the direction of the inequality symbol.

7. a. Graph the solution set of the following system of linear inequalities.

$$3x + y \geq 4$$

$$3x + y < 1$$

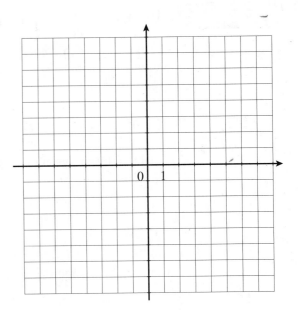

b. Does the system in part a have a solution? Explain why or why not.

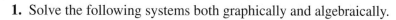

Activities 2.11–2.15 How Can I Practice?

1. Solve the following systems both graphically and algebraically.

a. $x + y = -3$
   $y = x - 5$

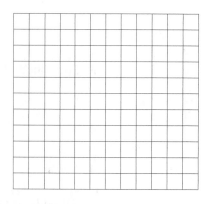

b. $x - 2y = -1$
   $4x - 3y = 6$

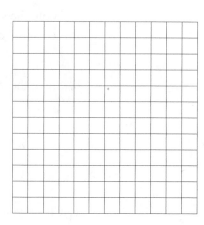

c. $2x - 3y = 7$
   $5x - 4y = 0$

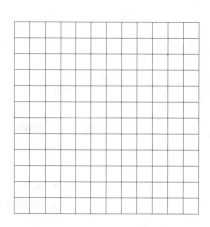

d. $x - y = 6$
   $y = x + 2$

2. Rewrite the systems in Exercise 1 in the form

$$y = ax + b$$
$$y = cx + d$$

and check your solutions numerically using the table feature of your graphing calculator.

3. Solve the following inequalities algebraically. Check your solutions graphically.

a. $2.5x + 9.8 \geq 14.3$ **b.** $-3x + 14 < 32$ **c.** $-5 \leq 3x - 8 < 7$

4. You are going to help your grandmother plant a garden of tulips and daffodils. She has space for approximately 80 bulbs. The florist tells you that tulips cost $0.50 per bulb and daffodils cost $0.75 per bulb. How many of each can you purchase if her budget is $52?

a. Write the system of equations.

b. Solve the system algebraically.

c. Check your solution graphically using your graphing calculator.

5. You need some repair work done on your truck. Towne Truck charges $80 just to examine the truck and $30 per hour for labor costs. World Transport charges $50 for the initial exam and $40 per hour for the labor.

a. Write a cost equation for each company. Use y to represent the total cost of doing the work and x to represent the number of hours of labor.

b. Complete the table of values for the cost functions.

x (NUMBER OF HOURS)	y, TOWNE TRUCK COST	y, WORLD TRANSPORT COST
2		
4		
6		
8		

c. Graph the functions.

d. From the graph, determine after how many hours the costs will be equal. What will be the total cost?

e. Check your solution in part d by solving the system algebraically.

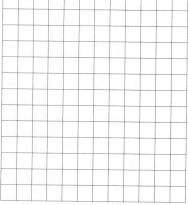

f. You think that you have a transmission problem that will take approximately 6 hours to fix. Determine from the graph which company you will hire for this job. Explain.

6. Translate each of the following into an inequality statement.

a. x is greater than -5 and at most 6.

b. x is less than -5 or x is at least 3.

c. x is greater than or equal to -3 and less than 4.

7. You own a hot dog cart in Daytona Beach. Your monthly profit is determined from the expression $1.50x - 50$, where x represents the number of hot dogs sold each month. The number 1.50 in the expression is the profit for each hot dog. The cost of leasing the hot dog stand is the number 50 in the expression $1.50x - 50$.

a. To ensure a profit of at least $2000 per month, approximately how many hot dogs do you have to sell? Write the inequality and solve.

b. Your profit has been fluctuating between $1500 and $2200 per month. Determine approximately between what two values your hot dog sales have to be to realize this range of profit. Write the inequality and solve.

8. The formula $A = P + Prt$ represents the value, A, of an investment of P dollars at a yearly simple interest rate, r, for t years.

    a. Write an equation to model the value, A, of an investment of $100 at 8% for t years.

    b. Write an equation to model the value A of an investment of $120 at 5% for t years.

    c. Assuming A has the same value, the equations in parts a and b form a system of two linear equations. Solve this system using an algebraic approach.

    d. Interpret your answer in part c.

9. Assuming equal costs, when warehouse workers use hand trucks to load a boxcar, it costs the management $40 for labor for each boxcar. After management purchases a forklift for $2000, it costs only $15 for labor to load each boxcar.

    a. Write an equation that models the cost, $C(n)$, of loading n boxcars with a hand truck.

    b. Write an equation that models the total cost, $C(n)$, including the purchase price of the forklift, of loading n boxcars with the forklift.

    c. The equations in parts a and b form a system of linear equations.
       Solve the system using an algebraic approach.

    d. Interpret your answer in part c in the context of the boxcar situation.

10. The sign on the elevator in a 10-story building states that the maximum weight the elevator can carry is 1500 pounds. As part of your work-study program, you need to move a large shipment of books to the sixth floor. Each box weighs 80 pounds.

    a. Let n represent the number of boxes that you place in the elevator. If you weigh 150 pounds, write an expression that represents the total weight, w, in the elevator. Assume that only you and the boxes are in the elevator.

    b. Using the expression in part a, write an inequality that can be used to determine the maximum number of boxes that you can place in the elevator at one time.

    c. Solve the inequality in part b.

11. Solve the following systems of linear inequalities.

    a. $y \geq \frac{1}{3}x - 2$

       $y < -x + 3$

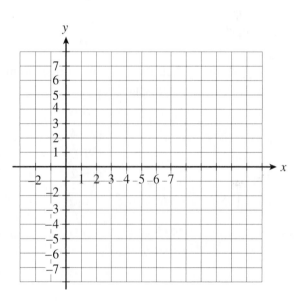

b. $x - y \le 0$

$y \ge -3x + 9$

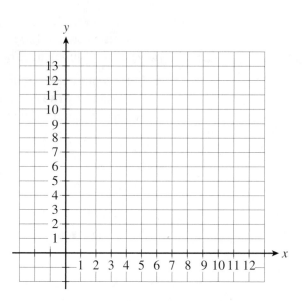

12. Determine the corner points of the solution set of the following system of linear inequalities.

$x \ge 0$

$x \le 4$

$y \ge 0$

$x + 2y \le 10$

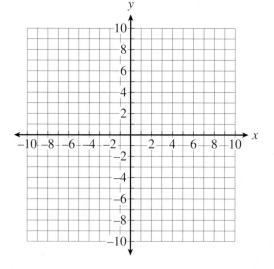

Summary

The bracketed numbers following each concept indicate the activity in which the concept is discussed.

CONCEPT / SKILL	DESCRIPTION	EXAMPLE
Delta notation for change [2.1]	Let y_1 and y_2 represent the values corresponding to x_1 and x_2, respectively. As the variable x changes in value from x_1 to x_2, the change is represented by $\Delta x = x_2 - x_1$ and the change in y is represented by $\Delta y = y_2 - y_1$.	Given the x-y pairs (4, 14) and (10, 32), $\Delta x = 10 - 4 = 6$ and $\Delta y = 32 - 14 = 18$.

Average rate of change over an interval [2.1]

The quotient

$$\frac{\Delta y}{\Delta x} = \frac{y_2 - y_1}{x_2 - x_1}$$

is called the average rate of change of y with respect to x over the x-interval from x_1 to x_2.

x	−3	4	7	10
y	0	14	27	32

The average rate of change over the interval from $x = 4$ to $x = 10$ is

$$\frac{\Delta y}{\Delta x} = \frac{32 - 14}{10 - 4} = \frac{18}{6} = 3.$$

Linear function [2.2]

A linear function is one whose average rate of change of y with respect to x from any one data point to any other data point is always the same (constant) value.

x	1	2	3	4
y	10	15	20	25

The average rate of change between any two of these points is 5.

Graph of a linear function [2.2]

The graph of every linear function is a line.

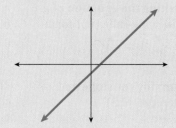

Slope of a line [2.2]

The slope of the line that contains the two points (x_1, y_1) and (x_2, y_2) is denoted by m;

$$m = \frac{\Delta y}{\Delta x} = \frac{y_2 - y_1}{x_2 - x_1}$$

The slope of the line containing the two points (2, 7) and (5, 11) is

$$m = \frac{11 - 7}{5 - 2} = \frac{4}{3}.$$

Positive slope [2.2]

The graph of every linear function with positive slope is a line rising to the right.

A linear function is increasing if its slope is positive.

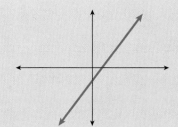

Negative slope [2.2]	The graph of every linear function with negative slope is a line falling to the right. A linear function is decreasing if its slope is negative.	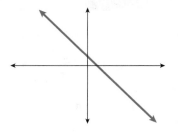
***x*-intercept of a graph** [2.3]	The *x*-intercept is the point at which the graph crosses the *x*-axis. Its ordered-pair notation is $(a, 0)$; that is, the *y*-value is equal to zero.	A line with *x*-intercept $(-3, 0)$ crosses the *x*-axis 3 units to the left of the origin.
***y*-intercept of a graph** [2.3]	The *y*-intercept is the point at which the graph crosses the *y*-axis. Its ordered-pair notation is $(0, b)$; that is, the *x*-value is equal to zero.	A line with *y*-intercept $(0, 5)$ crosses the *y*-axis 5 units above the origin.
Slope-intercept form of the equation of a line [2.3]	Represent the independent variable by *x*, the dependent variable by *y*. Denote the slope of the line by *m*, the *y*-intercept by $(0, b)$. Then the coordinate pair, (x, y), of *every* point on the line satisfies the equation $y = mx + b$.	The line with equation $y = 3x + 4$ has a slope of 3 and *y*-intercept $(0, 4)$. The point $(2, 10)$ is on the line because its coordinates satisfy the equation $$10 = 3(2) + 4.$$
Rewriting the equation of a line in slope-intercept form [2.3] **Identifying the slope and *y*-intercept** [2.3]	A nonvertical line whose equation is not in slope-intercept form can be rewritten in slope-intercept form by solving the equation for *y*. The slope can now be identified as the coefficient of the *x*-term. The *y*-intercept can be identified as the constant term.	The equation of the line $5x - 2y = 6$ can be rewritten by solving for *y*: $-2y = 6 - 5x$ Subtract 5*x*. $$\frac{-2y}{-2} = \frac{6}{-2} - \frac{5x}{-2} \quad \text{Divide by } -2.$$ $y = -3 + \dfrac{5}{2}x$ or $y = \dfrac{5}{2}x - 3$ The slope is $\dfrac{5}{2}$. The *y*-intercept is $(0, -3)$.
Zero slope [2.4]	The graph of every linear function with zero slope is a horizontal line. Every point on a horizontal line has the same *y*-value.	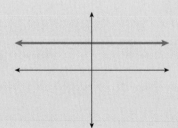
Equation of a horizontal line [2.4]	The slope, *m*, of a horizontal line is 0, and the *y*-value of each of its points is the same constant value, *c*. Its equation is $y = c$.	An equation of the horizontal line through the point $(-2, 3)$ is $y = 3$.

| **Undefined slope** [2.4] | A line whose slope is not defined (because its denominator is zero) is a vertical line.
A vertical line is the only line that does not represent a function.
Every point on a vertical line has the same input value. | 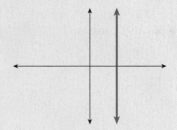 |

| **Equation of a vertical line** [2.4] | The graph of $x = a$ is a vertical line. | The graph of $x = 2$ is a vertical line 2 units to the right of the y-axis. |

| **Reflection across the x-axis** [2.5] | If the graph of $y = f(x)$ is reflected across the x-axis, then the equation of the resulting graph is $y = -1f(x)$. The graphs of $y = f(x)$ and $y = -1f(x)$ are mirror images across the x-axis. The y-values of each point in the original graph changes sign. The x-values remain the same. | 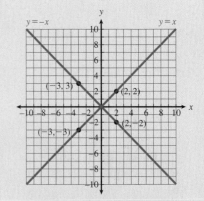
The graphs of $y = -1x$ is a reflection of $y = x$ across the x-axis. |

| **Vertical stretch and shrink** [2.5] | If the graph of $y = f(x)$ is vertically stretched (shrunk) by a factor of a, then the equation of the stretched (shrunk) graph is $y = af(x)$. The number a is called the stretch (shrink) factor. The y-value of each point in the graph of $y = f(x)$ is multiplied by a factor of a. The x-values remain the same. | 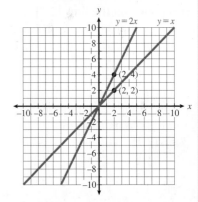
The graph of $y = 2x$ is a vertical stretch of the graph of $y = x$. The stretch factor is 2. The y-value of each point of the graph of $y = x$ is doubled to obtain the graph of $y = 2x$. |

Graph of $y = c \cdot f(x)$, where c is a positive constant [2.5]	If c is a positive constant, then the graph of $y = c \cdot f(x)$ is the graph of $y = f(x)$ **i.** vertically shrunk by a factor of c, if $0 < c < 1$. **ii.** vertically stretched by a factor of c, if $c > 1$.	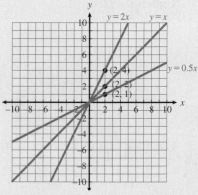 The graph of $y = 2x$ is a vertical stretch of the graph of $y = x$. The graph of $y = 0.5x$ is a vertical shrink of the graph of $y = x$.
Transformation [2.5]	Vertical and horizontal shifts (also called *translations*), reflections across the x-axis, and vertical stretches and shrinks are all examples of transformations.	The graph of $y = -2x + 1$ can be interpreted as a combination of transformations, including vertical shift, stretch, and reflection.
Using the slope and y-intercept to write an equation of the line [2.6]	Given a line whose slope is m and y-intercept is $(0, b)$, an equation of the line is $$y = mx + b.$$	An equation of the line with slope $\dfrac{2}{3}$ and y-intercept $(0, -6)$ is $$y = \frac{2}{3}x - 6.$$
Determining an equation of a line given the coordinates of two points on the line [2.7]	Given (x_1, y_1) and (x_2, y_2), calculate the slope, $m = \dfrac{\Delta y}{\Delta x} = \dfrac{y_2 - y_1}{x_2 - x_1}$. Substitute the coordinates of either given point for (h, k) and the value of the slope m into the equation $y - k = m(x - h)$. Then, solve for y.	See Example 1 in Activity 2.7.
Determining the x-intercept of a line given its equation [2.6], [2.7]	Because the x-intercept is the point whose y-coordinate is 0, set $y = 0$ in the equation and solve for x.	Given the line with equation $$y = 2x - 6,$$ set $y = 0$ to obtain equation $$0 = 2x - 6$$ $$6 = 2x$$ $$3 = x$$ The x-intercept is $(3, 0)$.
Linear regression equation [2.8], [2.9], [2.10]	The linear regression equation is the linear equation that best fits a set of data.	See Problem 2 in Activity 2.9.
Interpolation [2.9]	Interpolation is the process of using a regression equation to predict a value of output for an input value that lies within the range of the original data.	See Problem 2 in Activity 2.9.
Extrapolation [2.9]	Extrapolation is the process of using a regression equation to predict a value of output for an input value that lies outside the range of the original data.	See Problem 2 in Activity 2.9.

System of equations [2.11]	Two equations that relate the same variables are called a *system of equations*. The solution of the system is the ordered pair(s) that satisfies the two equations.	For the system of equations $$2x + 3y = 1$$ $$x - y = 3,$$ the ordered pair $(2, -1)$ is a solution of the system because $x = 2, y = -1$ satisfy both equations.
equations. **Graphical method for solving a system of linear equations**	[2.11]	Graph both equations on the same coordinate system. If the two lines intersect, then the solution to the system is the coordinates of the point of intersection.
	• Solve one equation for either variable, say y as an expression in x. • In the other equation, replace y by the expression in x. (This equation should now contain only the variable x.) • Solve this equation for x. • Use this value of x to determine y.	For the system of equations $$2x + 3y = 11$$ $$y = x - 3$$ • In the second equation, y is already written as an expression in x. • Rewrite the first equation $2x + 3(y) = 11$ as $2x + 3(x - 3) = 11.$ • Solve this equation for x: $$2x + 3x - 9 = 11$$ $$5x = 20$$ $$x = 4$$ • Solve for y: $y = x - 3$, so $y = 4 - 3 = 1.$
Consistent system [2.11]	A linear system is consistent if there is at least one solution.	$y = 3x - 10$ $y = 5x + 14$ is a consistent system.
Inconsistent system [2.11]	A linear system is inconsistent if there is no solution. The lines are parallel.	$y = 2x + 1$ $y = 2x - 3$
Solution set of an inequality [2.14]	The solution set of an inequality in one variable is the set of all values of the variable that satisfy the inequality.	$\{x \mid x \le 3\}$ is the solution set to the inequality $2x + 3 \le 9.$

Solving inequalities: direction of inequality sign [2.14]	**Property 1.** The direction of an inequality is not changed when
	  i. the same quantity is added to or subtracted from both sides of the inequality. Stated algebraically, if $a < b$ then $a + c < b + c$ and $a - c < b - c.$
		For example, because $-4 < 10$, then
		  i. $-4 + 5 < 10 + 5$ or $1 < 15$ is true.
		    $-4 - 3 < 10 - 3$ or $-7 < 7$ is true.

	ii. both sides of an inequality are multiplied or divided by the same positive number. If $a < b$ then $ac < bc$, where $c > 0$ and $\dfrac{a}{c} < \dfrac{b}{c}$, where $c > 0$.	ii. $-4(6) < 10(6)$ or $-24 < 60$ is true; $\dfrac{-4}{2} < \dfrac{10}{2}$ or $-2 < 5$ is true.
	Property 2. The direction of an inequality is reversed if both sides of an inequality are multiplied by or divided by the same negative number. These properties can be written symbolically as: i. if $a < b$, then $ac > bc$, where $c < 0$. ii. if $a < b$, then $\dfrac{a}{c} > \dfrac{b}{c}$, where $c < 0$.	Because $-4 < 10$, then $-4(-5) > 10(-5)$ or $20 > -50$. Because $-4 < 10$, then $\dfrac{-4}{-2} > \dfrac{10}{-2}$ or $2 > -5$.
	Properties 1 and 2 will still be true if $a < b$ is replaced by $a \le b$, $a > b$, or $a \ge b$.	These properties will be true if $a < b$ is replaced by $a \le b$, $a > b$, or $a \ge b$.
Solving inequalities of the form $f(x) < g(x)$ [2.14]	Inequalities of the form $f(x) < g(x)$ can be solved using three different methods. **Method 1** is a numerical approach, in which a table of input-output pairs is used to determine values of x for which $f(x) < g(x)$. **Method 2** is a graphical approach, in which values of x are located so that the graph of f is below the graph of g. **Method 3** is an algebraic approach, in which the two properties of inequalities are used to isolate the variable.	Solve $5x + 1 \ge 3x - 7$. 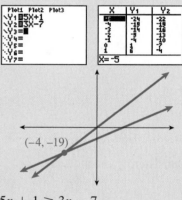 $(-4, -19)$ $5x + 1 \ge 3x - 7$ $2x \ge -8$ $x \ge -4$
A compound inequality [2.14]	A compound inequality is a statement that involves more than 1 inequality symbol $<$, $>$, $\le$, $\ge$, or $\ne$	$-3 < x + 7 \le 10$
Linear inequality in two variables [2.15]	An inequality of the form, $Ax + By < C$, where A and B can not both equal zero, is a linear inequality in two variables. The symbol $<$ can be replaced by $>$, $\le$, or $\ge$.	$2x + 3y \le 10$ is a linear inequality in two variables.

Graph of a linear inequality in two variables [2.15]	The graph is the collection all ordered pairs (x, y) whose coordinates satisfy the given inequality.	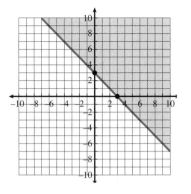
		All points on the solid line $y = -x + 3$ and above the line $y = -x + 3$ represent the graph of $x + y \geq 3$.
Half-plane [2.15]	A half-plane is the set of all points on one side of a line.	All the points above the line $y = -x + 3$ represented in the shaded region in the graph above.
System of linear inequalities in two variables [2.15]	A system of linear inequalities consists of two or more linear inequalities.	$x + y \leq 5$ $y \leq 2x - 6$ $x \geq 0, y \geq 0$ represents a system of linear inequalities.
Graphing a system of linear inequalities in two variables [2.15]	Step 1. Graph each linear inequality in the system. Step 2. The graph of the system is the intersection of the shaded regions representing the solutions of the linear inequalities in the system, and any solid line common to all the inequalities in the system.	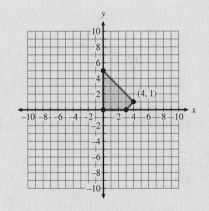
Corner points [2.15]	The points determined by the intersection of the boundary lines of the graph of a system of linear inequalities are called corner points.	The corner points in the region above are $(0, 0)$, $(0, 5)$, $(3, 0)$, and $(4, 1)$.

1. For a certain yard, the fertilizer costs $20. You charge $8 per hour to do yard work. If x represents the number of hours worked on the yard and f(x) represents the total cost, including fertilizer, complete the following table.

x	0	2	3	5	7
f(x)	20	36	44	60	76

a. Is the total cost a function of the hours worked? Explain.

b. Which variable represents the input?

c. Which is the dependent variable?

d. Which value(s) of the domain would not be realistic for this situation? Explain.

e. What is the average rate of change from 0 to 3?

f. What is the average rate of change from 5 to 7?

g. What can you say about the rate of change between any two of the points?

h. What kind of relationship exists between the two variables?

i. Write this relationship in the form $f(x) = mx + b$.

j. What is the practical meaning of the slope in this situation?

k. What is the y-intercept? What is the practical meaning of this point?

l. Determine $f(4)$.

m. For what value(s) of x does $f(x) = 92$? Interpret your answer in the context of the situation.

2. Which of the following sets of data represent a linear function?

a.

x	0	2	4	6	8
f(x)	14	22	30	38	46

b.

x	5	10	15	20	25
y	4	2	0	−2	−4

c.

x	1	3	4	6	7
g(x)	10	20	30	40	50

d.

t	0	10	20	30	40
d	143	250	357	464	571

3. a. Determine the slope of the line through the points $(5, -3)$ and $(-4, 9)$.

b. From the equation $3x - 7y = 21$, determine the slope.

c. Determine the slope of the line from its graph.

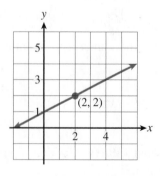

4. Write the equation of the line described in each of the following.

   a. A slope of 0 and passing through the point $(2, 4)$.

   b. A slope of 2 and a vertical intercept of $(0, 5)$.

   c. A slope of -3 and passing through the point $(6, -14)$.

   d. A slope of 2 and passing through the point $(7, -2)$.

   e. A line with undefined slope passing through the point $(2, -3)$.

   f. A slope of -5 and a horizontal intercept of $(4, 0)$.

   g. A line passing through the points $(-3, -4)$ and $(2, 16)$.

   h. Contains the point $(8, -3)$ and is parallel to $6x + 2y = 5$

   i. Contains the point $(-1, 5)$ and is perpendicular to $x - 4y = 4$

5. Given the following graph of the linear function, determine the equation of the line.

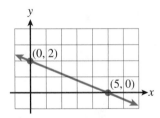

6. a. The building where your computer graphics store is located is 10 years old and has a value of $200,000. When the building was 1 year old, its value was $290,000. Assuming that the building's depreciation is linear, express the value of the building as a function, f, of its age, x, in years.

   b. What is the slope of the line? What is the practical meaning of the slope in this situation?

c. What is the *y*-intercept? What is the practical meaning of the *y*-intercept in this situation?

d. What is the *x*-intercept? What is the practical meaning of the *x*-intercept in this situation?

7. Determine the *y*-intercept of the following functions. Solve for *y* if necessary.

   a. $y = 2x - 3$

   b. $y = -3$

   c. $x - y = 3$

   d. What relationship do the graphs of these functions have to one another?

   e. Use your graphing calculator to graph the functions in parts a–c on the same coordinate axes. Compare your results with part d.

8. Determine the slopes and *y*-intercepts of each of the following functions. Solve for *y* if necessary.

   a. $y = -2x + 1$

   b. $2x + y = -1$

   c. $-4x - 2y = 6$

   d. What relationship do the graphs of these functions have to one another?

   e. Use your graphing calculator to graph the functions in parts a–c on the same coordinate axes. Compare your results with part d.

9. Determine the slopes and *y*-intercepts of each of the following functions. Solve for *y* if necessary.

   a. $y = -3x + 2$

   b. $3x + y = 2$

   c. $6x + 2y = 4$

   d. What relationship do the graphs of these functions have to one another?

   e. For two lines to be parallel to each other, what has to be the same?

   f. For two lines to lie on top of each other (coincide), what has to be the same?

   g. Use your graphing calculator to graph the functions in parts a–c on the same coordinate axes. Compare your results with part d.

10. **a.** Graph the function defined by $y = -2x + 150$. Determine the intercepts. Make sure to include some negative values of *x*.

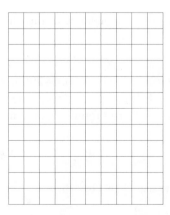

   b. Using your graphing calculator, verify the graph you have drawn in part a.

   c. Using the graph, determine the domain and range of the function.

   d. Assume that a 150-pound person starts a diet and loses 2 pounds per week for 15 weeks. Write the equation modeling this situation.

e. Compare the equation you found in part d with the one given in part a.

f. What is the practical meaning of the *x*- and *y*-intercepts you found in part a?

g. What is the practical domain and range of this function for the situation given in part d?

11. a. You pay a flat fee of $25 per month for your trash to be picked up, and it doesn't matter how many bags of trash you have. Use *x* to represent the number of bags of trash, and write a function, *f*, in symbolic form to represent the total cost of your trash for the month.

b. Sketch the graph of this function.

c. What is the slope of the line?

12. During the years 2005–2009, the number of finishers in a large marathon increased. The following table gives the total number of finishers (to the nearest hundred) each year, where *t* represents the number of years after 2005.

YEARS AFTER 2005, t	0	1	2	3	4
NUMBER OF FINISHERS, n	7900	9100	10,000	10,900	12,100

a. Enter the data from your table into your calculator. Determine the linear regression equation model and write the result.

b. What is the slope of the regression line? What is the practical meaning of the slope in this situation?

c. What is the t-intercept? What is the practical meaning of the t-intercept in this situation?

d. Use your graphing calculator to graph the regression line in the same screen as the scatterplot. How well do you think the line fits the data?

e. Use your regression model to predict the number of finishers in 2011.

f. Did you use interpolation or extrapolation to determine your result in part e? Explain.

g. Do you think that the prediction for the year 2024 will be as accurate as that in 2011? Explain.

13. Determine the equation of the perpendicular bisector of the line segment having endpoints $(2, 3)$ and $(-4, 7)$.

14. Which input value results in the same output value for $y_1 = 2x - 3$ and $y_2 = 5x + 3$?

15. Which point on the line given by $4x - 5y = 20$ is also on the line $y = x + 5$?

16. Solve the following system of two linear equations.

$y = 2x + 8$
$y = -3x + 3$

17. You sell centerpieces for $19.50 each. Your fixed costs are $500 per month, and each centerpiece costs $8 to produce.

    a. Let n represent the number of centerpieces you sell. Write an equation to determine the cost, C.

    b. Write an equation to determine the revenue, R.

    c. What is your break-even point (cost = revenue)?

18. Suppose you wish to break even (in Exercise 17) by selling only 25 centerpieces. At what price would you need to sell each centerpiece?

19. Solve the system algebraically.

$$y = -25x + 250$$
$$y = 25x + 300$$

20. Use the addition method to solve the following system.

$$4m - 3n = -7$$
$$2m + 3n = 37$$

21. Solve the following system graphically and algebraically.

$$y = 6x - 7$$
$$y = 6x + 4$$

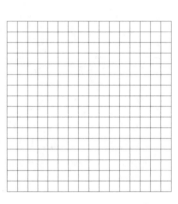

22. Consider the lines represented by the following pair of equations:
$3x + 2y = 10$ and $x - 2y = -2$.

a. Solve the system algebraically.

b. Determine the point of intersection of the lines by solving the system graphically.

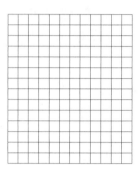

c. Determine the point of intersection of the lines by solving the system using the tables feature of your calculator, if available.

23. Use your graphing calculator to estimate the solution to the following system. *Note:* Both equations first must be written in the form $y = mx + b$.

$$342x - 167y = 418$$

$$-162x + 103y = -575$$

Use the window Xmin $= -10$, Xmax $= 0$,

Xscl $= 2$, Ymin $= -28$, Ymax $= 0$, Yscl $= 2$.

24. Solve the following systems of equations. Solve at least one system algebraically and at least one system graphically.

a. $3x - y = 10$
       $5x + 2y = 13$

b. $4x + 2y = 8$
       $x - 3y = -19$

c. $2x + y = 10$

$\quad y = -2x + 13$

d. $2x + 6y = 4$

$\quad x + 3y = 2$

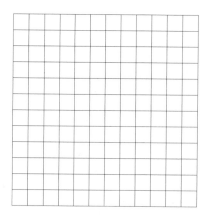

25. The employees of a video arcade order lunch two days in a row from the corner deli. Lunch on the first day consists of 5 small pizzas and 6 cookies for a total of $27. On the second day, 8 pizzas are ordered along with 4 cookies, totaling $39. To know how much money to pay, employees have to determine how much each pizza and each cookie cost. How much does the deli charge for each pizza and each cookie?

26. Solve the following inequalities algebraically.

    a. $2x + 3 \geq 5$ **b.** $3x - 1 \leq 4x + 5$

27. The weekly revenue, $R(x)$, and cost, $C(x)$, generated by a product can be modeled by the following equations:

$$R(x) = 75x$$
$$C(x) = 50x + 2500$$

Determine when $R(x) \geq C(x)$ numerically, algebraically, and graphically.

x	R(x)	C(x)
0		
50		
100		
150		
200		

28. Graph the solution set for each of the following systems of linear inequalities:

a. $x + y \geq 10$
$x + y \leq 12$
$3y \leq x$
$x \geq 0$
$y \geq 0$

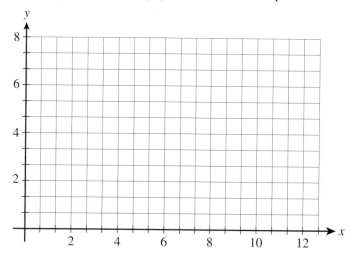

b. $x + y < 5$
$2x + y > 4$
$x > 0$
$y > 0$

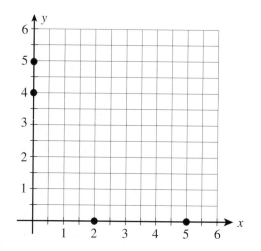

Problem Solving with Quadratic and Power Function Models

ACTIVITY 3.1

The Amazing Property of Gravity

OBJECTIVES

1. Evaluate functions of the form $y = ax^2$.

2. Graph functions of the form $y = ax^2$.

3. Interpret the coordinates of points on the graph of $y = ax^2$ in context.

4. Solve an equation of the form $ax^2 = c$ graphically.

5. Solve an equation of the form $ax^2 = c$ algebraically by taking square roots.

Note: $a \neq 0$ in Objectives 1–5.

In the sixteenth century, scientists such as Galileo were experimenting with the physical laws of gravity. In a remarkable discovery, they learned that if the effects of air resistance are neglected, any two objects dropped from a height above earth will fall at exactly the same speed. That is, if you drop a feather and a brick down a tube whose air has been removed, the feather and brick will fall at the same speed. Surprisingly, the function that models the distance fallen by such an object in terms of elapsed time is a very simple one:

$$s = 16t^2,$$

where t represents the number of seconds elapsed and s represents distance (in feet) the object has fallen.

The function defined by $s = 16t^2$ indicates a sequence of two mathematical operations:

Start with a value for $t \rightarrow$ *square the value* $\rightarrow$ *multiply by 16* $\rightarrow$ to obtain values for s.

1. Use the given equation to complete the table.

t (sec)	s (ft)
0	
1	
2	
3	

2. a. How many feet does the object fall one second after being dropped?

    b. How many feet does the object fall two seconds after being dropped?

3. a. Determine the average rate of change of distance fallen from time $t = 0$ to $t = 1$.

    b. What are the units of measurement of the average rate of change?

    c. Explain what the average rate of change indicates about the falling object.

4. Determine and interpret the average rate of change of distance fallen from time $t = 1$ to $t = 2$.

5. Is the function $s = 16t^2$ a linear function? Explain your answer.

6. a. If the object hits the ground after 5 seconds, determine the practical domain of the function.

    b. On the following grid, plot the points given in the table in Problem 1 and sketch a curve representing the distance function through the points.

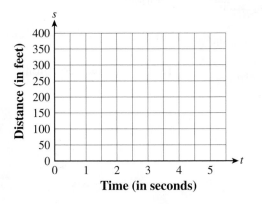

    c. Use your graphing calculator to verify the graph in part b. Your graph should resemble the one below to the right.

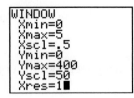 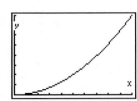

7. a. Confirm that the point (2.5, 100) lies on the graph. What do the coordinates of this point indicate about the falling object?

b. Confirm that the point (4.5, 324) lies on the graph. What do the coordinates of this point indicate about the falling object?

8. Use the graph to estimate the amount of time it takes the object to fall 256 feet.

9. Use $s = 16t^2$ to write an equation to determine the amount of time it takes the object to fall 256 feet.

To solve the equation in Problem 9, you need to reverse the order of operations indicated by the function rule, replacing each operation by its inverse. Here, one of the operations is "square a number." The inverse of squaring is to take a square root denoted by the symbol $\sqrt{}$, called a **radical sign**.

Start with a value for $s \rightarrow$ *divide by 16* $\rightarrow$ *take its square root* $\rightarrow$ to obtain t.

In particular, if $s = 256$ feet:

Start with 256 $\rightarrow$ *divide by 16* $\rightarrow$ *take its square root* $\rightarrow$ to obtain t.

$$256 \div 16 = 16 \qquad \sqrt{16} = 4 \qquad t = 4$$

Therefore, you can conclude that it takes four seconds for the object to fall 256 feet.

10. Reverse the sequence of operations indicated by $s = 16t^2$ to determine the amount of time it takes an object to fall 1296 feet, approximately the height of a 100-story building.

Graph of a Parabola

Some interesting properties of the function defined by $s = 16t^2$ arise when you ignore the falling object context and consider just the algebraic rule itself.

Replace t with x and s with y and consider the general equation $y = 16x^2$. First, by ignoring the context, you can allow x to take on a negative, positive, or zero value. For example, suppose $x = -5$. Then

$$y = 16(-5)^2 = 16 \cdot 25 = 400.$$

11. a. Use $y = 16x^2$ to complete the table.

x	−4	−3	−2.5	−2	−1.5	−1	−0.5	0	0.5	1	1.5	2	2.5	3	4
y								0		16		64		144	

    b. What pattern (symmetry) do you notice from the table?

12. a. Sketch the graph of $y = 16x^2$ by using the table in Problem 11. Plot the points and then draw a curve through them. Scale the axes appropriately.

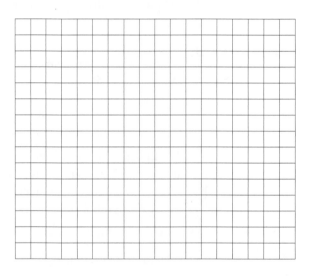

    b. Use a graphing calculator to produce a graph of this function in the window $-5 \le x \le 5$, $-100 \le y \le 400$. Your graph should resemble the one below.

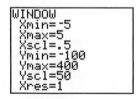
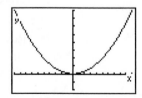

The U-shaped graph of $y = 16x^2$ is called a **parabola**.

13. a. The graph of the squaring function defined by $y = x^2$ is a parabola. How is the graph of $y = 16x^2$ related to the graph of $y = x^2$?

b. The graphs of $y = 16x^2$ and $y = x^2$ are both U-shaped. Is the graph of $y = 16x^2$ wider or narrower than the graph of $y = x^2$? Explain.

c. Is the graph of $y = 0.5x^2$ wider or narrower than the graph of $y = x^2$? Explain. Verify using a graphing calculator.

d. If $0 < a < 1$, then is the graph of $y = ax^2$ wider or narrower than the graph of $y = x^2$?

e. If $a > 1$, then is the graph of $y = ax^2$ wider or narrower than the graph of $y = x^2$?

Solving Equations of the Form

14. a. In the table in Problem 11a, how many points on the graph of $y = 16x^2$ lie 256 units above the x-axis?

b. Identify the points. What are their coordinates?

The x-values of the points on the graph of $y = 16x^2$ that lie 256 units above the x-axis can be determined algebraically by solving the equation $256 = 16x^2$.

Example 1   *Solve the equation $16x^2 = 256$ algebraically.*

SOLUTION

Step 1.   Divide both sides by 16:

$$\frac{16x^2}{16} = \frac{256}{16} \text{ to obtain } x^2 = 16$$

Step 2. Calculate the square root:

When x is no longer restricted to positive (or nonnegative) values only, there are *two* square roots of 16, one denoted by $\sqrt{16}$ and the other denoted by $-\sqrt{16}$. These two square roots are often written in condensed form as $\pm\sqrt{16}$. Since $\sqrt{16} = 4$ and $-\sqrt{16} = -4$, the solutions to the equation $x^2 = 16$ are $x = \pm 4$.

The solution to $16x^2 = 256$ can be written in the following systematic manner.

$16x^2 = 256$

$\dfrac{16x^2}{16} = \dfrac{256}{16}$ Divide both sides by 16.

$x^2 = 16$ Simplify.

$x = \pm\sqrt{16}$ Take the positive and negative square roots.

or equivalently, $x = \pm 4$

15. a. How many points on the graph in Problem 12b lie 400 units above the x-axis?

b. Identify the points. What are their coordinates?

c. Set up the appropriate equation to determine the values of x for which $y = 400$, and solve it algebraically.

16. Solve the following equations algebraically:

    a. $x^2 = 36$ **b.** $2x^2 = 98$

    c. $3x^2 = 375$ **d.** $5x^2 = 50$

17. a. Refer to the graph in Problem 12 to determine how many points on the graph of $y = 16x^2$ lie 16 units *below* the x-axis.

b. Set up an equation that corresponds to the question in part a.

c. How many solutions does this equation have? Explain.

18. What does the graph of $y = 16x^2$ (Problem 12) indicate about the number of solutions to the following equations? (You do not need to solve these equations.)

a. $16x^2 = 100$ **b.** $16x^2 = 0$ **c.** $16x^2 = -96$

19. Solve the following equations:

a. $5x^2 = 20$ **b.** $4x^2 = 0$ **c.** $3x^2 = -12$

SUMMARY
Activity 3.1

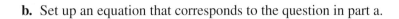

1. The graph of a function of the form $y = ax^2$, $a \neq 0$, is a U-shaped curve and is called a **parabola**.

2. If $a > 0$, then the larger the value of a, the narrower the graph of $y = ax^2$.

3. An equation of the form $ax^2 = c$, $a \neq 0$, is solved algebraically by dividing both sides of the equation by a and then taking the positive and negative square roots of both sides.

4. Every positive number a has two square roots, one positive and one negative. The square roots are equal in magnitude. The positive, or principal, square root of a is denoted by $\sqrt{a}$. The negative square root of a is denoted by $-\sqrt{a}$. The symbol $\sqrt{}$ is called the **radical sign**.

5. The **square root** of a number a is the number that when squared produces a. For example, the square roots of 25 are

$$\sqrt{25} = 5 \text{ because } 5^2 = 25$$

and

$$-\sqrt{25} = -5 \text{ because } (-5)^2 = 25.$$

The square roots of 25 can be written in a condensed form as $\pm\sqrt{25} = \pm 5$.

EXERCISES
Activity 3.1

1. On the Earth's Moon, gravity is only one-sixth as strong as it is on Earth, so an object on the Moon will fall one-sixth the distance it would fall on Earth in the same time. This means that the gravity distance function for a falling object on the Moon is

$$s = \left(\frac{16}{6}\right)t^2 \text{ or } s = \frac{8}{3}t^2,$$

where t represents time since the object is released, in seconds, and s is the distance fallen, in feet.

a. How far does an object on the Moon fall in 3 seconds?

b. How long does it take an object on the Moon to fall 96 feet?

c. Graph the Moon's gravity function on a properly scaled and labeled coordinate axis or on a graphing calculator for $t = 0$ to $t = 5$.

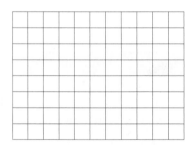

d. Use the graph to estimate how long it takes an object on the Moon to fall 35 feet.

e. Write an equation to determine the required time in part d. Solve the equation algebraically.

f. How does your answer in part e compare to your estimate in part d?

2. a. The graphs of $y = x^2$, $y = \dfrac{1}{3}x^2$, and $y = 5x^2$ appear in the following graphing calculator screen. Match the equation with the graph.

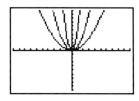

b. Is the graph of $y = 0.75x^2$ wider or narrower than the graph of $y = 10x^2$? Verify using a graphing calculator.

c. Is the graph of $y = 10x^2$ wider or narrower than the graph of $y = 5x^2$?

3. Solve the following equations:

   a. $5x^2 = 45$ **b.** $9x^2 = 0$

   c. $-25x^2 = 100$ **d.** $x^2 = 5$

   e. $2x^2 = 20$ **f.** $\dfrac{x^2}{2} = 32$

4. Solve the following by first writing the equation in the form $x^2 = c$:

   a. $x^2 - 49 = 0$ **b.** $15 + x^2 = 96$ **c.** $3a^2 - 21 = 27$

In a right triangle, as shown in the following diagram, the side c opposite the right angle is called the hypotenuse, and the other two sides a and b are called legs. The Pythagorean theorem states that in any right triangle, the lengths of the three sides are related by the equation $c^2 = a^2 + b^2$.

Use the Pythagorean theorem to answer Exercises 5–6.

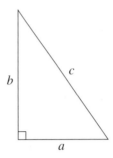

5. Determine the length of the hypotenuse in a right triangle with legs 5 inches and 12 inches.

6. One leg of a right triangle measures 8 inches and the hypotenuse 17 inches. Determine the length of the other leg.

Right triangles will be studied in more detail in Chapter 5.

ACTIVITY 3.2

Baseball and the
Sears Tower

OBJECTIVES

1. Identify functions of the
   form $y = ax^2 + bx + c$ as
   quadratic functions.

2. Explore the role of a as it
   relates to the graph of
   $y = ax^2 + bx + c$.

3. Explore the role of b as it
   relates to the graph of
   $y = ax^2 + bx + c$.

4. Explore the role of c as it
   relates to the graph of
   $y = ax^2 + bx + c$.

Note: $a \neq 0$ in Objectives 1–4.

Imagine yourself standing on the roof of the 1450-foot-high Sears Tower in Chicago. When you release and drop a baseball from the roof of the tower, *the ball's height above the ground, H (in feet), can be modeled as a function of the time, t (in seconds), since it was dropped.* This height function is defined by

$$H = -16t^2 + 1450.$$

1. a. Complete the following table:

Who Dropped the Ball?

TIME, t (sec)	$H = -16t^2 + 1450$
0	
1	
2	
3	
4	
5	
6	
7	
8	
9	
10	

b. How far does the baseball fall during the first second?

c. How far does it fall during the second second?

2. Using the height function, $H = -16t^2 + 1450$, determine the average rate of change of H with respect to t over the given interval.

a. $0 \leq t \leq 1$ **b.** $1 \leq t \leq 2$

c. Based on the results of parts a and b, do you believe that $H = -16t^2 + 1450$ is a linear function? Explain.

3. a. If the object hits the ground in approximately 9.5 seconds, what is the practical domain of the height function?

b. Determine the practical range of the height function.

c. On the following grid, plot the points in Problem 1 and sketch a curve representing the height function.

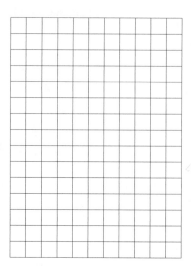

d. Is the graph of the height function the actual path of the object when the ball is dropped? Explain.

Some interesting properties of the function defined by $H = -16t^2 + 1450$ arise when you ignore the falling object context. Replace H with y and t with x and consider the general function defined by $y = -16x^2 + 1450$.

4. The graph of $y = -16x^2 + 1450$ can be obtained by performing three transformations on the graph of $y = x^2$. In parts a–c,

    i. Use a graphing calculator to sketch a graph resulting from the given transformation. Set the window parameters at Xmin $= -10$, Xmax $= 10$, Ymin $= -1000$, and Ymax $= 1500$.

    ii. Write the equation of the graph.

    a. A vertical stretch of the graph of $y = x^2$ by a factor of 16.

    b. A reflection of the graph in part a over the x-axis.

c. A vertical shift of the graph in part b upward 1450 units.

d. The graph of $y = x^2$ is U-shaped and is said to open upward. The graph of $y = -16x^2 + 1450$ is also U-shaped. Does the graph open upward or open downward?

5. The graph of $y = -16x^2 + 1450$ (setting the window parameters at Xmin $= -10$, Xmax $= 10$, Ymin $= -50$, and Ymax $= 1500$) should appear as follows:

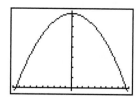

Describe the important features of the graph including the shape, symmetry, and intercepts.

The graph of $y = -16x^2 + 1450$ is a **parabola**. The graph of a parabola is a U-shaped figure that opens upward, ∪, or downward, ∩. Parabolas are graphs of a special category of functions called quadratic functions.

Quadratic Function

> **DEFINITION**
>
> Any function defined by an equation of the form $y = ax^2 + bx + c$ or $f(x) = ax^2 + bx + c$, where a, b, and c represent real numbers and $a \neq 0$, is called a **quadratic function**. The dependent variable y is defined by an expression having three terms: the **quadratic term**, ax^2, the **linear term**, bx, and the **constant term**, c. The numerical factors of the quadratic and linear terms, a and b, are called the **coefficients** of the terms.

Example 1   *$y = -16x^2 + 100$ defines a quadratic function. The quadratic term is $-16x^2$. The linear term is $0x$, although it is not written as part of the expression defining y. The constant term is 100. The numbers -16 and 0 are the coefficients of the quadratic and linear terms respectively. Therefore, $a = -16$, $b = 0$, and $c = 100$.*

6. For each of the following quadratic functions, identify the value of a, b, and c:

QUADRATIC FUNCTION	a	b	c
$y = 3x^2$			
$y = -2x^2 + 3$			
$y = x^2 + 2x - 1$			
$y = -x^2 + 4x$			

The Constant Term c

Consider once again the height function $H = -16t^2 + 1450$ from the beginning of the activity.

7. a. What is the H-intercept of the graph?

b. What is the practical meaning of the H-intercept in this situation?

c. Predict what the graph of $H = -16t^2 + 1450$ would look like if the constant term 1450 were changed to 800. That is, the baseball is dropped from a height of 800 feet rather than 1450 feet. Verify your prediction by graphing $H = -16t^2 + 800$. What does the constant term tell you about the graph of the parabola?

In general, the constant term c of a quadratic function $y = ax^2 + bx + c$ *always* indicates the y-intercept of the parabola. The y-intercept of any quadratic function is $(0, c)$.

8. Graph the parabolas defined by the following quadratic equations. Note the similarities and differences among the graphs, especially the y-intercepts.

a. $f(x) = 1.5x^2$

b. $g(x) = 1.5x^2 + 7$

c. $q(x) = 1.5x^2 + 4$

d. $s(x) = 1.5x^2 - 4$

The Effects of the Coefficient *a*

9. a. Using transformations, describe how to obtain the graph of $y = 16x^2 + 1450$ from the graph of $y = x^2$.

b. Compare the transformations used to graph $y = 16x^2 + 1450$ to the transformations used to graph $y = -16x^2 + 1450$ (see Problem 4). What is different?

c. Graph the quadratic function defined by $g(x) = 16x^2 + 1450$ on the same screen as $y = -16x^2 + 1450$. Use the window settings Xmin $= -10$, Xmax $= 10$, Ymin $= -50$, and Ymax $= 3000$.

d. What effect does the sign of the coefficient of x^2 appear to have on the graph of the parabola?

10. Graph the functions $h(x) = -16x^2 + 100, f(x) = -6x^2 + 100$, and $g(x) = -40x^2 + 100$ in the same window. What effect does the magnitude of the coefficients of x^2 (namely, $|-16| = 16, |-6| = 6$, and $|-40| = 40$) appear to have on the graph of that particular parabola?

The results from Problems 9 and 10 regarding the effects of the coefficient *a* can be summarized as follows:

The graph of a quadratic function defined by $f(x) = ax^2 + bx + c$ is called a *parabola*.

- If $a > 0$, the parabola opens upward.
- If $a < 0$, the parabola opens downward.
- The magnitude of *a* affects the width of the parabola. The larger the absolute value of *a*, the narrower the parabola.

11. a. Does the graph of $y = -3x^2 + 2x - 1$ open upward or downward?

   b. Is the graph of $h(x) = 0.3x^2$ wider or narrower than the graph of $f(x) = x^2$?

   c. How do the output values of h and the output values of f compare for the same input value?

   d. Is the graph of $g(x) = 3x^2$ wider or narrower than the graph of $f(x) = x^2$?

   e. How do the output values of g and f compare for the same input value?

The Effects of the Coefficient b

Assume for the time being that you are back on the roof of the 1450-foot Sears Tower. Instead of merely releasing the ball, suppose you *throw it down* with an initial velocity of 40 feet per second. Then the function describing its height above ground as a function of time is modeled by

$$H_{\text{down}} = -16t^2 - 40t + 1450.$$

> If you tossed the ball *up* with an initial velocity of 40 feet per second, then the function describing its height above ground as a function of time is modeled by
>
> $$H_{\text{up}} = -16t^2 + 40t + 1450.$$

12. Predict what features of the graphs of H_{down} and H_{up} have in common with $H = -16t^2 + 1450$.

13. a. Graph the three functions H, H_{down}, and H_{up} using the same window setting.

   b. What effect do the $-40t$ and $40t$ terms seem to have upon the graphs?

> In general, if $b = 0$, the turning point of the parabola is located on the y-axis. If $b \neq 0$, the turning point will not be on the y-axis.

14. Set the window of your graphing calculator to Xmin $= -8$, Xmax $= 8$, Ymin $= -20$, and Ymax $= 20$, and graph the parabolas defined by the following quadratic equations. Note the differences among the graphs, paying careful attention to the effects of the signs of the coefficients a, b, and c on the graph.

a. $y = x^2$

b. $y = x^2 - 4x$

c. $y = x^2 - 8x$

d. $y = x^2 + 6x$

e. $y = -x^2 + 6x$

f. $y = -x^2 - 8x$

15. Match each function with its corresponding graph below, and then verify using your graphing calculator.

a. $f(x) = x^2 + 4x + 4$ **b.** $g(x) = 0.2x^2 + 4$ **c.** $h(x) = -x^2 + 3x$

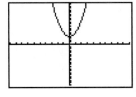
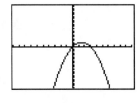

    i.   **ii.**   **iii.**

SUMMARY
Activity 3.2

1. The function that has a parabola as its graph is called a **quadratic function**. The equation of a quadratic function with x as the independent variable and y as the dependent variable has the standard form

$$y = ax^2 + bx + c,$$

where a, b, and c represent real numbers and $a \neq 0$.

2. The graph of a quadratic function is called a **parabola**.

3. For the quadratic function defined by $f(x) = ax^2 + bx + c$:

   • If $a > 0$, the parabola opens upward.

   • If $a < 0$, the parabola opens downward.

   The magnitude of a affects the width of the parabola. The larger the absolute value of a, the narrower the parabola.

4. If $b = 0$, the turning point of the parabola is located on the y-axis. If $b \neq 0$, the turning point will not be on the y-axis.

5. The constant term, c, of a quadratic function $y = ax^2 + bx + c$ always indicates the y-intercept of the parabola. The y-intercept of any quadratic function is $(0, c)$.

EXERCISES
Activity 3.2

1. **a.** Complete the following table for $y = x^2$:

x	y
−3	
−2	
−1	
0	
1	
2	
3	

   b. Use the results of part a to sketch a graph $y = x^2$.

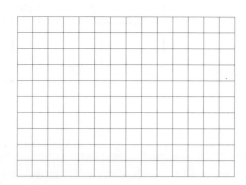

   c. Use your graphing calculator to compare and check the information for parts a and b. Are the graphs the same?

   d. What is the coefficient of the term x^2?

   e. From the graph, determine the domain and range of the quadratic function.

2. a. Create a table similar to the one in Exercise 1a for $y = -x^2$.

x	-3	-2	-1	0	1	2	3
y							

b. Sketch the graph of $y = -x^2$.

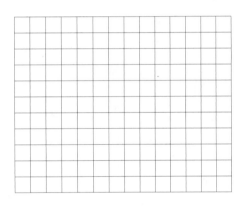

c. Use your graphing calculator to compare and check the information for parts a and b. Are the graphs the same?

d. What is the coefficient of the term $-x^2$?

e. How can the graph of $y = -x^2$ be obtained from the graph of $y = x^2$?

3. In each of the following functions defined by an equation of the form $y = ax^2 + bx + c$, identify the value of a, b, and c.

a. $y = -2x^2$

b. $y = \frac{2}{5}x^2 + 3$

c. $y = -x^2 + 5x$

d. $y = 5x^2 + 2x - 1$

4. Predict what the graph of each of the following quadratic functions will look like. Use your graphing calculator to verify your prediction.

a. $y = 3x^2 + 5$ **b.** $y = -2x^2 + 1$

   c. $y = 0.5x^2 - 3$

5. Graph the following pairs of quadratic functions and describe any similarities as well as any differences that you observe in the graphs:

   a. $f(x) = 3x^2, g(x) = -3x^2$ **b.** $h(x) = \frac{1}{2}x^2, f(x) = 2x^2$

   c. $g(x) = 5x^2, h(x) = 5x^2 + 2$ **d.** $f(x) = 4x^2 - 3, g(x) = 4x^2 + 3$

   e. $f(x) = 6x^2 + 1, h(x) = -6x^2 - 1$

6. Use your graphing calculator to graph the two functions $y_1 = 3x^2$ and $y_2 = 3x^2 + 2x - 2$.

   a. What is the vertical intercept of the graph of each function?

   b. Compare the two graphs to determine the effect of the linear term $2x$ and the constant term -2 on the graph of $y_1 = 3x^2$.

For Exercises 7–11, determine
   a. whether the parabola opens upward or downward and
   b. the y-intercept.

   7. $y = -5x^2 + 2x - 4$ **8.** $y = \frac{1}{2}x^2 + x$

9. $y = 2v^2 + v + 3$ **10.** $y = 3x^2 + 10$

11. $y = -x^2 + 6x - 7$

12. Does the graph of $y = -2x^2 + 3x - 4$ have any x-intercepts? Explain.

13. a. Is the graph of $y = \dfrac{3}{5}x^2$ wider or narrower than the graph of $y = x^2$?

   b. For the same x-value, which graph would have a larger y-value?

14. Put the following in order from narrowest to widest.
   a. $y = 0.5x^2$ **b.** $y = 8x^2$ **c.** $y = -2.3x^2$

15. Use transformations of the graph of $y = x^2$ to obtain a graph of each of the following. Verify using a graphing calculator.
   a. $y = -0.5x^2$

   b. $y = 2x^2 + 3$

   c. $y = -5x^2 - 2$

   d. $y = x^2 + 2x + 1$ *Note:* $x^2 + 2x + 1 = (x + 1)^2$

ACTIVITY 3.3
The Shot Put

OBJECTIVES

1. Determine the vertex or turning point of a parabola.

2. Identify the vertex as a maximum or minimum.

3. Determine the axis of symmetry of a parabola.

4. Identify the domain and range.

5. Determine the y-intercept of a parabola.

6. Determine the x-intercept(s) of a parabola using technology.

7. Interpret the practical meaning of the vertex and intercepts in a given problem.

8. Identify the vertex from the standard form $y = a(x - h)^2 + k$ of the equation of a parabola.

Parabolas are good models for a variety of situations that you encounter in everyday life. Examples include the path of a golf ball after it is struck, the arch (cable system) of a bridge, the path of a baseball thrown from the outfield to home plate, the stream of water from a drinking fountain, and the path of a cliff diver.

Consider the 2008 men's Olympic shot put event, which was won by Poland's Tomasz Majewski with a throw of 70.57 feet. The path of his winning throw can be approximately modeled by the quadratic function defined by

$$y = -0.015375x^2 + x + 6,$$

where x is the horizontal distance in feet from the point of the throw and y is the vertical height in feet of the shot above the ground.

1. **a.** After inspecting the equation for the path of the winning throw, which way do you expect the parabola to open? Explain.

   b. What is the y-intercept of the graph of the parabola? What practical meaning does this intercept have in this situation?

2. Use your graphing calculator to produce a plot of the path of the winning throw. Be sure to adjust your window settings so that all of the important features of the parabola (including x-intercepts) appear on the screen. Your graph should resemble the following:

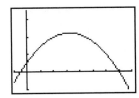

3. From the graph, what are the appropriate values for x (practical domain), and y (practical range)?

4. Use the table feature of your graphing calculator to complete the following table:

x	10	20	30	40	50
y					

Vertex of a Parabola

An important feature of the graph of any quadratic function defined by $f(x) = ax^2 + bx + c$ is its **turning point**, also called the **vertex**. The turning point of a parabola that opens downward or upward is the point at which the parabola changes direction from increasing to decreasing or decreasing to increasing.

5. a. Use the results of Problem 4 to estimate the coordinates of the vertex of the shot put function.

b. Use the Trace feature of your graphing calculator to approximate the vertex of the shot put function.

6. The vertex is often very important in a situation. What is the significance of the coordinates of the turning point in this problem?

The coordinates of the vertex of a parabola having equation $y = ax^2 + bx + c$ can be determined from the values of a and b in the equation.

DEFINITION

The **vertex** or turning point of a parabola having equation $y = ax^2 + bx + c$ has coordinates

$$\left(-\frac{b}{2a}, -\frac{b^2 - 4ac}{4a}\right),$$

where a is the coefficient of the x^2 term and b is the coefficient of the x term.

Note that the y-coordinate of the vertex is determined by substituting the x-coordinate of the vertex into the equation of the parabola and evaluating the resulting expression.

Example 1   *Determine the vertex of the parabola defined by the equation* $y = -3x^2 + 12x + 5.$

SOLUTION

Step 1. Determine the x-coordinate of the vertex by substituting the values of a and b into the formula $x = \frac{-b}{2a}$.

Because $a = -3$ and $b = 12$, you have

$$x = \frac{-(12)}{2(-3)} = \frac{-12}{-6} = 2.$$

Step 2. The y-coordinate of the vertex can be determined two ways.

i. Substitute $a = -3$, $b = 12$, and $c = 5$ into the expression $-\dfrac{b^2 - 4ac}{4a}$ and evaluate as follows.

$$-\frac{12^2 - 4(-3)(5)}{4(-3)} = -\frac{144 + 60}{-12} = \frac{-204}{-12} = 17$$

ii. The y-value of the vertex is the corresponding output value for $x = 2$. Substituting 2 for x in the equation, you have

$$y = -3(2)^2 + 12(2) + 5 = 17.$$

Therefore, the vertex is (2, 17).

Because the parabola in Example 1 opens downward ($a = -3 < 0$), the vertex is the high point (maximum) of the parabola as demonstrated by the following graph of the parabola.

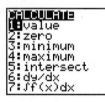

7. Determine the vertex of the parabola defined by $y = -0.015375x^2 + x + 6$ (the shot put function).

Rather than using the Trace feature to approximate the vertex of the parabola in Example 1, you can determine the vertex by selecting the maximum option in the Calc menu of your graphing calculator. Follow the prompts to obtain the coordinates of the maximum point (vertex).

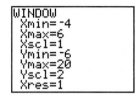 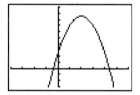

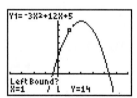 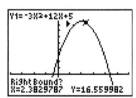

 For further help with the TI-83/84 Plus, see Appendix A.

8. a. Use your graphing calculator to determine the vertex of the parabola having equation $y = -0.015375x^2 + x + 6$ (the shot put function).

b. How do the coordinates you determined using the formula (see Problem 7) compare with your results in part a?

c. What is the practical meaning of the coordinates of the vertex in this situation?

Axis of Symmetry of a Parabola

> **DEFINITION**
>
> The **axis of symmetry** is a vertical line that divides the parabola into two symmetrical parts that are mirror images in the line.

Example 2 *Consider the parabola from Example 1 having equation* $y = -3x^2 + 12x + 5$. *The axis of symmetry of the parabola is* $x = 2$. *Note that the line of symmetry passes through the vertex of the parabola.*

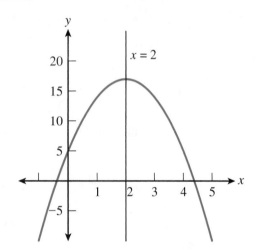

The vertex (turning point) of a parabola lies on the axis of symmetry. Because the x-value of the vertex is $x = \dfrac{-b}{2a}$, the equation of the axis of symmetry is

$$x = \frac{-b}{2a}.$$

9. What is the axis of symmetry of the shot put function?

Intercepts of the Graph of a Parabola

The y-intercept of the graph of the parabola defined by $y = -3x^2 + 12x + 5$ (see Example 1) can be determined directly from the equation. If $x = 0$, then

$$y = -3(0)^2 + 12(0) + 5 = 5$$

and the y-intercept is $(0, 5)$.

In general, the y-intercept of the parabola defined by $y = ax^2 + bx + c$ is $(0, c)$.

Because the vertex (2, 17) of the parabola having equation $y = -3x^2 + 12x + 5$ is a point above the x-axis (the y-coordinate is positive) and the parabola opens downward, the parabola must intersect the x-axis in two places. This is verified by the following graph:

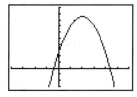

Appendix

The x-intercepts can be determined using the zero option in the Calc menu of the TI-83/84 Plus calculator (see Appendix A for details). Follow the prompts to obtain one x-intercept at a time. The screens should appear as follows:

   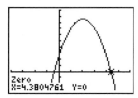   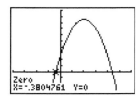

10. a. Use the zero option of your graphing calculator to determine the x-intercept(s) for the shot put function having equation $y = -0.015375x^2 + x + 6$. The right-most intercept appears in the following screen:

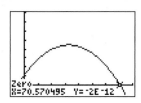

   b. Is either x-intercept determined in part a significant to the problem situation? Explain.

The graph of $y = -0.015375x^2 + x + 6$ has two x-intercepts. Does the graph of every parabola have x-intercepts? Problems 11 and 12 will help answer this question.

11. a. Use the values of a, b, and c to determine the coordinates of the vertex of the graph of $y = x^2 + 6x + 12$.

   b. Use the y-coordinate of the vertex to determine if the vertex is above or below the x-axis.

   c. Use the value of a in $y = x^2 + 6x + 12$ to determine if the parabola opens upward or downward.

d. Use the results from parts b and c to determine if the parabola has x-intercepts.

e. Use your graphing calculator to verify your answer to part d.

12. a. Use the values of a, b, and c to determine the coordinates of the vertex of the graph of $y = -x^2 + 8x - 21$.

b. Use the y-coordinate of the vertex to determine if the vertex is above or below the x-axis.

c. Use the value of a in $y = -x^2 + 8x - 21$ to determine if the parabola opens upward or downward.

d. Use the results from parts b and c to determine if the parabola has x-intercepts.

e. Use your graphing calculator to verify your answer to part d.

If a parabola opens upward and the vertex is above the x-axis, there are no x-intercepts. If a parabola opens downward and the vertex is below the x-axis, there are no x-intercepts.

13. a. Use your result from Problem 10 to determine the practical domain of the shot put function. How does this compare with your answer in Problem 3?

b. Sketch the path of the winning throw of the shot put. Be sure to label all key points, including the vertex and intercepts.

c. From the graph of the winning throw, over what horizontal distance (x-interval) is the height of the shot put increasing?

d. Determine the x-interval over which the height of the shot put is decreasing.

e. What is the practical range?

14. Now consider the function $y = -0.015375x^2 + x + 6$ as a general function that is not restricted by the physical situation in the activity.

a. What is the domain of the general function?

b. Over what x-interval does the general function increase?

c. Over what x-interval does the general function decrease?

d. What is the range?

Standard Form of an Equation of a Quadradic Function

15. a. Sketch a graph of the quadratic function defined by $y = 3x^2$.

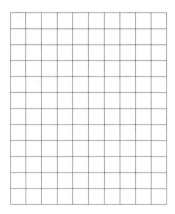

b. The graph of $y = 3x^2$ is shifted horizontally 2 units to the right. Sketch a graph of the new function. Write the equation of the transformed graph.

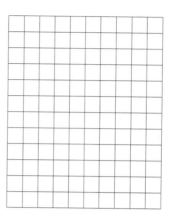

c. On the same coordinate axis, shift the graph in part b vertically 5 units upward. Write the equation of this new graph.

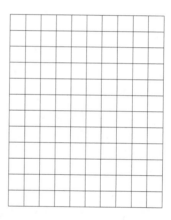

d. What is the vertex of the original parabola having equation $y = 3x^2$?

e. What is the vertex of the transformed parabola in part c?

The shift of the graph of $y = 3x^2$ horizontally 2 units to the right, followed by a vertical shift 5 units upward, moved the vertex of the parabola from $(0, 0)$ to $(2, 5)$. The resulting equation of the new parabola, $y = 3(x - 2)^2 + 5$, represents another way of writing the equation of a quadratic function.

> If (h, k) represents the vertex of a parabola, then $y = f(x) = a(x - h)^2 + k$, $a \neq 0$, is another form of the equation of a quadratic function. This form is especially convenient because the vertex (h, k) of the parabola is easily identified.

16. Determine the vertex of the graph of each of the following parabolas.

   a. $y = -2(x - 3)^2 + 4$

b. $y = 1.25(x + 4)^2 + 3$

c. $y = -3(x + 2)^2 - 4.5$

The sign of a in $y = f(x) = a(x - h)^2 + k$, as in $y = g(x) = ax^2$, determines the direction in which the parabola opens. If $a > 0$, then the parabola opens upward. If $a < 0$, the parabola opens downward.

17. a. Graph the quadratic function defined by $y = f(x) = 3(x - 1)^2 + 2$. Be sure to identify the vertex and y-intercept.

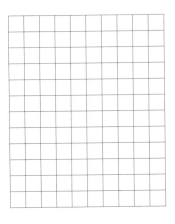

b. Graph the quadratic function defined by $y = g(x) = 3x^2 - 6x + 5$.

c. Compare the graphs in parts a and b.

d. Write the equation $y = 3(x - 1)^2 + 2$ in the form of $y = ax^2 + bx + c$. How does this equation compare to the equation of the parabola in part b?

SUMMARY
Activity 3.3

The following characteristics are commonly used in analyzing the quadratic function defined by $f(x) = ax^2 + bx + c, a \neq 0$, and its graph.

1. The **axis of symmetry** is a vertical line that separates the parabola into two mirror images. The equation of the vertical axis of symmetry is given by $x = \frac{-b}{2a}$.

2. The **vertex** (turning point) always falls on the axis of symmetry. The x-coordinate of the vertex is given by $\frac{-b}{2a}$. Its y-coordinate is determined by evaluating the function at this value. In other words, the y-coordinate of the vertex is given by $f\left(-\frac{b}{2a}\right)$.

3. If the parabola changes from increasing to decreasing at the turning point, then the vertex is a maximum point. If the parabola changes from decreasing to increasing at the turning point, then the vertex is a minimum point.

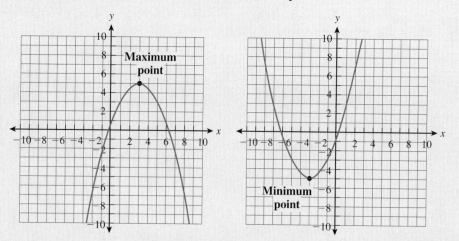

4. The **y-intercept**, the point where the parabola crosses the y-axis (that is, where its x-coordinate is zero), is always given by $(0, c)$.

5. The **x-intercept** is the point or points (if any) where the parabola crosses the x-axis (that is, where its y-coordinate is zero).

6. If a parabola opens upward and the vertex is above the x-axis, there are no x-intercepts. If a parabola opens downward and the vertex is below the x-axis, there are no x-intercepts.

7. The **domain** of the general quadratic function is the set of all real numbers.

8. If the parabola opens upward, the **range** is all real numbers greater than or equal to the y-value of the vertex. If the parabola opens downward, the *range* is all real numbers less than or equal to the y-value of the vertex.

9. The equation of a quadratic function can be written in the form $y = f(x) = a(x - h)^2 + k$, where (h, k) is the vertex and $a \neq 0$.

EXERCISES
Activity 3.3

For Exercises 1–8, determine the following characteristics of each quadratic function:

   a. the direction in which the graph opens

   b. the axis of symmetry

   c. the turning point (vertex); determine if maximum or minimum

   d. the y-intercept

1. $f(x) = x^2 - 3$

2. $g(x) = x^2 + 2x - 8$

3. $y = x^2 + 4x - 3$

4. $f(x) = 3x^2 - 2x$

5. $h(x) = x^2 + 3x + 4$

6. $g(x) = -x^2 + 7x - 6$

7. $y = 2x^2 - x - 3$

8. $f(x) = x^2 + x + 3$

For Exercises 9–16, use your graphing calculator to sketch the graphs of the functions and then determine each of the following:

   a. the coordinates of the x-intercepts for each function, if they exist

   b. the domain and range for each function

   c. the x-interval over which each function is increasing

   d. the x-interval over which each function is decreasing

9. $g(x) = -x^2 + 7x - 6$

10. $h(x) = 3x^2 + 6x + 4$

11. $y = x^2 - 12$

12. $f(x) = x^2 + 4x - 5$

13. $g(x) = -x^2 + 2x + 3$

14. $h(x) = x^2 + 2x - 8$

15. $y = -5x^2 + 6x - 1$

16. $f(x) = 3x^2 - 2x + 1$

17. You shoot an arrow straight into the air from a height of 5 feet with an initial velocity of 96 feet per second. The height, h, in feet above the ground, at any time, t (in seconds), is modeled by

$$h = 5 + 96t - 16t^2.$$

a. Determine the maximum height the arrow will attain.

b. Approximately when will the arrow reach the ground?

c. What is the significance of the h-intercept?

d. What are the practical domain and practical range in this situation?

e. Use your graphing calculator to determine the t-intercepts. Determine the practical meaning of these intercepts in this situation.

18. The city of Clewiston, Florida, plans to enclose a rectangular area along the waterfront of Lake Okeechobee and create a park and recreation area. The budget calls for the purchase of 3000 feet of fencing. *Note:* There is no fencing along the lake.

a. Draw a picture of the planned recreational area. Let x represent the length of one of the two equal sides that are perpendicular to the water.

b. Write an expression that represents the width (side opposite the water) in terms of x. *Note:* You have 3000 feet of fencing.

c. Write an equation that expresses the area A of this rectangular site as a quadratic function of x.

d. Determine the value of x for which A is a maximum.

e. What is the maximum area that can be enclosed?

f. What are the dimensions of the enclosed area?

g. Use your graphing calculator to graph the area function. What point on the graph represents the maximum area?

h. What is the A-intercept? Does this point have any practical meaning in this situation?

i. From the graph, determine the x-intercepts. Do they have any practical meaning in this situation? Explain.

19. The cost to produce metal statues for local parks is given by

$$C = 2x^2 - 120x + 2000,$$

where x represents the number of statues produced and C is the cost of producing them.

a. Use your graphing calculator to graph the cost function and determine the coordinates of the turning point.

b. Determine the vertex algebraically.

c. How do your answers in parts a and b compare?

d. Is the vertex a minimum or maximum point?

e. What is the practical meaning of the vertex in this situation?

f. What is the C-intercept? What is the practical meaning of this intercept?

20. You are manufacturing ceramic lawn ornaments. After several months, your accountant tells you that your profit P can be modeled by

$$P = -0.002n^2 + 5.5n - 1200,$$

where n is the number of ornaments sold each month.

a. Use your graphing calculator to produce a graph of this function. Use the table feature set at TblStart $= 0$ and ΔTbl $= 500$ to help you set your window. Include the n-intercepts and the vertex.

b. Determine the n-intercepts of the graph of the profit function.

c. Determine the practical domain of the profit function.

d. Determine the practical range of the profit function.

e. How many ornaments must be sold to maximize the profit?

f. Write the equation that must be solved to determine the number of ornaments that must be sold to produce a profit of $2300.

g. Solve the equation in part f graphically.

ACTIVITY 3.4

Per Capita
Personal Income

OBJECTIVES

1. Solve quadratic equations numerically.

2. Solve quadratic equations graphically.

3. Determine the zeros of a function using technology.

According to statistics from the U.S. Department of Commerce, the per capita personal income (or the average annual income) of each resident of the United States from 1960 to 2000 can be modeled by the equation

$$P = 15.1442x^2 + 98.7687x + 1831.6909,$$

where P represents the per capita income and x represents the number of years since 1960.

1. What is the practical domain for the model represented by the quadratic function?

2. Let $x = 0$ correspond to the year 1960. Use a graphing calculator to complete the following table of values for x, the number of years since 1960, and P, the per capita income. Round the output to the nearest dollar.

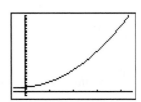

Earning Your Keep

YEAR	1960	1965	1970	1975	1980	1985	1990	1995	2000
x									
P ($)									

3. Sketch a graph of the function using a graphing calculator using the window Xmin = −5, Xmax = 45, Ymin = −2000, and Ymax = 35,000. The graph should appear as follows:

4. Estimate the per capita personal income in the year 1989 ($x = 29$).

5. You want to determine in which year the per capita personal income reached $20,500. Write an equation to determine the value of x when $P = 20,500$.

The equation in Problem 5 is called a **quadratic equation**. The standard form of a quadratic equation is $ax^2 + bx + c = 0$, $a \neq 0$. Examples of quadratic equations include $x^2 + 3x - 1 = 9$, $2x^2 - 4x + 1 = 0$, and $6x^2 = 18$.

One method of approximating a solution to an equation is numerical, using a table of appropriate data points. Example 1 demonstrates this method.

Example 1 *Solve the quadratic equation $x^2 + 3x - 1 = 9$ numerically (using tables of data).*

SOLUTION

Create a table in which x is the input and $y = x^2 + 3x - 1$ is the output. The solution is the x-value corresponding to a y-value of 9. Using the graphing calculator, one solution is $x = 2$.

A second solution is $x = -5$, try it for yourself.

6. Determine the solution to $20{,}500 = 15.1442x^2 + 98.7687x + 1831.6909$ numerically using a table of appropriate data points (see Problem 2). What is your approximation using this approach?

Solving Quadratic Equations Graphically

A second method of solving the quadratic equation in Problem 5 is graphical, using a graphing calculator. Recall that you can solve the equation $15.1442x^2 + 98.7687x + 1831.6909 = 20{,}500$ by solving the following system of equations graphically:

$$y_1 = 15.1442x^2 + 98.7687x + 1831.6909$$
$$y_2 = 20{,}500$$

The expression for y_1 gives the per capita personal income in any given year. The value y_2 is the specific per capita personal income in which you are interested. The solution to the equation is the x-value for which $y_1 = y_2$. To do this, determine the point of intersection of these two graphs. If you use the intersect option under the Calc menu, the graph should appear as follows:

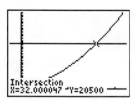

Another graphical method for solving the problem is to rearrange the quadratic equation

$$20{,}500 = 15.1442x^2 + 98.7687x + 1831.6909$$

so that the left-hand side is equal to zero. Subtracting 20,500 from each side, you have

$$0 = 15.1442x^2 + 98.7687x - 18{,}668.3091. \quad \text{(eq. 1)}$$

If you let $y = 15.1442x^2 + 98.7687x - 18{,}668.3091$, then the solution to the equation 1 is the x-value for which $y = 0$, if it exists. This is the x-value of the x-intercept of the graph, also called the **zero of the function**.

7. a. Use your graphing calculator to sketch a graph of
$$y = 15.1442x^2 + 98.7687x - 18{,}668.3091.$$

The graph should appear as follows:

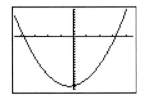

b. What are the x-intercepts of the new function defined by
$y = 15.1442x^2 + 98.7687x - 18{,}668.3091$?

c. Using the results from part b, determine the solutions to the equation $20{,}500 = 15.1442x^2 + 98.7687x + 1831.6989$. Are both of the values relevant to our problem? Explain.

8. Describe two different ways to solve the equation $2x^2 - 4x + 3 = 2$ using a graphing approach. Solve the equation using each graphing method. How do your answers compare?

SUMMARY
Activity 3.4

1. A **quadratic equation** is an equation having standard form $ax^2 + bx + c = 0$, $a \neq 0$.

2. To solve $f(x) = n$ **numerically**, construct a table for $y = f(x)$, and determine the x-values that produce n as y-value.

3. To solve $f(x) = n$ **graphically**:

   a. Graph $y_1 = f(x)$, graph $y_2 = n$, and determine the x-values of the points of intersection. ·

   b. Or graph $y = f(x) - n$, and determine the x-values of the x-intercepts of the graph (zeros of the function) using a graphing calculator.

In Exercises 1–4, solve the quadratic equation numerically (using tables of x- and y-values). Verify your solutions graphically.

1. $-4x = -x^2 + 12$

2. $x^2 + 9x + 18 = 0$

3. $2x^2 = 8x + 90$

4. $x^2 - x - 3 = 0$

In Exercises 5–8, solve the quadratic equation graphically using at least two different approaches. When necessary, give your solutions to the nearest hundredth.

5. $x^2 + 12x + 11 = 0$

6. $2x^2 - 3 = 2x$

7. $16x^2 - 400 = 0$

8. $4x^2 + 12x = -4$

In Exercises 9–12, solve the equation by using either a numeric or a graphic approach.

9. $x^2 + 2x - 3 = 0$

10. $x^2 + 11x + 24 = 0$

11. $x^2 - 2x - 8 = x + 20$

12. $x^2 - 10x + 6 = 5x - 50$

13. The stopping distance, d (in feet), for a car moving at a velocity (speed) v miles per hour is modeled by the equation

$$d = 0.04v^2 + 1.1v.$$

a. What is the stopping distance for a velocity of 55 miles per hour?

b. What is the speed of the car if it takes 200 feet to stop?

14. An international rule for determining the number, n, of board feet (usable finished lumber) in a 16-foot log is modeled by the equation

$$n = 0.22d^2 - 0.71d,$$

where d is the diameter of the log in inches.

a. How many board feet can be obtained from a 16-foot log with a 14-inch diameter?

b. Sketch a graph of this function. What is the practical domain of this function?

c. Use the graph to approximate the *d*-intercept(s). What is the practical meaning in this situation?

d. What is the diameter of a 16-foot log that has 200 board feet?

ACTIVITY 3.5
Sir Isaac Newton

OBJECTIVES

1. Factor expressions by removing the greatest common factor.

2. Factor trinomials using trial and error.

3. Use the zero-product principle to solve equations.

4. Solve quadratic equations by factoring.

Sir Isaac Newton XIV, a descendant of the famous physicist and mathematician, takes you to the top of a building to demonstrate a physics property discovered by his famous ancestor. He throws a softball straight up into the air. The ball's distance, s, above the ground as a function of time, x, is modeled by

$$s = -16x^2 + 16x + 32.$$

1. When the ball strikes the ground, what is the value of s?

2. Write the equation that you must solve to determine when the ball strikes the ground.

The quadratic equation in Problem 2 can be solved by using a numerical or a graphical approach. However, an algebraic technique is efficient in this case and will give an exact answer. The algorithm is based on the algebraic principle known as the **zero-product principle**.

Zero-Product Principle

If a and b are any numbers and $a \cdot b = 0$, then either a or b, or both, must be equal to zero.

Example 1   *Solve the equation $x(x + 5) = 0$.*

SOLUTION

The two factors in this equation are x and $x + 5$. The zero-product principle says one of these factors must equal zero. That is,

$$x = 0 \quad \text{or} \quad x + 5 = 0.$$

The first equation tells you that $x = 0$ is a solution. To determine a second solution, solve $x + 5 = 0$.

$$\begin{array}{r} x + 5 = 0 \\ \underline{-5 \quad -5} \\ x = -5 \end{array}$$

There are two solutions, $x = 0$ and $x = -5$.

Your graphing calculator verifies the solutions as follows.

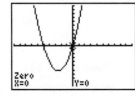 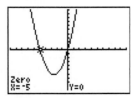

3. Solve each of the following equations using the zero-product principle.

  a. $3x(x - 2) = 0$ **b.** $(2x - 3)(x + 2) = 0$

c. $(x + 2)(x + 3) = 0$

For the zero-product principle to be applied, one side of the equation must be zero. Therefore, at first glance, the zero-product principle can be used to solve the quadratic equation $3x^2 - 6x = 0$. However, a second condition must be satisfied. The nonzero side of the equation must be written as a product.

The process of writing an expression such as $3x^2 - 6x$ as a product is called *factoring*.

>
> **DEFINITION**
> Rewriting an expression as a product is called **factoring**.

Factoring Common Factors

A **common factor** is a number or an expression that is a factor of each term of the entire expression. Whenever you wish to factor a polynomial, look first for a common factor.

> **PROCEDURE**
> **Removing a Common Factor from a Polynomial:** First, identify the common factor, and then apply the distributive property in reverse.

Example 2   *Given the binomial $3x + 6$, 3 is a common factor because 3 is a factor of both terms $3x$ and 6. Applying the distributive property in reverse, you write*

$$3x + 6 \text{ as } 3(x + 2).$$

You may always check the factored binomial by multiplying:

$$3(x + 2) = 3(x) + 3(2) = 3x + 6$$

When you look for a common factor, determine the largest or **greatest common factor** (or GCF). You can see that 3 is a common factor of $6x + 24$ because 3 is a factor of both 6 and 24. However, there is a larger common factor, 6. Therefore,

$$6x + 24 = 6(x + 4).$$

Example 3   *Given $6x^2 + 14x - 30$, you can see that 2 is a common factor. Is 2 the greatest common factor? Yes, because no larger number is a factor of every term.*

If you divide each term by 2, you obtain $3x^2 + 7x - 15$. The expression $6x^2 + 14x - 30$ can now be written in factored form as $2(3x^2 + 7x - 15)$. Check the factored trinomial by multiplying.

Example 4 *Factor $4x^3 - 8x^2 + 28x$.*

SOLUTION

Four is a factor of each term, but x is as well. Therefore, the greatest common factor is $4x$. You remove the GCF by dividing each term by $4x$. This leads to the factored form $4x(x^2 - 2x + 7)$.

You can check your factoring by applying the distributive property.

4. Factor the following polynomials by removing the greatest common factor.

   a. $9a^6 + 18a^2$ **b.** $21xy^3 + 7xy$

   c. $3x^2 - 21x + 33$ **d.** $4x^3 - 16x^2 - 24x$

Factoring Trinomials

With patience, you can factor trinomials of the form $ax^2 + bx + c$ by trial and error, using the FOIL method in reverse.

PROCEDURE: Factoring Trinomials by Trial and Error

1. Remove the greatest common factor, GCF.

2. To factor the resulting trinomial into the product of two binomials, try combinations of factors for the first and last terms in two binomials.

3. Check the outer and inner products to match the middle term of the original trinomial.

   a. If the constant term, c, is positive, both of its factors are positive or both are negative.

   b. If the constant term is negative, one factor is positive and one is negative.

4. If the check fails, repeat steps 2 and 3.

Example 5 *Factor $6x^2 - 7x - 3$.*

SOLUTION

Step 1. There is no common factor, so go to step 2.

Step 2. You could factor the first term, $6x^2$, as $6x(x)$ or as $2x(3x)$. The last term, -3, has factors $3(-1)$ or $-3(1)$. Try $(2x + 1)(3x - 3)$.

Step 3. The outer product is $-6x$. The inner product is $3x$. The sum is $-3x$, not $7x$. The check fails.

Step 4. Try $(2x - 3)(3x + 1)$. The outer product is $2x$. The inner product is $-9x$. The sum is $-7x$. It checks.

5. Factor the following trinomials.

    a. $x^2 - 7x + 12$ **b.** $x^2 - 8x - 9$

    c. $x^2 + 14x + 49$ **d.** $25 + 10w + w^2$

Solving Quadratic Equations by Factoring

The following example demonstrates the procedure for solving quadratic equations written in standard form, $ax^2 + bx + c = 0$, by factoring.

Example 6   *Solve the equation $3x^2 - 2 = -x$ by factoring.*

Step 1. Rewrite the equation in the form $ax^2 + bx + c = 0$ (called *standard form*).

$$3x^2 - 2 = -x$$
$$\underline{+ x \qquad\qquad + x}$$
$$3x^2 + x - 2 = 0$$

Step 2. Factor the expression on the nonzero side of the equation.

$$(x + 1)(3x - 2) = 0$$

Step 3. Use the zero-product principle to set each factor equal to zero, and then solve each equation.

$$(x + 1)(3x - 2) = 0$$

$$
\begin{array}{c|c}
x + 1 = 0 & 3x - 2 = 0 \\
x = -1 & 3x = 2 \\
& x = \frac{2}{3}
\end{array}
$$

Therefore, the solutions are $x = -1$ and $x = \frac{2}{3}$.

These solutions can be verified graphically as follows.

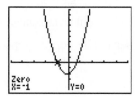 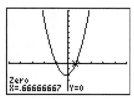

6. a. Returning to the ball problem from the beginning of this activity, solve the equation from Problem 2 by factoring.

    b. Are both solutions to the equation ($x = 2$ and $x = -1$) also solutions to the question, "At what time does the ball strike the ground"? Explain.

7. a. You want to know at what time the ball is 32 feet above the ground. Write a quadratic equation that represents this situation.

b. Solve the quadratic equation in part a by factoring.

8. Solve each of the following quadratic equations by factoring.

a. $2x^2 - x - 6 = 0$ **b.** $3x^2 - 6x = 0$

c. $x^2 + 4x = -x - 6$

9. Determine the zeros of the function defined by $f(x) = 2x^2 - 3x - 2$.

SUMMARY
Activity 3.5

1. To remove a **common factor** from a polynomial, first
  a. identify the common factor, and then
  b. apply the distributive property in reverse.

2. The **zero-product principle** says that if $ab = 0$ is a true statement, then either $a = 0$ or $b = 0$.

3. To factor trinomials of the form $ax^2 + bx + c$ by **trial and error**,
  a. remove the greatest common factor.
  b. try combinations of factors for the first and last terms in two binomials.
  c. check the outer and inner products to match the middle term of the original trinomial.

   • If the constant term, c, is positive, both factors of c are positive or both are negative.

   • If the constant term is negative, one factor is positive and one is negative.
  d. If the check fails, repeat steps 3b and 3c.

4. To solve equations by **factoring**,

   a. use the addition principle to remove all terms from one side of the equation; this results in a polynomial being set equal to zero.

   b. combine like terms, and then factor the nonzero side of the equation.

   c. use the zero-product principle to set each factor containing a variable equal to zero, and then solve the equations.

   d. check your solutions in the original equation.

EXERCISES
Activity 3.5

In Exercises 1–4, factor the polynomials by removing the GCF (greatest common factor).

1. $12x^5 - 18x^8$

2. $14x^6y^3 - 6x^2y^4$

3. $2x^3 - 14x^2 + 26x$

4. $5x^3 - 20x^2 - 35x$

In Exercises 5–13, completely factor the polynomials. Remember to look first for the GCF.

5. $x^2 + x - 6$

6. $p^2 - 16p + 48$

7. $x^2 + 7xy + 10y^2$

8. $x^2 - 4x - 32$

9. $12 + 8x + x^2$

10. $2x^2 + 7x - 15$

11. $3x^2 + 19x - 14$

12. $8x^4 - 47x^3 - 6x^2$

13. $20b^4 - 65b^3 - 60b^2$

In Exercises 14–21, solve each quadratic equation by factoring.

14. $x^2 - 5x + 6 = 0$

15. $x^2 + 2x - 3 = 0$

16. $x^2 - x = 6$

17. $x^2 - 5x = 14$

18. $3x^2 + 11x - 4 = 0$

19. $3x^2 - 12x = 0$

20. $x^2 - 7x = 18$

21. $3x(x - 6) - 5(x - 6) = 0$

22. Your neighbors have just finished installing a new swimming pool at their home. The pool measures 15 feet by 20 feet. They would like to plant a strip of grass of uniform width around three sides of the pool, the two short sides and one of the longer sides.

a. Sketch a diagram of the pool and the strip of lawn, using x to represent the width of the uniform strip.

b. Write an equation for the area, A, in terms of x that represents the lawn area around the pool.

c. They have enough seed for 168 square feet of lawn. Write an equation that relates the quantity of seed to the area of the uniform strip of lawn.

d. Solve the equation in part c to determine the width of the uniform strip that can be seeded.

ACTIVITY 3.6

Ups and Downs

OBJECTIVES

1. Use the quadratic formula to solve quadratic equations.

2. Identify the solutions of a quadratic equation with points on the corresponding graph.

3. Determine the zeros of a function.

Suppose a soccer goalie punted the ball in such a way as to kick the ball as far as possible down the field. The height of the ball above the field as a function of time can be approximated by

$$y = -0.017x^2 + 0.98x + 0.33,$$

where y represents the height of the ball (in yards) and x represents the horizontal distance (in yards) down the field from where the goalie kicked the ball.

In this situation, the graph of $y = -0.017x^2 + 0.98x + 0.33$ is the actual path of the flight of the soccer ball. The graph of this function appears below:

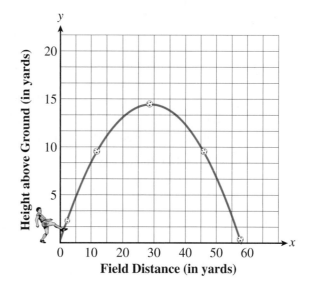

1. Use the graph to estimate how far downfield from the point of contact the soccer ball is 10 yards above the ground. How often during its flight does this occur?

2. **a.** Use $y = -0.017x^2 + 0.98x + 0.33$ to write the quadratic equation that arises in determining when the ball is 10 yards above the ground.

   b. Rewrite the equation in standard form and simplify if possible.

   c. What does the graph tell you about the number of solutions to this equation?

By some straightforward (but somewhat involved) algebraic manipulations, a quadratic equation can be turned into a formula that produces the solutions. This formula is called the **quadratic formula**.

> **The Quadratic Formula**
>
> For a quadratic equation in standard form, $ax^2 + bx + c = 0$, $a \neq 0$, the solutions are
>
> $$x = \frac{-b \pm \sqrt{b^2 - 4 \cdot a \cdot c}}{2 \cdot a}.$$
>
> The $\pm$ in the formula indicates that there are two solutions, one in which the terms in the numerator are added, and another in which the terms are subtracted.

When you use this formula, the quadratic equation *must* be in standard form so that the values (and signs) of the three coefficients a, b, and c are correct. You also want to be careful when you key the expression into your calculator. The square root and quotient computations need to be done carefully; you often must include appropriate sets of parentheses.

Example 1 *Use the quadratic formula to solve the quadratic equation $6x^2 - x = 2$.*

SOLUTION

$6x^2 - x - 2 = 0$ Write equation in standard form, $ax^2 + bx + c = 0$.

$a = 6, b = -1, c = -2$ Identify a, b, and c.

$x = \dfrac{-(-1) \pm \sqrt{(-1)^2 - 4(6)(-2)}}{2(6)}$ Substitute for a, b, and c in $x = \dfrac{-b \pm \sqrt{b^2 - 4ac}}{2a}$.

$x = \dfrac{1 \pm \sqrt{1 + 48}}{12} = \dfrac{1 \pm 7}{12}$

$x = \dfrac{1 + 7}{12} = \dfrac{2}{3}, x = \dfrac{1 - 7}{12} = \dfrac{-6}{12} = -\dfrac{1}{2}$

3. Use the quadratic formula to solve the quadratic equation in Problem 2b.

4. Solve $3x^2 + 20x + 7 = 0$ using the quadratic formula.

5. Determine the zeros of the function defined by $f(x) = -x^2 + 4x - 1$.

SUMMARY
Activity 3.6

The solutions of a quadratic equation in standard form, $ax^2 + bx + c = 0, a \neq 0$, are

$$x = \frac{-b \pm \sqrt{b^2 - 4 \cdot a \cdot c}}{2 \cdot a}.$$

The $\pm$ symbol in the formula indicates that there are two solutions, one in which the terms in the numerator are added and one in which the terms are subtracted.

EXERCISES
Activity 3.6

Use the quadratic formula to solve the equations in Exercises 1–5.

1. $x^2 + 2x - 15 = 0$ **2.** $4x^2 + 32x + 15 = 0$

3. $-2x^2 + x + 1 = 0$

4. $2x^2 + 7x = 0$ **5.** $-x^2 + 10x + 9 = 0$

6. a. Determine the x-intercepts, if any, of the graph of $y = x^2 - 2x + 5$.

b. Sketch the graph of $y = x^2 - 2x + 5$ using your graphing calculator and verify your answer to part a.

7. The following data from the National Health and Nutrition Examination Survey indicate that the number of American adults who are overweight or obese is increasing.

YEARS SINCE 1960, x	1	12	18	31	39
PERCENTAGE OF AMERICAN ADULTS WHO ARE OVERWEIGHT OR OBESE, P	45	47	47	56	64.5

The function defined by $P = 0.017x^2 - 0.174x + 45.493$ can be used to model these data.

a. Determine the percentage of overweight or obese Americans in the year 2015.

   b. Determine the year after 1960 when the model predicts that the percentage of overweight or obese Americans would have first exceeded 75%.

   c. Verify your results in part b using a graphing calculator.

8. The height of a bridge arch located in the Thousand Islands is modeled by the function $y = -0.04x^2 + 28$, where x is the distance, in feet, from the center of the arch and y is the height of the arch.

   a. Sketch a picture of this arch on a grid using the vertical axis as the center of the arch.

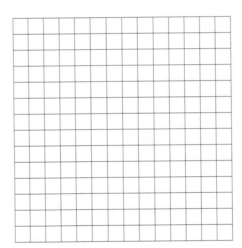

   b. Determine the y-intercept. What is the practical meaning of this intercept in this situation?

   c. Determine the x-intercepts algebraically using the quadratic formula.

d. Graph the function on your graphing calculator and check the accuracy of the intercepts you found in part c.

e. If the arch straddles the river exactly, how wide is the river?

f. A sailboat is approaching the bridge. The top of the mast measures 30 feet. Will the boat clear the bridge? Explain.

g. You want to install a flagpole on the bridge at an arch height of 20 feet. Write the equation that you must solve to determine how far to the right of center the arch height is 20 feet.

h. Solve the equation in part g using the quadratic formula. Use your graphing calculator to check your result.

9. The number, n (in millions), of cell phone subscribers in the United States from 1990 to 1999 is given in the following table:

YEAR	1990	1991	1992	1993	1994	1995	1996	1997	1998	1999
NUMBER OF SUBSCRIBERS (in millions)	5.28	7.56	11.03	16.01	24.13	33.79	44.04	55.31	69.20	86.05

This data can be approximated by the quadratic model

$$y = 0.846x^2 + 1.32x + 5.20,$$

where $x = 0$ corresponds to the year 1990.

a. Use your graphing calculator to sketch a graph of the function.

b. Use the graph in part a to estimate the year in which there will be 120 million cell phone subscribers.

c. Use the quadratic formula to answer part b. How does your answer compare to the estimate you obtained using a graphical approach?

d. How confident are you in your prediction? Explain.

You will return to the cell phone situation in the exercises of Activity 3.7.

ACTIVITY 3.7
Air Quality in
Atlanta

OBJECTIVES

1. Determine quadratic regression models using the graphing calculator.

2. Solve problems using quadratic regression models.

The Air Quality Index, or AQI, measures how polluted the air is by measuring five major pollutants: ground-level ozone, particulate matter, carbon monoxide, sulfur dioxide, and nitrogen oxide. Based on the amount of each pollutant in the air, the AQI assigns a numerical value to air quality, as follows.

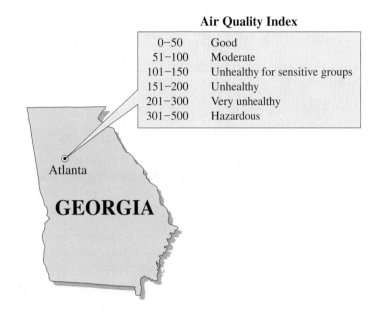

Air Quality Index

0–50	Good
51–100	Moderate
101–150	Unhealthy for sensitive groups
151–200	Unhealthy
201–300	Very unhealthy
301–500	Hazardous

Atlanta

GEORGIA

The following table indicates the number of days in which the AQI was greater than 100 in the city of Atlanta, Georgia.

YEAR	1990	1992	1994	1996	1998	1999
NUMBER OF DAYS AQI $>$ 100, n	42	20	15	25	50	61

1. Sketch a scatterplot of the data. Let t represent the number of years since 1990. Therefore, $t = 0$ corresponds to the year 1990. Does the data appear to be quadratic? Explain.

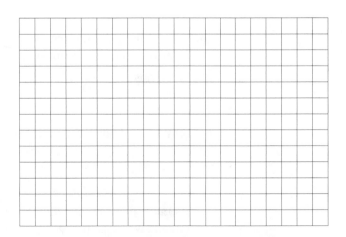

2. Use the regression feature of your graphing calculator to determine and plot a quadratic function that best fits these data. Your graph should appear as follows:

  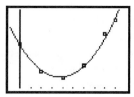

3. Do you believe that the quadratic regression model is a good model for the number of days the AQI exceeded 100 in Atlanta from 1990 to 1999?

The procedure used to develop the equation of a quadratic function that best fits a set of data is quite different from the least squares method used to develop a linear regression equation. Therefore, a correlation coefficient r cannot be calculated for quadratic regression equations. However, some statisticians use a value called the coefficient of multiple determination, denoted by R^2, to measure the goodness of fit of a quadratic model.

The values of R^2 vary from 0 to 1. The closer to 1, the better the likelihood of a good fit of the quadratic regression equation to the data. The value of R^2 is calculated using the graphing calculator and appears on the same screen as the quadratic regression equation.

4. What is the value of R^2 for the quadratic function determined in Problem 2? Does the value confirm your answer in Problem 3?

5. What is the practical domain of this function?

6. a. Use the quadratic regression equation to estimate the number of days the AQI exceeded 100 in Atlanta in each of the following years.

    i. 1995   **ii.** 1988   **iii.** 2002

  b. Which, if any, of these estimates do you think is most reliable? Explain.

7. Estimate the years in which the number of days that the AQI exceeded 100 in Atlanta was less than or equal to 30 using

  a. the given table (numerical method).

b. the graph of the quadratic regression equation (graphical method).

8. Use the quadratic formula (the algebraic method) to estimate the year in which the number of days that the AQI exceeded 100 in Atlanta was equal to 17.

9. Estimate graphically the years between 1990 and 1999 when the number of days that the AQI exceeded 100 in Atlanta was greater than 25.

10. **a.** The number of days that the AQI exceeded 100 in Atlanta in 1997 was 31. Does this agree with the prediction from the quadratic regression model?

    b. Include the data for 1997 from part a in the original data set, and then recalculate the quadratic regression equation.

    c. Predict the number of days that the AQI exceeded 100 in Atlanta in 1997 from this new quadratic regression equation from part b. Are the results any better?

11. The following data from the National Health and Nutrition Examination Survey appear in Exercise 7 of Activity 3.6. The data indicate that the number of American adults who are overweight or obese is increasing.

YEARS SINCE 1960, x	1	12	18	31	39
PERCENT OF OVERWEIGHT OR OBESE AMERICANS, $P(x)$	45	47	47	56	64.5

Use the regression feature of your graphing calculator to verify that this data can be modeled by the equation $P(x) = 0.017x^2 - 0.174x + 45.493$.

SUMMARY
Activity 3.7

Parabolic data can be modeled by a **quadratic regression equation**.

EXERCISES
Activity 3.7

1. During one game, the Florida State punter was called upon to punt the ball four times. On one of these punts, the punter struck the ball at his own 30-yard line. The height, *h*, of the ball above the field in feet as a function of time, *x*, in seconds can be partially modeled by the following table:

x	0	0.6	1.2	1.8	2.4	3.0
h(x)	2.50	28.56	43.10	46.12	37.12	17.60

   a. Sketch a scatterplot of the data using your graphing calculator. Your screen should appear as follows:

   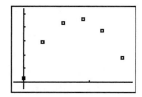

   b. Use your graphing calculator to obtain a quadratic regression function for these data. Round the values of *a*, *b*, and *c* to four decimal places.

   c. Graph the equation from part b on the same coordinate axes as the data points. Does the curve appear to be a good fit for the data? Explain.

   d. In this model, what is the practical domain of the quadratic regression function?

   e. Estimate the practical range of this model.

   f. How long after the ball was struck did the ball reach 35 feet above the field? Explain.

   g. How many results did you obtain for part f? Do you think you have all of the solutions? Explain.

2. Use the following data set to perform the tasks in parts a–e.

x	0	3	6	9	12
y	5	28	86	180	310

a. Determine an appropriate scale and plot these points.

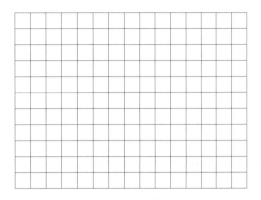

b. Use your graphing calculator to determine the quadratic regression equation for this data set.

c. Graph the regression equation on the same coordinate axes as the data points in part a.

d. Compare the predicted *y*-values with the *y*-values given in the table.

e. Predict the *y*-value for $x = 7$ and for $x = 15$.

3. The following table shows the stopping distance for a car at various speeds on dry pavement:

SPEED (mph)	25	35	45	55	65	75
DISTANCE (ft)	65	108	167	245	340	450

a. Use your graphing calculator to determine a quadratic regression equation that represents this data.

b. Use the regression equation to predict the stopping distance at 90 mph.

c. What speed would produce a stopping distance of 280 feet? (Round to the nearest tenth.) Explain how you arrived at your conclusion.

4. A downturn in the high-tech industry during the early 2000s caused a similar downturn in computer science and engineering enrollments for new undergraduates. The following data from the Computing Research Association represents new enrollments in computer science and engineering from 1995 to 2001.

YEARS SINCE 1995, x	0	1	2	3	4	5	6
NEW UNDERGRADS IN COMPUTER SCIENCE AND ENGINEERING (in thousands), N	8.2	11.9	16.2	17.1	16.6	18.9	18.0

Source: Computer Research Associates

a. Sketch a scatterplot of the data using your graphing calculator. Your screen should appear as follows:

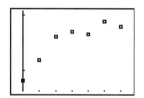

b. Use your graphing calculator to obtain a quadratic regression function for this data. Round the values of a, b, and c to four decimal places.

c. Graph the equation from part b on the same coordinate axes as the data points. Does the curve appear to be a good fit for the data? Explain.

d. What does the regression equation predict for the new undergraduate enrollments in computer science and engineering in 2010? Does this seem reasonable?

e. Use the model to determine the year in which the undergraduate computer science and engineering enrollments dropped below 15,000.

Collecting and Analyzing Data

5. The number, n (in millions) of cell phone subscribers in the United States from 1990 to 1999 is given in the following table.

YEAR	1990	1991	1992	1993	1994	1995	1996	1997	1998	1999
NUMBER OF SUBSCRIBERS (millions)	5.28	7.56	11.03	16.01	24.13	33.79	44.04	55.31	69.20	86.05

a. In Exercise 9 of Activity 3.6, this data was approximated by the quadratic model: $y = 0.846x^2 + 1.32x + 5.20$, where $x = 0$ corresponds to the year 1990. Use a graphing calculator to determine a quadratic regression equation for the given data. How does the equation compare to the quadratic model given in Exercise 9? How good is the fit?

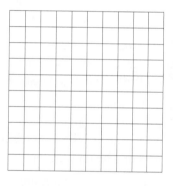

b. Use the model to predict the number of cell phone subscribers in the year 2005.

c. Find a website to determine the actual number of cell phone subscribers in the U.S. in each year from 2000 to 2006. How good was your prediction in part b? Is it what you expected? Explain.

d. Sketch a scatterplot of the data you found in part c (for years 2000–2006). Determine a new quadratic regression equation to predict the number of cell phone subscribers in a given year. How good is the fit?

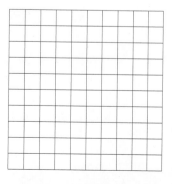

    e. Use the regression equation in part d to predict the number of cell phone subscribers in the year 2011. How confident are you in the prediction?

6. The shape of the main support cable in a suspension bridge is a parabola.

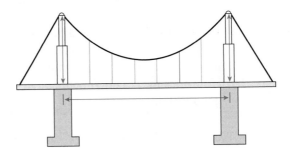

Use resources from the library or the Internet to determine specific dimensions, such as the distance between the main support columns, for one of the following bridges: Golden Gate Bridge, George Washington Bridge, or Verrazano-Narrows Bridge.

Use the dimensions to develop points that lie on the graph of the main support cable of the bridge you selected. Draw a sketch of the support cable on graph paper. The orientation of the coordinate system, especially the origin, is very important. You will need at least three points that lie on the graph of the support cable in your drawing.

Use the points to determine a quadratic regression equation to represent the main support cable of the bridge. Use the model to determine the minimum distance from the cable to the highway.

Be prepared to give a presentation of your findings.

Activities 3.1–3.7 What Have I Learned?

1. a. In order for the graph of the equation $y = ax^2 + bx + c$ to be a parabola, the value of the coefficient of x^2 cannot be zero. Explain.

b. What is the vertex of the parabola having an equation of the form $y = ax^2$?

c. Describe the relationship between the vertex and the y-intercept of the graph of $y = ax^2 + c$.

2. Determine if the vertex is a minimum point or a maximum point of $y = ax^2 + bx + c$ in each of the following situations.

a. $a < 0$ **b.** $a > 0$

3. a. What are the possibilities for the number of y-intercepts of a quadratic function?

b. What are the possibilities for the number of x-intercepts of a parabola?

4. What is the relationship between the vertex and the x-intercept of the graph of $y = x^2 - 4x + 4$?

5. a. The vertex of a parabola is $(3, 1)$. Using this information, complete the following table:

x	1	2	3	4	5
y	5	2			

b. If the vertex of a parabola is $(2, 4)$, complete the following table:

x	−2	0	2	4	6
y	0	3			

6. The vertex of the parabola having equation $g(x) = x^2 + 2x - 8$ is $(-1, -9)$.

a. The graph of g is shifted vertically upward 5 units. Write the equation of the resulting graph.

b. Determine the vertex of the graph in part a.

c. Compare the y-values of the vertex of the original parabola and the translated graph.

7. a. Given the following graph, explain why choices i, ii, and iii do not fit the curve:

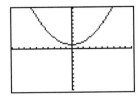

   i. $f(x) = ax^2 + bx$ with $a > 0, b < 0$

   ii. $g(x) = ax^2 + c$ with $a < 0, c > 0$

   iii. $h(x) = ax^2 + bx + c$ with $a < 0, b > 0, c < 0$

   b. What restrictions on a, b, and c are necessary to fit $y = ax^2 + bx + c$ to this graph?

8. Review the steps in the following solution. Is the solution correct? Explain why or why not.

$$x^2 - 3x - 4 = 6$$
$$(x - 4)(x + 1) = 6$$
$$x - 4 = 6 \qquad x + 1 = 6$$
$$x = 10 \qquad x = 5$$

Recognizing the correspondence among situations, equations, and graphs is an important skill. Exercises 9–13 contain a description of a free-falling object where s is the distance an object is above the ground at time t. Match the description to the quadratic models. Then match each description (and equation) to the graph that represents the situation, selecting from graphs i–vii.

9. A rock is thrown straight up with a velocity of 20 meters per second from a building that is 50 meters high.

10. A model rocket is shot straight up into the air from a launch pad at ground level with a velocity of 70 feet per second.

11. A telephone repairperson drops her vice grips from a 50-foot tower.

12. A ball is thrown directly upward with a velocity of 100 feet per second from a height of 6 feet above the ground on the Moon.

13. A bundle of shingles is thrown straight down with a velocity of 50 feet per second from the roof of a building that is 50 feet high.

a. $s(t) = -16t^2 + 50$

b. $s(t) = -4.9t^2 - 20t + 50$

c. $s(t) = -2.64t^2 + 100t + 6$

d. $s(t) = -16t^2 + 70t$

e. $s(t) = -16t^2 - 50t + 50$

f. $s(t) = -4.9t^2 + 20t + 50$

g. $s(t) = -16t^2 + 50t$

---

i.

ii.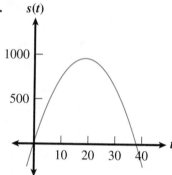

iii.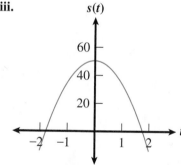

iv.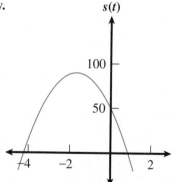

v.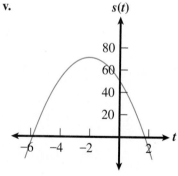

vi.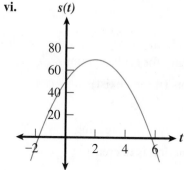

vii.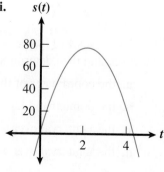

Activities 3.1–3.7   How Can I Practice?

1. Complete the following table:

EQUATION OF THE FORM $y = ax^2 + bx + c$	VALUE OF a	VALUE OF b	VALUE OF c
$y = 5x^2$			
$y = \frac{1}{3}x^2 + 3x - 1$			
$y = -2x^2 + x$			

For Exercises 2–7, determine the following characteristics for each graph:

   a. the direction in which the parabola opens

   b. the equation of the axis of symmetry

   c. the vertex; determine if maximum or minimum

   d. the y-intercept

2. $y = -2x^2 + 4$ **3.** $y = \frac{2}{3}x^2$

4. $f(x) = -3x^2 + 6x + 7$ **5.** $f(x) = 4x^2 - 4x$

6. $y = x^2 + 6x + 9$ **7.** $y = x^2 - x + 1$

For Exercises 8–11, use a graphing calculator to sketch the graph of each quadratic function, and then determine the following for each function.

   a. the coordinates of the x-intercepts (if they exist)

   b. the domain and range

   c. the x-interval over which the function is increasing

   d. the x-interval over which the function is decreasing

8. $y = -x^2 + 4$

9. $y = x^2 - 5x + 6$

10. $y = -3x^2 - 6x + 8$

11. $y = 0.22x^2 - 0.71x + 2$

12. Use a graphing calculator to approximate the vertex of the graph of the parabola defined by the equation

$$y = -2x^2 + 3x + 25.$$

13. Completely factor the following polynomials.

    a. $9a^5 - 27a^2$ **b.** $24x^3 - 6x^2$

    c. $4x^3 - 16x^2 - 20x$ **d.** $5x^2 - 16x + 6$

    e. $x^2 - 5x - 24$ **f.** $y^2 + 10y + 25$

14. Determine one solution of the following quadratic equations numerically. That is, construct a table of (x, y) ordered pairs, and estimate the value of x that results in the required y-value.

    a. $5x^2 = 7$ **b.** $x^2 - 7x + 10 = 5$ **c.** $3x^2 - 5x = 2$

a.

x	1	1.1	1.2	1.3	1.4	1.5
y						

b.

x	0.5	0.6	0.7	0.8	0.9	1
y						

c.

x	0	1	2	3	4	5
y						

15. Solve each of the equations from Exercise 14 using the quadratic formula. When necessary, round your solutions to the nearest tenth. Check your solutions by graphing.

16. Solve each of the following equations by factoring.

a. $4x^2 - 8x = 0$

b. $x^2 - 6 = 7x + 12$

c. $2x(x - 4) = -6$

d. $x^2 - 8x + 16 = 0$

e. $x^2 - 2x - 24 = 0$

f. $y^2 - 2y - 35 = -20$

g. $a^2 + 2a + 1 = 3a + 7$

h. $4x^2 + 4x - 3 = -3x - 1$

17. A fastball is hit straight up over home plate. The ball's height, h (in feet), from the ground is modeled by

$$h = -16x^2 + 80x + 5,$$

where t is measured in seconds.

a. What is the maximum height of the ball above the ground?

b. Write an equation to determine how long will it take for the ball to reach the ground. Solve the equation using the quadratic formula. Check your solution by graphing.

c. Write the equation you would need to determine when the ball is 101 feet above the ground.

d. Solve the equation you determined in part c algebraically to determine the time it will take for the ball to reach a height of 101 feet. Verify your results graphically.

18. A suspension bridge (shown below) is 100 meters long. The bridge is supported by cables attached to the tops of towers 35 meters high at each end of the bridge. The cables hang from the towers approximately in the shape of a parabola. The height, h (in meters), of the cables above the surface of the roadway is modeled by

$$h = 0.01x^2 - x + 35,$$

where x is the horizontal distance measured from the point where the tower and roadway meet.

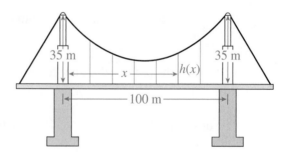

a. Use your graphing calculator to examine the height function. What is the practical domain of this function?

b. What is the minimum distance of the cables from the roadway?

19. Use the following data set to perform the tasks in parts a–f:

x	0	1	3	5	7	8
y	10	4	−18	−54	−107	−145

a. Determine an appropriate scale and plot these points.

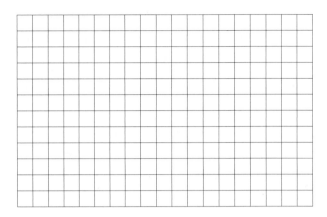

b. Use your graphing calculator to determine the quadratic regression equation for this data set.

c. Graph the regression equation on the same coordinate axes as the data points.

d. Compare the predicted outputs with the given outputs in the table.

e. What is the predicted output for $x = 4$ and for $x = 9$?

f. For what value of x is $y = -40$? Use the quadratic formula.

20. The average miles per gallon (mpg) for U.S. cars has steadily increased since 1950. The following graphic gives the average miles per gallon for selected years.

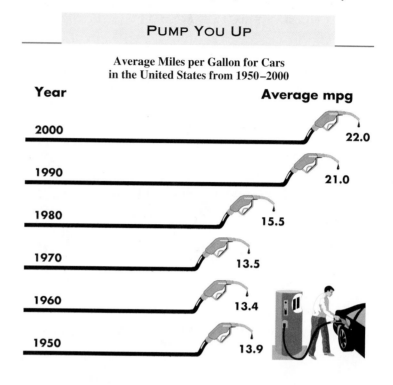

PUMP YOU UP

Average Miles per Gallon for Cars in the United States from 1950–2000

Year	Average mpg
2000	22.0
1990	21.0
1980	15.5
1970	13.5
1960	13.4
1950	13.9

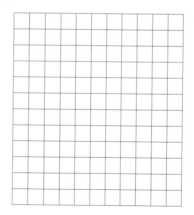

a. Draw a scatterplot of the data points, where x represents the number of years since 1950.

b. Determine the equation of a quadratic function that best fits the data.

c. Use the regression equation to predict the average miles per gallon in the year 2010.

d. Use your model to determine the year when the average miles per gallon is 30.

21. Use transformations to help describe the differences and the similarities in the graphs of the following quadratic functions. Verify using a graphing calculator.

   a. $y = 3x^2, y = 3x^2 + 5$

   b. $y = 2x^2, y = -2x^2$

   c. $y = 2x^2 + 1, y = 2x^2 - 4$

   d. $y = 4x^2, y = 4(x - 1)^2$

ACTIVITY 3.8
A Thunderstorm

OBJECTIVES

1. Recognize the equivalent forms of the direct variation statement.
2. Determine the constant of proportionality in a direct variation problem.
3. Solve direct variation problems.

One of nature's more spectacular events is a thunderstorm. The sky lights up, delighting your eyes, and seconds later your ears are bombarded with the boom of thunder. Because light travels faster than sound, during a thunderstorm you see the lightning before you hear the thunder. The formula

$$d = 1080t$$

describes the distance, d in feet, you are from the storm's center if it takes t seconds for you to hear the thunder.

1. Complete the following table for the model $d = 1080t$.

t, in seconds	1	2	3	4
d, in feet				

2. What does the ordered pair (3, 3240) from the above table mean in a practical sense?

3. As the value of t increases, what happens to the value of d?

The relationship between time t and distance d in this situation is an example of **direct variation**. As t increases, d also increases.

DEFINITION

Two variables are said to **vary directly** if as the magnitude of one increases, the magnitude of the other does as well.

4. Graph the distance, d, as a function of time, t, using the values in Problem 1.

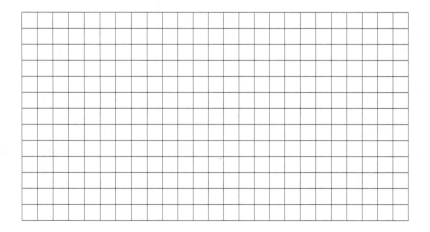

5. If the time it takes for you to hear the thunder after you see the lightning decreases, what is happening to the distance between you and the center of the storm?

If x represents the independent variable and y represents the dependent variable, then the following statements are equivalent.

a. y varies directly as x

b. y is directly proportional to x

c. $y = kx$ for some constant k.

The number represented by k is called the constant of proportionality or constant of variation.

---

6. The amount of garbage, G, varies directly with the population, P. The population of Coral Springs, Florida, is 0.13 million and creates 2.6 million pounds of garbage each week. Determine the amount of garbage produced by Jacksonville with a population of 0.81 million.

   a. Write an equation relating G and P and the constant of variation k.

   b. Determine the value of k.

   c. Rewrite the equation in part a using the value of k from part b.

   d. Use the equation in part c and the population of Jacksonville to determine the weekly amount of garbage produced.

7. Use Problem 6 to outline a procedure to solve direct variation problems. Let x represent the independent variable and y represent the dependent variable.

   a.

   b.

   c.

   d.

Note that direct variations are not always increasing. For example, $y = -1.2x$ is a direct variation. From the graph it is clear that the function is decreasing.

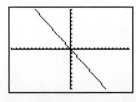

This does not contradict the definition of a direct variation.

The relationship $y = -1.2x$ is still of the form $y = kx$ and as x increases in value, the absolute value (the magnitude) of y is increasing.

8. A worker's gross wages, w, vary directly as the number of hours the worker works, h. The following table shows the relationship between the wages and the hours worked.

HOURS WORKED, h	15	20	25	30	35
WAGES, w	$172.50	$230.00	$287.50	$345.00	$402.50

a. Graph the gross wages, w, as a function of hours worked, h, using the values in the preceding table

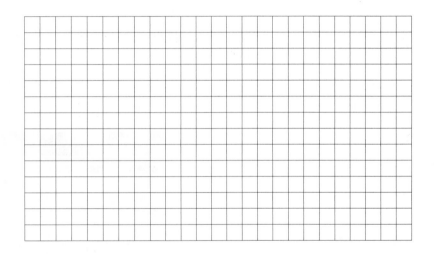

b. The relationship is defined by $w = kh$. Pick one ordered pair from the table and use it to determine the value of k.

c. What does k represent in this situation?

d. Use the formula to determine the gross wages for a worker who works 40 hours.

Direct variation can involve higher powers of x, like x^2, x^3, or in general, x^n.

9. The power P generated by a certain wind turbine varies directly as the square of the wind speed w. The turbine generates 750 watts of power in a 25 mph wind. Determine the power it generates in a 40 mph wind.

Functions defined by equations of the form $y = kx^n$, $k \neq 0$ and n is a positive integer, will be discussed in more detail in the next activity.

SUMMARY
Activity 3.8

1. Two variables are said to **vary directly** if as the magnitude of one increases, the magnitude of the other does as well.

2. The following statements are equivalent. The number represented by k is called the **constant of proportionality or constant of variation.**

   a. y varies directly as x

   b. y is directly proportional to x

   c. $y = kx$ for some constant x

EXERCISES
Activity 3.8

1. The amount of sales tax, s, on any item is directly proportional to the list price of an item, p. The sales tax in your area is 8%.

   a. Write a formula that relates the amount of sales tax, s, to the list price, p, in this situation.

   b. Use the formula in part a to complete the following table:

LIST PRICE, p ($)	SALES TAX, s ($)
10	
20	
30	
50	
100	

   c. Graph the sales tax, s, as a function of list price, p, using the values in the preceding table.

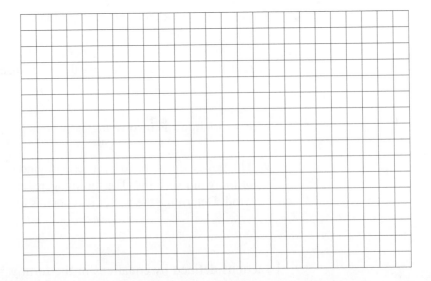

d. Determine the list price of an item for which the sales tax is $3.60.

2. The amount you tip a waiter, t, is directly proportional to the amount of the check, c.

a. Assuming you tip your waiter 15% of the amount of the check, write a formula that relates the amount of the tip, t, to the amount of the check, c.

b. Use the formula in part a to complete the following table:

AMOUNT OF CHECK, c ($)	AMOUNT OF TIP, t ($)
15	
25	
35	
50	
100	

c. Graph the amount of the tip, t, as a function of the amount of the check, c, using the values in the preceding table.

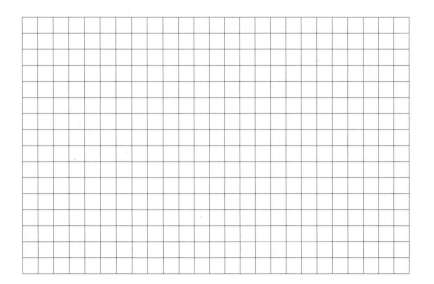

d. A company has a policy that no tip can exceed $12.00 and still be reimbursed by the company. What is the maximum cost of a meal for which all of the tip will be reimbursed if the tip is 15% of the check?

3. The distance, s, that an object falls from rest varies directly as the square of the time, t, of the fall. A ball dropped from the top of a building falls 144 feet in 3 seconds.

a. Write a formula that relates the distance the ball has fallen, s, in feet to the time, t, in seconds since it has been released.

b. Use the formula in part a to complete the following table:

TIME SINCE THE BALL WAS RELEASED, t (sec)	DISTANCE FALLEN, s (ft)
0.5	
1	
1.5	
2	
2.5	

c. Graph the distance fallen, s, as a function of the time since the ball was released, x, using the values in the preceding table.

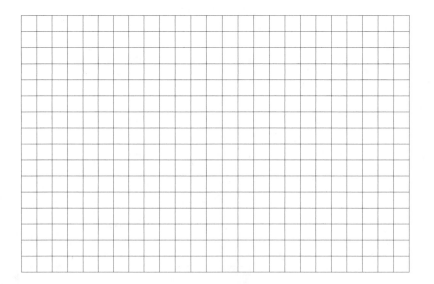

d. Estimate the height of the building if it takes approximately 2.3 seconds for the ball to hit the ground.

4. y varies directly as x, $y = 25$ when $x = 5$. Determine y when $x = 13$.

5. y varies directly as x, $y = 7$ when $x = 21$. Determine x when $y = 5$.

6. Given that y varies directly as x, consider the following table:

x	2	4	7		12
y	4	8		20	

a. Determine a formula that relates x and y.

b. Use the formula in part a to complete the table above.

ACTIVITY 3.9
The Power of
Power Functions

OBJECTIVES

1. Identify a direct variation function.

2. Determine the constant of variation.

3. Identify the properties of graphs of power functions defined by $y = kx^n$, where n is a positive integer and $k \neq 0$.

4. Graph transformations of power functions.

In Exercise 3 of Activity 3.8, you developed the formula $s = 16t^2$ to model the distance s, in feet, an object had fallen t seconds since it had been released. The equation $s = 16t^2$ is in the form

$$s = kt^n, \text{ where } k = 16 \text{ and } n = 2.$$

In general, the equation

$$y = kx^n,$$

where $k \neq 0$ and n is a positive integer, defines a **direct variation** function in which y varies directly as x^n. The constant, k, is called the **constant of variation** or the **constant of proportionality**.

Example 1 *The constant of variation, k, in the free-falling object situation defined by $s = 16t^2$ is 16.*

1. What is the constant of variation for the direct variation function defined by $V = \frac{4}{3}\pi r^3$?

Suppose you know only that the distance, s, varies directly as the square of t and one data pair. Are you able to determine the constant of variation k? Example 2 demonstrates the process discussed in Activity 3.8.

Example 2 *Let s vary directly as the square of t. If s = 64 when t = 2, determine the direct variation equation.*

SOLUTION

Because s varies directly as the square of t, you have
$$s = kt^2,$$
where k is the constant of variation. Substituting 64 for s and 2 for t, you have
$$64 = k(2)^2 \quad \text{or} \quad 64 = 4k \quad \text{or} \quad k = 16.$$
Therefore, the direct variation equation is
$$s = 16t^2.$$

2. For each table, determine the pattern and complete the table. Determine the constant k of variation and then write a direct variation equation for each table.

a. y varies directly as x.

x	1	2	4	8	12
y		12			

b. y varies directly as x^3.

x	1	2	3
y		32	

3. The length, L, of skid distance left by a car varies directly as the square of the initial velocity, v (in miles per hour), of the car.

   a. Write a general equation for L as a function of v. Let k represent the constant of variation.

   b. Suppose a car traveling at 40 miles per hour leaves skid distance of 60 feet. Use this information to determine the value of k.

   c. Use the function to determine the length of the skid distance left by the car traveling at 60 miles per hour.

Power Functions

The direct variation functions that have equations of the form $y = kx^n$, where n is a positive integer and $k \neq 0$, are also called **power functions**. The graphs of this family of functions are very interesting and are useful in problem solving.

4. Sketch a graph of each of the following power functions. Use a graphing calculator to verify the graph.

   a. $y = x$

   b. $y = x^2$

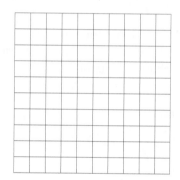 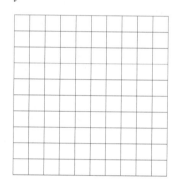

   c. $y = x^3$

   d. $y = x^4$

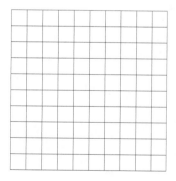 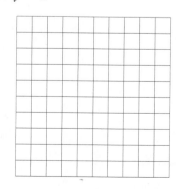

e. $y = x^5$

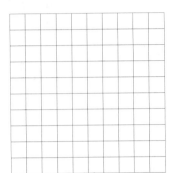

f. $y = x^6$

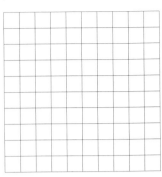

5. Each graph in Problem 4 has an equation of the form $y = x^n$, where n is a positive integer.

   a. What is the basic shape of the graph if

      i. n is even?   **ii.** n is odd?

   b. If n is even, what happens to the graph as n gets larger in value?

   c. If n is odd, is the function increasing or decreasing?

6. Use the patterns from Problem 5 in combination with graphing techniques you have learned previously to sketch a graph of each of the following without using a graphing calculator.

   a. $y = x^2 + 1$ **b.** $y = -2x^4$

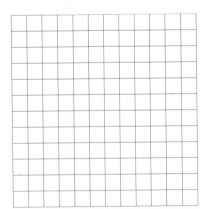

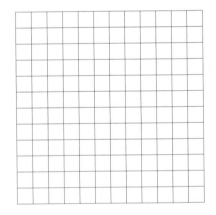

c. $y = 3x^8 + 1$

d. $y = -2x^5$

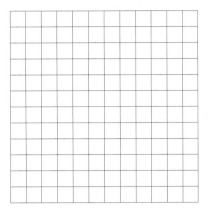

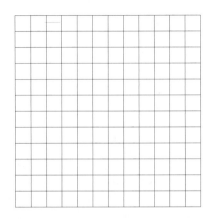

e. $y = x^{10}$

f. $y = 5x^3 + 2$

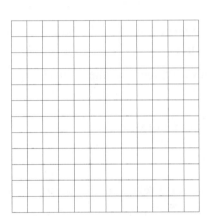

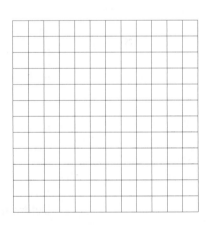

SUMMARY
Activity 3.9

1. The equation $y = kx^n$, where $k \neq 0$ and n is a positive integer, defines a **direct variation function**. The constant, k, is called the **constant of variation**.

2. The direct variation functions that have equations of the form $y = kx^n$, where n is a positive integer, are also called **power functions**.

   a. Power functions, in which n is even, resemble parabolas. As n increases in value, the graph flattens near the vertex.

   b. Power functions, in which n is odd, resemble the graph of $y = kx^3$. If k is positive, the graph is increasing. If k is negative, the graph is decreasing.

1. For each table, determine the pattern and complete the table. Then write a direct variation equation for each table.

a. y varies directly as x.

x	$\frac{1}{4}$	1	4	8
y		8		

b. y varies directly as x^3.

x	$\frac{1}{2}$	1	3	6
y		1		

2. The area, A, of a circle is given by the function $A = \pi r^2$, where r is the radius of the circle.

a. Does the area vary directly as the radius? Explain.

b. What is the constant of variation k?

3. Assume that y varies directly as the square of x, and that when $x = 2$, $y = 12$. Determine y when $x = 8$.

4. The distance, d, that you drive at a constant speed varies directly as the time, x, that you drive. If you can drive 150 miles in 3 hours, how far can you drive in 6 hours?

5. The number of meters, d, that a skydiver falls before her parachute opens varies directly as the square of the time, t, that she is in the air. A skydiver falls 20 meters in 2 seconds. How far will she fall in 2.5 seconds?

In Exercises 6–10, sketch a graph of the given power function. Verify your graphs using a graphing calculator.

6. $y = -3x^2$

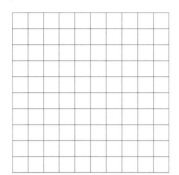

7. $y = x^4 + 1$

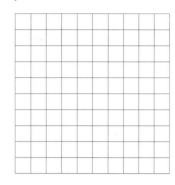

8. $y = -2x^5$

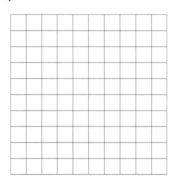

9. $f(x) = x^6$

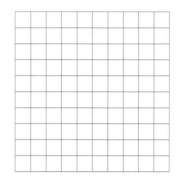

10. $g(x) = 3x^3 - 3$

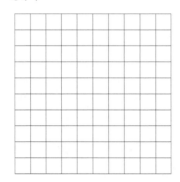

11. Determine the *x*-interval over which the function $f(x) = \frac{1}{2}x^4$ is increasing.

12. Does the function $g(x) = -\frac{1}{2}x^6$ have a maximum or a minimum point? Explain.

13. For $x > 1$, is the graph of $y = x^2$ rising faster or slower than the graph of $y = x^3$? Explain.

14. Is the graph of $y = \frac{3}{2}x^4$ wider or narrower than the graph of $y = x^4$?

15. How are the graphs of $y = -2x^3$ and $y = 2x^3 + 1$ different? How are the graphs similar?

ACTIVITY 3.10
Volume of a Storage Tank

OBJECTIVES

1. Use properties of exponents to simplify expressions and combine powers that have the same base.

2. Use the distributive property and properties of exponents to write expressions in expanded form.

3. Identify the greatest common factor (GCF) in an algebraic expression.

4. Factor algebraic expressions completely.

5. Use the distributive property to check factored algebraic expressions.

Mathematical models that involve expressions containing higher powers of x often need to be simplified and written in a more compact, usable form. Application of the various properties of exponents can be very helpful to accomplish this goal. For example, consider the following situation.

The volume v (in cubic feet) of the partially cylindrical propane storage tank pictured below is represented by the formula

$$v = r^2(4.2r + 78.54),$$

where r is the radius (in feet) of the cylindrical part of the tank.

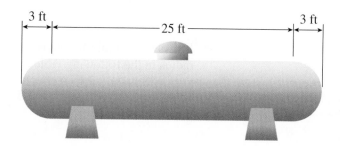

3 ft ← → ← 25 ft → ← → 3 ft

1. Determine the volume of the pictured tank if its radius is 3 feet.

Property 1 of Exponents: Multiplying Powers Having the Same Base

In Problem 1 you may have determined the volume by applying the order of operations procedure directly to the expression on the right side of the formula. You can also use the distributive property to first expand the expression and then evaluate the new expression.

Example 1   *Use the distributive property to expand the expression $r^2(4.2r + 78.54)$ and rewrite the formula for the volume. Then use the new formula to determine the volume for radius 3 feet.*

SOLUTION

Multiply each term within the parentheses of the expression by r^2.

$$r^2(4.2r + 78.54) = 4.2r \cdot r^2 + 78.54 \cdot r^2$$

Recall that in the expression r^2, the exponent 2 tells you that the base r is used as a factor 2 times. In the expression r, the exponent is 1, indicating that the base r is used as a factor once. Therefore,

$$4.2r \cdot r^2 = 4.2r \cdot r \cdot r = 4.2r^3$$

Base r is used as a
factor 3 times.

The formula for the volume in expanded form is $v = 4.2r^3 + 78.54r^2$.

For radius 3 feet, $v = 4.2 \cdot 3^3 + 78.54 \cdot 3^2 = 820.26$ cubic feet, which is the same result as in Problem 1.

2. a. Complete the following table. In column two, be sure to calculate r^2 first as indicated.

r	$r^2 \cdot r$	r^3
2		8
4		64
5		125

b. How does the table demonstrate that $r^2 \cdot r$ is equivalent to r^3?

c. Use each formula to determine the volume of the propane tank for each radius in the following table.

r	$v = r^2(4.2r + 78.54)$	$v = 4.2r^3 + 78.54r^2$
2		
4		

d. How does the table demonstrate that the two formulas are equivalent?

3. a. How many times does x appear as a factor in each of the following expressions?

    i. x^4 **ii.** x^2x^3

b. Multiply the following.

    i. $x \cdot x^4$ **ii.** $w^4 \cdot w^5$

    iii. $a^2 \cdot a^3 \cdot a^4$ **iv.** $x \cdot x^2 \cdot x^3$

4. What pattern do you observe in Problem 3?

The results of Problems 2, 3, and 4 lead to Property 1 of exponents.

> **Property 1 of Exponents: Multiplying Powers with the Same Base**
> For any number b, if m and n represent positive integers, then $b^m \cdot b^n = b^{m+n}$.

5. Show how you would evaluate the expression $2^4 \cdot 3^2$. Are you able to add the exponents first?

Problem 5 illustrates that when the bases are different, the exponential factors cannot be combined. For example, x^4y^2 cannot be simplified. However, a product such as $(x^3y^2)(x^2y^5)$ can be rewritten as $x^3x^2y^2y^5$, which can be simplified to x^5y^7.

6. Multiply the following:

    a. $(-3x^2)(4x^3)$ **b.** $(5a^3)(3a^5)$

    c. $(a^3b^2)(ab^3)(b)$ **d.** $(3.5x)(-0.1x^4)$

    e. $(r^2)(4.2r)$ **f.** $(4x^3y^6)(2x^3y)(3y^2)$

PROCEDURE

Multiply a Series of Monomial Factors

1. Multiply the numerical coefficients.

2. Use Property 1 of exponents to simplify the product of the variable factors that have the same base. That is, add their exponents and keep the base the same.

---

7. Use the distributive property and Property 1 of exponents to write each of the following expressions in expanded form.

    a. $x^3(x^2 + 3x - 2)$ **b.** $-2x(x^2 - 3x + 4)$

    c. $2a^3(a^3 + 2a^2 - a + 4)$

Greatest Common Factor

Recall from Activity 3.5, Sir Isaac Newton, a common factor is called **a greatest common factor (GCF)** if there are no additional factors common to the terms in the expression. For example, consider the expression $12x^3 + 30x^2$. Its two terms, $12x^3$ and $30x^2$, have several factors in common. The largest numerical factor common to both coefficients, 12 and 30, is 6. In addition, $12x^3$ contains three factors of x while $30x^2$ contains two factors of x. Therefore, the greatest common factor of $12x^3 + 30x^2$ is $6x^2$.

When an expression is written in factored form and none of its factors can themselves be factored any further, the expression is said to be in **completely factored form**. Therefore, $12x^3 + 30x^2$ is written in completely factored form as $6x^2(2x + 5)$.

8. Determine the greatest common factor of each expression and then rewrite the expression in completely factored form.

    a. $18x^7 + 27x^3 - 15x^2$ **b.** $-14y^8 - 21y^5$

    c. $2x^3y^4 - 2x^4y^3$ **d.** $100x^2y - 100xy^2$

Property 2 of Exponents: Dividing Powers Having the Same Base

9. a. Complete the following table for the given values of x:

x	$\dfrac{x^5}{x^2}$	x^3
2		
3		
4		

b. How does the table demonstrate that $\dfrac{x^5}{x^2}$ is equivalent to x^3?

In Problem 9, note that the exponent 3 in x^3 is the difference of the exponents 5 and 2 in $\dfrac{x^5}{x^2}$, that is, $5 - 2 = 3$. If you write both the numerator and denominator as a chain of multiplicative factors, you obtain

$$\frac{x^5}{x^2} = \frac{x \cdot x \cdot x \cdot x \cdot x}{x \cdot x}.$$

You can then divide out the two factors of x in the denominator with two of the factors of x in the numerator and are left with x^3. These computations suggest the following property of exponents.

Property 2 of Exponents: Dividing Powers Having the Same Base

For any nonzero number b, if m and n represent positive integers, then

$$\frac{b^m}{b^n} = b^{m-n}.$$

Example 2 *Use Property 2 of exponents to simplify the expression $\dfrac{15x^7}{6x^3}$.*

SOLUTION

$$\frac{15x^7}{6x^3} = \frac{\cancel{3} \cdot 5x^7}{\cancel{3} \cdot 2x^3} = \frac{5x^{7-3}}{2} = \frac{5x^4}{2}$$

10. Use Property 2 of exponents to simplify each of the following.

a. $\dfrac{3^4}{3^2}$

b. $\dfrac{y^{10}}{y^7}$

c. $\dfrac{10y^{10}}{5y^5}$

d. $\dfrac{x^6 y^{12}}{x^3 y^6}$

e. $\dfrac{15xy^9 z}{5xy^5}$

f. $\dfrac{5^2}{5^2}$

The result of Problem 10f using the division property is $\frac{5^2}{5^2} = 5^{2-2} = 5^0$. If you did the same problem by first writing 5^2 as 25, the result would be $\frac{5^2}{5^2} = \frac{25}{25} = 1$. Therefore, it must be true that $5^0 = 1$. In the same way it can be shown that $2^0 = 1$, $10^0 = 1$, and so on. This leads to the following definition.

> **DEFINITION**
>
> **Zero Exponents**
>
> $$a^0 = 1 \text{ if } a \neq 0.$$

Example 3 a. $16^0 = 1$

b. $\left(\frac{3}{x}\right)^0 = 1, \, x \neq 0$

c. $(3x)^0 = 1$ provided that $x \neq 0$. Note that $3x^0 = 3 \cdot 1 = 3$.

d. $5(x + 3)^0 = 5$

11. Simplify the following expressions. Assume $x \neq 0$.

a. 7^0

b. $2x^0$

c. $(5x)^0$

d. $\left(\dfrac{4}{x}\right)^0$

e. $-3(x^2 + 4)^0$

Property 3 of Exponents: Raising a Power to a Power

12. Suppose that you are in charge of decorations for a Monte Carlo Night benefit for the math club. Some of the decorations will be in the form of dice (cubes) that you will make out of foam material. You decide that if the length of each edge of the small die is a units, you want the edges of each large die to be a^2 units.

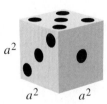

a. Recall that the volume V of a cube is $V = s^3$, where s is the length of a side. Determine the volume of a die for the edge lengths given in the table. Also evaluate the expression in the fourth column for the given lengths. The first row is done for you.

LENGTH OF EDGE a INCHES	SMALL DIE VOLUME a^3 CUBIC INCHES	LARGE DIE VOLUME $(a^2)^3$ CUBIC INCHES	a^6
2	8	$(2^2)^3 = 4^3 = 64$	$2^6 = 64$
3			
4			

b. How does the table demonstrate that $(a^2)^3$ is equivalent to a^6?

The results of Problem 12 suggest that the expression $(a^2)^3$ can be simplified. Note that $(a^2)^3$ indicates the base a^2 is used as a factor 3 times. Therefore,

$$(a^2)^3 = \underbrace{a^2 \cdot a^2 \cdot a^2} = \underbrace{a^{2+2+2}} = (a^{2 \cdot 3}) = a^6$$

This calculation shows that the simplified expression can be obtained by multiplying the exponents 2 and 3, and leads to the third property of exponents.

Property 3 of Exponents: Raising a Power to a Power

For any number b, if m and n represent positive integers, then $(b^m)^n = b^{m \cdot n}$.

---

13. Use the properties of exponents to simplify each of the following.

    a. $(t^3)^5$ **b.** $(y^2)^4$ **c.** $(3^2)^4$

    d. $2(a^5)^3$ **e.** $x(x^2)^3$

    f. $-3(t^2)^4$ **g.** $(5xy^2)(3x^4y^5)$

Example 4   *Multiply the series of factors $3x^4(x^2)^3 2x^3$.*

SOLUTION

$3x^4(x^2)^3 \cdot 2x^3$

$= 3x^4 x^6 \cdot 2x^3$ Remove parentheses by applying Property 3 of exponents.

$= 6x^4 x^6 x^3$ Multiply the numerical coefficients.

$= 6x^{13}$ Apply Property 1 of exponents to variable factors that have the same base.

14. Multiply the series of factors $2a^3(a^2)^4 7a^5$.

Property 4 of Exponents: Interpreting Negative Exponents

15. a. Evaluate the expression $\dfrac{2^3}{2^4}$ and write your result as a fraction in simplest form.

b. Use Property 2 of exponents to simplify $\dfrac{2^3}{2^4}$.

c. Use the result of part a to explain the meaning of the expression 2^{-1}.

In Problem 15c, the fact that $2^{-1} = \dfrac{1}{2}$ demonstrates that meaning can be given to negative exponents.

16. a. Simplify the expression $\dfrac{b^3}{b^5}$ by dividing out common factors.

b. Use Property 2 of exponents to simplify $\dfrac{b^3}{b^5}$.

c. Use the result of part a to explain the meaning of the expression b^{-2}.

Problems 15 and 16 lead to Property 4 of exponents.

Property 4 of Exponents: Interpreting Negative Exponents

For any nonzero number b, if n represents a positive integer, then $b^{-n} = \dfrac{1}{b^n}$.

17. Simplify each of the following expressions. Write the result in both exponential and fraction form.

a. $\dfrac{b^0}{b^3}$

b. $\dfrac{x^5}{x^9}$

c. $\dfrac{y^{10}}{y^{12}}$

d. $\dfrac{12x^2}{3x^4}$

Property 5 of Exponents: Raising a Product or a Quotient to a Power

18. a. Use the definition of an exponent to write the expression $(x \cdot y)^4$ as a repeated multiplication.

b. How many factors of x are in your expanded expression?

c. How many factors of y are in your expanded expression?

d. Regroup the factors in the expanded expression so that the x factors are written first, followed by the y factors.

e. Rewrite the expression in part d using exponential notation.

Problem 18 above demonstrates another property of exponents, that is, the power of a product is the same as the product of its factors each raised to that power.

> **Property 5 of Exponents: Raising a Product or a Quotient to a Power**
>
> For any numbers a and b, if n represents a positive integer, then
>
> $$(a \cdot b)^n = a^n \cdot b^n \quad \text{and} \quad \left(\frac{a}{b}\right)^n = \frac{a^n}{b^n}, \qquad b \neq 0.$$

19. Use Property 5 to simplify the following expressions.

a. $(2 \cdot a)^3$

b. $(3 \cdot m \cdot n)^2$

c. $\left(\dfrac{10}{p}\right)^6$

20. Use the properties of exponents to simplify each of the following.

　　a. $(5 \cdot x \cdot y)^2$　　　　　　　　**b.** $5(x \cdot y)^2$

　　c. $(2 \cdot a^4)^3$　　　　　　　　**d.** $\left(\dfrac{6 \cdot b^5}{c^2}\right)^4$

SUMMARY
Activity 3.10

Properties of Exponents.

1. Multiplying Powers Having the Same Base

For any number b, if m and n represent positive integers, then $b^m \cdot b^n = b^{m+n}$.

2. Dividing Powers Having the Same Base

For any nonzero number b, if m and n represent positive integers, then $\dfrac{b^m}{b^n} = b^{m-n}$.

3. Raising a Power to a Power

For any number b, if m and n represent positive integers, then $(b^m)^n = b^{mn}$.

4. Interpreting Negative Exponents

For any nonzero number b, if n represents a positive integer, then $b^{-n} = \dfrac{1}{b^n}$.

5. Raising a Product or a Quotient to a Power

For any numbers a and b, if n represents a positive integer, then

$$(a \cdot b)^n = a^n \cdot b^n \quad \text{and} \quad \left(\frac{a}{b}\right)^n = \frac{a^n}{b^n}, \qquad b \neq 0.$$

6. Interpreting Zero Exponents

For any nonzero number b, $b^0 = 1$.

EXERCISES
Activity 3.10

1. Refer to the properties of exponents, and explain how to simplify each of the following.

　　a. $x \cdot x \cdot x \cdot x \cdot x$

　　b. $x^3 \cdot x^7 \cdot x$

c. $\dfrac{x^6}{x^4}$

d. $(x^4)^3$

e. x^{-3}

f. y^0

g. $\dfrac{r^3}{r^8}$

h. $(5 \cdot w)^3$

In Exercises 2–22, use the properties of exponents to simplify the expressions.

2. $a \cdot a^3$ **3.** $3x \cdot x^4$

4. $y^2 \cdot y^3 \cdot y^4$ **5.** $3t^4 \cdot 5t^2$

6. $-3w^2 \cdot 4w^5$ **7.** $3.4b^5 \cdot 1.05b^3$

8. $(a^5)^3$ **9.** $4(x^2)^4$

10. $(-x^{10})^5$ **11.** $(-3x^2)(-4x^7)(2x)$

12. $(-5x^3)(0.5x^6)(2.1y^2)$ **13.** $(a^2bc^3)(a^3b^2)$

14. $(-2s^2t)(t^2)^3(s^4t)$ **15.** $\dfrac{16x^7}{24x^3}$

16. $\dfrac{10x^4y^6}{5x^3y^5}$ **17.** $\dfrac{9a^4b^2}{18a^3b^2}$

18. $\dfrac{x^4}{x^7}$ **19.** $\dfrac{4w^2z^2}{10w^2z^4}$

20. $11x^2(y^2)^0$ **21.** $5a(4 \cdot a^3)^2$

22. $\left(\dfrac{3 \cdot a^2}{2 \cdot b}\right)^4$

23. Use the properties of exponents and the distributive property to show how to simplify the expression $2x(x^3 - 3x^2 + 5x - 1)$.

In Exercises 24–31, use the distributive property and the properties of exponents to expand the algebraic expression.

24. $2x(x + 3)$

25. $y(3y - 1)$

26. $x^2(2x^2 + 3x - 1)$

27. $2a(a^3 + 4a - 5)$

28. $5x^3(2x - 10)$

29. $r^4(3.5r - 1.6)$

30. $3t^2(6t^4 - 2t^2 - 1.5)$

31. $1.3x^7(-2x^3 - 6x + 1)$

32. Simplify the expressions $4(a + b + c)$ and $4(abc)$. Are the results the same? Explain.

33. A rectangular bin has the following dimensions:

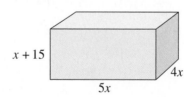

$x + 15$

$4x$

$5x$

    a. Write a formula that represents the area, A, of the base of the bin.

    b. Using the result from part a, write a formula that represents the volume, V, of the bin.

34. A cube measures b^4 units on a side. Write a formula in terms of b that represents the volume of the cube.

35. A square measures $3xy^2$ units on each side. Write an expression that represents the area of the square.

Activities 3.8–3.10 What Have I Learned?

1. In a direct variation situation, as the value of the independent variable, x, increases, what happens to the value of the dependent variable, y?

2. In a hurricane, the wind pressure varies directly as the square of the wind velocity (speed). If the wind speed doubles in value, what change in the wind pressure do you experience?

3. Is the graph of $y = 3x^4$ narrower or wider than the graph of $y = x^2$? Explain.

4. Explain the difference between the two expressions $-x^2$ and $(-x)^2$.

5. Simplify the product $x^3 \cdot x^3$. Explain how you obtained your answer.

6. Is there a difference between $(3x)^2$ and $3x^2$? Explain.

7. As you simplify the following expression, list each mathematical principle that you use.

$$(x - 3)(2x + 4) - 3(x + 7) - (3x - 2) + 2x^3x^5 - 7x^8 + (2x^2)^4 + (-x)^2$$

8. Is $(x + 3)^2$ equivalent to $x^2 + 9$? Explain why or why not.

Activities 3.8 – 3.10 **How Can I Practice?**

1. y varies directly as x and $y = 21$ when $x = 6$. Determine the value of y when $x = 14$.

2. y varies directly as x^2. When $x = 3$, $y = 45$. Determine y when $x = 6$.

3. Recall if d represents the distance (in feet) of the lightning from the observer, then d varies directly as the time, t (in seconds), it takes to hear the thunder. The relationship is modeled by

    $$d = 1080t.$$

    a. As the time t doubles (say from 3 to 6), the corresponding d-values _____ .

    b. What is the value of k, the constant of variation, in this situation? What significance does k have in this problem?

4. The velocity, v, of a falling object varies directly to the time, t, of the fall. After three seconds, the velocity of the object is 60 feet per second. What will be its velocity after four seconds?

5. A propane gas bill varies directly as the amount of gas used. The bill for 56 gallons of propane was \$184.80. What is the bill for 70 gallons of propane?

6. Select any three input values, and then complete the following table. Then determine numerically and algebraically which of the following expressions are equivalent.

    a. $4x^2$ **b.** $-2x^2$ **c.** $(-2x)^2$

x	$4x^2$	$-2x^2$	$(-2x)^2$

7. Use the properties of exponents to simplify the following.

a. $3x^3 \cdot x$

b. $-x^2 \cdot x^5 \cdot x^7$

c. $(2x)(-6y^2)(x^3)$

d. $8(2x^2)(3xy^4)$

e. $(p^4)^5 \cdot (p^3)^2$

f. $(3x^2y^3)(4xy^4)(x^7y)$

g. $\dfrac{w^9}{w^5}$

h. $\dfrac{z^5}{z^5}$

i. $\dfrac{15y^{12}}{5y^5}$

j. $\dfrac{x^8y^{11}}{x^3y^5}$

k. $\dfrac{21xy^7z}{7xy^5}$

l. $(a^4)^3$

m. $3(x^3)^2$

n. $(-x^3)^5$

o. $(-2x^3)(-3x^5)(4x)$

p. $(-5x^2)(0.3x^4)(1.2y^3)$

q. $(-3s^2t)(t^2)^3(s^3t^5)$

r. $\dfrac{a^8b^{10}}{a^9b^{12}}$

s. $\dfrac{6x^5z}{14x^5z^2}$

Summary

The bracketed numbers following each concept indicate the activity in which the concept is discussed.

CONCEPT / SKILL	DESCRIPTION	EXAMPLE
Parabola [3.1]	A parabola is the U-shaped graph described by a function of the form $y = ax^2 + bx + c$.	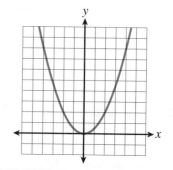
Solving an equation of the form $ax^2 = c$ [3.1]	Solve an equation of this form algebraically by dividing both sides of the equation by a and then taking the square root of both sides.	$2x^2 = 8$ $\dfrac{2x^2}{2} = \dfrac{8}{2}$ $x^2 = 4, x = \pm 2$
Quadratic function [3.2]	The quadratic function with x as the variable has the standard form $y = ax^2 + bx + c$, where a, b, and c represent real numbers and $a \neq 0$.	$y = 2x^2 - 3x - 2$
Graph a quadratic function (a parabola) [3.2]	For the quadratic function defined by $y = ax^2 + bx + c$; if $a > 0$, the parabola opens upward; if $a < 0$, the parabola opens downward.	The graph of $y = 2x^2 - 3x - 2$ is a parabola that opens upward.
y-intercept of the graph of a quadratic function [3.2]	The constant term c of a quadratic function $y = ax^2 + bx + c$ always indicates the y-intercept of the parabola. The y-intercept of any quadratic function is $(0, c)$.	The vertical intercept of the graph of $y = 2x^2 - 3x - 2$ is $(0, -2)$.
Axis of symmetry [3.3]	The axis of symmetry of a parabola is a vertical line that separates the parabola into two mirror images. The equation of the vertical axis of symmetry is given by $x = \frac{-b}{2a}$.	See Example 2, Activity 3.3.
Vertex (turning point) [3.3]	The vertex of a parabola defined by $y = ax^2 + bx + c$ is the point where the graph changes direction. It is given by $\left(\frac{-b}{2a}, f\left(-\frac{b}{2a}\right)\right)$.	See Example 1, Activity 3.3.
x-intercept(s) [3.3]	An x-intercept is the point or points (if any) where the parabola crosses the x-axis (that is, where its y-coordinate is zero).	The x-intercepts of the parabola defined by $y = 2x^2 - 3x - 2$ are $(2, 0)$ and $(-0.5, 0)$.

Domain of the quadratic function [3.3]	The domain of all quadratic functions is all real numbers.	The domain of $y = 2x^2 - 3x - 2$ is all real numbers.
Range of the quadratic function [3.3]	If the parabola opens upward, the range is $y \geq$ y-value of vertex. If the parabola opens downward, the range is $y \leq$ y-value of vertex.	The range of the parabola defined by $y = 2x^2 - 3x - 2$ is $y \geq \frac{-25}{8}$.
Solving $f(x) = c$ graphically [3.4]	Graph $y = f(x)$, graph $y = c$, and determine the x-values of the points of intersection. Or graph $y = f(x) - c$ and determine the x-intercepts.	See Example 1, Activity 3.4.
Greatest common factor (or GCF) [3.5]	The GCF is the largest factor common to all terms in an expression.	The GCF of $3x^4 - 6x^3 + 18x^2$ is $3x^2$.
Zero-product principle [3.5]	If a and b are any numbers and $a \cdot b = 0$, then either a or b, or both, must be equal to zero.	Example 1, Activity 3.5
Factoring trinomials by trial and error [3.5]	To factor trinomials by trial and error, 1. Remove the GCF. 2. Try combinations of factors for the first and last terms in two binomials. 3. Check the outer and inner products to match middle term of the original trinomial. 4. If the check fails, repeat steps 2 and 3.	Example 5, Activity 3.5
Solving quadratic equations by factoring [3.5]	To solve a quadratic equation by factoring, 1. Use the addition principle to remove all terms from one side of the equation. This results in a quadratic polynomial being set equal to zero. 2. Combine like terms and then factor the nonzero side of the equation. 3. Use the zero-product principle to set each factor containing a variable equal to zero and then solve the equations. 4. Check your solutions in the original equation.	Example 6, Activity 3.5
Quadratic formula [3.6]	$x = \dfrac{-b \pm \sqrt{b^2 - 4ac}}{2a}$	

Solving a quadratic equation of the form $ax^2 + bx + c = 0$, $a \neq 0$, **using the quadratic formula** [3.6]	To solve a quadratic equation of the form $ax^2 + bx + c = 0$, $a \neq 0$ using the quadratic formula $$x = \frac{-b \pm \sqrt{b^2 - 4ac}}{2a},$$ 1. Set the quadratic equation equal to zero. 2. Identify the coefficients a and b and the constant term c. 3. Substitute these values into the formula and simplify. 4. Check your solutions.	Example 1, Activity 3.6.
Direct variation [3.8], [3.9]	Two variables are said to vary directly if as the magnitude of one increases, the magnitude of the other does as well.	In the function $y = 2x$, y varies directly as x. As x increases in magnitude so does y.
The constant of proportionality or constant of variation, k [3.8], [3.9]	The following statements are equivalent: a. y varies directly as x b. y is directly proportional to x c. $y = kx$ for some constant k	In the direct variation function $y = 2x$, 2 is the constant of variation.
Power functions [3.9]	The direct variation function having an equation of the form $y = kx^n$, where n is a positive integer, is also called a power function.	$y = 4x^3$ is a third-power function.
Properties of exponents [3.10]	Property 1: $b^m \cdot b^n = b^{m+n}$ Property 2: $\dfrac{b^m}{b^n} = b^{m-n}$, $b \neq 0$ Property 3: $(b^m)^n = b^{m \cdot n}$ Property 4: $b^{-n} = \dfrac{1}{b^n}$, $b \neq 0$ Property 5: $(a \cdot b)^n = a^n b^n$ and $\left(\dfrac{a}{b}\right)^n = \dfrac{a^n}{b^n}$ Property 6: $b^0 = 1$, $b \neq 0$	1. $5^7 \cdot 5^6 = 5^{13}$ 2. $\dfrac{7^8}{7^5} = 7^3$ 3. $(3^2)^4 = 3^8$ 4. $2^{-3} = \dfrac{1}{2^3}$ 5. $(2 \cdot 3)^4 = 2^4 \cdot 3^4$ and $\left(\dfrac{3}{4}\right)^2 = \dfrac{3^2}{4^2}$ 6. $10^0 = 1$
Multiplying a series of factors [3.10]	1. If present, remove parentheses using property 3 of exponents. 2. Multiply the numerical coefficients. 3. Apply property 1 of exponents to variable factors that have the same base.	$3x^4(x^3)^2 \cdot 5x^3$ $= 3x^4 x^6 \cdot 5x^3$ $= 15x^{13}$

Writing an algebraic expression in expanded form [3.10]	Use the distributive property to expand, applying the properties of exponents.	$-2x^2(x^3 - 5x + 3)$ $= -2x^5 + 10x^3 - 6x^2$
Factoring completely [3.10]	Determine the GCF, and then use the properties of exponents to write the polynomial in factored form.	$24x^5 - 16x^3 + 32x^2$ $= 8x^2(3x^3 - 2x + 4)$
Multiplying a single term times an expression [3.10]	Multiply each term of the expression by the single term.	$2x(x^2 - 5x + 3)$ $= 2x \cdot x^2 - 2x \cdot 5x + 2x \cdot 3$ $= 2x^3 - 10x^2 + 6x$

Gateway Review

In Exercises 1–8, determine the following characteristics of each quadratic function by inspecting its equation.

    a. the direction in which the graph opens
    b. the equation of the axis of symmetry
    c. the vertex; maximum or minimum point
    d. the y-intercept

1. $y = x^2 + 2$ **2.** $y = -3x^2$

3. $y = -3x^2 + 4$ **4.** $y = 2x^2 - x$

5. $y = x^2 + 5x + 6$ **6.** $y = x^2 - 3x + 4$

7. $y = x^2 - 2x + 1$ **8.** $y = -x^2 + 5x - 6$

In Exercises 9–15, sketch the graph of each quadratic function using your graphing calculator. Then determine each of the following using the graph.

    a. the coordinates of the x-intercepts; if they exist
    b. the domain and the range of the function
    c. the x-interval in which the function is increasing
    d. the x-interval in which the function is decreasing

9. $y = x^2 + 4x + 3$ **10.** $y = x^2 + 2x - 3$

11. $y = x^2 - 3x + 1$

12. $y = 2x^2 + 8x + 5$

13. $y = -2x^2 + 8$

14. $y = -3x^2 + 4x - 1$

15. $y = 4x^2 + 5$

In Exercises 16–19, solve the quadratic equation numerically (using tables). Verify your solutions graphically.

16. $x^2 + 4x + 4 = 0$

17. $x^2 - 5x + 6 = 0$

18. $3x^2 = 18x + 10$

19. $-x^2 = 3x - 10$

In Exercises 20–21, solve the equation. Round your answer to the nearest tenth when necessary.

20. $8x^2 = 10$

21. $5x^2 + 25x = -5$

22. Completely factor the following polynomials.

    a. $9a^5 - 27a^2$ **b.** $24x^3 - 6x^2$ **c.** $4x^3 - 16x^2 - 20x$

    d. $5x^2 - 16x + 6$ **e.** $x^2 - 5x - 24$ **f.** $t^2 + 10t + 25$

In Exercises 23–27, solve each equation by factoring. Verify your answer graphically or by substitution of the solutions in the equations.

23. $x^2 - 9 = 0$ **24.** $-x^2 + 36 = 0$ **25.** $x^2 - 7x + 12 = 0$

26. $x^2 - 6x = 27$ **27.** $x^2 = -x$

In Exercises 28–32, write each of the equations in the form $ax^2 + bx + c = 0$. Then identify a, b, and c, and solve the equation using the quadratic formula. Verify your solutions by substitution.

28. $x^2 + 5x + 3 = 0$ **29.** $2x^2 - x = -3$ **30.** $x^2 = 81$

31. $3x^2 + 5x = 12$ **32.** $2x^2 = 3x + 5$

33. For the quadratic function $f(x) = 2x^2 - 8x + 3$, determine the zeros of the function. First, approximate the zeros using your graphing calculator. Second, solve the equation using the quadratic formula. Approximate your answers to the nearest hundredth.

34. The height, h (in feet), of a golf ball is a function of the time, t (in seconds), it has been in flight. A golfer strikes a golf ball with an initial velocity of 80 feet per second. The flight path of the ball is a parabola. The approximate height of the ball above the ground is modeled by

$$h = -16t^2 + 80t.$$

a. Sketch a graph of the function. What is the practical domain in this situation?

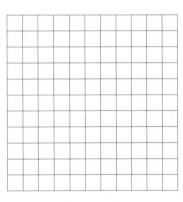

b. Determine the vertex of the parabola. What is the practical meaning of this point?

c. What is the h-intercept, and what is its practical meaning in this situation?

d. Determine the t-intercepts. What is the significance of these intercepts?

e. What assumption are you making in this situation about the elevation of the spot where the ball is struck and the point where the ball lands?

35. To use the regression feature of your calculator to determine the equation of a parabola, you need three distinct points. The stream of water flowing out of a water fountain is in the shape of a parabola. Suppose you let the origin of a coordinate system correspond to the point where the water begins to flow out of the nozzle (see figure).

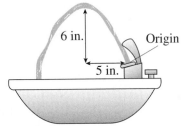

The maximum height of the water stream occurs approximately 5 inches measured horizontally from the nozzle. The maximum height of the stream of water is measured to be approximately 6 inches.

a. What is the vertex of the parabola?

b. You already have two points that lie on the parabola. What are they? Use symmetry to obtain a third point.

c. Using these three points and the regression feature of your graphing calculator, determine the equation of the stream of water.

36. A fastball is hit straight up over home plate. The ball's height, h (in feet), from the ground is modeled by

$$h(t) = -16t^2 + 80t + 5,$$

where t is measured in seconds.

a. What is the maximum height of the ball above the ground?

b. How long will it take for the ball to reach the ground?

37. Safe automobile spacing, S (in feet), is modeled by

$$S(v) = 0.03125v^2 + v + 18,$$

where v is average velocity in feet per second.

    a. Suppose a car is traveling at 44 feet per second. To be safe, how far should it be from the car in front of it?

    b. If the car is following 50 feet behind a van, what is a safe speed for the car to be traveling? How fast is this in miles per hour (60 miles per hour ≈ 88 feet per second)?

38. y varies directly as x and $y = 88$ when $x = 16$. Determine the value of x when $y = 77$.

39. The sales tax on an item varies directly as the cost of the item. The sales tax in your area is 7%. The sales tax on your item was $10.50. What was the cost of the item before the sales tax was applied?

40. County taxes vary directly with the assessed value of your property. Your tax bill indicated that you owed $1245 in taxes on your property assessed at $105,000.

    a. Determine the equation that relates the county tax due, t, to the assessed value of your property, v, in this case. Round k to three decimal places.

    b. Use the equation in part a to complete the following table:

ASSESSED VALUE OF YOUR PROPERTY, v	50,000	75,000	100,000	125,000	200,000	450,000
AMOUNT OF COUNTY TAXES, t						

    c. Explain how this table indicates that the relationship between v and t is a direct variation.

d. Graph the relationship between v and t using the first five pairs from the table in part b.

e. If the taxes on your property are $1164, what is the assessed value of your property.

41. $x^4(3x^3 + 2x^2 - 5x - 20)$

42. $-2x(3x^3 - 4x^2 + 8x - 5) + 3x(5x^3 - 8x^2 - 7x + 2)$

43. a. $(2x^3)^4$ **b.** $(5xy^3)^3$ **c.** $(-8a^2b^3)(-2a^3b^2)$

d. $\dfrac{y^{11}}{y^3}$ **e.** $\dfrac{45t^8}{9t^5}$ **f.** $(2x^0)(-3x^3)(x^5)$

Modeling with Exponential Functions

ACTIVITY 4.1
Going Shopping

OBJECTIVES

1. Define growth factor.
2. Determine growth factors from percent increases.
3. Use growth factors to solve problems involving percent increases.
4. Define decay factor.
5. Determine decay factors from percent decreases.
6. Use decay factors to solve problems involving percent decreases.

To earn revenue (income), many state and local governments require merchants to collect sales tax on the items they sell. In some localities, the sales tax is as much as 8% of the selling price and is passed on directly to the purchaser.

1. Determine the total cost (including the 8% sales tax) to the customer of the following items. Include each step of your calculation in your answer.

   a. A greeting card selling for $1.50

   b. An iPod priced at $300

Many people correctly determine the total costs for Problem 1 in two steps:

• They first compute the sales tax on the item.

• Then they add the sales tax to the selling price to obtain the total cost.

It is also possible to compute the total cost in one step by using the idea of a **growth factor**.

Growth Factors

2. **a.** If a quantity increases by 50%, how does its new value compare to its original value? That is, what is the ratio of the new value to the original value? The first row of the following table is completed for you. Complete the remaining rows to confirm or discover your answer.

A Matter of Values

ORIGINAL VALUE	NEW VALUE (INCREASED BY 50%)	RATIO OF NEW VALUE TO ORIGINAL VALUE		
		FRACTIONAL FORM	DECIMAL FORM	PERCENT FORM
20	$10 + 20 = 30$	$\frac{30}{20} = \frac{3}{2} = 1\frac{1}{2}$	1.50	150%
50				
100				
Your choice of an original value:				

b. Use the results from the preceding table to answer the question, "What is the ratio of the new value to the original value of any quantity that increases by 50%?" Express this ratio as a reduced fraction, a mixed number, a decimal, and a percent.

DEFINITION

For any specified percent *increase*, no matter what the original value may be, the ratio of the new value to the original value is always the same. This ratio $\frac{\text{new value}}{\text{original value}}$ is called the **growth factor** associated with the specified percent increase.

The growth factor is most often written in decimal form. As you saw previously, the growth factor associated with a 50% increase is 1.50.

PROCEDURE

The growth factor is formed by adding the specified percent increase to 100% and then changing this percent into its decimal form.

Example 1 *The growth factor corresponding to a 50% increase is*

$$100\% + 50\% = 150\%.$$

If you change 150% to a decimal, the growth factor is 1.50.

3. Determine the growth factor of any quantity that increases by the given percent.

a. 30%

b. 75%

c. 15%

d. 7.5%

4. A growth factor can always be written in decimal form. Explain why this decimal will always be greater than 1.

> ## PROCEDURE
>
> When a quantity increases by a specified percent, its new value can be obtained by multiplying the original value by the corresponding growth factor. That is,
>
> original value · growth factor = new value.

5. **a.** Use the growth factor 1.50 to determine the new value of a stock portfolio that increased 50% over its original value of $400.

   b. Use the growth factor 1.50 to determine the population of a town that has grown 50% over its previous population of 120,000 residents.

6. **a.** Determine the growth factor for any quantity that increases 20%.

   b. Use the growth factor to determine this year's budget, which has increased 20% over last year's budget of $75,000.

7. **a.** Determine the growth factor of any quantity that increases 8%.

   b. Use the growth factor to determine the total cost of each item in Problem 1.

In the previous problems, you were given an original (earlier) value and a percent increase and were asked to determine the new value. Suppose you are asked a "reverse" question: Sales in your small retail business have increased 20% over last year. This year you had gross sales receipts of $75,000. How much did you gross last year?

Using the growth factor 1.20, you can write

$$\text{original value} \cdot 1.20 = 75{,}000.$$

To determine last year's sales receipts, you divide both sides of the equation by 1.20.

$$\text{original value} = \frac{75{,}000}{1.20}$$

Therefore, last year's sales receipts totaled $62,500.

PROCEDURE

When a quantity has *already* increased by a specified percent, its original value is obtained by dividing the new value by the corresponding growth factor. That is,

$$\frac{\text{new value}}{\text{growth factor}} = \text{original value.}$$

---

8. You determined a growth factor for an 8% increase in Problem 7. Use it to answer the following questions.

   a. The cash register receipt for your new coat, which includes the 8% sales tax, totals $243. What was the ticketed price of the coat?

   b. The credit card receipt for your new sofa, which includes 8% sales tax, totals $1620. What was the ticketed price of the sofa?

Decay Factors

It's the sale you have been waiting for all season. Everything in the store is marked 40% off the original ticket price.

9. Determine the discounted price of a pair of sunglasses originally selling for $25.

Many people correctly determine the discounted price for Problem 9 in two steps:

• They first compute the actual dollar discount on the item.

• Then they subtract the dollar discount from the original price to obtain the sale price.

It is also possible to compute the sale price in one step by using the idea of a **decay factor**.

10. **a.** If a quantity decreases 20%, how does its new value compare to its original value? That is, what is the ratio of the new value to the original value? Complete the rows in the following table. The first row has been done for you.

Up and Down

ORIGINAL VALUE	NEW VALUE (DECREASED BY 20%)	RATIO OF NEW VALUE TO ORIGINAL VALUE		
		FRACTIONAL FORM	DECIMAL FORM	PERCENT FORM
20	16	$\frac{16}{20} = \frac{4}{5}$	0.80	80%
50				
100				
Choose any value:				

Notice that the new values are less than the originals, so the ratios of new values to original values will be less than 1.

b. Use the results from the preceding table to answer the question, "What is the ratio of the new value to the original value of any quantity that decreases 20%?" Express this ratio in reduced-fraction, decimal, and percent form.

DEFINITION

For a specified percent *decrease*, no matter what the original value may be, the ratio of the new value to the original value is always the same. This ratio $\frac{\text{new value}}{\text{original value}}$ is called the **decay factor** associated with the specified percent decrease.

As you have seen, the decay factor associated with a 20% decrease is 80%. For calculation purposes, a decay factor is usually written in decimal form, so the decay factor 80% is expressed as 0.80.

PROCEDURE

Note that a percent decrease describes the percent that has been *removed* (such as the discount taken off an original price), but the corresponding decay factor always represents the percent remaining (the portion that you still must pay). Therefore, a decay factor is formed by *subtracting* the specified percent decrease from 100% and then changing this percent into its decimal form.

Example 2 *The decay factor corresponding to a 10% decrease is*

$$100\% - 10\% = 90\%.$$

If you change 90% to a decimal, the decay factor is 0.90.

11. Determine the decay factor of any quantity that decreases by the following given percents:

a. 30%

b. 75%

c. 15%

d. 7.5%

Remember that multiplying the original value by the decay factor will *always* result in the amount remaining, not the amount that has been removed.

12. Explain why every decay factor will have a decimal format that is less than 1.

> **PROCEDURE**
>
> When a quantity *decreases* by a specified percent, its new value is obtained by multiplying the original value by the corresponding decay factor. That is,
>
> original value · decay factor = new value.

13. Use the decay factor 0.80 to determine the new value of a stock portfolio that has lost 20% of its original value of $400.

In the previous questions, you were given an original value and a percent decrease and were asked to determine the new (*smaller*) value. Suppose you are asked a "reverse" question: "Voter turnout in the local school board elections declined 40% from last year. This year, only 3600 eligible voters went to the polls. How many people voted in last year's school board elections?"

Using the decay factor 0.60 you can write

$$\text{original value} \cdot 0.60 = 3600.$$

To determine last year's voter turnout, divide both sides of the equation by 0.60.

$$\text{original value} = \frac{3600}{0.60}$$

Therefore, last year 6000 people voted in the school board elections.

> **PROCEDURE**
>
> When a quantity has already *decreased* by a specified percent, its original value is obtained by dividing the new value by the corresponding decay factor. That is,
>
> $$\frac{\text{new value}}{\text{decay factor}} = \text{original value.}$$

14. a. You purchased a scanner on sale for $150. The discount was 40%. What was the original price?

b. Determine the original price of a NordicTrack treadmill that is on sale for $1140. Assume that the store has reduced all merchandise by 25%.

SUMMARY
Activity 4.1

1. When a quantity increases by a specified percent, the ratio $\frac{\text{new value}}{\text{original value}}$ is called the **growth factor**. The growth factor is formed by adding the specified percent increase to 100% and then changing this percent into its decimal form.

2. **a.** When a quantity increases by a specified percent, its new value can be obtained by multiplying the original value by the corresponding growth factor. So,

$$\text{original value} \cdot \text{growth factor} = \text{new value}.$$

b. When a quantity has already increased by a specified percent, its original value can be obtained by dividing the new value by the corresponding growth factor. So,

$$\frac{\text{new value}}{\text{growth factor}} = \text{original value}.$$

3. When a quantity decreases by a specified percent, the ratio $\frac{\text{new value}}{\text{original value}}$ is called the **decay factor** associated with the specified percent decrease. The decay factor is formed by subtracting the specified percent decrease from 100% and then changing this percent into its decimal form.

a. When a quantity decreases by a specified percent, its new value can be obtained by multiplying the original value by the corresponding decay factor. So,

$$\text{original value} \cdot \text{decay factor} = \text{new value}.$$

b. When a quantity has already decreased by a specified percent, its original value can be obtained by dividing the new value by the corresponding decay factor. So,

$$\frac{\text{new value}}{\text{decay factor}} = \text{original value}.$$

EXERCISES
Activity 4.1

1. Complete the following table:

PERCENT INCREASE	5%		15%		100%	300%	
GROWTH FACTOR		1.35		1.045			11.00

2. The price your mother negotiated with a car dealer in Hillsborough County for a 2010 Nissan Altima is $17,944, excluding sales tax. The local sales tax rate is 7.00%.

   a. What growth factor is associated with the sales tax rate?

   b. Use the growth factor to determine the total cost of the car.

3. The cost of first-class postage in the United States increased approximately 5.4% in January of 2006 to 39 cents. What was the pre-January cost of the first-class stamp? Round your answer to the nearest penny.

4. A high school in southern Florida reported that its enrollment increased from 11,952 students in 2008–2009 to 12,144 students in 2009–2010.

   a. What is the ratio of the number of students in 2009–2010 to the number of students in 2008–2009?

   b. From your result in part a, determine the growth factor. Write it in decimal form to the nearest hundredth.

   c. By what percent did the high school's enrollment increase?

5. The 2000 United States Census showed that from 1990 to 2000, Florida's population increased by 23.5%. Florida reported its population in 2000 to be 15,982,378. What was Florida's population in 1990?

6. In 1967, your parents bought a house for $26,000. The United States Bureau of Labor Statistics reports that, due to inflation, the cost of the same house in 2001 was $138,563.

   a. What is the inflation growth factor of housing from 1967 to 2001?

   b. What is the inflation rate (percent increase to the nearest whole number percent) for housing from 1967 to 2001?

   c. In 2001, your parents sold their house for $245,000. What profit did they make in terms of 2001 dollars?

7. Your friend plans to move from Lubbock, Texas, to Miami. She earns $50,000 a year in Lubbock. How much must she earn in Miami to maintain the same standard of living if the cost of living in Miami is 35% higher?

8. You decide to invest $3000 in a one-year certificate of deposit that earns an annual percentage yield of 5.05%. How much will your investment be worth in a year?

9. Your company is moving you from the United States to one of the other countries listed in the following table. For each country, the table lists the cost of goods and services that would cost $100 in the United States.

Over There

COUNTRY	COST OF GOODS AND SERVICES ($)	GROWTH FACTOR IN COST OF LIVING	PERCENT INCREASE IN SALARY
United States	100		
Argentina	140		
Australia	114		
Belgium	127		
Canada	105		
Saudi Arabia	131		
Singapore	126		

a. Determine the growth factor for each cost in the table and list it in the third column.

b. Determine the percent increase in your salary that would allow you the same cost of living as you have in the United States. List the percent increase in the fourth column of the table.

c. You earn a salary of $45,000 in the United States. What would your salary have to be in Argentina for you to maintain the same standard of living?

10. Complete the following table:

PERCENT DECREASE	5%		15%		12.5%
DECAY FACTOR		0.45		0.94	

11. You wrote an eight-page article that will be published in a journal. The editor has asked you to revise the article and reduce the number of pages to six. By what percent must you reduce the length of your article?

12. In 1995, the state of California recorded 551,226 live births. In 2000, the number of live births dropped to 531,285. For the five-year period from 1995 to 2000, what was the decay factor for live births? What was the percent decrease (also called the decay rate)?

13. A car dealer will sell you a car you want for $18,194, which is just $200 over the dealer invoice price (the price the dealer pays the manufacturer for the car). You tell him that you will think about it. The dealer is anxious to meet his monthly sales quota, so he calls the next day to offer you the car for $17,994 if you agree to buy it tomorrow. You decide to accept the deal.

   a. What is the decay factor associated with the decrease in the price to you? Write your answer in decimal form to the nearest thousandths.

   b. What is the percent decrease of the price, to the nearest tenth of a percent?

   c. The sales tax is 6.5%. How much did you save on sales tax by taking the dealer's second offer?

14. Your company is moving you from the United States to one of the other countries listed in the following table. For each country, the table lists the cost of goods and services that would cost $100 in the United States.

COUNTRY	COST OF GOODS AND SERVICES ($)	DECAY FACTOR IN COST OF LIVING	PERCENT DECREASE IN COST OF LIVING
United States	100		
Colombia	83		
Hungary	80		
India	93		
Indonesia	98		
Poland	100		
South Africa	87		

   a. Determine the decay factor for each cost in the table and list it in the third column.

   b. Determine the percent decrease in the cost of living for each country compared to living in the United States. List the percent decrease in the fourth column of the table.

   c. You earn a salary of $45,000 in the United States. If you move to South Africa, what salary will you need for the cost of living there?

d. How much of your salary is available to save if you move to Hungary and your salary remains at $45,000?

15. You need a fax machine but plan to wait for a sale. Yesterday, the model you want was reduced by 30%. It originally cost $129.95. Use the decay factor to determine the sale price of the fax machine.

16. Your doctor advises you that losing 10% of your body weight will significantly improve your health.

   a. You weigh 175 pounds. Determine and use the decay factor to calculate your goal weight to the nearest pound.

   b. After six months, you reach your goal weight. However, you still have more weight to lose to reach your ideal weight range, which is 125–150 pounds. If you lose 10% of your new weight, will you be in your ideal weight range? Explain.

17. Aspirin is typically absorbed into the bloodstream from the duodenum (the beginning portion of the small intestine). In general, 75% of a dose of aspirin is eliminated from the bloodstream in an hour. A patient is given a dose of 650 milligrams. How much aspirin remains in the patient after one hour?

18. Airlines often encourage their customers to book online by offering a 5% discount on their ticket. You are traveling from Tampa to San Diego. A fully refundable fare is $558.60. A restricted, nonrefundable fare is $273.60. Determine and use the decay factor to calculate the cost of each fare if you book online.

ACTIVITY 4.2

Take an
Additional
20% Off

OBJECTIVES

1. Define consecutive growth and decay factors.

2. Determine a consecutive growth or decay factor from two or more consecutive percent changes.

3. Use consecutive growth and/or decay factors to solve problems involving percent changes.

Cumulative Discounts

Your friend arrives at your house. Today's newspaper contains a 20%-off coupon at Old Navy. The $100 jacket she had been eyeing all season was already reduced by 40%. She clipped the coupon, drove to the store, selected her jacket, and walked up to the register. The cashier brought up a price of $48; your friend insisted that the price should have been only $40. The store manager arrived and reentered the transaction, and, again, the register displayed $48. Your friend left without purchasing the jacket and drove to your house to tell you her story.

1. How do you think your friend calculated a price of $40?

2. You grab a pencil and start your own calculation. First, you determine the ticketed price that reflects the 40% reduction. At what price is Old Navy selling the jacket? Explain how you calculated this price.

3. To what price does the 20%-off coupon apply?

4. Apply the 20% discount to determine the final price of the jacket.

You are now curious: could you justify a better price by applying the discounts in the reverse order? That is, applying the 20% off coupon, followed by a 40% reduction. You start a new set of calculations.

5. Starting with the list price, determine the sale price after taking the 20% reduction.

6. Apply the 40% discount to the intermediate sale price.

7. Which sequence of discounts gives a better sale price?

The important point to remember here is that when multiple discounts are given, they are always applied sequentially, one after the other—never all at once.

In the following example, you will see how to use decay factors to simplify calculations such as the ones above.

Example 1   *A stunning $2000 gold and diamond necklace you saw was far too expensive to even consider. However, over several weeks you tracked the following successive discounts: 20% off list; 30% off marked price; and an additional 40% off every item. Determine the selling price after each of the discounts is taken.*

SOLUTION

To calculate the first reduced price, apply the decay factor corresponding to a 20% discount. Recall that you form a decay factor by subtracting the 20% discount from 100% to obtain 80%, or 0.80 as a decimal. Apply the 20% reduction by multiplying the original price by the decay factor.

The first sale price = $2000 · 0.80; the selling price is now $1600.

In a similar manner, determine the decay factor corresponding to a 30% discount by subtracting 30% from 100% to obtain 70%, or 0.70 as a decimal. Apply the 30% reduction by multiplying the already discounted price by the decay factor.

The second sale price = $1600 · 0.70; the selling price is now $1120.

Finally, determine the decay factor corresponding to a 40% discount by subtracting 40% from 100% to obtain 60%, or 0.60 as a decimal. Apply the 40% reduction by multiplying the most current discounted price by the decay factor.

$1120 · 0.60; the final selling price is $672.

You may have noticed that it is possible to calculate the final sale price from the original price using a single chain of multiplications:

$2000 · 0.80 · 0.70 · 0.60 = $672

The final sale price is $672.

8. Use the chain of multiplications in Example 1 to determine the final sale price of the necklace if the discounts are taken in the reverse order (40%, 30%, and 20%).

You can form a single decay factor that represents the cumulative effect of applying the three consecutive percent decreases; the single decay factor is the *product* of the three decay factors.

In Example 1, the effective decay factor is given by the product 0.80 · 0.70 · 0.6, which equals 0.336 (or 33.6%). The effective discount is calculated by subtracting the decay factor (in percent form) from 100% to obtain 66.4%. Therefore, the effect of applying 20%, 30%, and 40% consecutive discounts is identical to a single discount of 66.4%.

9. a. Determine a single decay factor that represents the cumulative effect of consecutively applying Old Navy's 40% and 20% discounts.

b. Use this decay factor to determine the effective discount on your friends's jacket.

10. a. Determine a single decay factor that represents the cumulative effect of consecutively applying discounts of 40% and 50%.

b. Use this decay factor to determine the effective discount.

Cumulative Increases

Your fast-food franchise is growing faster than you had ever imagined. Last year, you had 100 employees statewide. This year you opened several additional locations and increased the number of workers by 30%. With demand so high, next year you will open new stores nationwide and plan to increase your employee roll by an additional 50%.

To determine the projected number of employees next year, you can use growth factors to simplify the calculations.

11. a. Determine the growth factor corresponding to a 30% increase.

b. Apply this growth factor to calculate your current workforce.

12. a. Determine the growth factor corresponding to a 50% increase.

b. Apply this growth factor to your current workforce to determine the projected number of employees next year.

13. Starting from last year's workforce of 100, write a single chain of multiplications to calculate the projected number of employees.

You can form a single growth factor that represents the cumulative effect of applying the two consecutive percent increases; the single growth factor is the *product* of the two growth factors.

In Problem 13, the effective growth factor is given by the product $1.30 \cdot 1.50$, which equals 1.95 (an increase of 95%), nearly double the number of employees last year.

What Goes Up Often Comes Down

You purchased $1000 of a recommended stock last year and watched gleefully as it rose quickly by 30%. Unfortunately, the economy turned downward, and your stock recently fell 30% from last year's high. Have you made or lost money on your investment? The answer might surprise you. Find out by solving the following sequence of problems.

14. a. Determine the growth factor corresponding to a 30% increase.

   b. Determine the decay factor corresponding to a 30% decrease.

You can form a single factor that represents the cumulative effect of applying the consecutive percent increase and decrease—the single factor is the *product* of the growth and decay factors. In this example, the effective factor is given by the product $1.30 \cdot 0.70$, which equals 0.91.

15. Does 0.91 represent a growth factor or a decay factor? How can you tell?

16. a. What is the current value of your stock?

   b. What is the cumulative effect (as a percent change) of applying a 30% increase followed by a 30% decrease?

17. What is the cumulative effect if the 30% decrease had been applied first, followed by the 30% increase?

SUMMARY
Activity 4.2

1. The cumulative effect of a sequence of percent changes is the *product* of the associated growth or decay factors. For example,

   a. To calculate the effect of consecutively applying 20% and 50% increases, form the respective growth factors and multiply. The effective growth factor is
$$1.20 \cdot 1.50 = 1.80,$$
   which represents an effective increase of 80%.

   b. To calculate the effect of applying a 25% *increase* followed by a 20% *decrease*, form the respective growth and decay factors, and then multiply them. The effective factor is $1.25 \cdot 0.80 = 1.00$, which indicates neither growth nor decay. That is, the quantity has returned to its original value.

2. The cumulative effect of a sequence of percent changes is the same, regardless of the order in which the changes are applied. For example, the cumulative effect of applying a 20% *increase* followed by a 50% *decrease* is equivalent to having first applied the 50% *decrease*, followed by the 20% *increase*.

EXERCISES
Activity 4.2

1. A $300 suit is on sale for 30% off. You present a coupon at the cash register for an additional 20% off.

   a. Determine the decay factor corresponding to each percent decrease.

   b. Use these decay factors to determine the price you paid for the suit.

2. A union has just negotiated a three-year contract containing annual raises of 3%, 4%, and 5% during the term of contract. One union member's current salary is $42,000. What will she be earning in three years?

3. The manager of a toy store anticipates a large demand for a popular toy and increases her inventory of 1600 by 25%. She sold 75% of her inventory. How many toys remain?

4. You deposit a $2000 graduation gift in a five-year certificate of deposit that pays 4% interest compounded annually. Determine to the nearest dollar your account balance when your certificate comes due.

5. Budget cuts have severely affected your high school's athletics department over the last few years. The department's operating budget of $600,000 has decreased 5% in each of the last three years. What is the current operating budget?

6. When you became a manager, your $60,000 annual salary increased 25%. You found the new job too stressful and requested a return to your original job. You resumed your former duties at a 20% reduction in salary. How much more are you making at your old job after the transfer and return?

ACTIVITY 4.3

Inflation

OBJECTIVES

1. Recognize an exponential function as a rule for applying a growth factor or a decay factor.

2. Graph exponential functions from numerical data.

3. Recognize exponential functions from equations.

4. Graph exponential functions using technology.

Exponential Growth

Inflation means that a current dollar will buy less in the future. According to the U.S. Consumer Price Index, the inflation rate for 2005 was 4%. This means that a one-pound loaf of white bread that costs a dollar in January 2005 costs $1.04 in January 2006. The change in price is usually expressed as an annual percentage rate, known as the *inflation rate*.

1. **a.** At the current inflation rate of 4%, how much will a $20 pair of shoes cost next year?

   b. Assume that the rate of inflation remains at 4% next year. How much will the shoes cost in the year following next year?

2. Assume that the inflation rate is currently 5% per year and remains at 5% per year for the next decade. Calculate the cost of a currently priced $8 pizza for each of the next ten years. Complete the following table. Round to the nearest cent.

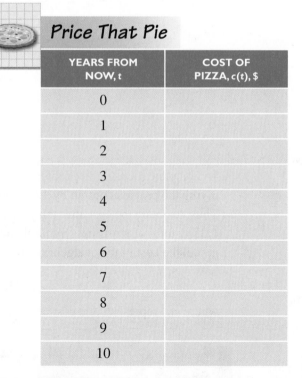

Price That Pie

YEARS FROM NOW, t	COST OF PIZZA, c(t), $
0	
1	
2	
3	
4	
5	
6	
7	
8	
9	
10	

3. Plot the data from Problem 2 on appropriately scaled and labeled axes. Use the variable t, years from now, as the independent variable and $c(t)$, the cost of pizza, as the dependent variable.

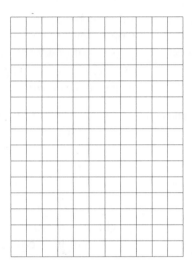

4. Determine the average rate of change of the cost of the pizza in the first year (from $t = 0$ to $t = 1$), the fifth year (from $t = 4$ to $t = 5$), and the tenth year (from $t = 9$ to $t = 10$). Explain what these results mean for the cost of pizza over the next ten years.

To complete the table in Problem 2, you could calculate each cost value by multiplying the previous output by 1.05, the inflation's growth factor (see Activity 4.1). Thus, to obtain the cost after ten years, you would multiply the original cost, $8, by 1.05, a total of ten times. Symbolically, you write $8(1.05)^{10}$. Therefore, you can model the cost of pizza algebraically as

$$c(t) = 8(1.05)^t,$$

where $c(t)$ represents the cost and t represents the number of years from now.

DEFINITION

When the independent variable of a function appears as an exponent of the growth factor, the function, in this case $c(t) = 8(1.05)^t$, is called an **exponential function**.

5. a. Under a constant annual inflation rate of 5%, what will a pizza cost after twenty years?

b. Use the cost function to calculate the cost of a pizza after five years.

6. a. A graph of the function $c(t) = 8(1.05)^t$ is shown below in a window for t between -20 and 20 and $c(t)$ between 0 and 20. Use the same window to graph this function on a graphing calculator.

b. Use the trace or table feature of the calculator to examine the coordinates of some points on the graph. Does your plot of the numerical data in Problem 3 agree with the graph shown here?

c. Is the entire graph in part a relevant to the original problem? Explain.

d. Resize your window to include only the first quadrant from $x = 0$ to $x = 20$ and $y = 0$ to $y = 20$. Regraph the function.

7. a. How many years will it take for the price of a pizza to double? Explain how you determined your answer.

b. How many years will it take for the price of a pizza to triple? Explain how you find your answer.

Exponential Decay

You have just purchased an automobile for $16,000. Much to your dismay, you have just learned that you should expect the value of your car to depreciate by 15% per year!

8. What is the decay factor (see Activity 4.1) for the yearly depreciation rate 15%?

9. Use the decay factor from Problem 8 to determine the car's values for the years given in the table. Record your results in the table.

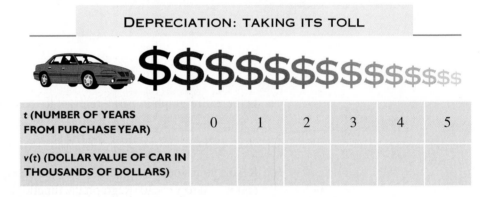

DEPRECIATION: TAKING ITS TOLL

t (NUMBER OF YEARS FROM PURCHASE YEAR)	0	1	2	3	4	5
v(t) (DOLLAR VALUE OF CAR IN THOUSANDS OF DOLLARS)						

In Problem 9, you could calculate the value of the car in any given year by multiplying the previous year's value by 0.85, the depreciation decay factor. Thus, to obtain the retail value after 5 years, you could multiply the original value by 0.85 a total of five times as follows:

$$16(0.85)(0.85)(0.85)(0.85)(0.85) \approx 7.1 \text{ thousand or } \$7100$$

or equivalently in exponential form,

$$16(0.85)^5 \approx \$7100$$

Therefore, you can model the value of the car, $v(t)$, algebraically by the formula

$$v(t) = 16(0.85)^t,$$

where t represents the number of years you own the car and $v(t)$ represents the car's value in thousands of dollars.

10. Determine the value of the car in 6 years.

11. Graph the depreciation formula for the car's value, $v(t) = 16(0.85)^t$, as a function of the time from the year of purchase. Use the following grid or a graphing calculator. Extend your graph to include 10 years from the date of purchase.

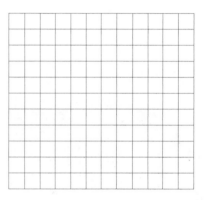

12. How long will it take for the value of the car to decrease to half its original value? Explain how you determined your answer.

SUMMARY
Activity 4.3

An **exponential function** is a function in which the independent variable appears as an exponent of the growth factor such as $c(t) = 8(1.05)^t$ or a decay factor such as $v(t) = 16(.85)^t$.

EXERCISES
Activity 4.3

1. a. Complete the following table, in which $f(x) = \left(\frac{1}{2}\right)^x$ and $g(x) = 2^x$.

x	−2	−1	0	1	2
f(x)					
g(x)					

b. Use the points in part a to sketch a graph of the given functions f and g on the same coordinate axes. Compare the graphs. List the similarities and differences.

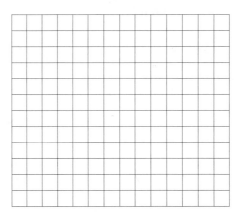

c. Use a graphing calculator to graph the functions $f(x) = \left(\frac{1}{2}\right)^x$ and $g(x) = 2^x$ given in part a in the window Xmin $= -2$, Xmax $= 2$, Ymin $= -2$, and Ymax $= 5$. Compare to the graphs you obtained in part b.

2. Suppose the inflation rate is 7% per year and remains the same for the next seven years.

a. Complete the following table for the cost of a pair of sneakers that costs $45 now. Round to the nearest cent:

t, YEARS FROM NOW	0	1	2	3	4	5	6	7
$c(t)$, COST OF SNEAKERS ($)	45							

b. Determine the growth factor for a 7% inflation rate.

c. If the yearly inflation rate remains at 7%, what exponential function would you use to determine the cost of $45 sneakers after t years?

d. What would be the cost of the sneakers in ten years if the inflation rate stayed at 7%?

3. An exponential function may be increasing or decreasing. Determine which is the case for each of the following functions. Explain how you determined each answer.

a. $y = 5^x$ **b.** $y = \left(\frac{1}{2}\right)^x$

c. $y = 1.5^t$ **d.** $y = 0.2^p$

4. a. Evaluate the functions in the following table for the input values, x:

INPUT x	0	1	2	3	4	5
$g(x) = 3x$						
$f(x) = 3^x$						

b. Compare the functions $f(x) = 3^x$ and $g(x) = 3x$ from $x = 0$ to $x = 5$ by comparing the output values in the table.

c. Compare the graphs of the functions f and g that are shown in the following window. Approximate the interval in which the exponential function f grows slower than the linear function g and the interval where it grows faster.

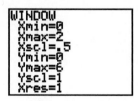
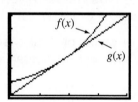

d. Compare the rate of increase of the functions $f(x) = 3^x$ and $g(x) = 3x$ from $x = 0$ to $x = 5$ by calculating the average rate of change for each function from $x = 0$ to $x = 5$. Determine which function grows faster on average in the given interval.

5. a. For investment purposes, your uncle recently bought a house for $100,000 in a neighborhood where the price of houses has been rising $10,000 a year. If the rise in housing prices continues in the same manner, how much will your uncle's investment be worth in a year and in two years?

b. Your uncle decides to buy a second investment property, again paying $100,000 for another house but in a different area. Here, the prices have been rising at a rate of 10% a year. If this rate of increase continues, how much will your investment be worth in a year and in two years?

c. Which investment will give the better return?

6. A radiology specialist uses the radioactive substance iodine-131 to diagnose conditions of the thyroid gland. Iodine-131 decays (loses radiation energy and changes to a nonradioactive form of iodine) at the rate of 8.3 percent per day. The hospital currently has a 20-gram supply of iodine-131.

a. What is the decay factor for the decay of the iodine?

b. Use the decay factor from part a to determine the number of grams remaining for the days listed in the following table. Record your results in the table to the nearest hundredth.

t (NUMBER OF DAYS STARTING FROM A 20-GRAM SUPPLY OF IODINE-131)	0	4	8	12	16	20	24
N, NUMBER OF GRAMS OF IODINE-131 REMAINING FROM A 20-GRAM SUPPLY	20.00						

c. Write an exponential decay formula for N, the number of grams of iodine-131 remaining, in terms of t, the number of days from the current supply of 20 grams.

d. Determine the number of grams of iodine-131 remaining from a 20-gram supply after 2 months (60 days).

e. Graph the decay formula for iodine-131, $N = 20(0.917)^t$, as a function of the time t (days). Use appropriate scales and labels on the following grid or an appropriate window on a graphing calculator.

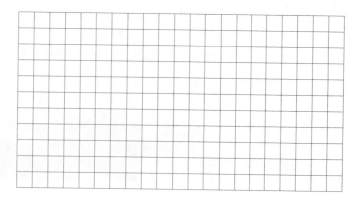

f. How long will it take for iodine-131 to decrease to half its original value? Explain how you determined your answer.

ACTIVITY 4.4

The Summer Job

OBJECTIVES

1. Determine the growth or decay factor of an exponential function.

2. Identify the properties of the graph of an exponential function defined by $y = b^x$, where $b > 0$ and $b \neq 1$.

Your brother will be attending college in the fall, majoring in mathematics. On July 1, he goes to your neighbor's house looking for summer work to help pay for college expenses. Your neighbor is interested since he needs some odd jobs done. Your brother can start right away and will work all day July 1 for 2 cents. This gets your neighbor's attention, but you wonder if there is a catch. Your brother says that he will work July 2 for 4 cents, July 3 for 8 cents, July 4 for 16 cents, and so on for *every* day of the month of July.

For Problems 1–2, assume that the neighbor hires your brother.

1. a. Complete the following table.

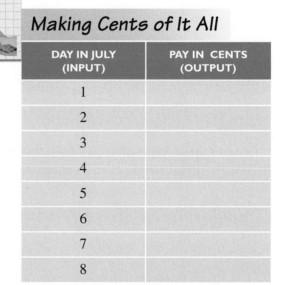

Making Cents of It All

DAY IN JULY (INPUT)	PAY IN CENTS (OUTPUT)
1	
2	
3	
4	
5	
6	
7	
8	

b. Do you notice a pattern in the output values? Describe how you can obtain the pay on a given day knowing the pay on the previous day.

c. Use what you discovered in part b to determine the pay on July 9.

2. a. The pay on any given day can be written as a power of 2. Write each pay entry in the output column of the table in Problem 1 as a power of 2. For example, $2 = 2^1$, $4 = 2^2$.

b. Let n represent the number of days worked. Write an equation for the daily pay, $P(n)$, (in cents) as a function of n, the number of days worked. Note that the number of days worked is the same as the July date.

c. Use the equation from part b to determine how much your brother will earn on July 20. That is, determine the value of $P(n)$ when $n = 20$. What are the units of measurement of your answer?

d. How much will he earn on July 31? Be sure to indicate the units of your answer.

Therefore, it was not a good idea for the neighbor to hire your brother! This situation demonstrates the growth power of exponential functions.

3. a. Determine the average rate of change of $P(n)$ as n increases from $n = 3$ to $n = 4$. What are the units of measurement of your answer?

b. Determine the average rate of change of $P(n)$ as n increases from $n = 7$ to $n = 8$. Include units in your answer.

c. Is the function linear? Explain.

4. a. What is the practical domain of the function defined by $P(n) = 2^n$?

b. Sketch a scatterplot of ordered pairs of the form $(n, P(n))$ from July 1 to July 10 on appropriately scaled and labeled axes.

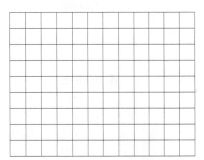

The function defined by $P(n) = 2^n$ gives the relationship between the pay $P(n)$ (in cents) and the given July date, n, worked. This function belongs to a family of **exponential functions**.

If x represents the independent variable and y represents the dependent variable, then some **exponential functions** can be defined by equations of the form $y = b^x$, where the base b is a constant such that b is a positive number not equal to 1 ($b > 0$ and $b \neq 1$). As discussed in Activity 4.3, the base b is a growth or decay factor.

Example 1   *Some examples of exponential functions are*

$g(x) = 10^x$, where $b = 10$, $h(x) = (1.08)^x$, where $b = 1.08$,

$V(x) = \left(\dfrac{1}{2}\right)^x$, where $b = \dfrac{1}{2}$, and $T(x) = (0.75)^x$, where $b = 0.75$.

Graphs of Increasing Exponential Functions

Because n in $P(n) = 2^n$ (the summer job situation) represents a given day in July, the practical domain (whole numbers from 1 to 31) limits the investigation of the exponential function.

5. a. Consider the general function defined by $f(x) = 2^x$. Use a graphing calculator to sketch a graph of this function. Use the window Xmin $= -10$, Xmax $= 10$, Ymin $= -2$, and Ymax $= 10$. Your screens should appear as follows:

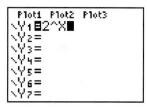 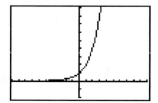

b. Because the graph of the general function $f(x) = 2^x$ is continuous (it has no holes or breaks), what appears to be the domain of the function f? What is the range of the function f?

c. Determine the y-intercept of the graph of f by substituting 0 for x in the equation $y = 2^x$ and solving for y.

d. Is the function f increasing or decreasing?

DEFINITION

If the base b of an exponential function defined by $y = b^x$ is greater than 1, then b is the **growth factor**. The graph of $y = b^x$ is increasing if $b > 1$. For each increase of 1 of the value of x, y increases by a factor of b.

Example 2 *The base 2 of $f(x) = 2^x$ is the growth factor because each time the input, x, is increased by 1, the output is multiplied by 2.*

6. Identify the growth factor, if any, for the given function.

a. $y = 1.08^x$

b. $h(x) = 0.8^x$

c. $y = 8x$

d. $g(x) = 10^x$

7. Return to the graph of $f(x) = 2^x$.

a. Does the graph of $f(x) = 2^x$ appear to have an x-intercept?

b. Use your calculator to complete the following table.

x	-1	-2	-4	-6	-8	-10
$f(x) = 2^x$						

Note: By definition, $b^{-n} = \dfrac{1}{b^n}$. Therefore,

$$2^{-1} = \frac{1}{2^1} = 0.5,\ 2^{-4} = \frac{1}{2^4} = 0.0625,\ \text{and}\ 2^{-10} = \frac{1}{2^{10}} \approx 0.000977.$$

c. As the values of the input variable x decrease, what happens to the output values?

d. Use the trace feature of your graphing calculator to trace the graph of $f(x) = 2^x$ for $x < 0$. What appears to be the relationship between the graph of $y = 2^x$ and the x-axis when x becomes more negative?

> **DEFINITION**
>
> A horizontal axis having equation $y = 0$ is called a **horizontal asymptote** of the graph of a function defined by $y = b^x$, where $b > 0$ and $b \neq 1$. The graph of the function gets closer and closer to the x-axis $(y = 0)$ as the input gets farther from the origin, in the negative direction.

Example 3   *The x-axis is the horizontal asymptote of $y = 3^x$ and $y = 7^x$ because, as x gets more negative, the graph gets closer and closer to the x-axis. See the graph that follows.*

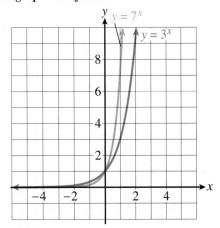

8. a. Complete the following table.

x	-3	-2	-1	0	1	2	3	4	5
$f(x) = 2^x$									
$g(x) = 10^x$									

b. Sketch the graph of the functions f and g on your graphing calculator. Use the window $\text{Xmin} = -5$, $\text{Xmax} = 5$, $\text{Ymin} = -2$, and $\text{Ymax} = 9$.

c. Use the results from parts a and b to describe how the graphs of $f(x) = 2^x$ and $g(x) = 10^x$ are similar and how they are different. Be sure to include domain, growth factor, x- and y-intercepts, and horizontal asymptotes. Also discuss whether the graph of g increases faster or slower than the graph of f.

Graphs of Decreasing Exponential Functions

9. a. Complete the following table.

x	-3	-2	-1	0	1	2	3	4	5
$y = \left(\frac{1}{2}\right)^x$									

b. Describe how you can obtain the y-value for $x = 6$, using the y-value for $x = 5$.

c. Sketch the graph of $y = \left(\frac{1}{2}\right)^x$. Verify your sketch using your graphing calculator.

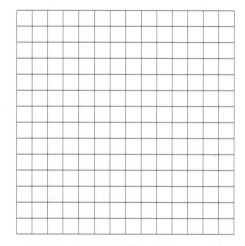

d. What are the domain and range of the exponential function?

e. Determine the y-intercept of the graph.

f. Is the function defined by $y = \left(\dfrac{1}{2}\right)^x$ increasing or decreasing?

DEFINITION

If the base b of an exponential function $y = b^x$ is between 0 and 1, then b is the **decay factor**. The graph of $y = b^x$ is decreasing if $0 < b < 1$. For each increase of 1 of the value of the input, the output decreases by a factor of b.

Example 4 *The base $\frac{1}{2}$ in the function $y = (\frac{1}{2})^x$ is the decay factor because each time x is increased by 1, the output value is multiplied by $\frac{1}{2}$.*

10. Identify the decay factor, if any, for the function defined by the given equation.

a. $y = 0.98^x$

b. $h(x) = 1.8^x$

c. $y = 0.8x$

d. $g(x) = \left(\dfrac{2}{7}\right)^x$

11. Return to the graph of $y = \left(\dfrac{1}{2}\right)^x$.

a. Does the graph of $y = \left(\dfrac{1}{2}\right)^x$ have an x-intercept?

b. Complete the following table.

x	1	3	5	7	10
$y = (\frac{1}{2})^x$					

c. As the values of the input variable x get larger, what happens to the y-values?

d. Does the graph of $y = \left(\dfrac{1}{2}\right)^x$ have a horizontal asymptote? Explain.

12. a. For each of the following exponential functions, identify the base, b, and determine whether the base is a growth or decay factor. Graph each function on your graphing calculator, and complete the table below.

FUNCTION	BASE, B	GROWTH OR DECAY FACTOR	x-INTERCEPT	y-INTERCEPT	HORIZONTAL ASYMPTOTE	INCREASING OR DECREASING
$h(x) = (1.08)^x$						
$T(x) = (0.75)^x$						
$f(x) = (3.2)^x$						
$r(x) = \left(\frac{1}{4}\right)^x$						

b. Without graphing, how might you determine which of the functions in part a increase and which decrease? Explain.

13. Examine the output pattern to determine which of the following data sets is linear and which is exponential. For the linear set, determine the slope. For the exponential set, determine the growth or decay factor.

a.

x	−2	−1	0	1	2	3	4
y	−8	−4	0	4	8	12	16

b.

x	−2	−1	0	1	2	3	4
y	$\frac{1}{16}$	$\frac{1}{4}$	1	4	16	64	256

14. Determine the decay factor of the function represented by the data and complete the table.

x	−2	−1	0	1	2
f(x)	16	4			

SUMMARY
Activity 4.4

Functions defined by equations of the form $y = b^x$, where $b > 0$ and $b \neq 1$, are called **exponential functions** and have the following properties.

1. The domain is all real numbers.

2. The range is $y > 0$.

3. If $0 < b < 1$, the function is decreasing and has the following general shape.

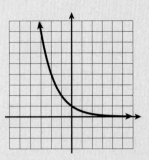

In this case, b is called the **decay factor**.

4. If $b > 1$, the function is increasing and has the following general shape.

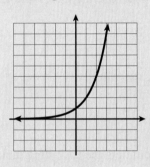

In this case, b is called the **growth factor**.

5. The y-intercept is $(0, 1)$.

6. The graph does not intersect the horizontal axis. There is no x-intercept.

7. The line $y = 0$ (the x-axis) is a **horizontal asymptote**.

8. The function is continuous.

EXERCISES
Activity 4.4

1. a. Complete the following tables.

x	-3	-2	-1	0	1	2	3
$h(x) = 5^x$							

x	-3	-2	-1	0	1	2	3
$g(x) = \left(\frac{1}{5}\right)^x$							

b. Sketch graphs of *h* and *g* on the following grid.

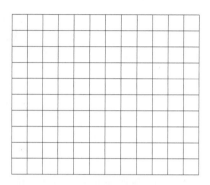

c. Use the tables and graphs in parts a and b to complete the following table.

$h(x) = 5^x$						
$g(x) = \left(\frac{1}{5}\right)^x$						

2. a. Complete the following table.

x	−3	−2	−1	0	1	2	3
$f(x) = 3^x$							
$g(x) = x^3$							
$h(x) = 3x$							

b. Sketch a graph of each of the given functions *f*, *g*, and *h*.

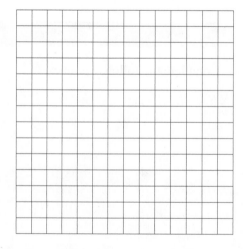

c. Describe any similarities or differences that you observe in the graphs.

3. Using your graphing calculator, investigate the graphs of the following families (groups) of functions. Describe any relationships within each family, including domain and range, growth or decay factors, vertical and horizontal intercepts, and asymptotes. Identify the functions as increasing or decreasing.

a. $f(x) = \left(\dfrac{3}{4}\right)^x$, $g(x) = \left(\dfrac{4}{3}\right)^x$

b. $f(x) = 10^x$, $g(x) = -10^x$

c. $f(x) = 3^x$, $g(x) = \left(\dfrac{1}{3}\right)^x$

4. Determine which of the following data sets are linear and which are exponential. For the linear sets, determine the slope. For the exponential sets, determine the growth factor or the decay factor.

a.

x	−2	−1	0	1	2	3	4
y	$\frac{1}{9}$	$\frac{1}{3}$	1	3	9	27	81

b.

x	−2	−1	0	1	2	3	4
y	2	2.5	3	3.5	4	4.5	5

c.

x	−2	−1	0	1	2	3	4
y	0.75	1.5	3	6	12	24	48

d.

x	−2	−1	0	1	2	3	4
y	6.25	2.5	1	0.4	0.16	.064	.0256

5. Assume that y is an exponential function of x.

   a. If the growth factor is 1.08, then complete the following table.

x	0	1	2	3
y	23.1			

   b. If the decay factor is 0.75, then complete the following table.

x	0	1	2	3
y	10			

6. a. Would you expect $f(x) = 3^x$ to increase faster or slower than $g(x) = 2.5^x$ for $x > 0$? Explain. (*Hint:* You may want to use your graphing calculator for help.)

   b. Would you expect $f(x) = \left(\frac{1}{2}\right)^x$ to decrease faster or slower than $g(x) = (0.70)^x$ for $x > 0$? Explain.

7. Determine the domain and range of each of the following functions.

a.

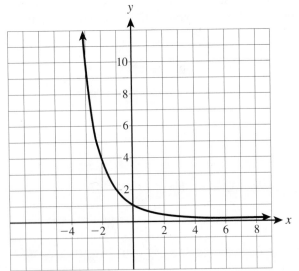

b.

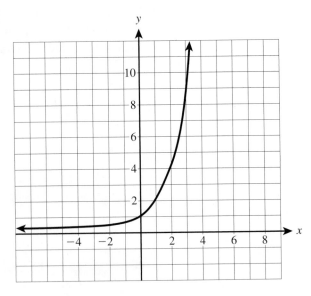

8. Take a piece of paper from your notebook. Let x represent the number of times you fold the paper in half and $f(x)$ represent the number of sections the paper is divided into after the folding.

   a. Complete the table of values.

x	0	1	2	3	4	5
f(x)						

   b. If you could fold the paper 8 times, how many individual sections will there be on the paper?

   c. Does this data represent an exponential function? Explain.

   d. What is the practical domain and range in this situation?

In Exercises 9–13, match each graph with its equation.

9. $y = 3^x$

10. $y = 3^{x+2}$

11. $y = 2 \cdot 3^x$

12. $y = -3^x$

13. $y = 3^{-x}$

a.

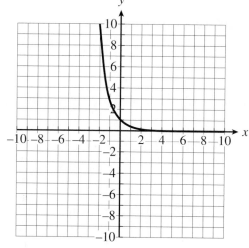

b.

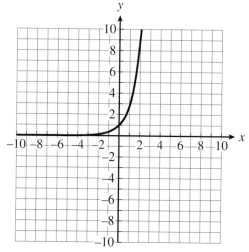

c.

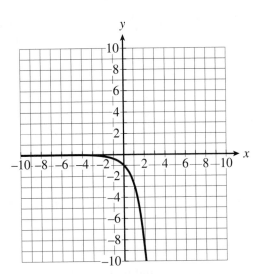

d.

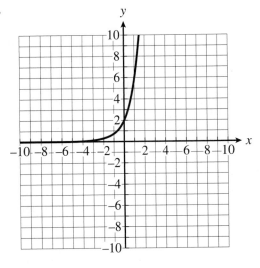

e.

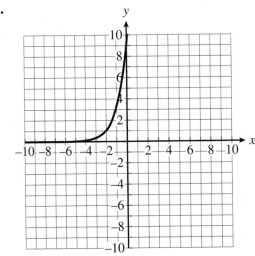

14. Identify if the exponential function is increasing or decreasing. Verify using a graphing calculator.

a. $y = 5^x$

b. $y = \left(\dfrac{4}{5}\right)^x$

c. $y = (2.5)^x$

d. $y = (0.65)^x$

ACTIVITY 4.5
Cell Phones

OBJECTIVES

1. Determine the growth or decay factor for an exponential function represented by a table of values or an equation.

2. Graph exponential functions defined by $y = ab^x$, where $a \neq 0$, $b > 0$, and $b \neq 1$.

3. Identify the meaning of a in $y = ab^x$ as it relates to a practical situation.

4. Determine the doubling and halving time.

During a meeting, you hear the familiar ring of a cell phone. Without hesitation, several of your friends reach into their jacket pockets, briefcases, and purses to receive the anticipated call. Although sometimes annoying, cell phones have become part of our way of life.

The following table shows the rapid increase in the number of cell phone users (figures are approximate) in the late 1990s. Note that the independent variable (year) increases in steps of one unit (year).

Calling All Cells

YEAR	NUMBER OF CELL PHONE USERS AS OF JAN. 1 (in millions)
1996	44.248
1997	55.312
1998	69.140
1999	86.425
2000	108.031

1. Is this a linear function? How do you know?

2. a. Evaluate the indicated ratios to complete the following table:

No. of phones in 1997 / No. of phones in 1996	No. of phones in 1998 / No. of phones in 1997	No. of phones in 1999 / No. of phones in 1998	No. of phones in 2000 / No. of phones in 1999

b. What do you notice about the values of the table?

In an exponential function with base b, equally spaced x-values yield y-values whose successive ratios are constant. If the x-values increase by increments of 1, the common ratio is the base b. If $b > 1$, b is the growth factor; if $0 < b < 1$, b is the decay factor.

3. a. Does the relationship in the table preceding Problem 1 represent an exponential function? Explain.

b. What is the growth factor?

c. As a consequence of the result found in part b, you can start with 44.248, the number of cell phone users in 1996, and obtain the number of cell phone users in 1997 by multiplying by the growth factor, $b = 1.25$. You can then determine the number of cell phone users in 1998 by multiplying the number of cell phone users in 1997 by b, and so on. Verify this with your calculator. Note that because the exponential function is a mathematical model, the results will vary slightly from the actual number of phones given in the table preceding Problem 1.

Once you know the growth factor ($b = 1.25$), you can determine the equation that gives the number of cell phone users as a function of t, the number of years since 1996. Note that $t = 0$ corresponds to 1996, $t = 1$ to 1997, and so on.

4. a. Complete the table.

t	CALCULATION FOR THE NUMBER OF CELL PHONE USERS	EXPONENTIAL FORM	NUMBER OF CELL PHONE USERS (in millions)
0	44.248	$44.248(1.25)^0$	44.248
1	(44.248)1.25	$44.248(1.25)^1$	
2			
3			

b. Use the pattern in the preceding table to help you write the equation of the form $N = a \cdot b^t$, where N represents the number of cell phones (in millions) in use at time t, the number of years since 1996.

c. What is the practical domain of the function N?

d. Graph the function N on your graphing calculator, and then sketch the result below on an appropriately scaled and labeled axis.

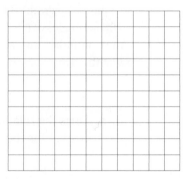

e. Using transformations, describe how the graph in part d is related to the graph of the increasing function $N = (1.25)^t$.

f. Determine the N-intercept of the graph of N by substituting 0 for t. What is the practical meaning of the vertical intercept in this situation?

g. What does the value of a in the equation in part b represent?

DEFINITION

Many exponential functions can be represented symbolically by $y = a \cdot b^x$, where a is the value of y when $x = 0$ and b is the growth or decay factor. If the x-variable of $y = a \cdot b^x$ represents time, then the coefficient a is called the *initial value*.

Example 1   *The exponential function defined by $y = 5 \cdot 2^x$ has y-intercept $(0, 5)$ and growth factor $b = 2$. The exponential function defined by $y = \frac{1}{2}(0.75)^x$ has y-intercept $\left(0, \frac{1}{2}\right)$ and decay factor $b = 0.75$.*

5. Use the function defined by $N = 44.248(1.25)^t$ to estimate the number of cell phone users in 2005. Do you think this is a good estimate? Explain.

6. a. Use the graph of the exponential function $N = 44.248(1.25)^t$ and the trace or table feature of your graphing calculator to estimate the number of years it takes for the number of cell phone users to double from 44.248 million to 88.496 million.

b. Estimate the time necessary for the number of cell phone users to double from 88.496 million to 176.992 million. Verify your estimate using your calculator.

c. How long will it take for any given number of cell phone users to double?

DEFINITION

The **doubling time** of an exponential function is the time it takes for an output to double. The doubling time is determined by the growth factor and remains the same for all output values.

Example 2 *The balance B(t), in dollars, of an investment account is defined by* $B(t) = 5500(1.12)^t$, *where t is the number of years. The initial value for this function is $5500. Determine the value of t when the balance is doubled or equal to $11,000.*

SOLUTION

If you use the table feature of your calculator, the doubling time is estimated at 6.1 years (see the following calculator graphic). The intersect feature on the graphing calculator shows the doubling time to be 6.12 years to the nearest hundredth.

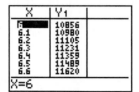
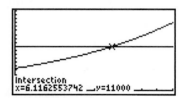

Decreasing Exponential Functions

You sold your used car and have just purchased a new car for $26,000. You have just learned that you should expect the value of your car to depreciate by 30% per year! The following table shows the book value of the car for the next several years, where *V* is the value in thousands of dollars:

DEPRECIATION: OF LITTLE VALUE

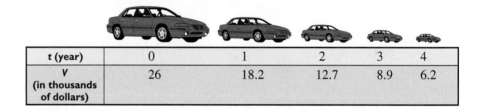

t (year)	0	1	2	3	4
V (in thousands of dollars)	26	18.2	12.7	8.9	6.2

The values of the independent variable, *t*, are incremented by 1, and a value of the *V* is obtained by multiplying the previous value by a constant factor. This is another example of an exponential function. However, because the value of the car is decreasing, the constant factor is a *decay factor* and its value will be between 0 and 1.

7. a. Calculate the decay factor, *b*, in this situation. Show the calculations you perform to determine the factor.

b. You can now start with 26, the initial value of the car (in thousands of dollars), and obtain the value after one year by multiplying by the decay factor, $b = 0.70$. The value of the car after two years is the value of the car after one year times the decay factor. Verify this on your calculator, and compare your results with the entries in the table prior to Problem 7.

8. a. Complete the following table.

t	CALCULATION OF THE VALUE OF THE CAR	EXPONENTIAL FORM	VALUE, $V = a \cdot b^t$ (in thousands of dollars)
0	26	$26(0.70)^0$	26
1	$26 \cdot 0.70$	$26(0.70)^1$	
2			
3			

b. Use the pattern in the preceding table to help you write an equation of the form $V = a \cdot b^t$, where V represents the value of the car as a function of time, t.

c. What is the practical domain of this function?

d. Graph this function on your graphing calculator, and sketch the result below on an appropriate scaled and labeled set of axes. Note that the graph is a vertical stretch of the graph of the decreasing function defined by $V = (0.70)^t$.

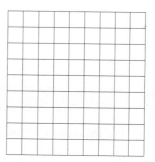

e. Determine the V-intercept of the graph by substituting 0 for the input t. What is the practical meaning of the intercept in this situation?

9. a. Use your graphing calculator to estimate the number of years it takes to halve the value of the automobile from $26,000 to $13,000.

b. Estimate the time necessary to halve the value from $13,000 to $6500. Verify your answer using your graphing calculator.

c. How long will it take for any specific value of the car to halve?

> DEFINITION
>
> The **half-life** of an exponential function is the time it takes for a y-value to decay by one-half. The half-life is determined by the decay factor and remains the same for all y-values.

10. Homemade chocolate chip cookies lose their freshness over time. Let the taste quality be 1 when the cookies are fresh. The taste quality decreases according to the function:

$$y = 0.8^x,$$

where x is the number of days since the cookies were baked.

Determine when the taste quality will be one-half of its value. Use the intersect feature of your calculator to determine when y is $\frac{1}{2}$ of 1 or 0.5.

SUMMARY
Activity 4.5

1. For **exponential functions** defined by $y = ab^x$, a is the value of y when $x = 0$ (sometimes called the initial value), and b is the growth or decay factor.

2. The y-intercept of these functions is $(0, a)$.

3. In an exponential function, equally spaced x-values yield y-values whose successive ratios are constant. If the x-values increase by one unit, then
   a. the constant ratio is the **growth factor** if the y-values are increasing.
   b. the constant ratio is the **decay factor** if the y-values are decreasing.

4. The **doubling time** of an increasing exponential function is the time it takes for y-values to double. The doubling time is set by the growth factor and remains the same for all y-values.

5. The **half-life** of a decreasing exponential function is the time it takes for y-values to decay by one-half. The half-life is determined by the decay factor and remains the same for all y-values.

EXERCISES
Activity 4.5

1. The population of Russia in selected years can be approximated by the following table.

YEAR	1995	1996	1997	2000
POPULATION (in millions)	148.0	147.6	146.9	146.0

   a. Let 1995 correspond to $t = 0$. Let b be the ratio between the population of Russia in 1996 and 1995. Determine an exponential function of the form $y = a \cdot b^t$ to represent the population of Russia symbolically. Round to four decimal places.

   b. Does the function in part a give an accurate value of the population of Russia in 2000? Explain.

2. Without using your graphing calculator, match each graph with its equation. Then check your answer using a graphing calculator.

   a. $f(x) = 0.5(0.73)^x$ **b.** $g(x) = 3(1.73)^x$ **c.** $h(x) = -2(1.73)^x$

   i.

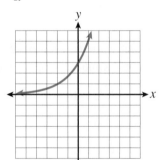

   ii.

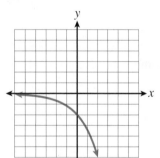

   iii.

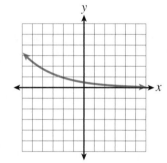

3. Which of the following tables represent exponential functions? Indicate the growth or decay factor for the data that is exponential.

   a.

x	0	1	2	3	4
y	0	2	16	54	128

   b.

x	0	1	2	3	4
y	1	4	16	64	256

c.

x	1	2	3	4	5
y	1750	858	420	206	101

4. a. Sketch a graph of $f(x) = 2^x$ and $g(x) = 3 \cdot 2^x$ on the same coordinate axis.

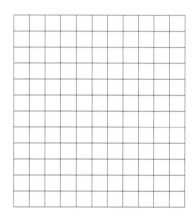

b. Describe how the graphs of f and g are similar and how they are different.

5. If $f(x) = 3 \cdot 4^x$, determine the exact value of each of the following, when possible. Otherwise, use your calculator to approximate the value to the nearest hundredth.

a. $f(-2)$ **b.** $f\left(\frac{1}{2}\right)$

c. $f(2)$ **d.** $f(1.3)$

6. In 1995, the U.S. emitted approximately 1400 million tons of carbon into the atmosphere. This represented about one-fourth of the world total. The U.S. emissions were increasing at about 1.3% per year. If t represents the number of years since 1995 and $A(t)$ represents the amount of carbon (in millions of tons) emitted in a given year, then $A(t) = 1400(1.013)^t$.

a. What is the initial amount of U.S. carbon emissions?

b. Complete the following table.

t, NUMBER OF YEARS SINCE 1995	0	1	2	3	4	5
A(t), AMOUNT OF U.S. CARBON EMISSIONS (in millions of tons)						

c. Determine the growth factor for carbon emissions.

d. Sketch a graph of this exponential equation. Use $0 \leq t \leq 25$ and $0 \leq A(t) \leq 2500$.

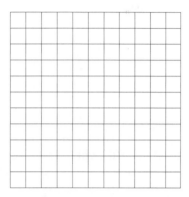

e. Use the equation $A(t) = 1400(1.013)^t$ to determine the amount of carbon emission in 2010. Include the units of measurement in your answer.

f. Use the graph and trace features of your graphing calculator to approximate the year in which carbon emissions in the U.S. will exceed 2000 million tons.

7. Chlorine is used to disinfect swimming pools. The chlorine concentration should be between 1.5 and 2.5 parts per million (ppm). On sunny, hot days, 30% of the pool's chlorine dissipates into the air or combines with other chemicals. The chlorine concentration, $A(x)$, (in parts per million) in a pool after x sunny days can be modeled by

$$A(x) = 2.5(0.7)^x.$$

a. What is the initial concentration of chlorine in the pool?

b. Complete the following table.

x	0	1	2	3	4	5
A(x)						

c. Sketch a graph of the chlorine function.

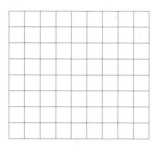

d. What is the chlorine concentration in the pool after three days?

e. Approximate graphically and numerically the number of days before chlorine should be added.

8. In the 1990s, there was a nationwide increase in the number of investment clubs. An investment club is a group of people who meet on a regular basis to invest in the stock market. By joining a club, members are able to share in a diverse portfolio and therefore reduce the risk of losing money.

The following table shows the rapid growth in the number of clubs from 1990 to 1996 (figures for the number of clubs are approximate). Note that the independent variable (year) increases in steps of one unit.

YEAR	NUMBER OF CLUBS AS OF JAN. I
1990	5820
1991	7180
1992	8860
1993	10,930
1994	13,480
1995	16,630
1996	20,510

a. Does the relationship in the table represent an exponential function? Explain.

b. What is the initial number of investment clubs?

c. What is the growth factor?

d. Determine the equation that gives the number of clubs N as a function of t, the number of years since 1990. Note that $t = 0$ corresponds to 1990.

e. Graph the function.

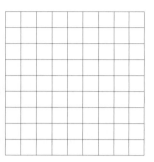

f. What is the N-intercept? What is the practical meaning of this intercept in this situation?

g. Use the equation to estimate the number of clubs in 2000. Do you think this is a good estimate? Explain.

h. Use the graph of the exponential function and the trace or table feature of your graphing calculator to estimate the number of years it takes for the number of clubs to double from 5820 to 11,640.

i. How long will it take for any given number of clubs to double?

Collecting and Analyzing Data

9. Find a website to determine the number of cell phone subscribers in the U.S. in each year from 2000 to 2006. Sketch a scatterplot of the data and determine a new exponential regression equation to predict the number of cell phone subscribers in a given year since 2000. How good is the fit?

ACTIVITY 4.6

Counting on
Florida

OBJECTIVES

1. Determine annual growth or decay rate of an exponential function represented by a table of values or an equation.

2. Graph an exponential function having equation $y = a(1 + r)^x$.

According to the 2000 U.S. Census, the metro area of Sarasota–Bradenton, Florida, had a population of approximately 541,000.

1. a. Assuming that the area's population increases at a constant rate of 3.2%, determine the population of Sarasota–Bradenton (in thousands) in 2001.

b. Determine the population of Sarasota–Bradenton (in thousands) in 2002.

c. Divide the population in 2001 by the population in 2000 and record this ratio.

d. Divide the population in 2002 by the population in 2001 and record this ratio.

e. What do you notice about the ratios in parts c and d? What do these ratios represent?

Linear functions represent quantities that change at a constant average rate (slope). Exponential functions represent quantities that change at a constant ratio, expressed as a percent.

Example 1 *Population growth, sales and advertising trends, compound interest, spread of disease, and concentration of a drug in the blood are examples of quantities that increase or decrease at a constant rate expressed as a percent.*

2. a. Let t represent the number of years since 2000 ($t = 0$ corresponds to 2000). Use the results from Problem 1 to complete the following table.

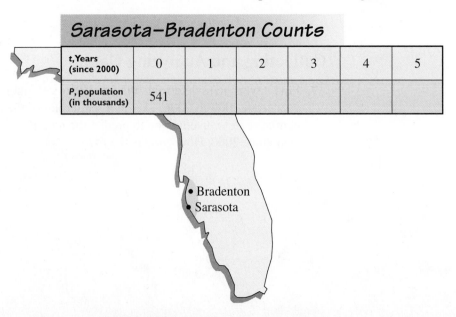

Sarasota–Bradenton Counts

t, Years (since 2000)	0	1	2	3	4	5
P, population (in thousands)	541					

Once you know the growth factor, b, and the initial value, a, you can write the exponential equation. In this situation, the initial value is 541, the population, in 1000s, in 2000 ($t = 0$). The growth factor is $b = 1.032$.

    b. Write the exponential equation, $P = a \cdot b^t$, for the metro-area population of Sarasota–Bradenton.

  3. a. Write the growth rate, $r = 3.2\%$, as a decimal.

    b. Add 1 to the decimal form of the growth rate r.

The growth factor, b, is determined from the growth rate, r, by writing r in decimal form and adding 1: $b = 1 + r$.

Example 2 *Determine the growth factor, b, for a growth rate of r = 8%.*

SOLUTION

$$r = 8\% = 0.08, \; b = 1 + r = 1 + 0.08 = 1.08$$

    c. Solve the equation for the growth factor, $b = 1 + r$, for r.

The growth rate, r, is determined from the growth factor, b, by subtracting 1 from b and writing the result in percent form.

Example 3 *Determine the growth rate, r, for a growth factor of b = 1.054.*

SOLUTION

$$r = b - 1 = 1.054 - 1 = 0.054 = 5.4\%$$

The growth rate is 5.4%

  4. a. Complete the following table.

t	CALCULATION FOR POPULATION (in thousands)	EXPONENTIAL FORM	P, POPULATION (in thousands)
0	541	$541(1.032)^0$	541
1	$(541)1.032$	$541(1.032)^1$	
2	$(541)(1.032)(1.032)$		
3			

    b. Use the pattern in the table in part a to help you write an equation for P, the metro-area population of Sarasota–Bradenton (in thousands), using t, the number of years since 2000, as the independent variable.

The equation $P = 541(1.032)^t$ has the general form $P = P_0(1 + r)^t$, where r is the annual **growth rate**, $(1 + r)$ is the **growth factor** or the base, b, of the exponential function, t is the time in years, and P_0 is the initial value, the population when $t = 0$.

Example 4

a. *Determine the growth factor and the growth rate of the function defined by* $y = 250(1.7)^x$.

SOLUTION

The growth factor $1 + r$ is the base 1.7. To determine the growth rate, solve the equation $1 + r = 1.7$ for r.

$$r = 0.7 \text{ or } 70\%$$

b. *If the growth rate of a function is 5%, determine the growth factor.*

SOLUTION

If $r = 5\%$ or 0.05, the growth factor is $1 + r = 1 + 0.05 = 1.05$.

5. **a.** Determine the growth factor in the Sarasota–Bradenton population function $P = 541(1.032)^t$.

   b. Determine the growth rate. Express your answer as a percent.

6. **a.** Using the function defined by $P = 541(1.032)^t$, determine the metro-area population of Sarasota–Bradenton in 2006. That is, determine P when $t = 6$.

   b. Graph the population function with a graphing calculator. Set the window to Xmin $= -50$, Xmax $= 100$, Ymin $= 0$, and Ymax $= 13,000$. The graph should appear as follows:

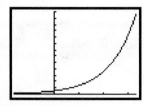

   c. Determine P when $t = 0$. What is the graphical and the practical meaning of this number?

7. a. Use the population model to predict the Sarasota–Bradenton population in 2010.

   b. Verify your prediction on the graph.

8. a. Use the graph to estimate when the Sarasota–Bradenton population will reach 700,000, assuming it continues to grow at the same rate. Remember, P is the number of thousands.

   b. Evaluate P when $t = 32$ and describe what it means.

9. Use the population model to estimate the population of Sarasota–Bradenton in 2002 and in 2020. In which prediction are you more confident? Why?

10. a. Assuming the growth rate remains constant, how long will it take for the Sarasota–Bradenton metro area to double its 2000 population?

   b. Explain how you reached your conclusion in part a.

Waste-Water Treatment Facility

You are working at a waste-water treatment facility. You are presently treating water contaminated with 18 micrograms of pollutant per liter. Your process is designed to remove 20% of the pollutant during each treatment. Your goal is to reduce the pollutant to less than 3 micrograms per liter.

11. a. What percent of pollutant present at the start of a treatment remains at the end of the treatment?

   b. The concentration of pollutant is 18 micrograms per liter at the start of the first treatment. Use the result of part a to determine the concentration of pollutant at the end of the first treatment.

c. Complete the following table. Round the results to the nearest hundredth.

n, NUMBER OF TREATMENTS	0	1	2	3	4	5
C, CONCENTRATION OF POLLUTANT, IN μg/l, AT THE END OF THE nTH TREATMENT	18	14.4				

d. Write an equation for the concentration, C, of the pollutant as a function of the number of treatments, n.

The equation $C = 18(0.80)^n$ has the general form $C = C_0(1 - r)^n$, where r is the **decay rate**, $(1 - r)$ is the **decay factor** or the base of the exponential function, n is the number of treatments, and C_0 is the initial value, the concentration when $n = 0$.

Example 5

a. *Determine the decay factor and the decay rate of the function defined by* $y = 123(0.43)^x$.

SOLUTION

The decay factor $1 - r$ is the base, 0.43. To determine the decay rate, solve the equation $1 - r = 0.43$ for r.

$$r = 0.57 \text{ or } 57\%$$

b. *If the decay rate of a function is 5%, determine the decay factor.*

SOLUTION

If $r = 5\%$ or 0.05, the decay factor is $1 - r = 1 - 0.05 = 0.95$.

12. a. If the decay rate is 2.5%, what is the decay factor?

b. If the decay factor is 0.76, what is the decay rate?

13. a. Use the function defined by $C = 18(0.8)^n$ to predict the concentration of contaminants at the waste-water treatment facility after seven treatments.

b. Sketch a graph of the concentration function on a graphing calculator. Use the table in Problem 11c to set a window. Does the graph look like you expected it would? Explain.

   c. What is the C-intercept? What is the practical meaning of the intercept in this situation?

   d. Reset the window of your graphing calculator to Xmin $= -5$, Xmax $= 15$, Ymin $= -10$, and Ymax $= 50$. Does the graph have a horizontal asymptote? Explain what this means in this situation.

14. Use the table or trace feature of a graphing calculator to estimate the number of treatments necessary to bring the concentration of pollutant below 3 micrograms per liter.

SUMMARY
Activity 4.6

1. **Exponential functions** are used to describe phenomena that grow or decay by a constant percent rate over time.

2. If r represents the **annual growth rate**, the exponential function that models the quantity, P, can be written as

$$P = P_0(1 + r)^t,$$

where P_0 is the initial amount, t represents the number of elapsed years, and $1 + r$ is the growth factor.

3. If r represents the **annual decay rate**, the exponential function that models the amount remaining can be written as

$$P = P_0(1 - r)^t,$$

where $1 - r$ is the decay factor.

EXERCISES
Activity 4.6

1. Determine the growth and decay factors and growth and decay rates in the following table.

GROWTH FACTOR	GROWTH RATE		DECAY FACTOR	DECAY RATE
1.02			0.77	
	2.9%			68%
2.23			0.953	
	34%			19.7%
1.0002			0.9948	

2. The 2000 U.S. Census reports the populations of Bozeman, Montana, as 27,509 and Butte, Montana, as 32,370. Since the 1990 census, Bozeman's population had been increasing at approximately 1.96% per year. Butte's population had been decreasing at approximately 0.29% per year. Assume that the growth and decay rates stay constant.

    a. Let P represent the population t years after 2000. Determine the exponential functions that model the populations of both cities.

    b. Use the population models to predict the populations of both cities in 2005.

    c. Estimate the number of years necessary for the population of Bozeman, Montana, to double.

    d. Using the table and/or graphs of these functions, predict when the populations will be equal.

3. You have just taken over as the city manager of a small city. The personnel expenses were $8,500,000 in 2010. Over the past five years, the personnel expenses have increased at a rate of 3.2% annually.

    a. Assuming that this rate continues, write an equation describing personnel costs, C, in millions of dollars, where $t = 0$ corresponds to 2010.

    b. Sketch a graph of this function up to the year 2020 $(t = 10)$.

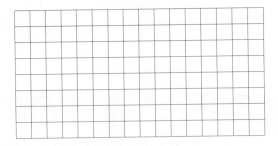

    c. What are your projected personnel costs in the year 2015?

    d. What is the C-intercept? What is the practical meaning of the intercept in this situation?

    e. In what year will the personnel expenses be double the 2010 personnel expenses?

4. According to the U.S. Bureau of the Census, the population of the United States from 1930 to 2000 can be modeled by $P = 120.6 \cdot 1.0125^t$, where t represents the number of years since 1930.

   a. Sketch a graph of the U.S. population model from 1930 to 2000.

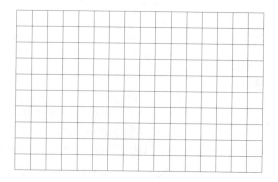

   b. Determine the annual growth rate and the growth factor from the equation.

   c. Use the population equation to determine the population (in millions) of the U.S. in 2000. How does your answer compare to the actual population of 281.4 million?

5. You have recently purchased a new truck for $20,000 by arranging financing for the next five years. You are curious to know what your new truck will be worth when the loan is completely paid off.

   a. Assuming that the value depreciates at a constant rate of 15%, write an equation that represents the value V of the truck t years from now.

   b. What is the decay rate in this situation?

   c. What is the decay factor in this situation?

   d. Use the equation from part a to estimate the value of your truck five years from now.

   e. Use the trace and table features of a graphing calculator to check your results in part d.

   f. Use the trace or table features of a graphing calculator to determine when your truck will be worth $10,000.

ACTIVITY 4.7
Bird Flu

OBJECTIVES

1. Determine the equation of an exponential function that best fits the given data.

2. Make predictions using an exponential regression equation.

3. Determine whether a linear or exponential model best fits the data.

In 2005, the avian flu, also known as bird flu, received international attention. Although there were very few documented cases of the avian flu infecting humans worldwide, world health organizations including the Centers for Disease Control in Atlanta expressed concern that a mutant strain of the bird flu virus capable of infecting humans would develop and produce a worldwide pandemic.

The infection rate (the number of people that any single infected person will infect) and the incubation period (the time between exposure and the development of symptoms) of this flu cannot be known precisely but they can be approximated by studying the infection rates and incubation periods of existing strains of the virus.

A very conservative infection rate would be 1.5 and a reasonable incubation period would be about 15 days or roughly half of a month. This means that the first infected person could be expected to infect 1.5 people in about 15 days. After 15 days, that person cannot infect anyone else. This assumes that the spread of the virus is not checked by inoculation or vaccination.

So the total number of infected people 0.5 months after the first person was infected would be 2.5, the sum of the original infected person and the 1.5 newly infected people. During the second half-month the 1.5 newly infected people would infect $1.5 \times 1.5 = 2.25$ new people. This means you have 2.25 people to add to the 2.5 people previously infected, or approximately 5 people infected with bird flu at the end of the first month.

The following table represents the total number of people who could be infected with a mutant strain of bird flu over a period of five months.

MONTHS SINCE THE FIRST PERSON WAS INFECTED	0	0.5	1	1.5	2	2.5	3	3.5	4	4.5	5
NUMBER OF NEWLY INFECTED PEOPLE		1.5	2.25	3.375	5						
TOTAL NUMBER OF PEOPLE INFECTED	1	2.5	5	8	13						

1. Complete the table above. Round each value to the nearest whole person.

2. Let t represent the number of months since the first person was infected and N represent the total number of people infected with the bird flu virus. Create a scatterplot of the data below.

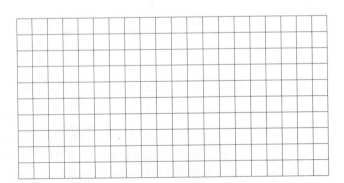

3. Does the scatterplot indicate a linear relationship between t and N? Explain.

4. a. Use your calculator to model the data with an exponential function. Use option 0: ExpReg in the STAT CALC menu to determine an exponential function that best fits the given data. Record that model below. Round a and b to the nearest 0.001.

    b. Sketch a graph of the exponential model using your calculator and add it to the scatterplot in Problem 2.

    c. What is the practical domain of this function?

    d. What is the N-intercept of the graph? How does it compare to the actual initial value ($t = 0$) from the table?

5. a. Use the exponential model to determine the total number of infected people one year after the initial infection ($t = 12$), provided the virus is unchecked. Round your result to the nearest whole person.

    b. Use the exponential function to write an equation that can be used to determine when the virus will first infect 2,000,000 people.

    c. Solve the equation in part b using a graphing approach. Use the intersect feature of your calculator; the screen containing the solution should resemble the following:

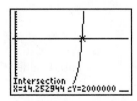

    d. Interpret the meaning of your solution in part c.

Increasing Exponential Model

According to the U.S. Department of Education, the number of college graduates increased significantly during the twentieth century. The following table gives the number (in thousands) of college degrees awarded from 1900 through 2000:

College Bound

YEAR	NUMBER OF COLLEGE GRADUATES (thousands)
1900	30
1910	54
1920	73
1930	127
1940	223
1950	432
1960	530
1970	878
1980	935
1990	1017
2000	1180

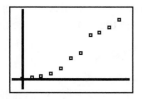

6. Let t represent the number of years since 1900 ($t = 0$ corresponds to 1900, $t = 10$ to 1910, etc.). Let N represent the number of college graduates (in thousands) at time t. Sketch a scatterplot of the given data on your graphing calculator. Your scatterplot should appear as seen to the left.

7. a. Use a graphing calculator to determine the equation of an exponential function that best fits the given data.

  b. Sketch a graph of the exponential model using a graphing calculator.

  c. What is the practical domain of this exponential function?

  d. What is the N-intercept of the graph? How does it compare to the actual initial value ($t = 0$) from the table?

8. a. What is the base of the exponential model? Is the base a growth or decay factor? How do you know?

  b. What is the annual growth rate?

9. a. Use the exponential model to determine the number of college graduates in 2010 ($t = 110$).

b. Use the exponential model to write an equation that can be used to determine the year in which there will be 2 million college graduates. Remember that the number of college graduates is measured in thousands.

c. Solve the equation in part a using a graphing approach. Use the intersect feature of your graphing calculator; the screen containing the solution should appear as follows. How confident are you in this prediction?

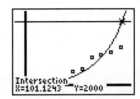

10. What is the doubling time for your exponential model? That is, approximately how many years will it take for a given number of college graduates to double?

Decreasing Exponential Model

Students in U.S. public schools have had much greater access to computers in recent years. The following table shows the number of students per computer in a large school district in selected years:

YEAR	1994	1995	1996	1998	2000	2003	2006	2010
NUMBER OF STUDENTS PER COMPUTER	125	75	50	32	22	16	10	5.7

11. a. Use your graphing calculator to determine the equation of an exponential function that models the given data. Let the independent variable, t, represent the number of years since 1994.

b. Sketch a graph of the exponential model using your graphing calculator.

c. What is the base of the exponential model? Is the base a growth or decay factor? How do you know?

d. What is the annual decay rate?

e. Does the graph have a horizontal asymptote? What is the practical meaning of this asymptote in the context of the situation?

EXERCISES
Activity 4.7

1. The total amount of money spent on health care in the United States is increasing at an alarming rate. The following table gives the total national health care expenditures in billions of dollars in selected years from 1975 through 2003.

Enough to Make You Sick

YEAR	1975	1980	1985	1990	1995	2000	2003
TOTAL SPENT (billions of dollars)	129.8	245.8	426.5	695.6	990.2	1309.9	1679.9

Source: National Center for Health Statistics

a. Would the data in the preceding table be better modeled by a linear model, $y = mx + b$, or an exponential model, $y = ab^x$? Explain.

b. Sketch a scatterplot of this data.

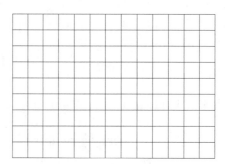

c. Does the graph reinforce your conclusion in part a? Explain.

d. Use a graphing calculator to determine the exponential regression equation that best fits the health care data in the preceding table. Let your input, t, represent the number of years since 1975.

e. Using the regression equation from part d, determine the predicted total health care expenditures for the year 1995.

f. According to the exponential model, what is the growth factor for the total health care costs per year?

g. What is the growth rate?

h. According to the exponential model, in what year did the total heath care costs first exceed $1 trillion?

i. What is the doubling time for your exponential model?

2. a. Consider the following data set for the variables x and y:

x	5	8	11	15	20
y	70.2	50.7	35.1	22.6	9.5

Plot these points on the following grid:

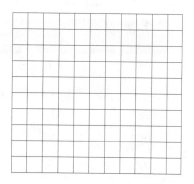

b. Use your graphing calculator to determine both a linear regression and an exponential regression model of the data. Record the equations for these models here.

c. Which model appears to fit the data better? Explain.

d. Use the better model to determine y when $x = 13$ and y when $x = 25$.

e. For the exponential model, what is the decay factor?

f. What does it mean that the decay factor is between 0 and 1?

g. What is the half-life for the exponential model?

3. Use the graph of $y = 5 \cdot 2^x$ as a check, and summarize the properties of the exponential function $y = a \cdot b^x$, where $a > 0$.

   a. What is the domain?

   b. What is the range?

   c. When is $y = a \cdot b^x$ positive?

   d. When is $y = a \cdot b^x$ negative?

   e. What is the y-intercept of the graph of $y = a \cdot b^x$?

4. The number of transistors that can be placed on a single chip has grown significantly between 1970 and 2004. The following table gives the number of transistors (in millions) that can be placed on a specific chip in a given year.

YEAR	x, NUMBER OF YEARS SINCE 1970	CHIP	TRANSISTORS (in millions)
1971	1	4004	0.0023
1986	16	386DX	0.275
1989	19	486DX	1.2
1993	23	Pentium	3.3
1995	25	P6	5.5
1997	27	Pentium II	7.5
1999	29	Pentium III	9.5
2000	30	Pentium IV	42
2004	34	Pentium IV Prescott	125

Source: Intel

   a. Use a graphing calculator to determine an exponential regression model of the data. Let the independent variable x represent the number of years since 1970.

   b. Assuming the rate of growth continues, approximate the number of transistors that can be placed on a chip in 2012?

Collecting and Analyzing Data

5. You need to find some real-world data that appears to be increasing exponentially. Newspapers, magazines, scientific journals, almanacs, and the Internet are good resources. Once the data has been obtained, model the data by an exponential function defined by $y = ab^x$. Explain why an exponential function would best represent the data. Be sure to describe the meaning of a and b in the exponential model in terms of the situation. Make a prediction about the dependent variable y for a specific value of the independent variable x. Describe the reliability of this prediction.

Activities 4.1–4.7   What Have I Learned?

1. **a.** Think of an example, or find one in a newspaper or magazine or on the Internet, and use it to show how to determine the growth factor associated with a percent increase. For instance, you might think of or find growth factors associated with yearly interest rates for a saving account.

   b. Show how you would use the growth factor to apply a percent increase twice, then three times.

2. Current health research shows that losing just 10% of body weight produces significant health benefits, including a reduced risk for a heart attack. Suppose a relative who weighs 199 pounds begins a diet to reach a goal weight of 145 pounds.

   a. Use the idea of a decay factor to show your relative how much he will weigh after losing the first 10% of his body weight.

   b. Explain to your relative how he can use the decay factor to determine how many times he has to lose 10% of his body weight to reach his goal weight of 145 pounds.

3. Consider a linear function defined by $g(x) = mx + b$, $m \neq 0$, and an exponential function defined by $f(x) = a \cdot b^x$. Explain how you can determine from the equation whether the function is increasing or decreasing.

4. Suppose you have an exponential function of the form $f(x) = a \cdot b^x$, where $a > 0$ and $b > 0$ and $b \neq 1$. By inspecting the graph of f, can you determine if $b > 1$ or if $0 < b < 1$? Explain.

5. You are given a function defined by a table, and the x-values are in increments of 1. By looking at the table, can you determine whether or not the function can be approximated by an exponential model? Explain.

6. Explain the difference between growth rate and growth factor.

7. An exponential function $y = a \cdot b^x$ passes through the point $(0, 2.6)$. What can you conclude about the values of a and b?

8. Explain why the base in an exponential function cannot equal 1.

Activities 4.1–4.7   How Can I Practice?

1. A suit with an original price of $300 was marked down 30%. You have a coupon good for an additional 20% off.

   a. What is the suit's final cost?

   b. What is the equivalent percent discount?

2. The Ford Motor Company released its Taurus sales figures for the month of October in 2001. Dealers sold a total of 28,000 new Taurus automobiles, a decrease of 14% from the same month in 2000. Approximately, how many 2001 Taurus cars were sold?

3. You are planning to purchase a new car and have your eye on a specific model. You know that new car prices are projected to increase at a rate of 4% per year for the next few years.

   a. Write an equation that represents the projected cost, C, of your dream car t years in the future, given that it costs $17,000 today.

   b. Identify the growth rate and the growth factor.

   c. Use your equation in part a to project the cost of your car three years from now.

   d. Use your graphing calculator to approximate how long it will take for your dream car to cost $30,000 if the price continues to increase at 4% per year.

4. Without using your graphing calculator, match the graph with its equation.

   a. $g(x) = 2.5(0.47)^x$ **b.** $h(x) = 1.5(1.47)^x$

   i. 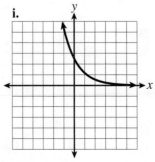   **ii.**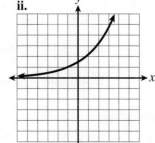

5. Explain the reasons for your choices in Problem 4.

6. Complete the following tables representing exponential functions. Round calculations to the nearest hundredth whenever necessary.

a.

x	0	1	2	3	4
y	2.00	5.10			

b.

x	0	1	2	3	4
y	3.50	2.10			

c.

x	0	1	2	3	4
y	$\frac{1}{6}$	6			

7. Write the equation of the exponential function that represents the data in each table in Problem 6.

a.   **b.**   **c.**

8. Without graphing, classify each of the following functions as increasing or decreasing and determine $f(0)$. (Use your graphing calculator to verify.)

a. $f(x) = 1.3(0.75)^x$ **b.** $f(x) = 0.6(1.03)^x$

c. $f(x) = 3\left(\frac{1}{5}\right)^x$

9. a. Given the following table, do you believe that it can be approximately modeled by an exponential function?

x	0	1	2	3	4	5	6
y	2	5	12.5	31.3	78.1	195.3	488.3

b. If you answered yes to part a, what is the constant ratio of successive y-values?

c. Determine an exponential equation that models this data.

10. a. Complete the following tables.

x	−3	−2	−1	0	1	2	3
$h(x) = 4^x$							

x	−3	−2	−1	0	1	2	3
$g(x) = \left(\frac{1}{4}\right)^x$							

b. Sketch graphs of h and g on the following grid.

c. Use the tables and graphs in part a and b to complete this table.

FUNCTION	BASE, b	GROWTH OR DECAY FACTOR	x-INTERCEPT	y-INTERCEPT	HORIZONTAL ASYMPTOTE	INCREASING OR DECREASING
$h(x) = 4^x$						
$g(x) = \left(\frac{1}{4}\right)^x$						

11. The starting salary at your new job is $22,000 per year. You are offered two options for salary increases:

Plan 1: an annual increase of $1000 per year or

Plan 2: an annual percentage increase of 4% of your salary.

Your salary is a function of the number of years of employment at your job.

a. Write an equation to determine the salary S after x years on the job using plan 1; using plan 2;

b. Complete the following table using the equations from part a:

x	0	1	3	5	10	15
S, PLAN 1						
S, PLAN 2						

c. Which plan would you choose? Explain.

12. You have just obtained your first credit card. You immediately purchase a stereo system for $415. Your credit limit is $500. Let's assume that you make no payments and purchase nothing more and there are no other fees. The monthly interest rate is 1.18%.

   a. What is your initial credit card balance?

   b. What is the growth rate of your credit card balance?

   c. What is the growth factor of your credit card balance?

   d. Write an exponential function to determine how much you will owe (represented by y) after x months with no more purchases or payments.

   e. Use your graphing calculator to graph this function. What is the y-intercept?

   f. What is the practical meaning of this intercept in this situation?

   g. How much will you owe after ten months? Use the table feature on your graphing calculator to determine the solution.

   h. When you reach your credit limit of $500, the bank will expect a payment. How long do you have before you will have to start paying the money back? Use the trace feature on your graphing calculator to approximate the solution.

13. You are working part-time for a computer company while going to high school. The following table shows the hourly wage, w, in dollars, that you earn as a function of time, t. Time is measured in years since the beginning of 2005 when you started working.

TIME, t, YEARS, SINCE 2005	0	1	2	3	4	5
HOURLY WAGE, w, ($)	12.50	12.75	13.01	13.27	13.53	13.81

   a. Calculate the ratios of the w-values to determine if the data in the table is exponential. Round each ratio to the nearest hundredth.

b. What is the growth factor?

c. Write an exponential equation that models the data in the table.

d. What percent raise did you receive each year?

e. For approximately how many years will you have to work for the company in order for your hourly wage to double? (Assume you will receive the same percentage increase each year.)

14. The number of farms in the U.S. has declined from 1940 to 2000, as the data in the following table shows. The data is estimated from National Agricultural Statistics Service, U.S. Department of Agriculture.

YEAR	1940	1950	1960	1970	1980	1990	2000
NUMBER OF FARMS (in millions)	6.2	5.8	4	3	2.5	2.2	2

a. Make a scatterplot of this data.

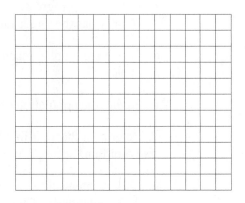

b. Does the scatterplot show that the data would be better modeled by a linear model or by an exponential model? Explain.

c. Use a graphing calculator to determine the exponential regression equation that best fits the U.S. farm data. Let x represent the number of years since 1940.

d. Use the regression equation to predict the total number of farms in the U.S. in 2010.

    e. According to your exponential model, what is the decay factor for the total number of farms in the U.S.?

    f. What is the decay rate?

    g. Use a graphing calculator to determine the halving time for your exponential model.

Collecting and Analyzing Data

15. The combined populations of China and India currently represent 38% of the world's population. Go to the United Nations' Population Database website http://esa.un.org/unpp to obtain the population of each country for every five years from 1960 to 2005.

    a. Beginning with 1960, make a scatterplot of the data from each country's population. Let the independent variable represent the number of years since 1960 and the dependent variable represent the population of the country in billions. Describe any patterns you observe.

    b. Determine whether a linear or exponential function best fits each set of data. Explain.

    c. Determine a regression equation for each set of population data. Which country has the larger rate of increase in population?

    d. Sketch the graph of each regression equation on the appropriate scatterplot in part a.

    e. Predict the population of each country in 2010.

    f. Determine the year in which the population of each country should reach 1.5 billion.

    g. Use the intersect feature of a graphing calculator to estimate the year when the populations of China and India will be equal.

Summary

The bracketed numbers following each concept indicate the activity in which the concept is discussed.

CONCEPT / SKILL	DESCRIPTION	EXAMPLE
Growth factor [4.1]	When a quantity increases by a specified percent, the ratio of its new value to the original value is called the growth factor associated with the specified percent increase. The growth factor is formed by adding the specified percent increase to 100% and then changing this percent into its decimal form.	To determine the growth factor associated with a 25% increase, add 25% to 100% to obtain 125%. Change 125% into a decimal to obtain the growth factor 1.25.
Applying a growth factor to an original value [4.1]	original value × growth factor = new value	A $120 item increases by 25%. Its new value is $120 × 1.25 = $150.
Applying a growth factor to a new value [4.1]	new value ÷ growth factor = original value	An item has already increased by 25% and is now worth $200. Its original value was $200 ÷ 1.25 = $160.
Decay factor [4.1]	When a quantity decreases by a specified percent, the ratio of its new value to the original value is called the *decay factor* associated with the specified percent decrease. The decay factor is formed by subtracting the specified percent decrease from 100% and then changing this percent into its decimal form.	To determine the decay factor associated with a 25% decrease, subtract 25% from 100% to obtain 75%. Change 75% into a decimal to obtain the decay factor 0.75.
Applying a decay factor to an original value [4.1]	original value · decay factor = new value	A $120 item decreases by 25%. Its new value is $120 × 0.75 = $90.
Applying a decay factor to a new value [4.1]	new value ÷ decay factor = original value	An item has already decreased by 25% and is now worth $180. Its original value was $180 ÷ 0.75 = $240.
Applying a sequence of percent changes [4.2]	The cumulative effect of a sequence of percent changes is the product of the associated growth or decay factors.	The effect of a 25% increase followed by a 25% decrease is 1.25 × 0.75 = 0.9375. That is, the item is now worth only 93.75% of its original value. The item's value has decreased by 6.25%.

Exponential function [4.3]	An exponential function is a function whose y-values exhibit a constant percent growth (or decay). In an equation defining an exponential function, $y = ab^x$, $b > 0$, $b \neq 1$, the x-values variable always occurs as the exponent on the growth (decay) factor.	$y = 16 \cdot (2.1)^x$
Decay factor of an exponential function [4.3]	If $0 < b < 1$, the function is decreasing, and b is called the decay factor.	The exponential function $y = \left(\frac{1}{2}\right)^x$ has a decay factor of $\frac{1}{2}$.
Growth factor of an exponential function [4.3]	If $b > 1$, the function is increasing, and b is called the growth factor.	The exponential function $y = 3^x$ has a growth factor of 3.
y-intercept of an exponential function [4.3]	The y-intercept of an exponential function $y = a \cdot b^x$ is $(0, a)$.	The graph of $y = 5 \cdot 2^x$ passes through the point $(0, 5)$.
Horizontal asymptote of an exponential function [4.3]	The line $y = 0$ is a horizontal asymptote of an exponential function $y = b^x$.	As x gets smaller, the output values of $y = 3^x$ approach 0.
Doubling time [4.5]	The doubling time of an exponential function is the time it takes for an output to double. The doubling time is set by the growth factor and remains the same for all output values.	Example 2, Activity 4.5.
Half-life [4.5]	The half-life of an exponential function is the time it takes for an output to decay by one-half. The half-life is determined by the decay factor and remains the same for all output values.	Problem 10, Activity 4.5.
Growth model [4.6]	If r represents the annual growth rate, the exponential function that models the quantity P can be written as $P(t) = P_0(1 + r)^t$, where P_0 is the initial amount, t represents the number of elapsed years, and $1 + r$ is the growth factor.	Example 2, Activity 4.6.
Decay model [4.6]	If r represents the annual percent that decays, the exponential function that models the amount remaining can be written as $P(t) = P_0(1 - r)^t$, where $1 - r$ is the decay factor.	Example 3, Activity 4.6.

Gateway Review

1. Due to inflation, your tuition will increase 6% each year.

   a. If tuition is $300 per credit now, determine how much it will be in five years, in ten years.

   b. Calculate the average rate of change in tuition over the next five years.

   c. Calculate the average rate of change in tuition over the next ten years.

   d. If the inflation stays at 6%, approximately when will the tuition double?

2. a. Determine some of the output values for the function $f(x) = 8^x$ by completing the following table.

x	-1	$-\frac{1}{3}$	0	1	$\frac{4}{3}$	2	3
$f(x) = 8^x$							

   b. Sketch the graph of the function, f.

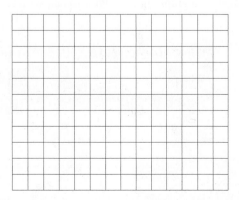

c. Is this function increasing or decreasing? Explain how you know this by looking at the equation of the function.

d. What is the domain?

e. What is the range?

f. What are the x- and y-intercepts?

g. Are there any asymptotes? If yes, write the equations of the asymptotes.

h. Compare the graph of f to the graph of $g(x) = \left(\frac{1}{8}\right)^x$. What are the similarities and the differences?

i. In what way does the graph of $h(x) = 8^x + 5$ differ from that of $f(x) = 8^x$?

3. Complete the table for each exponential function. Use a graphing calculator to check your work.

FUNCTION	BASE, b	GROWTH OR DECAY FACTOR	x-INTERCEPT	y-INTERCEPT	HORIZONTAL ASYMPTOTE	INCREASING OR DECREASING
$h(x) = 6^x$						
$g(x) = \left(\frac{1}{3}\right)^x$						
$p(x) = 5(2.34)^x$						
$q(x) = 3(0.78)^x$						
$r(x) = 2^x - 4$						

4. Use a graphing calculator to help you determine the domain and range for each function.

FUNCTION	$f(x) = 0.8^x$	$h(x) = 6^x + 2$	$t(x) = 3^x - 5$
DOMAIN			
RANGE			

5. **a.** Given the following table, determine whether the given data can be approximately modeled by an exponential function. If it can, what is the growth or decay factor?

x	0	1	2	3	4
y	10	15.5	24	36	55.5

   b. Determine an exponential equation that models this data.

6. **a.** Your salary has increased at the rate of 1.5% annually for the past 5 years, and your boss projects this will continue for the next 5 years. You were making $15,000 annually in 2008. Complete the following table.

2008	2009	2010	2011	2012	2013

   b. Write the exponential growth function that models your annual salary during this period of time. Let x represent the number of years since 2008.

   c. If your increase in salary continues at this rate, how much will you make in 2016? Is this realistic?

   d. You would like to double your salary. How many years will you have to work before your salary will be twice the salary you made in 2008?

7. Complete the following tables representing exponential functions. Round calculations to two decimal places whenever necessary.

   a.

x	0	1	2	3	4
y	3.00	6.12			

   b.

x	0	1	2	3	4
y	4.50	3.15			

   c.

x	0	1	2	3	4
y	$\frac{1}{4}$	4			

8. Write the equation of the exponential function that represents the data in each table in Problem 7.

9. The number of multiple births (triplets or higher) in the United States between 1990 and 1999 is listed in the following table, with 0 representing the year 1990.

NUMBER OF YEARS SINCE 1990	0	2	3	4	5	6	7	8	9
NUMBER OF MULTIPLE BIRTHS	3028	3883	4168	4594	4973	5939	6737	7625	7321

Source: National Center for Health Statistics

  a. Plot the data on an appropriately scaled and labeled coordinate axis.

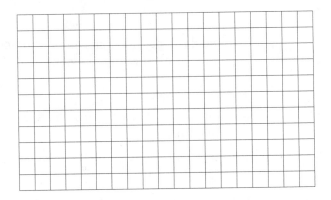

  b. Does the scatterplot show that the data would be better modeled by a linear or an exponential model?

  c. Use a graphing calculator to determine the exponential regression equation that best fits the multiple births data.

  d. According to your model, what is the growth factor for the multiple births data?

  e. Estimate the growth rate (written as a percent) in multiple births each year.

  f. Use the regression equation to determine the predicted total number of multiple births in 2012.

  g. Use your graphing calculator to determine the doubling time for your exponential model.

Using Geometric Models to Solve Problems

ACTIVITY 5.1

Walking around
Bases, Gardens,
Trusses, and
Other Figures

OBJECTIVES

1. Recognize perimeter as a geometric property of plane figures.

2. Write formulas for, and calculate perimeters of, squares, rectangles, triangles, parallelograms, trapezoids, kites, rhombi, and polygons.

3. Use unit analysis to solve problems involving perimeter.

4. Write and use formulas for the circumference of a circle.

In this first group of activities, you will explore the properties of geometric figures or shapes that are two dimensional. This means they exist in a **plane**—a surface like the floor beneath your feet or the walls in your classroom. To make sure you understand these various shapes, some preliminary definitions are needed.

DEFINITION

A **ray** is a portion of a line that starts from a point and continues indefinitely in one direction, much like a ray of light coming from the Sun.

Example:

An **angle** is formed by two rays that have a common starting point. The common starting point is called the **vertex** of the angle.

Example:

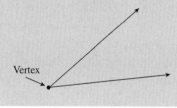

Vertex

Squares

DEFINITION

A **square** is a closed plane figure whose four sides have equal length and are at right angles to each other. A right angle measures 90 degrees.

Examples:

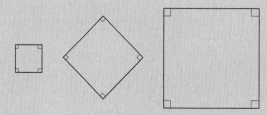

1. You are at bat in the middle of an exciting baseball game. You are a pretty good hitter and can run the bases at a speed of 15 feet per second. Further, you know that the baseball diamond has the shape of a square, measuring 90 feet on each side.

   a. What is the total distance in feet you must run starting from home plate and running the bases back to home? Recall that the total distance around the square is called the *perimeter* of the square.

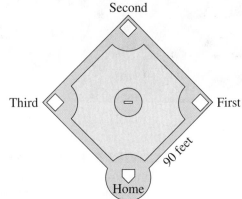

   b. How many seconds will it take you to run this total distance?

2. Your brother plays Little League baseball. The baseball diamond is still in the shape of a square but measures 60 feet on each side. What is the total distance if he ran all of the bases?

DEFINITION

The **perimeter of a square** is the total distance around all its edges or sides.

PROCEDURE: **Calculating the Perimeter of a Square**

The formula for the perimeter, P, of a square whose sides have length s is

$$P = s + s + s + s = 4s.$$

Rectangles

DEFINITION

A **rectangle** is a closed plane figure whose four sides are at right angles to each other.

Examples:

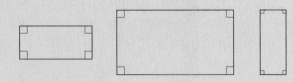

3. You are interested in planting a rectangular garden, 10 feet long by 15 feet wide. To protect your plants, you decide to purchase a fence to enclose your entire garden.

a. How many feet of fencing must you buy to enclose your garden?

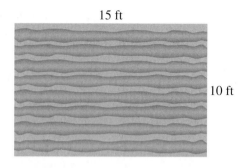

15 ft

10 ft

b. A friend suggests first surrounding the garden with a 2-foot-wide path and then enclosing the garden and path with fencing. If you do this, how many feet of fencing must you buy? Explain by including a labeled sketch of the garden and path.

DEFINITION

The **perimeter of a rectangle** is the total distance around all its edges or sides.

PROCEDURE: **Calculating the Perimeter of a Rectangle**

The formula for the perimeter, P, of a rectangle with length l and width w is

$$P = l + w + l + w = 2l + 2w.$$

Triangles

DEFINITION

A **triangle** is a closed plane figure with three sides.

Examples:

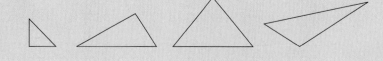

Most houses and garages have roofs supported by trusses. Trusses provide the greatest strength in building design. See accompanying figure.

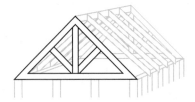

4. Why would a builder need to know about the perimeter of a triangular truss?

5. The dimensions of the three sides of a triangular truss are 13 feet, 13 feet, and 20 feet. What is the perimeter of the truss?

6. If the sides of a triangle measure *a*, *b*, and *c*, write a formula for the perimeter, *P*, of the following triangle.

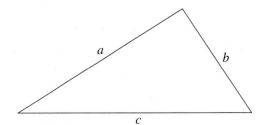

Parallelograms

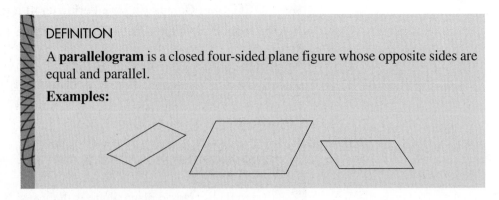

DEFINITION

A **parallelogram** is a closed four-sided plane figure whose opposite sides are equal and parallel.

Examples:

7. Where do you see parallelograms in the real world?

8. You decide to install a walkway diagonally from the street to your front steps. The width of your steps is 3 feet, and you determine that the length of the walkway is 23 feet. What is the perimeter of your walkway?

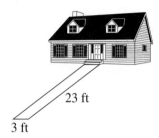

23 ft

3 ft

9. If the sides of a parallelogram measure a and b, write the formula for the perimeter, P, of a parallelogram.

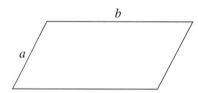

b

a

Trapezoids

DEFINITION

A **trapezoid** is a closed four-sided plane figure that has two sides parallel and two other sides that are not parallel.

Examples:

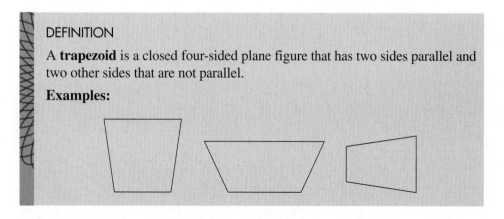

10. The sides of a trapezoid measure a, b, c, and d. Write a formula for the perimeter, P, of a trapezoid.

11. You buy a piece of land in the shape of a trapezoid with sides measuring 100 feet, 40 feet, 130 feet, and 50 feet. Draw the trapezoid and calculate its perimeter.

Kites

DEFINITION

A kite is a four-sided plane figure that has two distinct pairs (do not share a common side) of equal adjacent sides.

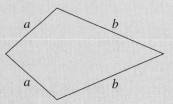

PROCEDURE: Calculating the Perimeter of a Kite

The formula for the perimeter, P, of a kite with short side a and long side b is

$$P = a + a + b + b = 2a + 2b.$$

12. The short side of a kite measures 20 inches and the long side measures 30 inches. Determine the perimeter, P, of the kite.

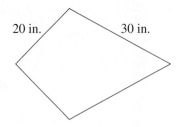

13. You wish to add a decorative thin red cord to the edge of a homemade kite with a short side of 18 inches and a long side of 27 inches. Draw the kite and calculate the length of cord that you need to buy.

Rhombus

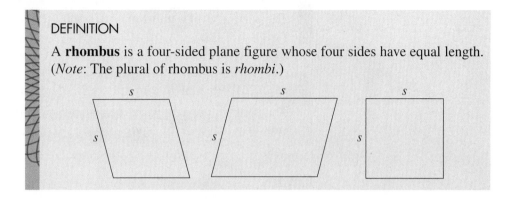

DEFINITION

A **rhombus** is a four-sided plane figure whose four sides have equal length. (*Note*: The plural of rhombus is *rhombi*.)

14. Each side of a rhombus measures, *s*. Write a formula for the perimeter, *P*, of a rhombus.

15. Many gemstones have a rhomboid shape. Determine the perimeter of a gemstone where the edges measure 0.5 millimeters.

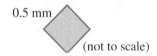

0.5 mm (not to scale)

Polygons

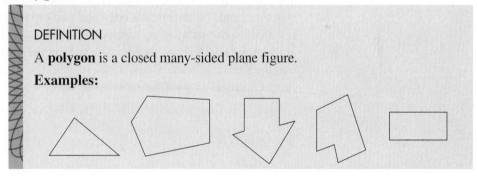

DEFINITION

A **polygon** is a closed many-sided plane figure.

Examples:

16. Calculate the perimeter of the following polygon.

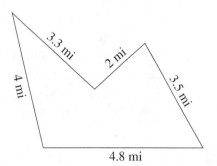

3.3 mi   2 mi   3.5 mi   4 mi   4.8 mi

DEFINITION

The **perimeter of a polygon** is the total distance around all its edges or sides.

PROCEDURE: **Calculating the Perimeter of a Polygon**

The perimeter of a polygon is calculated by adding all of the lengths of the sides that make up the figure.

Circles

DEFINITION

A **circle** is a collection of points that is equidistant from a fixed point called the center of the circle.

Examples:

Objects in the shape of circles of varying sizes are found in abundance in everyday life. Coins, dartboards, and ripples made by a raindrop in a pond are just a few examples.

The size of a circle is customarily described by the length of a line segment that starts and ends on the circle's edge and passes through its center. This line segment is called the **diameter** of the circle. The **radius** of a circle is a line segment that starts at its center and ends on its edge. Therefore, the length of the radius is one-half the length of the diameter. The distance around the edge of the circle is the perimeter, more commonly called the **circumference.**

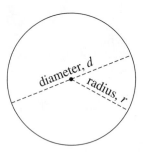

In every circle, the ratio of the circumference, C, to the diameter, d, is always the same $\left(\text{approximately } 3.14 \text{ or } \frac{22}{7}\right)$ and is represented by the Greek letter pi, or π. Most calculators have π keys.

> **PROCEDURE: Calculating the Circumference of a Circle**
>
> The formula for the circumference, C, of a circle with diameter d is
>
> $$\frac{C}{d} = \pi \quad \text{or} \quad C = \pi d.$$
>
> Since $d = 2r$, where r is the radius of the circle, the circumference formula may also be written as
>
> $$C = 2\pi r.$$

17. Use the circumference formulas to calculate the circumference of the following circles (not drawn to scale): Use π on your calculator and round your answers to the nearest hundredths.

a. If the radius is 8 miles, then the circumference = ____.

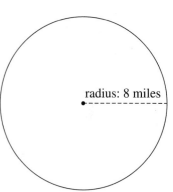

radius: 8 miles

b. If the diameter is 10 meters, then the circumference = ____.

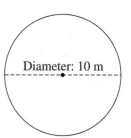

Diameter: 10 m

c. If the radius is 3 inches, then the circumference = ____.

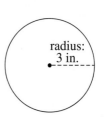

radius: 3 in.

SUMMARY
Activity 5.1

Two-Dimensional Figure	Labeled Sketch	Perimeter Formula
Square	s ... s	$P = 4s$

continued

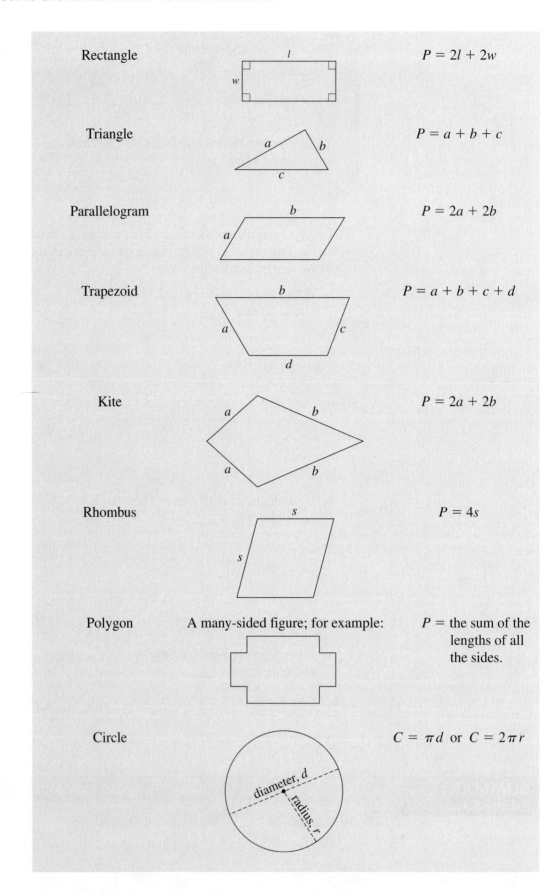

Rectangle $\qquad P = 2l + 2w$

Triangle $\qquad P = a + b + c$

Parallelogram $\qquad P = 2a + 2b$

Trapezoid $\qquad P = a + b + c + d$

Kite $\qquad P = 2a + 2b$

Rhombus $\qquad P = 4s$

Polygon — A many-sided figure; for example: $\quad P =$ the sum of the lengths of all the sides.

Circle $\qquad C = \pi d$ or $C = 2\pi r$

diameter, d

radius, r

EXERCISES
Activity 5.1

1. During your summer internship at an architecture firm, the first thing you learn about older homes is that they frequently have had additions put on over the years and the floor plans often have the shape of a polygon.

   a. In the case of one house the architects are redesigning, it is discovered that when the house was built one hundred years ago, it had a simple rectangular floor plan.

   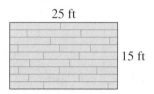

   Calculate the perimeter of the floor plan.

   b. Sixty years ago, a rectangular 10-foot by 25-foot garage was added to the original structure.

   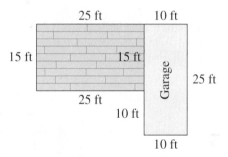

   Calculate the perimeter of the floor plan.

   c. Twenty-five years ago, a new master bedroom, with the same size and shape of the garage, was added onto the other side of the original floor plan.

   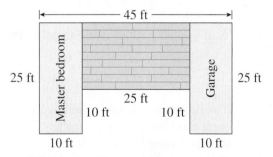

   Calculate the perimeter of the remodeled floor plan.

d. The architects have been asked to design a triangular family room as shown in the following floor plan.

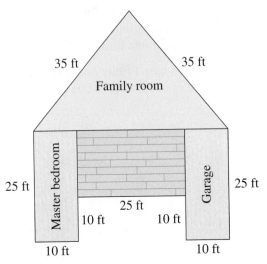

Calculate the new perimeter of the floor plan of the house.

2. A standard basketball court has the following dimensions:

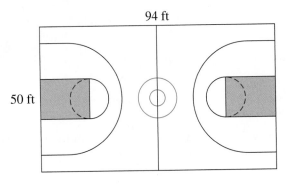

a. Calculate the perimeter of the court.

b. If you play a half-court game, calculate the perimeter of the half-court.

3. The Bermuda Triangle is an imaginary triangular area in the Atlantic Ocean in which there have been many unexplained disappearances of boats and planes. Public interest was aroused by the publication of a popular and controversial book, *The Bermuda Triangle*, by Charles Berlitz in 1974. The triangle starts at Miami, Florida, goes to San Juan, Puerto Rico (1038 miles), then to Bermuda (965 miles), and back to Miami (1042 miles).

a. What is the perimeter of this triangle?

b. If you were on a plane that was averaging 600 miles per hour, how long would it take you to fly the perimeter of the Bermuda Triangle?

4. Leonardo da Vinci's painting of *The Last Supper* is a 460 cm by 880 cm rectangle.

   a. Calculate the painting's perimeter.

   b. Would the painting fit in your living room? Explain.

5. Calculate the perimeter for each of the following figures:

a.

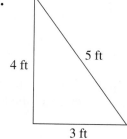

4 ft   5 ft

3 ft

b.

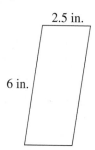

2.5 in.

6 in.

c.

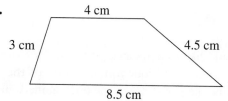

4 cm

3 cm   4.5 cm

8.5 cm

d.

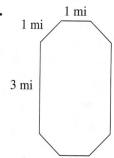

1 mi

1 mi   1 mi

3 mi

6. If a square has a perimeter of 64 feet, calculate the length of each side of the square.

7. A rectangle has a perimeter of 75 meters and a length of 10 meters. Calculate its width.

8. The short side of a kite measures 15 inches and the long side is twice as long. Determine the perimeter, P, of the kite.

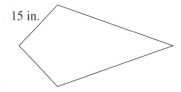

15 in.

9. You have 124 inches of edging for your kite. The short side of your kite measures 24 inches. What is the length of the long side of your kite?

24 in.

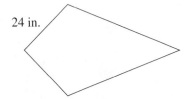

10. You would like to build a silver frame for a rhombus-shaped stained-glass ornament to hang in your room. A side of the ornament measures 6 inches. Determine the perimeter of the 6 in. stained-glass ornament.

6 in.

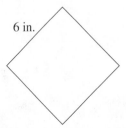

11. What is the length of one side of a rhombus-shaped hiking-trail marker that has a perimeter of 66 inches?

For calculations in Exercises 12–17, use π on your calculator and round your answers to the nearest hundredths.

12. You order a pizza in the shape of a circle with diameter 14 inches. Calculate the "length" of the crust (that is, find the circumference of the pizza).

13. United States coins are circular. Choose a quarter, dime, nickel, and penny.

    a. Use a ruler to estimate the diameter of each coin in terms of centimeters. Record your results to the nearest tenth of a centimeter.

    b. Use a ruler to estimate the circumference of each coin in terms of centimeters. Record your results to the nearest tenth of a centimeter.

    c. Check your estimates by using the formulas derived in this lab.

14. Use the appropriate geometric formulas to calculate the circumference for each of the following figures:

    a.

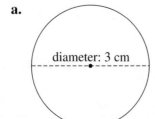

diameter: 3 cm

    b.

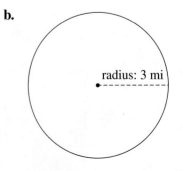

radius: 3 mi

c.

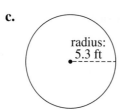

radius:
5.3 ft

d.

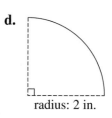

radius: 2 in.

15. If a circle has a circumference of 63 inches, approximate its radius.

16. The number π has an extraordinary place in the history of mathematics. Many books and articles have been written about this curious number. Using the Internet or your local library, research π and report on your findings.

ACTIVITY 5.2

Lance Armstrong
and You

OBJECTIVES

1. Calculate the perimeter of many-sided plane figures using formulas and combinations of formulas.

2. Use unit analysis to solve problems involving perimeter.

3. Determine how changes in dimensions affect the perimeter of plane figures.

1. Inspired by Lance Armstrong's remarkable performance in the Tour de France, you decide to experiment with long-distance biking and choose the following route shown by the solid path in the following figure, made up of partial rectangles and a quarter circle:

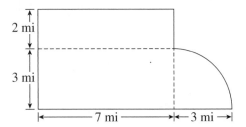

a. Calculate the total length of your bike trip in miles (that is, determine the perimeter of the figure). Use π on your calculator and round to the nearest hundredth.

b. If you can average 9 miles per hour on your bike, how long will it take you to complete the trip?

c. If your bike tires have a diameter of 2 feet, calculate the circumference of the tires to the nearest hundredth.

d. To analyze the wear on your tires, calculate how many rotations of the tires are needed to complete your trip.

e. Participants in the Tour de France bike 3454 kilometers (km). How many days would it take you to complete the race if you average 9 miles per hour?

f. Compare your time with the 2001 time by Lance Armstrong: 86 hours, 17 minutes, 28 seconds

Predicting the Change in Perimeter

The following problems demonstrate how certain changes in the dimensions of a plane figure affect its perimeter in a predictable way.

2. A celebration is scheduled at the end of a long-distance bike race you have entered. A local baker has donated a three-tiered cake with square layers. The top layer measures 12 inches on each side. The baker plans to decorate each layer with a ribbon of red, white, and blue frosting around the edges.

   a. How long a ribbon of frosting do you need for the top layer?

   b. Each side of the middle layer will be 18 inches long. How long a ribbon of frosting is needed for the middle layer?

   c. In part b, notice that each side of the middle layer is 6 inches longer than the top layer. Is the perimeter of the middle layer also 6 inches longer than the top layer?

   d. Each side of the bottom layer will be 24 inches. How long a ribbon of frosting is needed for the bottom layer?

   e. The length of each side of the bottom layer is twice the length of a side of the top layer. Is the perimeter of the bottom layer twice the perimeter of the top layer?

3. In Problem 2e, it appears that if the side of a square is multiplied by a certain positive number, its perimeter is affected in a predictable way. You can use algebra to prove this observation. Let the side of a square with length s be increased by a factor of $n > 0$. That is, multiply the length s of the side of the square by a positive number n.

   a. Write an expression that represents the perimeter of the new square.

b. Compare the result in part a with the expression for the perimeter of the original square.

c. Complete the following statement: If the side of a square is increased by a factor of n, then its perimeter is _____ .

4. Recall that the length of the side of the middle square layer (12 inches) was 6 inches longer than the side of the top layer (18 inches). Although the perimeter of the middle layer (72 inches) is not 6 inches more than the perimeter of the top layer (48 inches), there is a relationship between the perimeters of these two squares. Determine this relationship. *Hint:* Substitute $s + 6$ for s in the formula for the perimeter of a square.

5. Your neighbor has a rectangular garden plot that measures l feet by w feet.

   a. Write an expression for the perimeter of the garden?

   b. She would like to enlarge the garden by increasing the length by 5 feet and the width by 3 feet. Write an expression that represents the amount of fencing she would need for her new garden.

   c. From your observations in parts a and b, complete the following: If $a > 0$ is added to the length of a rectangle and $b > 0$ is added to its width, then the perimeter increases by _____ .

   d. Suppose your neighbor decides to enlarge the rectangular garden by doubling the length and width of the garden instead. Write an expression that represents the amount of fencing she would need to fence in her new garden.

   e. Compare the amount of fencing used in the original garden (see part a) with the amount needed for the garden with dimensions doubled (see part d).

   f. If both the length and width of a rectangle are multiplied by the same positive number n, how is the perimeter affected?

SUMMARY
Activity 5.2

1. A many-sided closed plane figure is a composite of basic plane figures: squares, rectangles, parallelograms, triangles, trapezoids, and circles.

2. To calculate the perimeter of a many-sided plane figure,
   i. Determine the length of each composite part of the perimeter.
   ii. Add the composite lengths to obtain the figure's total perimeter.

3. a. If the side of a square is increased by a factor of $n > 0$, then its perimeter is multiplied by n.

   b. If a number $n > 0$ is added to the length of a square, its perimeter is increased by $4n$ units.

   c. If $a > 0$ is added to the length of a rectangle and $b > 0$ is added to its width, then the perimeter increases by $2a + 2b$.

EXERCISES
Activity 5.2

1. You plan to fly from New York City to Los Angeles via Atlanta and return from Los Angeles to New York City via Chicago.

Determine the perimeter of the polygon that describes your trip.

2. A Norman window is rectangular on three sides with a semi-circular top. You decide to install a Norman window in your family room with the dimensions indicated in the diagram. What is its perimeter?

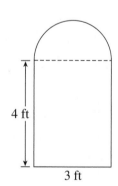

3. Stonehenge is an ancient site on the plains of southern England consisting of a collection of concentric circles (circles with the same center) outlined with large sandstone blocks. Carbon-dating has determined the age of the stones to be approximately 5000 years. Much curiosity and mystery has surrounded this site over the years. One theory about Stonehenge is that it was a rit-ualistic prayer site. However, even today, there is still controversy over what went on there. The one thing everyone interested in Stonehenge can agree on is the mathematical description of the circles:

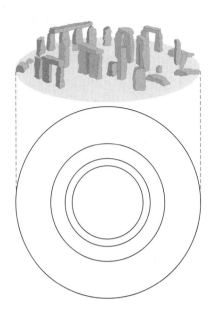

The diameters of the four circles are 288 feet for the largest circle, 177 feet for the next, 132 feet for the third, and 110 feet for the innermost circle.

    a. For each time you walked around the outermost circle, how many times could you walk around the innermost circle?

    b. What is the ratio of the diameter of the outermost circle to that of the innermost circle?

    c. How does this ratio compare to the ratio of their circumferences from part a?

    d. What is the ratio of the diameter of the larger intermediate circle to that of the smaller intermediate circle?

    e. Predict how much longer the trip around the larger intermediate circle would be than around the smaller intermediate circle?

4. Calculate the perimeter for each of the following figures:

a.

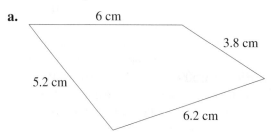

b.

c.

d.

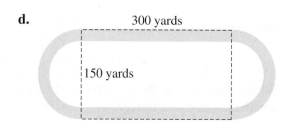

5. a. Use the perimeter formula to calculate the perimeter of a square with side 5 cm.

b. From your answer to part a, what do you expect to be the perimeter of a square with side 30 cm?

c. Use the perimeter formula to calculate the perimeter of a square with side 30 cm.

d. Was your prediction correct? That is, does your answer to part c match your answer to part a?

6. a. Determine the ratio of the length and width of the larger rectangle to the length and width of the smaller rectangle.

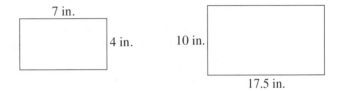

7 in.

4 in.   10 in.

17.5 in.

b. What relationship do you expect the perimeters of the two rectangles to have?

c. Calculate the two perimeters and check your prediction.

7. You enjoy playing darts. You decide to make your own dartboard consisting of four concentric circles (that is, four circles with the same center). The smallest circle, C_1 (the "bull's-eye"), has radius 1 cm, the next largest circle, C_2, has radius 3 cm, the third circle, C_3, has radius 6 cm, and the largest circle, C_4, has radius 10 cm. You decide to compare the circumferences of the circles.

a. What are these circumferences?

b. Compare the radius of circles C_1 and C_2. Compare their circumferences. Is there a connection between the relationship of the radii and the relationship of the circumferences?

c. Compare the radius of circles C_3 and C_2. Compare their circumferences. Is there a connection between the relationship of the radii and the relationship of the circumferences?

d. Compare the radius of circles C_1 and C_4. What would you predict the circumference of C_4 to be? Compare their circumferences. Was your prediction correct?

e. Complete the following: If the radius of a circle is multiplied by a positive number n, then the circumference is _____ .

8. a. Calculate the circumference of a circle of radius 4.

b. Use part a to predict the circumference of a circle of radius 6, without using the circumference formula.

c. Use the circumference formula to calculate the circumference of a circle of radius 6.

d. Does your answer to part c match your answer to part a?

ACTIVITY 5.3
Walking around, Revisited

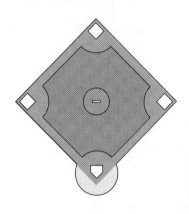

In previous activities, you ran the bases of a baseball diamond, fenced in a rectangular garden, and explored the perimeters of triangular trusses, parallelograms, trapezoids, kites, rhombi, and circles. Now, you will look at those same geometric figures, but from a different perspective.

Squares

As groundskeeper for the local baseball team, you need to guarantee good-quality turf for the infield, that is, the space enclosed by the base lines. In order to plant and maintain this turf, you need to measure this space. It makes sense to count the number of square units needed to cover the space and label this total number as the area of the figure.

1. Recall that a regulation baseball diamond is a square with 90-foot sides. A square unit (or unit square) in this case is a square with each side measuring 1 foot. How many square units are needed to cover this baseball diamond? Your answer in square feet is called the area of the square.

2. The Little League diamond has sides measuring 60 feet. Calculate the area of the Little League baseball diamond.

DEFINITION

The **area of a square,** or any polygon, is the measure, in square units, of the region enclosed by the sides of the polygon.

PROCEDURE: Calculating the Area of a Square

The formula for the area, A, of a square with sides of length s is

$$A = s \cdot s = s^2.$$

3. Your home has hardwood floors throughout the entire house. In the living room, there is a square carpet measuring 3 feet on each side under a table.

   a. What is the area of the carpet?

   b. There is a square carpet with sides 3 times as long under the dining room table. What is the area of the second carpet?

   c. Compare the areas of the two carpets. Is there a connection between the relationship of the sides and the relationship of the areas?

d. In general, how does multiplying the length of a square by $n > 0$ affect its area? Explain by replacing s with ns in the area formula for a square and comparing the results.

e. Complete the following: If the side of a square is multiplied by $n > 0$, then the area is _____ .

Rectangles

Planting your rectangular 15-foot by 10-foot garden requires that you know how much space it contains.

4. How many square feet are required to cover your garden? Include a sketch to explain your answer.

5. Will doubling the length and width of your garden double its area? Explain.

> **PROCEDURE: Calculating the Area of a Rectangle**
> The formula for the area of a rectangle with length l and width w is
> $$A = lw.$$

Parallelograms

Once you know the formula for the area of a rectangle, then you have the key for determining the formula for the area of a parallelogram. A parallelogram is formed by two intersecting pairs of parallel sides.

6. If you "straightened up" the parallelogram into the shaded rectangle, is the area changed? Explain.

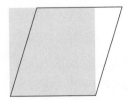

7. Use your observations from Problem 6 to calculate the area of the parallelogram with height 4 inches and base 7 inches. Note that the height of a parallelogram is defined as the perpendicular (right angle) distance from the base to its parallel side.

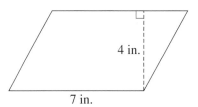

4 in.

7 in.

PROCEDURE: Calculating the Area of a Parallelogram

The formula for the area of a parallelogram with base b (the length of one side) and height h (the perpendicular distance from the base b to its parallel side) is

$$A = bh.$$

Triangles

Triangles can always be thought of as one-half a rectangle or parallelogram.

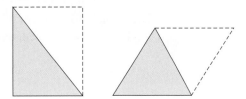

8. For each of the following triangles, draw the rectangle or parallelogram that encloses the triangle.

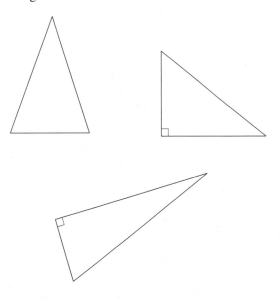

9. Use the idea that a triangle is $\frac{1}{2}$ of a rectangle to write a formula for the area of a triangle in terms of its base b and height h. Note that the height is the perpendicular distance from the base to the vertex, v, opposite it and that a vertex is a point where two sides of a triangle intersect. Explain.

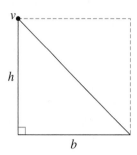
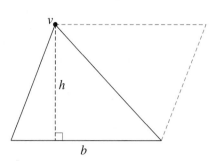

PROCEDURE: **Calculating the Area of a Triangle**

The formula for the area of a triangle with base b (the length of one side) and height h (the perpendicular distance from the base b to the vertex opposite it) is

$$A = \tfrac{1}{2}bh.$$

---

10. Use your formula from Problem 9 to calculate the area for each of the following triangles:

a.

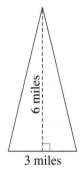

3 miles

b.

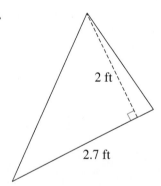

2 ft

2.7 ft

c.

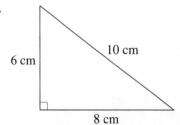

6 cm

10 cm

8 cm

d.

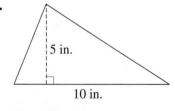

5 in.

10 in.

Trapezoids

Trapezoids may be viewed as one-half of the parallelogram that is formed by adjoining the trapezoid to itself turned upside down, as shown.

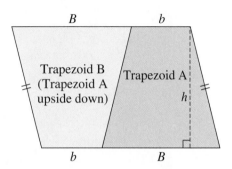

11. a. The parallelogram shown above has base $b + B$ and height h. Determine the area of this parallelogram.

b. Use the idea that a trapezoid is $\frac{1}{2}$ of a parallelogram to write a formula for the area A of a trapezoid in terms of its bases b and B and its height h.

PROCEDURE: **Calculating the Area of a Trapezoid**

The formula for the area of a trapezoid with bases b and B and height h is

$$A = \tfrac{1}{2}h(b + B).$$

---

12. Calculate the area of the trapezoid with height 5 feet and bases 6 feet and 11 feet.

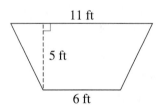

13. If one of the bases of the trapezoid in Problem 12 is increased by 2 feet and the other base is decreased by 2 feet, draw the new trapezoid and compute its new area.

Kites

PROCEDURE: **Calculating the Area of a Kite**

The formula for the area, A, of a kite with short diagonal, d, and long diagonal, D, is

$$A = \tfrac{1}{2}d \cdot D.$$

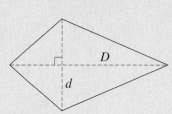

14. Calculate the area for each of the following kites.

   a.

   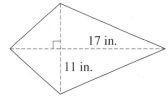

   b.

   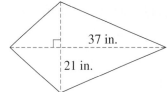

15. You need to make a kite as part of a school project. You are given two straight sticks measuring 24 inches and 12 inches to use for diagonals. Determine the area of your kite.

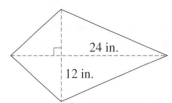

Rhombus

PROCEDURE: Calculating the Area of a Rhombus

A rhombus is a parallelogram with four equal sides. So the formula for the area of a rhombus is

$$A = bh.$$

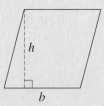

16. Calculate the area of the rhombus with height 6 feet and base 7 feet.

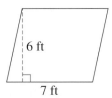

6 ft

7 ft

17. Suppose that you are given that the longer diagonal of a rhombus is 8 inches and that the shorter diagonal is 6 inches. Can you determine the area of the rhombus?

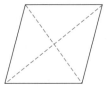

Polygons

You can determine the area of a polygon by seeing that polygons can be broken up into other more familiar figures, such as rectangles and triangles. For example, the garage shown below is a polygon that can also be viewed as a triangle sitting on top of a rectangle:

To determine the area of this polygon, use the appropriate formulas to determine each area, and then sum your answers to obtain the area of the polygon.

18. Calculate the area of the front of the garage:

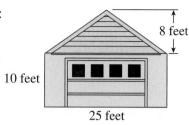

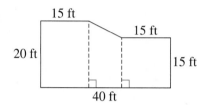

19. You are planning to build a new home with the following floor plan:

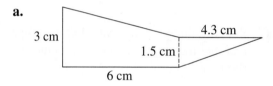

Calculate the total floor area.

20. Calculate the area for each of the following polygons:

a.

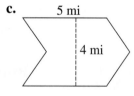

b.

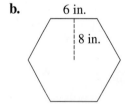

c.

SUMMARY
Activity 5.3

Two-Dimensional Figure	Labeled Sketch	Area Formula
Square		$A = s^2$
Rectangle		$A = lw$
Triangle		$A = \dfrac{1}{2}bh$
Parallelogram		$A = bh$
Trapezoid		$A = \dfrac{1}{2}h(b + B)$
Kite		$A = \dfrac{1}{2}d \cdot D$
Rhombus		$A = bh$
Polygon	A many-sided figure that is subdivided into familiar figures whose areas are given by formulas in this summary.	$A = $ sum of the areas of each figure

EXERCISES
Activity 5.3

1. You are carpeting your living room and sketch the following floor plan:

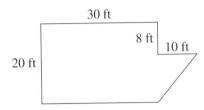

a. Calculate the area that you need to carpet.

b. Carpeting is sold in 10-foot-wide rolls. Calculate how much you need to buy. Explain.

2. You need to buy a solar cover for your 36-foot by 18-foot rectangular pool. A pool company advertises that solar covers are on sale for $1.77 per square foot. Determine the cost of the pool cover before sales tax.

3. Calculate the area for each of the following figures:

a.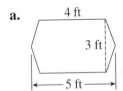

b.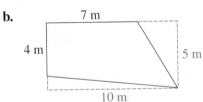

4. How would you break up the following star to determine what dimensions you need to know in order to calculate its area? Explain.

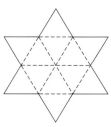

5. A standard basketball court is a rectangle with length 94 feet and width 50 feet. How many square feet of flooring would you need to purchase in order to replace the court?

6. You are planning to build a new garage on your home and need to measure the length and width of your cars to help you estimate the size of the double garage. Your car measurements are

  Car 1: 14 ft. 2 in. by 5 ft. 7 in.

  Car 2: 14 ft. 6 in. by 5 ft. 9 in.

  a. Based on these measurements, what would be a reasonable floor plan for your garage? Explain.

  b. What is the area of this floor plan?

7. You need to make a kite as part of a community contest. You are given two straight sticks measuring 35 in. and 18 in. to use for diagonals. Determine the surface area of your kite.

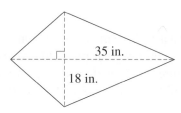

8. You wish to make a kite out of a piece of material that is 2 feet by 4 feet.

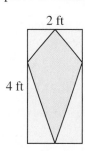

  a. Calculate how much material you have by finding the area of the rectangle.

b. Calculate the area of the kite.

c. How many square feet of material will you have left over?

9. Two neighbors, Ahmad and Marisa, are having their rectangular driveways paved.

   a. Ahmad's driveway measures 10 feet by 75 feet. What is the area of his driveway?

   b. Marisa has decided to pave a large rectangular parking area to accommodate the many cars in the family. This space is twice as long and three times as wide as Ahmad's driveway. Calculate the length, width, and the area of Marisa's new parking area.

   c. What is the ratio of the area of Ahmad's parking area to that of Marisa's driveway?

   d. Can you predict the area of Marisa's parking area from that of Ahmad's driveway by multiplying an amount related to the change in width and length?

   e. The results in part d suggest that if one side of a rectangle is multiplied by $a > 0$, and the other side is multiplied by $b > 0$, then its area is multiplied by ab. Prove this conjecture by comparing the area of a rectangle having length l and width w to the area of a new rectangle formed by multiplying the width by a and the length by b.

10. Your family has purchased a new A-frame vacation home in the mountains. The house contains several triangular windows that match the shape of the roof. In the living room, there is a large picture window shaped like an isosceles triangle (two sides of equal length). The base of the window is 12 feet long and the equal sides measure 10 feet.

    a. What is the perimeter of the living room window?

    b. What is the area of the living room window?

c. In the back of the house, there is a bedroom with a smaller isosceles triangle–shaped window that measures 6 feet across the base and 4 feet in height. What is the perimeter of the bedroom window?

d. What is the area of the bedroom window?

e. What is the relationship between the length of the sides of the bedroom window and the sides of the living room window?

f. What is the relationship between the perimeter of the bedroom window and the perimeter of the living room window?

g. What is the relationship between the area of the bedroom window and the area of the living room window?

h. Complete the following: If all sides of a triangle are multiplied by the same value $n > 0$, then the perimeter is _____ and the area is _____ .

ACTIVITY 5.4

How Big Is
That Circle?

OBJECTIVES

1. Develop a formula for the area of a circle.

2. Use the formula to determine areas of circles.

Determining the area of a circle becomes a challenge because there are no straight sides. No matter how hard you try, you cannot neatly pack unit squares inside a circle to completely cover the area of a circle. The best you can do in this way is to get an approximation of the area. In this activity you will explore methods for estimating the area of a circle and develop a formula to calculate the exact area.

> **DEFINITION**
>
> The **area of a circle** is the measure of the region enclosed by the circumference of the circle.

1. **a.** To help understand the formula for a circle's area, start by folding a paper circle in half, then in quarters, and finally halving it one more time into eighths.

b. Cut a circle into eight equal pieces (called *sectors*) and rearrange these sectors into an approximate parallelogram (see accompanying figure).

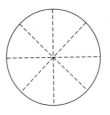

c. What measurement on the circle approximates the height of the parallelogram? Explain.

d. What measurement on the circle approximates the base of the parallelogram?

e. Recall that the area of a parallelogram is given by the product of its base and its height. Use your answers to parts b and c to determine the area of the parallelogram and the resulting area of the circle.

Imagine cutting a circle into more than eight equal sectors. Each sector would be thinner. When reassembled, as in Problem 1, the resulting figure will more closely approximate a parallelogram. Hence, the formula for the area of a circle, $A = \pi r^2$, is even more reasonable and accurate.

> **PROCEDURE: Calculating the Area of a Circle**
>
> The formula for the area A of a circle with radius r is
> $$A = \pi r^2.$$

2. You own a circular dartboard of radius 1.5 feet. To figure how much space you have as a target, calculate the area of the dartboard. Be sure to include the units in your answer.

3. The diameter of a circle is twice its radius. Use this fact, with the formula $A = \pi r^2$, to derive a formula for the area of a circle in terms of its diameter. Show the steps you took.

4. Calculate the area for each of the following circles:

   a.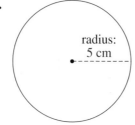

   radius:
   5 cm

   b.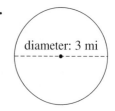

   diameter: 3 mi

5. a. **True or False:** If you double the size of the diameter of a circle, then you double the area of the circle.

   b. If the radius of a circle is multiplied by $a > 0$, then its area is multiplied by _____ .

SUMMARY
Activity 5.4

Two-Dimensional Figure	Labeled Sketch	Area Formula
Circle	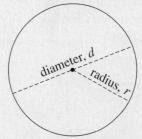	$A = \pi r^2$ (involving the radius) $A = \dfrac{\pi d^2}{4}$ (involving the diameter)

1. You order a pizza with diameter 14 inches. Your friend orders a pizza with diameter 10 inches. Compare the areas of the two pizzas to estimate approximately how many of the smaller pizzas can fit into the larger pizza.

2. You enjoy playing darts and decide to make your own simplified dartboard consisting of four concentric circles (that is, four circles with the same center, as shown in the diagram below). The smallest circle (the bull's-eye) has radius 1 cm, the next largest circle has radius 3 cm, the third has radius 6 cm, and the largest circle has radius 10 cm. In order to assign point values to the dartboard, you decide to compare the areas of the annular regions (the space between circles) on the board. There are two rules for your game:

   i. The three annular regions and the innermost circle on the board are assigned point values, based on the size of their areas, with the most points given to the smallest area, and

   ii. The winner is the person to score the highest number of points.

   a. What are the areas of the four circles?

   b. Using the areas from part a, compute the areas of each of the annular areas on the dartboard.

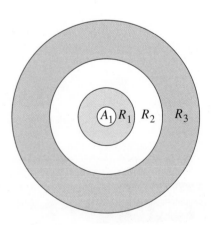

   c. Based on the areas of the annular regions, assign reasonable point values to each of the regions. Explain how you used the areas to assign the point values to each of the regions.

3. United States coins are circles of varying sizes. Choose a quarter, dime, nickel, and penny and

    a. Use a ruler to estimate the diameter of each coin.

    b. Calculate the area of each coin.

4. Use an appropriate formula to calculate the area for each of the following figures:

    a.

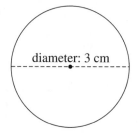

diameter: 3 cm

    b.

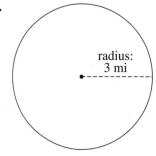

radius: 3 mi

    c.

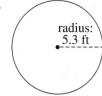

radius: 5.3 ft

    d.

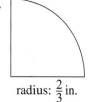

radius: $\frac{2}{3}$ in.

5. You need to polish your circular dining room table whose diameter is 7 feet. The label on the polish can claims coverage for 100 square feet, but you notice that the can is only about one-half full. Will you have enough polish to finish your table? Explain.

LEMON
G
L
O
W

6. a. Calculate the area of a circle of radius 4 inches.

b. Use part a to predict the area of a circle of radius 6 inches, without using the area formula.

c. Use the area formula to calculate the area of a circle of radius 6 inches.

d. Does your answer to part c match your answer to part a?

ACTIVITY 5.5

A New Pool and
Other Home
Improvements

OBJECTIVES

1. Solve problems in context
   using geometric models.

2. Distinguish between
   problems requiring area
   formulas and perimeter
   formulas.

Your family are the proud owners of a new circular swimming pool with a diameter of 25 feet and you are eager to dive in. However, you quickly discover that having a new pool requires making many decisions about other purchases.

1. The first concern is a solar pool cover. Online research indicates that circular pool covers come in the following sizes: 400, 500, and 600 square feet. Friends recommend that you buy a pool cover with very little overhang. Which size is best for your needs? Explain.

2. You decide to build a circular concrete patio 6 feet wide all around the pool. Draw a sketch of your pool with the patio. What is the area covered by your patio? Explain.

3. State law requires that all pools be enclosed by a fence to prevent accidents. You decide to completely enclose the pool and patio with a stockade fence. How many feet of fencing do you need? Explain.

4. Next, you decide to stain the new fence. The paint store recommends a stain that covers 500 square feet per gallon. If the stockade fence has a height of 5 feet, how many gallons of stain should you buy? Explain.

5. Last, you decide to plant a circular flower garden near the pool and patio but outside the fence. You measure that a circle of circumference 30 feet would fit. What is the length of the corresponding diameter of the flower garden?

Other Home Improvements

Now that the new pool, patio, and flower garden are finished, your parents want to do some other home improvements in anticipation of enjoying the new pool with family and friends.

They have budgeted $1000 for this purpose and the to-do list looks like this:

• replace the kitchen floor

• add a wallpaper border to the third bedroom

• paint the walls in the family room

To stay within the budget, your parents ask you to determine the cost of each of these projects. Your parents, along with you, expect to do the work yourselves, so the only monetary cost will be for materials.

6. The kitchen floor is divided into two parts. The first section is rectangular and measures 12 by 14 feet. The second section is a semicircular breakfast area that extends off the 14-foot side. The cost of vinyl flooring is $21 per square yard plus 6 percent sales tax. The vinyl is sold in 12-foot widths.

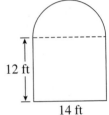

12 ft

14 ft

a. How long a piece of vinyl flooring will need to be purchased if you want only one seam where the breakfast area meets the main kitchen, as shown? Remember that the vinyl is 12 feet wide.

b. How many square feet of flooring must be purchased? How many square yards is that? (9 square feet = 1 square yard)

c. How much will the vinyl flooring cost including tax?

d. How many square feet of flooring will be left over after it's installed? Explain.

7. The third bedroom is rectangular in shape and has dimensions of $8\frac{1}{2}$ by 13 feet. On each 13-foot side, there is a window that measures 3 feet 8 inches wide and 4 feet high. The door is located on an $8\frac{1}{2}$-foot side and measures 3 feet wide from edge to edge. Your parents plan to put up a decorative horizontal wallpaper stripe around the room about halfway up the wall.

a. How many feet of wallpaper stripe will need to be purchased?

b. The border comes in rolls 5 yards in length. How many rolls will need to be purchased?

c. The wallpaper border costs $10.56 per roll plus 6% sales tax. Determine the cost of the border.

d. How many feet of wallpaper will be left over after it's installed?

8. The family room needs to be painted. It has a cathedral ceiling with front and back walls that measure the same, as shown in the diagram on right. The two side walls measure 14 feet long and 12 feet high. Each of the walls will need two coats of paint. The ceiling will not be painted.

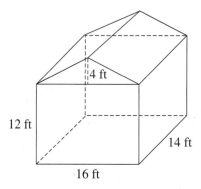

a. How many square feet of wall surface will be painted? (Remember, all walls will need two coats.)

b. Each gallon of paint covers approximately 400 square feet. How many gallons of paint will need to be purchased?

c. The paint costs $19.81 per gallon plus 6 percent sales tax. What is the total cost of the paint you need for the family room?

9. What is the cost for all of these home-improvement projects (not including the new pool, patio, and flower garden)?

10. Additional costs for items such as paint rollers and wallpaper paste amount to approximately $30. Can you afford to do all the projects? Explain.

1. Area formulas are used when you are measuring the amount of region *inside* a plane figure.

2. Perimeter or circumference formulas are used when you are measuring the length *around* a plane figure.

1. The driveway is rectangular in shape and measures 15 feet wide and 25 feet long. Calculate the area of the driveway.

2. A flower bed in the corner of the yard is in the shape of a right triangle. The perpendicular sides of the bed measure 6 feet 8 inches and 8 feet 4 inches. Calculate the area of the flower bed. What are the units of this area?

3. The front wall of the storage shed is in the shape of a trapezoid. The bottom measures 12 feet, the top measures 10 feet, and the height is 6 feet. Calculate the area of the front wall of the shed.

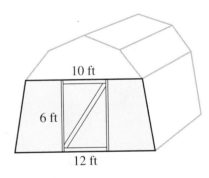

4. Your grandmother lives in a small, one-bedroom condo. Your parents want to surprise her with new wall-to-wall carpeting, but first they need to know the area of the floor space. The bedroom is 10 by 12 feet, the living room is 12 by 14 feet, the kitchen is 8 by 6 feet, and the bathroom is 5 by 9 feet. Calculate the total floor space (area) of her condo.

5. There is a large rectangular window in the living room with dimensions of 10 feet wide by 6 feet tall. In order to fit a new digital TV on the wall, your mother wants to redesign the window so that it admits the same amount of light but is only 8 feet wide. How tall should the redesigned window be?

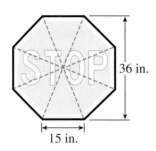

36 in.

15 in.

6. A stop sign is in the shape of a regular octagon (an eight-sided polygon with equal sides and angles). A regular octagon can be created using eight triangles of equal area. One triangle that makes up a stop sign has a base of 15 inches and a height of 18 inches. Calculate the area of the stop sign.

7. How does the area of the stop sign in Exercise 6 compare with the area of a circle of radius 18 inches? Explain.

8. Your uncle and aunt are buying plywood to board up their windows in preparation for Hurricane Euclid. In the master bedroom, they have a Norman window (in the shape of a rectangle with a semicircular top). So, they need your help to calculate the area of the window.

a. If the rectangular part of the window is 4 feet wide and 5 feet tall, what is the area of the entire window?

b. The master bathroom also has a Norman window whose dimensions are half the size of the one in the master bedroom. Without using the area formula again, determine how much plywood will be needed to board up both windows.

9. The diameter of the Earth is 12,742 km; the diameter of the Moon is 3476 km.

a. If you flew around Earth by following the equator at a height of 10 km, how many trips around the Moon could you take in the same amount of time, at the same height from the Moon, and at the same speed? Explain.

b. The circle whose circumference is the equator is sometimes called the "great circle" of the Earth or of the Moon. Compare the areas of the great circles of Earth and the Moon.

ACTIVITY 5.6
*How Big Is
That Angle?*

OBJECTIVES

1. Measure the size of angles with a protractor.
2. Classify triangles as equiangular, equilateral, right, isosceles, or scalene.

EQUIPMENT

In this laboratory activity, you will need the following equipment:

1. A 12-inch ruler
2. A protractor

You may have wondered why a right angle measures 90 degrees. Why not 100 degrees? As with much of the mathematics that we use today, the measurement of angles has a rich history, going back to ancient times when navigation of the oceans and surveying the land were priorities. The ancient Babylonian culture used a base 60 number system, which at least in part led to the circle being divided into 360 equal sectors. The angle of each sector was simply defined to measure 1 degree and so today we say there are 360 degrees (abbreviated 360°) in a circle. In this activity you will be using degrees to measure angles. The illustration shows a sector having an angle of 20 degrees ($\frac{1}{18}$ of a circle).

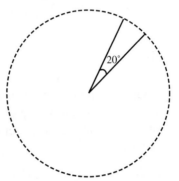

In the following diagram, the circle is divided into four equal sectors by two perpendicular lines. The angles of the four sectors must add up to 360 degrees. Since the angles are equal, dividing 360° by 4 results in each angle measuring 90°. Recall that 90° angles are called *right* angles.

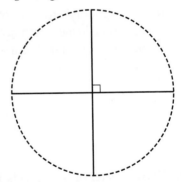

1. How many degrees are in the angle of a sector that is exactly half of a circle? Such an angle is called a *straight angle*.

Measuring Angles

> **PROCEDURE: Measuring Angles with a Protractor**
>
> A protractor is a device for measuring the size of angles in degrees. Place the vertex of the angle at the center of the protractor (often a hole in the center of the baseline) and place one side of the angle along the baseline of the protractor. Where the other side of the angle meets the appropriate scale on the semicircle is the measure of the angle in degrees.

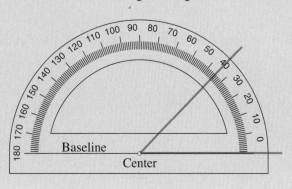

Example 1   *The following angle measures 75°.*

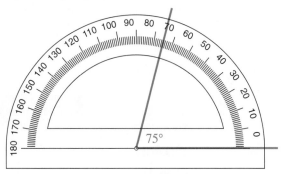

2. Use a protractor to measure the size of each of the following angles.

   a.

   b.

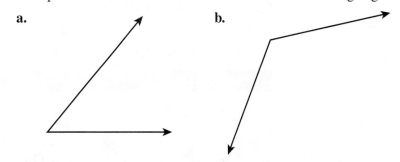

> **DEFINITIONS**
>
> An **acute angle** is any angle that is smaller than a right angle. Its degree measure is less than 90°.
>
> An **obtuse angle** is any angle that is larger than a right angle. Its degree measure is greater than 90°.

It is a well-known theorem in geometry that the sum of the measures of the angles of a triangle *must* equal 180°.

3. Verify this theorem by carefully measuring the angles of each of the following triangles, recording the results in the table below. You will have to extend the sides of each triangle to use your protractor effectively.

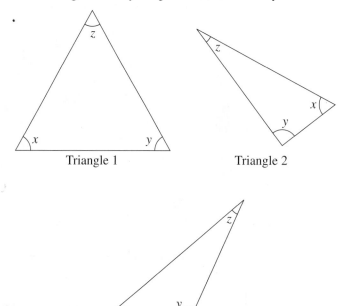

Triangle 1   Triangle 2

Triangle 3

	ANGLE *x*	ANGLE *y*	ANGLE *z*	SUM
TRIANGLE I				
TRIANGLE 2				
TRIANGLE 3				

Classifying Triangles

Sometimes, it is useful to classify triangles in terms of special properties of their sides or angles. These classifications are summarized in the following table.

TRIANGLE CLASSIFICATIONS	DEFINITION
Equilateral	All three sides have the same length.
Isosceles	Exactly two sides have the same length. The two angles opposite the equal sides will also have the same measure.
Scalene	None of the sides have the same length.
Equiangular	All three angles have the same measure. An equiangular triangle is also an equilateral triangle.
Right	One angle measures 90°.
Acute	All angles measure less than 90°.
Obtuse	One angle measures greater than 90°.

4. Use your protractor to measure the acute angles in the following right triangles, recording your results in the table. What is the sum of the two acute angles in each triangle?

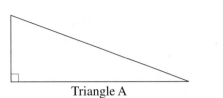

Triangle A

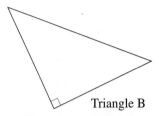

Triangle B

	ONE NONRIGHT ANGLE	OTHER NONRIGHT ANGLE	SUM
TRIANGLE A			
TRIANGLE B			

5. In a right triangle, what must be true about the two angles that are not right angles? Explain your answer.

6. a. In an equiangular triangle, what is the measure of each angle?

b. In an isosceles triangle, if one angle measures 110°, what is the measure of the other two equal angles?

c. Consider the following three triangles:

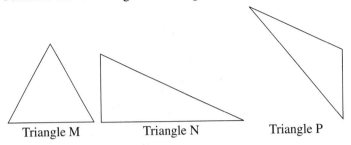

Triangle M   Triangle N   Triangle P

i. Choose the triangles that are scalene, and explain why. Then use a protractor to measure the angles.

ii. Choose the triangle(s) that is (are) obtuse and explain why.

iii. Choose the triangle(s) that is (are) acute and explain why.

SUMMARY
Activity 5.6

Concept/Skill	Description	Example
1. Using a protractor	Place the vertex of the angle to be measured at the center of the protractor and line up one side with the base line. Read the protractor scale to measure the angle.	See Example 1, page 599
2. Equilateral triangle	A triangle in which all three sides have the same length (also equiangular).	
3. Isosceles triangle	A triangle in which two sides have the same length. The two angles opposite the equal sides will also have the same measure.	
4. Scalene triangle	A triangle in which all the sides have different lengths.	
5. Equiangular triangle	A triangle in which all three angles are the same measure (also equilateral).	

6. Right triangle   A triangle in which one angle measures 90°.

7. Acute triangle   A triangle in which all angles measure less than 90°.

8. Obtuse triangle   A triangle in which one angle measures greater than 90°.

9. Angle sum   The sum of the measures of
   of a triangle   the angles of a triangle
                            equals 180°.

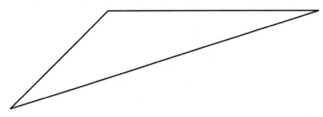

EXERCISES
Activity 5.6

1. Use a protractor to measure the angles in this triangle. Verify that the sum of the angles is 180°.

2. In a right triangle, one of the acute angles measures 47°. What is the size of the other acute angle?

3. In an isosceles triangle one of the angles measures 102°. What is the size of the other two angles?

4. What is true about the sizes of the three angles in a scalene triangle?

5. Give an example of the possible sizes of the three angles in a scalene triangle that is also an acute triangle.

6. What must be the sum of the four angles in a parallelogram? (*Hint:* Consider dividing the parallelogram into two triangles.)

7. a. Extend the idea of Exercise 6 to a pentagon (a five-sided polygon) to determine the sum of all 5 angles by dividing the pentagon into 3 triangles that all meet at one point on the pentagon.

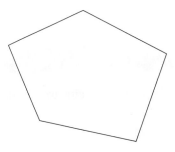

b. Extend the idea of part a to determine the sum of all eight angles in an octagon (an eight-sided polygon).

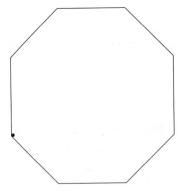

ACTIVITY 5.7

How about
Pythagoras?

OBJECTIVES

1. Verify and use the
   Pythagorean theorem
   for right triangles.

2. Use the Pythagorean
   theorem to solve
   problems.

3. Determine the distance
   between two points using
   the distance formula.

In this activity you will experimentally verify the Pythagorean theorem for right triangles. This formula is used by surveyors, architects, and builders to check whether or not two lines are perpendicular or if a corner truly forms a right angle.

Recall that a right triangle is simply a triangle that has a right angle. In other words, one of the angles formed by the triangle measures 90°. The two sides that are perpendicular and form the right angle are called the **legs** of the right triangle. The third side, opposite the right angle, is called the **hypotenuse**.

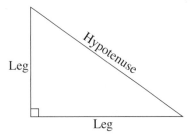

1. Use a protractor to construct three right triangles, one with legs of length 1 inch and 5 inches, a second with legs of length 3 inches and 4 inches, and a third with legs of length 2 inches each.

Triangle 1

Triangle 2

Triangle 3

Pythagorean Theorem

2. For each triangle in Problem 1, complete the following table. The first triangle was done for you as an example. Note that the lengths of the legs of the triangles are represented by a and b. The letter c represents the length of the hypotenuse.

   a. Use a ruler to measure the length of each hypotenuse, in inches. Record the lengths in column c.

   b. Square each length a, b, and c and record in the table.

	a	b	c	a^2	b^2	c^2
TRIANGLE 1	1	5	5.1	1	25	26.0
TRIANGLE 2	3	4				
TRIANGLE 3	2	2				

3. There does not appear to be a relationship between a, b, and c, but investigate further. What is the relationship between a^2, b^2, and c^2?

The relationship demonstrated in Problem 2 has been known since antiquity. It was known by many cultures but has been attributed to the Greek mathematician Pythagoras, who lived in the sixth century B.C.

The **Pythagorean theorem** states that, in a right triangle, the sum of the squares of the leg lengths is equal to the square of the hypotenuse length.

Symbolically, the Pythagorean theorem is written as

$$c^2 = a^2 + b^2 \text{ or } c = \sqrt{a^2 + b^2},$$

where a and b are leg lengths and c is the hypotenuse length.

Note that this relationship is true for any right triangle. Also, if this relationship is true for a triangle, then the triangle is a right triangle.

Example 1 *If a right triangle has legs a = 4 centimeters and b = 7 centimeters, you can calculate the length of the hypotenuse as follows:*

$$c = \sqrt{a^2 + b^2} = \sqrt{(4)^2 + (7)^2}$$
$$= \sqrt{16 + 49} = \sqrt{65} \approx 8.06 \text{ cm}$$

4. A popular triangle with builders and carpenters has dimensions 3 units by 4 units by 5 units.

   a. Use the Pythagorean theorem to show that this triangle is a right triangle.

   b. Builders use this triangle by taking a 12-unit-long rope and marking it in lengths of 3 units, 4 units, and 5 units (see figure below.)

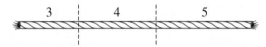

   Then, by fitting this rope to a corner, they can quickly tell if the corner is a true right angle. Another special right triangle has legs of length 5 units and 12 units. Determine the perimeter of this right triangle. Explain how a carpenter can use this triangle to check for a right angle.

5. Suppose you wish to measure the distance across a pond but don't wish to get your feet wet! By being clever and knowing the Pythagorean theorem, you can estimate the distance by taking two measurements on dry land, as long as your two distances lie along perpendicular lines. (See figure below.)

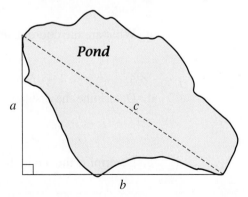

If your measurements for legs *a* and *b* are 260 feet and 310 feet, respectively, what is the distance, *c*, across the pond?

Distance Formula

Archaeologists need to keep precise records of locations of their findings. To accomplish this, some landmark point at the archaeological site is selected. From this key point, a grid of squares, usually made of rope, is laid out over the site to form a coordinate system. This system provides a method in which the location of artifacts, bones, and other items can be located and distances between points can be calculated.

By using the coordinates of the points in the coordinate system and the Pythagorean theorem, you can determine the distance between any two points in a plane.

6. The following graph shows the points P (1, 7) and Q (4, 2).

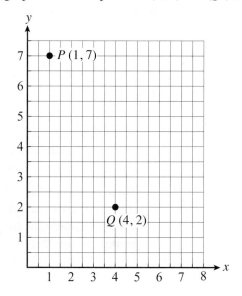

Complete a right triangle as follows:

a. Draw a line segment with P and Q as endpoints.

b. Using P as an endpoint, draw a vertical segment downward that intersects with a horizontal segment drawn to the left from endpoint Q. Label this point C. The angle formed by the horizontal and vertical segments is a right angle.

c. What are the coordinates of the point of intersection in part b?

d. Determine the distance of the vertical segment PC.

e. Determine the length horizontal segment CQ.

f. The distance between the points P (1, 7) and Q (4, 2) is the length of the hypotenuse of the right triangle PCQ. Use the Pythagorean theorem to determine this distance.

To develop a general formula for the distance, d, between two points, let (x_1, y_1) and (x_2, y_2) represent two points in the plane that do not lie on the same horizontal or vertical line. With these two points, a right triangle can be formed as shown in the following diagram.

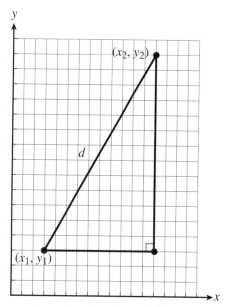

7. a. What are the coordinates of the vertex of the right angle?

b. Write an expression that represents the length of the horizontal side of the right triangle.

c. Write an expression that represents the length of the horizontal side of the right triangle.

Applying the Pythagorean theorem to determine the length, d, of the hypotenuse, you have

$$\begin{array}{ccc}\text{Square of the length} & = \text{Square of the length} & + \text{Square of the length}\\ \text{of the hypotenuse} & \text{of horizontal side} & \text{of vertical side}\end{array}$$

$$d^2 = (x_2 - x_1)^2 + (y_2 - y_1)^2$$

$$d = \sqrt{(x_2 - x_1)^2 + (y_2 - y_1)^2}$$

Distance Formula

Let $P(x_1, y_1)$ and $Q(x_2, y_2)$ represent two points in the plane. The distance, d, between P and Q is given by

$$d = \sqrt{(x_2 - x_1)^2 + (y_2 - y_1)^2}.$$

8. a. Use the distance formula to determine the distance between $P(-8, 4)$ and $Q(3, -2)$.

b. Use the distance formula to determine the distance between the 2 points in Problem 6 and then compare your results.

9. a. Plot the points $P\,(2, 1)$, $Q\,(4, 0)$, and $R\,(5, 7)$ on the following grid. Connect the points to form a triangle.

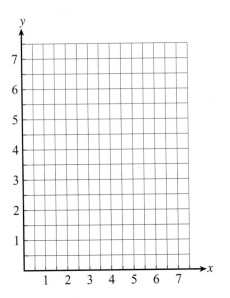

b. Use the distance formula to determine the length of each of the following

i. side PQ **ii.** side PR **iii.** side QR

c. Use the Pythagorean theorem to verify that the points P, Q, and R are vertices of a right triangle. Be sure to identify which vertex represents the right angle and which side represents the hypotenuse.

SUMMARY
Activity 5.7

Concept/Skill	Description	Example
1. Pythagorean theorem	In a right triangle, $c^2 = a^2 + b^2$.	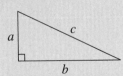

2. Let $P\,(x_1, y_1)$ and $Q\,(x_2, y_2)$ represent two points in the plane. The distance, d, between P and Q is given by

$$d = \sqrt{(x_2 - x_1)^2 + (y_2 - y_1)^2}.$$

EXERCISES
Activity 5.7

1. New cell phone towers are being constructed on a daily basis throughout the country. Typically, they consist of a tall, thin tower supported by several guy wires. Assume the ground is level in the following. Round answers to the nearest foot.

   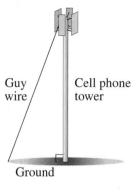

   a. The guy wire is attached on the ground at a distance of 100 feet from the base of the tower. The guy wire is also attached to the phone tower 300 feet above the ground. What is the length of the guy wire?

   b. You move the base of the guy wire so that it is attached to the ground at 120 feet from the base of the tower. Now how much wire do you need for the one guy wire?

   c. Another option is to attach the base of the guy wire 100 feet from the base of the tower and to the tower 350 feet above the ground. How much wire do you need for this option?

2. A building inspector needs to determine if two walls in a new house are built at right angles, as the building code requires. He measures and finds the following information. Wall 1 measures 12 feet, wall 2 measures 14 feet, and the distance from the end of wall 1 to the end of wall 2 measures 18 feet. Do the walls meet at right angles? Explain.

   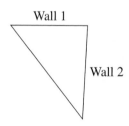

3. Trusses used to support the roofs of many structures can be thought of as two right triangles placed side by side.

   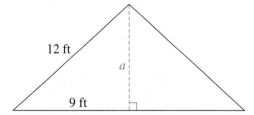

   a. If the hypotenuse in one of the right triangles of a truss measures 12 feet and the horizontal leg in the same right triangle measures 9 feet, how high is the vertical leg of the truss?

b. To make a steeper roof, you may increase the vertical leg to 10 feet. Keeping the 9-foot horizontal leg, how long will the hypotenuse of the truss be now?

4. You can consider the truss in Exercise 3 as a single triangle. In this case, it is a good example of an isosceles triangle.

    a. If the top angle of the truss is 120°, then what are the measures of the other two angles?

    b. If you wish to have a steeper roof, with the base angles of the isosceles truss each measuring 42°, what is the measure of the top angle?

5. For the following right triangles, use the Pythagorean theorem to compute the length of the third side of the triangle:

a.

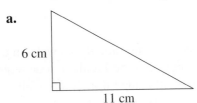

6 cm

11 cm

b.

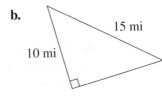

15 mi

10 mi

6. You are buying a ladder for your 30-foot-tall house. For safety, you would always like to ensure that the base of the ladder be placed at least 8 feet from the base of the house. What is the shortest ladder you can buy and still be able to reach the top of your house?

7. Pythagorean triples are three positive integers that could be the lengths of three sides of a right triangle. For example, 3, 4, 5 is a Pythagorean triple because $5^2 = 3^2 + 4^2$.

    a. Is 5, 12, 13 a Pythagorean triple? Why or why not?

    b. Is 5, 10, 15 a Pythagorean triple? Why or why not?

c. Is 1, 1, 2 a Pythagorean triple? Why or why not?

d. Name another Pythagorean triple. Explain.

8. You own a summer home on the east side of Lake George in New York's Adirondack Mountains. To drive to your favorite restaurant on the west side of the lake, you must go directly south for 7 miles and then directly west for 3 miles. If you could go directly to the restaurant in your boat, how far is the boat trip?

9. You are decorating a large evergreen tree in your yard for the holidays. The tree stands 25 feet tall and 15 feet wide. You want to hang strings of lights from top to bottom draped on the outside of the tree. How long should the strings of lights be? Explain.

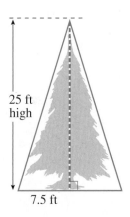

25 ft high

7.5 ft

10. Is it possible to have a right triangle with sides measuring 7 inches, 10 inches, and 15 inches?

11. Determine the distance between the given points.

   a. $(3, -11), (-12, -3)$

   b. $(-7, 3), (2, -9)$

12. Determine the length of the hypotenuse in the following two ways:
i. use the Pythagorean theorem and **ii.** use the distance formula

a.

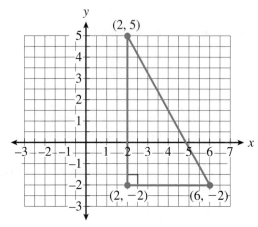

b.

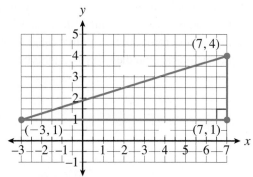

13. a. Plot the points $A\ (1, -3)$, $B\ (3, 2)$, and $C\ (-2, 4)$ on the following:

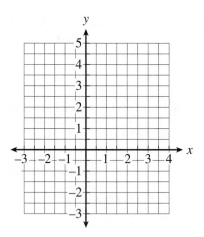

b. Use the distance formula to verify that those points are vertices of an isosceles triangle.

ACTIVITY 5.8
Not Exactly
the Same

OBJECTIVES

1. Identify similar geometric figures.
2. Solve problems involving similar figures.
3. Identify congruent geometric figures.

You are planning a surprise anniversary party for your parents and want to prepare a large poster of their wedding picture. The original picture has width 4 inches and height 6 inches. You want to enlarge the picture without distorting it. Mathematically, this means you want to create a rectangular enlargement that is **similar** to the original rectangular photograph.

> **DEFINITION**
>
> **Similar** geometric figures have identical *shape* but different *size*. It is often necessary to rotate or flip one similar figure so that it is in the same position as the other. In this case, "corresponding" means in the same relative position.
>
> Similar geometric figures have corresponding angles of equal measure and corresponding sides that have identical ratios (proportional). Equivalently, the ratio of any two sides of a given figure is equal to the ratio of the two corresponding sides of a similar figure.

For example, consider the two triangles *ABC* and *XYZ* below. The two triangles are similar because $\angle A = \angle X$, $\angle B = \angle Y$, and $\angle C = \angle Z$. Note that sides *a* and *x* are corresponding sides, sides *b* and *y* are corresponding sides, and sides *c* and *z* are corresponding sides.

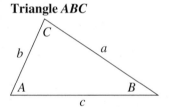

Triangle *ABC*   **Triangle *XYZ***

The proportionality of the corresponding sides can be described algebraically as

$$\frac{a}{x} = \frac{b}{y}, \quad \frac{a}{x} = \frac{c}{z}, \quad \frac{b}{y} = \frac{c}{z}.$$

1. The lengths of the sides of two triangles appear in the following diagram:

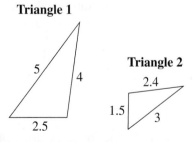

Triangle 1

Triangle 2

a. Rotate triangle 2 so that it is in the same position as triangle 1. What is the ratio of the corresponding sides (of triangle 1 to triangle 2)? Express this ratio in reduced fraction form.

b. What is the perimeter of each triangle?

c. What is the ratio of the perimeters? Express this ratio in reduced fraction form.

d. Compare the ratios in parts a and c.

The **proportionality constant** $\frac{5}{3}$ in Problem 1 applies to *all* corresponding linear measurements associated with the same similar figures—sides, diagonals, perimeters, heights, and so forth. Therefore, the ratio of the altitudes of similar triangles 1 and 2 is also $\frac{5}{3}$.

2. a. The following figure contains two similar triangles. Identify these triangles.

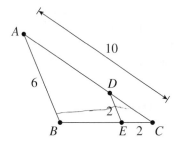

In parts b–e, determine the length of the given side.

b. *BC*   **c.** *DC*   **d.** *AD*   **e.** *BE*

f. Determine the proportionality constant of the larger triangle to the smaller triangle.

Let us return to the poster problem.

3. a. Suppose the standard poster size is 36 inches by 48 inches. Are the original 4-inch by 6-inch photograph and the full poster similar rectangles?

b. If the width and height of the original 4-inch by 6-inch photograph is increased by a factor of 5, what are the dimensions of the enlargement?

c. Are the original photograph and enlargement in part b similar?

d. By what maximum factor can you enlarge the original photograph so that it fits in the standard 36 inch by 48 inch poster?

e. What are the dimensions of the enlarged picture?

f. Is the enlarged picture similar to the original photograph?

Indirect Measurement

4. A 5-foot-tall woman casts a shadow of 4 feet while a nearby tree casts a shadow that measures 30 feet. This situation can be represented by two similar right triangles as shown in the following diagram (not drawn to scale). Let h represent the height of the tree.

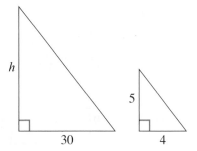

Use the proportionality of corresponding sides to determine the height of the tree.

Purchasing a New TV

5. You are getting ready to buy a new television. One of the most important considerations you need to make is whether to buy a 16:9 HD television or a more conventional 4:3 television set. These ratios are the width to height ratios of each TV screen. Do these two screens represent similar rectangles?

6. The displayed size of a TV actually represents the length of the screen diagonal. Suppose you decide to purchase a 32-inch TV. You are curious which TV, the conventional or the HD, will give you a larger screen area.

a. Use the diagram below and your understanding of similarity to determine the width, height, and area of the conventional TV screen.

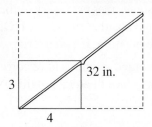

Note that the width-to-height ratio $\frac{4}{3}$ for the conventional television represents a reduced fraction of the actual width and height measurements of the TV. As you encountered in Problem 3, you need to determine the factor to multiply 4 and 3 by to acquire the actual width and height.

b. Determine the width, height, and area of the HD TV.

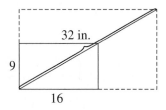

32 in.

9

16

c. Which TV are you going to buy?

Congruent Figures

7. The following two right triangles are congruent.

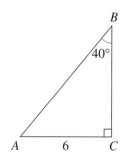
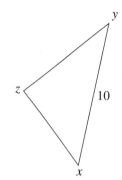

Determine each of the following:

a. The length of the side *AB*.

b. The measure of the angle *YXZ*.

c. The length of side *YZ*.

SUMMARY
Activity 5.8

1. Similar geometric figures have *identical shape* but *different size*. It is often necessary to rotate or flip one similar figure so that it is in the same position as the other. In this case, *corresponding* means in the same relative position.

2. Similar geometric figures have corresponding angles of equal measure and corresponding sides that have identical ratios (proportional). Equivalently, the ratio of any two sides of a given figure is equal to the ratio of the two corresponding sides of a similar figure.

3. Congruent geometric figures have *identical shape* and *size*. As with similar figures, it is sometimes necessary to rotate or flip one congruent figure so that it is in the same position as the other. Once again, *corresponding* means in the same relative position. If you overlap congruent figures, they will coincide.

4. Congruent geometric figures have corresponding angles of equal measure and corresponding sides of equal length.

EXERCISES
Activity 5.8

1. The following two triangles are similar.

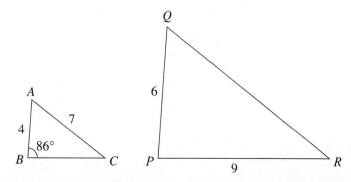

    a. Determine the length of the sides BC and QR.

    b. Determine the measure of angle P.

2. At 10 A.M. a 6-foot-tall man casts a 4.5-foot shadow. How long a shadow is cast by a 50-foot tree?

3. An architectural blueprint is drawn to a scale of 1:20.

    a. A window on the blueprint measures $2\frac{1}{4}$ inches by $1\frac{3}{8}$ inches. What are the dimensions of the actual window?

    b. What are the dimensions of a square room whose diagonal on the sketch measures $10\frac{3}{4}$ inches?

4. You want to place a 20-inch by 15-inch watercolor painting on a mat so that a 2-inch-wide strip of matting shows on all four sides of the painting. Do the mat and painting form similar rectangles?

5. Determine the length x in each figure:

    a.   **b.**   **c.**

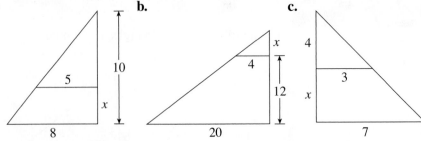

6. Standing 20 feet from a streetlight, a 5-foot-tall woman casts an 8-foot shadow. How tall is the streetlight?

7. You and your friends decide to set up an experiment to estimate the height of the high school gym. You wait until dark and then use a flashlight to project shadows onto the building. One of your friends sets the flashlight on the ground 50 feet from the building and shines it at you as you (6 feet tall) walk away from the flashlight and towards the building. Another friend tells you to stop when the height of your shadow reaches the top of the building; you have walked 12 feet.

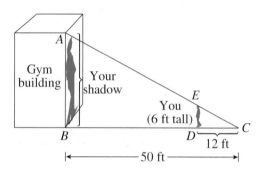

a. Where do you see two similar right triangles in the diagram? Explain.

b. Use the properties of similar right triangles to estimate the height of the gym.

8. You measure an isosceles triangle and label the lengths, as shown.

In a similar isosceles triangle the longest side is 14 feet. Compute the lengths of its two equal sides.

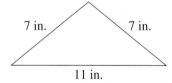

9. A triangle has legs that measure 3 feet, 5 feet, and 7 feet.

    a. Calculate the dimensions of a similar triangle whose longest side measures 13 inches.

    b. Calculate the dimensions of a similar triangle whose shortest side measures 2 meters.

10. The following two trapezoids are congruent:

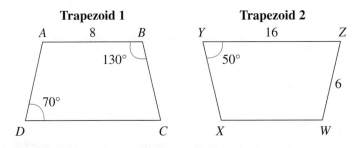

    a. Rotate trapezoid 2 so that it is in the same position as trapezoid 1.

In parts b–d, determine the length of the given side.

    b. side *XW*   **c.** side *AD*   **d.** side *DC*

In parts e–g, determine the measure of the given angle.

    e. angle *C*   **f.** angle *Z*   **g.** angle *A*

ACTIVITY 5.9
The Skylight

OBJECTIVES

1. Identify properties of 45-45-90 triangles and 30-60-90 triangles.

2. Use special right triangles (30-60-90 and 45-45-90) to solve problems.

You are employed by a construction firm that is bidding on a large home to be constructed in the area. Specifically, you are assigned the task of pricing the cost of building a skylight for the master bedroom. The skylight is to be in the shape of a triangular pyramid (see diagram) with a square base, measuring 1 meter on one side.

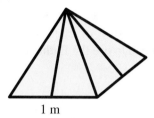

1 m

You start with the metal base, which is 1 meter square with one reinforcing piece on the diagonal.

Figure 5.1

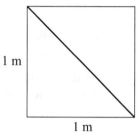

1 m

1 m

Before you can determine the cost of the materials, you need to know the length of the diagonal. The diagonal divides the square base into two congruent triangles that resemble the following.

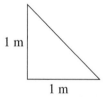

1 m

1 m

Because the two triangles are congruent, the two triangles formed by the diagonal have the same measures for the length of their sides and their angles.

1. **a.** Determine the measure of each angle for one of the triangles. Describe how you determined these measurements. Record your results on the accompanying figure.

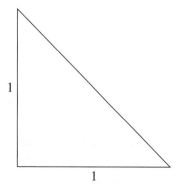

1

1

b. Is the triangle in part a, a right triangle? Explain.

Recall that the side opposite the 90° angle of a right triangle is called the **hypotenuse** and the two other sides are called the **legs.**

2. Determine the measure of each side of the right triangle in Problem 1. *Note:* You will need to use the Pythagorean theorem to determine the length of the hypotenuse.

The triangle in Problem 1 is a special right triangle known as a **45-45-90 triangle** because the two angles formed by the legs and the hypotenuse measure 45 degrees and the angle formed by the two legs is a 90 degree angle. This triangle is also known as an **isosceles right triangle,** because the legs are equal in length and the legs form a right angle.

There is a special relationship between the length of the legs of a 45-45-90 triangle and the length of the hypotenuse. Problem 3 demonstrates this property.

3. a. Determine the length of the hypotenuse in a 45-45-90 triangle in which the lengths of the legs are 3.5 cm. Round your result to the nearest hundredth.

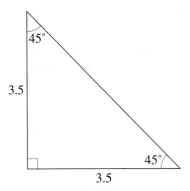

b. If the length of one of the legs of a 45-45-90 triangle is represented by s, determine the length of the hypotenuse. Label the sides of the triangle in terms of s.

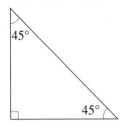

c. Use the result in part b to complete the following statement: If the length of the legs of a 45-45-90 triangle is represented by s, then the length of the hypotenuse is _____.

d. Use the conclusion in part c to determine the length of the hypotenuse in part a. Compare the results.

You can now determine the cost of the base of the skylight.

4. a. Determine the length of the diagonal of the metal base (see Figure 5.1).

  b. Determine the length of the metal material needed to construct the base of the skylight.

  c. The cost of the metal for the base is $16 per meter. Determine the cost of the base of the skylight.

30-60-90 Triangles

Now that you have the base of the skylight priced out, you begin to work on the skylight itself. Each side of the pyramid is made up of two congruent triangular glass sections (see diagram). Each glass section is enclosed in a metal frame.

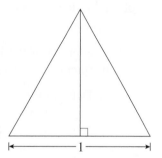

5. Together, the two triangular sections form one equilateral triangle.

  a. Determine the length of each side of the equilateral triangle. Explain.

  b. Determine the measure of each of the angles of the equilateral triangle. Explain.

You now have two calculations to make. First, you must price out the metal frame for each piece. Second, you must price out the glass needed. In either case, you need to determine the dimensions of each of the two congruent triangles that make up the side of the pyramid.

6. Each triangular section can be represented by the following, where *a* and *b* represent the lengths of the legs of the right triangle.

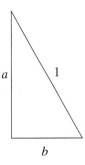

a. Determine the measures of each angle of the triangle. Recall this is one-half an equilateral triangle. Record your results in the given figure.

b. Determine the lengths of each side of the triangle. Note you will need the Pythagorean theorem to determine the length of side *a*. Record your results in the given figure.

The triangle in Problem 6 is an example of a second special right triangle known by its angles as a **30-60-90 triangle**. Remember, this 30-60-90 triangle is one-half of an equilateral triangle that makes up one side of the skylight. Therefore, the hypotenuse of the 30-60-90 triangle is a side of the equilateral triangle.

7. The length of the legs in a 30-60-90 triangle are related to the length of the hypotenuse in special ways.

a. Determine the length of each side of a 30-60-90 triangle whose hypotenuse measures 3 feet. Let *a* represent the length of the side opposite the 60° angle. Let *b* represent the length of the side opposite the 30° angle.

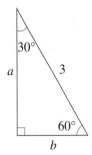

b. Determine the length of each side of a 30-60-90 triangle whose hypotenuse measures s feet. Label the sides of the triangle in terms of s.

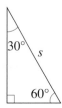

c. Use the results from part b to complete the following statements.

If the length of the hypotenuse of a 30-60-90 triangle is represented by s, then

i. the length of the side opposite the 30° angle is _____.

ii. the length of the side opposite the 60° angle is _____.

d. Use the conclusions in part c to determine the length of each side of the triangle in part a. Compare the results.

Before you determine the cost of the skylight itself, let's investigate special area and perimeter formulas for the 45-45-90 and 30-60-90 triangles.

Area and Perimeter Formulas for Special Right Triangles

8. a. Write a formula for the perimeter of a 45-45-90 triangle whose legs measure s feet. Use the triangle below that you labeled in Problem 3b. Simplify your answer.

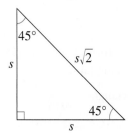

b. Use the triangle below that you labeled in Problem 7c to write a formula for the perimeter of a 30-60-90 triangle whose hypotenuse measures s feet.

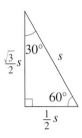

9. a. Write a formula for the area of a 45-45-90 triangle whose legs measure s. Use the triangle in Problem 8a. Recall the formula for the area of a triangle, $A = \frac{1}{2}bh$, where b represents the base and h is the height.

b. Recall that two congruent 45-45-90 triangles form the square base of the skylight. Using the formula for the area of a square having side s, compare the area of the square base and the area of the triangle in part a. Does the result seem reasonable? Explain.

10. a. Write a formula for the area of a 30-60-90 triangle whose hypotenuse measures s. Use the triangle in Problem 8b.

b. Recall that two 30-60-90 triangles form an equilateral triangle that makes up a side of the pyramid. Using the formula for the area of an equilateral triangle having side s, compare the area of this equilateral triangle with the 30-60-90 triangle in part a. Explain.

The perimeter and area formulas for 45-45-90 and 30-60-90 triangles are summarized in the accompanying table.

45-45-90 triangle   **30-60-90 triangle**

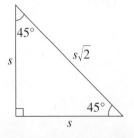
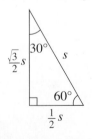

	SQUARE	45-45-90 TRIANGLE	EQUILATERAL TRIANGLE	30-60-90 TRIANGLE
PERIMETER	$4s$	$s(2 + \sqrt{2}) \approx 3.41s$	$3s$	$\frac{1}{2}s(3 + \sqrt{3}) \approx 2.37s$
AREA	s^2	$\frac{1}{2}s^2 = 0.5s^2$	$\frac{1}{4}s^2\sqrt{3} \approx 0.43s^2$	$\frac{1}{8}s^2\sqrt{3} \approx 0.22s^2$

Now, let's finish the skylight problem.

11. How many 30-60-90 triangles are contained in the pyramid skylight?

12. a. What is the perimeter of each of the 30-60-90 triangles in the skylight?

   b. What is the total length of metal needed in the construction of the sides of the skylight? Recall, each triangular glass section is enclosed in a metal frame.

   c. What is the cost for the metal used in the sides of the skylight? The cost of the metal frame enclosing the glass triangular sections is $12 per meter.

13. a. What is the area of each of the 30-60-90 glass triangles used in the construction of the sides of the pyramid?

   b. What is the total area of the glass used in the construction of the skylight?

   c. What is the total cost of the glass used in the construction of the skylight? The cost of the glass is $32 per square meter.

14. What is the total cost of the skylight including the metal base, the metal framing for the glass, and all of the glass?

SUMMARY
Activity 5.9

1. A **45-45-90 triangle** is an isosceles right triangle, that is, the two legs have equal measure. The measure of the hypotenuse is $\sqrt{2}$ times the measure of one of the legs.

45-45-90 triangle

2. In a **30-60-90 triangle** the measure of the side opposite the 30° angle is one-half the measure of the hypotenuse. The measure of the side opposite the 60° angle is

$$\frac{\sqrt{3}}{2}$$ times the measure of the hypotenuse.

30-60-90 triangle

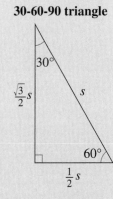

3.

	45-45-90 TRIANGLE	30-60-90 TRIANGLE
PERIMETER	$s(2 + \sqrt{2}) \approx 3.41s$	$\frac{1}{2}s(3 + \sqrt{3}) \approx 2.37s$
AREA	$\frac{1}{2}s^2 = 0.5s^2$	$\frac{1}{8}s^2\sqrt{3} \approx 0.22s^2$

EXERCISES
Activity 5.9

1. Determine the perimeter and area of the following 45-45-90 triangles.

4 cm

2 ft

2. Determine the perimeter and area of the following 30-60-90 triangles.

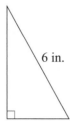

6 in.

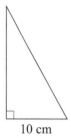

10 cm

3. The side of a storage shed is in the shape of a 45-45-90 triangle on top of a square. Determine the area of the side of the shed.

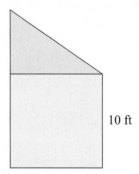

10 ft

4. If an equilateral triangle has a side with length $10\sqrt{6}$, find the length of the altitude of the triangle to the nearest tenth.

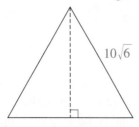

$10\sqrt{6}$

5. The baseball diamond is a square with each side having a length of 90 feet. The third baseman throws the ball from third base to first base. How far, to the nearest foot, does the player have to throw the ball to reach first base? Draw a diagram.

6. A kitten was caught in a tree at a height of 26 feet from the ground. A ladder was placed against the tree at the height of the kitten. The angle of the ladder with the ground was at 60 degrees. How long a ladder, to the nearest foot, was needed in order to reach the kitten in the tree? Draw a picture.

7. Two ships are stationed so that they form a 90 degree angle with their port. They are each a distance of 360 feet away from the port. How far, to the nearest foot, are they away from each other? Draw a picture.

8. The Bermuda Triangle from the map looks very much like an equilateral triangle. It extends from Miami to Bermuda and from Bermuda to San Juan, Puerto Rico, and back to Miami. The area of this triangle is 500,000 square miles. If indeed it is an equilateral triangle, then what is the distance of each of its sides?

9. My brother and I have just purchased a square plot of land with a side measuring 200 feet. We plan to divide the land into two triangular parcels by drawing a diagonal through the square. I will be fencing in my property. How many feet of fencing will I need to fence in my piece of property?

10. Draw a clock with a radius of 4 cm. Draw a line segment, *AB*, from the center of the circle to 6 o'clock. Draw another line segment, *AC*, from the center to 3 o'clock. Connect points *B* and *C*. What is the length of line segment *BC*?

Activities 5.1–5.9 · What Have I Learned?

1. What are the differences and similarities between the area and perimeter of a figure? Explain.

2. If the perimeter of a figure is measured in feet, then what are the units of the area of that figure? Explain.

3. If the area of a circular figure is measured in square centimeters, then what are the units of the diameter of that circle? Explain.

4. A racetrack can be described as a long rectangle with semicircles on the ends.

   a. At a racetrack, who would be interested in its perimeter? Why?

   b. At a racetrack, who would be interested in knowing its area? Why?

5. If different figures have the same perimeter, must their areas be the same? Explain.

6. If different figures have the same area, must their perimeters be the same? Explain.

7. Construct a nonright triangle, measure the sides, and show that the square of the length of the longest side is not equal to the sum of the squares of the lengths of the shorter sides.

8. Explain why the equation $x^2 = -81$ has no solution.

9. You have put on weight, and the radius of your waist has increased by an inch (assume that your waist is approximately circular). How much has your waist measurement increased? Explain.

10. On the high school's campus, there is a very tall tree. Your math teacher challenges the class to devise a way to use similar triangles to indirectly measure the height of the tree. Be specific in explaining your best problem-solving strategy.

Activities 5.1–5.9 **How Can I Practice?**

1. Calculate the area and the perimeter for each of the following figures.

   a.

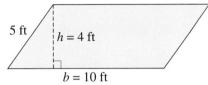

5 ft
$h = 4$ ft
$b = 10$ ft

   b.

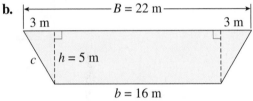

$B = 22$ m
3 m   3 m
c $h = 5$ m
$b = 16$ m

2. Calculate the area and the perimeter for each of the following figures:

   a. Rectangle topped by a semicircle:

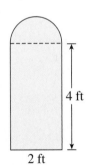

4 ft

2 ft

   b. Rectangle topped by a right triangle:

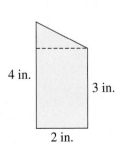

4 in.

3 in.

2 in.

c. Three-quarters of a circle with a square "corner":

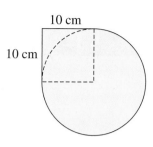

3. Determine the area of the shaded region in each of the following:

a.

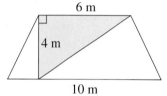

b.

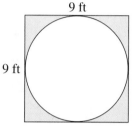

4. a. You have 150 inches of edging for your kite. The short side of a kite measures 28 inches. What is the length of the long side of your kite?

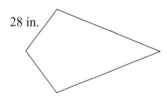

b. What is the length of one side of a rhombus-shaped sign that has a perimeter of 96 inches?

5. a. Calculate the circumference of a circle of radius 2.3 feet.

b. Use part a to predict the circumference of a circle of radius 9.2 feet, without using the circumference formula.

c. Use the circumference formula to calculate the circumference of a circle of radius 9.2 feet.

d. Does your answer to part c match your answer to part b?

e. Determine the area of the circle having radius 2.3 feet.

f. Without using the area formula, predict the area of a circle of radius 9.2 feet.

g. Use the area formula to verify your result in part f.

6. a. Use the area formula to calculate the area of a square with side 5 cm.

b. From your answer to part a, what do you expect to be the area of a square with side 30 cm?

c. Use the area formula to calculate the area of a square with side 30 cm.

d. Was your prediction correct? Does your answer to part c match your answer to part b?

7. Consider the right triangle with dimensions as shown.

a. Determine the length of the third side of the triangle. Round to the nearest tenth.

b. Determine the perimeter of the triangle.

c. Determine the area of the triangle.

    d. Give an example of another right triangle that is similar to the given triangle.

8. A triangle has two angles measuring 42° and 73°.

    a. Make a sketch of the triangle.

    b. Calculate the third angle of the triangle.

    c. Give the angle measurements of a triangle similar to this triangle.

9. You intend to put in a 4-foot-wide concrete walkway along two sides of your house, as shown.

    a. Determine the area covered by the walkway only.

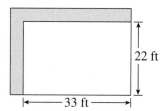

    b. If you decide to place a narrow flower bed along the outside of the walkway, how many feet of flowers should you plan for?

10. Triangle *A* has sides measuring 3 feet, 5 feet, and 7 feet; triangle *B* has sides measuring 4 feet, 4 feet, and 5 feet; triangle *C* has sides measuring 5 inches, 12 inches, and 13 inches.

    a. Which of the three triangles is a right triangle? Explain.

b. A fourth triangle, *D*, is similar to triangle *B* but not identical to it. What are some possibilities for the lengths of the sides of triangle *D*? Explain.

c. If 2 feet are added to the lengths of each side of triangle *A*, will the resulting triangle be similar to triangle *A*? Explain.

d. If the length of each side of triangle *C* is tripled, will the resulting triangle be similar to triangle *C*?

e. Which of the three triangles, *A*, *B*, or *C*, are scalene? Explain.

11. a. Calculate the perimeter and area of isosceles triangle 1.

Triangle 2

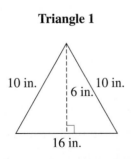

Triangle 1

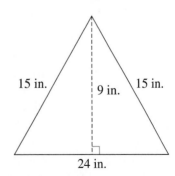

b. The sides of triangle 2 are formed by multiplying the sides of triangle 1 by a constant factor. What is that factor?

c. Without using the perimeter and area formulas, predict the perimeter and area of triangle 2.

d. How long is the base of triangle 2?

e. Calculate the perimeter and area of triangle 2 and check the prediction made in part b.

12. Determine the distance between the points $(-2, -3)$ and $(4, 2)$.

13. Verify that the points $(-4, 3)$, $(3, 5)$, and $(5, -2)$ are vertices of a right triangle.

14. A softball diamond is in the shape of a square. The bases are 60 feet apart. What is the distance a catcher would have to throw a ball from home plate to second base?

15. Answer the following questions about right triangles.

a. Is it possible for a right triangle to be isosceles? Scalene? Equilateral? Explain.

b. Is it possible for a right triangle to be acute? Obtuse? Equiangular? Explain.

16. If you measure the circumference of a circle to be 20 inches, estimate the length of its radius.

17. You want to know how much space is available between a basketball and the rim of the basket. One way to find out is to measure the circumference of each and then use the circumference formula to determine the corresponding diameters. The distance you want to determine is the difference between the diameter of the rim and the diameter of the ball. Try it!

18. a. Determine the ratio of the sides of the *similar* rectangles shown below.

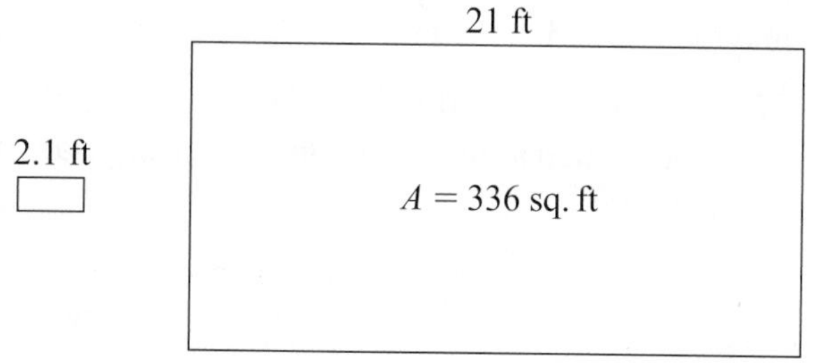

21 ft

2.1 ft

$A = 336$ sq. ft

b. Determine the width of the smaller rectangle.

19. Standing 15 feet from a streetlight, a 5-foot-tall woman casts an 3-foot shadow. How tall is the streetlight?

ACTIVITY 5.10

Painting Your
Way through the
Summer

You decide to paint houses for summer employment. To determine how much to charge, you do some experimenting to discover that you can paint approximately 100 square feet per hour. To pay upcoming college expenses, you need to make at least $900 per week during the summer to cover your profit and the cost of paint, and brushes. You figure that it is reasonable to paint for approximately 40 hours per week. Armed with these facts, you are ready to start your painting business.

1. Use the appropriate information from above to determine your hourly fee.

Your first job is to paint the exteriors of a three-building farm complex (a small barn, a storage shed, and a silo) with the following dimensions:

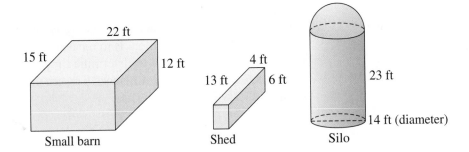

In order to determine your fee to the farmer, you need to estimate how many square feet of surface must be painted. Since there are few windows in the buildings, they may be ignored.

2. To paint the small barn and the shed, use the formula for the surface area S of a box. Such a figure is called a **rectangular prism,** with length l, width w, and height h.

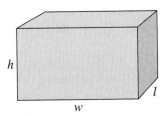

a. To determine the surface area of the rectangular prism, you first write the surface areas of each of the six rectangular surfaces:

Area of front = _____.   Area of back = _____.

Area of one side = _____.   Area of other side = _____.

Area of top = _____.   Area of bottom = _____.

b. Sum these six areas from part a to obtain the formula for the surface area of a rectangular prism.

c. How is the surface area of a rectangular prism affected if you double each of the prism's three dimensions?

3. Assume that you will not paint the floors of the small barn and storage shed (but you *will* paint the special flat roofs), and use the appropriate formulas to compute the total surface area for the exteriors of these two buildings.

4. To paint the cylinder part of the silo, you need to use the formula for the surface area S of a can, with height h and radius r. Such a figure is called a **right circular cylinder**.

a. To determine the surface area S of the right circular cylinder, you compute the surface areas of the circular top and bottom, and the surface area of the "sides."

Area of circular top = _____

Area of circular bottom = _____

Area of side = _____

Hint: To determine the area of the side, think about cutting off both circular ends and cutting the side of the can perpendicular to the bottom. Then, uncoil the side of the can into a big rectangle with height h and width the circumference of the circle.

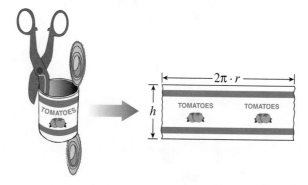

b. Sum the three areas from part a to obtain the formula for the surface area of a right circular cylinder.

c. The roof of the silo is half of a sphere with radius r. The surface area, S, for a ball, or sphere, with radius r, is a little more difficult to derive. You may study the formula in future courses. It is provided here:

$$S = 4\pi r^2$$

The formula seems to be the sum of the areas of four circles of radius r. Explain why this formula is reasonable.

5. Carefully use the surface area formulas for a sphere and a cylinder to compute the total exterior surface area for the silo. Again, assume you will not paint the floor but will paint the semispherical roof.

6. What is the total surface area that you must paint?

7. How long will it take you paint all three buildings?

8. What will you charge for the job?

SUMMARY
Activity 5.10

Figure	Labeled Diagram	Surface Area Formula
Box (rectangular prism)		$S = 2wl + 2hl + 2wh$
Can (right circular cylinder)		$S = 2\pi \cdot r^2 + 2\pi \cdot r \cdot h$
Sphere (ball)		$S = 4\pi \cdot r^2$

EXERCISES
Activity 5.10

1. A basketball has a radius of approximately 4.75 inches.

   a. Compute the basketball's surface area.

   b. Why would someone want to know this surface area?

2. Hot air balloons require large amounts of both hot air and fabric material. A hot air balloon is spherical with a diameter of 25 feet.

   a. Does finding the surface area help you determine the amount of the hot air or the fabric material? Explain.

   b. Compute that surface area. What are the units?

3. Compute the surface area for each of the following figures:

   a. diameter = 7 in.

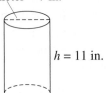

   $h = 11$ in.

   b.

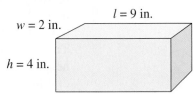

   $l = 9$ in.
   $w = 2$ in.
   $h = 4$ in.

   c.

   $r = 2$ m

4. You need to wrap a rectangular box with dimensions 2 ft by 3.5 ft by 4.2 ft. What is the least amount of wrapping paper you must buy in order to complete the job?

5. A can of soup is 3 inches in diameter and 5 inches in height. How much paper is needed to make a label for the soup can?

6. Calculate the height of a right circular cylinder with a surface area of 300 square inches and a radius of 5 inches.

7. As part of your senior project, your class has volunteered to paint all of the fire hydrants in your community. You need to estimate how much paint you will need. As you look at one hydrant, you can see a cylinder with two small cylinders on each side. You think the top of the hydrant resembles a half of a sphere. The town engineer tells you that the diameter of each hydrant is 7 inches and the height to the top of the cylinder is 30 inches. The two side cylinders have a diameter of 3 inches and a length of 4 inches.

   You know that one gallon of paint covers approximately 400 square feet of surface and will cost $23 per gallon. The firefighters have GPS technology in their fire trucks to determine where each hydrant is located. You are told that there are 514 fire hydrants in your community. What will be the cost of the project?

8. Complete the following statement: If the radius of a sphere is multiplied by $a > 0$, then its surface area is _____.

ACTIVITY 5.11
Truth in Labeling

OBJECTIVES

1. Write formulas for and calculate volumes of boxes and cans.

2. Recognize geometric properties of three-dimensional figures.

When buying a half-gallon of ice cream or a 12-ounce can of Coke, have you ever wondered if the containers actually hold the amounts advertised? In this activity, you will learn how to answer this question. The space inside a three-dimensional figure such as a box (rectangular prism) or can (right circular cylinder) is called its *volume* and is measured in cubic units (or unit cubes).

1. A half-gallon of ice cream has estimated dimensions as shown in the figure.
   In order to determine the number of unit cubes (1 inch by 1 inch by 1 inch) in this box, explain why it is reasonable to multiply the area of the top or bottom by the height.

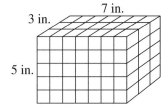

> ## DEFINITION
> The **volume** of a box (rectangular prism) is the measure, in cubic units, of the space enclosed by the sides, top, and bottom of a three-dimensional figure.

> ## PROCEDURE: Calculating the Volume of a Box (Rectangular Prism)
> The formula for the volume V of a rectangular prism with length l, width w, and height h is
> $$V = lwh.$$

2. Use the formula to calculate the volume of the half-gallon of ice cream.

3. One cubic inch contains 0.554 fluid ounces of ice cream. Estimate the amount of fluid ounces of ice cream in the carton.

4. There are 64 fluid ounces in a half gallon. How close is your estimate to the half gallon?

5. In a way similar to the volume of a box, it is reasonable to define the volume of a right circular cylinder (can) as the product of the area of its circular bottom and its height. If a can has height h and radius r, write a formula for its volume. Explain.

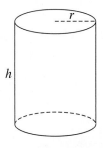

> **PROCEDURE: Calculating the Volume of a Can (Right Circular Cylinder)**
> The formula for the volume V of a can (right circular cylinder) with height h and radius r is
> $$V = \pi r^2 h.$$

6. A 12-ounce can of Coke is estimated to be $2\frac{1}{2}$ inches in diameter and $4\frac{3}{4}$ inches high. Use the volume formula to calculate the volume of a can of Coke.

7. One cubic inch contains 0.554 fluid ounces of Coke. Estimate the amount of Coke in a can. How close to 12 ounces is your estimate?

8. Supermarkets are a wonderful place to find geometric shapes such as boxes and cans. Walk up and down the aisles to notice all the various shapes and sizes of containers. Assume that you need a container that can store 100 cubic inches of a product.

   a. Design a long, slim container (like a spaghetti box) to store your product. What are the dimensions? *Hint:* Use a length of 2 inches and a width of 4 inches and solve for the height, h.

   b. Design a long but higher container (like a box of tissues) to house your volume. What are the dimensions?

c. Design a cube (length = width = height) to store your 100-cubic-inch volume.

   i. Let x represent the length = width = height. Write an equation for a volume of 100 cubic inches.

   ii. To solve the equation in part i, you need to "uncube," that is, take the cube root of, both sides. You are looking for a number whose cube is 100. You note that 4 is too small, because $4^3 = 64$. Is 5 too large or too small?

   iii. Estimate the cube root of 100.

   iv. Most calculators have a cube root key or menu to calculate cube roots. The cube root of 100 is denoted as $\sqrt[3]{100}$. Use your calculator to compute the cube root of 100.

d. Design a "tall" can (like a juice can) to store your volume. What are the dimensions?

e. Design a "short" can (like a can of tunafish) to store your volume. What are the dimensions?

f. Why do you suppose that there are so many different shapes and sizes of containers?

SUMMARY
Activity 5.11

Three-Dimensional Figure	Labeled Sketch	Volume Formula
Rectangular prism		$V = lwh$
Right circular cylinder		$V = \pi r^2 h$

EXERCISES
Activity 5.11

1. Compute the volume for each of the following figures:

   a. diameter = 7 in.

   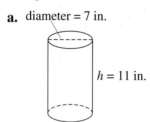

   $h = 11$ in.

   b.

   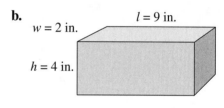

   $l = 9$ in.

   $w = 2$ in.

   $h = 4$ in.

2. A landscaper wants to buy a pickup truck and is interested in one with a large carrying capacity. One model features a rectangular prism shaped cargo space, measuring 6 feet by 10 feet by 2 feet; another has a space with dimensions 5 feet by 11 feet by 3 feet. Which truck provides the landscaper with the most space (that is, the most volume)? Explain.

3. A can of soup is 3 inches in diameter and 5 inches high. How much soup can fit into the can?

4. You construct a box from a rectangular piece of cardboard measuring 2 feet by 3 feet. You do this by cutting out identical squares from each of the corners and folding up the sides. Experiment with several possibilities to determine which dimensions will make a box with the largest volume.

5. Automobile engines come in many different shapes and sizes but the amount of area occupied by all the engine's cyclinders is usually measured in either cubic inches, cubic centimeters, or liters. Research the shapes of engines and describe how their volume is measured. Prepare a report for the class.

6. If the volume of a cube is given as 42 cubic feet, estimate its dimensions.

7. If the volume of a right circular cylinder is given as 50 cubic cm and if its radius measures 2 cm, calculate its height.

8. Which melts faster: a block of ice with dimensions 6 × 3 × 2 inches or 36 one-inch cubes of ice?

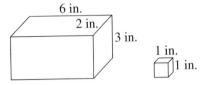

a. Determine the volume of the large ice block.

b. Determine the total volume of the individual cubes.

c. Compare the volume of the cubes with that of the volume of the large block of ice.

It is the exposure of surface area that melts the ice; the more surface area exposed the faster the ice will melt.

d. What is the total surface area of the block of ice?

e. What is the total surface area of the 36 cubes?

f. Compare the surface area of the large block of ice with that of the 36 cubes.

g. Do you think the block of ice or the cubes will melt faster. Explain.

9. There is a special on a cylinder of M&Ms at the movie theater. You can bring in your own homemade cardboard cylinder. The dimensions of the piece of cardboard that you use to make the cylinder, excluding the top and the bottom, must be the size of a piece of paper $\left(8\frac{1}{2} \times 11\right)$.

You need to experiment. Roll the cardboard into a cylinder making its height 8.5 inches and determine the volume of the cylinder. Now roll the cardboard into a cylinder with the height 11 inches and determine the volume.

Do you think it matters which cylinder you have filled with M&Ms at the theater?

10. In this exercise, you will explore what happens to the volume of a cube if you double the length of each edge of the cube.

   a. Determine the volume of a cube having 3 units as the measure of each edge. Record your result in the following table where s represents the length and V_1 represents its volume.

   TABLE 1

s	V_1
3	$3^3 = 27$

   TABLE 2

$2s$	V_2
$2 \cdot 3 = 6$	$6^3 = 216$

   b. Choose several numbers between 1 and 10 for s and calculate the corresponding volume. Record your results in table 1.

   c. Double each value of s in table 1 and calculate the volume of the resulting cube. Record your results in the appropriate column in table 2.

   d. Compare your results from parts b and c and explain how the volume of the cube changes if you double the length of each edge.

   e. Replace $2s$ with s in the formula for the volume of a cube. Does the resulting formula confirm your results in part d?

ACTIVITY 5.12

Analyzing an
Ice Cream Cone

A popular summertime treat is the ice cream cone. The geometry of this treat is interesting, since it involves a three-dimensional cone topped with spheres (of ice cream). Let's begin our analysis of the ice cream cone with the geometry of spheres.

OBJECTIVE

1. Write formulas for, and calculate volumes of, spheres and cones.

Spheres

1. Visually, it seems clear that a golf ball is smaller than a tennis ball, which is smaller than a baseball, which is smaller than a basketball. One way to compare these balls is by their radii, r. Another way is to measure the volume, V, of each ball. Determining a formula for V in terms of r is an involved process, but it can be estimated visually.

   a. Think about one-half of a sphere that just fits inside a right circular cylinder.

   The area of the "great circle" running through the center of the sphere at the base of the cylinder is given by $A = \pi r^2$. The height of the cylinder is r. What is a formula for the volume of the cylinder?

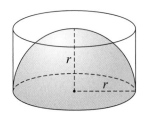

   b. Doubling the formula from part a produces a formula for the cylinder that just encloses the entire sphere. What is that formula?

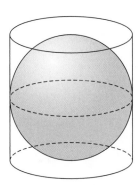

   c. It is visually clear that the formula from part b is an overestimate of the volume of the sphere. However, what is not so clear is that the exact volume for the sphere is given by the formula $V = \dfrac{4}{3}\pi r^3$. Explain why this formula for the volume of a sphere is reasonable.

PROCEDURE: **Calculating the Volume of a Sphere**

The formula for the volume, V, of a sphere with radius r is

$$V = \frac{4}{3}\pi r^3.$$

2. The accompanying table contains the radii of golf balls, tennis balls, baseballs, and basketballs.

Round and Round

TYPE OF BALL	RADIUS, r	VOLUME, V
Golf	0.84 inch	
Tennis	1.28 inches	
Baseball	1.45 inches	
Basketball	4.75 inches	

   a. Use the formula for volume of a sphere to compute the volume for each ball and write your answers in the table.

   b. How many baseballs would "fit" inside a basketball?

3. You notice that the spherical scoop of ice cream on your cone has diameter 2 inches. How much ice cream does the scoop contain?

4. You read an ad for a beach ball that claims it has a volume of 50 cubic inches. Estimate its radius. Explain the procedure you used to determine your estimate.

5. A sphere has a circumference of 20 cm (as measured by the circumference of the "great circle" around the center of the sphere). Estimate its volume.

Cones

6. Determining the formula for the volume of a cone of radius r and height h is also involved, but the formula can be estimated visually.

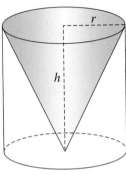

a. Think about a cone of height h and radius r that *just* fits inside a right circular cylinder. The area of the "great circle" at the top of the cone is given by $A = \pi r^2$. The height of the cylinder is h. What is a formula for the volume of the cylinder?

b. It is clear that $V = \pi r^2 h$ is an overestimate for the volume of the cone in the cylinder. Guess what fractional part of $\pi r^2 h$ is the volume of the cone and explain why your guess is reasonable.

c. The correct formula for the volume of a cone is $V = \dfrac{1}{3}\pi r^2 h$. Compare this with your answer to part b.

PROCEDURE: Calculating the Volume of a Cone

The formula for the volume, V, of a cone with radius r and height h is

$$V = \frac{1}{3}\pi r^2 h.$$

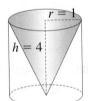

7. Your ice cream cone has a radius of 1 inch and is 4 inches high.

a. Determine its volume.

b. If you filled the cone with soft ice cream so the ice cream is level with the top of the cone, would you have more ice cream than the spherical scoop in Problem 3?

8. Cones are also used to mark highway construction. To stabilize these cones, which measure diameter 1 foot and height 2.5 feet, one option is to fill the cones with various materials. Compute the volume of the cone.

9. If you want to double the volume of the cone from Problem 7 without changing the radius, how high must the new cone be?

SUMMARY
Activity 5.12

Three-Dimensional Figure	Labeled Sketch	Volume Formula
Sphere		$V = \dfrac{4}{3}\pi r^3$
Cone		$V = \dfrac{1}{3}\pi r^2 h$

EXERCISES
Activity 5.12

1. Hot air balloons require lots of hot air and lots of fabric material. Suppose a hot air balloon is spherical with a diameter of 25 feet.

   a. Does finding the volume help you determine the amount of hot air or fabric material?

   b. Compute the volume.

2. Earth has a radius of approximately 6378 km; the radius of Mars is approximately 3397 km.

   a. Compute the volumes of Earth and Mars.

b. The volume of Earth is how many times larger than the volume of Mars?

3. Write the formula for the volume of a sphere in terms of its diameter.

4. Compute the volumes for four spheres of radii 1 foot, 2 feet, 3 feet, and 4 feet and compare the answers. How many of the smallest sphere can be fit into the largest sphere?

5. A basketball has a radius of approximately 4.75 in. How many cubic inches of air would you need to inflate the ball?

6. Write the formula for the volume of a cone in terms of its diameter and height.

7. You decide to start a soft ice cream cone business. You pack the cones with soft ice cream and then top off each one with a "cone shaped" amount of ice cream swirled on top, measuring about one-third the height of the cone.

　a. If a regular size cone has dimensions diameter 1.5 in. and height 3 in., determine the volume of ice cream inside and on top of the cone.

b. What size would you make a cone that contains twice as much ice cream as the regular sized cone in part a?

8. Determine the volume for each of the following cones and spheres:

a.

diameter = 2 ft

height = 6.2 ft

b.

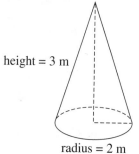

height = 3 m

radius = 2 m

c.

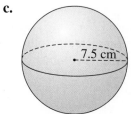

7.5 cm

d.

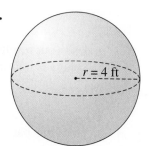

r = 4 ft

9. What other real-world examples of cones can you think of? Estimate their volumes.

10. An inflatable beach ball has a radius of 18 inches.

  a. What is the exact volume (in terms of π) of the beach ball?

  b. What is the exact volume of the beach ball when the radius is doubled?

  c. What is the exact volume of the beach ball when the radius is tripled?

  d. Complete the following table. Select several of your own values for the radius.

1. RADIUS	2. VOLUME	3. RADIUS DOUBLED	4. VOLUME	5. RADIUS TRIPLED	6. VOLUME
18	7776π	36	62208π	54	209952π

  e. Compare columns 2 and 4. When the radius is doubled, by how many times did the volume increase?

  f. Compare columns 2 and 6. When the radius is tripled, by how many times is the volume increased?

  g. Use your results in parts e–f to complete the following sentence: If the radius of a sphere is multiplied by $n > 0$, then its volume is _____.

  h. Does this pattern work with the beach ball in parts a–c?

ACTIVITY 5.13

Summertime

OBJECTIVES

1. Use geometry formulas to solve problems.

2. Use scale drawings in the problem-solving process.

EQUIPMENT

In this activity, you will need the following equipment:

1. A 12-inch ruler

With summer approaching, your neighbor decides to invest in a new in-ground swimming pool with the dimensions given in the following scale drawing:

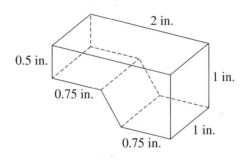

2 in.

0.5 in.

1 in.

0.75 in.

1 in.

0.75 in.

Scale: $\frac{1}{2}$ in. = 6 ft

1. Use the scale drawing measurements to determine the dimensions (in feet) of your neighbor's new pool.

2. Calculate the perimeter of the top view of the pool.

3. Calculate the surface area of the top of the pool.

4. Calculate the area of the side view of the pool.

5. Calculate the total volume of the pool. (*Hint:* Remember that to obtain the volume of a prism or cylinder, you multiply the area of top or bottom by the height—the distance between the parallel top and bottom.) What is the distance between the two side views?

6. If the pool is to be filled with water to within 6 inches of the pool's top edge, calculate the amount of water needed to fill the pool. What are your units?

7. Determine the number of gallons of water needed to fill the pool. (There are 7.48 gallons in 1 cubic foot of water.)

8. A garden hose can fill the pool at the rate of 4.5 gallons per minute. How many minutes will it take to fill the pool? How many hours? How many days?

9. A pool-filling company charges $0.03 per gallon for water delivered in a big tanker truck. How much will this company charge to fill the pool?

10. Because of the soil conditions in your area, your neighbor needs to know the weight of the water in the pool. Water weighs 62.4 pounds per cubic foot. Calculate the weight of the water in the pool to the nearest pound. Compare it with the weight of an average car.

11. To prevent accidents, state law requires that all pools be enclosed by a fence. How many feet of fencing are needed, if a fence will be placed around the pool 4 feet from each side?

12. You decide to buy some beach balls of 100 cubic feet volume for playing in the pool. What is the diameter of these balls?

13. To decorate the area around the pool with flowers, your neighbor purchases conical urns of radius 1.5 ft and height 3 ft. How much soil must he buy to fill each urn?

ACTIVITY 5.14

Math in Art

The visual arts have always been influenced by nature and mathematical ideas. In this activity, you will explore one of the classic relationships that has been applied to architecture and design since antiquity. The golden rectangle has been considered to have the most perfect proportion, to be the most pleasing to the eye. An example from ancient Greece, the Parthenon (pictured below), was constructed with the golden rectangle as a design guideline.

1. Consider the following rectangles.

a. Just for fun, which one do you think is the most pleasing to the eye?

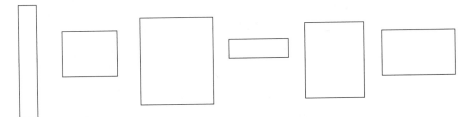

b. Measure the lengths of the sides of each rectangle, in millimeters. Calculate the ratio of the long to short side for each rectangle, rounding to two decimal places.

The golden rectangle has the interesting property that when a square is cut off, the rectangle that remains is still a golden rectangle. We can use algebra to determine precisely what the ratio of sides must be.

2. Assuming the longer side is x, and the shorter side is one unit, solve the proportion $\dfrac{x}{1} = \dfrac{1}{x-1}$.

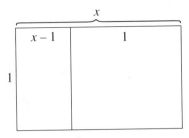

(*Hint:* You will need to apply the quadratic formula.)

3. Because the shorter side of the rectangle is one, the value you found for x in Problem 2 is the exact value for the **golden ratio**, namely $\dfrac{1 + \sqrt{5}}{2}$. This is the ratio for every golden rectangle. Approximate the golden ratio to three decimal places. Which rectangle in Problem 1 is closest to a golden rectangle? Was it the one you chose as most pleasing?

4. Calculate the ratio of width to height for DaVinci's *Last Supper* (1498). How close is it to the golden ratio? Do you think that it was an accident?

The golden ratio has been utilized for centuries in artistic design, perhaps on purpose or sometimes by accident. But the golden ratio does show up in nature, sometimes quite surprisingly. If the process of cutting off a square from a golden rectangle is repeated indefinitely, a quarter circle drawn in each square will trace out a spiral that appears frequently in nature.

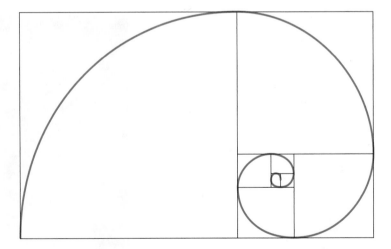

Chambered Nautilus

The Perfect Spiral Galaxy

Such spirals often appear in plant forms, in tightly bound rows. Look carefully at a pine cone or a flower head, like a sunflower. Notice that in the photo in Problem 4 of the sunflower you can pick out rows of spirals going in two directions (or more!).

4. Carefully count the rows of spirals in at least *two* directions. Record what you find, and check that your count agrees with that of your classmates.

You may recall the Fibonacci sequence of numbers: 1, 1, 2, 3, 5, 8, 13, 21, 34, 55, . . . (see Exercise 6, Activity 1.2). As a sequence, the numbers in this pattern keep going forever.

5. Do you notice a relationship between the sunflower's spirals and the Fibonacci numbers? Again could it be simply an accident? Check it out with other seed forms, especially pine cones—the rows are easy to count.

Consider again the golden ratio. Sometimes called the *divine proportion*, it appears in nature and throughout mathematics in some unpredictable places, much like the number π. In fact, the Greek letter ϕ (phi) is often used to represent the golden ratio. Here it is again, accurate to thirty digits:

$$\phi = \frac{1 + \sqrt{5}}{2} \approx 1.618033988749894848204586834336$$

6. An interesting pattern develops when you calculate the ratios of successive numbers in the Fibonacci sequence. That is, $\frac{1}{1}, \frac{2}{1}, \frac{3}{2}, \frac{5}{3}, \frac{8}{5}$, and so on. Complete the table, and express the ratio as a decimal accurate to eight decimal places. (Your calculator is essential here!)

FIBONACCI NUMBER	RATIO OF SUCCESSIVE NUMBERS
1	—
1	1
2	2
3	1.5
5	1.6666667
8	1.6
13	1.625

Can you guess what these ratios are getting closer and closer to?

It can be proven in higher mathematics that, in fact, the ratios are indeed getting as close as you like to ϕ. It is the limit of the infinite string of ratios.

One- and Two-Point Perspectives

Let's look at a different aspect of mathematics in art. During the Renaissance in Europe (16th century), artists were very interested in portraying the physical world realistically, to create an illusion of three-dimensional space in a two-dimensional painting. To accomplish this, artists have developed many techniques over the past several centuries. The laws of perspective, an application of geometry, are probably the most significant development. To help understand how perspective works, Renaissance artists developed mechanical devices such as that illustrated in the wood engraving below by Albrecht Durer (1471–1528), the German Renaissance artist.

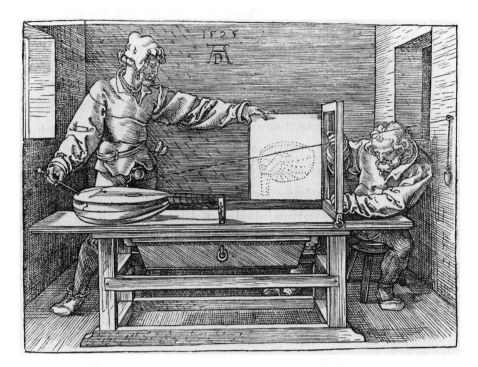

Perspective is most easily illustrated with the aid of vanishing points. Consider the horizontal line below the horizon line where earth meets sky in the distance. **One-point perspective** refers to a single point on the horizon line where all parallel lines moving away from the viewer will appear to converge to that vanishing point.

7. With a straightedge, draw a line segment from point *A* to point *P*. Repeat for points *B* and *P*. By drawing short horizontal line segments across your two lines, can you visualize a straight railroad track going through the desert? Embellish your drawing with a few cacti to make it appear more "real." Which point is the vanishing point?

P

A  *B*

8. Now go back and look more closely at Leonardo DaVinci's *Last Supper*. Where is the vanishing point located? Do you see how Leonardo used one-point perspective to emphasize the central point?

Two-point perspective utilizes two vanishing points to create the illusion of depth.

9. With a straightedge, lightly draw line segments connecting point A to both point P and Q. Repeat the process for point B. Also connect points A and B with a line segment. Now draw two line segments, parallel to segment AB, on either side of AB, stopping at the original line segments that you drew.

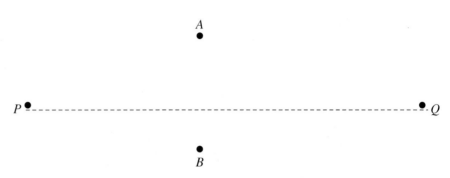

Can you visualize a three-dimensional block, maybe a building on a deserted street? Embellish the illusion by erasing the guideline leading to the vanishing points, darken the horizon line, and use the vanishing points to draw a few lines to represent tops and bottoms of rows of windows.

The geometry that underlies these visual tricks was developed shortly after the Renaissance. Here is an example of an important theorem from projective geometry.

DEFINITION

If corresponding vertices of two triangles form three lines that intersect in a single point, the two triangles are in **perspective**.

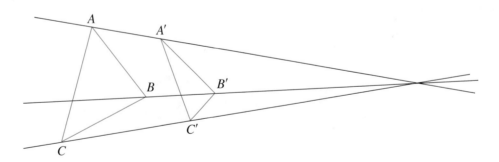

Desargues' Theorem (1636)

If two triangles are in perspective, then the intersection points of corresponding sides of the two triangles will be collinear (be on a single line).

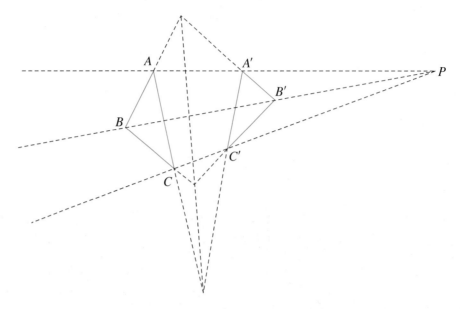

In the illustration you can see the triangles are in perspective, and the intersection points of AC–$A'C'$, AB–$A'B'$, and BC–$B'C'$ all line up.

10. In the illustration below, where the triangles ABC and $A'B'C'$ are in perspective, carefully extend the sides of each triangle. Mark the three intersection points of the corresponding sides to verify that Desargues' theorem works in this case.

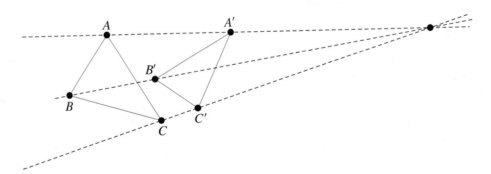

Desargues' theorem was developed, at least in part, to allow architectural drawings to be completed accurately when a vanishing point is well outside the boundary of the paper.

SUMMARY
Activity 5.14

1. A rectangle is golden when removing a square from one end results in a rectangle that has the same proportion as the original rectangle.

2. A golden rectangle's sides are in the ratio, $\dfrac{1 + \sqrt{5}}{2} \approx 1.618$, called the **golden ratio**.

3. The ratios of successive terms of the Fibonacci sequence {1, 1, 2 , 3, 5, 8, 13, ...} approach the golden ratio as a limit.

4. One- and **two-point perspective** are geometry techniques that can give the illusion of depth to a two-dimensional figure.

5. Desargues' theorem states that if two triangles are in **perspective**, then the intersection points of corresponding sides of the two triangles will be collinear (be on a single line).

EXERCISES
Activity 5.14

1. The golden ratio is also sometimes expressed as the golden mean, the ratio of two line segments cut from a single line segment. For example, suppose line segment AB is one unit long. If point C cuts AB so that $AC = 0.618$, what is the ratio of AB to AC? What is the ratio of AC to CB?

2. The common five-pointed star, as seen on an American flag, gives us another example of the golden mean. Consider one of the five line segments that compose such a star. Segment AB is cut at two points, J and K. Carefully measure, in millimeters, the length of AB, AJ, and AK. Are the ratios $\dfrac{AB}{AJ}$, $\dfrac{AJ}{AK}$, and $\dfrac{AK}{JK}$ the same?

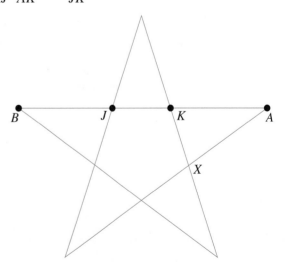

3. It is possible to verify the golden mean in the star on the previous page by using geometry and trigonometry. Assume that $JK = 1$ unit, and show that $AK = 1.618$. (*Hints:* You need the size of the interior angles of a regular pentagon, supplementary angles, and the bisection of an isosceles triangle. Then apply trigonometry to a right triangle.)

4. The Fibonacci sequence is defined by what is called a recursive process. Each number in the sequence is determined by adding the two previous terms. But the sequence is also determined by the first two numbers. In the Fibonacci sequence the first two numbers are both one. Another well-known sequence, the Lucas sequence, starts with 1 and 3.

a. Determine the next five numbers in the Lucas sequence:

1, 3, 4, 7, 11, ___, ___, ___, ___, ___

b. Determine your own sequence by picking different numbers for the first two and listing the first ten numbers in the sequence.

5. Which of the following points are the vanishing points for this two-point perspective drawing?

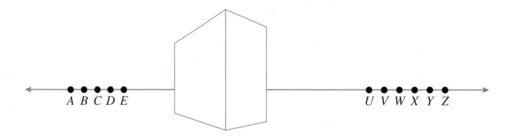

6. If triangles *ABC* and *XYZ* are in perspective (that is, lines *AX*, *BY*, and *CZ* all meet in a single point), name or describe the points that must be collinear (be on a single line) according to Desargues' theorem.

What Have I Learned?

1. What are the differences and similarities between the *surface area* and *volume* of a figure? Explain.

2. If the surface area of a figure is measured in square feet, then what are the units of the volume of that figure? Explain.

3. If the volume of a spherical figure is measured in cubic cm, then what are the units of the surface area of that sphere? Explain.

4. If different figures have the same surface areas, must their volumes be the same? Explain using an example.

5. If different figures have the same volume, must their surface areas be the same? Explain, using an example.

6. If you double the height of a can and keep all other dimensions the same, does the volume double? Explain, using an example.

7. If you double the diameter of a can and keep all other dimensions the same, does the volume double? Explain, using an example.

8. If you triple the radius of a sphere, what effect does that have on the volume? Explain, using an example.

9. If you take two identical cubes and insert the largest possible sphere into one of the cubes and the largest possible cone into the other, which figure has the larger volume? Explain, using an example.

Activities 5.10–5.14 How Can I Practice?

1. Compute the volume and surface area for each of the following figures:

   a.

   6 in.

   b. diameter = 4.5 ft

   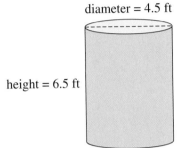

   height = 6.5 ft

   c.

   $w = 4\frac{1}{2}$ ft

   $l = 14.3$ ft

   $h = 5\frac{1}{3}$ ft

2. Compute the volume of the cone with dimensions given.

   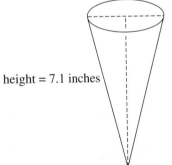

   diameter = 2.3 inches

   height = 7.1 inches

3. Draw each of the following figures with the desired property. In each case, provide the dimensions for the radius length or height of the figure as appropriate.

    a. A sphere with a volume of 20 cubic feet:

    b. A sphere with a surface area of 53 square cm:

    c. A can with a surface area of 20 square feet and radius 1 foot:

    d. A can with a volume of 20 cubic feet:

e. A cone with a volume of 20 cubic feet:

f. A box with a surface area of 20 square feet:

g. A box with a volume of 20 cubic feet:

Summary

The bracketed numbers following each concept indicate the activity in which the concept is discussed.

CONCEPT / SKILL	DESCRIPTION	EXAMPLE
Perimeter formulas [5.1]	Perimeter measures the length around the edge of the figure.	
Square [5.1]	$P = 4s$	$P = 4 \cdot 1 = 4$ ft 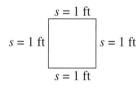
Rectangle [5.1]	$P = 2l + 2w$	$P = 2 \cdot 2 + 2 \cdot 3 = 10$ in.
Triangle [5.1]	$P = a + b + c$	$P = 3 + 4 + 6 = 13$ meters 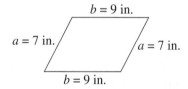
Parallelogram [5.1]	$P = 2a + 2b$ 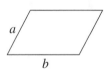	$P = 2 \cdot 7 + 2 \cdot 9 = 32$ inches 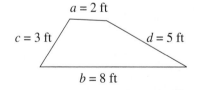
Trapezoid [5.1]	$P = a + b + c + d$ 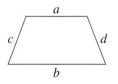	$P = 2 + 8 + 3 + 5 = 18$ feet 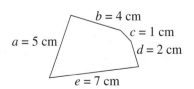
Polygon [5.1]	$P =$ sum of the lengths of all the sides $= a + b + c + d + e$ 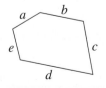	$P = 1 + 4 + 5 + 7 + 2 = 19$ cm

CONCEPT / SKILL	DESCRIPTION	EXAMPLE
Circle [5.1]	$C = 2\pi r$ For circles, perimeter is usually called *circumference*. $C = \pi d$	$C = 2\pi \cdot 3 = 6\pi \approx 18.85$ ft $r = 3$ ft $C = \pi \cdot 5 \approx 15.71$ m $d = 5$ m
Area formulas [5.3]	Area is the measure of the region inside a plane figure.	
Square [5.3]	$A = ss = s^2$ 	$A = 1 \cdot 1 = 1$ sq. ft $s = 1$ ft $s = 1$ ft
Rectangle [5.3]	$A = lw$ 	$A = 2 \cdot 3 = 6$ sq. in. $w = 2$ in. $l = 3$ in.
Triangle [5.3]	$A = \dfrac{1}{2}bh$ 	$A = \dfrac{1}{2} \cdot 4 \cdot 6 = 12$ sq. m 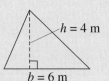 $h = 4$ m $b = 6$ m
Parallelogram [5.3]	$A = bh$ 	$A = 6 \cdot 3 = 18$ sq. in. 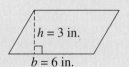 $h = 3$ in. $b = 6$ in.

CONCEPT / SKILL	DESCRIPTION	EXAMPLE
Trapezoid [5.3]	$A = \frac{1}{2}h(b + B)$	$A = \frac{1}{2} \cdot 6 \cdot (4 + 9) = 39$ sq. ft 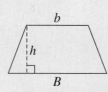
Polygon [5.3]	$A =$ sum of the areas of all the parts of the figure.	$A = 2 \cdot \frac{1}{2} \cdot 4 \cdot (6 + 12) = 72$ sq. m 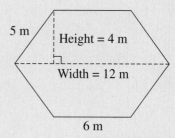
Circle [5.4]	$A = \pi r^2$	$A = \pi \cdot 3^2 = 9\pi \approx 28.27$ sq. ft
Circle [5.4]	$A = \dfrac{\pi d^2}{4}$	$A = \pi\left(\frac{5}{2}\right)^2 = \dfrac{\pi \cdot 5^2}{4} \approx 19.63$ sq. m

Classification of triangles [5.6]

Equilateral [5.6]	All three sides have the same length.	
Isosceles [5.6]	Two sides have the same length and the corresponding angles are identical.	
Scalene [5.6]	None of the sides have the same length.	

CONCEPT / SKILL	DESCRIPTION	EXAMPLE
Equiangular [5.6]	All three angles have the same size.	
Right [5.6]	One angle measures 90°.	
Acute [5.6]	All angles measure less than 90°.	
Obtuse [5.6]	One angle measures greater than 90°.	
The sum of the angles of a triangle [5.6]	The sum of the angles of a triangle is 180°.	$a + b + c = 180°$

Similar triangles [5.8]	Two triangles are similar provided their corresponding angles are equal; the lengths of their corresponding sides must be proportional (that is, their ratios must be equal).	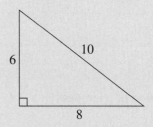 $\dfrac{3}{6} = \dfrac{4}{8}$ and $\dfrac{3}{6} = \dfrac{5}{10}$

Surface area formulas [5.10]	Surface area is the measure in square units of the area on the outside of the three-dimensional figure.	
Box (rectangular prism) [5.10]	$S = 2lw + 2lh + 2wh$	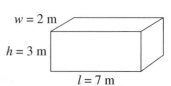 $S = 2 \cdot 7 \cdot 2 + 2 \cdot 7 \cdot 3 + 2 \cdot 2 \cdot 3$ $S = 28 + 42 + 12 = 82$ sq. m

CONCEPT / SKILL	DESCRIPTION	EXAMPLE

Can (right circular cylinder) [5.10]

$$S = 2\pi r^2 + 2\pi rh$$

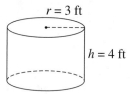

$$S = 2\pi \cdot 3^2 + 2\pi \cdot 3 \cdot 4 = 42\pi$$
$$S \approx 131.95 \text{ sq. ft}$$

Sphere [5.10]

$$S = 4\pi r^2$$

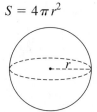

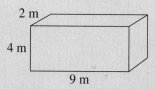

$$S = 4\pi \cdot 6^2 = 144\pi \approx 452.39 \text{ sq. in.}$$

Volume formulas [5.11], [5.12]

Volume is the measure in cubic units of the space inside a three-dimensional figure.

Box (rectangular prism) [5.11]

$$V = lwh$$

$$V = 2 \cdot 4 \cdot 9 = 72 \text{ cu. m}$$

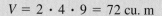

Can (right circular cylinder) [5.11]

$$V = \pi r^2 h$$

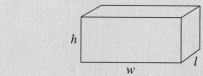

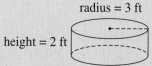

$$V = \pi \cdot 3^2 \cdot 2 = 18\pi \approx 56.55 \text{ cu. ft}$$

Sphere [5.12]

$$V = \frac{4}{3}\pi r^3$$

$$V = \frac{4}{3} \cdot \pi \cdot 7^3 \approx 1436.76 \text{ cu. cm}$$

CONCEPT / SKILL	DESCRIPTION	EXAMPLE

Cone [5.12]

$V = \frac{1}{3}\pi r^2 h$

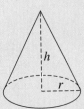

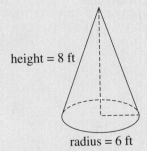

height = 8 ft

radius = 6 ft

$V = \frac{1}{3}\pi \cdot 6^2 \cdot 8 \approx 301.59$ cu. ft

1. Consider the following two-dimensional figures:

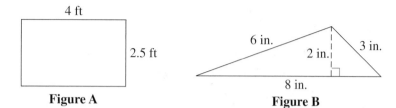

4 ft

2.5 ft

Figure A

6 in.   2 in.   3 in.

8 in.

Figure B

4.5 miles

2 miles

4 miles

Figure C

   a. The area of figure A = _____.

   b. The perimeter of figure B = _____.

   c. The area of figure B =
_____.

   d. The area of figure C =
_____.

2. Draw a circle of area 23 square inches and label the length of its radius. Explain.

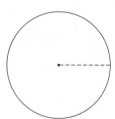

3. You buy a candy dish with a 2-inch by 2-inch square center surrounded on each side by attached semicircles.

  a. Draw the candy dish described above and label its dimensions.

  b. Determine its perimeter and area.

  c. If you place the dish on a 1 foot by 1 foot square table, how much space is left on the table for other items? Explain.

4. a. The short side of a kite measures 12 inches and the long side is two and a half times as long. Find the perimeter, P, of the kite.

12 in.
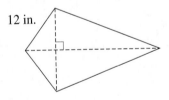

  b. You would like to build a frame for a rhombus-shaped math award to hang in your family room. A side of the ornament measures 4.5 inches. Find the perimeter of the award.

Math Award

5. You buy a kite in the shape shown. When you open the box, you discover a tear in the kite's fabric. You decide to buy new fabric to place over the entire frame.

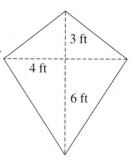

a. How much fabric do you need to buy?

b. You also decide to buy gold ribbon to line the perimeter of the kite. How much ribbon must you buy?

6. You are in the process of building a new home and the architect sends you the following blueprint for your approval:

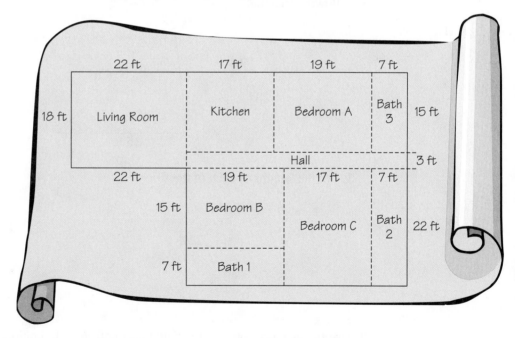

a. What is the perimeter of this floor plan?

b. What is the floor space, in square feet, of the floor plan?

c. Which bedroom has the largest area?

d. If you decide to double the area of the living room, what change in dimensions should you mark on the floor plan that you send back to the architect?

7. Your home is located in the center of a 300-foot by 200-foot rectangular plot of land. You are interested in measuring the diagonal of that plot. Use the Pythagorean theorem to make that indirect measurement.

8. Construct a triangle with its shortest side measuring 3 inches and similar to the following triangle:

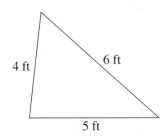

Label the lengths of each of the sides.

9. Use the distance formula to show that the following points are vertices of a right triangle: $P(-2, 5)$, $Q(12, 3)$, and $R(10, -11)$.

10. You plan to decorate a rhombus-shaped banner for a school play. The banner has a height of 3.8 feet and a base that is 4 feet long.

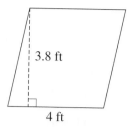

a. Determine the perimeter and area of the banner.

b. Suppose that you double the length of each side of the banner so that it now has a height of 7.6 feet and a base of 8 feet. Determine the new perimeter and area.

c. Compare the perimeter and area of the larger banner to the perimeter and area of the smaller banner.

11. a. Calculate the perimeter and area of triangle T1.

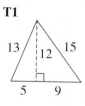
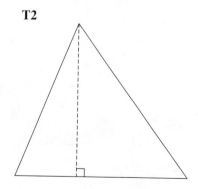

b. The sides of the second triangle, T2, are formed by multiplying the sides of T1 by a factor of 2.5. Without using the perimeter and area formulas, predict the perimeter and area of T2.

c. Determine the lengths of the sides and the height of T2 and write them in on the drawing above.

d. Calculate the perimeter and area of T2 and check the prediction made in part b.

12. At 5 P.M., a 6-ft-tall man casts a 7.5-ft shadow. How long a shadow is cast by a 40-ft tree?

13. An architectural sketch is drawn to a scale of $\frac{1}{2}$ inch : 1 foot. A room on the drawing measures $8\frac{1}{4}$ inches by $10\frac{3}{4}$ inches. What are the dimensions of the actual room?

14. Calculate the volume for each of the following three-dimensional figures:

a.

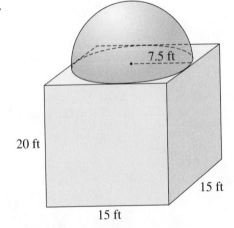

7.5 ft

20 ft

15 ft

15 ft

b.

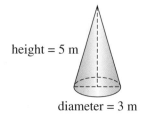

height = 5 m

diameter = 3 m

c.

diameter = 5 inches

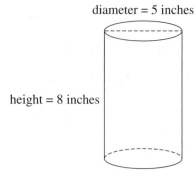

height = 8 inches

15. Biologists studying a lake determine that the lake's shape is approximately circular with a diameter of 1 mile and an average depth of 187 feet. Estimate how much water is in the lake.

Note that for consistency in units, 1 mile = 5280 feet.

16. The Alaska pipeline is a cylindrical pipeline with diameter 48 inches that carries oil for 800 miles through Alaska. It is an engineering marvel, with many safety and business concerns.

   a. What is the total capacity of the pipeline for oil at any given time, assuming that it could be filled to capacity? Explain.

   b. Estimate the amount of material needed to construct the pipeline. Explain.

CHAPTER 6

Problem Solving with Graphical and Statistical Models

ACTIVITY 6.1
Visualizing Trends

OBJECTIVE

1. Recognize how scaling of the axes of a graph can misrepresent the data.

The overwhelming amount of data available to the American public has become an integral part of our information society. Newspapers, magazines, television news, and especially the Internet provide us with data collected from a wide variety of sources. The United States Census Bureau collects a vast amount of data. For example, each month the United States Census Bureau's American Community Survey collects data from 250,000 households. The survey asks a wide range of questions about the household and each person in the household.
(See www.bls.census.gov/ACS.)

Statistics

Statistics is the science of gathering, analyzing, and making predictions from data (numerical information). Statistics has become an indispensable tool in the study of such diverse areas as medicine and health issues, the economy, marketing, manufacturing, population trends, and the environment.

An important part of a statistical study is organizing and displaying the data collected. Throughout this textbook, you have observed how useful graphs can be for identifying patterns and trends. However, graphs can also be misleading. For example, consider the following three linear graphs:

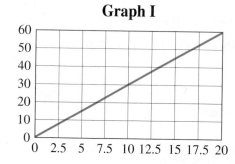

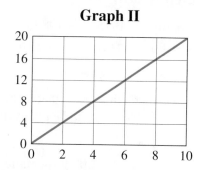

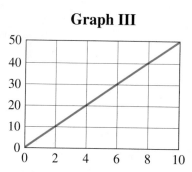

At first glance, the three graphs appear to represent the same line. However, with closer examination, the scale along the x- and y-axis is not the same. This results in the deception that the lines are identical. The lines have different slopes as shown below:

Line I: $\quad m = \dfrac{\Delta y}{\Delta x} = \dfrac{60 - 0}{20 - 0} = \dfrac{60}{20} = 3$

Line II: $\quad m = \dfrac{\Delta y}{\Delta x} = \dfrac{20 - 0}{10 - 0} = \dfrac{20}{10} = 2$

Line III: $\quad m = \dfrac{\Delta y}{\Delta x} = \dfrac{50 - 0}{10 - 0} = \dfrac{50}{10} = 5$

1. The following graphs show the performance of two stocks over the first five months of the year. In statistical terminology, these graphs are usually called *line graphs* because straight line segments connect adjoining data points. They are also known as broken-line graphs.

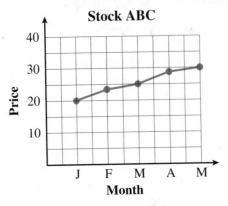

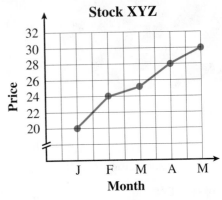

   a. Use the graphs to determine the performances of each stock. How do they compare?

   b. The graphs have different scales along the *y*-axis. Which scale makes the graph appear to be rising more slowly?

As a matter of fact, the graphs in Problem 1 display the same information.

2. The following table shows the life expectancy for women in the United States for selected years in the period 1975–2000.

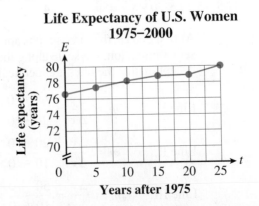

Living Longer

YEAR	1975	1980	1985	1990	1995	2000
WOMEN	76.6	77.4	78.2	78.8	78.9	80.0

Data: U.S. Bureau of the Census

   a. Construct a line graph that makes the increase in the life expectancy from 1975–2000 appear to be relatively small.

Life Expectancy of U.S. Women 1975–2000

b. How would you change the vertical scale to make the increase seem larger?

3. The following graphs are examples of *bar graphs*. Bar graphs are a very popular way of displaying data in print media such as newspapers and magazines. The graphs show the increase in the use of the Internet for homework in a certain school district.

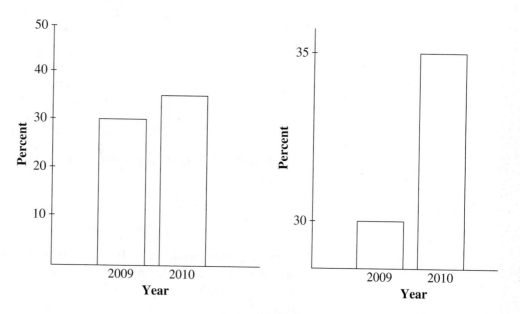

a. At your first glance, what does each graph tell you about the increase in the use of the Internet for homework in the district?

b. If you take a closer look at each graph, what do you notice about the vertical axes?

c. Having made the above observations of the graphs, which one do you think best represents the increase in the use of the Internet for homework in the school district. Explain.

4. Sometimes a single symbol or picture is used instead of a bar, its size indicating the quantity being measured. For example, the graph below (sometimes called a **pictograph**) is meant to show the growth in sales for a carpet retailer.

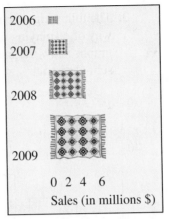

The length of the symbol represents the amount of sales, just like the length of a bar in a bar graph. Approximately how much did sales grow from 2006 to 2009?

5. There is a possible deception, however, in the graph of Problem 4. The size or area of the picture can be misleading. For example, if the width and length of a rectangle both increase by a factor of three, by how much does the area of the rectangle increase?

Applying this idea to the smallest and largest symbol in the pictograph above, it appears visually that sales have increased nine times as much from 2006 to 2009.

Another illusion may appear when bars are represented in 3-D instead of as simple rectangles. Since representing three dimensions requires perspective, a graph may be manipulated to appear different than it really is. This situation is demonstrated in Problem 6.

6. The three variations of bar graphs on the following page display waste collection for three Florida counties, all based on exactly the same data. The first graph is looked at directly and appears flat or two-dimensional. The second and third graphs are each viewed from angles different from straight ahead and therefore appear three-dimensional. Which graph could be misinterpreted in comparing the waste collection of the three counties? Explain how someone could be misled because of the visual effect.

2006 County Municipal Solid Waste Collection Pounds Per Capita

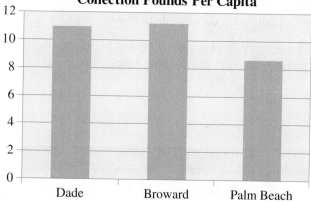

2006 County Municipal Solid Waste Collection Pounds Per Capita

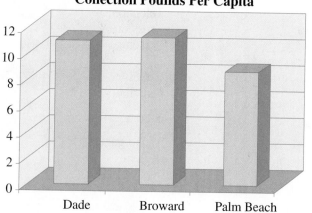

2006 County Municipal Waste Collection Pounds Per Capita

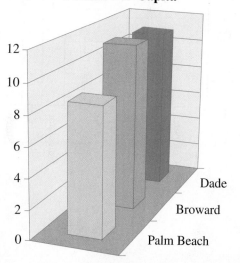

SUMMARY
Activity 6.1

1. **Line graphs**, also known as broken-line graphs, are straight line segments that connect adjoining data points to display data.

2. A **pictograph** uses a single symbol or picture to display data. The size of the symbol or picture indicates the quantity being measured.

EXERCISES
Activity 6.1

1. In the late 1990s, students in grades 7 through 12 were asked about their familiarity with and use of various technologies. The results of the survey are summarized in the following table and corresponding bar graph.

TECHNOLOGY	USE DAILY
Computer	44%
Telephone answering machine	46%
VCR	39%
Calculator	67%
Stereo	85%
Video games	46%

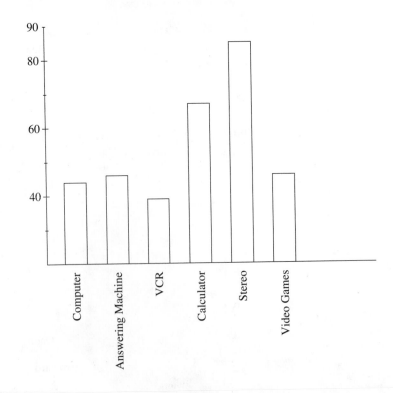

a. Use the table to determine the actual difference in the percentages between daily calculator use and daily video game use.

b. Use *only* the graph shown to estimate the difference in the percentages between daily calculator use and daily video game use?

c. From your work in part a and part b, and for other reasons you may have, how well do you think the graph presents the data in the table? Explain.

2. The following pictograph shows sales for a local furniture store.

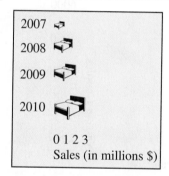

a. How much did sales grow from 2007 to 2010?

b. How is the graph potentially deceptive?

3. Look through a newspaper or magazine for an article containing a line graph or bar graph. Do you think the graph accurately depicts the data described in the article? Does the scaling of the axis misrepresent the data? Explain.

ACTIVITY 6.2

Bald Eagle
Population

OBJECTIVES

1. Read tables.

2. Read and interpret bar graphs.

The bald eagle has been the national symbol of the United States since 1782, when its image with outspread wings was placed on the country's Great Seal. Bald eagles were in danger of becoming extinct about thirty years ago, but efforts to protect them are working. In 1999, President Clinton announced a proposal to remove this majestic bird from the list of threatened species. The bald eagle was eventually declared recovered and was delisted in July 2007.

Bar Graphs

The following bar graph displays the numbers of nesting bald eagle couples in the lower 48 states for the years from 1963 to 2000. The horizontal direction represents the years from 1963 to 2000. The vertical direction represents the number of nesting pairs.

 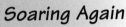

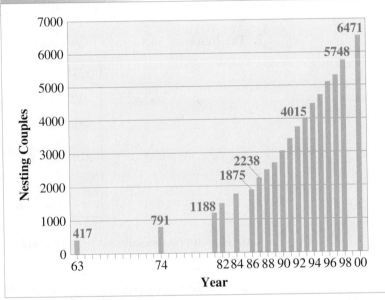

Source: U.S. Fish and Wildlife Service

1. a. What was the number of nesting couples in 1963? In 1986? In 2000?

b. Explain how you located these numbers on the bar graph.

2. a. Estimate the number of nesting couples in 1982. In 1988. In 1996.

b. Explain how you estimated the numbers from the bar graph.

c. To what place value did you estimate the number of nesting couples in each case?

d. Compare your estimates with the estimates of some of your classmates. Briefly describe the comparisons.

3. a. Estimate the number of nesting couples in 1983 and 1985.

b. Explain how you determined your estimate from the graph.

c. Estimate to the nearest thousand the number of nesting couples in 1977.

d. From 1986 to 1998, what do the bars indicate about the growth trend in the number of eagle couples?

Bar graphs can be oriented either vertically or horizontally.

4. Approximately how many more bald eagle couples were observed in Louisiana compared to Texas in 2000?

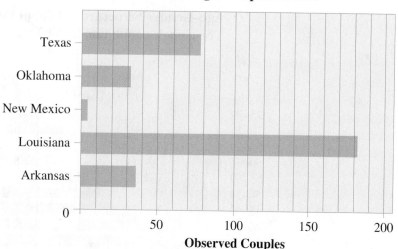

Bald Eagle Couples in 2000

Source: U.S. Fish and Wildlife Service

Grouped Bar Graph

Bar graphs can also show paired data for each category. In Problem 5 on the following page, a **grouped bar graph** shows the number of endangered and threatened species for four animal categories (groups) and for each of the two years, 1995 and 2005.

5. a. Which animal group actually saw a drop in the number of endangered and threatened species between 1995 and 2005?

Number of U.S. Endangered and Threatened Species

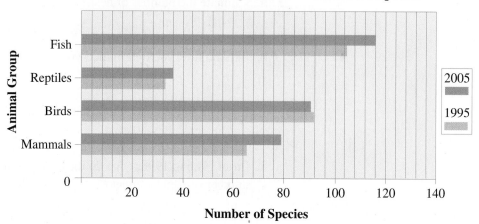

Source: U.S. Fish and Wildlife Service

b. Which animal group showed the largest increase between 1995 and 2005 and by approximately how many species?

The following is an example of a **paired bar graph** from the U.S. Census Bureau that appeared in a local newspaper.

Age–Gender Structure of Global Population: 2002
The globe's population in 2002 was relatively young.

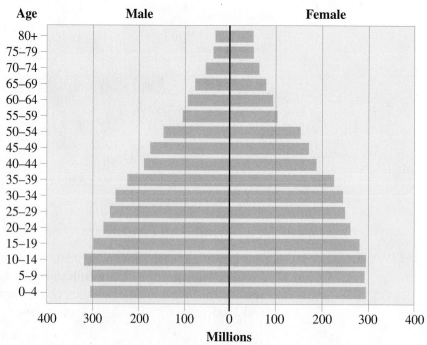

Source: U.S. Census Bureau, International Programs Center, International Database

6. A number of conclusions can be drawn about the age–gender structure of the global population in 2002. For each of the following claims, give specific data from the bar graph that either supports or refutes the claim.

   a. No matter what the age group, there are more females than males.

   b. The largest age group, regardless of gender, was 10–14-year-olds.

   c. Males and females were very close in number for all age groups between 40 and 59.

   d. The worldwide birthrate appears to have increased dramatically during the 1988–2002 period.

Stacked or subdivided bar graphs are another way to show paired data. The U.S. Census Bureau uses mathematical models to project what the world's population will look like in the coming decades. The projections are illustrated in the stacked bar graph that follows. Note that a percentage given within a bar represents the proportion of the population that is between 0 and 14 years of age in that year.

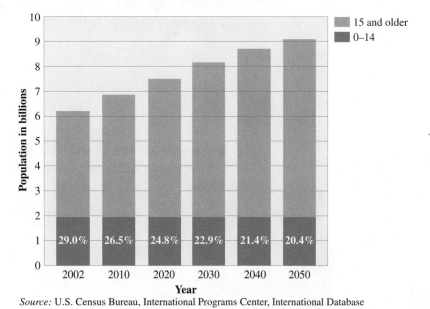

Global Population 0–14 Years of Age Compared to Total Global Population: 2002–2050
The percent of children across the globe is projected to decline by one-third over the next 5 decades.

Source: U.S. Census Bureau, International Programs Center, International Database

7. The preceding stacked bar graph provides information about the global populations both directly and indirectly. For example, you can read *directly* the total population counts predicted for the listed years between 2010 and 2050. You can obtain information *indirectly* by reasoning from specific information that you read directly. Keep this in mind as you answer the following questions.

   a. What was the total population for 2002 and the total population predicted for the year 2050?

   b. What is the expected increase in global population from 2002 to 2050?

   c. The graph shows that 29.0% of the population was between the ages of 0 and 14 in the year 2002. Use this information and your answers from part a to determine how many children were in the 0–14 age group.

   d. What is the number of children, ages 0 to 14 years, that is projected for the year 2050?

   e. What do you observe about the percents of children, ages 0–14, in the years from 2002 to 2050?

   f. The caption above the graph states that the percent of children 0–14 years of age will decrease by one-third over the next 5 decades. Do you agree or disagree with this statement? Support your answer by reasoning from the information provided in the graph.

   g. The percent of children relative to the whole population will decrease. Does this mean that the actual population of the 0–14 year-olds will be decreasing also?

SUMMARY
Activity 6.2

1. A **bar graph** presents data in the form of bars or columns, drawn either horizontally or vertically on a scale of values. Each bar or column represents a category and the height or length of the column or bar represents the data value for the category. See graph in Problem 1.

2. Sometimes, bar graphs compare categories in more than one aspect such as populations in two different years or smoking habits of men and of women in different age categories. These bar graphs have a number of different styles.

   a. One style is called a **grouped bar graph.** This style allows the comparison of categories in two (or three or more) aspects at the same time. This is done by drawing the category bars for each aspect attached next to each other. See graph in Problem 5.

   b. Another style of grouped bar graphs is called a **paired bar graph.** These graphs compare data categories in two respects at the same time by placing the bars for each aspect in each category opposite from each other, base to base. See the graph for Problem 6.

   c. A third type of grouped bar graph is called a **stacked** or **subdivided bar graph** where each category bar is divided into two or more component parts, each of which represents a different aspect. Most often the largest or most important component is put next to the zero line. See graph for Problem 7.

EXERCISES
Activity 6.2

1. The following chart presents the number of new and abandoned hazardous waste sites found in various regions in the United States by the 1990s.

Down in the Dumps

U.S. Hazardous Waste Sites by Region

a. How many regions are represented in the chart?

b. Which region has the greatest number of hazardous waste sites? Estimate the number.

c. Which region has the least number of hazardous waste sites? Estimate the number.

d. What feature of this chart aids in estimating the number of waste sites for a given region?

e. Based on this data, in what region(s) would you advise someone to live (or not live)?

f. From the chart, estimate the total number of waste sites found in the United States by the 1990s.

2. The following bar graph provides the annual rainfall in San Antonio, Texas, from 1934 to 2000.

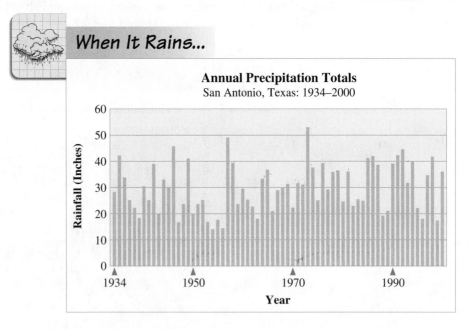

Source: National Weather Service

a. In which year(s) was there the greatest rainfall? Estimate the number of inches.

b. In which year(s) was there the least rainfall? Estimate the number of inches.

c. How many years did San Antonio have 20 to 30 inches of rain per year? Is this more or less than the number of years that San Antonio had 30 to 40 inches of rain per year? Explain.

3. The bar graph below shows some interesting projections for the world's population.

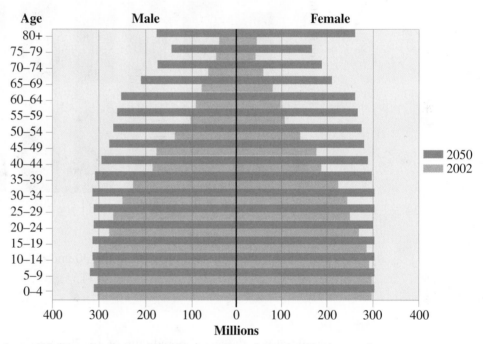

Pyramids of Global Population: 2002 and 2050
The globe's population is expected to grow at progressively higher rates at higher ages.

Source: U.S. Census Bureau, International Programs Center, International Database

a. Which age group of females shows the greatest increase from 2002 to 2050, and by approximately how much?

b. In 2002, the age groups for males decreased in size consistently from age 10 and older. The projections for 2050 show decreases in size from age 35 to 79, but the 80+ age group shows an increase. What does this mean, compared to 2002?

c. In 2050, over what age groups would there be very close to the same number of women?

d. Which age group shows the smallest change in size between 2002 and 2050?

4. Use this stacked bar graph of population projections to answer the following questions.

Global Population 15–29 Years of Age Compared to Total Global Population: 2002–2005
The percent of youth across the globe is projected to decline steadily over the next 50 years.

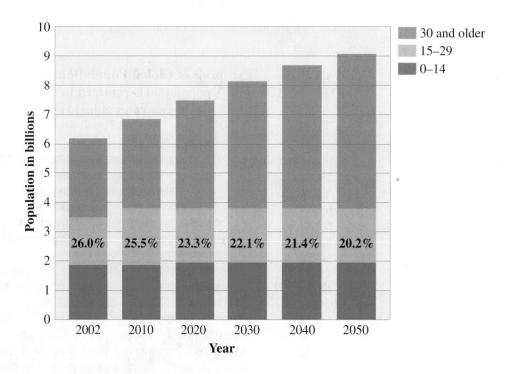

a. What is the projected increase in the 30 and older population between 2002 and 2050?

b. What was the actual population of 15–29-year-olds in 2002, and how much is it expected to change by 2050?

c. In light of your answer to part b, why are the percents decreasing for the 15–29-year-olds?

d. The 0–14-year-old population is projected to change very little through 2050. Which of the following statements provides the best explanation?

  i. The birthrate (births per year) will level off and remain constant.

  ii. The birthrate will actually be decreasing.

  iii. Due to overpopulation, famine, and disease, the death rate in this age group will increase.

  iv. It is not possible to know the individual birthrate and death rate trends, but the combined rates will result in no significant change.

ACTIVITY 6.3
Florida
Demographics

OBJECTIVES

1. Construct line, bar, picture, and circle graphs.

2. Determine an appropriate graph to display data.

Many government agencies and research institutions depend upon statistical reports to understand the demographics of a population. Demographics refers to the characteristics of a human population. Good demographic information allows for an informed decision making process.

The Florida Youth Tobacco Survey is administered each spring by the state Department of Health. From this survey the following projections were made for all high school students in Florida.

Table 6.1. Percent of Florida High School Students Having Tried Smoking at Least Once

YEAR	1998	1999	2000	2001	2002	2003	2004	2005	2006	2007	2008
% OF HS STUDENTS	68.1	60.7	56.9	53.7	52.2	50.4	46.7	44.3	43.6	40.7	37.9

Source: Florida Dept. of Health (http://www.doh.state.fl.us)

1. a. Using the data in Table 6.1, construct a line graph and a bar graph that displays the percent of high school students that have tried smoking at least once between 1998 and 2008.

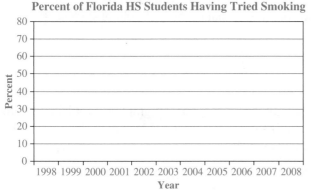

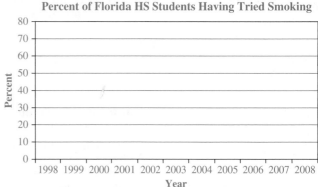

b. What trend do you observe from your graphs?

c. Which graph do you think better displays the data? Give a reason for your answer.

2. The Florida Youth Tobacco Survey also includes middle school students, as shown in Table 6.2 below.

Table 6.2. Percent of Florida Middle School Students Having Tried Smoking at Least Once

YEAR	1998	1999	2000	2001	2002	2003	2004	2005	2006	2007	2008
% OF MS STUDENTS	43.6	41.0	30.7	32.1	30.6	26.4	26.7	25.5	23.0	21.1	18.0

Source: Florida Dept. of Health (http://www.doh.state.fl.us)

This data could be graphed separately from the high school data, but to better compare the two age groups, a single graph is preferred.

a. Include the middle school data with your previous line graph from Problem 1 using the same grid.

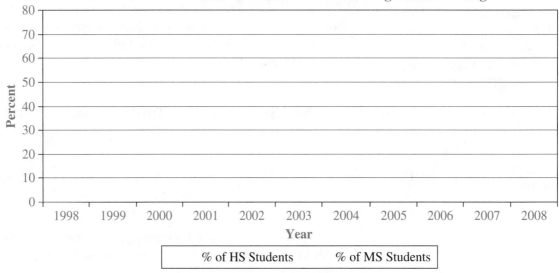

Percent of Florida MS & HS Students Having Tried Smoking

b. Each line graph displays a trend over the same time period. How does the middle school trend compare to that of the high school students?

3. a. Include the middle school data with your bar graph in Problem 1 for high school students by creating new bars side-by-side with the high school bars. Clearly indicate which is which.

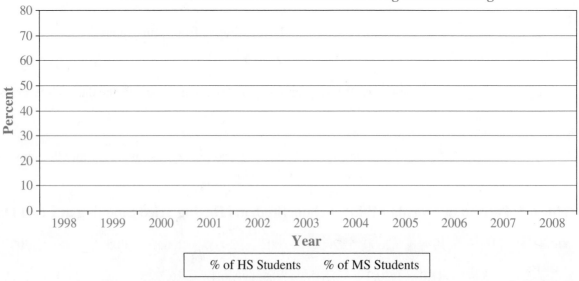

Percent of Florida HS & MS Students Having Tried Smoking

b. Compare this paired bar chart to your paired line graph in Problem 2. Do you find one display easier to read and/or interpret? Is there any significant difference?

In Problems 1–3, the **actual number** of students that had tried smoking in the years between 1998 and 2008 was not represented in your graphs but rather the percents or portions of the high school populations for those years that had tried smoking.

Sometimes, actual population counts are included, as in the data in Table 6.3 for the Orlando metropolitan area. The U.S. Census asked questions about language use at home to locate groups of people who speak a language other than English. This data is from the 1990 and 2000 census.

Table 6.3. Language Spoken at Home, 1990–2000

	1990		2000	
	NUMBER	PERCENT	NUMBER	PERCENT
ONLY ENGLISH	1,002,656	88%	1,201,764	79%
SPANISH	88,373	8%	235,140	15%
OTHER INDO-EUROPEAN	33,069	3%	67,369	4%
ASIAN LANGUAGE	11,227	1%	25,067	2%

Source: www.censusscope.org

The number column in Table 6.3 refers to the actual number of people in each language category. The percent column refers to the percent of the total number of people in the Orlando metro area that make up that language group.

4. a. Using the data in Table 6.3, make a side-by-side bar graph for the actual number of people in each language category, for the given years.

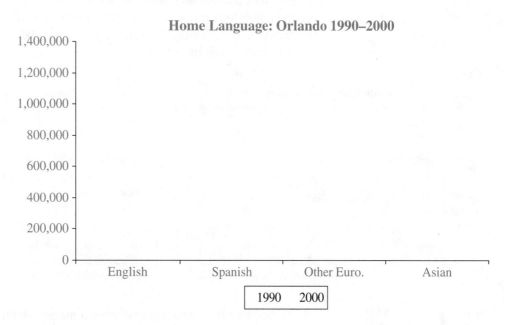

b. Draw another side-by-side bar graph for the two given years, this time using the percentages.

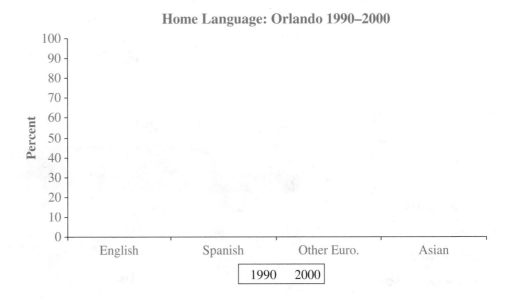

c. How do your graphs compare?

A line graph is usually used when a trend over time is being observed (such a graph is sometimes called a **time plot**). When the counts do not take place over time, connecting points to create a line graph may not have as much meaning or significance. For example, the following two line graphs display the same information for the 2000 home language data in Table 6.3.

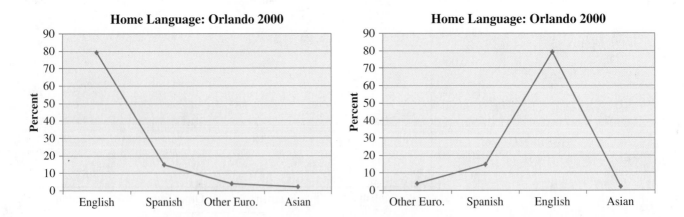

5. For the two line graphs above, does it matter which order you use to place the languages on your axis? Is there any significance to the shape of the line segments making up the graph? Explain.

Circle Graphs

Circle graphs, also called pie charts, are a convenient way to display data when you are interested in showing the relative sizes of the various categories. The size of each piece ("slice") of the pie is proportional to the percentage of the whole for that category. For example, the 1990 home language data in Table 6.3 can be displayed by the following circle graph.

Home Language: Orlando 1990

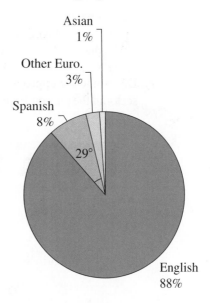

The percent gives the relative size of each piece (or sector) in the circle as well as the fractional part of each group compared to the total number of people in the population. For example, the total number of people from Spanish-speaking homes in 1990 was 88,373. The total number of people in the survey was 1,135,325. So the percent of people from Spanish-speaking homes was 88,373/1,135,325 = 0.0778, or approximately 8%. Therefore, the sector representing Spanish-speaking homes is 8% of the total area of the circle. The central angle of the sector representing the number of people from Spanish-speaking homes is 8% of 360 degrees or 0.08(360) = 28.8, or approximately 29 degrees.

6. Using the 2000 home language data from Table 6.3, label each sector of the following pie chart accordingly.

Home Language: Orlando 2000

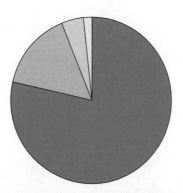

7. Using the preceding side-by-side bar graph (Problem 4b) and the circle graphs, describe how home language usage had changed in the Orlando area from 1990 to 2000. In your opinion, which graphs were most useful in answering this question, and why?

> Circle graphs must always represent the whole collection, or population, of whatever is being displayed. When expressed as percents, those percents must add up to 100%, the whole amount.

8. Determine the appropriate percents for each region of the world, and label each sector of the pie chart accordingly. The sectors for each category are already drawn.

2010 World Population

WORLD REGION	2010 POPULATION (in millions)
Africa	977.413
Near East	211.969
Asia	3838.247
Latin America	595.988
Europe	810.142
North America	343.546
Oceania	34.705

Data: U.S. Census Bureau

2010 World Population

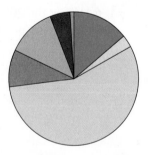

SUMMARY
Activity 6.3

1. A **circle graph**, or pie chart, displays the relative number of data values in each category by the size of the corresponding sector, or slice. Circle graphs require that all the categories that make up the whole are included.

EXERCISES
Activity 6.3

1. a. Use the data in the following table to construct a bar graph and a line graph.

AVERAGE 2004 EARNINGS BY EDUCATIONAL ATTAINMENT FOR WORKERS 18 YEARS OF AGE AND OLDER						
EDUCATIONAL LEVEL	Not high school graduates	High school graduates	Some college	Associate's degree	Bachelor's degree	Master's degree	All workers combined
AVERAGE INCOME LEVEL	$19,041	$28,631	$30,173	$36,021	$51,568	$67,073	$37,897

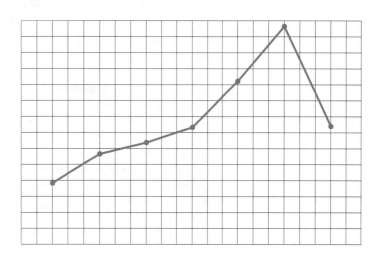

b. Which graph is the most appropriate display of the data? Explain.

2. There were approximately 7,964,950 male Texans 15 years or older in 2003. Use the circle graph below to estimate the number of males in each category.

Marital Status: Males 15 Years and Over in Texas, 2003

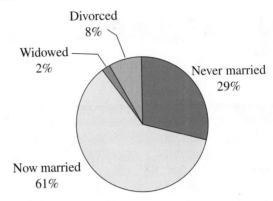

Source: U.S. Census Bureau

3. A pictograph can use pictures or symbols of the same size, instead of lines or bars, to give the visual image more meaning. A key is given to indicate how many items are represented by each symbol. In the pictograph below, each picture or symbol represents 10,000 cars.

Registered Vehicles in Broward County

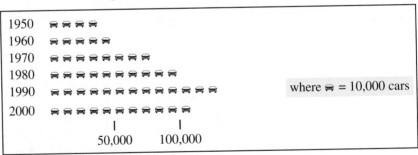

a. Approximately how many more cars were registered in Broward County in 1990 compared to 1950?

b. Do you think a pictograph is more like a bar graph or line graph?

4. The line graph below shows population growth in Duval County.

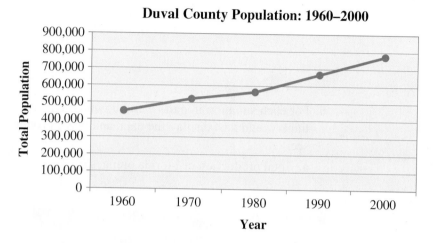

Duval County Population: 1960–2000

Source: Duval County (www.censusscope.org)

a. Could a bar graph be used just as effectively? Explain.

b. Could a circle graph be used just as effectively? Explain.

5. In the late 1990s, students in grades 7 through 12 were asked about their familiarity with and use of various technologies. The results of the survey are summarized in the following table.

TECHNOLOGY	USE DAILY
Computer	44%
Telephone answering machine	46%
VCR	39%
Calculator	67%
Stereo	85%
Video games	46%

The following circle graph displays the percentages of students who use the technologies on a daily basis.

List the errors in the circle graph.

6. For each situation in parts a and b, which type of graph (line, bar, or circle) do you think would best display the data, and why? Produce a graph and interpret what you see.

a. Total production of Florida oranges (in millions of 90-pound boxes)

SEASON	2000–1	2001–2	2002–3	2003–4	2004–5	2005–6	2006–7
COUNT	224.55	231.55	204.3	243.4	150.45	148.4	129.0

Source: http://www.floridajuice.com

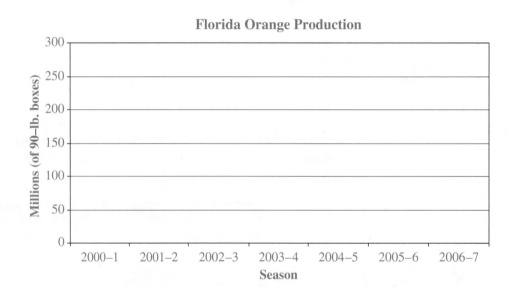

b. In a report from the Florida attorney general, the number of hate crimes was reported in the state during 2007.

HATE CRIMES BY MOTIVATION				
MOTIVATION	Race/Color	Religion	Ethnicity	Sexual Orientation	Total
COUNT	104	28	33	28	193

Source: http://myfloridalegal.com

Use the following headlines as a guide for creating the necessary circle graph on the left and bar graph on the right.

Hate Crimes in Florida 2007   **Hate Crimes in Florida 2007**

ACTIVITY 6.4
The Class Survey

OBJECTIVES

1. Organize data with frequency tables, dotplots, and histograms.

2. Organize data using stem-and-leaf plots.

Decisions that are made in business, government, education, engineering, medicine, and many other professions depend on analyzing collections of data. As a result, data analysis has become an important topic in many mathematics classes.

In this activity, you will collect and organize data from your class.

1. Record the requested data for your entire class.

GENDER	NUMBER OF SIBLINGS	MILES FROM SCHOOL	TIME DOING HOMEWORK YESTERDAY (TO THE NEAREST HALF HOUR)

2. Using the data collected in Problem 1, determine the following characteristics of your entire class.

   a. The most common number of siblings

   b. The average number of miles from school

   c. More females or males

   d. The most hours studied last night

The data can be organized in several different ways to help you arrive at your answers. One visual approach is to produce a **dotplot** for each category. To illustrate, consider the following data representing the size of 20 families.

Family sizes: 4, 6, 2, 8, 3, 5, 6, 4, 7, 2, 5, 6, 4, 6, 9, 4, 7, 5, 6, 3

The data values appear on the horizontal scale of the dotplot. The number of occurrences of each data value (called the **frequency**) is recorded on the vertical scale. Each dot represents one data value.

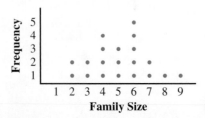

The following frequency table for these data shows another way to organize the data.

FAMILY SIZE	2	3	4	5	6	7	8	9
FREQUENCY	2	2	4	3	5	2	1	1

3. Draw dotplots for each of the four data categories from Problem 1.

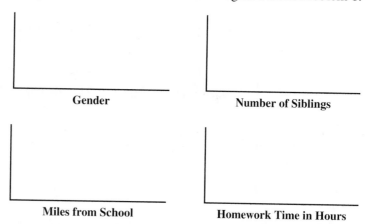

Gender   Number of Siblings

Miles from School   Homework Time in Hours

4. Explain how you can use the dotplots to answer each of the following questions.

   a. What is the most common number of siblings?

   b. What is the average number of miles from school?

   c. Are there more girls or boys in your class?

   d. What was the most number of hours studied?

In the study of statistics, the dotplot and frequency table are usually called **frequency distributions**. They describe how the data are distributed over all possible values.

5. Looking at your dotplots in Problem 3, describe in a few sentences how the frequency distributions compare with each other visually. Note any similarities and differences.

6. Of the four frequency distributions, which one is really quite different because of the nature of the data values?

Histograms

Histograms are statistical graphs that can be used to display a frequency distribution. The data values are located on the horizontal axis of the histogram. The frequencies are located on its vertical axis. A rectangle is constructed above each data value and its height indicates the frequency of the specific data value. Therefore, in a histogram, the column of data in a dotplot is replaced by a rectangle.

Example 1 *Construct a histogram of the following frequency distribution.*

FAMILY SIZE	2	3	4	5	6	7	8	9
FREQUENCY	2	2	4	3	5	2	1	1

SOLUTION

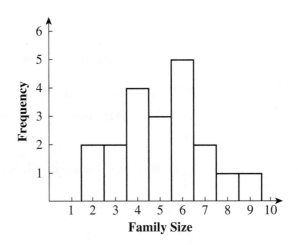

Note that the vertical scale should start at 0. The rectangles are centered at the data value and have the same width. The height of a rectangle represents the frequency of the data value.

The rectangles in a histogram should always touch.

7. Construct a histogram to show the frequency distribution from Problem 3 of the number of miles from school.

Your graphing calculator can also be used to generate a graph of a frequency distribution. Using the sample family size data in Example 1, the following **histogram** can be generated.

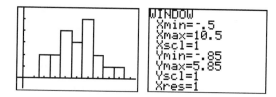

8. Use a graphing calculator to produce the histogram for the class miles from the school distribution. Refer to Appendix A for detailed instructions for the TI-83/84 plus calculator.

Grouped Data

In the Class Survey problems, you learned that a histogram is a very useful method to display numerical data in order to visualize how individual values of data are distributed. Often, data are grouped together in order to provide information about the distribution that would be difficult to observe if the data were treated individually.

For example, suppose your mathematics teacher wants to analyze the grades on the last test for the students in his two math classes. In this situation, rather than determining the frequency for a specific test grade, such as 82, your teacher is interested in the number of 80's, as well as the number of 60's, 70's, and so forth. Therefore, the test scores are **grouped** into intervals. The interval for the number of 80's is 80–89. The frequency table for the test scores is given as follows:

FREQUENCY INTERVAL	FREQUENCY
50–59	2
60–69	6
70–79	16
80–89	18
90–100	8

Note that the **frequency intervals**, also called **classes**, for the grouped data should be of the same width. The numbers 50, 60, 70, 80, and 90 are called the **lower class limits**. The numbers 59, 69, 79, 89 are called the **upper class limits**. The difference between any two consecutive lower class (or upper class limits) is the class width. In this case, the **class width** is 10. The frequency intervals should not overlap, and each piece of data should belong to only one interval.

9. a. How many students are in the two courses?

b. How many students had a test grade in the 80's?

The grouped test scores for the students in the two mathematics sections is displayed by the following histogram:

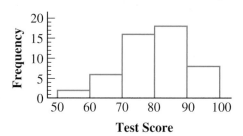

10. What specific information can you gather by examining the preceding histogram?

Although you are able to easily identify the frequency of test scores within each frequency interval, the original test scores cannot be identified from the frequency table or the histogram. For example, you know that there are eight scores in the 90's, but there is no way to determine what they are. As a result, you are not able to calculate the exact values for statistical measures.

Stem-and-Leaf Plots

A stem-and-leaf plot is a way to organize and display groups of data as well as displaying the actual data values. In a stem-and-leaf plot, each data value is split into two parts called the **stem** and the **leaf**. The *stem* is the digit or group of digits *with the greatest place value*. The remaining digits on the right of the stem form the leaf for the data value. For example, the number 517 can be split into a stem and leaf as follows:

Stem: 5   Leaf: 17

The number 517 could also be split with the stem 51 and the leaf 7. The single-digit number, 5, which can be written as 05, would have stem 0 and leaf 5.

The following example demonstrates the procedure for constructing a stem-and-leaf plot.

Example 2   *Construct a stem-and-leaf plot for the following test scores on a 50-point quiz:*

26 29 32 34 35 37 39 40 42 43 43 46 47 48 50 50

SOLUTION

Step 1. Write the data in numerical order. Although this step is not required, it makes working with the data more convenient.

The data is already in numerical order.

Step 2. Identify which part of the number is the *stem* and which part is the *leaf*.

Since the scores consist of two digits, use the first digit, the tens digit, as the stem and the units digit as the leaf. For example, the test score 26 has stem 2 and leaf 6.

Step 3. List the stems in numerical order as follows. Note that a vertical line separates the stem from the leaf.

Stem	Leaf
2	
3	
4	
5	

Step 4. Proceeding in numerical order, place the leaf of each data value on the right of the vertical line next to the appropriate stem. Proceed until all the leaves of the data values are displayed.

Stem	Leaf
2	6 9
3	2 4 5 7 9
4	0 2 3 3 6 7 8
5	0 0

Step 5. Determine a legend (key) to indicate how the numbers are represented by the stem and leaves.

Legend: 2 | 6 represents the number 26

Note that if the data in Example 2 is listed line by line, in groups, you have

26 29
32 34 35 37 39
40 42 43 43 46 47 48
50 50

The stem-and-leaf plot of this data reduces the repetition of the tens digits and displays the data in a more compact fashion. The stem-and-leaf plot gives the same visual display as a sideways histogram.

11. The test scores from the two math classes are listed below:

57 58 62 64 64 68 69 69 70 70 71 71 71 72 73 73 75 76 76 78 78
78 79 79 81 81 82 82 83 83 84 84 85 85 85 85 85 86 86 87 88 89
91 92 92 94 95 95 98 99

Construct a stem-and-leaf plot for this data. Use the tens digit for the stem and the ones digit for the leaf.

Suppose your teacher wants to analyze the test scores from each of the math classes separately. When comparing two similar collections of data, a **back-to-back stem-and-leaf plot** can be constructed.

12. The test scores for each math class are as follows:

Class 1: 57 58 64 69 70 70 71 72 73 73 76 78 79 82 85 85 85 88
91 92 95

Class 2: 62 64 69 71 71 75 76 78 78 79 81 81 82 83 83 84 84 85
85 86 86 87 89 92 94 95 98 99

Complete the following back-to-back stem-and-leaf plot for the two classes.

CLASS I		CLASS 2
LEAF	STEM	LEAF
8 7	5	
9 4	6	2 4 9

13. Construct a stem-and-leaf plot for the following data collected in a science experiment: 7.6 8.3 9.4 6.7 5.4 6.3 6.1 5.7 7.5 8.4 8.6 7.3 7.7 8.8 9.1

a. Write the data values in ascending order.

While these values have a decimal point, a stem-and-leaf plot would display these numbers without a decimal point. The legend (key) of the plot is used to show the position of decimal points in the original data.

b. Ignore the decimal point in the data values, and construct a stem-and-leaf plot for these numbers. Use the ones digit for the stem and the tenths digit for the leaf.

c. Write a legend for this plot.

SUMMARY
Activity 6.4

1. A **frequency distribution,** usually displayed in a frequency table, or visually in a dot-plot or histogram, describes how frequently each of the data values occurs.

2. A grouped histogram is useful when there is a wide range of data. In a grouped histogram, data are grouped into intervals of the same class width.

3. A stem-and-leaf organizes data by splitting each data value into two parts called the stem and leaf.

EXERCISES
Activity 6.4

1. A large publishing company wants to review the ages of its sales representatives. The ages of a sample of 25 sales reps are as follows:

50 42 32 35 41 44 24 46 31 47 36 32 30

44 22 47 31 56 28 37 49 28 42 38 45

Construct a histogram for the ages.

2. The scores on the last math quiz are summarized in the following frequency table.

SCORE	10	9	8	7	6	5	4	3	2	1	0
FREQUENCY	5	7	6	4	2	0	1	0	0	0	0

Construct a dotplot for the scores.

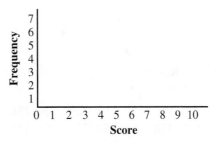

3. The frequency distribution for a collection of data is given in the following table:

CLASS	FREQUENCY
9.5–11.4	3
11.5–13.4	7
13.5–15.4	10
15.5–17.4	15
17.5–19.4	9
19.5–21.4	2

a. Determine the total number of data.

b. What is the width of each class?

c. If an additional class were to be added, what are its class limits?

d. Construct a histogram of the frequency distribution.

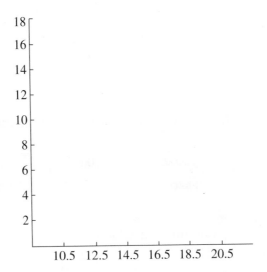

4. The following collection of data gives the weights (in pounds) of 45 male high school gym students:

105 112 115 118 125 129 130 132 135 135 137 138 138 139 141 144 145
148 148 151 154 154 156 158 158 160 161 161 162 165 166 166 169 172
174 174 176 181 184 185 192 195 206 209 218

a. Use this data to construct a frequency table having the first interval (class) 100–109.

FREQUENCY INTERVAL	FREQUENCY

b. Construct a histogram of the frequency distribution from the table above.

5. Construct a stem-and-leaf plot of the original data in Exercise 4. Use the hundreds and the tens digit for the stem and the ones digit for the leaf.

6. The scores on a 60-point exam are given in the following stem-and-leaf plot. List the original data.

Stem	Leaf
0	9
1	3 7
2	1 6 8 9
3	3 7 7 8
4	2 2 3 5 5 6 6 6 9
5	1 3 4 5 5 8 9
6	0 0

Legend: 1 | 3 represents 13

7. Subjects in a psychology study were timed while completing a certain task. Complete a stem-and-leaf plot for the following list of times (to the nearest tenth of a minute):

7.5 8.2 9.3 6.8 5.9 6.4 6.1 7.9 5.8 7.3 8.2 8.7 7.4 7.8 8.2 9.2 7.7

ACTIVITY 6.5
Class Survey
Continued

OBJECTIVES

1. Determine measures of central tendency, including the mean, median, mode, and midrange.

2. Recognize symmetric and skewed frequency distributions.

3. Distinguish between percentiles and quartiles.

In Activity 6.4, The Class Survey, you worked with the following data representing the size of 20 families.

Family sizes: 4, 6, 2, 8, 3, 5, 6, 4, 7, 2, 5, 6, 4, 6, 9, 4, 7, 5, 6, 3

The frequency distribution of the data was displayed graphically using a dotplot and a histogram.

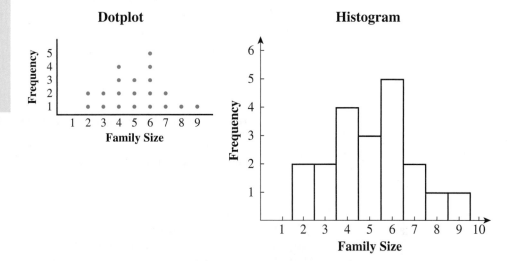

1. By observing the graphs, estimate where you think the center of the frequency distribution lies.

2. Look at the three frequency distributions with numerical data values in Problem 3 in Activity 6.4 (page 721). Estimate on each dotplot where you think the center of the frequency distribution lies. Record your estimates and compare with your classmates.

FREQUENCY DISTRIBUTION	ESTIMATE OF THE CENTER
Siblings	
Miles from school	
Time doing homework	

Measuring the center of a frequency distribution is a basic starting point in many statistics applications. There are several different ways to measure the center, including the mean, the median, the mode, and the midrange. Since each will result in a number near the center of the data, these statistics are said to measure the **central tendency** of a frequency distribution. The term "average" is often used to describe these measures of central tendency.

Measures of Central Tendency

The **arithmetic mean**, or simply **mean**, is the most commonly used "average." The mean of a sample of a population is represented by the symbol $\bar{x}$, read "x bar." The mean of the entire population is represented by the Greek letter mu, μ. Unless specified, you can assume that the data used in this activity represent samples.

The mean is calculated by adding the data values and dividing the sum by the number of values. The notation Σx, read the "sum of x," is used to represent the sum of all the data. The symbol Σ is the Greek letter sigma, used to indicate summation. The formula for calculating the mean $\bar{x}$ is

$$\bar{x} = \frac{\Sigma x}{n},$$

where n represents the number of data values in the sample.

3. Determine the mean of the 20 family sizes in the introduction of this activity.

A second average is the **median**. The median is in the exact middle of the numerically ordered (ranked) data. Half of the data lies above (is greater than) the median. Half of the data lies below (is less than) the median.

To calculate the median:

Step 1. Rank the data from the smallest to the largest (or largest to the smallest).

Step 2. **i.** If there is an odd number of data, the median is the number in the middle of the ranked data.

ii. If there is an even number of data, the median is halfway between the two middle data values. Expressed as a formula,

$$\text{median} = \frac{\text{Sum of middle data values}}{2}.$$

4. Determine the median of the 20 family sizes in the introduction of this activity.

The next commonly used measures of central tendencies are the **mode** and **midrange**.

- The mode is the data value that occurs most frequently.
- The midrange is the exact midpoint between the lowest and highest data values. Expressed as a formula,

$$\text{midrange} = \frac{\text{lowest value} + \text{highest value}}{2}.$$

5. Determine the mode and midrange of the 20 family sizes.

6. a. Now determine the following statistics for the class survey distributions, where possible.

DISTRIBUTION	MEAN	MEDIAN	MODE	MIDRANGE
Number of siblings				
Miles from school				
Time studying				

b. On your original dotplots in Problem 3, page 721, clearly mark with a vertical line each of the above statistics from the preceding table.

c. For each distribution, circle the statistic (mean, median, mode, midrange) that is closest to the estimate of the center that you made in Problem 2. Which type of statistic did you have in mind when you made your estimates?

7. Which statistic would you choose to best describe the "average" number of siblings among your classmates, and why?

8. Do any of these measurements of central tendency make sense for the gender distribution? Explain.

The commonly used "averages" can give very different results for the same set of data. Problem 9 demonstrates how the averages can be used to misrepresent the given situation.

9. A small company pays its president $200,000. The vice president receives $150,000. There are five employees in the company: the foreman who earns $30,000; three workers, earning $25,000, $22,000, $22,000 respectively; and a secretary who earns $19,000.

a. Determine the mean, median, and mode income in this company.

b. The union representative wants to negotiate new wages for the workers. In the negotiation, should the union representative emphasize the mean, median, or mode? Explain.

c. Which of the three measures would the president of the company stress in the negotiations? Explain.

   d. Which do you think best represents this sample? Explain why in a paragraph.

   e. Do you think that the measure you chose in part d is always the best to use? Explain.

10. Which measure of central tendency is most affected by extreme data values? Explain.

11. Consider the following set of scores from a science test:

   10, 16, 21, 62, 62, 62, 68, 70, 71, 72, 74, 77, 78, 79, 80, 85, 88, 93

   a. Determine the mean, median, and mode of the science test scores.

   b. Which of the "averages" in part a best represents the grades on the science exam? Explain.

Using Technology to Determine Measures of Central Tendency

Once the data are stored in your calculator, you can generate a variety of statistics for the data, including the measures of central tendency. For example, the following windows of the TI-83/84 Plus calculator result from the 20-sample family size data. Refer to Appendix A for detailed instructions for the TI-83/84 Plus calculator.

The mean $(\bar{x})$ and median (Med) are given, n is the number of data values, and minX and maxX are the smallest and largest data values respectively. From these you can calculate the midrange.

12. Use a graphing calculator to produce the measures of central tendency for the siblings distribution from the Class Survey.

Types of Frequency Distributions

13. a. The three frequency distributions pictured here have the same range of data values. What is it?

i.

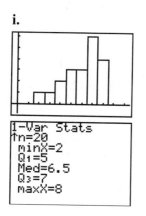

```
1-Var Stats
↑n=20
 minX=2
 Q1=5
 Med=6.5
 Q3=7
 maxX=8
```

ii.

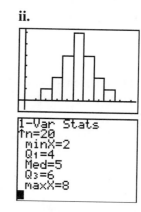

```
1-Var Stats
↑n=20
 minX=2
 Q1=4
 Med=5
 Q3=6
 maxX=8
```

iii.

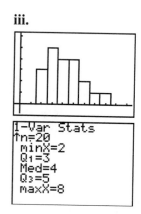

```
1-Var Stats
↑n=20
 minX=2
 Q1=3
 Med=4
 Q3=5
 maxX=8
```

b. Describe in your own words the visual differences among the distributions in part a.

c. The means for the distributions in part a are as follows:

$$\overline{x}_i = 6.0 \quad \overline{x}_{ii} = 5.0 \quad \overline{x}_{iii} = 4.2$$

Compare these to the median for each distribution.

Some distributions are symmetrical (like distribution ii in Problem 13). Others are slightly "off," as if they have been stretched to one side or the other. Distribution i is **skewed to the left**, while distribution iii is **skewed to the right**.

14. a. If a distribution is perfectly symmetrical, what do you think will be true about the relationship between the mean and median?

b. Based on your results in Problem 13, what is the relation between the mean and median of a skewed distribution?

c. Enter in your calculator a skewed distribution with ten data values. Record your data, sketch the histogram (or dotplot), and calculate the mean and median. Does this result help confirm your answer in part b?

Measure of Position

Two measures of position of data within a distribution are **quartiles** and **percentiles**. Quartiles divide a set of data into four equal parts. Percentiles divide a set of data into 100 equal parts.

For a given set of data, your calculator generates the data values corresponding to the quartiles. For example, for the 20 sample family size data, the 1-Var Stats screen of the TI 83/84 Plus calculator gives the following information:

$$Q_1 = 4$$
$$\text{Med} = 5$$
$$Q_3 = 6$$

Q_1 represents the first quartile and has a value of 4. This means that 25% of the data has a value less than 4.

15. a. Explain the meaning of $Q_3 = 6$.

b. What is the second quartile?

Such measures are often used to make comparisons of scores of individuals when the amount of data is large. For example, suppose you scored 500 on the math portion of the Scholastic Aptitude Test (SAT). If this score is at the 80th percentile, denoted P_{80}, it does **not** mean that you answered 80% correct on the test. It means that 80% of the high school students who took the test scored less than you. That is, 80% of the students scored less than 500.

SUMMARY
Activity 6.5

A **frequency distribution**, usually displayed in a frequency table, or visually in a dot-plot or histogram, describes how frequently each of the data values occurs.

There are four typical measures of the **central tendency** of a frequency distribution:

1. The **mean** is the usual average found by adding the data values and dividing by the number of values.

2. The **median** is in the exact middle of the numerically ordered data—half the data values lie above and half lie below the median. If there is an even number of data values, the median is the mean of the two middle values.

3. The **mode** is the data value that occurs most frequently.

4. The **midrange** is the exact midpoint between the lowest and highest data values.

EXERCISES
Activity 6.5

1. A large publishing company wants to review the ages of its sales representatives. The ages of a sample of 25 sales reps are as follows:

50 42 32 35 41 44 24 46 31 47 36 32 30

44 22 47 31 56 28 37 49 28 42 38 45

    a. Construct a histogram for the ages.

    b. Calculate the mean and median ages.

    c. Determine the midrange.

    d. Is there a mode for this distribution?

2. Suppose the scores of seven members of a men's golf team are 68, 62, 60, 64, 70, 66, and 72. Determine the mean, median, and midrange.

3. The scores on the last math quiz are summarized in the following frequency table:

SCORE	10	9	8	7	6	5	4	3	2	1	0
FREQUENCY	5	7	6	4	2	0	1	0	0	0	0

Calculate the mean, median, mode, and midrange of this quiz distribution.

4. a. Create a set of ten data values whose distribution is perfectly symmetrical.

    b. Verify that the mean, median, and midrange are identical.

    c. Change two data values so that the resulting distribution is skewed to the left.

    d. Predict how this will change the mean and median. Then verify by doing the calculations.

5. A set of data has a mean of 32.4 and a median of 38.9. Would you expect the distribution for this data to be symmetrical, skewed to the left, or skewed to the right?

6. Find a collection of at least 25 data values from a real-world source. Use your calculator to create a histogram, and calculate the four measures of central tendency.

7. The mean is the most affected by any change in the data.

   a. Determine the mean, median, mode, and midrange of the following data:

   $$10, 11, 12, 14, 14, 15, 16, 20$$

   b. Change the 16 to 19 in part a. Determine the mean, median, mode, and midrange of the resulting set of data.

   c. Which measure of central tendency was affected by changing the 16 to 19?

   d. In addition to the mean, which measure would be affected if the 20 was changed to 19 in part a?

8. The salaries of 10 employees of a small company are listed below:

   $$33,000, \quad 28,000, \quad 36,000, \quad 31,000, \quad 31,000,$$
   $$68,000, \quad 29,000, \quad 32,000, \quad 86,000, \quad 34,000.$$

   a. Determine the mean, median, mode, and midrange of the 10 salaries. Verify your results using the statistics feature of the graphing calculator.

   b. Which average would the employees use to demonstrate that they were underpaid? Explain.

   c. Which average would management use if they did not want to give a raise to the employees? Explain.

9. Reports about incomes and other highly skewed distributions usually give the median rather than the mean as the measure of the "average." Explain.

10. Locate an article in a newspaper or magazine that discusses an "average."

    a. Is the average used the mean, median, or mode? Explain.

    b. Is the choice of the average used in the article appropriate for the situation? Explain.

ACTIVITY 6.6
Course Grades
and Your GPA

OBJECTIVE

1. Recognize and calculate a
weighted average.

You are a college freshman and the end of the semester is approaching. You are concerned about keeping a B− (80 through 83) average in your English literature class, in which your grade will be determined by computing a **simple average** or mean of your exam scores. To calculate a simple average, you add all your scores and divide the sum by the number of exams. So far, you have scores of 82, 75, 85, and 93 on four exams. Each exam has a maximum score of 100.

1. What is your current average for the four exams?

2. There is another way you can view simple averages that will lead to the important concept of weighted average. First note that the fraction $\frac{82 + 75 + 85 + 93}{4}$ also means that 4 divides into each of the test scores in the numerator. Therefore you can write,

$$\frac{82 + 75 + 85 + 93}{4} = \frac{82}{4} + \frac{75}{4} + \frac{85}{4} + \frac{93}{4}.$$

   a. The sum $\frac{82}{4} + \frac{75}{4} + \frac{85}{4} + \frac{93}{4}$ can be calculated by first dividing each numerator by 4 and then adding the results to obtain the average score 83.75. Do this calculation.

   b. Part a shows that the average 83.75 is the sum of 4 values, each one of which is $\frac{1}{4}$ of a test. This means that each test contributed $\frac{1}{4}$ of its value to the average and you say that each test contributed equally to the average. For example, the first test score 82 contributed 20.5 to the average. How much did each of the other tests contribute?

3. The calculation of averages can be viewed by yet another way that allows you to calculate more complex weighted averages. You should recall that dividing by an integer is the same as multiplying by its reciprocal. In this case, dividing by 4 is the same as multiplying by $\frac{1}{4}$. So you can rewrite the fraction from Problem 2 as follows:

$$\frac{82}{4} + \frac{75}{4} + \frac{85}{4} + \frac{93}{4} = \frac{1}{4} \cdot 82 + \frac{1}{4} \cdot 75 + \frac{1}{4} \cdot 85 + \frac{1}{4} \cdot 93$$

   a. Calculate the expression $\frac{1}{4} \cdot 82 + \frac{1}{4} \cdot 75 + \frac{1}{4} \cdot 85 + \frac{1}{4} \cdot 93$ by first multiplying each test score by $\frac{1}{4}$ and then adding the terms to get the average 83.75.

From the point of view of Problem 3, the ratio $\frac{1}{4}$ is called the **weight** of a test score. It means that a test with a weight of $\frac{1}{4}$ contributes $\frac{1}{4}$ (or 0.25 or 25%) of its score to the overall average. In the preceding problems, each test had the same weight. However there are many other situations where not every score contributes the same weight. One such situation occurs when your college determines an average for your semester's work. The average is called a grade point average or GPA.

Weighted Averages

The semester finally ended and your transcript has just arrived in the mail. As a part-time student this semester you took eight credits—a 3-credit English literature course and a 5-credit biology course. You open the transcript and discover that you earned an A (numerically equivalent to 4.0) in biology and a B (numerically 3.0) in English.

4. Do you think that your biology grade should contribute more to your semester average (GPA) than your English literature grade? Discuss this with your classmates and give a reason for your answer.

Perhaps you recognized and wrote in Problem 4 that a course that has more credit usually means more time and effort spent on more material. So, it seems fair that you should earn more points towards your GPA from a higher credit course.

5. a. One way to give your 5-credit biology course more weight in your GPA than your literature course is to consider what part of your 8 total credits is your biology course. Write that ratio.

b. Write the ratio that represents the weight your 3-credit literature grade contributes to your GPA.

c. Calculate the sum of the two weights from part a and part b.

As you continue learning more about weighted averages, you will discover that the sum of the weights for a set of scores will always total one, as it did in Problem 5c.

6. In Problem 3, you multiplied each test score by its weight and then summed the products to obtain your test average. Do the same kind of calculation here to obtain your GPA; that is, multiply each grade (4.0 for biology and 3.0 for literature) by its respective weight (from Problem 5) and then sum the products. Write your GPA to the nearest hundredths.

Problem 6 illustrates the procedure for computing a weighted average. The general procedure is given in the following.

PROCEDURE: Computing the Weighted Average of Several Data Values

1. Multiply each data value by its respective weight, and then

2. Sum these weighted data values.

Example 1 *You will have a 12-credit load next semester as a full-time student. You will have a 2-credit course, two 3-credit courses and a 4-credit course. Determine the weights of each course.*

SOLUTION

The 2-credit course will have a weight of $\dfrac{2}{12} = \dfrac{1}{6}$; the 3-credit courses will each have a weight of $\dfrac{3}{12} = \dfrac{1}{4}$. Finally, the 4-credit course has a weight of $\dfrac{4}{12} = \dfrac{1}{3}$.

7. Do the weights in Example 1 sum to 1? Explain.

Your letter grade for a course translates into a numerical equivalent according to the following table:

LETTER GRADE	A	A−	B+	B	B−	C+	C	C−	D+	D	D−	F
NUMERICAL EQUIVALENT	4.00	3.67	3.33	3.00	2.67	2.33	2.00	1.67	1.33	1.00	0.67	0.00

Suppose you took 17 credit-hours this past semester, your third semester in college. You earned an A− in psychology (3 hours), a C+ in economics (3 hours), a B+ in chemistry (4 hours), a B in English (3 hours), and a B− in mathematics (4 hours).

8. a. Use the first four columns of the following table to record the information regarding the courses you took. As a guide, the information for your psychology course has been recorded for you.

1 COURSE	2 LETTER GRADE	3 NUMERICAL EQUIVALENT	4 CREDIT HOURS	5 WEIGHT	6 CONTRIBUTION TO GPA
Psychology	A−	3.67	3	$\dfrac{3}{17}$	$\dfrac{3}{17} \cdot 3.67 \approx .648$

b. Calculate the weight for each course and enter it in column 5.

c. For each course, multiply your numerical grade (column 3) by the course's weight (column 5). Round to three decimal places and enter this product in column 6, the course's contribution to your GPA.

d. You can now calculate your semester's GPA by summing the contributions of all your courses. What is your semester GPA?

9. ESR Manufacturing Corporation of Tampa, Florida, makes brass desk lamps that require three levels of labor to make and finish. The table shows the number of hours each level of labor is needed to make each lamp and how much each level of labor costs per hour.

LEVEL OF LABOR	LABOR HOURS REQUIRED	HOURLY WAGE ($)
Skilled	6	10.00
Semiskilled	3	8.00
Unskilled	1	6.00
Total: 10		

a. What are the weights for each level of labor?

b. Determine the average hourly wage.

SUMMARY
Activity 6.6

1. To calculate a simple average (also called a **mean**), add all your scores and divide the sum by the number of exams.

2. To compute a weighted average of several data values:
    i. Multiply each data value by its respective weight, and then
    ii. Sum the weighted data values.

3. The sum of the weights used to compute a weighted average will always be equal to 1.

EXERCISES
Activity 6.6

1. A grade of W is given if you withdraw from a course before a certain date. The W appears on your transcript but is not included in your grade point average. Suppose that instead of a C+ in economics in Problem 8, you receive a W. Use this new grade to recalculate your GPA.

2. Now suppose that you earn an F in economics. The F is included in your grade point average. Recalculate your GPA from Problem 8.

3. In your first semester in college, you took 13 credit hours and earned a GPA of 2.13. In your second semester, your GPA of 2.34 was based on 12 credit hours. You calculated the third semester's GPA in Problem 8.

    a. Explain why the calculation of your overall GPA for the three semesters requires a weighted average.

    b. Calculate your overall GPA for the three semesters.

SEMESTER	GPA	CREDITS	WEIGHT	NUMERICAL EQUIVALENT
1				
2				
3				
				Total:

4. You are concerned about passing your economics class with a C– (70) average. Your grade is determined by averaging your exam scores. So far, you have scores of 78, 66, 87, and 59 on four exams. Each exam is based on 100 points. Your economics teacher uses the simple average method to determine your average.

   a. What is your current average for the four exams?

   b. What is the lowest score you could achieve on the fifth exam to have at least a 70 average?

5. Suppose you took 15 credit hours last semester. You earned an A– in English (3 hours), a B in mathematics (4 hours), a C+ in chemistry (3 hours), a B+ in health (2 hours), and a B– in history (3 hours). Calculate your GPA for the semester.

COURSE	LETTER GRADE	NUMERICAL EQUIVALENT	CREDIT HOURS	WEIGHT	WEIGHT × NUM. EQUIV.

6. Suppose your history professor discovers an error in his calculation of your grade from last semester. Your newly computed history grade is a B+. Use this new grade and the information in Exercise 5 to recalculate your GPA.

7. In baseball, weighted averages may lead to surprising results. For example, this happened in 1995 and 1996 in the comparison of batting averages for Derek Jeter of the New York Yankees and David Justice of the Atlanta Braves. In 1995, Derek Jeter made 12 hits and each hit that he made was weighted $\frac{1}{48}$ because he went up to bat 48 times in 1995. Therefore, his batting average was $\frac{1}{48} \cdot 12 = 12 \div 48 = 0.250$ to the nearest thousandths.

a. In 1995, David Justice of the Atlanta Braves went up to bat 411 times, so each of his 1995 hits was weighted $\frac{1}{411}$. He made 104 hits. Calculate his batting average and record your answer to the nearest thousandths in the table in part c.

b. In the 1996 baseball season, Jeter made 183 hits in 582 times at bat. Justice made 45 hits in 140 at bats. Calculate each of their batting averages for 1996 and record in the table.

c. Other statistics that could be of interest to ballplayers, managers, team owners, and fans would be batting averages over two years, over three years, over entire careers. For example, over the two year period, 1995 and 1996, Justice had $104 + 45 = 149$ hits in $411 + 140 = 511$ at bats. Therefore, his batting average combining the two years is $\frac{1}{551} \cdot 149 = 0.270$. Similarly, calculate Jeter's combined batting average combining the two years. Record your result in the table.

	BATTING AVERAGE		
	1995	1996	1995 & 1996 COMBINED
DEREK JETER	0.250		
DAVID JUSTICE			0.270

d. According to the statistics in the above table, who was the better hitter in 1995? In 1996? Give a reason for each answer.

e. Is David Justice a better hitter according to the combined 1995–1996 baseball seasons?

f. As it turned out, these contradictory results continued for Jeter and Justice into the 1997 baseball season. In 1997, Jeter had 190 hits in 654 at bats; Justice hit 163 times in 495 at bats. Calculate their batting averages to the nearest thousandths and record in the following table.

	BATTING AVERAGES		
	1995	1996	1997
DEREK JETER	0.250	0.314	
DAVID JUSTICE	0.253	0.321	

g. Use the appropriate data from parts a, b, and c to determine the total number of hits and at bats for each player. Then use those totals to determine the batting averages over the three-year period. Record your results here.

	BATTING AVERAGE FOR COMBINED DATA FOR 1995 THROUGH 1997		
	TOTAL HITS	TOTAL AT BATS	BATTING AVERAGE
DEREK JETER	12 + 183 + 190 = 385	48 + 582 + 654 = 1284	385/1284 = 0.300
DAVID JUSTICE	104 + 45 + 163 = 312	411 + 140 + 495 = 1046	312/1046 = 0.298

h. What conclusions would you draw from the results you recorded in part g?

You may want to research these curious results further to find out what else baseball followers and statisticians have to say about this result (which is known as the Simpson-Yule paradox in statistics).

Activities 6.1–6.6   What Have I Learned?

1. Bar graphs and circle graphs can be used to visualize the same collection of data. What advantage does each display have over the other?

2. Determine if the mean and median accurately represent an "average" of the following set of numbers:

   a. Zip codes: 12303, 13601, 32703, 52104

   b. Ranks of different brands of a product in a taste test: 1, 3, 5, 2

3. A small supply company employs a supervisor at $1200 a week, an inventory manager at $700 a week, six stock boys at $400 a week, and four drivers at $500 a week.

   a. Determine the mean and median wage.

   b. Which "average" best describes a typical wage at this company? Explain.

4. If a distribution is skewed to the right, then which average is generally larger, the mean or the median? Explain.

5. Polk County is about to impose a 4.5% property tax increase on its residents. Is the county legislature concerned about the *mean* or *median* home assessment of its residents?

Activities 6.1–6.6 How Can I Practice?

1. The number line in the following graphic represents net exports in billions of dollars for six countries. Net exports are obtained by subtracting total imports from total exports; a negative net export means the country imported more goods than it exported.

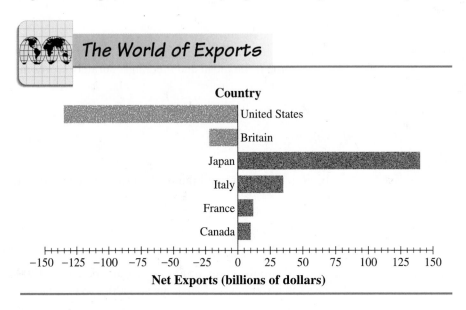

The World of Exports

Country

Net Exports (billions of dollars)

   a. Estimate the net amount of exports for Japan. Is your answer a positive or negative integer? Explain what this number tells you about the imports and exports of Japan.

   b. Estimate the net amount of exports for the United States. Is your answer a positive or negative integer? Explain what this number tells you about the imports and exports of the United States.

   c. What is the difference between net exports from Japan and Italy?

   d. What is the difference between the net exports from Britain and France?

   e. What is the total sum of net exports for the six countries listed?

2. In the bar graphs below, a projection of world population by age groups and gender for six different regions is given as a percent of the region's population at the time.

Population Pyramids for Regions and Selected Countries: 2002 and 2050
In 2050, the elderly are expected to be a substantially larger part of national and regional populations.

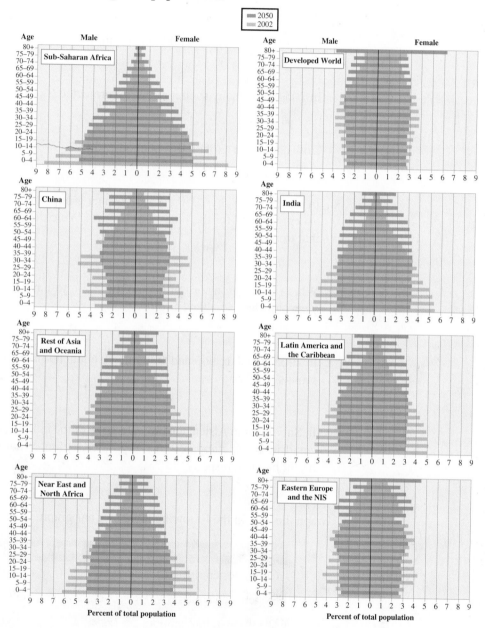

Source: U.S. Census Bureau, International Programs Center, International Database

a. In 2002, which region had the largest portion of its population in the 0–4-year-old age group, and what was that percent?

b. What is the 2050 projection for the 10–14 age group of the region you identified in part a?

c. In 2002, which region's 80+ age group is larger than the 75–79 age group?

In 2050, how many such regions are projected?

How could you explain this phenomenon?

d. In most regions, by 2050 the various age groups have become fairly equal in size, except perhaps for the oldest age groups. Which region does not appear to follow that trend?

e. Which two regions are projected, in 2050, to have larger populations of 60–64-year-olds than 45–49-year-olds?

f. In 2002, which region had pretty much equal numbers in the 0–39 and 40–80+ age groups?

g. In Sub-Saharan Africa, the projected size of the elderly population will remain quite small in 2050, compared to every other region. What single factor do you think might be most responsible?

3. Graph the data in the following table as a bar graph. Use the grid that follows.

OCCUPATION	MEDIAN ANNUAL SALARY ($)
Computer engineers	62,000
Systems analysts	52,000
Database administrators	48,000
Physician assistants	47,000

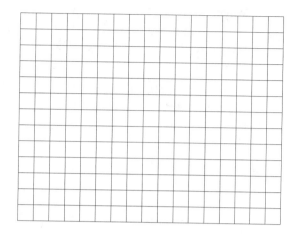

4. The educational attainment of Texans age 25 and older in 2003 is summarized below.

EDUCATION	ATTAINED BY
Less than 9th grade	1,416,434
9th to 12th grade, no diploma	1,516,837
High school graduate	3,473,633
Some college, no degree	2,773,964
Associate's degree	778,403
Bachelor's degree	2,163,749
Graduate or professional degree	1,065,672

Source: U.S. Census Bureau

Identify each category on the following circle graph.

Education: Texans 25 years and older

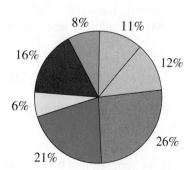

5. Wayne Gretzky scored 50% more points than anyone who ever played professional hockey. He accomplished this by playing in 280 fewer games than Gordie Howe, the second leading record holder. The number of games played by Gretzky during each season of his career are listed:

   79, 80, 80, 80, 74, 80, 80, 79, 64, 78, 73, 78, 74, 45, 81, 48, 80, 82, 82, 70

   Create a stem-and-leaf display.

6. The traveling times in minutes for 15 workers randomly chosen at High Tech Manufacturing are as follows:

   30, 20, 15, 15, 25, 20, 35, 60, 20, 40, 10, 30, 15, 35, 20

   a. Create a dotplot of the frequency distribution of the traveling times.

   b. Determine the mean, median, mode, and midrange of the set of traveling times.

   c. Which measure best represents the set of data? Explain.

7. The body mass index (BMI) is a measure based on height and weight of a person. The BMI of randomly selected males and females are listed below:

   Males: 23.6, 23.4, 24.6, 26.5, 24.2, 31.0, 28.1, 26.3, 22.5, 27.9, 29.2
   Females: 19.6, 22.8, 20.6, 28.1, 25.5, 21.1, 27.5, 20.5, 27.9, 18.7, 29.8

   a. Determine the mean of each group of BMI measures.

   b. In general, it is believed that males weigh more than females, and males are taller than females. Do the sample means in part a support this general belief? Explain.

8. The following data is the number of cancellations on a certain commuter flight on 12 randomly selected days in the past 6 months.

$$5, \ 5, \ 6, \ 9, \ 9, \ 11, \ 12, \ 12, \ 13, \ 13, \ 13, \ 14$$

a. Construct a dotplot of the data.

b. Does the distribution seem skewed? Explain.

c. Determine the mean and median of the number of cancellations.

d. When the data is skewed, the mean is "pulled" from the center to the direction of the skew. The median tends to remain near the center of the distribution. The following diagram illustrates the relationship between the mean and median in a distribution that is skewed to the right.

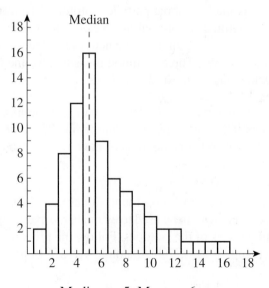

Median = 5; Mean = 6

Identify the location on the *x*-axis of the mean and median in the following distribution that is skewed to the left.

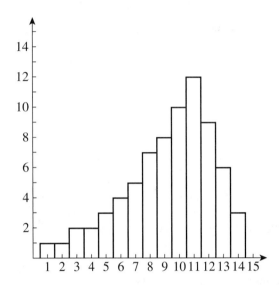

e. Do the results in parts b and c confirm the observation in part d?

9. In chemistry, measuring the masses of chemical elements is an important activity. An atom of an element is made of three particles; protons, electrons, and neutrons. For example, an atom of boron has 5 protons and 5 electrons. However, some boron atoms have 5 neutrons (boron 10) and some have 6 neutrons (boron 11). Each of these forms of boron is called an isotope. Three common measures for the mass of boron are the mass of boron 10, the mass of boron 11, and the average weighted mass of boron.

a. The mass of an atom is measured by the sum of its protons and neutrons. The unit of measurement is called an atomic mass unit (amu). Therefore, the boron 10 isotope has a mass of 10 amu. What is the mass of the boron 11 isotope?

b. Approximately 1/5 (20%) of boron found in nature is boron 10 and 4/5 (80%) is boron 11. These estimates can be used to estimate the average atomic mass of boron from the atomic masses of the isotopes. Follow the procedure given previously in this activity to compute the weighted atomic average of boron.

c. One check that your answer (10.8 amu) in part b is reasonable is to be sure the relative weights add up to one or alternatively to 100%. Do this check.

d. The atomic masses of other elements are calculated in the same way that you calculated the atomic mass for boron. The average atomic mass of magnesium (Mg) can be estimated from the atomic masses and relative natural occurrences of three isotopes as listed in the following table. Check that the weights add up to 100% and then calculate the average mass of magnesium to the nearest tenth

MAGNESIUM ISOTOPE	Mg 24	Mg 25	Mg 26
RELATIVE OCCURRENCE (%)	79%	10%	11%

ACTIVITY 6.7

Sampling a
Population

Suppose you have a need to know the average weight of every adult in the United States, or the mean age of every blue crab in the Chesapeake Bay, or the median income of every household in Miami. To determine such measures of central tendency, it is not usually practical to obtain the data for every individual in the population. If every individual in the population is measured it is called a **census**.

1. Do you think it is possible to conduct a census to determine each of the measures mentioned above? Give specific reasons for each case.

Conducting a census to determine the characteristics of an entire population is usually either too costly or time consuming. If even possible, other ways have been devised to achieve the same objective with a high degree of certainty. By taking a relatively small sample from the entire population, a great deal can be determined about that population. A **sample** consists of any portion of a population, no matter how large or small. Once a sample is chosen, this smaller collection can be measured and a central tendency can be recorded.

2. Since a sample can be of any size, how would you compare the practicality and usefulness of samples of size 1, 25, and 2 million when attempting to estimate the income of Florida households?

The process of collecting data from some fraction of a population is called **sampling**. It allows us to learn about the entire population by studying a relatively small portion of the population. The size of the sample along with the method used to select individuals for the sample can have a big effect on the results.

3. Suppose you are interested in knowing the mean average height for everyone in your school. A census would give the exact value while a sample will result in an estimate.

   a. Assume you got a sample of size one student less than the population. How close do you think the mean height for the sample will be to the mean of the population?

   b. If you got another sample, this time with ten fewer students than the population, do you think this sample mean would be as close to the population mean as the sample in part a?

c. If you took a sample of size 100 and another sample of size 10, which sample's mean do you think will be closer to the population's mean?

In general, a larger sample size will result in a more accurate estimate of the population. But when the population is very large, larger samples will not produce significantly better results and are usually more expensive or difficult to obtain. A decision is normally made that will balance these two tendencies, not too small to sacrifice accuracy, and not too large to sacrifice cost.

As a general rule, for very large populations, a sample in the size of hundreds is normally sufficient.

To help illustrate some of these ideas you will explore some relatively small populations. The table below shows the current grades (0–100) for all the 20 students in Mr. Horton's economics class.

ID NUMBER	LAST NAME	CURRENT GRADE
1	Adams	78
2	Baker	84
3	Cooper	82
4	Davenport	95
5	Elacqua	71
6	Flanagan	83
7	Grant	97
8	Haught	65
9	Jacobs	80
10	Kim	78
11	Lee	67
12	Moloney	91
13	Naraparaju	69
14	O'Brochta	74
15	Park	81
16	Reeves	79
17	Snider	62
18	Thoreson	88
19	Vilece	93
20	Whiting	63

4. Consider this class as the entire population. In this case, a census is quite feasible. Determine both the median and mean for this population.

5. Now suppose you did not have access to all the grades, but could be given the grades for five students. In other words, you can take a sample of size five. Choose any five students you like and calculate the mean and median grade for your sample. Such measurements taken from a sample are called **statistics**. How far are your statistics from the population mean and median?

6. Now compare your statistics to those of others in your group, or even the entire class. If you found the average of all your sample means, would you expect it to be close to the population mean? Find this average and check.

7. Describe how you chose the five students for your sample, and compare your method with others in your group and/or class.

If you chose your sample by looking at the grades and then tried to pick a balanced set of grades (not too high, not too low), or purposely picked all high scores or all low scores, you would introduce a bias to the selection process. **Bias** simply means that some individuals are somehow favored over others in the population. This is a critically important idea when attempting to select a sample that is representative of the entire population.

There is a classic example that helps illustrate this point. In 1936, *Literary Digest* magazine conducted a survey to predict the outcome of the U.S. presidential election. They had conducted similar surveys the five previous presidential elections, and had correctly predicted the winner each time. In 1936, ten million postcards were distributed to a list of voters, generated primarily from owners of automobiles and telephones. Over two million of the postcards were returned, and on that basis the Republican governor of Kansas, Alf Landon, was predicted to beat the incumbent Democratic president, Franklin Roosevelt, by an overwhelming margin, with 57% of the popular vote. The election was actually won by Roosevelt, with over 61% of the popular vote!

8. There was a bias in this presidential election survey. What do you think could have been the cause?

Simple Random Sample (SRS)

Many methods have been devised to select samples in a way that eliminates, or at least minimizes, any form of bias. To achieve this, the most basic idea is the random selection of the individuals in the sample. To select randomly means every individual in the population has an equal chance of being selected. A **simple random sample** (SRS for short) is the result of a sampling method that assures every possible sample of the same size has an equal chance or probability of being selected.

9. Describe a method that would ensure your sample of five students from Mr. Horton's class will be a simple random sample. Compare and discuss your method with others in your class.

10. Use your calculator to generate five random integers between 1 and 20. Use these numbers to identify the five students for your sample, by simply counting each student's position in the alphabetical class list.

    a. Suppose one of your random numbers is repeated. Since you need five different numbers, what could you do next?

    b. Record your five random numbers and the student associated with each number.

    c. Does the same chance or probability apply to every possible sample of size five using this method? Why?

    d. Calculate the mean and median grade for your sample.

    e. As you did in Problem 5, use the mean and median from part d for all the samples to find the average mean and average median for your class. Compare your averages this time to what you found in Problem 5. Which are closer to the population mean and median?

In general, all the possible sample means will naturally vary, both above and below the population mean. But the average of several sample means will generally be very close to the population mean, an idea that is useful for further statistical analysis.

Random numbers are a primary tool in selecting simple random samples. There are several ways to get random numbers, in addition to using your calculator. Books of random numbers have been published (especially useful before computers became commonplace), and websites exist that provide truly random numbers, based upon physical phenomena, like the weather. (See www.random.org)

SUMMARY
Activity 6.7

1. A **census** is the result of measuring or counting every individual in a population.

2. A **sample** is the result of measuring or counting any portion of a population.

3. **Sampling** is the process of collecting a sample from a population.

4. The larger the sample size, the more accurate the estimate for the population.

5. A **bias** occurs when some individuals in a population have a greater chance of being selected for a sample than others.

6. A **statistic** is a measurement derived from a sample, usually intended to be representative of an entire population.

7. A **simple random sample** (**SRS** for short) is a sample that is selected by a method that ensures every possible sample of a given size has an equal chance of being selected.

EXERCISES
Activity 6.7

1. The following list of digits was taken from a table of random numbers.

   39 63 46 23 49 74 08 86 55 64 16 37 91 97 13 39 15 39 45 91 79 86 45 37

   59 53 50 50 40 46 92 74 78 44 52 66 73 31 93 36 55 45 26 22 35 69 08 32

   30 73 47 15 71 83 72 27 97 12 25 77 56 51 78 07 76 32 92 81 13 13 01 96

   62 88 91 26 91 25 42 40 90 25 75 20 30 91 39 41 17 31 46 06 08 91 56 30

   83 19 51 13 43 51 14 20 82 15 14 03 47 33 68 07 61 82 92 69 48 68 04 68

   70 58 37 03 61 41 04 72 67 92 84 66 90 43 24 33 01 49 39 09 86 54 59 06

   54 09 20 83 00 19 11 60 76 75 52 48 79 25 31 23 17 84 12 07 77 72 50 10

   95 83 62 25 30 91 78 58 02 10 34 36 15 22 28 33 86 99 43 32 38 68 61 67

   a. Since there are 20 students in Mr. Horton's class, think of each student's ID number as a two digit sequence (the ID number for Baker is 02). Start at the beginning of the table, looking at each two-digit number, and record the first eight numbers that are between 01 and 20. These give the student ID numbers. (If there is a repeated number, simply ignore the repetition.) What students would make a sample of size 8, using this table?

b. If you wanted a different sample, you would of course need to use different random numbers. But there is another way to use the table without bypassing so many numbers. Since there are 100 possible two digit numbers in the table (00 through 99), and 100 is a multiple of 20, each student could be assigned five numbers, their student ID plus a multiple of 20. So, for example, Jacobs would be identified by 09, 29, 49, 69 and 89. Use the first row of the table to choose a different sample of size 8, and identify the students by name.

2. A sample of size 100 is to be selected from each of the following populations. In which cases do you think a simple random sample is possible? Give a reason for your answer.

a. All the adult blue crabs in the Chesapeake Bay

b. All the students enrolled in your school

c. All the passenger cars registered in the state of Florida

d. All the passenger cars on the road in Florida on December 25, 2008

e. All the homeless people in the United States

3. The data below (10 rows by 20 columns) gives the weights, in pounds, of 200 chickens at a poultry farm.

5.9	6.4	4.3	5.9	5.3	6.0	5.5	5.4	5.3	4.8	6.0	4.0	5.1	4.9	5.5	6.0	4.6	4.1	4.8	6.7
5.7	6.1	6.1	6.2	5.9	4.1	4.7	5.2	6.7	6.5	5.1	5.4	5.8	4.1	5.8	5.1	5.0	6.0	5.3	6.2
5.8	6.5	6.9	6.7	5.9	4.6	4.9	6.3	6.6	5.4	5.3	5.2	6.9	6.7	4.7	6.9	5.5	6.6	5.7	5.2
6.8	5.2	4.9	4.9	6.8	6.7	6.7	6.7	5.6	6.9	6.9	6.8	5.1	5.3	7.0	4.9	4.2	4.5	6.7	4.4
5.7	6.2	6.8	5.8	4.5	4.7	5.8	4.4	4.7	5.1	4.5	5.1	6.1	4.6	5.2	4.7	4.2	4.9	6.2	6.8
4.4	4.9	6.1	6.9	6.1	6.9	4.3	4.8	4.8	4.9	6.2	4.3	4.4	4.4	5.2	5.0	6.2	6.3	6.7	6.0
6.1	5.3	6.3	5.8	4.8	7.0	6.7	4.3	6.6	6.7	5.3	6.2	6.6	6.4	6.4	5.8	5.2	5.3	4.0	6.6
4.2	4.8	5.9	4.5	6.7	5.5	5.7	6.2	4.1	6.5	5.8	4.8	5.3	6.2	5.4	5.8	6.9	5.5	6.4	5.0
6.1	4.1	4.3	6.9	6.3	4.2	6.6	5.8	6.6	5.1	4.6	4.8	4.1	6.9	4.4	6.5	6.7	4.8	5.5	6.1
5.5	4.7	5.9	5.3	5.8	5.9	4.8	6.1	6.9	6.4	5.0	4.3	5.7	7.0	5.4	6.2	6.4	5.2	4.9	5.6

a. Generate random numbers from your calculator to select a SRS of size 10. (Use integers between 1 and 200.) Explain exactly how you chose your sample, showing your random numbers and the associated weights. Calculate the mean weight for your sample.

b. Now select a SRS of size 25 and calculate the mean weight for this sample.

c. Which of your samples do you think has a mean closer to the population mean, and why?

d. Calculate the population mean to check your answer to part c.

e. If your larger sample was closer to the population mean, that was to be expected, but was not a certainty. Hand pick ten weights that result in a sample mean further from the population mean than your size 25 sample mean.

4. The random numbers generated on your calculator are not quite as random as you might think. It is possible that two different calculators could generate the same random list of numbers in the same order. The random number generator (rand) used in the calculators relies on what is known as a seed value. The default seed value is 0. With each rand execution, the calculator will generate the same random number sequence for a given seed value. To obtain a different random number sequence, store any nonzero number to rand. (from http://epsstore.ti.com)

This sort of random number is called a **pseudorandom number**. For most random sampling purposes, pseudorandom numbers work fine. Truly random numbers can be generated from truly random processes, like the weather or the physical behavior of atomic particles. Such random numbers are available on the web, at sites such as www.random.org. Visit this website, generate a list of ten different random integers between 1 and 200, and report on the process that was used to generate the numbers.

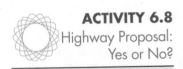

ACTIVITY 6.8

Highway Proposal:
Yes or No?

OBJECTIVES

1. Identify the characteristics of a well-defined sample survey.

2. Understand how to collect a stratified sample.

3. Identify ways in which a sample might be biased.

Opinion polls are everywhere these days, on TV and the Internet, in all print media, and at meetings of decision makers in business and government. Such polls generally attempt to measure the percentage of a population that holds a certain opinion or will make a certain decision (like for whom they plan to vote). Such a poll is an example of a **sample survey**, a methodical process of collecting a sample that is representative (hopefully) of the larger population. A simple random sample, as defined in the previous activity, results from one of several different methods that can be employed to attain an unbiased sample. In this activity you will explore different sampling methods and sources of bias.

Highway Proposal

In your capacity as an administrative assistant for your county government, you need to assess the attitude of your community for a new highway proposal. Some people will favor the highway in the belief it will provide greater mobility and promote business. Others will argue that it will bring even more congestion and will negatively impact the environment. An opinion poll will be helpful for government leaders in making final decisions.

1. Since you have been asked to submit your preliminary report as soon as possible, there is no time to even consider a census of the 100,000 plus adult residents of your county. So you turn to one of the more convenient tools at your disposal, the phone book. Describe a plan you could use to come up with a sample of 50 adult residents using the phone book. Do you think your method results in a simple random sample?

Even if you did truly randomize the process of selecting names from the phone book, the overall process of using a phone book is flawed. For example, will every adult resident of your community have an equal chance of being included in the sample?

2. Give several reasons why your sampling plan of using a phone book to create the sample and then calling each person in the sample is biased and will not result in a SRS of the entire population of adult residents.

One of the biggest difficulties with whatever plan you might employ in your poll is the same as the bias created with the *Literary Digest* poll in 1936. A significant number of adult residents didn't even have a chance to be included. It is possible that all the individuals in the phone book really are representative of the entire adult population, but you don't know that. Therefore, you have to assume there is a bias in the sampling results.

3. Can you think of other ways to obtain a complete list of adult residents of your county, so a true SRS could be attained?

Whatever list is used for sampling purposes, usually not the entire population, is called the **sampling frame**. The closer the sampling frame comes to the actual population, the better. At best, it should be representative of the entire population.

Nonrespondents

The issue of **nonrespondents** also will create a bias. No matter how you select individuals for the sample, some will not answer their phone, or will refuse to participate, or will simply forget to return the questionnaire. That group of individuals may not be representative of the whole population, so their exclusion will definitely result in inaccurate results.

4. It is important for any sampling plan to include how to deal with nonrespondents. What do you think are some possibilities?

Mean of the Sample Means

Now let's turn to a sample survey that you can do with your classmates. You may wonder how much television the students in your school watch each day. It would probably be feasible to do a census in this case, but for the sake of understanding the sampling process, let's assume it is best to take a sample. In fact, let's first limit the population to your math class.

5. Using a list of all students in your math class, devise and describe a plan to take a SRS of size ten. Take the poll by asking each selected student to estimate how many hours of television they watch each week, and then calculate the mean for your sample.

6. Now determine the mean of all the sample means from the samples in your class. Compare your sample mean to the class's mean of all the sample means.

7. Since the population (your math class) is relatively small, you can take a census to determine the population mean number of TV hours watched each week. How close is the class mean of the sample means to this population mean?

You should have discovered that the mean of all the sample means comes very close to the population mean. This basic fact of statistics is very powerful and is used to make inferences and decisions about entire populations based upon relatively small samples. This phenomenon will be studied in great detail if and when you take an elementary statistics course.

Stratified Sampling

Now suppose you suspect there may be a real difference in boys' and girls' TV watching habits. (If you happen to be in a class with all girls, or all boys, you will need to use a different distinction, maybe based on age or ethnicity.) If there is a real difference, and your sample just happened to be almost all girls, or almost all boys, it will not be very representative of the population.

8. What is the ratio of boys in your class to the total number of students in the class (the population)? Express as a decimal number.

9. a. What fraction of your sample of size ten, from Problem 5, consisted of boys?

   b. If you round the population ratio you determined in Problem 8, is it the same as the sample ratio?

You want the ratios in Problems 8 and 9 to be nearly the same. Then your sample would be proportional to the population. But it is entirely possible your SRS could result in almost all boys, or almost all girls. To try to remove any gender bias in your sample, you could devise your sampling method to assure the sample ratio of boys and girls is the same as, or at least as close as possible to, the population ratios.

10. With a sample size of ten, how many boys should be in your sample to closely match (as close as possible) the ratio of boys to students in your class?

Once you know how many boys and how many girls need to be in your sample, you can then separate the class into two groups, called **strata**, the boys and the girls. From each group you then randomly select the required number. Such a method is called **stratified sampling**.

11. Use your result in Problem 10 to produce a stratified sample, and then calculate the mean.

Self-selection

You will end this activity by considering one of the most prevalent types of opinion polls. Whether on the web, TV, the radio, or in a print magazine or newspaper, you often are offered the chance to make your opinion known.

12. You hear on a TV news show that the results of a phone-in poll revealed that 83% of the callers prefer text-messaging over in-person talking. This seems like an overwhelming majority.

   a. How would you describe this method of sampling?

   b. Why do you think this sample is biased?

   c. Do you think there is a way to design this method to eliminate a bias?

The previous problem illustrates a classic form of bias, called **self-selection**. The individuals in the sample who chose to take part in the poll were motivated to do so. That motivation will most likely be more prevalent among those that hold one opinion over another. Of course, it also means everyone in the population will not have the same probability of being included, even if everyone hears of the poll. There will be some individuals with no motivation to respond, hence no likelihood of being included in the sample. Self-selection as a method may be cheap and easy to do (hence their prevalence), but as a sampling method is deeply flawed.

SUMMARY
Activity 6.8

1. A **sample survey** is a methodical process of collecting a sample from a larger population.

2. A **statistical experiment** consists of a well-defined process that applies statistical analysis to answer a question about some given population.

3. A **sampling plan** refers to the detailed step-by-step procedure to collect data through a specific sampling method.

4. A **sampling frame** is the collection of individuals from which a sample is drawn. It may or may not be the entire population.

5. There are several common sources of **bias** that can occur, even with a well established sampling method.

   Selected individuals for a sample may be unavailable or choose to not respond. Such **nonrespondents** do not have the same likelihood of being included, hence creating a bias.

   A sample composed of individuals that voluntarily respond, a **self-selected** sample, creates a bias since everyone in the population is not equally likely to be included.

6. A **stratified sample** results when a population is separated into two or more subgroups, called **strata**, and simple random samples are selected from each strata in proportion to the relative size of the strata.

1. Use your local phone book to select a sample of ten people in your community.

   a. Precisely describe the method you used.

   b. Is your sample random? Explain.

2. One way to reduce the number of nonrespondents in a survey is to make face-to-face contact. This is more expensive than phoning or mailing, due to additional travel time, especially if the population is spread over a large geographic area. One method that helps reduce this expense is called **cluster sampling**. For example, to personally interview a representative sample of all residents of Florida, a simple random sample of 500 residents would most likely be spread far and wide across the state. Creating a plan to efficiently visit 500 different locations would be a costly challenge. With cluster sampling, the plan would be to randomly select a small number of geographic regions, or clusters, and then find a fixed size SRS within each cluster.

   a. In designing a cluster sampling plan, what do you think would be a reasonable choice for the clusters?

   b. If you chose the counties of Florida for the clusters, how many clusters would there be? (A resource for the geography of Florida: www.floridacountiesmap.com)

   c. If your plan is to include ten clusters, what size SRS should be selected from each cluster?

   d. Find a list of all the counties in Florida and randomly select ten counties for your clusters. Describe your process. On the map of Florida below, shade in the selected counties.

e. Assuming you then generate the required SRS for each cluster, in what ways might your resulting overall sample have a bias? Could a bias be fixed?

3. When a sample is to be drawn from a list, such as a phone book, it is sometimes easiest to select one individual at random, and then count from that first individual a fixed number to pick the next individual. The fixed number is also randomly chosen, and is used to continue counting until the sample size is completed. Such a method is called **systematic sampling**. For example, the random number 134 might be chosen, to select the 134th individual on the list for the sample. Then if the random number 20 was chosen, the 154th individual on the list would be the next one chosen.

a. With these numbers, what positions would the third, fourth, and fifth chosen individual's position be?

b. Suppose you desire a sample of size 50, chosen from a list of students at your school. If you randomly generate 58 for the first student chosen, and 15 for the count to the next student, what will be the positions of the second, third, and fourth students chosen?

c. By the time the last student is chosen, what would their position be?

d. Suppose there are not that many students in your school? How could you still complete your sample of size 50 using this method?

e. As long as the order of the list will in no way influence the response, as in an alphabetic listing, a representative sample will be acquired. Suppose the listing is by age. Can you think of a question and random numbers that would result in a bad sample (meaning not representative of the population)?

4. The principal of a high school wants to determine the "average" number of children in the families of students who attend the high school. The principal visits each classroom in the building and selects the four students who are seated closest to the corners of the classroom. The principal then asks each student how many children are in his family. Will this sampling technique result in an unbiased sample? Explain.

5. A **convenience sample** uses data that is easily or readily available. However, this type of sampling can be extremely biased. For example, suppose the city council wants to raise taxes in order to build a new science wing on the high school. In order to obtain the opinion of the city residents on the issue, the first 50 adults leaving the local shopping mall are asked if they are in favor of raising taxes to build the new wing.

    a. Discuss the possible cause of a bias in the sample.

    b. Describe a sampling technique that would be less biased.

6. The student council at your high school wants to survey students about the quality of food in the school cafeteria. It is decided that students leaving the cafeteria will be given a short questionnaire. Is this method of sampling unbiased? Explain.

7. Your student council desires a quick and representative poll of student attitudes toward a dress code proposed by the administration. In case there are differences in opinion among students in the various grades, you recommend that a stratified sample be used. You know there are 212 seniors, 273 juniors, 255 sophomores, and 320 freshmen in your high school. To get a sample of 50 students, using the four classes as your strata, what number of students from each class should be in your sample?

8. The Addison-Wesley Publishing Company wants you to obtain a sample of 100 students who use this textbook. Describe the procedure to obtain the required data for parts a–d.

    a. a simple random sample

    b. a stratified sample

    c. a cluster sample

    d. a systematic sample

9. *Buyer's Market* magazine mailed a questionnaire to its subscribers about cars and other consumer products. Also included were a request for a voluntary contribution and a ballot for the board of directors. Responses were to be mailed back in envelopes that required postage. Discuss potential problems with this sampling technique.

10. Identify each of the following as simple random sampling, stratified sampling, systematic sampling, cluster sampling, or convenience sampling.

    a. Randomly select high schools from different geographic regions and survey all students at each of the chosen schools.

    b. Survey each 10th student who walks in the front entrance of the school.

    c. Obtain a list of students enrolled in a high school. Number these students and then use a random number table to obtain the sample.

d. Obtain a list of students enrolled at a high school. Draw a random sample from each of the freshman, sophomore, junior, and senior classes, proportional to the size of each class.

e. At a local tire manufacturing plant, every 20th tire coming off the assembly line is checked for defects.

f. Survey the first five students who enter the classroom.

g. Elementary school children in a large city are classified based on the neighborhood school they attend. A random sample of five elementary schools is selected. All the children from each selected school are included in the sample.

h. A teacher at the high school teaches five classes of Spanish. Two of the classes are chosen by the principal and all the students in those classes fill out a teacher evaluation form about that Spanish teacher.

i. The first 50 people entering a museum are asked if they support the city council's increase in funding for the arts.

j. Students in your senior class obtain the voting records for the county. You randomly select 50 Democrats, 40 Republicans, and 8 Independents. (The numbers chosen are based on the percentage of registered voters in each category in the county.) You survey them concerning their favorite candidate for county commissioner in the upcoming fall election.

k. A state is divided into regions using Zip codes. A random sample of 15 Zip code areas is selected.

l. Every 10th person in line to purchase tickets to a rock concert is asked their age.

m. At a Key Club meeting, the names of all members are written on identical slips of paper and placed in a bowl. The names of five members are drawn. These five people will participate in face-to-face interviews with a pollster.

n. You are approached by a person at a local mall who asks you to answer a few questions about the security at the mall.

o. Numbered ping-pong balls are placed in a bin. The bin is shaken. A ball is then selected from the bin.

p. A marketing expert for MTV is planning a survey in which 500 people will be randomly selected from each of the following age groups: 10–14, 15–19, 20–24, 25–29.

ACTIVITY 6.9
Statistical
Survey

OBJECTIVE

1. Design and execute a statistical survey.

Many different sampling methods were described in Activities 6.7 and 6.8. Efficiency in cost and time is usually an important factor in deciding which sampling method is appropriate. Designing a sample survey requires a well-defined, step-by-step process, as outlined below.

1. Formulate the problem and devise a plan.

   • State what you need to know.

   • Identify the population and what is to be measured.

   • Decide on an appropriate sampling method and sample size.

   • Think carefully about the exact form of all questions and responses.

2. Execute the plan.

   • Follow the plan to gather the data.

   • Specify all the details of the methodology.

3. Analyze and organize the results in a report.

   • Discuss all elements of the sampling process.

   • Interpret the results and state final conclusions.

To illustrate this process, let us return to the highway proposal situation introduced in Activity 6.8. Suppose your county executive decides that you should survey only registered voters in your community to determine whether the majority of county residents favor a new highway proposal. You do have a complete list of registered voters, with their party affiliation (34% are Republicans, 45% are Democrats, and 21% are independent). In Problems 1–3 use complete sentences to record your design for this sample survey.

1. You can save money by using a sample of size 100 instead of doing a census. Record a plan for this sample survey.

   a. State what you need to know.

   b. Identify the population that is to be measured and the sampling frame.

   c. Which sampling method, simple random sample or stratified sample, do you think would be best? Give a reason for your choice.

2. Since you are only discussing a hypothetical sample survey, you are not actually going to execute the survey. However, describe precisely all the details of what you would need to do.

3. The report for your survey will include all the difficulties that were encountered, the actual results of the survey, how the results might be biased, and an interpretation of those results. Use your imagination to write a feasible report for this sample survey. (*Hint:* Start by assuming you used a stratified sample, and fill in the table to help create your report.)

RESPONSE	REPUBLICAN	DEMOCRAT	INDEPENDENT	TOTAL
Favors proposal				
Doesn't favor				

In a real sample survey, the results will be subjected to more advanced statistical analysis, which include the notion of margins of error and confidence levels. For example, if you concluded that 58% of residents favor the highway proposal, the sample size would yield an error of $\pm 10\%$, at the .05 confidence level. This means that you expect the real percentage of residents favoring the proposal to be between $58 - 10 = 48\%$ and $58 + 10 = 68\%$, with a .05 probability that you are wrong. These topics are studied fully in a statistics course.

EXERCISES
Activity 6.9

1. Conduct your own sample survey to determine how many hours per week students at your school spend using the Internet during the week. In your sampling plan, be sure to follow the step-by-step process outlined in this activity:

   a. Formulate the problem and devise a plan.

   State what you need to know.
   Identify the population and what is to be measured.
   Decide on an appropriate sampling method and sample size.
   Think carefully about the exact form of all questions and responses.

   b. Execute the plan.

   Follow the plan to gather the data.
   Specify all the details of the methodology.

   c. Analyze and organize the results in a report.

   Discuss all elements of the sampling process.
   Interpret the results and state final conclusions.

2. Depending upon what sampling method you used in Exercise 1, discuss how you could have applied either stratified or systematic sampling to conduct your survey.

3. With a group of your classmates, come up with an issue concerning some particular population that you would like to know about.

    a. Clearly state the following, as a preliminary proposal.

        i. What would you like to find out?

        ii. Precisely what population would be involved?

        iii. How would you go about collecting a sample?

    b. Is your proposal feasible? (That is, is it something you and your classmates could actually do?)

        i. If feasible, clear your idea with your teacher, and proceed to conduct your statistical survey. Be sure to follow all steps in the process outlined in this activity.

        ii. If your proposal is not feasible (or your teacher does not approve it), go back and revise the proposal, or start all over.

ACTIVITY 6.10

What's the
Cause?

OBJECTIVES

1. Understand the purpose and principles of experimental design.

2. Know when a causal relationship can be established.

3. Understand the importance of randomization, control treatments, and blinding.

In Activity 2.8, Body Fat Percentage, you learned how to recognize a linear correlation between two variables. Recall that finding a correlation does not necessarily establish a cause-and-effect relationship between two variables. Problem 1 demonstrates such a situation.

1. Suppose a survey of elementary school students in your county results in the following scatterplot of reading level versus shoe size.

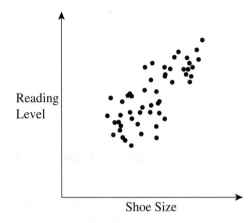

a. How would you describe the association between reading level and shoe size?

b. Based upon your response in part a, would you be willing to conclude that an increase in shoe size causes a higher reading level? Why or why not?

c. If your answer in part b was no, can you think of a lurking variable that might explain the correlation?

Experimental Design

Scientists and statisticians have developed methods to determine causal relationships. **Experimental design** involves a very meticulous procedure for controlling the environment surrounding two variables. The goal is to determine whether changing one variable actually causes a change in the second variable.

2. The mathematics lab at your school has started using a new computerized study program for Algebra I. After the first semester, the average scores on the midterm test were 5% higher than last year. The principal thinks that the computer program caused the increase in test scores.

a. Do you think there is enough evidence to justify this claim? Explain the reason for your answer.

b. What other factors might be involved that could also result in higher scores?

c. What groups of students are being compared, and how might that affect the results?

Treatment and Control Groups

When attempting to establish a causal relationship, a good experimental design will always try to control outside variables. That means, in this example, any other influence beyond using the computer program (or not), and the test scores should be kept constant for all students, as much as is possible. For example, to better establish the principal's claim, all Algebra I students could be divided into two groups. One group would use the computer program (or receive the **treatment**, as it is usually called). The other group would not (usually called the **control group**).

3. If a control group is used for the Algebra I experiment, what outside influences (that you may have identified in Problem 2) could be controlled so they do not vary between the groups?

Another critically important aspect of a good experimental design is randomization. Recall how collecting a sample randomly is essential to assure unbiased results. In a similar way, selecting members for the control group must be done randomly to help even out any unforeseen variables that could affect the results.

4. Suppose the group to receive the computer program treatment in Algebra I is selected on a voluntary basis instead of being selected by a random process. How might this invalidate the results of the experiment?

> To summarize, a **good experimental design** will consist of a **control group** and at least one **treatment group** that will receive the treatment being studied. The selection of subjects for the groups must be **selected through a random process**.

The real point of a control group is to try to minimize the possibility that some unanticipated factor might be at least part of the cause for the results you see. If everyone receives the treatment, maybe the real cause of the improved test scores is a subtly improved test. Students may do better on the test simply because they now understand the questions. The average scores would improve, but not necessarily because of the treatment. With a control group, the improvement would be seen in both the treatment group and the control group, so there would be no reason to believe the computer program was the cause of the improved test scores.

This methodology has been used for research in the sciences for many years, credited to the psychologist Gustav Fechner in the mid-1800s. Medical research has benefited greatly, whether in testing the effectiveness and safety of new drugs or searching for new innovative treatments of dangerous diseases. A classic example of the later occurred over fifty years ago, as medical researchers were seeking a cure for polio, a devastating disease that has since been nearly defeated.

5. Dr. Jonas Salk is credited with discovering a polio vaccine. This successful discovery depended upon many years of experimentation with control groups. To further control for unseen variables, subjects in both the control group and the treatment group were not allowed to know which group they were in. This is called **blinding**.

   a. What kind of influence do you think blinding would eliminate?

   b. During the course of this lengthy experiment, many children participated. Some were treated and some were not. The treatment eventually proved to be effective in preventing the spread of polio. What ethical problem comes to mind as a result of this experiment?

You may have heard of the **placebo effect**. A placebo is a false treatment. In other words, if the treatment is a medicine that is given as a pill, a fake pill (a sugar pill) would be given to the control group so they would not know they were not given the treatment (they would think they were given the treatment). The placebo effect is the real power of the human mind/body to affect positive results without a treatment, just by believing a treatment has been received! Compare this with your answer in Problem 5a.

6. Suppose you are involved in a study to determine whether a new drug is effective in lowering blood pressure. A placebo is administered to the control group.

   a. How important is it that the control group not know they are given a placebo?

   b. Should the treatment group be allowed to know that they are given the real treatment? Why or why not?

   c. What should be done so the administrator/technician does not inadvertently tip off the subject?

To assure that the subject does not know which group they are in, the personnel administering the treatment (or placebo) are also blinded (don't know which they are giving). This makes the experiment **single-blind**. To further assure there is no subjective influence among any involved parties, the evaluators are also blinded to group membership. This will make an experiment **double-blind**.

7. There have been cases where experimenters have influenced the results by evaluating the subjects without double-blinding. Suppose a researcher is trying to establish a new herb from the Amazon rainforest as a remedy for dry skin. The experiment is single-blind, but not double-blind. The study results in the claim that there was a remarkable improvement in skin condition. What might be wrong with this conclusion?

Replication

It is critical that an experiment include enough participants for the results to be statistically significant. Providing a treatment to one or two individuals will prove nothing. But to truly establish a causal relationship the entire experiment must be repeatable by others. It is very possible that positive results occurred by chance. Repeating the experiment will help verify, or deny, the claim. This feature is usually called **replication**. If researchers in another laboratory can't duplicate the results independently, then the entire study is brought into question. A classic example occurred in 1989 when physicists at the University of Utah produced what they called cold fusion. Fusion is a nuclear process that produces vast amounts of energy but is very difficult to control. After many years of research, it is not currently feasible as an energy source. But the claim of cold fusion (fusion that could take place very inexpensively) appeared to be a breakthrough and caused quite a stir in the mass media. As it turned out, no other physicists could replicate the results, so the excitement was short lived.

SUMMARY
Activity 6.10

1. To establish a **cause-and-effect relationship** between two variables an **experimental design** must include a **control group**, **randomization**, and be **replicable**.

- A **control group** includes individuals that do not receive the treatment under study.
- To be valid, assignment of members to the control and treatment groups must be done through a **random** process.
- An experiment should include as many subjects as possible, and the results should be **replicated** with further experiments with different study groups.

2. Most good experiments are **double-blind**, meaning neither the participants (subjects and administrators) nor the evaluators know which subjects received the treatment and which are in the control group.

3. A **placebo** is a treatment having no effect (a false treatment) given to the control group so all subjects experience the same conditions.

4. Many humans will respond positively to a placebo, even though the treatment being tested is not present. This **placebo effect** could fool the researcher into thinking the treatment caused a positive result unless a placebo is used with the control group.

1. **a.** Suppose a city passes a gun control law, and two years later the number of violent crimes increases. Can you conclude that the gun control law caused the crime rate to go up? Explain.

   b. If the crime rate had decreased, can you conclude that the gun control law caused the crime rate to go down? Explain.

2. A study skills company claims their SAT prep program will increase your overall SAT score by 45 points. Their claim is based upon 2350 students that completed their course and scored on average 45 points higher than their first attempt at the SAT. Do you accept their inferred claim that their program caused the higher scores?

3. In the 1990s, a study was designed to determine if listening to Mozart's music would improve performance on an IQ test. Subjects were randomly assigned to two groups. One group listened to Mozart; the second group was not given any instructions or music. The sample mean scores on the IQ test were 119 for the Mozart group and 110 for the no instructions group. Describe how well this experiment was designed, and whether you think a causal relationship was established. How could the experiment be improved, in your opinion?

4. Over the past twenty years, mathematics educators have been very busy reforming the way algebra is taught. The goal has been to improve the basic conceptual understanding required to successfully apply algebra in other courses and work. Suppose you wish to determine how well a particular reformed algebra course accomplishes this goal, compared to a traditionally taught algebra course. In other words, does taking a reformed algebra course cause a higher level of learning than the traditional course?

   a. Classes using the reformed course materials take a standardized algebra test. Standardized means the test has been given to many other algebra students and the mean and standard deviation are known. If the reformed class scores higher than the mean for this test, would you be able to conclude the reformed course caused the higher scores? Explain.

b. Describe how you could design an experiment to better assess whether the goal is being met.

5. A research doctor has developed a new medication to relieve the joint swelling of arthritis. Twenty patients have volunteered to take part in an experiment to determine if the new medication is more effective than their old medication.

    a. Describe how this experiment should be conducted. Carefully describe how each aspect of a good experiment can be accomplished.

    b. How can the control group and placebo effect be managed so patients still receive some medication?

6. Does filling the gas tank of a car with premium gasoline result in better fuel efficiency than with regular unleaded gasoline? Design an experiment to determine whether premium gasoline causes a car to get better gas mileage.

7. Sometimes a very strong belief can influence how the results of an experiment are interpreted, hence the need for double-blinding. Many popular beliefs and superstitions have not been subject to rigorous testing with good experimental design. Dowsing is a widely held belief that the use of a forked stick (called a dowsing rod) can be used to detect underground water. The dowser holds the two ends of the forked part, leaving the main stem pointing in front. When walking along with the dowsing rod held horizontally in front, if the pointer dips down, that is interpreted to mean underground water has been detected. Many people have employed dowsers over the years to help find the best location to dig a well, for example. In attempting to prove that hidden water is causing the dowsing rod to dip the following experiment is performed. Twenty buckets are laid out in a field, half are filled with water, the other half are empty. Boards are placed over each bucket, so no one can see inside. The dowser proceeds to walk around, passing the dowsing rod over each bucket. The evaluator, who also was responsible for filling and laying out the buckets, records the reaction of the rod in each case. The dowser goes over all the buckets a second time and reconfirms the choices from the first round. The dowser has picked out twelve buckets that he claims contain water, and in fact nine of them do. This means the dowser has correctly identified the contents of 16 out of 20, or 80%, of the buckets. A pretty good score, since the expected result by randomly guessing would be 50%. Are you convinced? Explain.

8. Think of something that interests you. Try to find two variables that are related to your interests and to each other. Pose a question about how one variable might cause a change in the other variable. Design an experiment that could test this situation, being sure to address how your experiment would address all aspects of a good design. If possible, conduct the experiment and report on the results.

ACTIVITY 6.11
A Switch Decision

OBJECTIVE

1. Measure the variability of a frequency distribution.

Statistical analysis is useful when important decisions need to be made. The following sets of data are the result of testing two different switches that can be used in the life-support system on a submarine. Two hundred of each type of switch were placed under continuous stress until they failed, the time recorded in hours. Switch A and switch B have approximately the same means and medians, as displayed by the following histograms. (The displays are from a TI-83/84 Plus.)

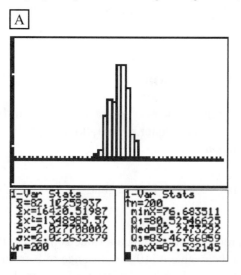

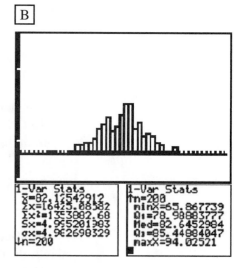

1. Verify that the means and medians for both switches are approximately the same. What does this tell you about the general shapes of the distributions?

2. Which distribution is the most spread out?

3. Which distribution is packed more closely around its center?

4. Based on these tests, which switch would you choose to use and why?

Like the central tendency of a distribution, the spread, or **variability,** of a distribution is also measured several different ways. The **range** is simply the difference between the minimum and maximum data values.

5. Determine the range for each set of switch data to the nearest hour. Do these ranges confirm your answers to Problems 2 and 3?

6. The range is of limited value in describing the variability (or spread) of a distribution. Consider these two data sets.

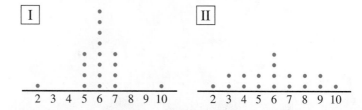

a. Which distribution has greater variability?

b. Calculate the range for each distribution.

c. What is your conclusion about the range as a measure of variability?

Standard Deviation

The most common measure of spread is the **standard deviation** (symbol σ, the Greek lowercase letter sigma). It measures how much the data deviates from the mean.

7. Calculate the mean for distributions I and II of Problem 6.

Deviation refers to how far a data value is from the mean. For example, if the mean is 7, then a data value of 10 is a distance of 3 from the mean, and you would say that the data value 10 has a deviation of 3 from the mean. If the data value is 4, it is still a distance of 3 from the mean, but its deviation is -3, indicating that it is below the mean.

8. a. Calculate the deviations for every data value in both distributions I and II of Problem 6. Record your results in the column having heading $x - \bar{x}$. Then add all the deviations for each distribution.

<table>
<tr><td colspan="3" align="center">**DISTRIBUTION I**</td><td colspan="3" align="center">**DISTRIBUTION II**</td></tr>
<tr><td>x</td><td>$x - \bar{x}$</td><td>$(x - \bar{x})^2$</td><td>x</td><td>$x - \bar{x}$</td><td>$(x - \bar{x})^2$</td></tr>
<tr><td></td><td></td><td></td><td></td><td></td><td></td></tr>
<tr><td></td><td></td><td></td><td></td><td></td><td></td></tr>
<tr><td></td><td></td><td></td><td></td><td></td><td></td></tr>
<tr><td></td><td></td><td></td><td></td><td></td><td></td></tr>
<tr><td></td><td></td><td></td><td></td><td></td><td></td></tr>
<tr><td></td><td></td><td></td><td></td><td></td><td></td></tr>
<tr><td></td><td></td><td></td><td></td><td></td><td></td></tr>
<tr><td></td><td></td><td></td><td></td><td></td><td></td></tr>
<tr><td></td><td></td><td></td><td></td><td></td><td></td></tr>
<tr><td></td><td></td><td></td><td></td><td></td><td></td></tr>
<tr><td></td><td></td><td></td><td></td><td></td><td></td></tr>
<tr><td></td><td></td><td></td><td></td><td></td><td></td></tr>
<tr><td></td><td></td><td></td><td></td><td></td><td></td></tr>
<tr><td></td><td></td><td></td><td></td><td></td><td></td></tr>
<tr><td></td><td></td><td></td><td></td><td></td><td></td></tr>
<tr><td></td><td></td><td></td><td></td><td></td><td></td></tr>
<tr><td></td><td></td><td></td><td></td><td></td><td></td></tr>
<tr><td>**Total**</td><td></td><td></td><td>**Total**</td><td></td><td></td></tr>
</table>

b. Is the sum of the deviations, denoted by $\sum (x - \bar{x})$, a good measure of the spread of the data? Explain.

To overcome the deficiency of the total deviation, you could simply take the absolute value of each deviation. The more conventional method is to calculate the **standard deviation**. The standard deviation of a distribution involves summing the squares of the deviations, denoted by $\sum (x - \bar{x})^2$.

9. For each distribution, calculate the standard deviation using the following procedure.

   a. Square each deviation in both of the tables of Problem 8 and then record your results in the column $(x - \bar{x})^2$.

   b. Add the squares of all the deviations: _____ _____

   c. Divide by the number of data values: _____ _____

   d. Take the square root: _____ _____

   In a single formula, the standard deviation is $\sigma = \sqrt{\dfrac{\sum (x - \bar{x})^2}{n}}$, where σ is the standard deviation, $\sum$ is short for "the sum of," x is a single data value, $\bar{x}$ is the mean, and n is the number of data values.

   e. Does distribution I or distribution II have greater variability? Explain using the standard deviation of each distribution.

10. Verify that your standard deviations in Problem 9d agree with those in the following display, from the TI-83/84 Plus. (The TI-83/84 Plus uses σx for σ.)

Distribution I

```
1-Var Stats
 x̄=6
 Σx=108
 Σx²=688
 Sx=1.533929978
 σx=1.490711985
↓n=18
```

Distribution II

```
1-Var Stats
 x̄=6
 Σx=108
 Σx²=736
 Sx=2.275185836
 σx=2.211083194
↓n=18
```

11. What do you think a standard deviation of zero would mean?

12. a. Return to the testing of switches A and B. The standard deviations of each distribution are given by the calculator output screen in the introduction of the activity. Record the standard deviations here.

b. Which distribution has the greater variability? Explain using the standard deviation of each distribution.

Boxplots

Another type of statistical graph, the **boxplot**, helps you to visualize the variability of a distribution. Five statistics form a boxplot: the minimum data value, the **first quartile (Q₁)**, the median, the **third quartile (Q₃)**, and the maximum data value, in order from smallest to largest. These are often referred to as the **five-number summary** for the distribution.

Quartiles refer to values that separate the data into quarters. The lowest 25% of all the data falls between the minimum and the first quartile. The next lowest 25% of the data falls between the first quartile and the median. Hence, 75% of the data is above the first quartile.

13. a. How much of the data is below the third quartile?

b. How much of the data is between the first and third quartiles?

The five-number summaries are displayed here for the switch A and B data.

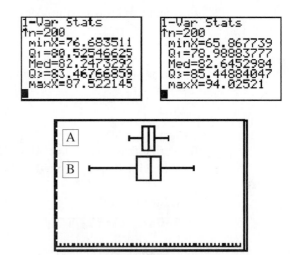

Sometimes called box-and-whisker plots, the preceding boxplots show visually how the quartiles for the switch data compare. The box represents the middle 50% of the data. The whiskers represent the extent of the lower and upper quarters of the data.

Appendix

See Appendix A for details to obtain a boxplot using the TI-83/84 Plus calculator.

14. Consider the following boxplots for three distributions.

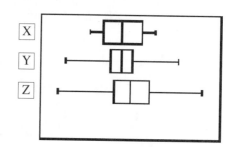

a. Compare the minimum, first quartile, median, third quartile, and maximum for the three distributions.

b. Compare the ranges for each of the three distributions.

c. Which distribution do you think has the least variability? Explain.

SUMMARY
Activity 6.11

1. The **variability** of a frequency distribution refers to how spread out the data is, away from the center.

2. The **range** of a frequency distribution is the difference between the lowest and highest data values.

3. The **deviation** of a data value is how far it is from the mean of the data set.

4. The **standard deviation** is a measure of how far all the data collectively is from the mean.

5. A **boxplot** is a graph that displays the **five-number summary** (the minimum, first quartile, median, third quartile, and maximum data value) for a distribution.

EXERCISES
Activity 6.11

Do the calculations in each of the following exercises. Fill in the table as part of your calculation. Then check your work by using the statistics features of your calculator.

1. Consider the following data: 5   8   2   1   7   1

Determine the standard deviation by filling in the table as part of your calculation.

x_i	$\bar{x}$	$x - \bar{x}$	$(x - \bar{x})^2$

2. Eight adults are surveyed and asked how many credit cards they possess. Their responses are 4, 0, 3, 1, 5, 2, 2, and 3. Determine the standard deviation for these data. Fill in the table as part of your calculation.

x_i	$\bar{x}$	$x - \bar{x}$	$(x - \bar{x})^2$

3. A student takes ten exams during a semester and receives the following grades: 90, 85, 97, 76, 89, 58, 82, 102, 70, and 67. Find the five-number summary.

4. In a year-long music course, you are required to attend 12 concerts. Last season, the lengths of the concerts were 92, 101, 98, 112, 80, 119, 92, 90, 116, 106, 78, and 65 minutes. Find the five-number summary for these data. Decide on a scale and draw a boxplot.

5. The weights, in pounds, of a group of workers are as follows:

173 123 171 175 188 120 177 160 151 169 162 128 145

140 158 132 202 162 154 180 164 166 157 171 175

Find the five-number summary for these data. Decide on a scale and draw a boxplot.

6. Joe DiMaggio played center field for the New York Yankees for 13 years. Mickey Mantle, who played for 18 years, succeeded him. Here is the number of home runs by DiMaggio and Mantle:

DiMaggio: 29, 46, 32, 30, 31, 30, 21, 25, 20, 39, 14, 32, 12

Mantle: 13, 23, 21, 27, 37, 52, 34, 42, 31, 40, 54, 30, 15, 35, 19, 23, 22, 18

a. Compute the five-number summary for each player.

	Min	Q_1	Median	Q_3	Max
DiMaggio:	_____	_____	_____	_____	_____
Mantle:	_____	_____	_____	_____	_____

b. Using the same scale, draw a box-and-whisker plot for each player. (Draw one boxplot above the other.)

c. Discuss the similarities or differences of the two boxplots.

7. Given the following boxplots of three distributions, which do you think will have the smallest standard deviation?

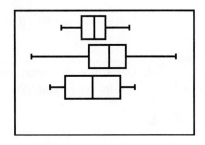

ACTIVITY 6.12

What Is Normal?

OBJECTIVES

1. Identify a normal distribution.

2. List the properties of a normal curve.

3. Determine the z-score of a given numerical data value in a normal distribution.

4. Identify the properties of a standard normal curve.

5. Solve problems using the z-scores of a standardized normal curve.

The following collection of data gives the heights, in inches, of 35 randomly selected eleventh grade male students. The measurement was made to the nearest inch.

63 64 65 65 66 66 66 67 67 67 67 67 68 68 68 68 68 68
69 69 69 69 69 70 70 70 70 71 71 72 72 73 74 75 76

1. a. Complete the following frequency distribution.

HEIGHT (in inches)	NUMBER OF ELEVENTH GRADE MALES

b. Construct a histogram from the frequency distribution in part a.

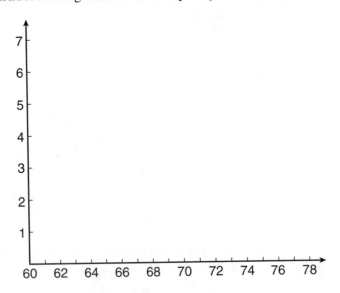

c. Does the distribution appear to be skewed or symmetrical? Explain.

d. Determine the mean, median, and mode of the given set of data. Do your results verify your conclusion in part c?

Normal Distribution

One of the most important distributions is called the **normal distribution**. The histogram for a normal distribution has the following general shape:

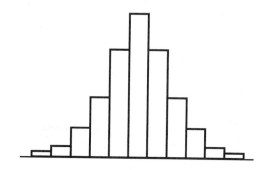

The normal distribution is important because many sets of data are normally distributed, or nearly so. Such distributions include heights and weights of males and females, measures of reading ability, intelligence quotients, scores on standardized tests, and wear-out mileage of car tires. Much of the theory in the study of statistics is based on normal distributions.

2. Is the distribution in Problem 1 normal? Explain.

When the histogram of a normal distribution is smoothed to form a curve, the curve is **bell-shaped**. This curve is called a **normal curve** and is used to model the normal distribution.

The bell can vary in size. It can be high and narrow, or short and wide. For example, each of the following graphs represents a normal curve.

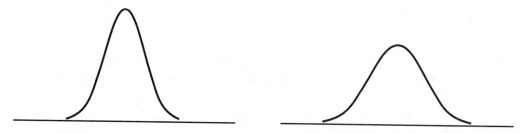

Although normal curves have a variety of sizes, all normal curves have the same basic properties. Use the normal curve given in Problem 3 to help identify some of these properties.

3. Assume the heights of all 16-year-old males are normally distributed with mean $\mu = 68$ and standard deviation $\sigma = 2$. The following normal curve represents this distribution, where x represents the height in inches.

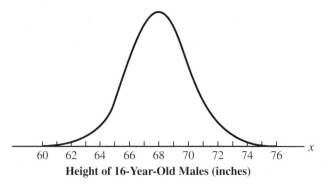

Height of 16-Year-Old Males (inches)

a. For what value of x does the maximum or highest point of the curve occur? What does this value of x correspond to in this distribution?

b. Each tick mark along the x-axis presents one inch. Locate the point on the x-axis that is one standard deviation greater than the mean.

c. If $\mu + \sigma$ represents the x-value that is one standard deviation greater than the mean, what does $\mu - \sigma$ represent? Locate the point on the graph.

d. The curve is symmetric about a vertical line through the mean μ. Describe this symmetry property of the given normal curve. What is the equation of the vertical line in this situation?

e. Since the curve is symmetrical about the mean, what is the median and mode of the height distribution? What percentage of the data points is greater than the mean? Less than the mean?

f. Approximately 68% of the data values in any normal distribution fall between $\mu - \sigma$ and $\mu + \sigma$. What percent of the data values are between μ and $\mu + \sigma$?

g. The horizontal axis is an asymptote for every normal curve. Describe what this means.

Summary of the properties of a normal curve:

1. The curve is bell-shaped with the highest point at the mean μ.

2. The curve is symmetrical about a vertical line $x = \mu$.

3. The mean, median, and mode are all equal.

4. 50% of the data values of the distribution are to the right of the mean μ; 50% of the data values are to the left of the mean μ.

5. Approximately 68% of the data values fall between $\mu - \sigma$ and $\mu + \sigma$; that is, 68% of the data values in the normal distribution are between $x = \mu - \sigma$ (one standard deviation less than the mean) and $x = \mu + \sigma$ (one standard deviation greater than the mean).

6. The normal curve model approaches the horizontal axis, but never touches or crosses the axis.

4. Use the following normal curves to answer parts a–d.

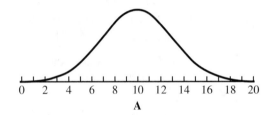

A

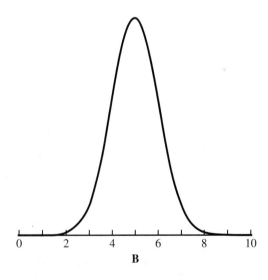

B

a. Determine the mean, median, and mode of each normal distribution.

b. One of the curves corresponds to a normal distribution with $\sigma = 3$ and the other with $\sigma = 1$. Match each curve with the correct standard deviation.

   c. For curve A, what value corresponds to each of the following:

      i. one standard deviation less than the mean, represented by $\mu - \sigma$

      ii. one standard deviation greater than the mean, represented by $\mu + \sigma$

   d. What percentage of the data in the distribution represented by curve A is between the values determined in part c?

Standard Scores

Different normal distributions vary from each other based on the values of the mean μ and standard deviation σ. The mean μ may be located anywhere on the x-axis. The bell-shape may be wide or narrow, depending on the value of the standard deviation σ. But no matter how large or small the standard deviation might be, about 68% of the data values in the normal distribution will fall within one standard deviation of the mean. Therefore, the standard deviation σ is often used as a standard unit of measurement that will allow you to compare different normal distributions.

Standard scores, also called z-scores, give the number of standard deviations that the original measurement x is from the mean, μ. The z-score formula is

$$z = \frac{x - \mu}{\sigma},$$

where $z = z$-score,

      $x = $ given data value,

      $\mu = $ mean of the x-score distribution,

      $\sigma = $ standard deviation of the x-score distribution.

Example 1   *The heights of 16-year-old males are normally distributed with mean 68 inches and standard deviation 2 inches. Determine the z-score for:*

   a. 70 inches.

   b. 66 inches.

SOLUTION

   a. Let $x = 70$, $\mu = 68$, and $\sigma = 2$. Substituting, you have

$$z = \frac{x - \mu}{\sigma} = \frac{70 - 68}{2} = \frac{2}{2} = 1.$$

   b. Let $x = 66$, $\mu = 68$, and $\sigma = 2$.

$$z = \frac{x - \mu}{\sigma} = \frac{66 - 68}{2} = \frac{-2}{2} = -1$$

Therefore, in the 16-year-old male height distribution with mean 68 and standard deviation 2, a height of 70 has a z-score of 1. This means that a height of 70 inches is one standard deviation greater than the mean of 68 inches. Similarly, a height of 66 inches has a corresponding z-score of -1. This indicates that 66 inches is one standard deviation less than the mean of 68 inches.

5. Determine the z-score for each of the following heights of 16-year-old males. Recall that this population is normally distributed with mean 68 inches and standard deviation 2 inches.

   a. 71 inches

   b. 74 inches

   c. 68 inches   **d.** 64 inches   **e.** 62 inches

6. The mean of the normal 16-year-old male height distribution is 68. The corresponding z-score (see Problem 5c) for 68 is 0. Will the mean of every normal distribution have a z-score of 0? Explain.

Data below the mean will always have negative z-scores. Data above the mean will always have positive z-scores. The mean will always have a z-score of 0.

7. Suppose the test scores on the last exam in the Liberal Arts Mathematics course are normally distributed. The z-scores for some of the students in your class were:

$$1.5, 0, -1.2, -2, 1.95, 0.5.$$

   a. List the z-scores of students that scored below the mean.

   b. List the z-scores of students that scored above the mean.

   c. If the mean of the exam was $\mu = 80$, did any of the students selected above have an exam score of 80? Explain.

    d. Which z-score represents the student that scored the highest among the students selected above? Explain.

    e. If the standard deviation of the exam was $\sigma = 5$, what was the actual test score for the student having z-score 1.95?

If the original distribution of x-values is normal, then the corresponding z-values will be normally distributed. The z-distribution will have a mean of $\mu = 0$ and a standard deviation of $\sigma = 1$.

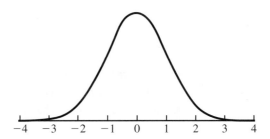

The resulting curve is called the **standard normal curve**.

SUMMARY
Activity 6.12

1. **Normal curve** is a **bell-shaped** curve that is symmetric about its mean. The mean, mode, and median in a normal distribution are the same. Each normal distribution can be modeled by a corresponding normal curve.

2. 50% of the data values of a normal distribution are greater than the mean μ; 50% of the data values are less than the mean μ.

3. Approximately 68% of the data values fall between $\mu - \sigma$ and $\mu + \sigma$; that is, 68% of the data values in the normal distribution are between $x = \mu - \sigma$ (one standard deviation less than the mean) and $x = \mu + \sigma$ (one standard deviation greater than the mean).

4. The normal curve model approaches the horizontal axis, but never touches or crosses the axis.

5. A normal curve can have any mean and any standard deviation; however, a **standardized normal curve** has $\mu = 0$ and $\sigma = 1$.

6. **Standard scores,** also called z-scores, indicate the number of standard deviations that the original measurement x is from the mean μ of the normal distribution.

7. The z-score formula is: $z = \dfrac{x - \mu}{\sigma}$,

     where $z = z$-score,

           $x =$ given data value,

           $\mu =$ mean of the x-score distribution,

           $\sigma =$ standard deviation of the x-score distribution.

8. The mean of a normal distribution always has z-score 0. The values in any normal distribution that are below the mean have negative z-scores; those above the mean have positive z-scores.

EXERCISES
Activity 6.12

1. A normal distribution has a mean $\mu = 100$ and standard deviation $\sigma = 10$. Determine the z-score for each of the following x-values.

   a. 110   **b.** 125   **c.** 100

   d. 90   **e.** 85

2. The high school physical education department offers an advanced first-aid course. The scores of the first exam were normally distributed. The z-scores for some of the students are shown below:

$$1.10,\ 1.70,\ -2.00,\ 0.00,\ -0.80,\ 1.60$$

   a. Which of these students scored above the mean?

   b. Which of these students had a test score equal to the mean of the exam?

   c. Which of these students scored below the mean?

   d. If the mean score was $\mu = 150$ with standard deviation $\sigma = 20$, what was the exam score for the student having z-score 1.70?

3. Students who drive to school are randomly selected. Each participant is asked the "arrival" time (in minutes) it takes to drive from their home, park the car, and enter the high school building. After analyzing the data, it is determined that the data is normally distributed with mean 20 minutes and standard deviation 3 minutes.

   a. If the arrival time is 26 minutes, determine the corresponding z-score.

   b. If the arrival time is 14 minutes, determine the corresponding z-score.

   c. If the arrival time is 20 minutes, determine the corresponding z-score. Is this answer to be expected? Explain.

   d. If the arrival time is 25 minutes, determine the corresponding z-score.

   e. If the arrival time is less than 20 minutes, is the corresponding z-score positive or negative?

   f. If the z-score for a certain arrival time is positive, then what can you determine about the value of the arrival time?

4. Your z-score on a college entrance exam is 1.3. If the x-scores on the exam have a mean of 480 and a standard deviation of 70 points, what is your x-score?

5. If a z-score is less than -2 ($z < -2$) or more than 2 ($z > 2$), the corresponding x-value is considered "unusual." If $z < -3 \; or \; z > 3$, then the corresponding x-value is considered "very unusual."

   a. Assume the white blood cell count per cubic millimeter of whole blood has a distribution that is approximately normal with mean $\mu = 7500$ and standard deviation $\sigma = 1750$. If someone had a white blood count of 3500, would that be considered unusually low?

b. If the red blood cell count in millions per cubic millimeter has an approximately normal distribution with mean $\mu = 4.8$ and standard deviation $\sigma = 0.3$, would a red blood count of 5.9 or higher be considered unusually high?

6. a. You score 680 on the mathematics portion of the SAT. If the math scores on the SAT are normally distributed with mean $\mu = 518$ and standard deviation $\sigma = 114$, determine the corresponding z-score for $x = 680$.

b. Your friend scores 27 on the ACT assessment mathematics test. If the ACT math scores are normally distributed with mean $\mu = 20.7$ and standard deviation 5.0, determine the corresponding z-score for $x = 27$.

c. Assume the tests both measure the same kind of ability. Compare the z-scores in parts a and b to determine who scored higher.

Activities 6.7–6.12 What Have I Learned?

1. A voluntary response sample (or self-selected sample) is one in which individuals decide to be included in the sample. Will such a sampling technique result in a biased example? Explain.

2. You want to determine the average family size of households in Florida. You collect data consisting of the number of siblings from students in your high school. Regardless of the sampling technique used, is the sample representative of all households in the state?

3. Determine if the following sampling techniques result in a random sampling. Explain why or why not.

   a. Your teacher obtains a sample by selecting the first six students entering the classroom.

   b. Your math classroom consists of 30 students in six different rows. Your teacher rolls a die to determine a row, then rolls the die again to select a particular student in the row. This process is repeated until a sample of 6 students is obtained.

4. Which do you think has more variation: the IQ scores of 20 randomly selected graduating college seniors or the IQ scores of 20 randomly selected adults entering the local mall? Explain.

5. Does adding the same number to each value of a set of data affect the measure of variability for that set of data?

6. Which distribution has greater variability?

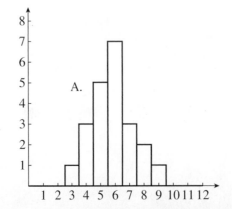
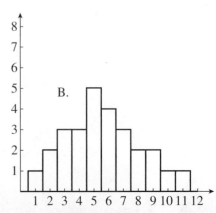

7. a. Use a graphing calculator to determine the mean and standard deviation of the following two data sets:

DATA I	9.14	8.14	8.74	8.77	9.26	8.10	6.13	3.10	9.13	7.26	4.74
DATA 2	6.58	5.76	7.71	8.84	8.47	7.04	5.25	5.56	7.91	6.89	12.50

b. Construct a stem-and-leaf plot of each distribution and compare the shapes of the distribution.

8. For a given data set, is the second quartile, Q_2, always the same as the median of the data? Explain.

9. Does the following histogram represent a distribution that is approximately normal? Explain.

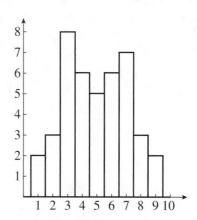

10. Identify the following distributions as skewed to the left, normal, or skewed to the right.

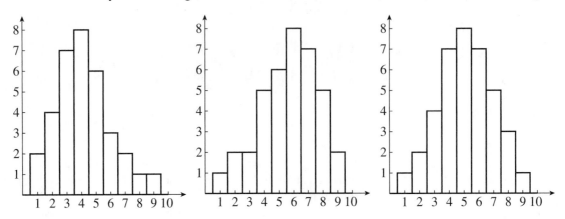

11. A value from a large data set has a corresponding z-score of -2. Is the data value greater than or less than the mean of the data set?

12. For a standard normal distribution:

  a. What is the mean μ and standard deviation σ of the distribution?

  b. Determine the positive z-score that is two standard deviation from the mean on the z-axis.

  c. Determine the percentage of z-scores that are within 1 standard deviation of the mean. That is, the percentage of z-scores between $z = -1$ and $z = 1$?

13. Heights of males are normally distributed. If the heights (x-values) are measured in units of inches, what are the units for the z-scores that correspond to specific heights?

Activities 6.7–6.12   How Can I Practice?

1. Consider the following data: 12, 8, 9, 10, 12, 9

   Determine the standard deviation by filling in the table as part of your calculation.

x	$\bar{x}$	$x - \bar{x}$	$(x - \bar{x})^2$

2. The following speeds of 21 cars are recorded as they pass a concealed marker on an interstate highway that has a legal speed limit of 65 mph: 73, 67, 69, 65, 64, 77, 59, 74, 71, 67, 70, 58, 67, 69, 71, 70, 69, 64, 85, 67, and 64. Determine the five-number summary and produce the boxplot.

3. The management of Disney World would like to determine the amount of waiting time for the rides at Space Mountain. The following data represents a random sample of waiting times in minutes (rounded to the nearest half-minute):

   4.0 5.5 9.5 5.0 13.5 6.5 8.5 9.0 9.5 12.0 8.0 7.5

   a. What is the mean waiting time for the ride?

   b. What is the standard deviation?

4. Sandy Allen is the world's tallest woman having a height of 91.25 inches (7 feet, 7.25 inches). The heights of adult females are normally distributed with mean $\mu = 63.6$ inches and a standard deviation $\sigma = 2.5$ inches. Determine the z-score corresponding to Sandy Allen's height.

The bracketed numbers following each concept indicate the activity in which the concept is discussed.

CONCEPT / SKILL	DESCRIPTION	EXAMPLE
Line graph [6.1]	When data points are plotted and connected with line segments to better show a trend.	
Bar graph [6.1], [6.2], [6.3]	A plot of data where the number of data values falling in a category is represented by the height or length of a rectangle, or bar.	
Circle graph [6.3]	Displays the relative number of data values in each category by the size of the corresponding sector, or slice.	
Stacked bar graph [6.2]	When paired data separates a bar into two parts, to show relative sizes for each category.	
Frequency table [6.4]	A table that displays the number of times (the frequency) a data value occurs.	Score: 6 7 8 9 10 Freq.: 2 6 8 5 3
Dot plot [6.4]	The frequency is measured on the vertical scale, one dot for each data value.	
Histogram [6.4]	Displays the frequency of each category of data, with each rectangle's height giving the frequency.	

Frequency distribution [6.4]	Any collection of data that has been organized according to how frequently each data value occurs, in a table or graph.	
Measures of the central tendency of a frequency distribution [6.5]	An indication, or measurement, of the approximate location of the center or middle of a collection of data.	Mean, median, mode, and midrange are all different ways of measuring the center.
Mean [6.5]	The usual average found by adding the data values and dividing by the number of values.	The mean of $\{1, 3, 4, 8, 10\}$ is $(1 + 3 + 4 + 8 + 10)/5 = 5.2$.
Median [6.5]	The exact middle of the numerically ordered data; half the data values lie above and half lie below the median. (If there is an even number of data values, the median is the mean of the two middle values.)	The median of $\{1, 3, 4, 8, 10\}$ is 4.
Mode [6.5]	The data value that occurs most frequently.	The mode of $\{1, 3, 3, 3, 5, 7, 7\}$ is 3.
Midrange [6.5]	The exact midpoint between the lowest and highest data values.	The midrange of $\{1, 3, 4, 8, 10\}$ is $(1 + 10)/2 = 5.5$.
Simple random sample (SRS) [6.7]	A sample that is selected where every possible sample of a given size has an equal chance of being selected.	
Bias in a sample [6.7], [6.8]	When some individuals in a population have a greater chance of being selected for a sample than others.	
Sampling plan [6.7], [6.8], [6.9]	A detailed step-by-step procedure to collect data through a specific sampling method.	
Stratified sample [6.8]	When a population is separated into two or more strata, with a SRS selected from each, proportional to the relative size of each strata.	
Experimental Design [6.10]	To establish a cause-and-effect relationship between two variables through control, randomization, and replication.	
Control group [6.10]	The individuals in an experiment that do not receive the treatment.	

Double-blind [6.10]	Desirable in a good experiment, when all individuals involved in the study, subjects, administrators and evaluators, have no knowledge of which subjects are receiving the treatment.	
Placebo-effect [6.10]	When a human responds positively to a false treatment (normally in the control group).	
Variability of a frequency distribution [6.10]	Refers to how spread out the data is, away from the center.	$\{1, 4, 7, 13, 25, 34\}$ has greater variability than $\{3, 3, 3, 4, 4, 5\}$.
Range of a frequency distribution [6.10]	The difference between the minimum and maximum data values.	The range of $\{1, 3, 4, 8, 10\}$ is $10 - 1 = 9$.
Deviation of a data value [6.11]	Refers to how far a data value is from the mean.	In the data set $\{1, 3, 4, 8, 10\}$, the deviation of 10 is $10 - 5.2 = 4.8$.
Standard deviation [6.11]	A measure of how far all the data collectively is from the mean. A standard deviation of zero means all the data is the same number (the mean); there is no variation.	$\sigma = \sqrt{\dfrac{\sum (x - \bar{x})^2}{n}}$ For $\{1, 3, 4, 8, 10\}$, $\sigma \approx 3.31$.
Five-number summary for a distribution [6.11]	The minimum, first quartile, median, third quartile, and maximum data value for a distribution.	
Boxplot [6.11]	A graph that displays the five-number summary for a distribution.	
Standard normal curve (distribution) [6.12]	A bell-shaped curve representing a normal distribution with $\mu = 0$ and $\sigma = 1$.	
Standard (z) scores [6.12]	The number of standard deviations a data value is from the mean of normal distribution.	$z = \dfrac{x - \mu}{\sigma}$, where $x =$ data value, $\mu =$ mean, $\sigma =$ standard deviation

1. The weights, in pounds, of a group of workers are as follows:

173	123	171	175	188	120	177	160	151	169
162	128	145	140	158	132	202	162	154	180
164	166	157	171	175					

Determine the mean, standard deviation, and five-number summary for these data. Decide on a scale and draw a boxplot. Check your answers with your calculator.

2. **a.** Determine the mean, median, mode, and midrange for this collection of class test scores:

88	82	97	76	79	92	65	84	79
90	75	82	78	77	93	88	95	73
69	89	93	78	60	95	88	72	80
94	88	74						

   b. From these measures of central tendency, would you guess that the distribution is symmetrical, skewed to the left, or skewed to the right? Check your answer by displaying the histogram and/or boxplot on your grapher.

3. The ages of 10 randomly selected NASCAR drivers are listed.
33, 48, 41, 29, 40, 48, 44, 42, 49, 28

   a. Determine the mean age of the 10 drivers.

   b. Determine the median age.

   c. Determine the mode, if it exists.

   d. Determine the midrange of the ages of the 10 drivers.

e. Determine the standard deviation of the ages of the 10 NASCAR drivers.

f. Verify your results in parts a–d using a graphing calculator.

4. A company is receiving complaints from customers about the amount of time waiting on hold when attempting to contact customer service. A sample of 40 customers are randomly selected and the amount of time on hold when calling customer service is recorded (in minutes).

0.5	4.6	5.5	6.3	6.8	7.8	8.9	10.1
1.6	4.6	5.6	6.3	6.9	8.0	9.2	10.5
3.2	4.9	6.0	6.4	7.0	8.3	9.3	10.6
3.7	5.1	6.0	6.5	7.2	8.6	9.4	11.0
4.3	5.3	6.2	6.5	7.5	8.6	9.7	11.3

a. Using 0–1.9 as the first class width, construct a histogram of the data.

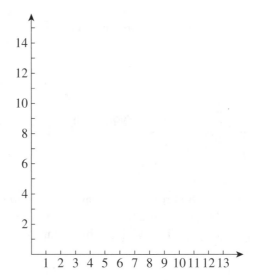

b. Describe the shape of the distribution.

c. Determine the mean of the sample.

d. Determine the standard deviation.

CHAPTER 7

Problem Solving with Financial Models

ACTIVITY 7.1
Income and
Expenses

OBJECTIVE

1. Solve problems involving
   personal finances.

You are starting your first job in Syracuse, New York, as a salesperson at a sporting goods store. Your income consists of a base salary of $8.00 per hour with time and a half for more than 40 hours per week and double time for holidays. You also receive a 3% commission on total sales.

1. Based on a 5-day week, 8-hour day, and 52-week year, determine your annual gross base salary.

2. You are paid biweekly. What is your gross base salary per pay period?

Example 1 *If the Social Security tax is 6.2% of gross income, determine the amount of your Social Security deduction (6.2% = 0.062) in each pay period.*

SOLUTION

$0.062(640) = 39.68$ The amount of the Social Security deduction is $39.68.

3. **a.** If Medicare is 1.45% of gross income, determine your Medicare deduction (1.45% = 0.0145) in each pay period.

   b. Use the tax tables on the following three pages to determine the federal and state biweekly deductions for a single person earning $640 biweekly and claiming zero for withholding allowances.

   c. Union dues of ten dollars per pay period are also deducted. Determine the total of all deductions in each pay period.

   d. What is your net base salary per pay period?

SINGLE Persons—BIWEEKLY Payroll Period

If the wages are—		And the number of withholding allowances claimed is—										
At least	But less than	0	1	2	3	4	5	6	7	8	9	10
		The amount of income tax to be withheld is—										
$0	$105	$0	$0	$0	$0	$0	$0	$0	$0	$0	$0	$0
105	110	1	0	0	0	0	0	0	0	0	0	0
110	115	1	0	0	0	0	0	0	0	0	0	0
115	120	2	0	0	0	0	0	0	0	0	0	0
120	125	2	0	0	0	0	0	0	0	0	0	0
125	130	3	0	0	0	0	0	0	0	0	0	0
130	135	3	0	0	0	0	0	0	0	0	0	0
135	140	4	0	0	0	0	0	0	0	0	0	0
140	145	4	0	0	0	0	0	0	0	0	0	0
145	150	5	0	0	0	0	0	0	0	0	0	0
150	155	5	0	0	0	0	0	0	0	0	0	0
155	160	6	0	0	0	0	0	0	0	0	0	0
160	165	6	0	0	0	0	0	0	0	0	0	0
165	170	7	0	0	0	0	0	0	0	0	0	0
170	175	7	0	0	0	0	0	0	0	0	0	0
175	180	8	0	0	0	0	0	0	0	0	0	0
180	185	8	0	0	0	0	0	0	0	0	0	0
185	190	9	0	0	0	0	0	0	0	0	0	0
190	195	9	0	0	0	0	0	0	0	0	0	0
195	200	10	0	0	0	0	0	0	0	0	0	0
200	205	10	0	0	0	0	0	0	0	0	0	0
205	210	11	0	0	0	0	0	0	0	0	0	0
210	215	11	0	0	0	0	0	0	0	0	0	0
215	220	12	0	0	0	0	0	0	0	0	0	0
220	225	12	0	0	0	0	0	0	0	0	0	0
225	230	13	0	0	0	0	0	0	0	0	0	0
230	235	13	1	0	0	0	0	0	0	0	0	0
235	240	14	1	0	0	0	0	0	0	0	0	0
240	245	14	2	0	0	0	0	0	0	0	0	0
245	250	15	2	0	0	0	0	0	0	0	0	0
250	260	15	3	0	0	0	0	0	0	0	0	0
260	270	16	4	0	0	0	0	0	0	0	0	0
270	280	17	5	0	0	0	0	0	0	0	0	0
280	290	18	6	0	0	0	0	0	0	0	0	0
290	300	19	7	0	0	0	0	0	0	0	0	0
300	310	20	8	0	0	0	0	0	0	0	0	0
310	320	21	9	0	0	0	0	0	0	0	0	0
320	330	22	11	0	0	0	0	0	0	0	0	0
330	340	23	11	0	0	0	0	0	0	0	0	0
340	350	24	12	0	0	0	0	0	0	0	0	0
350	360	25	13	1	0	0	0	0	0	0	0	0
360	370	26	14	2	0	0	0	0	0	0	0	0
370	380	27	15	3	0	0	0	0	0	0	0	0
380	390	29	16	4	0	0	0	0	0	0	0	0
390	400	30	17	5	0	0	0	0	0	0	0	0
400	410	32	18	6	0	0	0	0	0	0	0	0
410	420	33	19	7	0	0	0	0	0	0	0	0
420	430	35	20	8	0	0	0	0	0	0	0	0
430	440	36	21	9	0	0	0	0	0	0	0	0
440	450	38	22	10	0	0	0	0	0	0	0	0
450	460	39	23	11	0	0	0	0	0	0	0	0
460	470	41	24	12	0	0	0	0	0	0	0	0
470	480	42	25	13	0	0	0	0	0	0	0	0
480	490	44	26	14	1	0	0	0	0	0	0	0
490	500	45	27	15	2	0	0	0	0	0	0	0
500	520	47	29	16	4	0	0	0	0	0	0	0
520	540	50	32	18	6	0	0	0	0	0	0	0
540	560	53	35	20	8	0	0	0	0	0	0	0
560	580	56	38	22	10	0	0	0	0	0	0	0
580	600	59	41	24	12	0	0	0	0	0	0	0
600	620	62	44	26	14	2	0	0	0	0	0	0
620	640	65	47	29	16	4	0	0	0	0	0	0
640	660	68	50	32	18	6	0	0	0	0	0	0
660	680	71	53	35	20	8	0	0	0	0	0	0
680	700	74	56	38	22	10	0	0	0	0	0	0
700	720	77	59	41	24	12	0	0	0	0	0	0
720	740	80	62	44	26	14	1	0	0	0	0	0
740	760	83	65	47	28	16	3	0	0	0	0	0
760	780	86	68	50	31	18	5	0	0	0	0	0
780	800	89	71	53	34	20	7	0	0	0	0	0

SINGLE Persons—BIWEEKLY Payroll Period

If the wages are—		And the number of withholding allowances claimed is—										
At least	But less than	0	1	2	3	4	5	6	7	8	9	10
		The amount of income tax to be withheld is—										
$800	$820	$92	$74	$56	$37	$22	$0	$0	$0	$0	$0	$0
820	840	95	77	59	40	24	11	0	0	0	0	0
840	860	98	80	62	43	26	13	1	0	0	0	0
860	880	101	83	65	46	28	15	3	0	0	0	0
880	900	104	86	68	49	31	17	5	0	0	0	0
900	920	107	89	71	52	34	19	7	0	0	0	0
920	940	110	92	74	55	37	21	9	0	0	0	0
940	960	113	95	77	58	40	23	11	0	0	0	0
960	980	116	98	80	61	43	25	13	1	0	0	0
980	1,000	119	101	83	64	46	27	15	3	0	0	0
1,000	1,050	122	104	86	67	49	30	17	5	0	0	0
1,050	1,040	125	107	89	70	52	33	19	7	0	0	0
1,040	1,060	128	110	92	73	55	36	21	9	0	0	0
1,060	1,080	131	113	95	76	58	39	23	11	0	0	0
1,080	1,100	134	116	98	79	61	42	25	13	0	0	0
1,100	1,120	137	119	101	82	64	45	27	15	2	0	0
1,120	1,140	140	122	104	85	67	48	30	17	4	0	0
1,140	1,160	143	125	107	88	70	51	33	19	6	0	0
1,160	1,180	146	128	110	91	73	54	36	21	8	0	0
1,180	1,200	149	131	113	94	76	57	39	23	10	0	0
1,200	1,220	152	134	116	97	79	60	42	25	12	0	0
1,220	1,240	157	137	119	100	82	63	45	27	14	2	0
1,240	1,260	162	140	122	103	85	66	48	29	16	4	0
1,260	1,280	167	143	125	106	88	69	51	32	18	6	0
1,280	1,300	172	146	128	109	91	72	54	35	20	8	0
1,300	1,320	177	149	131	112	94	75	57	38	22	10	0
1,320	1,340	182	152	134	115	97	78	60	41	24	12	0
1,340	1,360	187	157	137	118	100	81	63	44	26	14	2
1,360	1,380	192	162	140	121	103	84	66	47	29	16	4
1,380	1,400	197	167	143	124	106	87	69	50	32	18	6
1,400	1,420	202	172	146	127	109	90	72	53	35	20	8
1,420	1,440	207	177	149	130	112	93	75	56	38	22	10
1,440	1,460	212	182	152	133	115	96	78	59	41	24	12
1,460	1,480	217	187	156	136	118	99	81	62	44	26	14
1,480	1,500	222	192	161	139	121	102	84	65	47	28	16
1,500	1,520	227	197	166	142	124	105	87	68	50	31	18
1,520	1,540	232	202	171	145	127	108	90	71	53	34	20
1,540	1,560	237	207	176	148	130	111	93	74	56	37	22
1,560	1,580	242	212	181	151	133	114	96	77	59	40	24
1,580	1,600	247	217	186	155	136	117	99	80	62	43	26
1,600	1,620	252	222	191	160	139	120	102	83	65	46	28
1,620	1,640	257	227	196	165	142	123	105	86	68	49	31
1,640	1,660	262	232	201	170	145	126	108	89	71	52	34
1,660	1,680	267	237	206	175	148	129	111	92	74	55	37
1,680	1,700	272	242	211	180	151	132	114	95	77	58	40
1,700	1,720	277	247	216	185	154	135	117	98	80	61	43
1,720	1,740	282	252	221	190	159	138	120	101	83	64	46
1,740	1,760	287	257	226	195	164	141	123	104	86	67	49
1,760	1,780	292	262	231	200	169	144	126	107	89	70	52
1,780	1,800	297	267	236	205	174	147	129	110	92	73	55
1,800	1,820	302	272	241	210	179	150	132	113	95	76	58
1,820	1,840	307	277	246	215	184	153	135	116	98	79	61
1,840	1,860	312	282	251	220	189	158	138	119	101	82	64
1,860	1,880	317	287	256	225	194	163	141	122	104	85	67
1,880	1,900	322	292	261	230	199	168	144	125	107	88	70
1,900	1,920	327	297	266	235	204	173	147	128	110	91	73
1,920	1,940	332	302	271	240	209	178	150	131	113	94	76
1,940	1,960	337	307	276	245	214	183	153	134	116	97	79
1,960	1,980	342	312	281	250	219	188	158	137	119	100	82
1,980	2,000	347	317	286	255	224	193	163	140	122	103	85
2,000	2,020	352	322	291	260	229	198	168	143	125	106	88
2,020	2,040	357	327	296	265	234	203	173	146	128	109	91
2,040	2,060	362	332	301	270	239	208	178	149	131	112	94
2,060	2,080	367	337	306	275	244	213	183	152	134	115	97
2,080	2,100	372	342	311	280	249	218	188	157	137	118	100

New York State Tax Table

T-4

Method I

Table II

NY STATE
Income Tax

SINGLE

BIWEEKLY
Payroll Period

WAGES		EXEMPTIONS CLAIMED										10 or more
At Least	But Less Than	0	1	2	3	4	5	6	7	8	9	
		TAX TO BE WITHHELD										
$0	$200	$0.00										
200	210	0.00										
210	220	0.00										
220	230	0.00	$0.00									
230	240	0.00	0.00									
240	250	0.00	0.00									
250	260	0.00	0.00									
260	270	0.00	0.00	$0.00								
270	280	0.30	0.00	0.00								
280	290	0.70	0.00	0.00								
290	300	1.10	0.00	0.00								
300	320	1.70	0.10	0.00	$0.00							
320	340	2.50	0.90	0.00	0.00							
340	360	3.30	1.70	0.20	0.00	$0.00						
360	380	4.10	2.50	1.00	0.00	0.00						
380	400	4.90	3.30	1.80	0.30	0.00	$0.00					
400	420	5.70	4.10	2.60	1.10	0.00	0.00					
420	440	6.50	4.90	3.40	1.90	0.30	0.00	$0.00				
440	460	7.30	5.70	4.20	2.70	1.10	0.00	0.00	$0.00			
460	480	8.10	6.50	5.00	3.50	1.90	0.40	0.00	0.00			
480	500	8.90	7.30	5.80	4.30	2.70	1.20	0.00	0.00	$0.00		
500	520	9.70	8.10	6.60	5.10	3.50	2.00	0.40	0.00	0.00		
520	540	10.50	8.90	7.40	5.90	4.30	2.80	1.20	0.00	0.00	$0.00	
540	560	11.30	9.70	8.20	6.70	5.10	3.60	2.00	0.50	0.00	0.00	
560	580	12.10	10.50	9.00	7.50	5.90	4.40	2.80	1.30	0.00	0.00	$0.00
580	600	12.90	11.30	9.80	8.30	6.70	5.20	3.60	2.10	0.60	0.00	0.00
600	620	13.80	12.10	10.60	9.10	7.50	6.00	4.40	2.90	1.40	0.00	0.00
620	640	14.70	13.00	11.40	9.90	8.30	6.80	5.20	3.70	2.20	0.60	0.00
640	660	15.60	13.90	12.20	10.70	9.10	7.60	6.00	4.50	3.00	1.40	0.00
660	680	16.50	14.80	13.10	11.50	9.90	8.40	6.80	5.30	3.80	2.20	0.70
680	700	17.40	15.70	14.00	12.30	10.70	9.20	7.60	6.10	4.60	3.00	1.50
700	720	18.50	16.60	14.90	13.10	11.50	10.00	8.40	6.90	5.40	3.80	2.30
720	740	19.50	17.50	15.80	14.00	12.30	10.80	9.20	7.70	6.20	4.60	3.10
740	760	20.60	18.60	16.70	14.90	13.20	11.60	10.00	8.50	7.00	5.40	3.90
760	780	21.60	19.60	17.60	15.80	14.10	12.40	10.80	9.30	7.80	6.20	4.70
780	800	22.80	20.70	18.60	16.70	15.00	13.30	11.60	10.10	8.60	7.00	5.50
800	820	24.00	21.70	19.70	17.70	15.90	14.20	12.50	10.90	9.40	7.80	6.30
820	840	25.20	22.90	20.70	18.70	16.80	15.10	13.40	11.70	10.20	8.60	7.10
840	860	26.40	24.10	21.80	19.80	17.80	16.00	14.30	12.50	11.00	9.40	7.90
860	880	27.50	25.30	23.00	20.80	18.80	16.90	15.20	13.40	11.80	10.20	8.70
880	900	28.70	26.50	24.20	21.90	19.90	17.80	16.10	14.30	12.60	11.00	9.50
900	920	29.90	27.60	25.40	23.10	20.90	18.90	17.00	15.20	13.50	11.80	10.30
920	940	31.10	28.80	26.50	24.30	22.00	19.90	17.90	16.10	14.40	12.70	11.10
940	960	32.30	30.00	27.70	25.50	23.20	21.00	19.00	17.00	15.30	13.60	11.90
960	980	33.40	31.20	28.90	26.60	24.40	22.10	20.00	18.00	16.20	14.50	12.70
980	1,000	34.60	32.40	30.10	27.80	25.50	23.30	21.10	19.00	17.10	15.40	13.60
1,000	1,020	35.80	33.50	31.30	29.00	26.70	24.50	22.20	20.10	18.10	16.30	14.50
1,020	1,040	37.00	34.70	32.40	30.20	27.90	25.60	23.40	21.10	19.10	17.20	15.40
1,040	1,060	38.30	35.90	33.60	31.40	29.10	26.80	24.50	22.30	20.20	18.20	16.30
1,060	1,080	39.60	37.10	34.80	32.50	30.30	28.00	25.70	23.50	21.20	19.20	17.20
1,080	1,100	41.00	38.40	36.00	33.70	31.40	29.20	26.90	24.60	22.40	20.30	18.20
1,100	1,120	42.40	39.80	37.20	34.90	32.60	30.40	28.10	25.80	23.50	21.30	19.30
1,120	1,140	43.80	41.10	38.50	36.10	33.80	31.50	29.30	27.00	24.70	22.50	20.30
1,140	1,160	45.10	42.50	39.90	37.30	35.00	32.70	30.40	28.20	25.90	23.60	21.40
1,160	1,180	46.50	43.90	41.20	38.60	36.20	33.90	31.60	29.40	27.10	24.80	22.50
1,180	1,200	47.90	45.20	42.60	40.00	37.30	35.10	32.80	30.50	28.30	26.00	23.70
1,200	1,220	49.20	46.60	44.00	41.30	38.70	36.30	34.00	31.70	29.40	27.20	24.90
1,220	1,240	50.60	48.00	45.30	42.70	40.10	37.40	35.20	32.90	30.60	28.40	26.10
1,240	1,260	52.00	49.30	46.70	44.10	41.40	38.80	36.30	34.10	31.80	29.50	27.30
1,260	1,280	53.30	50.70	48.10	45.40	42.80	40.20	37.50	35.30	33.00	30.70	28.40
1,280	1,300	54.70	52.10	49.50	46.80	44.20	41.50	38.90	36.40	34.20	31.90	29.60
1,300	3,460	6.85% (.0685) of the excess over $1,300 plus:										
		55.40	52.80	50.10	47.50	44.90	42.20	39.60	37.00	34.80	32.50	30.20
$3,460 & OVER		Use Method II, "Exact Calculation Method," on page T-13 of this booklet										

4. During the first pay period of a certain month, you work 10 days. Two of these days are holidays (HOL). During the second pay period, you work 10 days, and on four occasions you work overtime (OT), accumulating $2\frac{1}{4}$, $4\frac{2}{3}$, $5\frac{1}{2}$, and $3\frac{3}{4}$ hours overtime. Calculate your net pay for these pay periods by filling in the accompanying table.

Reminder: Use 6.2% (6.2% = 0.062) for Social Security, 1.45% (1.45% = 0.0145) for Medicare, and the tables for federal and state taxes. Don't forget the union dues.

Where Does It All Go?	FIRST PAY PERIOD	SECOND PAY PERIOD
Gross Base ($)		
Gross OT/Hol. ($)		
Total Gross ($)		
Federal Income Tax ($)		
State Income Tax ($)		
Social Security Tax ($)		
Medicare ($)		
Union Dues ($)		
Total Net ($)		

5. You sell $10,000 worth of merchandise during each pay period this month.

   a. What is your total commission (3% = 0.03)?

   b. Your commission is paid to you in a separate paycheck. Calculate your take-home pay for commission for this month. (Remember that federal and state tax tables are based on biweekly payroll periods.)

   c. What is your total take-home pay for the month in Problem 4, including commission?

6. a. You want to purchase a new TV that costs $549 plus 7% sales tax. You plan to save your overtime pay to purchase the TV outright and not pay monthly installments on the bill. Estimate the number of hours you need to work to yield enough net overtime pay to purchase the TV.

(Use 3% = 0.03 state income tax and 13% = 0.13 federal income tax, plus 6.2% = 0.062 Soc. Sec. and 1.45% = 0.0145 Medicare.)

b. Your overtime hours for the month in Problem 4 are a reasonable estimate of the hours you work each month. How many months of saving will it take for you to purchase the TV?

7. You are trying not to go any further into debt, and you want to pay off some of your debts. Each month you analyze how you spend your money and categorize your expenses under the following headings: (1) household, (2) medical, (3) entertainment, (4) loans, (5) insurance, (6) personal, and (7) miscellaneous.

You recorded the actual expenses you incurred for a previous month in the following list. The number in parentheses indicates the category of the expense.

car payment (4), $125	rent (1), $300
car insurance (5), $72	utilities (1), $140
parking (7), $50	movies (3), $20
bowling (3), $60	towels (1), $22
shoes (6), $43	student loan (4), $60
dentist (2), $30	film (7), $5
groceries (1), $150	savings (6), $100
credit-card debt (4), $50	medicines (2), $47
bank charges (7), $7	clothes (6), $110
gas/car (7), $80	restaurant/fast food (3), $80

a. If computers are accessible, create a spreadsheet; otherwise, use the accompanying table to group the information. List the given expenses in the appropriate columns in the table.

Life by the Numbers

HOUSEHOLD (1)	MEDICAL (2)	ENTERTAINMENT (3)	LOANS (4)	INSURANCE (5)	PERSONAL (6)	MISC. (7)
Totals:						

b. Do you think that the expenses you incurred this month will be consistent with the month in part a? Explain.

c. What are your total expenses for the month?

d. Will you have enough income to cover your expenses this month? Explain.

e. You are considering a move to another apartment that has two bedrooms. How much more do you think you can afford to pay, based on your calculated income and expenses? Will the move be possible?

ACTIVITY 7.2

Time Is Money

1. a. Suppose $10,000 is deposited in a bank at 6.5% annual interest. What is the interest earned after one year?

b. Suppose you left the money in the account for 10 years. Can the total amount of interest on your investment be calculated by multiplying your answer in part a by 10? What assumption are you making if you said yes?

If you have money invested at **simple interest**, the interest earned during the first period does not earn interest for the rest of the life of the investment. Therefore, at 6.5% simple annual interest, an investment of $10,000 would earn a total interest of $10,000(0.065)(10) = \$6,500$.

The interest paid on savings accounts in most banks is **compound interest**. The interest earned for each period is added to the previous principal before the next interest calculation is made. Simply stated, interest earns interest.

For example, if you deposit $10,000 in the bank at 6.5%, the balance after one year is

$$10,000 + 0.065(10,000) = 10,000 + 650 = \$10,650.$$

The interest, $650, earned during the year becomes part of the new balance. At the end of the second year, your balance is

$$10,650 + 0.065(10,650) = 10,650 + 692.25 = \$11,342.25.$$

Note that you made interest on the original deposit, plus interest on the first year's interest. In this situation, we say that interest is compounded. Usually, the compounding occurs at fixed intervals (typically at the end of every year, quarter, month, or day). In this example, interest is compounded annually.

If interest is compounded, then the current balance is given by the formula

$$A = P\left(1 + \tfrac{r}{n}\right)^{nt},$$

where A is the current balance or compound amount in the account,
   P is the principal (the original amount deposited),
   r is the annual interest rate (in decimal form),
   n is the number of times per year that interest is compounded, and
   t is the time in years the money has been invested.

The given formula for the compound amount A is called the **compound interest formula**.

Example 1   *You invest $2000 at 8% compounded quarterly. How much money do you have after five years?*

SOLUTION

The principal is $2000; so $P = 2000$. The annual interest rate is 8%; so $r = 0.08$. Interest is compounded quarterly; that is, four times per year, so $n = 4$. The money is invested for five years; so $t = 5$. Substituting numbers for the variables in the preceding formula, you have

$$A = 2000(1 + \tfrac{0.08}{4})^{4 \cdot 5} = \$2971.89.$$

The amount $A = \$2971.90$ in Example 1 is called the **future value** of the investment.

2. **a.** Suppose you deposit $10,000 in an account that has a 6.5% annual interest rate and whose interest is compounded annually ($n = 1$). Substitute the appropriate values for the variables into the compound interest formula to verify that the balance A at the end of the second year is $11,342.25.

   b. Suppose you deposit the $10,000 into an account that has the same interest rate of 6.5%, with compounding quarterly ($n = 4$) rather than annually ($n = 1$). Write a new formula for your balance, A, as a function of time.

   c. What would be your balance after 5 years?

   d. Now deposit your $10,000 into a 6.5% account with *monthly* compounding ($n = 12$). Use your graphing calculator and the appropriate formula to determine your balance after 5 years.

Future Value Using Technology

Your TI-83/84 Plus graphing calculator has several built-in functions to help you solve many of the finance problems encountered in this chapter. To access the finance applications menu, press APPS,

followed by (ENTER).

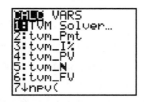

Next, press (ENTER) to select option 1: TVM Solver . . . The following screen will appear:

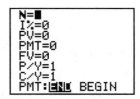

where the time-value-of-money (TVM) variables represent the following:

N   = total number of compounding periods;

I%   = r, where r% is the annual interest rate;

PV   = present value (amount invested or principal);

PMT = payment;

FV   = future value;

P/Y   = number of payments per year;

C/Y   = number of compounding periods per year;

PMT:END = payment due at the end of the period; and

PMT:BEGIN = payment due at the beginning of the period.

Example 2   *Determine the future value of $2000 invested at 8% compounded quarterly for five years (see Example 1).*

SOLUTION

Use the up and down arrow keys to enter the following information:

$$N = 20, I\% = 8, PV = -2000, PMT = 0, P/Y = 4, C/Y = 4$$

The value of N is 20 because 5 years $\times$ 4 periods/year = 20 compounding periods. The present value is entered as a negative value since it is a cash outflow; 0 is entered for PMT to specify no payments; P/Y and C/Y are set to 4 to indicate 4 periods/year. Now, arrow up to FV to highlight FV = ■ and press (ALPHA) followed by (ENTER) to select [SOLVE]. The future value appears next to ■FV.

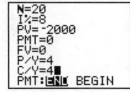 

Therefore, after five years the investment will grow to $2971.89.

3. When you were born, your parents invested the cash gifts that they received from friends and relatives into a certificate of deposit (CD). Cash gifts received on birthdays were also added to this account. Currently, there is a total balance of $4500. If this money were invested into an account at 6% compounded semiannually, use your graphing calculator to determine the future value in seven years.

Effective Annual Yield

4. **a.** Determine the interest earned on an investment of $1200 at 10% simple annual interest for one year.

   b. Determine the interest earned on an investment of $1200 at 10% compounded monthly for one year.

   c. Which investment option earned more? Is this what you expected? Why?

   d. The interest in part b is what percent of the $1200 investment?

The annual interest rate of 10.47% is called the **effective annual yield** of an investment at 10% compounded monthly. Most financial institutions refer to the effective annual yield as the **annual percentage yield (APY)**. The effective interest yield can be determined using several different methods. Example 3 demonstrates the use of the graphing calculator.

Example 3   *Determine the annual percentage yield (APY) on an investment of $1200 at 10% annual interest compounded monthly.*

SOLUTION

Press (APPS), followed by (ENTER). Use ↓ to select option C:▶Eff(.

Press (ENTER) to select the Eff option. Enter the annual interest rate 10 (for 10%), followed by a comma, followed by the number of compounding periods 12. Press (ENTER) and the effective annual rate will appear on the screen.

Therefore, the APY is 10.47%.

5. Your local credit union is offering a one-year certificate of deposit (CD) at an annual interest rate of 5.25% compounded daily. Determine the APY.

Present Value

A local bank is offering a 60-month CD at a rate of 5.70% APY compounded monthly. How much must be invested now in the CD to accumulate $6000 at the end of five years?

In previous problems, the amount to be invested, called the **present value**, was known and you needed to determine the future value. In this problem, the **future value** (amount needed in the future) is known and you must determine the present value.

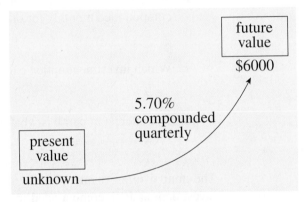

A formula for the present value can be determined by solving the compound interest formula for the principal P (present value).

6. a. Solve the compound interest formula $A = P\left(1 + \dfrac{r}{n}\right)^{nt}$ for P. Replace the amount accumulated, A, with the future value FV and the principal P with the present value PV. The new formula is called the **present value formula**. Check your result with the formula given in the Activity 7.2 Summary.

b. Use the present value formula from part a to determine how much must be invested now (present value PV) in the 60-month CD at 5.70% APY compounded monthly in order to have $6000 at the end of five years.

The present value for a known future value can also be determined using a graphing calculator.

Example 4   *Determine how much money must be invested now (present value) at 6.5% APY compounded daily if $5000 is due in three years.*

SOLUTION

Using the TI-83/84 Plus TVM SOLVER, enter the following values:

N = 1095, I% = 6.5, PMT = 0, FV = 5000, P/Y = 365, C/Y = 365

Note: You can input 3 · 365 for the value of N and the calculator will determine the product, 1095.

Now, arrow up to PV and press (ALPHA) followed by (ENTER) to select [SOLVE]. The screen should appear as follows:

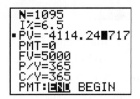

```
N=1095
I%=6.5
▪PV=-4114.24▪717
PMT=0
FV=5000
P/Y=365
C/Y=365
PMT:END BEGIN
```

Therefore, $4114.24 must be invested now in order for the investment to accumulate to $5000 in three years.

7. Use the TVM feature of the TI-83/84 Plus to determine how much must be invested now in a 60-month CD at 5.70% APY compounded monthly in order to have $6000 at the end of five years. How does your answer compare to your result in Problem 6b?

SUMMARY
Activity 7.2

1. **Compound interest** is interest paid on interest as well as the principal.

2. The **compound amount**, also called **future value**, is the total amount of compound interest and principal at the end of the investment.

3. The compound amount (future value) can be calculated using the **compound interest formula**:

$$A = P\left(1 + \frac{r}{n}\right)^{nt},$$

where A is the compound amount, or future value, in the account,
P is the principal (the original amount deposited),
r is the annual interest rate (annual percentage rate in decimal form),
n is the number of times per year that interest is compounded, and
t is the time in years the money has been invested.

4. The compound amount (future value) can be calculated using the TVM Solver feature of the TI-83/84 Plus graphing calculator.

5. **Effective interest yield** as on an investment (called **annual percentage yield** or **APY**) is the true rate of return on an investment.

6. **Present value** (or **principal**) is the amount that must be invested now at compound interest to reach a given future value.

continued

7. **Present value formula** is

$$PV = \frac{FV}{(1 + \frac{r}{n})^{nt}},$$

where PV is present value (principal),
FV is future value (amount accumulated),
r is the annual interest rate (annual percentage rate in decimal form),
n is the number of times per year that interest is compounded, and
t is the time in years the money has been invested.

EXERCISES
Activity 7.2

1. Your high school freshman class had a total of $1200 from fund-raisers during the year. To help pay for a class trip at the end of your senior year, the class deposits the money into a 30-month CD paying 4.2% interest compounded monthly.

   a. Determine the amount the class will receive after 30 months.

   b. How much interest did the class earn on the investment?

2. a. You have just graduated from high school and received $1500 in gifts from family and friends. You also received scholarships in the amount of $800. If you deposit the total amount received into a 24-month CD at 5.5% compounded daily, how much will you receive at the end of 24 months?

   b. How much interest did you earn on the investment?

3. You started a new job and received a $2000 signing bonus. In order to save for a new car, you decide to deposit the money into an account earning 6.75% compounded monthly. How much will you have saved after five years?

4. Determine the effective annual yield for $100 invested for one year at 6.75% compounded monthly.

5. An advertisement in the local newspaper claims that the APY on a CD that paid 4.5% interest compounded quarterly was 4.58%. Is this claim accurate?

6. a. You are the beneficiary of a trust fund established by your grandparents 21 years ago, when you were born. The original amount of the fund was $15,000. If the money earned interest at the rate of 6% compounded annually, what is the current amount in the fund?

b. How much money would be in the fund if it had been invested at 6% compounded monthly?

7. The parents of a child have just received a large inheritance and want to put a portion of the money into a college fund. They estimate that they will need $75,000 in 12 years. If they invest the money at 7% annual interest compounded quarterly, how much should they deposit into the fund?

8. You have two investment options:

   Option 1: Invest $10,000 at 10% compounded semiannually.

   Option 2: Invest $10,000 at 9.5% compounded daily.

   Which option has the greater return after five years?

9. When you graduate from law school in four years, you estimate that you will need $20,000 to set up a law office.

   a. How much money must you invest now at 9% interest compounded quarterly to achieve this goal?

   b. How much interest will you have earned on your investment?

10. You are a member of the town planning board. The town intends to pay off a $4,000,000 bond issue that comes due in 6 years. How much must the town set aside now in order to accumulate the necessary amount of money? Assume the money is invested in an account that earns 8% compounded quarterly.

11. Your car is for sale. You have received two offers:

   Offer 1: The first buyer offers you $6000. He wants to pay you $2000 now, $2000 in six months, and $2000 in one year.

   Offer 2: The second buyer offers to pay you $5600 in cash now.

   a. What is the present value of offer 1? Assume you can earn 10% interest compounded monthly on your money.

   b. Which offer is the better deal? Explain.

ACTIVITY 7.3

Saving for
Retirement

OBJECTIVES

1. Distinguish between an ordinary annuity and an annuity due.

2. Determine the future value of an ordinary annuity using a formula.

3. Determine the future value of an annuity due using technology.

4. Determine the present value of an ordinary annuity using technology.

5. Solve problems involving annuities.

You have a discussion in your business class regarding a retirement plan, including Social Security, company pension plans, 401(k) accounts, and individual accounts such as Roth IRA. Your business teacher asks you to determine how much money will accumulate for retirement if you deposit $500 each year at 6% interest compounded annually for the next 40 years.

So far, you have dealt with problems that involve the future value of a lump-sum investment or payment. To answer your teacher's question, you need to determine the future value of payments of $500 per year. If the payment for each period is fixed, and the compound interest rate is fixed over a specified amount of time, the payment is called an **annuity payment**. Such accounts are called **annuities**. Note that the number of annuity payments made each year will be the same as the number of compounding periods each year.

Before you answer your teacher's question, you need to investigate how an annuity grows over time.

1. A deposit of $1000 is made at the end of every six months (semiannually) for two years at 8% annual interest compounded semiannually.

   a. Determine the amount in the account at the end of the first six-month period.

   b. Determine the amount in the account at the end of the second six-month period. Note that the period interest rate is 8% ÷ 2 = 4%.

   c. Enter your results from parts a and b into the following table. Then complete the table.

PERIOD	END-OF-PERIOD VALUE IN THE ACCOUNT
1	
2	
3	
4	

   d. What is the future value of the annuity described in part a in two years?

In Problem 1, the payment is made at the end of each period. Such an annuity is called an **ordinary annuity**. If the payment is made at the beginning of each period, the annuity is called an **annuity due**. Therefore, the first annuity payment in an annuity due will earn interest. The difference in the future value of an ordinary annuity and an annuity due is one additional period's worth of interest for the length of the loan period.

2. Suppose the $1000 annuity payment in Problem 1 is made at the beginning of every six months for two years at 8% compounded semiannually.

   a. Determine the amount in the account at the end of period 1.

   b. Determine the amount in the account at the end of period 2.

   c. Record your results from part a and b into the following table. Then complete the table by filling the information for periods 3 and 4.

PERIOD	END-OF-PERIOD VALUE IN THE ACCOUNT
1	
2	
3	
4	

   d. What is the future value of this annuity due account at the end of two years?

   e. Compare the future value of the ordinary annuity in Problem 1d to your result in Problem 2d. Is this what you expected?

Future Value of an Annuity

The future value of an annuity is the total accumulation of the payments and interest earned. The formulas to determine the future value of an annuity are:

Future Value of an Ordinary Annuity	**Future Value of an Annuity Due**
$FV = P \cdot \dfrac{(1 + i)^n - 1}{i}$	$FV = P \cdot \dfrac{(1 + i)^n - 1}{i} \cdot (1 + i),$

where FV = future value,
   P = annuity payment,
   i = interest rate per period (written as a decimal), and
   n = total number of periods.

3. Consider the ordinary annuity in Problem 1: A deposit of $1000 made at the end of every six months for two years at 8% annual interest compounded semi-annually.

   a. Determine the interest rate-per-period and the number of periods.

b. Use the appropriate formula above to determine the future value of this annuity.

You may be wondering if the TVM Solver feature of your graphing calculator can be used to determine the future value. The answer is yes.

4. Redo Problem 3 using the TI-83/84 Plus graphing calculator.

    a. Enter the values for the TVM Solver variables into the calculator.

Be careful. The value for I% is the annual interest rate; the PMT (payment) value is entered as a negative number since the payment is a cash outflow. Since the annuity is ordinary, the payment is made at the end of the period. Therefore, the END *must* be highlighted. Simply move the cursor to END and press (ENTER).

    b. Determine the future value of the annuity. How does your result compare to the answer in Problem 3b using a formula?

5. a. Suppose $1000 is deposited at the beginning of every six months for two years at 8% compounded semiannually. Determine the future value of this annuity by using the appropriate formula.

    b. Redo Problem 4a using the TVM calculator application.

    c. Compare the result with the future value of the ordinary annuity in Problem 2d.

6. You are now ready to answer your business teacher's question: How much money will accumulate if you deposit $500 at the beginning of each year for 40 years at 6% compounded annually?

Present Value of an Annuity

One of the requirements in your business class is to write a report describing your retirement plans. You estimate that you will need $20,000 a year at the beginning of each year for 20 years to supplement your pension and Social Security during retirement. How much money (lump sum) will you need at the time of retirement so that you can make the $20,000 annual payment for 20 years? You assume that the lump-sum amount needed will earn 5% annual interest compounded annually during the payout period.

Until now, you have considered annuities in which you start with a zero balance. Then, by making equal annuity payments for a given period of time at compound interest, a future value or accumulation is reached. This new situation starts with a lump-sum amount (unknown) so that equal payments ($20,000 per year) can be made over a specified time (20 years).

The starting lump-sum amount will earn interest (5% compounded annually) while annuity payments are being made. However, the starting amount will continue to decline to a zero balance at the end of 20 years. The lump sum that must be present in the beginning is called the **present value of an annuity**.

> DEFINITION
>
> The **present value of an annuity** is a lump sum that is put into a fund in order for the fund to payout a specified regular payment for a specified amount of time.

7. Now, let us review the details of the problem just given.

As part of your retirement plan, you want to set up an annuity in which a regular payment of $20,000 is made at the end of each year. You need to determine how much money must be deposited (present value) in order to make the annuity payment for 20 years. Assume the money is earning 5% compounded annually.

a. What is the annuity payment? What is the number of payments?

b. What is the annual interest rate?

c. What is the future value?

d. Is the annuity ordinary or due?

e. Use the TVM feature of your graphing calculator to determine the present value of the annuity.

Formulas to determine the present value of an annuity are given in Exercise 8 of this activity.

Applications

8. Your business teacher asks the class to consider the following retirement plans. Assume that the money is invested at 7% compounded annually and that all annuities are ordinary. If the annuity payments stop, the money will continue in the account at 7% compounded annually.

Plan 1: Invest $500 per year for 25 years and then stop the payments.

Plan 2: Wait to invest for 15 years, and then invest $500 per year for 25 years.

a. Determine the total accumulation of money for retirement plan 1 over the next 40 years.

b. Determine the total accumulation of money for plan 2 over the next 40 years.

c. Which retirement plan results in the largest accumulation? Does this seem reasonable? Why?

9. Your parents began depositing $500 at the beginning of each year into a college fund. The fund paid 8% annual interest compounded annually for the first 10 years. For the last eight years, your parents have increased the payments to $1000 per year, but the interest has dropped to 6% interest compounded annually. Determine the amount of money in the college fund after 18 years.

SUMMARY
Activity 7.3

1. An **annuity** is the payment (or receipt) of equal cash payments per period for a given period of time.

2. **Ordinary annuity** is an annuity in which the payments are made at the end of the period.

3. **Annuity due** is an annuity in which the payments are made at the beginning.

4. **Future value** of an annuity is the total accumulation of the payments and interest earned.

5. Future value of an ordinary annuity

$$FV = P \cdot \frac{(1 + i)^n - 1}{i}$$

Future value of an annuity due

$$FV = P \cdot \frac{(1 + i)^n - 1}{i} \cdot (1 + i),$$

where FV = future value,
P = annuity payment,
i = interest rate per period (written as a decimal), and
n = total number of periods.

6. A **present value** of an annuity is a lump sum that is put into a fund in order for the fund to pay out a specified regular payment for a specified amount of time.

7. The future value (and present value) of an annuity can be determined using the TVM solver feature of the TI-83/84 Plus graphing calculator.

EXERCISES
Activity 7.3

1. A college fund is established in which $100 is deposited at the end of every month at 6% per year compounded monthly. If the account started when you were five years old, how much will be in the account when you turn 18?

2. After making a $1500 down payment on a truck, you paid $210 per month for 36 months for a loan. The interest rate for the loan was 10.5% compounded monthly.

   a. What was the amount of the loan?

   b. What was the original cost of the truck?

3. As part of your retirement plan, at the beginning of each year you want to invest $2000 into an IRA. If you plan to retire in 25 years, how much will be in the IRA if it earns 8% compounded annually?

4. Suppose you have $100,000 in a retirement account at your current place of employment. Since you are beginning work at a new company, you plan to roll over the $100,000 into a new account earning 7.5% per year compounded quarterly. You plan to deposit an additional $2000 at the end of each quarter into a second account until you retire. The second account also pays 7.5% per year compounded quarterly.

   a. If you plan to retire in 20 years, what amount of money will be in the first retirement account?

   b. How much money will be in the second retirement account?

5. The winner of the $2,000,000 state lottery will receive 20 payments of $100,000 per year. The payments are to be made as follows:

   1. The first payment of $100,000 is to be made immediately.

   2. The next 19 payments of $100,000 will be made at the end of each year.

   Determine the amount of money that the state needs to have on deposit in order to make the payments. Assume that the balance on deposit will earn 5% per year compounded annually.

6. As part of your retirement plan, you have decided to deposit $2500 at the beginning of each year into an account paying 5.5% interest compounded annually. How much will be in the account after 10 years?

ACTIVITY 7.4

Buy or Lease?

OBJECTIVES

1. Determine the amortization payment on a loan using a formula.

2. Determine the amortization payment on a loan using technology.

3. Solve problems involving repaying a loan or liquidating a sum of money by amortization model.

You are interested in purchasing a new car. You have decided to buy a 2010 Honda Accord for $20,995. The credit union requires a 10% down payment and will finance the balance with an 8% interest loan for 36 months. The sales tax in your city is 7%, and the license and title charges are $80.

1. a. What is the total purchase price of the car including tax, license, and title?

b. What is the amount of the down payment?

c. What is the total amount of the car loan?

Many large-sum loans, such as business loans for new equipment, home mortgages, and car loans are repaid through amortization. Generally, a loan is repaid by a series of equal periodic payments over a specific period of time. Each payment typically includes an amount for interest and a principal reduction (amortization).

When amortizing a loan, the original amount of the loan is known (present value). Since amortization is actually an application of an annuity, you can use a variation of the present value formula for annuities (see Exercise 8 in Activity 7.3) to develop a new formula for determining the amortization payment. Assume the payments are made at the end of each period (ordinary annuity).

Calculating Amortization Payments by Formula

The formula to determine the amount of the payment, *Amt*, is

$$Amt = PV \cdot \frac{i}{1 - (1 + i)^{-n}}$$

or equivalently

$$Amt = PV \cdot \frac{i}{1 - \dfrac{1}{(1 + i)^n}},$$

where Amt = amortization payment,
  PV = amount of loan (present value),
  i = interest rate per period, and
  n = number of periods.

Example 1   *What monthly amortization payment at 12% interest is required to pay off an $8000 loan in two years?*

SOLUTION

To use the amortization formula, you need to first determine the interest rate per period and the number of periods *n*.

$$n = 2 \text{ years} \times 12 \text{ periods per year} = 24$$

$$i = \frac{12\%}{12} = 1\% \text{ or } 0.01$$

Now, substituting 8000 for *PV*, 24 for *n*, and 0.01 for *i*, you have

$$Amt = PV \cdot \frac{i}{1 - (1 + i)^{-n}}$$

$$= 8{,}000 \cdot \frac{0.01}{1 - (1 + 0.01)^{-24}}$$

$$= 8{,}000 \cdot \frac{0.01}{1 - (1.01)^{-24}}.$$

Using your graphing calculator to perform the calculations, the screen should appear as follows:

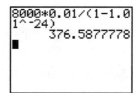

Therefore, the monthly amortization payment is $376.59.

2. Determine the monthly amortization payment on your car loan in Problem 1c using the amortization payment formula.

3. Redo Problem 2 using the TMV Solver feature of your graphing calculator. How does the calculator result compare to the answer obtained by the formula in Problem 2?

College Fund

Your parents and grandparents have been contributing to your college fund for many years. The fund currently has a total of $16,000. The decision has been made to amortize (liquidate) that amount so you will receive equal monthly payments over the next four years of college. At the end of the four years, there will be no funds in the account. If the single college account earns 6% annual interest, how much money will you receive each month?

4. a. What is the number of payments?

b. What is the annual interest rate?

c. What is the present value of the annuity?

d. Assume that payments will be made at the beginning of each month. Use your graphing calculator to determine the monthly payment.

Leasing a Car

Rather than purchasing the car, you have the option of **leasing**. The car salesperson explains to you that a lease is an agreement in which you make equal monthly payments for a specific period of time. At the end of this period, you return the car to the leasing dealer. You do not have ownership of the car and, therefore, have no equity or asset at the end of the leasing period. You have the option of purchasing the car at a predetermined price. There can be end-of-lease termination fees as well as charges for excess mileage or damage.

She gives you the following advertisement that the dealership just placed in the local newspaper:

> ### Lease a 2010 Honda Accord
>
> **Only $249 per month for 36 months**
>
> **WITH NO SECURITY DEPOSIT**
>
> $2500 at signing plus tax, license, and title with approved credit

5. a. What is the leasing monthly payment?

b. How does the monthly leasing payment compare to the monthly purchase payment determined in Problem 2?

Since the monthly leasing payment is much lower than the monthly amortization payment, it seems like you are getting more for your money. Rather than comparing the monthly payments, you decide to compare the total cost of purchasing (Problem 6) to the total cost of leasing the car (Problem 7).

6. a. What is the down payment if you purchase the car?

b. If the monthly amortization payment is $635.82 (see Problem 2), what is the total of the loan payments?

c. Your down payment could have earned interest if you did not purchase the car. If your money currently earns 4% compounded annually in a savings account, how much interest would have been earned in the three-year period?

d. Because you own the car after the loan is paid off, you have equity in the car. You search the Internet and discover that the 2010 Honda Accord should depreciate about $1850 dollars per year. What is the value of the car at the end of the loan?

e. Using parts a–d, determine the total cost of purchasing the car.

7. a. What is the down payment and security deposit if you lease the car?

b. If the monthly leasing payment is $249, what is the total of the lease payments?

c. How much interest is lost if the amount in part a had been deposited at 4% compounded annually for three years?

d. Assume there are no end-of-lease termination fees or charges for excess mileage or damage. If a full refund of the security deposit (if any) is made, what is the total cost of leasing?

8. Is it better to purchase or lease your new car? Explain.

SUMMARY
Activity 7.4

1. **Amortization** is the process of repaying a loan by a series of equal periodic payments over a specific period of time. Amortization can also be used to liquidate a fund down to a zero balance.

2. The **amortization payment** can also be determined using the following formula:

$$Amt = PV \cdot \frac{i}{1 - (1 + i)^{-n}}$$

or equivalently

$$Amt = PV \cdot \frac{i}{1 - \dfrac{1}{(1 + i)^n}},$$

where Amt = amortization payment,
PV = amount of loan,
i = interest rate per period, and
n = number of periods.

1. Your grandmother borrows $5000 from the credit union to purchase a car. She agrees to repay the loan in 36 equal monthly payments. The credit union charges 12% per year compounded monthly.

   a. What is the monthly payment? Use the amortization formula and then verify your result using your graphing calculator.

   b. How much interest was charged for the loan?

2. Your parents buy a new high-definition (HD) TV for $3000 and finance the purchase at 14% interest compounded monthly for 24 months.

   a. What is the monthly payment?

   b. What was the total finance charge?

3. A dealership offers two options to finance $22,500 for a new truck:

   Option 1: 0% financing for 48 months
   Option 2: A $3000 rebate

   If a customer chooses the rebate, she can obtain a loan for the balance at 8.5% compounded annually for 48 months.

   a. If the customer chooses option 1, what is the monthly payment?

   b. If the customer chooses option 2, what is the monthly payment?

   c. Which option should the buyer choose? Explain.

4. The outstanding balance on your credit card is $4000. The bank issuing the credit card is charging 18.5% per year compounded monthly. You decide you must pay off the balance before you get married in 18 months. If you make equal monthly payments for the next 18 months, determine the monthly payment. Assume no additional charges are made.

5. Your cousin makes a profit of $30,000 on the sale of her small business. She deposits the money into an account paying 7.2% interest compounded annually. She wants to make equal annual withdrawals from the account over the next five years. At the end of the five years, there will be no funds in the account.

   a. Determine the amount of each withdrawal. Assume the withdrawal is made at the beginning of each year.

   b. Determine the amount of each withdrawal if the money must last 10 years.

6. Find an advertisement in your local newspaper for a lease offer on a vehicle you would like to own. Obtain the information necessary to determine whether it is better to lease or purchase the vehicle. Use your local dealership, banks, and the Internet. Submit a report of your findings and conclusions.

ACTIVITY 7.5

Buy Now,
Pay Later

Significant price cuts have recently taken place in the cost of high-definition televisions. Your parents have decided that now is the time to take the plunge. After researching the features of different types of HD TVs, including LCD, plasma, rear-projection, and picture-tube, they have selected a 60-inch HD plasma TV at a cost of $4000.

The electronics store salesperson informs them that the store is offering a 36-month installment plan to finance the TV. They are interested and discuss the details of the plan with the salesperson.

Closed-End Installment Loan

The installment loan that is being offered by the electronics store is an example of **closed-end installment loan**. The amount borrowed is repaid plus interest in equal payments (usually monthly) over a certain period of time. Such loans are commonly used to purchase furniture, appliances, and computers. The length of the loans can vary from a few months to several years.

1. The store requires no down payment. The salesperson tells your parents that they can finance the HD plasma TV with 36 monthly payments of $132.86.

   a. Determine the total amount paid. This total is called the **installment price**.

   b. Determine the finance charge (interest) of the installment loan. Remember that the monthly payment includes payment of interest as well as repayment of some of the amount borrowed (principal).

Annual Percentage Rate (APR)

The results from Problem 2 can be used to demonstrate a hidden cost when borrowing money on an installment plan.

2. a. Suppose you borrowed $1000 for a year and had an interest charge of $100. If you repaid the amount borrowed plus interest at the end of the year, what is the annual interest rate on the loan?

   b. Suppose you paid the amount borrowed plus interest on a 12-month installment plan, what is the monthly payment?

In Problem 2a, you would have the use of the $1000 for the entire year. In part b, you are losing the use of some of the $1000 because you are using some of it to pay

$91.67 each month. Therefore, when paying a loan on an installment plan, the actual interest rate charged is more than 10% (the actual rate charged if you paid off the loan at the end of the year). The true annual interest rate charged is called the **annual percentage rate (APR)**.

DEFINITION

The **annual percentage rate (APR)** is the *true rate of interest* charged for the loan.

The APR can be calculated using the formula:

$$APR = \frac{72i}{3P(n + 1) + i(n - 1)},$$

where   APR = annual percentage rate,
i = interest (finance) charge on the loan,
P = principal or amount borrowed, and
n = number of months of the loan.

3. a. In Problem 2, $1000 was borrowed at an interest rate of 10%. If the loan is paid off in 12 monthly payments and $100 interest was charged, determine the APR using the APR formula.

b. Verify your result in part a using the TVM Solver feature of the TI-83 Plus graphing calculator. Your screen should appear as follows:

4. Let us return to your parents' TV loan. They are borrowing $4000 to purchase a 60-inch HD plasma TV using a 36-month installment plan. Determine the annual percentage rate (APR) using the APR formula. Round your answer to the nearest whole percent. Recall that the interest charge was $782.96 (see Problem 1b).

In 1969, Congress passed the **Truth in Lending Act**. This legislation required the lender to provide the borrower with the finance charge and APR of the loan. In order to help lending institutions and businesses to provide this information, the Federal Reserve Board has published APR tables. A portion of one of these tables appears in Table 7.1.

The following example demonstrates the process for using APR Table 7.1 to determine the APR for a loan.

Table 7.1
Interest per $100 of Amount Financed

NUMBER OF MONTHLY PAYMENTS	APR (ANNUAL PERCENTAGE RATE)											
	10.00%	10.50%	11.00%	11.50%	12.00%	12.50%	13.00%	13.50%	14.00%	14.50%	15.00%	15.50%
1	0.83	0.87	0.92	0.96	1.00	1.04	1.08	1.12	1.17	1.21	1.25	1.29
2	1.25	1.31	1.38	1.44	1.50	1.57	1.63	1.69	1.75	1.82	1.88	1.94
3	1.67	1.76	1.84	1.92	2.01	2.09	2.17	2.26	2.34	2.43	2.51	2.59
4	2.09	2.20	2.30	2.41	2.51	2.62	2.72	2.83	2.93	3.04	3.14	3.25
5	2.51	2.64	2.77	2.89	3.02	3.15	3.27	3.40	3.53	3.65	3.78	3.91
6	2.94	3.08	3.23	3.38	3.53	3.68	3.83	3.97	4.12	4.27	4.42	4.57
7	3.36	3.53	3.70	3.87	4.04	4.21	4.38	4.55	4.72	4.89	5.06	5.23
8	3.79	3.98	4.17	4.36	4.55	4.74	4.94	5.13	5.32	5.51	5.71	5.90
9	4.21	4.43	4.64	4.85	5.07	5.28	5.49	5.71	5.92	6.14	6.35	6.57
10	4.64	4.88	5.11	5.35	5.58	5.82	6.05	6.29	6.53	6.77	7.00	7.24
11	5.07	5.33	5.58	5.84	6.10	6.36	6.62	6.88	7.14	7.40	7.66	7.92
12	5.50	5.78	6.06	6.34	6.62	6.90	7.18	7.46	7.74	8.03	8.31	8.59
13	5.93	6.23	6.53	6.84	7.14	7.44	7.75	8.05	8.36	8.66	8.97	9.27
14	6.36	6.69	7.01	7.34	7.66	7.99	8.31	8.64	8.97	9.30	9.63	9.96
15	6.80	7.14	7.49	7.84	8.19	8.53	8.88	9.23	9.59	9.94	10.29	10.64
16	7.23	7.60	7.97	8.34	8.71	9.08	9.46	9.83	10.20	10.58	10.95	11.33
17	7.67	8.06	8.45	8.84	9.24	9.63	10.03	10.44	10.82	11.22	11.62	12.02
18	8.10	8.52	8.93	9.35	9.77	10.19	10.61	11.03	11.45	11.87	12.29	12.72
19	8.54	8.98	9.42	9.86	10.30	10.74	11.18	11.63	12.07	12.52	12.97	13.41
20	8.98	9.44	9.90	10.37	10.83	11.30	11.76	12.23	12.70	13.17	13.64	14.11
21	9.42	9.90	10.39	10.88	11.36	11.85	12.34	12.84	13.33	13.82	14.32	14.82
22	9.86	10.37	10.88	11.39	11.90	12.41	12.93	13.44	13.96	14.48	15.00	15.52
23	10.30	10.84	11.37	11.90	12.44	12.97	13.51	14.05	14.59	15.14	15.68	16.23
24	10.75	11.30	11.86	12.42	12.98	13.54	14.10	14.66	15.23	15.80	16.37	16.94
25	11.19	11.77	12.35	12.93	13.52	14.10	14.69	15.28	15.87	16.46	17.06	17.65
26	11.64	12.24	12.85	13.45	14.06	14.67	15.28	15.89	16.51	17.13	17.75	18.37
27	12.09	12.71	13.34	13.97	14.60	15.24	15.87	16.51	17.15	17.80	18.44	19.09
28	12.53	13.18	13.84	14.49	15.15	15.81	16.47	17.13	17.80	18.47	19.14	19.81
29	12.98	13.66	14.33	15.01	15.70	16.38	17.07	17.75	18.45	19.14	19.83	20.53
30	13.43	14.13	14.83	15.54	16.24	16.95	17.66	18.38	19.10	19.81	20.54	21.26
31	13.89	14.61	15.33	16.06	16.79	17.53	18.27	19.00	19.75	20.49	21.24	21.99
32	14.34	15.09	15.84	16.59	17.35	18.11	18.87	19.63	20.40	21.17	21.95	22.72
33	14.79	15.57	16.34	17.12	17.90	18.69	19.47	20.26	21.06	21.85	22.65	23.46

Table 7.1 *(continued)*
Interest per $100 of Amount Financed

NUMBER OF MONTHLY PAYMENTS	APR (ANNUAL PERCENTAGE RATE)											
	16.00%	16.50%	17.00%	17.50%	18.00%	18.50%	19.00%	19.50%	20.00%	20.50%	21.00%	21.50%
1	1.33	1.37	1.42	1.46	1.50	1.54	1.58	1.62	1.67	1.71	1.75	1.79
2	2.00	2.07	2.13	2.17	2.26	2.32	2.38	2.44	2.51	2.57	2.63	2.70
3	2.68	2.76	2.85	2.93	3.01	3.10	3.18	3.27	3.35	3.44	3.52	3.60
4	3.36	3.46	3.57	3.67	3.78	3.88	3.99	4.10	4.20	4.31	4.41	4.52
5	4.04	4.16	4.29	4.42	4.54	4.67	4.80	4.93	5.06	5.18	5.31	5.44
6	4.72	4.87	5.02	5.17	5.32	5.46	5.61	5.76	5.91	6.06	6.21	6.36
7	5.40	5.58	5.75	5.92	6.09	6.26	6.43	6.60	6.78	6.95	7.12	7.29
8	6.09	6.29	6.48	6.67	6.87	7.06	7.26	7.45	7.64	7.84	8.03	8.23
9	6.78	7.00	7.22	7.43	7.65	7.87	8.08	8.30	8.52	8.73	8.95	9.17
10	7.48	7.72	7.96	8.19	8.43	8.67	8.91	9.15	9.39	9.63	9.88	10.12
11	8.18	8.44	8.70	8.96	9.22	9.49	9.75	10.01	10.28	10.54	10.80	11.07
12	8.88	9.16	9.45	9.73	10.02	10.30	10.59	10.87	11.16	11.45	11.74	12.02
13	9.28	9.89	10.20	10.50	10.81	11.12	11.43	11.74	12.05	12.36	12.67	12.99
14	10.29	10.67	10.95	11.28	11.61	11.95	12.28	12.61	12.95	13.28	13.62	13.95
15	11.00	11.35	11.71	12.06	12.42	12.77	13.13	13.49	13.85	14.21	14.57	14.93
16	11.71	12.09	12.46	12.84	13.22	13.60	13.99	14.37	14.75	15.13	15.52	15.90
17	12.42	12.83	13.23	13.63	14.04	14.44	14.85	16.25	15.66	16.07	16.48	16.89
18	13.14	13.57	13.99	14.42	14.85	15.28	15.71	16.14	16.57	17.01	17.44	17.88
19	13.86	14.31	14.76	15.22	15.67	16.12	16.58	17.03	17.49	17.95	18.41	18.87
20	14.59	15.06	15.54	16.01	16.49	16.97	17.45	17.93	18.41	18.90	19.38	19.87
21	15.31	15.81	16.31	16.81	17.32	17.82	18.33	18.83	19.34	19.85	20.36	20.87
22	16.04	16.57	17.09	17.62	18.15	18.68	19.21	19.74	20.27	20.81	21.34	21.88
23	16.78	17.32	17.88	18.43	18.98	19.54	20.09	20.65	21.21	21.77	22.33	22.90
24	17.51	18.09	18.66	19.24	19.82	20.40	20.98	21.56	22.15	22.74	23.33	23.92
25	18.25	18.85	19.45	20.05	20.66	21.27	21.87	22.48	23.10	23.71	24.32	24.94
26	18.99	19.62	20.24	20.87	21.50	22.14	22.77	23.41	24.04	24.68	25.33	25.97
27	19.74	20.39	21.04	21.69	22.35	23.01	23.67	24.33	25.00	25.67	26.34	27.01
28	20.48	21.16	21.84	22.52	23.20	23.89	2.458	25.27	25.96	26.65	27.35	28.05
29	21.23	21.94	22.64	23.35	24.06	24.27	25.49	26.20	26.92	27.64	28.37	29.09
30	21.99	22.72	23.45	24.18	24.92	25.66	26.40	27.14	27.89	28.64	29.39	30.14
31	22.71	23.50	24.26	25.02	25.78	26.55	27.32	28.09	28.86	29.64	30.42	31.20
32	23.50	24.28	25.07	25.86	26.65	27.44	28.24	29.04	29.84	30.64	31.45	32.26
33	24.26	25.07	25.88	26.70	27.52	28.34	29.16	29.99	30.82	31.65	32.49	33.33

Table 7.1 (*continued*)
Interest per $100 of Amount Financed

NUMBER OF MONTHLY PAYMENTS	APR (ANNUAL PERCENTAGE RATE)											
	10.00%	10.50%	11.00%	11.50%	12.00%	12.50%	13.00%	13.50%	14.00%	14.50%	15.00%	15.50%
34	15.25	16.05	16.85	17.64	18.46	19.27	20.08	20.90	21.72	22.54	23.37	24.19
35	15.70	16.53	17.35	18.18	19.01	19.85	20.69	21.53	22.38	23.23	24.08	24.94
36	16.16	17.01	17.86	18.71	19.57	20.43	21.30	22.17	23.04	23.92	24.80	25.68
37	16.62	17.49	18.37	19.25	20.13	21.02	21.91	22.81	23.70	24.69	25.51	26.42
38	17.08	17.98	18.88	19.78	20.69	21.61	22.52	23.45	24.37	25.30	26.24	27.17
39	17.54	18.46	19.39	20.32	21.26	22.20	23.14	24.09	25.04	26.90	26.96	27.92
40	18.00	18.95	19.90	20.86	21.82	22.79	23.76	24.73	25.71	26.70	27.69	28.68
41	18.47	19.44	20.42	21.40	22.39	23.38	24.38	25.38	26.39	27.40	28.41	29.44
42	18.93	19.93	20.93	21.94	22.96	23.98	25.00	26.03	27.06	28.10	29.15	30.19
43	19.40	20.42	21.45	22.49	23.53	24.57	25.62	26.68	27.74	28.81	29.88	20.96
44	19.86	20.91	21.97	23.03	24.10	25.17	26.25	27.33	28.42	29.52	30.62	31.72
45	20.33	21.41	22.49	23.58	24.67	25.77	26.88	27.99	29.11	30.23	31.36	32.49
46	20.80	21.90	23.01	24.13	25.25	26.37	27.51	28.65	29.79	30.94	32.10	33.26
47	21.27	22.40	23.53	24.68	25.82	26.98	28.14	29.31	30.48	31.66	32.84	34.03
48	21.74	22.90	24.06	25.23	26.40	27.58	28.77	29.97	31.17	32.37	33.59	34.81
49	22.21	23.39	24.58	25.78	26.98	28.19	29.41	30.63	13.86	33.09	34.34	35.59
50	22.69	23.89	25.11	26.33	27.56	28.80	30.04	31.29	32.55	33.82	35.09	36.37
51	23.16	24.40	25.64	26.89	28.15	29.41	30.68	31.96	33.25	34.54	35.84	37.15
52	23.64	24.90	26.17	27.45	28.73	30.02	31.32	32.63	33.95	35.27	36.60	37.94
53	24.11	25.40	26.70	28.00	29.32	30.64	31.97	33.30	34.65	36.00	37.36	38.72
54	24.59	25.91	27.23	28.56	29.91	31.25	32.61	33.98	35.35	36.73	38.12	39.52
55	25.07	26.41	27.77	29.13	30.50	31.87	33.26	34.65	36.05	37.46	38.88	40.31
56	25.55	26.92	28.30	29.69	31.09	32.49	33.91	35.33	36.76	38.20	39.65	41.11
57	26.03	27.43	28.84	30.25	31.68	33.11	34.56	36.01	37.47	38.94	40.42	41.91
58	26.51	27.94	29.37	30.82	32.27	33.74	35.21	36.69	38.18	39.68	41.19	42.71
59	27.00	28.45	29.91	31.39	32.87	34.36	35.86	37.37	38.89	40.42	41.96	43.51
60	27.48	28.96	30.45	31.96	33.47	34.99	36.52	38.06	39.61	41.17	42.74	44.32

Table 7.1 (continued)
Interest per $100 of Amount Financed

NUMBER OF MONTHLY PAYMENTS	APR (ANNUAL PERCENTAGE RATE)											
	16.00%	16.50%	17.00%	17.50%	18.00%	18.50%	19.00%	19.50%	20.00%	20.50%	21.00%	21.50%
34	25.03	25.86	26.70	27.54	28.38	29.24	30.09	30.95	31.80	32.67	33.53	34.40
35	25.79	26.66	27.52	28.39	29.27	30.14	31.02	31.91	32.79	33.68	34.58	35.47
36	26.57	27.46	28.35	29.25	30.15	31.05	31.96	32.87	33.79	34.71	35.63	36.56
37	27.34	28.26	29.18	30.10	31.03	31.97	32.90	33.84	34.79	35.74	36.69	37.64
38	28.11	29.06	30.01	30.96	31.92	32.88	33.85	34.82	35.79	36.77	37.75	38.73
39	28.89	29.87	30.85	31.83	32.81	33.80	34.80	35.80	36.80	37.81	38.82	39.83
40	29.68	30.68	31.68	32.69	33.71	34.73	35.75	36.78	37.81	38.85	39.69	40.93
41	30.46	31.49	32.52	33.56	34.51	35.66	36.71	37.77	38.83	39.89	40.96	42.04
42	31.25	32.31	33.37	34.44	35.51	36.59	37.67	38.76	39.85	40.95	42.05	43.15
43	32.04	33.13	34.22	35.31	36.42	37.52	38.63	39.75	40.87	42.00	43.13	44.27
44	32.83	33.95	35.07	36.19	37.33	38.46	39.60	40.75	41.90	43.06	44.22	45.39
45	33.63	34.77	35.92	37.08	38.24	39.41	40.58	41.75	42.94	44.13	45.32	46.52
46	34.43	35.60	36.78	37.96	39.16	40.35	41.55	42.76	43.98	45.20	46.42	47.65
47	35.23	36.43	37.64	38.86	40.08	41.30	42.54	43.77	45.02	46.27	47.53	48.79
48	36.03	37.27	38.50	39.75	41.00	42.26	43.52	44.79	46.07	47.35	48.64	49.93
49	36.84	38.10	39.37	40.65	41.93	43.22	44.51	45.81	47.12	48.43	49.75	51.08
50	37.65	38.94	40.24	41.55	42.86	44.18	45.50	46.83	48.17	49.52	50.87	52.23
51	38.46	39.79	41.11	42.45	43.79	45.14	46.50	47.86	49.23	50.61	51.99	53.38
52	39.28	40.63	41.99	43.36	44.73	46.11	47.50	48.89	50.30	51.71	53.12	54.55
53	40.10	41.48	42.87	44.27	45.67	47.08	48.50	49.93	51.37	52.81	54.26	55.71
54	40.92	42.33	43.75	45.18	46.62	48.06	49.51	50.97	52.44	53.91	55.39	56.88
55	41.74	43.19	44.64	16.10	47.57	49.04	50.52	52.02	53.52	55.02	56.54	58.08
56	42.57	44.05	45.53	47.02	48.52	50.03	51.54	53.06	54.60	56.14	57.68	59.24
57	43.40	44.91	46.42	47.94	49.47	51.01	52.56	54.12	55.68	57.25	58.84	60.43
58	44.23	45.77	47.32	48.87	50.43	52.00	53.58	55.17	56.77	58.38	59.99	61.62
59	45.07	46.64	48.21	49.80	51.39	53.00	54.61	56.23	57.87	59.51	61.15	62.81
60	45.91	47.51	49.12	50.73	52.36	54.00	55.64	57.30	58.96	60.64	62.32	64.01

Example 1   *In Problems 2 and 3, you financed $1000 for a year and agreed to repay the loan with 12 monthly payments of $91.67. The interest charge was $100. Use the APR Table 7.1 to determine the annual percentage rate (APR).*

SOLUTION

Step 1. Determine the total finance charge (interest) on the loan. The finance charge is given as $100.

Step 2. Determine the finance charge per $100 of the amount financed.

$$\frac{\text{finance charge}}{\text{amount financed}} \cdot 100 = \frac{100}{1000} \cdot 100 = 10$$

Therefore, you pay $10 for each $100 being financed.

Step 3. Using APR Table 7.1, determine the row for the given number of payments (12) and then move across to locate the number nearest to 10. Next, move to the top of the column to determine the APR of the loan.

Therefore, the APR is 18%

5. Redo Problem 4 (TV loan) using APR Table 7.1. How does your answer compare to the APR determined in Problem 4?

Calculating Monthly Installment Payment

If you know the APR and the number of monthly payments, the APR Table 7.1 can be used to determine the monthly payment.

6. Suppose the salesperson at a competing electronics store offers the same model 60-inch HD plasma TV, but at a lower price of $3800. With no down payment required, your parents can borrow $3800 at 14% APR for 32 months.

   a. Use the APR Table 7.1 to determine the finance charge per $100 financed.

   b. Determine the total finance charge of the loan. Note that if you divide the table value of 20.40 by 100, you get the finance charge for $1 borrowed. Multiplying this number by the amount financed will give the total finance charge of the $3800 loan.

   c. What is the total of the amount financed and finance charge for the HD plasma TV at this competing store?

d. What is the monthly payment on the loan?

Using the TVM Solve feature, where N = 32, I% = 14, PV = 3800, FV = 0, P/Y = 12, C/Y = 12, PMT: END, you obtain $142.98 for the monthly payment.

  e. Complete the following table to summarize the information you have calculated for each of the installment plans to purchase the 60-inch HD plasma TV.

	INSTALLMENT PLAN I	INSTALLMENT PLAN 2 AT COMPETING STORE
PURCHASE PRICE		
DOWN PAYMENT		
MONTHLY PAYMENT		
NUMBER OF MONTHLY PAYMENTS		
APR		
FINANCE CHARGE		
TOTAL COST		

  f. Which installment plan represents the better deal? Explain.

Paying an Installment Loan before It Is Due

Your parents purchase the HD plasma TV at the second electronics store (installment plan 2). Recall from Problem 6b that the total finance charge for plan 2 is $775.20. Suppose your parents pay the first 20 payments and then decide to pay off the loan. Would you have to pay the total finance charge of $775.20?

The answer is no. Your parents are entitled to a finance charge rebate. At the time of the loan pay off, the lender must return any unearned interest that is saved by paying off the loan early.

The most commonly used method to determine the unearned interest is the **actuarial method**.

The actuarial method formula is

$$u = \frac{npv}{100 + v},$$

where u = unearned interest,
  n = number of remaining monthly payments,
  p = monthly payment, and
  v = value from the APR table that corresponds to the
    APR for the number of remaining payments.

7. Recall that your parents' monthly payments for the 32-month installment plan 2 to purchase the HD plasma TV is $142.98.

    a. If you pay off the loan after 20 payments, how many payments remain?

    b. Determine the value v in the actuarial method formula. *Hint:* Using the APR table, find the intersection of the number of remaining payments now (12) with the APR column headed by the loan APR (14%).

    c. Substitute the appropriate values for n, p, and v into the actuarial formula to determine the unearned interest u.

    d. Determine the total amount due to pay off the loan after 20 payments.

Open-end Installment Loans

You are enjoying the new HD plasma TV. Your parents purchase a $450 cabinet to contain the TV equipment and store your large collection of DVDs. They charge the cabinet on their credit card.

Use of a credit card to purchase goods is a type of **open-end installment loan**. Rather than making fixed equal payments over a specific period time, you make variable monthly payments. There is generally no specific period of time to pay off the loan. As a matter of fact, you can actually borrow additional money to purchase merchandise while you still have unpaid loans in the account.

Interest rates for open-ended accounts are generally given as annual rates. The interest on most open-end accounts is calculated using the **average daily balance method**. In this method, a balance is determined for each day of the billing period and then the total is divided by the number of days in that billing period. This gives an average of all the daily balances.

The following example demonstrates the process:

Example 2   *The balance on your credit card on March 1, the billing date, is $242.50. The following transactions were made during the month of March.*

March 6	Payment	$50.00
March 15	Charge: clothing	37.00
March 20	Charge: car tire	85.00
March 25	Charge: music CDs	41.50

Determine the balance due on April 1.

SOLUTION

i. Determine the average daily balance for the month of March as follows:

Step 1.   Determine the balance due for each transaction date:

March 1   242.50

March 6 $242.50 - 50.00 = 192.50$

March 15 192.50 + 37.00 = 229.50
March 20 229.50 + 85.00 = 314.50
March 25 314.50 + 41.50 = 356.00

Step 2. Determine the number of days that the balance did not change between each transaction.

March 1–March 5 5
March 6–March 14 9
March 15–March 19 5
March 20–March 24 5
March 25–March 31 7

Step 3. Multiply the balance due times the number of days it did not change.

5(242.50) = 1212.50
9(192.50) = 1732.50
5(229.50) = 1147.50
5(314.50) = 1572.50
7(356.00) = 2492.00

Step 4. Determine the sum of the products in step 3 and divide by the number of days in the billing cycle (month).

$$\frac{1212.50 + 1732.50 + 1147.50 + 1572.50 + 2492.00}{31} = \$263.13$$

Therefore, the average daily balance is $263.13.

ii. Determine the finance charge for the month. Assume that the interest rate is 1.25% per month. The finance charge is

$$0.0125 \times 263.13 = 3.29$$

iii. Determine the balance due on April 1.

$$\text{finance charge} + \text{balance} = 3.29 + 356 = \$359.29$$

SUMMARY
Activity 7.5

1. A **closed-end installment** loan is one in which you pay a fixed amount of money for a specified number of payments.

2. The **finance charge** is the total amount of money that the borrower must pay for its use.

3. The **finance charge** is the amount borrowed subtracted from the total monthly payments.

4. The **annual percentage rate (APR)** is the true rate of interest charged for the loan.

5. The APR can be calculated using the following formula

$$\text{APR} = \frac{72i}{3P(n + 1) + i(n - 1)},$$

where APR = annual percentage rate,
 i = interest (finance) charge on the loan,
 P = principal or amount borrowed, and
 n = number of months of the loan.

The APR can also be calculated using Table 7.1 or the TVM Solver on the TI-83/84 Plus.

continued

6. The **installment payment** is the amount that is paid (including interest) in regular payments.

7. The total **installment price** is the down payment plus the total of monthly payments.

8. An **open-end installment loan** is one in which you make variable payments each month.

9. The **actuarial method** is used to determine the amount of the unearned interest of an installment loan if it is paid off before it is done. The actuarial method formula is

$$u = \frac{npv}{100 + v},$$

where u = unearned interest,
n = number of remaining monthly payments,
p = monthly payment, and
v = value from the APR table that corresponds to the APR for the number of remaining payments.

10. The interest on most credit card accounts is calculated using the **average daily balance method** (see Example 2).

EXERCISES
Activity 7.5

1. The high school's computer lab purchases a new laptop computer for $1200. They pay a 5% down payment and $55 per month on a 24-month purchase plan.

   a. What is the amount of the down payment?

   b. Determine the amount financed.

   c. Determine the total finance charge.

   d. Use the APR formula to determine the annual percentage rate to the nearest half percent.

   e. Use the TVM Solver feature of the TI-83/84 Plus to verify your result in part d.

2. Ever Green Landscaping wants to finance a used dump truck for $8000. The dealership requires a $1000 down payment and offers a 36-month installment plan to finance the balance. If the monthly payment is $235, use APR Table 7.1 to determine the APR. Verify your result using the calculator.

3. The senior class is planning a fund-raiser to purchase a new refrigerator for a local daycare center. The refrigerator's total cost is $950. In order to finance the purchase, the appliance store requires a 10% down payment, with the balance being financed with a 24-month installment plan having an APR of 10.5%.

    a. What is the amount of the down payment?

    b. What is the amount to be financed?

    c. Determine the finance charge. Use the APR table.

    d. Determine the monthly payment. Verify using the TVM Solver.

4. Your sister bought a new sport utility vehicle for $34,000. She received $8000 for her trade-in and used that money as a down payment. She financed the vehicle at 10% APR over 48 months. She received a bonus check at work and paid off the loan after making the 30th payment.

    a. Determine the total interest that would have been paid if she had made all 48 payments.

    b. What were her monthly payments?

    c. How many payments are left?

    d. Use the actuarial method formula to determine the amount of unearned interest.

    e. Determine the total amount due to pay off the loan after 30 payments.

ACTIVITY 7.6
Home Sweet Home

You are the loan officer at a bank that specializes in long-term loans, called **mortgages**, in which property is used as security for a debt. A young couple, recently married, has decided to purchase a townhouse at a negotiated price of $120,000. They have applied for a conventional mortgage from your bank. Because the townhouse is older, the bank is requiring a 20% down payment. A special interest mortgage loan of 5.5% is being offered.

The bank is also requiring 2 points for their loan at the time of closing (the final step in the sale process). You explain to the couple that charging points enables the bank to reduce the amount of interest on the mortgage loan and, therefore, will reduce the amount of monthly payment.

1. Determine the amount of the down payment. This amount is paid to the seller at closing.

2. **a.** If the couple agrees to pay the premium for private mortgage insurance (PMI), the bank can lend up to 95% of the value of the property. What would be the down payment if the bank required a 5% down payment?

   b. Assuming they agree to purchasing the PMI, what is the amount to be mortgaged?

   c. A point is 1% of the amount to be borrowed. Determine the amount of the points. This amount is paid to the bank at closing.

Calculating the Monthly Mortgage Payment

In Activity 7.4, you learned that amortization is a special type of annuity in which a large loan is paid off with equal periodic payments over a period of time. Mortgages are loans that are paid off using amortization. The amount of the mortgage is actually the present value of an annuity.

The amount of the monthly mortgage payments can be calculated by using a table. Since mortgages often run for a period of 5 to 30 years, there is a special present value table in which the periods are listed in years. Also, since mortgage loans involve large sums of money, the table values represent the monthly payment per $1000 of mortgage.

Example 1 illustrates the procedure to calculate the monthly mortgage payment using Table 7.2 on page 850.

Example 1 *Determine the monthly payment and total interest on a $250,000 mortgage at 7.5% for 20 years.*

SOLUTION

Step 1. Divide the amount to be mortgaged by 1000. This gives the number of thousands of dollars to be mortgaged.

$$\frac{250,000}{1000} = 250$$

Step 2. Using Table 7.2, locate the table value, monthly payment per $1000 financed, at the intersection of the number of years row (20) and annual interest rate column (7.5%).

Table value is 8.06.

Step 3. Multiply the amount to be mortgaged (step 1) by the table value (step 2) to determine the monthly mortgage payment.

$$250 \cdot 8.06 = \$2015$$

Using Table 7.2, the monthly mortgage payment in Example 1 is $2015. The TVM Solver feature of your TI-83/84 Plus can be used to determine the monthly mortgage payment. Let N = 240, I% = 7.5, PV = 250,000, FV = 0, P/Y = C/Y = 12, PMT:END, you obtain PMT = −2013.98. Your screen should appear as follows:

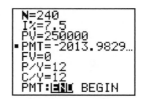

Note that there is a small difference between the results obtained from the graphing calculator and the result using the mortgage table. This is a result of rounding numbers in the calculations.

3. a. Recall from Problem 2c that the couple is applying for a mortgage amount of $114,000 at 5.5% APR. Determine the monthly payment for a 30-year mortgage.

    b. What is the total interest paid? Use the monthly payment obtained by the TVM Solver.

4. a. The couple would like to compare the monthly payment and total interest paid for different lengths of time, in years. Complete the following table:

$114,000 MORTGAGE AT 5.5% ANNUAL INTEREST		
LENGTH OF MORTGAGE	MONTHLY PAYMENT	TOTAL INTEREST
15		
20		
25		
30		

Table 7.2
Monthly Payments per $1000 of Mortgage (including principal and interest)

INTEREST RATE (%)	5 YEARS	10 YEARS	15 YEARS	20 YEARS	25 YEARS	30 YEARS	35 YEARS	40 YEARS
5	18.88	10.61	7.91	6.60	5.85	5.37	5.05	4.83
$5\frac{1}{4}$	18.99	10.73	8.04	6.74	6.00	5.53	5.21	4.99
$5\frac{1}{2}$	79.11	10.86	8.18	6.88	6.15	5.68	5.38	5.16
$5\frac{3}{4}$	19.22	10.98	8.31	7.03	6.30	5.84	5.54	5.33
6	19.34	11.11	8.44	7.17	6.45	6.00	5.71	5.51
$6\frac{1}{4}$	19.45	11.23	8.58	7.31	6.60	6.16	5.88	5.68
$6\frac{1}{2}$	19.57	11.36	8.72	7.46	6.76	6.33	6.05	5.86
$6\frac{3}{4}$	19.69	11.49	8.85	7.61	6.91	6.49	6.22	6.04
7	19.81	11.62	8.99	7.76	7.07	6.66	6.39	6.22
$7\frac{1}{4}$	19.92	11.75	9.13	7.91	7.23	6.83	6.57	6.40
$7\frac{1}{2}$	20.04	11.88	9.28	8.06	7.39	7.00	6.75	6.59
$7\frac{3}{4}$	20.16	12.01	9.42	8.21	7.56	7.17	6.93	6.77
8	20.28	12.14	9.56	8.37	7.72	7.34	7.11	6.96
$8\frac{1}{4}$	20.40	12.27	9.71	8.53	7.89	7.52	7.29	7.15
$8\frac{1}{2}$	20.52	12.40	9.85	8.68	8.06	7.69	7.47	7.34
$8\frac{3}{4}$	20.64	12.54	10.00	8.84	8.23	7.87	7.66	7.53
9	20.76	12.67	10.15	9.00	8.40	8.05	7.84	7.72
$9\frac{1}{4}$	20.88	12.81	10.30	9.16	8.57	8.23	8.03	7.91
$9\frac{1}{2}$	21.01	12.94	10.45	9.33	8.74	8.41	8.22	8.11
$9\frac{3}{4}$	21.13	13.08	10.60	9.49	8.92	8.60	8.41	8.30
10	21.25	13.22	10.75	9.66	9.09	8.78	8.60	8.50
$10\frac{1}{4}$	21.38	13.36	10.90	9.82	9.27	8.97	8.79	8.69
$10\frac{1}{2}$	21.50	13.50	11.06	9.99	9.45	9.15	8.99	8.89
$10\frac{3}{4}$	21.62	13.64	11.21	10.16	9.63	9.34	9.18	9.09
11	21.75	13.78	11.37	10.33	9.81	9.53	9.37	9.29
$11\frac{1}{4}$	21.87	13.92	11.53	10.50	9.99	9.72	9.57	9.49
$11\frac{1}{2}$	22.00	14.06	11.69	10.67	10.17	9.91	9.77	9.69
$11\frac{3}{4}$	22.12	14.21	11.85	10.84	10.35	10.10	9.96	9.89
12	22.25	14.35	12.01	11.02	10.54	10.29	10.16	10.09
$12\frac{1}{4}$	22.38	14.50	12.17	11.19	10.72	10.48	10.36	10.29
$12\frac{1}{2}$	22.50	14.64	12.33	11.37	10.91	10.68	10.56	10.49
$12\frac{3}{4}$	22.63	14.79	12.49	11.54	11.10	10.87	10.76	10.70
13	22.76	14.94	12.66	11.72	11.28	11.07	10.96	10.90
$13\frac{1}{4}$	22.89	15.08	12.82	11.90	11.47	11.26	11.16	11.10
$13\frac{1}{2}$	23.01	15.23	12.99	12.08	11.66	11.46	11.36	11.31
$13\frac{3}{4}$	23.14	15.38	13.15	12.26	11.85	11.66	11.56	11.51
14	23.27	15.53	13.32	12.44	12.04	11.85	11.76	11.72

b. What is the effect on the monthly payment and total interest paid as the length of the mortgage increases?

Amortization Schedule

The couple decides on a 30-year mortgage in order to have the lowest monthly payments. You explain to them that the monthly payment is applied to pay interest on the loan and to reduce the amount owed. The couple asks you if the $647.28 monthly payment is divided equally between reducing the amount owed (principal) and paying the interest. They are surprised that this is not the case.

Example 2 *The calculated monthly payment for the couple's 30-year $114,000 mortgage at 5.5% annual interest is $647.28 (using TVM). Determine the outstanding balance at the start of the second month.*

SOLUTION

Step 1. Determine the amount of interest in the first month using $i = Prt$, where P is the outstanding balance of the loan for given month, r is the annual interest rate (fixed at 5.5%), and t is time (fixed at 1/12).

For the first payment, $P = 114,000$, $r = 0.055$, $t = \frac{1}{12}$

$$i = Prt = 114,000(0.055)\left(\tfrac{1}{12}\right) = \$522.50$$

Step 2. Determine the portion of the payment used to reduce the amount of the principal by subtracting the amount of interest owed (from step 1) from the monthly payment.

$$647.28 - 522.50 = \$124.78$$

Step 3. Calculate the outstanding balance for the next month by subtracting the amount to reduce the principal (step 2) from the outstanding balance of the current month.

$$114,000 - 124.78 = \$113,875.22$$

5. a. Repeat steps 1–3 in Example 2 to complete the following table:

PAYMENT NUMBER	MONTHLY PAYMENT	INTEREST	AMOUNT USED TO REDUCE PRINCIPAL	END-OF-MONTH BALANCE OF LOAN
1	$647.28	$522.50	$124.78	$113,875.22
2				
3				
4				

b. Using the results in part a, determine whether each of the following gradually increases, gradually decreases, or remains the same, as monthly payments are made over the years.

i. monthly payment   _____

ii. interest   _____

iii. amount that reduces principal   _____

iv. end-of-month balance   _____

The table in Problem 5a is a partial **amortization schedule** for the first four payments. An amortization schedule for the entire loan would require 360 lines. (Why?) Therefore, such schedules are usually done by spreadsheet programs and calculator websites. For example, see the monthly mortgage payment site at www.hsh.com.

Qualifying for a Mortgage

An important responsibility of a mortgage loan officer is to determine the borrower's ability to repay the loan. To determine if the couple is qualified for the mortgage, you obtain the following information:

Couple's combined gross annual income:	$60,000
Estimated annual property taxes on house:	$ 2200
Annual house insurance:	$ 670

6. a. Determine the total monthly housing expenses by adding the monthly mortgage payment and the monthly expenses for property taxes and house insurance.

b. Determine the couple's combined gross monthly income.

Most lenders of conventional loans use the qualifying rule that the monthly housing expenses should not be more than 28% of the monthly gross income. The ratio

$$\frac{\text{monthly housing expense}}{\text{monthly gross income}}$$

is called the **housing expense ratio**.

7. a. Using the results in Problem 6, determine the housing expense ratio for the couple applying for the loan.

b. Do they qualify for the loan?

8. The couple has just closed on the townhouse. Determine the total cost of the house by summing the down payment, the principal, the interest, and the points.

There are usually many other expenses every home buyer needs to pay when purchasing a house. These expenses include the cost of a lawyer, loan application fees, state and local real estate taxes, and title search fees.

SUMMARY
Activity 7.6

1. A **mortgage** is a long-term loan in which the property is used as security for the debt.

2. **Amortization** is a special type of annuity in which a large loan is paid off with equal regular payments over a specified time.

3. The monthly mortgage payment can be determined by using a table (see Example 1) or the TVM Solver feature of the TI-83 Plus graphing calculator.

4. An **amortization schedule** is a list containing the payment number, payment on the interest, payment on the principal, and balance of the loan.

5. A borrower qualifies for a mortgage if the **monthly housing expense** is no more than 28% of the monthly gross income.

EXERCISES
Activity 7.6

1. A house is purchased at a selling price of $285,000. The bank requires a 15% down payment. The current mortgage rate is 6.5%.

   a. Determine the amount of the down payment.

   b. What is the amount to be financed?

   c. What is the monthly payment for a 20-year mortgage on the amount in part b?

    d. What is the total interest paid?

2. Your aunt is buying a new condominium for $210,000. A 20% deposit is required. In order to obtain a 5.75% mortgage rate, she must pay 2 points at the time of the closing.

    a. What is the amount of the down payment?

    b. What is the amount to be financed?

    c. What is the cost of the 2 points?

    d. What is the monthly payment for a 30-year mortgage on the amount in part b?

    e. What is the total interest paid?

3. **a.** How much money in interest would your aunt save in mortgaging the condominium in Problem 2 if she obtained a 20-year mortgage?

    b. By how much would her monthly payments increase if she chose the 20-year mortgage?

4. The monthly payment for a 30-year, $185,000 conventional mortgage at 6.75% is $1199.91.

    a. Determine the amount of interest in the first payment.

    b. How much of the first payment is applied to the principal?

    c. What is the outstanding balance at the start of the second month of the loan?

5. You are looking for a mortgage to purchase a house selling for $300,000. You have gathered the following information about mortgage offers at two local banks:

First Bank: 10% down payment, an interest rate of 5.75%, a 30-year conventional mortgage, and 2 points to be paid at the time of closing

Second Bank: 20% down payment, an interest rate of 6.5%, a 25-year conventional mortgage, and no points

a. Determine the total cost of the house if the first bank is selected.

b. What is the total cost of the house if the mortgage offer from the second bank is chosen?

c. Based on the results from parts a and b, which bank should you select? Explain.

6. For new homeowners, banks often require that 1/12 of the estimated property taxes and house insurance premiums be included in the monthly payment. Each month, the taxes and insurance portions of the payment are deposited into a type of savings account called an **escrow account**. The bank pays the property taxes and insurance premiums when they are due.

A new townhouse is purchased with a mortgage of $95,000 at 6.75% for 30 years.

a. What is the monthly payment needed to pay principal and interest?

b. If the property taxes are $2100 per year and the insurance premium is $675.70, what amount must be added to the monthly payment?

c. Determine the total monthly payment for principal, interest, taxes, and insurance (called the PITI payment).

7. Your parents sold their house for a profit of $65,000 and have just received $30,000 from your grandparents' estate. They offer $310,000 on a new house, which has been accepted by the seller.

    a. Your parents plan to make a large down payment, including the monies from the sale of their old house, your grandparents' estate, and $15,000 from savings. What will be the amount of their down payment?

    b. What is the amount they will be financing?

    c. The lender has offered a 30-year mortgage at 5.65% with no points. The estimated property tax is $4500 and hazard insurance costs $1200. Determine the PITI payment.

8. You have enough money saved for the down payment for a new home. The monthly mortgage payment will be $850.40. All that is left is whether you qualify for the mortgage. Your annual gross earnings are $45,000. The estimated annual property taxes on the home are $1500 and the annual house insurance is $350.

    a. Determine your total housing monthly expenses including the monthly mortgage payment and the property taxes and the insurance.

    b. Determine your combined gross monthly income.

    c. Determine your housing expense ratio.

    d. Do you qualify for the loan?

PROJECT ACTIVITY 7.7
Which Is the Best Option?

OBJECTIVE

1. Use the financial models developed in this chapter to solve problems.

Each of the following problems presents a financial situation in which you must select the best option. Work with a group and be prepared to give an oral presentation of your findings to the class. The presentation should include visual displays showing any tables, equations, or graphs used in the problem-solving process.

1. You are 25 years old and begin to work for a large company that offers you two different retirement options.

   Option 1: You will be paid a lump sum of $20,000 for each year you work for the company.

   Option 2: The company will deposit $10,000 annually into an account that will pay you 12% compounded monthly. When you retire, the money will be given to you.

   Which option is the best? Explain.

2. Congratulations! You have just won $50,000 in the state lottery. You decide to invest half of the money into a savings account in order to start your own business when you graduate from college. You have three investment options:

   Option 1: Open a savings account that pays 6.5% simple interest.

   Option 2: Open a savings account that pays 3% compounded annually.

   Option 3: Open a savings account that pays 2.7% compounded daily.

   Which option will result in having the most money in six years? Explain.

3. You have just purchased a new computer for $2400. The store offers you two options to pay off the computer:

   Option 1: Apply for a store credit card and make payments of $150 per month until paid off. Assume you will make no additional purchases using the card and that there is no annual fee. The interest on the card is 1.5% per month. Payment is due at the beginning of each month.

   Option 2: Apply for a fixed installment loan of $2,400 at 6.55% APR for two years.

   Which is the best option? Explain.

Activities 7.1–7.7 What Have I Learned?

1. You invest $1000 at 4% compounded annually.

    a. Use the simple interest formula to determine the amount accumulated after three years.

    b. Use the compound interest formula to determine the amount after three years.

2. Which option would result in a greater return on your investment?

    Option 1: Invest at 10% interest compounded quarterly.

    Option 2: Invest at 10% interest compounded monthly.

    Explain.

3. If you invest $100 every month for five years, will you earn more interest if you made the payments at the beginning of each month or at the end of each month? Explain.

4. Banking regulations require that the effective interest rate (APR for loans, APY for deposits) be stated on all loan or investment contracts. Explain why.

5. A recent promotion for a credit card made the following introductory offer:

    • 0% fixed APR on all purchases and balance transfers for the first 12-month period

    • a low 8.5% APR thereafter

    However, if the minimum payment is not received by the due date on the billing statement or if the outstanding balance exceeds your credit limit, then your interest rate becomes a so-called default rate of 24.99%.

    a. What is the interest for the month on an average daily balance of $8000 at 8.5% APR?

Indigo Rodriquez

5/15/11

Indigo Rodrigue
5/13/11

1a.)

    b. What is the interest for the month on an average daily balance of $8000 at 24.99% APR?

    c. How much more did you pay in the month at the default rate of 24.99% APR?

6. For a mortgage having a given amount and interest rate,

    a. What happens to the total amount of interest paid if the number of years of the mortgage increases?

    b. What happens to the monthly payments as the number of years increase?

Activities 7.1–7.7   How Can I Practice?

1. You just started a new job and received a $5000 bonus. You decide to invest this money so that you can purchase a new car in four years. Your local credit union offers a CD paying 6% annual interest compounded semiannually. How much money will you have at the end of four years?

2. You are a freshman in high school and plan to attend the local community college in four years. Your father said he would pay for your college tuition, fees, and books for the first year. You estimate that $4500 will be needed to cover these expenses. Your father has done some research and has decided on a four-year CD with an interest rate of 4.65% compounded monthly. How much will he have to invest now to have $4500 in 48 months?

3. You plan to start a consulting business for computer networking. You deposit $200 at the beginning of each month into an account paying 4.75% compounded monthly.

   a. How much will be in the account after five years?

   b. How much interest was earned?

4. You notice the following advertisement in the local newspaper:

   > **24-foot motorboat for sale: $30,000**
   > **$6000 down and $555 per month**
   > **for 60 months.**

   a. Determine the total finance charge.

   b. What is the APR of the loan?

5. You are ready to purchase your first home. This home sells for $160,000. You must put a 10% down payment and you are required to pay 3 points at the time of closing. The conventional mortgage will be for 30 years at an interest rate of 6.5%. You wonder if you can afford this home.

   a. Determine the amount of the down payment.

b. What is the amount of the mortgage?

c. Determine the cost of the 3 points.

d. Determine the monthly mortgage payment.

e. What is the total cost of the house including the down payment and points?

f. What is the total interest that you will pay over the life of the loan?

g. Determine how much of the first payment on the loan is applied to the principal.

Summary

The bracketed numbers following each concept indicate the activity in which the concept is discussed.

CONCEPT / SKILL	DESCRIPTION	EXAMPLE
Compound amount [7.2]	The compound amount, also called future value, is the total amount of principal and compound interest at the end of an investment.	The compound amount of a $1000 investment at 6% interest compounded annually for two years: Original principal $1000.00; Interest first year +60.00; Balance after first year 1060.00; Interest (.06 × 1060) +63.60; Balance after 2 years $1123.60
Calculating compound amount (future value) using the compound interest formula [7.2]	The compound interest formula is $A = P\left(1 + \frac{r}{n}\right)^{nt}$, where A is the compound amount, P is the principal, r is the annual interest rate (decimal form), n is the number of compounding periods per year, and t the number of years money invested.	See Example 1 in Activity 7.2.
Calculating compound amount (future value) using technology [7.2]	The TI-83 Plus graphing calculator has a finance applications feature (TVM Solver).	See Example 2 in Activity 7.2.
The annual percentage yield (APY) or effective interest rate [7.2]	The APY is the true rate of return on an investment. One method to calculate the APY is the Eff(feature of the TI-83 Plus.	See Example 3 in Activity 7.2.
Calculating the present value of a compound amount (future value) using a formula [7.2]	Present value is the amount that must be invested now at a compound interest to reach a given future value. The present value formula is $$PV = \frac{FV}{\left(1 + \frac{r}{n}\right)^{nt}}.$$	The amount that must be invested now in order to have $6000 in five years, at 5.7% compounded monthly is $$P = \frac{6000}{\left(1 + \frac{0.057}{12}\right)^{5 \cdot 12}}$$ $$= \frac{6000}{(1 + 0.00475)^{60}}$$ $$= \$4515.13.$$
Calculating the present value using technology [7.2]	The present value for a given future value of an investment can be calculated using the TVM Solver feature of the TI-83 Plus.	See Example 4 in Activity 7.2.

Calculating the future value of an ordinary annuity using a formula [7.3]	An annuity is the payment (or receipt) of equal cash payments per period for a given period of time. For an ordinary annuity, the payments are made at the end of each period. The future value of ordinary annuity formula is $$FV = P \cdot \frac{(1+i)^n - 1}{i},$$ where FV is future value, P is annuity payment, i is interest rate per period (written as a decimal), and n is total number of periods.	The future value of a deposit of \$1000 made at the end of every six months for two years at 8% compounded semiannually is $$FV = 1000 \cdot \frac{(1+.04)^4 - 1}{0.04}$$ $$= \$4246.46.$$
Calculating the future value of an annuity due using a formula [7.3]	For an annuity due, the payments are made at the beginning of each period. The future value of an annuity due formula is $$FV = P \cdot \frac{(1+i)^n - 1}{i} \cdot (1+i).$$	The future value of a deposit of \$1000 made at the beginning of every six months for two years at 8% compounded semiannually is $$FV = \frac{1000(1+0.04)^4 - 1}{0.04}(1+0.04)$$ $$= \$4416.32.$$
Calculating the future value of an annuity using technology [7.3]	The future value of an ordinary annuity or annuity due can be calculated using the TVM Solver feature of the TI-83 Plus graphing calculator.	What is the future value of an ordinary annuity of \$500 per month, for three years, at 10% compounded monthly? Using N = 36, I% = 10, PMT = −500, PV = 0, P/Y = C/Y = 12, PMT:END, you have FV = 20,890.91
Calculating the present value of an annuity using technology [7.3]	The present value of annuity is a lump sum that is deposited now to yield a pay out of equal periodic payments for a given time. Present value can be calculated using the TVM Solver feature of TI-83 Plus.	How much must be deposited now, at 6% compounded annually, to yield an annuity payment of \$5000 at the end of each year, for five years? Using N = 5, I% = 6, PMT = −5000, FV = 0, P/Y = C/Y = 1, PMT:END, PV = 21,061.82.

Calculating the amortization payment by formula [7.4]	Amortization is repaying a loan by a series of equal periodic payments over a specified period of time. The amount Amt of the amortization payment can be calculated using the formula $$\text{Amt} = PV \cdot \frac{i}{1 - (1 + i)^{-n}}$$ or equivalently $$Amt = PV \cdot \frac{i}{1 - \dfrac{1}{(1 + i)^n}},$$ where Amt is amortization payment, PV is amount of loan, i is interest rate	per period, and n is number of periods. See Example 1 in Activity 7.4.
Calculating the amount of the equal period payments to amortize (liquidate) a lump sum with equal periodic payments over specified period of time [7.4]	The TVM Solver feature of the TI-83/84 Plus graphing calculator can be used to determine the amount of the payments to liquidate a lump sum.	What payment is required at the end of each month, at 8% interest compounded monthly, to liquidate $2000 in two years? Using N = 24, I% = 8 PV = 2000, FV = 0, P/Y = C/Y = 12, PMT:END, you obtain PMT = −90.45.
Finance charge [7.5]	The finance charge on an installment loan is the total amount that the borrower must pay for its use.	The finance charge on an installment loan of $2000 with 24 monthly payments of $95 is the total amount of payments minus the amount financed: $$24(95) - 2000 = \$280$$
Annual percentage rate (APR) [7.5]	The APR is the true rate of interest charged for the loan. The APR formula is $$\text{APR} = \frac{72i}{3P(n + 1) + i(n - 1)},$$ where APR is annual percentage rate, i is interest (finance) charge on the loan, P is principal or amount borrowed, and n is number of months of the loan.	The APR on a 12-month installment loan of $1000 having finance charge of $100 is $$\text{APR} = \frac{72(100)}{3(1000)(12 + 1) + 100(12 - 1)}$$ $$= \frac{7200}{39000 + 1.1}$$ $$= 0.18 \text{ or } 18\%.$$
Calculating the APR using tables [7.5]	The APR of a loan can be determined using APR Table 7.1 in Activity 7.5.	See Example 1 in Activity 7.5.
Calculating the monthly installment payment using tables [7.5]	If you know the APR and the number of monthly payments, the APR Table 7.1 can be used to determine the monthly payment.	See Problem 6, parts a–d, in Activity 7.5.

The amount of unearned interest when an installment loan is paid off before it is due [7.5]	The unearned interest can be determined by the actuarial method formula $$u = \frac{npv}{100 + v},$$ where u is unearned interest, n is number of remaining monthly payments, p is monthly payment, and v is value from the APR table that corresponds to the APR for the number of remaining payments.	See Problem 7, parts a–c, in Activity 7.5. The answer in part c is: Let $n = 12$, $p = 142.98$, and $v = 7.74$. $$u = \frac{npv}{100 + v}$$ $$= \frac{12(142.98)(7.74)}{100 + 7.74}$$ $$= \$123.26$$
Interest on an open-ended installment loan, such as a credit card [7.5]	The interest on most credit card accounts is calculated using the average daily balance method.	See Example 2 in Activity 7.5.
Calculating the monthly mortgage payment using a table [7.6]	The monthly mortgage payment can be determined using Table 7.2.	See Example 1 in Activity 7.6.
Calculating the monthly mortgage payment using technology [7.6]	The TVM Solver feature of the TI-83/84 Plus can be used to determine the monthly mortgage payment.	What is the monthly payment on a $200,000 mortgage at 5.5% APR for 25 years? Let N = 300, I% = 5.5, PV = 200,000, FV = 0, P/Y = C/Y = 12, PMT:END, you obtain PMT = −1228.17
Amortization schedule [7.6]	An amortization schedule displays, for a given monthly payment, the amount of interest paid and the amount used to reduce principal.	See Example 2 in Activity 7.6 for a partial amortization schedule.
Housing expense ratio [7.6]	A borrower qualifies for a mortgage if the monthly housing expenses do not exceed 28% of the borrower's monthly gross income. The housing expense ratio is $$\frac{\text{monthly housing expense}}{\text{monthly gross income}}.$$	The housing expense ratio for borrowers having $910 monthly housing expenses and $4800 monthly gross income is $$\frac{910}{4800} = 0.190 = 19\% < 28\%.$$ The borrower qualifies.

1. If $100 is invested in a bank in the year the *Declaration of Independence* was signed, how much would it be worth in the year 2010? Assume the investment earned 3.5% compounded monthly.

2. You deposit $2000 at the start of each year in a Roth IRA that earns 6.85% compounded annually. After 10 years, you stop making payments, but the money in the account continues to earn interest.

   a. Determine the amount in the Roth IRA after 10 years.

   b. If you withdraw the money 10 years after you stopped making payments, how much money did you receive?

3. Your older brother and his wife just had a baby boy. They want to establish a college fund for their son. If they decide to deposit $2000 at the beginning of each year at 4.5% compounded annually, how much money will be in the fund after 18 years?

4. Your parents are planning to retire and want to set aside a lump sum, earning 6.5% compounded quarterly, in order to have a pay out of $5000 per quarter for 20 years. What lump sum should your parents put aside when they retire? Assume payments are made at the beginning of each quarter.

5. a. What lump sum of money must a 20-year-old invest today at 5.75% compounded monthly in order for the investment to have a value of $1,000,000 at age 55?

   b. For this same 20-year-old, what would their monthly payments be in an ordinary annuity at 5.75% compounded monthly in order to accumulate $1,000,000 at age 55?

6. A landscaper needs to finance $27,000 in order to purchase a 4-by-4 truck. The dealer offers him the option of 0% financing for 60 months or a $4500 rebate.

   a. What is the monthly payment if he chooses the 0% financing?

b. If the rebate is chosen, the buyer can finance the balance for 60 months at 8% compounded monthly. What is the monthly payment? Assume payments are made at the end of each month.

c. Which option is the best? Explain.

7. Your passion is flying remote control model airplanes. You find the ultimate plane in a hobby shop for $675. The terms of the sale include a down payment of $175 and 12 monthly payments of $44.83.

   a. Determine the total amount paid or the installment price.

   b. Determine the finance charge of the installment loan.

   c. Use the formula and determine the APR.

8. You are going to college in the fall. You have just heard from your roommate who asks you to bring the stereo system for the dorm room. You find the perfect system for $1750. You have to put 25% down and you can pay the balance in 18 equal installments. The clerk tells you that you will pay a total finance charge of $112. You wonder if that is a good rate and if you can afford the monthly payments.

   a. How much is the down payment?

   b. What is the total amount financed including the finance charge?

   c. What is the monthly payment on the loan?

   d. Use the formula and determine the APR.

9. A house is selling for $250,000. The bank requires a 15% down payment, but no points. The current fixed mortgage rate is 5.75%.

    a. Determine the amount of the down payment.

    b. What is the amount of the mortgage?

    c. If a 25-year mortgage is obtained, what is the monthly mortgage payment?

    d. What is the total interest that will be paid on the loan?

    e. How much of the first payment on the loan is applied to principal?

The TI-83/84 Plus Graphing Calculator

A Basic Primer for Necessary Features and Routines

Contents

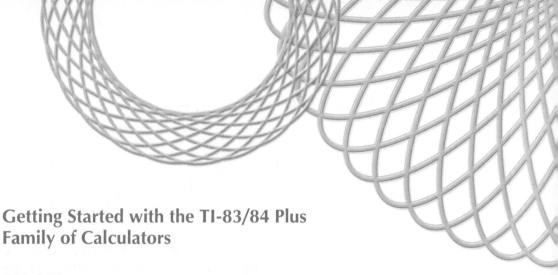

Getting Started with the TI-83/84 Plus Family of Calculators

ON-OFF

To turn on the TI-83/84 Plus, press the (ON) key. To turn off the calculator, press (2nd) and then (ON).

Most keys on the calculator have multiple purposes. The number or symbolic function/command written directly on the key is accessed by simply pressing the key. The symbolic function/commands written above each key are accessed with the aid of the (2nd) and (ALPHA) keys. The command above and to the left is color coded to match the (2nd) key. That command is accessed by first pressing the (2nd) key and then pressing the key itself. Similarly, the command above and to the right is color coded to match the (ALPHA) key and is accessed by first pressing the (ALPHA) key and then pressing the key itself.

Contrast

To adjust the contrast on your screen, press and release the (2nd) key and hold (▲) to darken and (▼) to lighten.

Mode

The (MODE) key controls many calculator settings. The activated settings are highlighted. For most of your work in this course, the settings in the left-hand column should be highlighted.

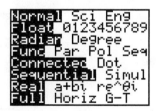

To change a setting, move the cursor to the desired setting and press (ENTER).

The Home Screen

The home screen is used for calculations.

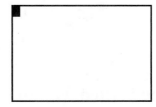

You may return to the home screen at any time by using the QUIT command. This command is accessed by pressing (2nd) (MODE). All calculations in the home screen are subject to the order of operations.

Enter all expressions as you would write them. Always observe the order of operations. Once you have typed the expression, press (ENTER) to obtain the simplified result. Before you press (ENTER), you may edit your expression by using the arrow keys, the delete command (DEL), and the insert command (2nd) (DEL).

Three keys of special note are the reciprocal key (X⁻¹), the caret key (^), and the negative key (−).

Typing a number and then pressing the reciprocal command key (X⁻¹) will give the reciprocal of the number. The reciprocal of a nonzero number, n, is $\frac{1}{n}$. As noted in the screen below, when performing an operation on a fraction, the fraction MUST be enclosed in parentheses before accessing this command.

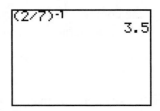

The caret key (^) is used to raise numbers to powers

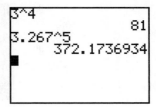

The negative key (−) on the bottom of the keyboard is different from the subtraction key (−). They cannot be used interchangeably. The negative key is used to change the sign of a single number or symbol; it will not perform a subtraction operation. If you mistakenly use the negative key in attempting to subtract, you will likely obtain an ERROR message.

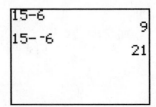

A table of keys and their functions follows.

KEY	FUNCTION DESCRIPTION
ON	Turns calculator on or off.
CLEAR	Clears the current line on the text screen.
ENTER	Executes a command.
(−)	Calculates the additive inverse.
MODE	Displays current operating settings.
DEL	Deletes the character at the cursor.
^	Symbol used for exponentiation.
ANS	Storage location of the last answer, or calculation.
ENTRY	Retrieves the previously executed expression.

ANS and ENTRY

The last two commands in the table can be real time savers. The result of your last calculation is always stored in a memory location known as ANS. It is accessed by pressing (2nd) (−) or it can be automatically accessed by pressing any operation button.

Suppose you want to evaluate $12.5\sqrt{1 + 0.5 \cdot (0.55)^2}$. It could be evaluated in one expression and checked with a series of calculations using ANS.

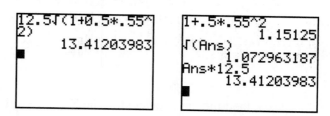

After you have keyed in an expression and pressed (ENTER), you cannot move the cursor back up to edit or recalculate this expression. This is where the ENTRY ((2nd) (ENTER)) command is used. The ENTRY command retrieves the previous expression and places the cursor at the end of the expression. You can use the left and right arrow keys to move the cursor to any location in the expression that you wish to modify.

Suppose you want to evaluate the compound interest expression $P\left(1 + \frac{r}{n}\right)^{nt}$, where P is the principal, r is the interest rate, n is the number of compounding periods annually, and t is the number of years, when $P = \$1000$, $r = 6.5\%$, $n = 1$, and $t = 2, 5$, and 15 years.

Using the ENTRY command, this expression would be entered once and edited twice.

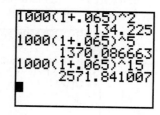

Note that there are many last expressions stored in the ENTRY memory location. You can repeat the ENTRY command as many times as you want to retrieve a previously entered expression.

Functions and Graphing

"Y =" Menu

Functions of the form $y = f(x)$ can be entered into the TI-83/84 Plus using the "Y =" menu. To access the "Y =" menu press the Y= key. Type the expression $f(x)$ after Y_1 using the X,T,θ,n key for the variable x and press ENTER.

For example, enter the function $f(x) = 3x^5 - 4x + 1$.

```
Plot1 Plot2 Plot3
\Y1■3X^5-4X+1
\Y2=
\Y3=
\Y4=
\Y5=
\Y6=
\Y7=
```

Note the = sign after Y_1 is highlighted. This indicates that the function Y_1 is active and will be graphed when the graphing command is executed and will be included in your table when the table command is executed. The highlighting may be turned on or off by using the arrow keys to move the cursor to the = symbol and then pressing ENTER. Notice in the screen below that Y_1 has been deactivated and will not be graphed nor appear in a table.

```
Plot1 Plot2 Plot3
\Y1=3X^5-4X+1
\Y2=
\Y3=
\Y4=
\Y5=
\Y6=
\Y7=
```

Once the function is entered in the Y = menu, function values may be evaluated in the home screen.

For example, given $f(x) = 3x^5 - 4x + 1$, evaluate $f(4)$. In the home screen, press VARS.

```
VARS Y-VARS
1:Window…
2:Zoom…
3:GDB…
4:Picture…
5:Statistics…
6:Table…
7:String…
```

Move the cursor to Y-VARS and press ENTER.

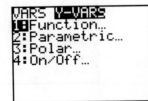
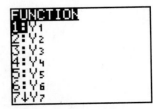

Press (ENTER) again to select Y_1. Y_1 now appears in the home screen.

To evaluate $f(4)$, press (⃞) (4) (⃞) after Y_1 and press (ENTER).

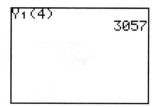

Tables of Values

If you are interested in viewing several y-values for the same function, you may want to construct a table.

Before constructing the table, make sure the function appears in the "Y =" menu with its "=" highlighted. You may also want to deactivate or clear any functions that you do not need to see in your table. Next, you will need to check the settings in the Table Setup menu. To do this, use the TBLSET command ((2nd) (WINDOW)).

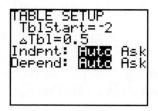

As shown in the screen above, the default setting for the table highlights the Auto options for both the independent (x) and dependent (y) variables. Choosing this option will display ordered pairs of the function with equally spaced x-values. TblStart is the first x-value to be displayed, and here is assigned the value -2. ΔTbl represents the equal spacing between consecutive x-values, and here is assigned the value 0.5. The TABLE command ((2nd) (GRAPH)) brings up the table displayed in the screen below.

Use the (▲) and (▼) keys to view other values in the table.

If the input values of interest are not evenly spaced, you may want to choose the ask mode for the independent variable from the Table Setup menu.

The resulting table is blank, but you can fill it by choosing any values you like for *x* and pressing ENTER after each.

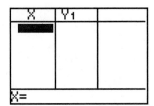 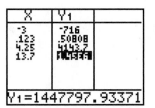

Note that the number of digits shown in the *y*- is limited by the table width, but if you want more digits, move the cursor to the desired output and more digits appear at the bottom of the screen.

Graphing a Function

Once a function is entered in the "Y =" menu and activated it can be displayed and analyzed. For this discussion, we will use the function $f(x) = -x^2 + 10x + 12$. Enter this as Y_1, making sure to use the negation key (–) and not the subtraction key (–).

The Viewing Window

The viewing window is the portion of the rectangular coordinate system that is displayed when you graph a function.

Xmin defines the left edge of the window.

Xmax defines the right edge of the window.

Xscl defines the distance between horizontal tick marks.

Ymin defines the bottom edge of the window.

Ymax defines the top edge of the window.

Yscl defines the distance between vertical tick marks.

In the standard viewing window, Xmin $= -10$, Xmax $= 10$, Xscl $= 1$, Ymin $= -10$, Ymax $= 10$, and Yscl $= 1$.

To select the standard viewing window, press ZOOM and 6.

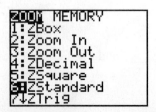

You will view the following:

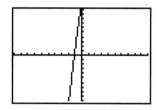

Is this an accurate and or complete picture of your function, or is the window giving you a misleading impression? You may want to use your table function to view the *y*-values for $x = -10$ to 10.

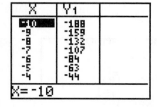

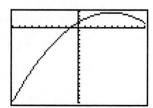

The table indicates that the minimum *y*-value on the interval from $x = -10$ to $x = 10$ is -188 and the maximum *y*-value is 37. Press WINDOW and reset the settings to approximately the following;

$$\text{Xmin} = -10, \text{Xmax} = 10, \text{Xscl} = 1, \text{Ymin} = -190, \text{Ymax} = 40, \text{Yscl} = 10$$

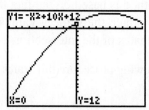

The new graph gives us a much more complete picture of the behavior of the function for $-10 \leq x \leq 10$.

The coordinates of specific points on the curve can be viewed by activating the trace feature. While in the graph window, press TRACE. The function equation will be displayed at the top of the screen, a flashing cursor will appear on the curve at the middle of the screen, and the coordinates of the cursor location will be displayed at the bottom of the screen.

The left arrow key, ◀, will move the cursor toward smaller x-values. The right arrow key, ▶, will move the cursor toward larger x-values. If the cursor reaches the edge of the window and you continue to move the cursor, the window will adjust automatically.

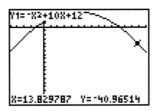

Zoom Menu

The Zoom menu offers several options for changing the window very quickly.

The features of each of the commands are summarized in the following table:

ZOOM COMMAND	DESCRIPTION
1: ZBox	Draws a box to define the viewing window.
2: Zoom In	Magnifies the graph near the cursor.
3: Zoom Out	Increases the viewing window around the cursor.
4: ZDecimal	Sets a window so that Xscl and Yscl are 0.1.
5: ZSquare	Sets equal size pixels on the x and y axes.
6: ZStandard	Sets the window to standard settings.
7: ZTrig	Sets built-in trig window variables.
8: ZInteger	Sets integer values on the x and y axes.
9: ZoomStat	Sets window based on the current values in the stat lists.
0: ZoomFit	Replots graph to include the max and min output values for the current Xmin and Xmax.

Solving Equations Graphically

The Intersection Method

This method is based on the fact that solutions to the equation $f(x) = g(x)$ are values of x that produce the same y-values for the functions f and g. Graphically, these are the x-coordinates of the intersection points of $y = f(x)$ and $y = g(x)$.

The following procedure illustrates how to use the intersection method to solve $x^3 + 3 = 3x$ graphically:

Step 1. Enter the left-hand side of the equation as Y_1 in the "Y =" editor and the right-hand side as Y_2. Select the standard viewing window.

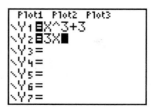

Step 2. Examine the graphs to determine the number of intersection points.

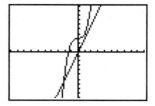

You may need a couple of windows to be certain of the number of intersection points.

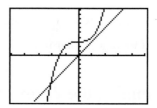

Step 3. Access the Calculate menu by pushing (2nd) (TRACE), then choose option 5: intersect.

 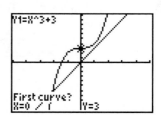

The cursor will appear on the first curve in the center of the window.

Step 4. Move the cursor close to the desired intersection point and press (ENTER).

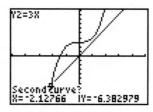

The cursor will now jump vertically to the other curve.

Step 5. Repeat step 4 for the second curve.

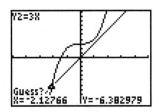

Step 6. To use the cursor's current location as your guess, press (ENTER) in response to the question on the screen that asks Guess? If you want to move to a better guess value, do so before you press (ENTER).

The coordinates of the intersection point appear below the word Intersection

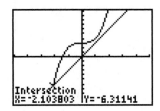

The *x*-coordinate is a solution to the equation.

If there are other intersection points, repeat the process as necessary.

Determining the Zeros of a Function

Graph the function and size the window so the *x*-intercept is visible.

For example: The zero of $y = x^3 + 2x^2 - x - 5$ is visible in the standard window, between $x = 1$ and $x = 2$. To determine the zero approximately, follow these steps.

1. Press (2nd) $\boxed{\text{CALC}}$ to go to the CALCULATE menu, then select 2:zero.

2. Move the cursor on the graph until it is clearly to the left of the *x*-intercept, then press (ENTER).

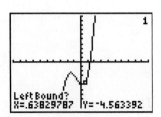

3. Move the cursor on the graph until it is clearly to the right of the *x*-intercept, then press (ENTER).

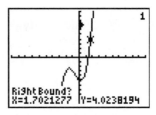

4. For the guess you can simply press (ENTER). (If you move the cursor outside of the [left,right] interval you will get an error message).

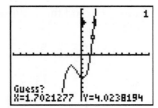 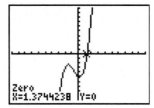

The zero is *x* ≈ 1.3744.

If there are more zeros, each must be determined separately by following the same procedure.

Alternative Method to Determine a Zero

If the constant function $y = 0$ is entered as a second function, the zeros can be found by using the intersection method discussed previously.

Determining the Linear Regression Equation for a Set of Data

Example:

x	y
2	2
3	5
4	3
5	7
6	9

Enter the data into the calculator as follows:

1. Press (STAT) and choose EDIT.

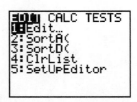

2. The TI-83/84 Plus has six built-in lists, L1, L2, . . . , L6. If there is data in L1, clear the list as follows:

   a. Use the arrows to place the cursor on L1 at the top of the list. Press CLEAR followed by ENTER, followed by the down arrow.

   b. Follow the same procedure to clear L2 if necessary.

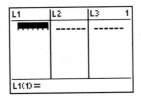

   c. Enter the *x*-values into L1 and the *y*-values into L2.

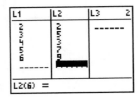

To see a scatterplot of the data proceed as follows.

1. STAT PLOT is the 2nd function of the Y= key. You must press 2nd before pressing Y= to access the STAT PLOT menu.

2. Select Plot 1 and make sure that Plots 2 and 3 are Off. The screen shown below will appear. Select On and then choose the scatterplot option (first icon) on the Type line. Confirm that your *x* and *y* values are stored, respectively, in L_1 and L_2. The symbols L_1 and L_2 are 2nd functions of the 1 and 2 keys, respectively. Finally, select the small square as the mark that will be used to plot each point.

3. Press Y= and clear or deselect any functions currently stored.

4. To display the scatterplot, have the calculator determine an appropriate window by pressing `ZOOM` and then `9` (ZoomStat).

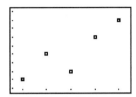

The following instructions will calculate the linear regression equation and store it in Y_1.

1. Press `STAT` and right arrow to highlight CALC.

2. Choose 4: LinReg($ax + b$). LinReg($ax + b$) will be pasted to the home screen. To tell the calculator where the data is, press `2nd` and `1` (for L1), then `,`, then `2nd` and `2` (for L2) because the x list and y list are stored in L_1 and L_2 respectively. The display looks like this:

3. Press `,` and then press `VARS`.

4. Right arrow to highlight Y-VARS.

5. Choose 1, FUNCTION.

6. Choose 1 for Y_1 (or 2 for Y_2, etc.).

7. Press ENTER.

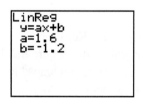

The linear regression equation for this data is $y = 1.6x - 1.2$.

8. To display the regression line, press GRAPH.

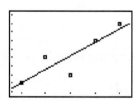

9. Press the Y= key to view the equation.

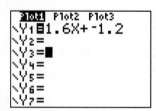

Determining the Correlation Coefficient and Residuals

10. If the correlation coefficient, r, does not appear with the linear regression equation, as in step 7 on page A-16, press [2nd] and [9] (CATALOG), scroll down to select DiagnosticOn, press [ENTER] twice. This will allow you to see r whenever you find a linear regression equation.

```
LinReg
 y=ax+b
 a=1.6
 b=-1.2
 r²=.7804878049
 r=.8834522086
■
```

11. Whenever a regression equation is calculated, the residuals are automatically stored in a list. To see the residuals, go to [STAT] [EDIT] and highlight L3 at the top of the list. Press [2nd] [DEL] (for INSERT) which will open a new list. At the flashing cursor, press [2nd] [STAT] (for LIST) and scroll down to select RESID. Press [ENTER] twice and the list of residuals will appear.

```
L1      L2      RESID  4
 2       2       0
 3       5       1.4
 4       3       -2.2
 5       7       .2
 6       9       .6
------  ------  ------
RESID ={0,1.4,-2.…
```

Histograms, Boxplots, and Statistics

Entering a Collection of Data

Press [STAT], then choose [EDIT]. You will see a table with heading L1, L2, L3, (L is for List). If there is a list of numbers already stored under L1, move the cursor to the L1 heading, then press [CLEAR] and [ENTER]. When the list is empty start entering the data one number at a time. If you wish to store more than one set of data values, simply repeat the process for any of list L2 through L6.

Example:

COLLECTION OF DATA				
18	20	19	23	20
19	25	21	18	27
20	35	23	19	21
28	18	21	28	33

1. Press [STAT] and choose [EDIT].

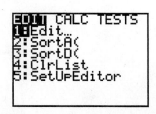

```
EDIT CALC TESTS
1:Edit…
2:SortA(
3:SortD(
4:ClrList
5:SetUpEditor
```

2. To enter one variable data, you will need only one list.

    a. If there is data in L1, clear the list.

    b. Enter the data into L1.

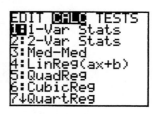

Calculating One-Variable Statistics

Press (STAT), then choose (CALC). From the calculate menu, press (ENTER) to choose the one-variable statistics. When you see 1-Var Stats on your home screen, enter the name of the list where your data is stored (the second function of 1 through 6).

1. To calculate the one variable statistics using the example data in L1, press (STAT), highlight CALC, then choose option 1: 1-Var Stats.

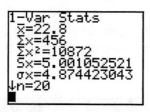

2. When 1-Var Stats appears on the home screen, enter (2nd) and (1) (for L1). The following basic statistics appear. Scroll down to see the second screen.

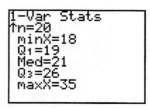

The statistics you should note are:

    mean, $\overline{x}$ = 22.8

    standard deviation, σ_x = 4.874423043

    number of data values, n = 20

    median, med = 21

Creating a Histogram for One-Variable Data

1. Using the example data in L1, press ⟨2nd⟩ and ⟨Y=⟩ to get the STAT PLOT menu. Choose any of Plot1, Plot2, or Plot3, making sure the two you *don't* choose are Off.

2. In the plot menu, highlight and select On, histogram type of plot, L1 for the Xlist, and 1 for the Freq, as shown:

3. To see a histogram, press ⟨ZOOM⟩ and choose option 9: ZoomStat. The following histogram shows the domain of the distribution, grouping data values into classes.

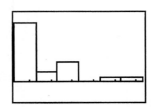

4. To show the histogram where each rectangle represents one data value, press ⟨WINDOW⟩ and set Xscl to 1, then press ⟨GRAPH⟩.

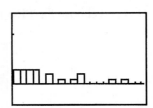

5. Pressing ⟨TRACE⟩ allows you to see the frequency for each data value.

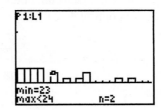

Creating a Boxplot for One-Variable Data

1. In the plot menu, highlight and select On, boxplot type of plot, L1 for the Xlist, and 1 for the Freq, as shown below:

2. To see a boxplot, press ⬚ZOOM⬚ and choose option 9: ZoomStat.

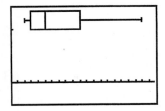

3. Pressing ⬚TRACE⬚ allows you to see the five-number summary for this distribution.

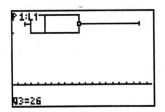

Factorials, Permutations, and Combinations

All are found by selecting the probability menu.

Press ⬚MATH⬚ and choose the PRB menu.

1. To calculate ten factorial, enter the integer followed by ⬚MATH⬚, choose the PRB menu, and select option 4: !, then ⬚ENTER⬚.

2. To calculate the number of permutations of ten things taken four at a time, enter 10 followed by (MATH), choose the PRB menu, and select option 2: nPr, followed by 4, then (ENTER).

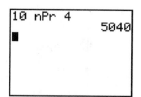

To calculate the number of combinations of ten things taken four at a time, or the binomial coefficient $\binom{10}{4}$, enter 10 followed by (MATH), choose the PRB menu, and select option 3: nCr, followed by 4, then (ENTER).

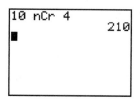

Generating a List of Random Numbers

1. Press (STAT) and choose (EDIT).

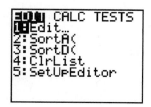

2. Clear list L1 and highlight the L1 heading. Press (MATH), choose the PRB menu, and select option 5: randInt(.

3. To randomly generate integers between 0 and 1, enter this domain, followed by the quantity of numbers desired, separated by commas. The following command generates a list of 50 zeros and ones. (Note that the command is too long to fit on the screen at once.)

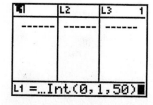 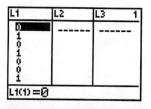

4. To quickly add the numbers in a list, from the home screen, press ⟨2nd⟩ and ⟨STAT⟩ (for LIST), choose the MATH menu, and select option 5: sum(. Enter the name of the list, L1, and the sum will be displayed, as shown.

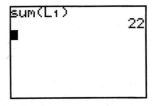

In this example, 22 of the 50 integers were ones.

Metric–U.S. Conversions

Length

1 meter = 3.28 feet

1 meter = 1.094 yards

1 centimeter = 0.394 inches

1 kilometer = 0.6214 miles

1 foot = 0.305 meters

1 yard = 0.914 meters

1 inch = 2.54 centimeters

1 mile = 1.6093 kilometers

Temperature

Celsius (C) to Fahrenheit (F)

$F = \frac{9}{5}C + 32$

Fahrenheit (F) to Celsius (C)

$C = \frac{5}{9}(F - 32)$

Weight

1 gram = 0.03527 ounces

1 kilogram = 2.205 pounds

1 gram = 0.002205 pounds

1 ounce = 28.35 grams

1 pound = 0.454 kilograms

1 pound = 454 grams

Volume

1 liter = 1.057 quarts

1 liter = 0.2642 gallons

1 quart = 0.946 liters

1 gallon = 3.785 liters

U.S. System of Measurement

Length

1 foot = 12 inches

1 yard = 3 feet

1 mile = 5280 feet

Weight

1 pound = 16 ounces

1 ton = 2000 pounds

Volume

1 cup = 8 fluid ounces

1 pint = 2 cups

1 quart = 2 pints

1 gallon = 4 quarts

Metric System of Measurement

Length

1 kilometer (km) = 1000 meters (m)

1 hectometer (hm) = 100 m

1 dekameter (dam) = 10 m

1 decimeter (dm) = $\frac{1}{10}$ m = 0.1 m

1 centimeter (cm) = $\frac{1}{100}$ m = 0.01 m

1 millimeter (mm) = $\frac{1}{1000}$ m = 0.001 m

Mass

1 kilogram (kg) = 1000 grams (g)

1 hectogram (hg) = 100 g

1 dekagram (dag) = 10 g

1 decigram (dg) = $\frac{1}{10}$ g = 0.1 g

1 centigram (cg) = $\frac{1}{100}$ g = 0.01 g

1 milligram (mg) = $\frac{1}{1000}$ g = 0.001 g

Volume

1 kiloliter (kl) = 1000 liters (L)

1 hectoliter (hl) = 100 L

1 dekaliter (dal) = 10 L

1 deciliter (dl) = $\frac{1}{10}$ L = 0.1 L

1 centiliter (cl) = $\frac{1}{100}$ L = 0.01 L

1 milliliter (ml) = $\frac{1}{1000}$ L = 0.001 L

APPENDIX C

Glossary of Geometric Formulas

Perimeter and Area of a Triangle, and Sum of Measures
of the Angles

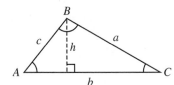

$$P = a + b + c$$
$$A = \tfrac{1}{2}bh$$
$$A + B + C = 180°$$

Pythagorean Theorem

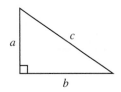

$$a^2 + b^2 = c^2$$

Perimeter and Area of a Rectangle

$$P = 2l + 2w$$
$$A = lw$$

Perimeter and Area of a Square

$$P = 4s$$
$$A = s^2$$

Area of a Trapezoid

$$A = \tfrac{1}{2}h(b_1 + b_2)$$

Circumference and Area of a Circle

$$C = 2\pi r$$
$$A = \pi r^2$$

Volume and Surface Area of a Rectangular Solid

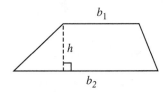

$$V = lwh$$
$$SA = 2lw + 2lh + 2wh$$

Volume and Surface Area of a Sphere

$$V = \tfrac{4}{3}\pi r^3$$
$$SA = 4\pi r^2$$

Volume and Surface Area of a Right Circular Cylinder

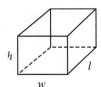

$$V = \pi r^2 h$$
$$SA = 2\pi r^2 + 2\pi rh$$

Volume and Surface Area of a Right Circular Cone

$$V = \tfrac{1}{3}\pi r^2 h$$
$$SA = \pi r^2 + \pi rl$$

Interval Notation

$(a, b) = a < x < b$ $(-\infty, a) = x < a$

$(a, b] = a < x \leq b$ $(-\infty, a] = x \leq a$

$[a, b) = a \leq x < b$ $(a, \infty) = x > a$

$[a, b] = a \leq x \leq b$ $[a, \infty) = x \geq a$

Glossary of Functions

Constant Function
$f(x) = b$

Linear Function
$f(x) = mx + b$

Quadratic Function
$f(x) = ax^2 + bx + c,$
$a \neq 0$

Cubic Function
$f(x) = x^3$

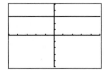
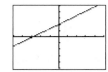
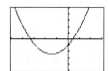

Exponential Function
$f(x) = ab^x$
$a > 0, b > 1$

Exponential Function
$f(x) = ab^x$
$a > 0, 0 < b < 1$

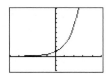
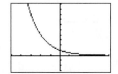

Index

A

Absolute value function, 126–127
Actuarial method formula, 843, 846
Acute angles, 599
Acute triangle, 600, 603, 682
Addition method, 296–297, 299
Air Quality Index (AQI), 417–418
Algebraic approach
  to problem solving, 11–14
  solving equations using, 87–89, 95
    undoing operations, 88
  for solving inequalities, 305–306, 308, 310
  for solving systems of equations, 281
Algebraic expressions
  evaluating, 78, 152
  in expanded form, 466
Algebraic solutions
  to solving inequalities, 305–306
  to 2 × 2 systems of linear equations, 295–299
American National Standards Institute (ANSI), 189
Amortization
  applications, 831–833
  calculating payments for, by formula, 830–831, 833, 865
  definition of, 833, 853
  of lump sum, 865
  mortgages using process of, 848–851
  schedule, 851–852, 853, 866
Angles, 600–604
  acute, 597
  in congruent geometric figures, 618, 619
  defined, 551
  measuring, 599–600
  obtuse, 599
  right, 233, 600
  in similar geometric figures, 615, 619
  straight, 600
  sum of measures of, A25
  sum of triangle's, 600, 603, 682
  of triangle, 600
Annual decay rate, 527
Annual growth rate, 527
Annual percentage rate (APR), 836–842, 863, 865
  calculating, 837, 845
    using tables, 842–843, 865
  definition of, 837, 845
  tables, 838–841
Annual percentage yield (APY), 819, 821
Annuities, 824, 828. *See also* Amortization
  future value of, 825–826, 828
    using formula to calculate, 864
    using technology to calculate, 826, 864
  present value of, 826–827
    using technology to calculate, 827
Annuity due, 824, 828
  calculating future value of, 825, 828, 864

Annuity payment, 824
ANSI. *See* American National Standards Institute (ANSI)
APR. *See* Annual percentage rate (APR)
APY. *See* Annual percentage yield (APY)
AQI. *See* Air Quality Index (AQI)
Area
  of circle, 588–589, 679, A25
  distinguishing between problems requiring formulas for perimeter and, 596
  formulas, 680–681, A25
  of kite, 580, 583
  of parallelogram, 576–577, 583, 680
  of polygons, 575, 581–582, 583, 681
  of rectangle, 576, 583, 680, A25
  of rhombus, 581, 583
  of special right triangles, 627–629
  of square, 575–576, 583, 680, A25
  of trapezoid, 579, 583, 681, A25
  of triangle, 577–578, 583, 680, A25
Argument. *See* Function(s)
Arithmetic mean, 732
Arithmetic sequence, 6
Armstrong, Lance, 567
Art, math in, 664–671
Asymptotes, horizontal, 501, 505, 546
Average, 731, 732
  simple, 739, 743
  weighted, 739–742, 743
Average daily balance method, 844–845, 846
Average rate of change, 166–167, 169
  graphical interpretation of, 168–169
  linear functions and, 175–176
  over an interval, 341
  of weight, 167, 168
Axes of graph, data misrepresentation and, 693
Axis of symmetry, 463
  of parabola, 387, 392

B

Back-to-back stem-and-leaf plot, 726
Balance, 305
Bar graphs, 695, 697, 700–701, 705, 709–710, 804
  definition of, 705
  grouped, 701–704, 705
  paired, 702, 705
  side-by-side, 711–712
  stacked (subdivided), 703, 705, 804
Basketball court dimensions, 97
Bell-shaped curve, 791, 796, 806
Bermuda Triangle, 562
Bias, 758, 760, 765, 767, 805
  nonrespondents and, 765
  self-selection, 767
Bird flu, 530–531
Blinding, 778
Body fat percentage, 242–244

Bone length, prediction of height from, 264–266
Box. *See* Rectangular prism
Box-and-whisker plots. *See* Boxplots
Boxplots, 786–787, 806
  for one-variable data, creating, on graphing calculator, A20
Break-even point, 291
Broken-line graphs, 694, 698
Business modeling, 290–294

C

Calculators. *See also* Graphing calculator
  determining measures of central tendency with, 734–735
  generating random numbers with, 762
Can. *See* Right circular cylinders
Car leasing, 832–833
Cause-and-effect relationships, 251, 776, 779
Celsius (C) scale, conversion to Fahrenheit (F) scale, 194–195, A23
Census, 756, 760
Centers for Disease Control, 530
Central tendency (of frequency distribution), 731
  measures of, 732–735, 736, 805
Change, average rate of, 166–167, 341
Circle graphs, 713–715, 804
Circles, 558–559, 560
  area of, 588–589, 681, A25
  circumference of, 558–559, 560, 680
  defined, 558
Circumference, 558–559, 560, 680, A25
  formulas, 559, 596
Classes, 723
Class width, 723
Closed-end installment loan, 836, 845
Closed interval, 309
Cluster sampling, 768–769
Coefficient(s)
  a, effects of, 377–378
  b, effects of, 378–379
  of term, 375
College fund, 831–832
Collinear, 670, 671
Combinations, A21
Common factors, 404–405, 407
  factoring, 404
  removing, from a polynomial, 404
Completely factored form, 451
Compound amount, 863. *See also* Future value
  calculating, 863
Compound inequality, 307–309, 346
  algebraic approach to solving, 308
  graphical method for solving, 308
  phrases that indicate, 307
  symbolic representation of, 307
Compound interest, 816, 821
Compound interest formula, 816, 821, 863